HENRY GARNET

HENRY GARNET
From a portrait by Jan Wiericx

HENRY GARNET

1555 – 1606

and the

Gunpowder Plot

by

PHILIP CARAMAN

FARRAR, STRAUS & COMPANY

New York

To
MARGARET FITZHERBERT

CONTENTS

ILLUSTRATIONS

Plates

ix

LIST OF ABBREVIATIONS
used in footnotes

C.A.   Claudius Aquaviva

C.R.S.   *Catholic Record Society*

E.H.R.   *English Historical Review*

Foley   *Records of the English Province of the Society of Jesus,* by Henry Foley, S.J. (1877–83)

F.G.   Fondo Gesuitico (Papers in the Jesuit Archives, Rome. The folio reference is always to the first sheet of Garnet's letters. The letters of Robert Southwell contained in this volume are arranged in chronological order and numbered one to thirteen.) All the letters written to Aquaviva are translated from the Latin or French; the letters to Robert Persons were written in English

Hat. Cal.   Calendar of Manuscripts of the Marquess of Salisbury preserved at Hatfield House

Humble Supplication   *An Humble Supplication to Her Majestie,* by Robert Southwell (edited by R. C. Bald, Cambridge University Press, 1953)

John Gerard   *John Gerard, the Autobiography of an Elizabethan,* by Philip Caraman (1951)

Narrative   *A Narrative of the Gunpowder Plot,* by John Gerard, printed from the original at Stonyhurst in *The Condition of English Catholics* (ed. John Morris) 1871

S.P.D.   *State Papers Domestic,* Public Record Office, London

William Weston   *William Weston, the Autobiography of an Elizabethan,* by Philip Caraman (1955)

PREFACE

THIS is the first biography of Henry Garnet. For more than fourteen years I gathered materials for it, transcribing and translating from the Latin more than a hundred and fifty letters or fragments of letters written by Henry Garnet as well as a number of letters sent to him. Several of Garnet's letters were between five and ten thousand words in length; some were already known; another fifty or more I had the good fortune to discover in 1952 in Rome, where they had first been used by Fr Robert Persons in his historical works, and later by Fr Henry More, whose *History of the English Province* was completed in 1630, though it waited another thirty years for publication. The material I gathered was so abundant that I was compelled to be selective in my use of it. But during this time of preparation I came gradually to form an appreciation of Garnet's character that was both consistent and compulsive. The crux of the interpretation lay in the last months of his life, for it had often been asserted that he behaved then in a baffling, if not reprehensible, manner. For this reason I determined to follow his behaviour, from his arrest to his execution, day by day, exclusively from the primary sources. Only then did his conduct appear logical and consistent.

At the end of the last century Fr John Gerard, at the time Editor of *The Month*, began a biography of Garnet but had written no more than the first chapter when he was appointed Superior of the Jesuit English Province. He never returned to the task, but in 1898 he published his first chapter together with notes he had made, mainly transcripts of letters he had taken from the archives at Stonyhurst.[1] Gerard correctly judged that it was impossible to assess Garnet's guilt or innocence in the Gunpowder Plot without taking into account his whole career; but it was, perhaps, fortunate that he got no further than he did, for since his time much more information has become available; and, what is more important, it is possible to get a clearer view of Garnet now that the Gunpowder Plot has ceased to be a subject of acrimonious debate among historians.

An earlier attempt to write at least a sketch of Garnet was planned by another Fr John Gerard, Garnet's friend and fellow-Jesuit. In his *Narrative*

[1] Cf. *The Month*, January to May 1898.

of the Gunpowder Plot, Gerard, after describing with unimpeachable accuracy
the examinations and arraignment of Garnet, began: 'I will here set down
as much of his course (in life) as I could learn from some of those that have
been intimate with him'; but he wrote no more than two sentences on his
birth and early education. He gave no explanation for breaking off his
biography. What he knew would have been of inestimable value, since he
was an intimate friend both of Fr Robert Southwell and Anne Vaux,
Garnet's closest associates.

In earlier books, *John Gerard* and *William Weston*, and in my anthology,
The Other Face, there have been frequent references to Fr Garnet. Over the
greater part of sixteen years he has never been long absent from my work.
Perhaps because of this and of the extensive sources I gathered, I hesi-
tated to begin this biography; there were always excuses at hand to do other
things, even to write other books. Certainly I should never have started,
still less finished, had it not been for the constant but kindly taunts of my
research assistant, Margaret FitzHerbert, who, impatient of my talking,
goaded me into writing. The book is dedicated to her in affectionate appreciation also of her sharp interest and sustaining curiosity.

It is impossible after a decade to recall all to whom I have become
indebted for help. Always I have received exemplary courtesy from the
librarians at the British Museum, the Public Record Office, the Bodleian,
Stonyhurst, Hatfield House, Canterbury, Rome, Gravesend, Nottingham
and the Bibliothèque Royale at Brussels. Among previous workers in this
patch of history I manifestly owe a great deal to Fr Christopher Devlin
and Fr Godfrey Anstruther as well as to the editors of the Catholic Record
Society. Mr Patrick Barry has done much work for me in London libraries;
Mr Thomas Raworth has always been at hand to type my transcripts and to
help me in other ways. As I followed, so to speak, the footsteps of Fr Garnet
in the field, I had the cooperation of Fr I. St Lawrence, Fr A. Powell and
Fr John Skinner. I am particularly grateful to Fr Bernard Basset, Dr David
Mathew and Fr Joseph Barrett, who read the book in typescript and sug-
gested many changes which I have done my best to carry out.

Writing as I did at intervals of leisure over two and a quarter years I have
incurred debts of hospitality to many friends in England and Ireland, in
whose houses I found most happy conditions for work while I was both
their elusive chaplain and eremitical guest; and, most particularly to Mr and
Mrs Evelyn Waugh who, for days on end, many times suffered my moods
and depressions as I strove to continue the book when it was in danger of
dying; to the Lady Honor Svejdar, and also to her secretary, Mrs Beatty,
who made the first typed copy from a manuscript that would have baffled

most typists; to Mrs K. Scheunert, the Hon Mrs Aubrey Herbert and also to many priests with whom I stayed and worked. The second typescript was made by Eliane de Miramon and Tessa Fraser in circumstances that demanded much patience and endurance.

P. C.

I

EARLY LIFE

HENRY GARNET, son of Brian and Alice Garnet, was born at Heanor, a market town of east Derbyshire, in the second half of the year 1555.

A recent history of the family[1] traces the Garnets from Ralph de Gernet, a literate gentleman, possibly a clerk, who followed Duke William from Normandy and was employed to witness several grants of land in Lancashire during the years following the battle of Hastings. From the twelfth to the sixteenth century the name, in a number of variants — Gurin, Guerin and Guerinet — occurs in the north-west of England, especially on the borders of Westmorland and Lancashire. There, Garnets became small landholders and acquired the right to bear arms. Only under the Tudors does the name appear farther south in the immediate forebears of Henry Garnet, 'the most famous, certainly the most spectacular of all the family'.[2]

The Garnets prospered moderately in the Middle Ages, but made their mark more in learning than in politics. Throughout the sixteenth century, the name recurs in the registers of Oxford colleges. John Garnet received his B.A. in 1522; another John Garnet was fellow of Merton in 1545; and Anthony, Master of Balliol for two years from 1560 to 1562. In 1591, when a Grammar School in Westmorland was granted a charter, two Garnets were among its Governors. Brian Garnet, Henry's father, became master of the Grammar School at Nottingham in 1565. Apart from Henry he had at least two sons who distinguished themselves academically, and four daughters.[3]

The earliest parish register of Heanor dates from 1559, four years after Henry's birth. It can be presumed that a day or two after his birth Henry

---

[1] Carolyn G. Heilbrun, *The Garnett Family* (Allen & Unwin 1961).

[2] *Ibid.*, 20.

[3] A treatise on mathematics, written probably by this brother, is among the unpublished manuscripts in the possession of the University Library of Nottingham. One of his sisters married a Mr Heathcote of Kirby, Derbyshire: their son John entered the English College, Rome, in 1609. Cf. *C.R.S.*, vol. 54, 200.

was christened by the vicar, Richard Arnold, in the parish church of St Laurence. No suggestion has been made why he received the name 'Henry'; nor in later life did he show any devotion to the emperor-saint. Possibly he was born or baptised on or near his feast day, 15 July; indeed this may explain why he was not given the name Laurence, the saint second only to John the Baptist in popularity in Marian England. It was no accident that Prince Philip, the consort of the reigning Queen, on his return to Spain, designed his great palace at the Escurial in the shape of a gridiron in honour of St Laurence.

In Heanor church Laurence is commemorated in a window of the north aisle. From the tower there is a wide view extending to the foothills of the peak district and beyond to Sherwood Forest.

Henry's mother, Alice Jay, was a lady of less staunch religious conviction than her husband. Nothing is known of her family. Her son, Henry, re-tained for her all his life a tender affection, and as a priest in England had the comfort of receiving her back into the Church in which she was born and had educated her young children. She may have been connected with the Jays of Nottingham; possibly she was the sister of a Master Jay, burgess of the city and a member of Parliament.[1]

It is unfortunate that Fr John Gerard's *Narrative of the Gunpowder Plot* stops abruptly at the point where he begins his sketch of Henry Garnet.[2] 'His parents were well esteemed', writes Gerard, 'and well able to maintain charge of their family. His father was given to learning, insomuch that he made profession thereof and taught in the Free School in the next shire town, which was Nottingham.' When Henry entered the school it was under its fourth Master, Henry Cockrane, an Oxford scholar and bach-elor of Canon Law. Nothing is known of him; but in 1565 he gave place to Brian Garnet two years before his son, Henry, entered Winchester College.

The original foundation charter of the school, dated 22 November 1512, now hangs framed in the office of the governing body in Peter Gate. The ornamental initial letter *H* is elaborated into a sketch that shows the pious foundress, Agnes Mellers, kneeling near Henry VII, who is seated, robed and crowned, as he hands her the charter of foundation. By this deed Alice, a widow and 'vowess', was entitled to establish a free school of one scholar master and one usher to teach grammar in the parish of Our Lady. It was

[1] W. H. Stevenson, *Records of the Borough of Nottingham* (1914), vol. 4, 142. The Chamberlain's accounts mention a Master Jay of Selston, Notts., who may have been the brother of Alice Jay.

[2] *Narrative of the Gunpowder Plot* (ed. Morris, 1872), 297.

to be called 'the free school of Nottingham',[1] and its Master, elected by the Guardians of the school, along with the Mayor, aldermen and Council, was to be a 'man of good and honest conservation'. He was charged carefully to educate the pupils in religion and to observe annually in the church of Our Lady on 16 June, the feast of the translation of St Richard, the obiits of Richard Mellers and later of Alice herself. Every morning schools were to open with the recital in a 'high voice' of the whole *Credo in Deum Patrem*.

The first master was John Smith, the parson of Bilborough. He and his successors retained the devout customs laid down in the charter until the accession of Elizabeth I. Brian Garnet, the school's fifth master, was a classical scholar, a conformist in practice but a Catholic by conviction.

Nottingham fell within the northern Province of York. Nicholas Heath, who had been translated from Rochester to York in January 1555, was tolerant, gentle, religious and firm. Persecution had never been to his liking and he had successfully put every obstruction in the way of making martyrs of men and women for their conscientious beliefs. On the accession of Elizabeth I he had been imprisoned. When on 28 April 1559 the revision of the book of Common Prayer became law, Nottingham was among the first towns to be visited by the commissioners appointed to enforce the new worship. Those who declined to conform in the parish of St Mary's were few. Both in the town and the country, and in the parts of Derbyshire, like Heanor, bordering on Nottingham, there was no opposition; only the peak district of Derbyshire held out vigorously for the old faith. In this atmosphere Brian Garnet conformed, and with him his son Henry and his daughters.[2]

On 24 August 1567 Henry Garnet, with twenty-two others, was elected a scholar of Winchester on the Foundation.[3] At the time he was eleven years old on his last birthday; but as he was low on the roll, twentieth out of twenty-three, he was not admitted until exactly a year later, on 24 August 1568. He was then over twelve, but not yet thirteen, years old.

Among the schools founded in the fifteenth century Winchester was the

---

[1] *Records of the Borough of Nottingham*, vol. 3, 453–6.

[2] The recusants of Nottingham, however, did not forget the association of Garnet with the city. During the year 1623–4, when Catholics were allowed an unwonted freedom, it was reported that Garnet was venerated as a saint. In the presentations in the borough that year (under the date 19 January 1624) there is the following entry: 'It was reported by Master Foxe, in Saint James' Lane, and his wife to some of our jury that there is an altar made with diver idolatrous pictures upon it; and we intreat that it may be severely looked unto and sharply punished; and with a picture of a profane traitor [viz. Henry Garnet] that was executed in the Gunpowder treason and, as they said, was canonised for a saint.' (*op. cit.*, vol. 4, 389).

[3] T. F. Kirby, *Winchester Scholars* (1888), 141.

last to accept the change in religion. Too little is known about Brian Garnet's beliefs even to guess his motives in sending Henry there rather than to Eton. Although there is no recorded association between the Garnet family and the school, he may well have known the headmaster, Christopher Johnson, a Derbyshire man from Kedleston. Possibly Winchester's high reputation for scholarship and its Catholic sympathies determined his choice. Indeed, six years before Garnet's election there had been a riot in the school, and the then headmaster, Thomas Hyde, had been imprisoned for his refusal to accept the new religion. 'A most fierce hater of vice and a capital enemy to sects and heresies',[1] he had the esteem of the boys, who refused the summons of his successor, the poet Christopher Johnson, to chapel for a sermon and shut themselves up in the dormitories. 'When the headmaster found fault with their disobedience', writes Nicholas Sanders,[2] who was on the staff with Hyde, 'the boys asked if he wished to destroy the souls of the innocents.' They remained obstinate and Johnson was compelled to call in the military commander from the 'nearest seaport', Portsmouth, to restore order. Either from fear of retaliation or from loyalty to their religion, 'about twelve boys took to flight'.[3]

Winchester remained strongly Catholic into the second decade of the reign. Hyde's example endured. On his escape from prison many of the masters and pupils later followed him into exile.[4] Christopher Johnson, his successor, was a person of parts and a gentleman; and it was under him that Garnet passed his years at the college. A brilliant teacher, he produced a series of excellent scholars for the universities and inspired in Henry Garnet an interest both in classics and the sciences. Johnson himself was a Latin poet, the best of his period,[5] but his chief pride was his medical work. 'All the time he could get at vacant hours, he spent on his beloved study of physic, which he practiced in the city of Winchester, but not to the neglect of the school.'[6] An author himself, he formed a generation that was prolific and varied in its

---

[1] A. Wood, *Athenae Oxonienses* (ed. Bliss 1813), vol. 1, 695.

[2] *Dr Nicholas Sanders' Report to Cardinal Moroni* (1561) in *C.R.S.*, vol. 1, 44–5.

[3] *Ibid.*

[4] Hyde, whom John Pits (*De Illustribus Angliae Scriptoribus*, Paris, 1619) praises for his strict life, lived first at Louvain and then at Douai, where he died on 9 May 1597. Of the eighteen Catholic writers on the Continent who wrote in defence of their faith in the years Garnet was at school, ten were Wykehamists; their combined output (apart from new editions) was thirty-one books; the leaders among them were Thomas Stapleton, Nicholas Sanders and Thomas Harding.

[5] *Poetis omnibus coaetaneis facile antecelluit:* he easily surpassed all his contemporary poets. F. Tanner, *Bibl. Brit.*, 442.

[6] A. Wood, *op. cit.*, vol. 1, 660.

literary output. Apart from Latin poems, he wrote a medical treatise on the plague, and another entitled *Whether a Man for Preservation may be purged on the Dog-days or no?* From him Garnet learnt to be industrious with his pen during his own 'vacant hours', and acquired also a scientific curiosity which, had his life followed a different course, might have made him eminent as an astronomer.

The second strong influence on Garnet at Winchester was Thomas Stempe, the warden, a man with a national reputation for his skill in music, both vocal and instrumental.[1] He had charge of the cathedral choristers and it was thanks to him that Garnet developed his appreciation of music and love of the sung liturgy. Stempe had no difficulty in conforming to the new religion: he remained in office until his retirement.

Shortly before Garnet left the school, Christopher Johnson resigned as headmaster in 1571 in order to become a physician in Winchester. Before relinquishing his post he left in Latin hexameters a description of life at Winchester during his headmastership.

The peal of bells for rising was rung at five o'clock; half an hour later the boys assembled in chapel for prayers. At six o'clock they were in school. Breakfast was at nine and at eleven middle school, followed by dinner at midday. Afternoon school was from two o'clock until five, when all, including the Warden, Fellows and Masters went *circum* in the cloisters; supper was then taken and at eight o'clock the day closed with evening chapel. On Wednesday and Thursday were morning 'hills', Friday was flogging morning. The order had changed little from the days of foundation and was to remain unaltered for a long period.[2]

Little is known about Garnet's schooldays. From his later career it can be assumed that he was an able scholar. In his last year he was a 'prepositor' with certain responsibility for the supervision of the studies and behaviour of junior boys. Mathematics and science, in which Garnet became more than competent and might have become eminent, appear not to have been taught in any form at this time: at best the knowledge that he acquired at school would have been scanty and derived from the teaching of the Roman classics. But there is little doubt that, thanks to his father, he received the best education then available in England. Moreover, true to the school motto, *Manners Makyth Man*, he was educated in moral uprightness that even his enemies acknowledged. Although his most bitter detractors

---

[1] Walter P. Smith, *Henry Garnet, Wykehamist, Jesuit, Traitor?* (Winchester, no date), 7.

[2] Walter P. Smith, *op. cit.*, 7–8; A. F. Leach, *A History of Winchester College* (1899), 272.

attempted, as will be seen, to denigrate him, he was perhaps the most moral and saintly of the alumni. There was nothing violent or headstrong about him, although certain of his calumniators, after his death, as part of the national campaign to vilify him, invented tales about his outrageous and immoral conduct at school; tales that have been rebutted by all historians of the College.

If the tradition is true that Elizabeth I visited Winchester in 1570, Garnet would have been among the boys who welcomed her; but unfortunately there is no record of the visit beyond an entry in the bursar's books that on the order of the vice-warden, the sum of seven shillings and fourpence was paid for refreshments for the royal minstrels. The fullest statement on Garnet's career at this time comes from Fr Thomas Stanney, a Jesuit who served under him in England. 'He was the prime scholar of Winchester College,' wrote Fr Stanney, 'very skilful in music and playing upon instruments, very modest in his countenance and in all his actions, so much so that the schoolmasters and wardens offered him very great friendship, to be placed by their means in New College, Oxford.' He adds, probably basing himself on conversations he had with Garnet, 'Two of them [the schoolmasters] were Catholics at heart, to wit, Dr Stempe and Dr Johnson, and the other who was there, Dr Bilson, was not at that time malicious.'[1] Possibly it was these men who influenced Garnet in his decision to become a Catholic. It is said[2] that he was in 'high favour' with his masters, who responded to his friendly disposition and high ability; and that both Stempe and Johnson took an exceptional interest in their promising pupil.

It was probably at the close of 1571 that Garnet left Winchester. In October 1570 Robert Horne, a Marian exile from Zurich, now Bishop of Winchester, began his visitation of the College. He had already purged Corpus Christi, Christ's and St John's College, Cambridge, of the old religion. When he arrived on 25 October 1570 twelve boys, including Henry Garnet, were absent.[3] Perhaps owing to the intervention of Christopher Johnson, the Bishop pardoned their non-attendance; but they were commanded to appear before him on 25 August following. This they did. Six weeks later, on 7 October 1571, Horne issued injunctions based on his findings at the visitation. The abuses he attempted to stop show the strength of Catholic sympathy in Winchester in Garnet's schooldays. Henceforth no one who had been compelled to leave Oxford for his attachment to

[1] Stonyhurst, Grene *P.*, 580

[2] M. Tanner *Soc. Jesu usque ad sanguinis profusionem militans* (Prague, 1675), 65.

[3] This was a large proportion of the school, for William of Wykeham's foundation was for seventy scholars.

Catholicism could accept the hospitality of the college. Any scholar who received from friends abroad letters encouraging him to become a Papist and failed to inform the authorities, was to be instantly expelled; and likewise all scholars, fellows and boys visiting any Papist household in the city. All Catholic relics, statues and books were to be destroyed; frequent sermons were to be preached to the boys denouncing the Pope. In Chapel scholars were no longer to turn to the place where the high altar had once stood at the moment when the *Gloria Patri* was sung at the end of each psalm.[1]

After these injunctions had been promulgated, Christopher Johnson retired from the headmastership. At the same time there was an exodus of scholars. Between September 1570 and the close of 1571 thirty-two new scholars, rather more than half the total number of the school, were admitted. As Garnet's name no longer appears on the register, it can be presumed that he left at the same time as Johnson.

The fact that Garnet did not go up to New College, the normal course for a Winchester scholar, is explained by his doubts on religion. 'No one', he wrote twenty years later,[2] 'could enter a university unless he was or pretended to be a heretic.' Moreover, in 1570, during his last year at school, his brother, Richard Garnet, had been compelled to relinquish his fellowship at Balliol.[3] The commissioners for religion had been at work in the University and had summoned before them all 'that smelt of Popery or were Popishly affected, suspending imprisoning or expelling them'.[4] Tanner says that on leaving Winchester Henry was reconciled to the Church, but had not yet determined to become a priest. On the recommendation of his former headmaster, he was taken into employment by Richard Tottel, Johnson's publisher and the best known legal printer in England. For three years he acted as Tottel's 'corrector for the press', an apprenticeship which later stood him in good stead and gave him a sense of accuracy in statement that is marked throughout his long correspondence. Moreover, under Tottel

---

[1] New College, which also remained staunchly Papist, was given similar injunctions: *Neque socii, scholares aut ministri chori se convertant in Divinis, more Papistico, ad orientem cum cantatur* Gloria Patri. Neither fellows, scholars nor choristers should turn to the east after the manner of Papists, when the *Gloria Patri* is sung.

[2] H. G. to C. A. 25 May 1590. F.G. 651, f. 25.

[3] Richard Garnet later went abroad to study for the priesthood but returned to England before ordination, married in London and later settled at Trottam, near Midhurst. He is later listed among the prisoners in Horsham gaol 'with his wife and poor children'. *C.R.S.*, vol. 22, 107.

[4] A. Wood, *Historia et Antiquitates Universitatis Oxoniensis* (Oxford 1674), vol. 2, 290.

he learned the technicalities of printing which enabled him later to supervise the establishment of his own secret press.

It is not known whether Garnet on leaving Winchester returned to Heanor to visit his parents. It has been suggested that he was immediately compelled to earn his living. This would perhaps imply that his father did not approve of his reluctance to go to Oxford and so declared himself irrevocably a Protestant. While Henry was at Winchester and for some time afterwards his father still taught at Nottingham, for the records of the school seem to indicate that he ceased teaching in 1574, when his son Henry was preparing to go abroad.[1]

Tottel had set up his press under Edward VI and at this time occupied a house and shop known as *The Head and Star* within Temple Bar between the gates of the Temple in Fleet Street. He had held in succession all the principal offices in the Stationers' Company, of which he was a founder member. Although he dealt mainly in books of law — he possessed a lucrative patent, renewed several times, to print 'all duly authorised books on common law' — he also published in 1557 the first literary anthology in the English language. It was known as *Tottel's Miscellany*, and was followed by others. The first Miscellany included two hundred and seventy-one poems, all of them unpublished. Among them were forty poems of Henry Howard, Earl of Surrey, ninety-six poems of Sir Thomas Wyatt; others were by Thomas Lord Vaux and John Heywood, father of the eccentric Jesuit Jasper Heywood.[2] Thus in Tottel's offices or at his table, Garnet met many distinguished persons in the London world of letters and law. Frequently he dined there with John Popham[3] who, thirty-five years later as the Lord Chief Justice was to pronounce sentence of treason on him. 'There', recalled Garnet, 'I dined often with him and told him that I was beginning the law.' At the time Garnet could not have suspected that his fellow-guest would attain eminence, for Popham was then already forty. He had recently reformed his conduct and was living down a reputation for a dissolute life. In his youth he had been 'as skilful a man at sword and buckler as any in that age and wild in his recreation'.[4] Now in early middle life, he was an industrious lawyer. Being 'a strong, stout' man, as Aubrey says,[5] he 'could endure to sit at it all his life'. The two, both then and later, could not have

[1] Adam W. Thomas, *A History of Nottingham High School* (1958), 30, 273

[2] Jasper Heywood (1535–98): page of honour to Princess Elizabeth, later fellow of Merton (1554) and All Souls (1558); he became a Jesuit at Rome in 1562. He contributed poems to the *Paradyse of Daynty Devices* (1576).

[3] H. G. to Anne Vaux. *S.P.D. James I*, vol. 19, no. 11.

[4] John Aubrey, *Brief Lives* (1813 ed.), vol. 2, 492.

[5] *Ibid.*

been more contrasted in temperament and appearance: Garnet a slender, gentle and delicate young scholar, Popham 'a coarse, huge, heavy, ugly man'. Only in the keenness of their intellect was there any resemblance, and in their industry. Both now were at the beginning of their careers, for Popham's advancement dates from these years. When he became Attorney-at-Law in 1571, he celebrated his promotion with a feast and fine old Gascony wine. That year also, in the Parliament that was so critical of the old religion, Popham was returned as member for Bristol. He had now set out on the way of royal favour; the same year also he was appointed Privy Councillor. There was no doubting his acumen, which, ironically, was best illustrated in Garnet's trial. Even the Attorney-General, Sir Edward Coke, another actor in the trial, excepted him from the sneer he levelled at his legal contemporaries, including Francis Bacon.

The proceedings of the Parliament in the seventies brought Garnet to the decision to quit the country and return only as a priest. It was a step already taken by many of his most distinguished predecessors at Winchester. The Bull *Regnans in Excelsis*, excommunicating the Queen, had laid down that it was no longer permissible for Catholics to attend the services of the established religion. As the Parliamentary journalist, Sir Simonds D'Ewes noted: 'Most of the Papists of England did come to our Church and heard the divine service until the eleventh year of the Queen, when the Bull of Pius Quintus enforced not only their wilful obstinate separation, but drew in and necessitated many of these laws that were afterwards made against them.'[1] The new enactments of Parliament were discussed at Tottel's table by Popham: they constituted the Queen's reply to Pius V. Henceforth Catholics who held to their religion were termed 'recusants' for their refusal to go to church quarterly and Communion annually, and paid instead a fine amounting to a hundred marks.[2] Only one strong voice was raised against the measure in the House of Commons. Edward Aglionby, member for Warwick, argued that no positive human law could enforce conscience, which was not to be constrained even by the greatest monarchy in the world.[3] It was a noble plea for toleration, but it received no support. The bill had episcopal approval, at least by silence, and became law on 25 May 1571.

For three years at least Garnet remained with Tottel. It was probably early in 1575 that he decided to seek admission into the Society. At the time there was no Jesuit in England; but it has been reported, by papers sent from France, that Thomas Wodehouse, the first priest to be executed in London

---

[1] Sir Simonds D'Ewes, *Journal of all the Parliaments of Elizabeth* (1682), 30.
[2] This is reckoned at roughly £66 in current money.
[3] Sir Simonds D'Ewes, *op. cit.*, 177.

under Elizabeth, had been accepted as a Jesuit. In a letter written many years later there is a suggestion that Garnet may have been influenced by this priest's example. 'I happened to be in London at the time of his martyrdom', he wrote,[1] 'and I heard it said by many Catholics there and elsewhere that when in prison he was received into the Society by the Provincial of Paris.' Certainly Wodehouse's death and the report of his being a Jesuit was widely discussed.[2] Anyhow, Garnet made straight for Rome instead of going first to Douai, an unexpected course to take during the first twelve months that the newly-ordained men from Allen's seminary were working in England. With him went Giles Wallop, a fellow-Wykehamist who had passed from school to New College. Sailing to Portugal, they made their way overland via Compostella to Rome, which they reached in the late summer.[3]

[1] H. G. to C. A., 11 March 1601. Stonyhurst, *Anglia* 2, 172.

[2] Thomas Wodehouse, a Marian priest was executed at Smithfield on 19 or 20 June 1573. He was notorious in London for the simple, fearless and abrupt profession of his faith. On one occassion he had been set in the stocks for refusing to uncover his head when a Protestant said grace; when asked by Burghley whether he would become his chaplain he agreed on condition that the Treasurer did not himself attend his Mass. From his prison he wrote letters to persons of distinction (exhorting them to submit to the Pope), tied the letters to stones and dropped them from his cell into the street below.

[3] H. G. to Robert Persons, 2 June 1601. Stonyhurst, Grene *P.*, 553

2
ROME

On 11 September 1575 Henry Garnet entered the novitiate of the Society of Jesus at Sant' Andrea, Rome. He was then twenty-one years old or near his twenty-first birthday.

The novitiate of the Roman Province was situated across the street from the summer palace of the Popes on the Quirinal Hill. Ten years before Garnet's arrival charge of the small parish church there had been given to the Jesuits by the Bishop of Tivoli. Attached to the church was a small house which Francis Borgia, then General of the Society, used for the convalescence of sick priests from the city, its high position, exposed to breezes from the campagna, being considered beneficial to their health. The following year, 1556, the Duchess of Tagliacozzo, mother of Marco Colonna, presented to Borgia part of a large adjoining house with its garden, a gift which made it possible for him to move to Sant' Andrea from the Gesù as many novices as the house would contain. When Garnet joined the community in 1574 the novitiate was well established and under the direction of a Roman Jesuit, Fabio di Fabiis.

Garnet's arrival is noted thus:[1] 'Garnet, an Englishman, came on the eleventh day of September 1575 and was examined as an "indifferent".' This last phrase refers to his preliminary interview with four priests who, after conversation with the candidate, gave their views on his suitability for the life he proposed to undertake. At this time and for many years later the applicant was asked whether, at the end of his novitiate, he would be prepared at the decision of his superiors to become a lay-brother or to study for the priesthood. On his agreement he was described as *indifferens*, or indifferent to his grade in the Society. The entry concerning Garnet adds that there was nothing to impede his admission; he was considered a good candidate and in his previous career had incurred no canonical obstruction to priestly orders.

It was customary for newcomers, on the day following their arrival, to

[1] Archives of the Roman Province S.J., 171 A, f. 38, no. 306.

11

sign an inventory of their clothes and possessions, which were then put in the custody of the Minister, who would return them to the candidate if he should fail to persevere in the noviceship. Then after ten days or more as the guest of the house he was accepted as a novice. The register states that Garnet had arrived in a cloak and an old worn pair of brown seaman's trousers with a second pair of rough blue material. The list of his belongings includes among other trivial objects a felt hat, two shirts, a pair of red stockings, another brown pair, and an embroidered vest of black fustian. Apart from his own statement that he made his way to Rome through Portugal and Spain, no details of Garnet's journey are known. The Minister's book[1] suggests that he had travelled roughly and lightly, spending on food and lodgings whatever money he had saved during his last year with Tottel. When candidates arrived on horse, an exact note was made of the charges for stabling it and the sum realised later by its sale. Garnet had come on foot, perhaps begging part of his expenses in the manner of a poor pilgrim. All he had in his pocket was twenty pence, the balance of a small sum given to him by a Jesuit on his reaching Rome.

Fr Fabio di Fabiis, the novice-master who gave Garnet the black clerical habit in exchange for an assortment of coloured garments he left in the wardrobe at Sant' Andrea, was one of the more remarkable Jesuits of his day. To the end of his life Garnet revered him as a saint and, no matter how preoccupied with the business of the English mission, found time to correspond with him. The man's sanctity had a universal appeal, and there was magic attached to his name. He belonged to the most ancient Roman family, and it was acknowledged that he was last in direct line of descent from the famous Roman general, Quintus Fabius Cunctator, who had fought Hannibal to a stalemate in the second Carthaginian war. Immediately Gregory XIII learnt that Fabio had taken his vows as a Jesuit, the Pope proposed that he should be released from his undertaking in order to continue his family. Fabio refused.

Fabio himself had been a novice with St Stanislaus Kostka and Fr Claudio Aquaviva, the General of the Society. It was through the introduction of Fabio that Garnet soon formed with Aquaviva a close personal friendship that was to be his main source of strength during his twenty years in England. Both priests, the Neapolitan General and the Roman novice-master were to outlive their English friend by many years. Fabio died nine months after Aquaviva, on 12 February 1615. He was returning from a pilgrimage to St Paul's-outside-the-walls, when he was attacked and gored by a bull on the Via Ostia. Several messages and an extract from a single letter[2] written

[1] *Ibid.*   [2] Stonyhurst, Grene *P.*, 554

in May 1602 are all that survive from a frequent exchange of news between Fabio and Garnet.

Fabio's novices were drawn from every nation and class in Europe, and he appears to have won the esteem of them all. Several were older than Garnet; many, from Poland, Austria and eastern Germany, had been attracted by the preaching of Peter Canisius. Every month, particularly in the weeks before Christmas, young men came to Sant' Andrea seeking admission into the Society; for instance, on 20 November there arrived Paul Boxa from Sluck in Ruthenia. He was already in minor orders but, nevertheless, along with his copy of *The Imitation of Christ*, he carried sword and dagger.[1] More typical perhaps was Simon Nikowski, from Lobzenica, a Master of Arts at Cracow, with a load of spiritual books in his saddle-pack.

Less than two months after Garnet's arrival came another Englishman, clothed similarly to him, but rather more expensively, with a fair sum in cash and a copy of Cicero's *Officia*.[2] This was William Weston, from King's School, Canterbury and Christ Church, Oxford. He had left the University in the same year as Campion, and for a time had been a member of Lincoln's Inn. Scholarly, gentle and friendly, he closely resembled Garnet, who was five years his junior. Later, for a few important weeks, he was to be Garnet's Superior in England; then, after his capture, Garnet's subject for eighteen years. Soon after his entry into Sant' Andrea he also formed a great affection for Fabio. In a moment of crisis in England, when Garnet's enemies attempted to estrange him from his former fellow-novice, Weston recalled their days together at Sant' Andrea and the ties that united them. 'There was never a man', he wrote,[3] referring to Garnet, 'to whom I was more closely united in bonds of peace and friendship. . . . I will say nothing of our noviceship together, when in the same city, at the same time, in the same house of Sant' Andrea, under the same teacher, we had set before us the same ideals we share today in common.'

Robert Persons was already a novice of three months' standing when Garnet entered.[4] Before the close of the year, they were joined by William Holt and Thomas Stephens. Holt, the 'Fr William' of Garnet's letters, was to tutor Prince James in Edinburgh and later become the agent for the English Jesuits in the Netherlands. Stephens,[5] from Bushton in Wiltshire, was

[1] Archives of Roman Province S.J., 171 A, f. 38.

[2] *Ibid.*

[3] Stonyhurst, *Anglia* 2, 34: Weston to Fr Oliver Manares 27 March 1598. Cf. *William Weston*, 250.

[4] Archives of Roman Province S.J., 171 A, f. 35.

[5] Cf. 'Thomas Stephens, 1549–1619' by Georg Schurhammer in *The Month*, April 1955, 197–210.

the first Englishman known to have reached India via the Cape, a brilliant missionary whose writings are still among the classics of the Murathi language. This was the year of jubilee and it brought yet other Englishmen to Rome before its close. Persons, reflecting later on the large entry from England into Sant' Andrea that year, wrote:[1]

'And so upon the year of jubilee, which was 1575, met and entered at Rome divers at one time, as by name Persons, Henry Garnet, William Weston, William Holt, all Oxford men[2] and afterwards employed in the mission of England. Thomas Stephens also, a painful and fruitful labourer in the East Indies, and John Lane, Master of Arts of Corpus Christi College, Oxford,[3] and of great expectation, that died afterwards at Alcala in Spain. Gallop, fellow of New College, that died in Rome:[4] all which, I say, coming as it were together from divers parts and joining in that resolution to abandon the world and all hopes thereof, and to follow our Lord Jesus in that his Society, gave a certain abodement to all men of some matter of importance to ensue. And so did Fr Campion write from Prague in divers letters unto Fr Persons in Rome that had advertised him of their number and entrance together in the Society.'

While Persons saw 'abodement' for his country in the large group of English novices, Campion, then at Prague, observed:[5] 'You are seven; I congratulate you; I wish you were seventy times seven. Considering the goodness of the cause, the number is small.'

The manner of training novices was already well established by custom and legislation. At Sant' Andrea the two years of prayer, housework and ascetical reading that constituted the novices' routine was interrupted by four so-called experiments, designed to test the aptitude and character of candidates for the Society.[6] Usually, in his first twelve months the novice followed the *Spiritual Exercises* of Ignatius in total seclusion for a period of four weeks. It was then that the ideals intended to guide his conduct in life were first set before him. The effects of this 'experiment' can be seen time and again in Garnet's letters, and most of all in his behaviour during the last three critical months of his life. Any construction put on his speech

---

[1] *Fr Persons' Memoirs*, in *C.R.S.*, vol. 2, 191–2.

[2] Persons is wrong in stating that Garnet had studied at Oxford.

[3] John Lane, scholar and fellow of Corpus Christi, Oxford; a fellow-convert of Persons, whom he accompanied to Padua with the intention of studying law, he entered Sant' Andrea on 2 February 1576 and died at D'Alcaba, Spain, in 1578.

[4] Giles Gallop died in Rome in 1579.

[5] Campion to Persons, 25 June 1577. Cf. Richard Simpson, *Edmund Campion* (1867), 85.

[6] In so far as circumstances allow, these tests continue unchanged today.

and action at his trial and death must take into account the *Exercises* which he learnt first from Fr Fabio. Much depended during this month on the direction of his novice-master, who used this period of retreat to get intimate knowledge of Garnet and instruct him in the practice of prayer, in which he himself, through long experience of dryness and desolation, had become an acknowledged master in Rome.

After this 'retreat', or sometimes before it, the novices were assigned an exercise or 'experiment' in the catechetical instruction of children. Usually it was carried out in one of the poorer parishes of the city. In groups of two or three they went out from Sant' Andrea twice a week and put themselves at the service of the parish priest. For men like Garnet, still imperfect in the Italian language, it was a test also of their humility, for Roman children would laugh at the faulty accent of their foreign preceptors. More intense and indeed testing was the hospital 'experiment' assigned to the second year of noviceship. For a period of a month or more the novices acted as servants in the hospital belonging to the Arch-confraternity of the Holy Trinity, which cared chiefly for pilgrims and permanent convalescents, and was situated off the Piazza Farnese in the via Regola.[1] A few years after the time of Garnet's novitiate, the Englishmen, during this 'experiment' lodged at the neighbouring English College in the via di Monserrato. From there they went daily to the hospital to nurse the sick, doing, according to their instructions, all the most menial and distasteful tasks.

Before Christmas 1576 Garnet received news of the death of his brother John. Apart from the entry in the register of St Laurence's Church, Heanor — 'John, the son of Brian Garnet, was buried on the XIX day of June' (1576) — nothing is known of him. Six months later his father died and was likewise buried at Heanor on 21 December.[2]

During their second twelve months at Sant' Andrea, the novices in groups of three were sent on pilgrimage to some distant shrine. Every morning the novice in charge of his brethren opened his sealed orders for the day. Often in the winter they begged their board and food. Every member of the company in turn took the part of leader. Men who had not the physical strength for the journey were given instead the task of begging in the streets of Rome. In this way they were tested in the lessons they had learnt from their reading of ascetical writers. While there is no record of Garnet's life at this time, two enduring effects of these experiments are perhaps traceable later: first, a lifelong interest in the catechism, which led him to translate from the

[1] Cf. Archives of the Roman Province S.J., 171 A: under entry for Albert Mroshowski, 3 December 1574

[2] An unprinted register in the parish church of St Laurence, Heanor.

Italian a standard catechetical book for the use of English Catholics and, secondly, after his appointment as Superior of the English mission, a constant concern for the health of the priests working under him.

At the end of two years at Sant' Andrea, Garnet, on 12 September 1577, was received into the Society. Immediately he began his studies for the priesthood at the Roman College, a seminary founded by St Ignatius in 1551. For the last seventeen years it had occupied a bleakly functional brick building, a former monastery, now adjoining the Church of Sant' Ignacio. It had little money and few endowments, and the life of the Jesuit students was hard. In 1560, the first year in these new premises, one hundred and fifty young Jesuits lived and studied in the College, while another six hundred students, quartered elsewhere in the City, followed the courses it provided. By 1577 the extern students numbered several thousands. Already, after the ancient universities, it was recognised as the most celebrated educational establishment on the Continent. It combined school, university and seminary; boys learning the rudiments of grammar entered along with young men studying for doctorates; every nation in Europe was represented and the teachers were men of international reputation: *intra pusillam domum mundi quasi compendium*:[1] a microcosm within the walls of a small house. The Roman College, moreover, set a pattern for other seminaries in the city. Gregory XIII, in the year Garnet began his ecclesiastical studies, established also a Greek College and another for convert Jews and infidels. The English College followed in 1579, the Marionite College in 1582. As well as founding or assisting a number of seminaries in Switzerland and Germany, Gregory also endowed the English seminary at Douai and the Scotch College at Pont-à-Mousson.

Each year Gregory's own benefactions to the Roman College increased and he was rightly considered its second founder. Its professors, often selected by the Pope himself, were the best in Europe. In 1577, the staff included Suarez, Bellarmine, Vasquez and Pereira, great men by any intellectual measure, besides many lesser celebrities drawn from every Province of the Society.

Along with fundamental metaphysics and logic, the course in the first year included mathematics, which at this time embraced astronomy, physics and geography. Garnet's ability in the sciences caught the notice of his teacher, perhaps the most brilliant mathematician in Europe, the German Jesuit, Fr Christopher Clavius. Aristotle's *De Coelo* and *Meteorologica* were no more than texts that he used to expound his own theories of the universe. By now Clavius had been teaching for over ten years; and already there had

[1] *Historia Societatis Jesu* (1620), pars. 2, 225.

passed through his lecture room a generation of Jesuits, including the celebrated Matteo Ricci, the Mandarin priest, who were to make the Society
famous for its scientific achievements. Ricci had sat under Clavius in 1574,
the year Garnet entered Sant' Andrea. After leaving Rome for the east he
corresponded regularly with his former master.

Joining the same class two years later, Garnet succeeded to Ricci's
favoured position. Although he and Clavius became close friends, there is
no extant correspondence between them;[1] nor is there any direct reference
to Clavius in Garnet's numerous letters written from England to friends in
Rome. Garnet's precision of mind and his intellectual curiosity made him
an ideal pupil. It was the decade in which Galileo attained fame by his skilful
development and use of the telescope. When astonishing discoveries were
made with this instrument concerning the appearance, composition and
movement of the heavenly bodies, Clavius encouraged the young Galileo,
who was only twenty-three when they first met; later he used his great
influence in Rome to protect him there and eventually to secure the acceptance of his views in the learned world of Europe. Clavius at this time was
completing his own calculations on which Gregory XIII was to base his
reform of the Julian Calendar.[2]

From his first year at the Roman College, Garnet, with the rest of the
pupils, took part in the regular weekly 'disputations' conducted by the students under the supervision of their professor. This scholastic debate, confined in the Middle Ages to theological questions, was now extended and
adapted to deal with the new sciences. It served both as a useful repetition
of the subject taught in the classroom and as an instrument to develop
talent for public speaking. It was also an exercise in self-control. Perhaps it is
not fanciful to trace in the accounts of Garnet's own defence at his trial
something of the Roman manner of debate, accurate and rigid in its pro-
cesses of establishing truth but unsuited to the cut and thrust of an English
court determined to secure, at all costs, a prisoner's condemnation.

After two years of philosophical studies, Garnet in 1579 began his course
of theology. It was the year in which the English College was founded by
Gregory XIII and Cardinal Allen. In the space of the next twelve months
the number of English students attending lectures at the Roman College
more than doubled. It was also a memorable year for Garnet, for he now
received his first introduction to the famous lectures of Robert Bellarmine,

[1] Cf. *Archivum Historicum* S.J., vol. 8, 193–222.
[2] The fifth volume of Clavius's collected mathematical and astronomical works
printed at Mainz, deals with the reform of the calendar; volume four with gnomonics, or
the art of constructing sundials.

who, three years earlier, had been summoned from Louvain by Gregory XIII to fill the chair of Controversy at the Roman College. The first attempt made to establish this course had been unsuccessful and the lecture-ship had lapsed. However, soon after his arrival, Bellarmine made it one of the most important and discussed courses in Europe. Primarily he set out to equip students from Germany, England and other northern countries to hold their own in theological debate, and by means of both the written and the spoken word to refute the ablest Protestant antagonists. Echoes of his instruction can be found in the printed reports of debates held between English priests and Anglican divines, common in the middle years of Eliza-beth's reign, and often an inescapable preliminary of martyrdom. Bellar-mine's gifts as a teacher were so outstanding that the Queen soon gave orders for these public discussions to cease.

In his inaugural lecture given on 26 November 1576 Bellarmine sketched the scope of his course. Since the heresies of the age were for the most part directed against the ninth and tenth articles of the Creed, he proposed to confine himself to them: the first part of his course would deal with Christ as head of the Church and with his vicar, the Pope; then he would pass on to the Church in purgatory and in heaven. At this point he would 'speak of the veneration and invocation of the saints, of relics, sacred images and similar matters'; and pass from there to the communion of the saints and the sacraments, and 'last of all, under the tenth article, to various debatable matters concerning grace, justification, free-will and merit'.[1]

Fr Tanner says that Garnet, after ordination, joined the staff of the Roman College, teaching first Hebrew and Mathematics and then, for two years 'scientific questions' during the absence of Clavius through ill-health; he adds that Aquaviva had destined him to succeed his master should he not recover from his sickness.[2] It is likely therefore that Garnet was ordained not later than 1582.[3]

To the end of his life Garnet acknowledged his indebtedness to his fellow professors at the Roman College. Tanner speaks of the great esteem in which he was held for the simple holiness of his life and of the sorrow his departure for England caused the College. More than once Bellarmine, in writing about Englishmen, expresses a very tender affection for Garnet, who was his penitent and spiritual child. Lecturing in Rome after Garnet's death, he told his students: 'One man, particularly, and a person of importance and,

[1] James Brodrick, *Robert Bellarmine* (1928), vol. 1, 122.

[2] M. Tanner, *Soc. Jesu usque ad sanguinis profusionem militans* (Prague 1675), 65.

[3] Since Garnet's name does not occur in the ordination register of the Roman vicariate, it is possible that he was made priest outside Rome.

moreover, not a priest or Jesuit, or alumnus of a seminary,[1] who was in court near to Garnet himself, told me solemnly, and I readily believe it, that he had it from Garnet himself that he knew nothing of the Gunpowder plot except under the seal of confession.' This, Bellarmine asserted, he was ready to believe because he himself had been associated with Garnet for many years and knew what an upright and innocent man he was, a person also of very great talent and erudition.[2]

There is evidence also that Garnet was esteemed highly by two young Spaniards who had already won international renown, Francesco Suarez and Benedict Pereira. There is no surviving letter between Garnet and these two men. Suarez made Garnet's death the occasion of a famous lecture in which he paid public tribute to his former pupil; Pereira, one of the most assiduous exegetists of his day, particularly in the field of the Old Testament, had considerable influence on him and, a little later, on Robert Southwell also. The two young Englishmen, both in their books and in their letters, used Scripture to advantage, often quoting from memory long passages and drawing from them illustrations at every level of legitimate exegesis.[3]

After landing in England in 1586 Garnet was never to see them again. They are the 'brethren in Rome' whose advice he urges Aquaviva to ask on points of moral theology and canon law whenever he sought an authoritative interpretation. Occasionally there is direct mention of them by a name, more frequently he sends his greetings to 'all his friends in Rome', thanks them for their interest in the English mission and begs their prayers.

[1] The reference is to Sir Tobie Mathew.
[2] R. Bellarmine, *Apologiae*, cap. 13.
[3] Southwell's translations from Scripture are particularly beautiful, and make an interesting comparison with Campion's. It is easy to understand the sense of regret experienced by Gregory Martin when these two Englishmen were lost to him as translators of the Douai Scriptures.

3

THE ROAD TO LONDON

On 8 May, the feast of St Michael Archangel, Garnet left Rome for England in company with Robert Southwell, six years his junior.[1] Southwell had entered Sant' Andrea three years after Garnet and had been a fellow novice with Simon Hunt, once Shakespeare's schoolmaster at Stratford. While studying for the priesthood at the Roman College he had lived at the newly-founded English seminary, and had acted there, both before and after ordination, as tutor in philosophy. He was now two years a priest and his request to be sent to England had come at the time Aquaviva was being pressed by Allen and Persons to send his best English subjects back to work in their own country. Weston supported their plea. Writing from London in April 1586, he had urged the need for more priests: 'If we were given freedom to preach and teach publicly, I believe we should hardly see a thousand heretics left within a year.... Pray send men to help us and someone to take charge. Then we shall gather in sheaves on sheaves with laden arms. ... But I beg you to examine the men through and through, since the need for prudence is very great.' Reluctantly the General consented, murmuring that he was sending 'lambs to the slaughter';[2] Southwell saw it differently: 'We are two arrows shot at the same mark', he said of himself and Garnet.[3]

Before taking leave of Aquaviva Garnet had been given instructions for his work.[4] Dated 24 March 1586, they supplemented instructions drawn up for Fr Campion and Fr Persons.[5] The fresh recommendations were designed to meet the changed circumstances of the day. The spiritual character of their mission was beyond cavil. In no circumstances were they to 'mix themselves

[1] Southwell was the son of Sir Richard Southwell of Horsham St Faith's, Norwich; his mother was the daughter of Sir Roger Copley of Roughway, Sussex; through Sir Henry Belknap, his mother's great-grandfather, he claimed cousinship with Sir Francis Bacon, Lord Burghley and Sir Edward Coke.

[2] M. Tanner, *op. cit.*, 65.

[3] Christopher Devlin, *Robert Southwell* (1956), 89-90.

[4] Leo Hicks, *Letters and Memorials of Father Robert Persons*, C.R.S., vol. 39, 361-2.

[5] *Ibid.*

in the affairs of state'; they were not even allowed to recount political news in their letters to Rome. In conversation they were to refrain from all talk against the Queen, and were not to permit others to talk against her in their presence. As long as no regular community life was possible in England, the Fathers were to meet as often as conditions allowed. Nothing they did was to endanger Catholics, whose spiritual good was their only concern. Thus they were to dress in laymen's costume, but in a modest and sober manner. Except for Mass and for the administration of the sacraments, the soutane was allowed only when it could be worn with perfect safety. None of the articles prescribed by law under penalty of death — *Agnus Dei*s, rosaries or blessed grains[1] — were to be carried on their person. Both for security and for effectiveness they were to deal, at the start, with the upper classes rather than the common people; converts were to be made first of the entire family and then among its connections and friends. Only in this way, in a hierarchical society, could their work be enduring. They should have as little dealing as possible with heretics: if forced into debate with them, they were to argue, not wrangle, give evidence of charity rather than be caught out using intemperate or biting words. In summary, they were to behave in such a way that it might always be seen that their sole purpose was to gain souls.

In drafting these instructions Aquaviva set the pattern of work for the English Jesuits, and at the same time determined in some measure the shape of the Catholic community for the next two hundred and fifty years. The country houses of the gentry became the churches of the people, each with its congregation, consisting largely of friends, relatives, retainers and servants. Only in London and half a dozen other cities was the organisation different.

Garnet's own work during his twenty years of freedom was inspired by these general instructions. The personal orders given to himself and Southwell are interesting but less important. On their way to England Garnet was to act as Superior; on their arrival both were to place themselves under obedience to William Weston, the only Jesuit then at liberty. Should Weston be captured, Garnet was to succeed him. If ever it became necessary to fly the country they should go where they could, but not to Scotland without

---

[1] *Agnus Dei*: discs of wax impressed with a cross and the figure of a lamb and blessed by the Pope. The *Agnus Dei* was usually worn like a medal round the neck. In origin it goes back to the fifth century and symbolises Christ, the Lamb of the New Testament. The cross associated with the lamb suggests that its purpose was to protect those who wore it from evil influences, as the blood of the paschal lamb protected the households of the Jews from the destroying angel. *Blessed grains* were a form of chaplet or rosary made of cereal seeds or at least of some material so perishable that no examples survive.

consulting the Jesuit Superior there, nor to Ireland without Weston's agreement. On their journey they had faculties to preach and hear confessions, with leave of the local priests; but they were not to create any suspicion about their mission. If necessary, they were to stay away from Jesuit houses, wear lay dress while travelling and sleep in public hostelries.[1] Permission, usually reserved to the General, was given to the Superior to print and publish 'some small books' for the defence of the faith and for 'the edification of Catholics'.

During their two months' journey Garnet and Southwell discussed and perhaps planned the 'small books' which both were shortly to write: Southwell minor masterpieces of prose and a few enduring poems, Garnet some slight apologetical works. There is no letter of Garnet's extant that describes the journey; Southwell, however, recorded their route and incidents on the road. In these and later letters Southwell's poetic temperament is manifest, and from the start of their journey it can be seen how well Garnet understood and nursed it. Probably never again in the story of the counter-reformation in England were there two men who, working together, had such an intimate mutual understanding and became so necessary for each other's best effort. When Southwell was eventually caught Garnet's life manifestly changed. Yet it is clear even from these early letters of Southwell that Aquaviva showed wisdom in his preference of Garnet as Superior. Southwell, true poet and giant-hearted young priest that he was, suffered alternating moods of exaltation and depression; by turns he was excited, alarmed, apprehensive, exhilarated; his reaction to every encounter was deeply personal. Garnet, less sensitive yet always sympathetic, was his perfect friend and leader, dependent on the affection and advice of his companion, and seldom far removed from him for any length of time.

On the morning of 8 May Fr Persons had ridden with them two miles out of Rome to the Milvian Bridge. There he took his leave.[2]

Instead of striking north along the via Cassia to Florence, the two priests made for Ancona in order to visit the shrine of Loretto. Thence they rode to Modena, Parma and Piacenza, and reached Milan at the end of May. From the Jesuit College of Brera Southwell reported their progress in a letter to Rome on 26 May.[3] They had arrived on the eve of Whitsunday and were leaving for Como on the following Tuesday morning. At Modena they had met an English priest, Jonas Meredith, who had lodged there with them at

[1] These last instructions were given to Fr Joseph Creswell and Fr William Holt in writing and orally to Garnet and Southwell. *C.R.S.*, vol. 39, 361–2.

[2] Henry More, *Historia Provinciae Anglicanae* (1660), 182.

[3] R. S. to Fr Alfonso Agazzari, 26 May 1586. *C.R.S.*, vol. 5, 306–7.

the Jesuit College. He had associations with Sir Francis Walsingham, the organiser of the English spy system on the Continent, and was to arrive in England two weeks ahead of the Jesuits. Southwell related innocently that they met him again at Piacenza.[1]

At Milan, if not earlier, they were joined by a Flemish lay-brother, William, who as their guide, servant and interpreter accompanied them the rest of their way to the Channel coast. Probably it was intended that he should arrange their passage to England, for at the time of their leaving Rome it was known there that a special watch for priests had been set on all ships entering England from Continental ports.

Nothing is recorded of their journey from Milan to Flanders. Southwell, perhaps recalling these days some years later, mused:[2] 'to the wayfaring pilgrim wandering in the dark and misty night, every light, though never so little, is comfortable; and to the stranger that travelleth in a land of divers languages any that can, though it be but brokenly, speak his country's tongue, doth not a little rejoice him'.

Anxious about the condition of their horses, that had done 'good service' thus far, they left for Como, but 'the sore on William's mount is not yet healed', wrote Southwell, 'and I am afraid for the chestnut, too, which has been galled by the baggage since we left Loretto'.[3]

Garnet was silent. He called at the English seminary in Rheims and there met again Dr William Allen. It was their first conversation since Allen had been in Rome in 1579. From Garnet's later letters it is clear that the financial condition of the seminary was discussed, probably also means of communication between England and Flanders. Then they continued their journey to Douai where Southwell secretly visited the College of the Belgian Jesuits and took his farewell of his friend, the young Flemish priest, John Decker, who seven years earlier had gone with him on foot from Paris to Rome to enter the Society of Jesus.

From Douai they rode together to St Omer, lying some twenty-seven miles back from Dunkerque and Calais and a little further distant from Boulogne: from there it was not more than a morning's ride to all three ports. The two missionaries hoped to remain concealed there until they got word to embark. While they awaited their final instructions based on the latest information of English conditions available in Paris or Rome, Southwell, at Garnet's prompting, wrote on 2 July to John Decker. He began:

'I promised, five days ago, I think, to write to you: and I am doing so now

[1] Devlin, *op. cit.*, 97.
[2] *Epistle of Comfort*, Introduction.
[3] R. S. to Alfonso Aggazzari, 26 May, 1586. *C.R.S.*, vol. 5, 307.

in case there is delay in the post. We have heard nothing of the letters we expected from Rome and this is most inconvenient, for we may have to delay longer than we can safely lie hid. If they do not come, we shall be off on our journey. Meanwhile, I beg of you, do not let any English people know where we are or that we have been there at Douai, until I write to you from the port.'

Both Garnet and Southwell were nervous of discovery by English spies placed at the French ports. Excitedly Southwell repeated to Decker: 'In case any English people should hear of our coming, keep secret at least where we are now; and if they already know that, conceal the reason for it until I write to you again with my own hand.' Then he added: 'Father Henry sends his greetings.'[1]

They did not have to wait long for the expected letters from Rome: their attack was to be frontal like that of Persons and Campion six years earlier. Persons still believed in the principle of making brazenly for the places where the watch was closest, even though in the past year twelve priests had been captured on entering England by the Kentish and Sussex ports. There were already rumours that Southwell had landed with an unknown companion on the Norfolk coast. Fr Meredith, who had ridden with them through Italy, had perhaps given this false information to Gilbert Gifford, an English spy in Flanders. It had reached Walsingham on 3 July. 'There are two Jesuits sent into England', he wrote, 'both very young men, Father Southwell and Father Garnet.'[2]

On 15 July the two priests were told they were to sail the following day. Immediately Southwell despatched his promised letter to Fr Decker. This was the most tense moment of his life: 'the flesh is weak and can do nothing and even now revolts from what is proposed'. Then he stirred himself to confidence in words that echo St Paul: 'He will not fail the challengers who himself has framed the challenge.' He begged his friend to pray for him now that he was 'confronted with death', so that he might either 'usefully escape, or manfully endure it'; he did not dare to hope for what he so ardently desired.[3] Garnet again was silent.

After reciting the first Vespers of the feast of St Alexis, they set sail from Calais at 2 o'clock in the afternoon of 17 July. 'The wind was blowing against us', wrote Garnet in his first letter from England less than two weeks later,[4] 'and we had to use the oars . . . to hold the ship on her course

---

[1] Devlin, *op. cit.*, 98.
[2] *S.P.D. Eliz.*, vol. 18, no. 31.
[3] Devlin, *op. cit.*, 99.
[4] H. G. to C. A. 30 July 1586. F.G. 651, f. 211.

to the point where we proposed to land. However, after sunset the wind changed direction; the sea became calm, the surface undisturbed. We sailed as smoothly as on a river. Shortly before sunrise we reached the [English] coast. Some portent in the weather had led the sailors to expect the change of wind, but we ourselves ascribed it to divine providence; and to some extent the sailors did also, for they asserted that we were good men whom God had been pleased to help on their way. And we escaped a number of freebooters.'

On a high mound overlooking the shore stood a man eyeing the two priests intently.[1] 'Perhaps he was wondering what kind of people we were', says Garnet in the same letter, 'to put in at this unusual point far away from any port: the sight filled us with considerable foreboding.'

Nevertheless the two priests landed. The Flemish lay-brother carried them ashore on his shoulders and then waded back to the boat. The 'point' was probably about a mile east of Folkestone. Garnet is imprecise; he was more concerned with the curious figure on the hill than with the contours of the coast. Then as now, the only place where the steep cliff made a landing possible was the section of the shore less than a mile from Folkestone known as 'the warren'; behind it was some rising ground called Copt Hill that would have hidden their landing from the small fishing village of Folkestone, then no more than a cluster of houses gathered on the site of the present fish-market. As they stepped ashore from the cockboat, Garnet and Southwell would have been seen by no one but the shepherd who, they feared, was a special watcher posted specially against their coming. 'But the die was cast', Garnet decided; and he comforted himself with the reflection that whatever fate awaited them it did not 'hang on turn of the blind forces of darkness, but on the provident disposition of the divine goodness'.[2]

The fear he experienced was fresh in his mind when he wrote to Aquaviva ten days later. Boldly the two priests approached the menacing figure on the hill: they grumbled to him against the ship's captain who had landed them so far away from the port to which he had contracted to take them; they did not know where they were.

The watcher was a simple shepherd, and he showed them sympathy. As Garnet wrote with relief: 'he felt the imagined injury done to us more than we did ourselves: he told us the names of several places in the district; then pointed out our way, and finally swore an oath that he had been as honest with us as he would have been with his own mother and father' had they been in the same distress.[3]

[1] *Ibid.*   [2] *Ibid.*   [3] *Ibid.*

It was Garnet's first piece of good fortune in England. For twenty years he was to have many astonishing escapes from capture. The charm and simplicity of his character had immediately allayed suspicion. Always there was something in his approach to strangers that quickly won him their sympathy. He reflected later: 'We were happy with the result of our first encounter.'

The contrary winds, followed by the calm, had disturbed their first sailing plan. Raising anchor at two o'clock from Calais, they had expected to land about ten hours later on an open beach under cover of darkness.

Fifteen years afterwards Garnet remembered every detail of his first day ashore; he recalled, perhaps for Fr Clavius's interest, the gap of ten days that separated the English from the Gregorian calendar he had followed on the Continent. 'I remember that we said the first vespers of St Alexis (17 July)', he wrote, 'but on the following morning as the sun was rising, we landed on the feast of St Thomas — ten days earlier! Also we were in his diocese between Dover and Folkestone, so we were under his holy protection, though at the time we did not realise it.'[1]

As they walked away from the shore the two priests made their confessions to each other; then, to escape arrest together, they separated. They had decided to meet again as soon as they reached London.[2]

Garnet quickened his step; he imagined he was being followed; he skirted every hamlet on his route, for he told himself that an unseen spy had ridden ahead to raise the alarm in the first populated place through which he would pass. After long empty days of waiting at St Omer his nerves were tense; at sea he had remained apparently self-possessed, while Southwell had betrayed his anxiety. Now, separated from Southwell his self-control briefly deserted him. On their first day in England Southwell showed the greater resourcefulness.

'Avoiding the towns on the coast like the plague', Garnet struck inland; he spoke to no one. After he had covered ten miles he was exhausted and hungry and still anxious. 'I was compelled to rest awhile in some town or other', he says. Deliberately he avoided the inn of the hamlet he happened to be passing and approached a private house. 'There with assumed ignorance I enquired whether or not the town possessed an inn. The answer

[1] July 7 was the feast of the translation of the body of St. Thomas of Canterbury. On this day, 1220, in the presence of Cardinal Stephen Langton, Henry III and Cardinal Pandulf, the papal legate, and of the Archbishop of Rheims, St Thomas's remains were transferred from his tomb in the crypt to a shrine behind the high altar, which for its wealth and beauty soon became one of the most famous in Christendom. It was destroyed in September 1538. On the feast of the translation a great fair was held in Canterbury.

[2] H. G. to C. A. 30 July 1596. F.G. 651, f. 211.

naturally was that I had just passed it.' Feigning simplicity — the same device which saved him earlier that day — he asked the daughter of the house whether she could give him a drink, for he was too fatigued to retrace his steps. He was invited to enter, asked to sit down and answer questions about himself. 'So cleverly and cunningly were the questions put', Garnet wrote, 'that I might have been in a court of law.' Then he recalled how St Paul at Athens, puzzled at first by the persistence of his questioners, had realized of a sudden that his hosts were anxious merely to gather and retail news. Garnet took courage. The girl had no sinister motive; she was simply curious. After a very short while both she and her father put Garnet at his ease. Sustaining the part of a traveller in an unfamiliar district Garnet said he would welcome the chance of returning their hospitality in London in his own father's home, if ever they had occasion to visit the city.

However, something in his speech and in the cut of his clothes almost betrayed him: after more than twelve years abroad he had become a foreigner in his own country; his English accent sounded strange in the ears of his Kentish hosts, his suit had a distinctly foreign look. He was taken first for a Fleming, and asked why he was making for London at a time when 'all stray persons on the road were being intercepted and sent abroad to the wars in Flanders'. The people of Kent were accustomed to strangers: from the beginning of the reign Protestant refugees from the Continent had been welcomed there. In a number of towns Flemings had already set up factories for baize, linen and flannels; with the sack of Antwerp in 1576 there had been many fresh immigrants; by the end of the century Sandwich contained more foreigners than natives. It was a calculated policy, backed by Acts of Parliament, to repair the economy of the county, so severely damaged by the dissolution of the monasteries. Canterbury, which had lived largely on its pilgrim traffic, had suffered most severely; twenty-six wagons had removed the treasures of St Thomas's shrine; the grounds of St Augustine's had been converted into a deer park, the Franciscan friary into a cloth factory. Lambarde,[1] writing of the end of Henry's VIII's reign, says that Kent was then a waste. The appearance of foreigners was common and welcome; Garnet's host was clearly accustomed to them. Unaware of this, Garnet congratulated himself that he had not provoked any suspicion of his priestly character; he continued his journey with a prayer of Moses on his lips: *fiant immobiles sicut lapis, donec pertranseat populus tuus, Domine, populus tuus quem possedisti.*[2]

---

[1] William Lambarde, *The Perambulation of Kent* (1570).

[2] *Let them become immovable as a stone, until thy people, O Lord, pass by: thy people whom thou hast possessed.* Ex. xv, 16.

During the rest of his journey through Kent, St Thomas sheltered him. For many miles around Canterbury all the roads leading to the city were crowded with travellers to St Thomas's fair, and he mingled with them unnoticed. It was then that he realised what feast it was by the English calendar. 'We had St Thomas's protection, though we did not realise it at once. This was the reason for our safe journey — the crowds that flocked to the fair.'[1]

Garnet does not say where he passed his first night as a priest in England. The next morning on the road to Gravesend he was hailed by a gentleman on horseback. It was Robert Southwell. This was the first stretch of highroad Garnet had used; till then he had 'followed tracks which a horse could not negotiate'. They stayed together just long enough to exchange congratulations that 'neither had thus far met with misfortune'. Then Garnet, following Southwell's lead, purchased a horse at the next farm and arrived the same evening at Gravesend. From Gravesend to the Tower Wharf there was a regular service of tilt-boats: Southwell was already on his way up river.

Southwell reached London in the early morning, then anxiously walked the streets until dawn. Garnet followed on a later boat. 'There immediately and to my great joy, I met my companion in the street. For five or six hours we walked about the city but we did not see a single friend. Then by chance we met the man we were looking for'. Their unidentified guide took them to a prison where they breakfasted and immediately afterwards, as Garnet relates, 'we were safely hidden away'. The young Jesuits lay quietly in London until William Weston, 'the person whom above all others we desired to see', was able to seek them out. They could not have reached the city at a more inauspicious moment, nor could they have been more fortunate in meeting Fr Weston, whose careful shepherding saved them from arrest at the very start of their enterprise.

[1] H. G. to C. A., 30 July 1596. F.G. 651, f. 102. For Garnet's route from the coast to Canterbury, see Appendix A, p. 441.

4

HURLEYFORD

THE year 1586 was the severest yet for English Catholics. The worst days followed midsummer, and the climax of those days came almost at the very hour that Garnet and Southwell reached London.

During the previous six months seven priests, all from the seminary at Rheims, had been condemned for their priesthood and executed at Tyburn, York and in the Isle of Wight. On Ladyday, 25 March, Margaret Clitherow had been pressed to death at York. There were two more executions in the last fortnight of July; and another in Gloucester in August. In June a systematic clearance of the London prisons prepared the way for the 'discovery' in August of the Babington plot, which, as Weston saw it, was itself the prelude to the execution of Mary Queen of Scots early the following year. Lists of all Catholics in prison were drawn up for Secretary Walsingham. The priests among them were divided into categories; some 'most dangerous men' were marked for execution, others for transportation abroad, yet others, young still and active, for perpetual internment at Wisbech or Ely castles or one of the newly created prison camps. By the end of July the old prisons were ready to receive their intake of fresh inmates.[1]

Weston in London, like Allen at Rheims and Persons in Rome, knew nothing of the snares set to catch his new subjects. On the day Garnet embarked at Calais, Anthony Tyrrell, a priest who had recently worked with Weston, was arrested and promptly sold his services to Lord Burghley as a spy. On the same day the government made its first organised attempt to seal the English ports against incoming priests; simultaneously all priests inside the country were to be expelled, imprisoned or rendered incapable of work. This very same day also, the government ordered a general search of Catholic houses. In the early morning of the following days pursuivants were roving the London streets in organised bands. Thus Southwell wrote that he 'met with Catholics first amid swords and then in a prison'.[2]

[1] Prisons Lists (Midsummer 1586), *C.R.S.*, vol. 2, 241–78.
[2] R. S. to C. A. 25 July 1586. *C.R.S.*, vol. 5, 307.

On the same fateful 6 July Walsingham drew in his net on the Babington conspirators. For that day the famous letter, allegedly written by Anthony Babington, was despatched to Mary Queen of Scots: the letter which was to implicate her in the Plot and provide the crucial evidence against her at her trial. Its authenticity has often been questioned.[1] It ran:

'Myself with ten gentlemen and a hundred . . . followers will undertake to deliver your royal person from the hands of our enemies. For the despatch of the usurper [Elizabeth] . . . there shall be six noble gentlemen, all my private friends, who . . . will undertake that tragical execution.'[2]

Through Catholics in the Clink prison, Southwell and Garnet found lodgings in a safe inn, known to Weston. On 13 July, Weston met them there. 'We greeted one another', he wrote,[3] 'and had dinner in the same place.' Weston was nervous. He had earnestly petitioned Aquaviva for the despatch of these recruits and was determined at all costs not to risk their safety. The same evening, after dinner, he removed his two charges to a private house, probably Mrs Francis Browne's in Hog Lane, on the boundaries of Bishopsgate and Shoreditch. That same night or the next morning Anthony Babington called there to see Weston. At that moment none of the three priests knew how near they were to arrest: 'I myself might have seen them',[4] wrote Babington later about Southwell and Garnet, suggesting that the two newcomers were in an adjoining room while Weston was speaking with Babington. Weston recorded his conversation, which illustrates both the naivety of the gay young conspirator and his own instinctive caution. Babington was still unaware that he was the prey of Walsingham's duplicity. Weston suspected it; already the Secretary had summoned Babington.[5] 'He asked him many questions about the Queen of Scotland; said he knew every detail of his design, and, if he chose, could reveal many secrets; and he claimed, for instance, certain information that frequent letters had passed between him and the other party. In conclusion, he used threatening words. . . . Finally Walsingham sent him away, very dejected (I think) and anxious over many things.

[1] At this point it is necessary to revert to the old calendar, which was still in force in England. Henceforth the English, not the Continental dating will be used. It was on 16 July N.S. (6 July O.S.) that Garnet sailed from Calais.

[2] *Mary Stuart and the Babington Plot* (ed. J. H. Pollen), Scottish Historical Society (1922), 21–2. It is noteworthy that Southwell, who later gathered inside information about the Plot, learned and believed that this critical letter 'was brought him [Babington] ready penned by Pooley from Master Secretary [Walsingham]'. *Humble Supplication*, 21.

[3] *William Weston*, 69.

[4] *Ibid.*, 75

[5] *Ibid.*, 101.

'A few days passed and he [Walsingham] summoned him again . . . using gentle words to soothe him.' He tried to win him over: for what purpose Weston did not know, since, as he commented, 'I would have thought that he had him already well entangled in his net.'

It was after this second interview with Walsingham that Babington called on Weston, who was then sheltering Southwell and Garnet. Babington had been promised complete freedom from his entanglement on condition that he revealed the whereabouts of the two recently arrived Jesuits. To his credit the offer was rejected. He 'could have seen them': indeed have betrayed them. On his side Weston never forgot his debt to Babington, 'a young man, not yet thirty, good-looking, with a fine presence, quick intelligence, enchanting manners and wit; . . . gallant, adventurous, daring in defence of the Catholic faith in its day of stress and ready for any arduous enterprise whatsoever that might advance the Catholic cause'.[1]

In distress, Weston now gave his friend hard counsel. He told him there was no way he could escape the snare set for him. 'If you accept [Walsingham's] offer', he said, 'you deny your religion; if you hold him off . . . you expose yourself to inevitable death; you cannot dissimulate and waver between the two without endangering your salvation; nor if you did, would you keep for any length of time your Catholic name among Catholic gentlemen.'

This was his argument. There followed a discussion overheard perhaps by Garnet and Southwell in the next room. Babington protested solemnly: 'No man who has ever known me will ever suspect that I am anything but a Catholic, even if occasionally I have acted and spoken rather more freely than I should.'

Weston congratulated him on his loyalty, but was anxious not to inform himself of Babington's schemes. This was the last time he saw him, not, as he said, because he 'was afraid of him or of anything he might do, for he was always a most honourable youth and most faithful to his religion': nor was he apprehensive that Walsingham might 'deflect him to perform the smallest action which would discredit a Catholic'; but it was impossible now for him to consort with Babington and at the same time honour the instructions given him by Aquaviva to keep himself aloof from politics. As he justly remarks, Babington was 'certain to ask my advice on many questions and to give me secret information'.

Surrounded by plotters, yet unacquainted with their designs, Weston was impeccably prudent. After his arrest he was to be examined time and again. Desperately as the Council tried, it could not implicate him on his

[1] *Ibid.*, 99.

conduct during these days. Weston, moreover, succeeded in shielding his recruits. Garnet makes no allusion to his escape, nor in his letters does he refer directly to Babington; Southwell, on the other hand, had much to say about him in his *Humble Supplication*, and after extensive investigation firmly believed in his innocence.

On the morning Weston took his farewell of Babington, he conducted Garnet and Southwell to a friend's house in Buckinghamshire. After five days in London Catholics in the city and the Council as well knew of their arrival. They had no choice but to seek safety, watch events and wait their opportunity for work. 'We have to conceal the fact that we are members of the Society', wrote Garnet in his first letter to Aquaviva, 'lest the whole of Jerusalem be disturbed; such is the opinion people have of us.'[1] Southwell was sensitive to the same atmosphere: 'our coming has marvellously cheered and inspirited Catholics; for previously they were complaining that they were practically deserted by the Society, and they were full of misgivings that their shepherds, dismayed by difficulties, were abandoning a flock that never stood in greater need of their care.'[2]

This was the first and last time the three Jesuits rode together. Although Weston and Garnet had been fellow-novices at Sant' Andrea, their paths had separated after their first two years of training. Garnet passed on to the Roman College, while Weston completed his studies at Cordova and Seville. Doubtless there was much talk about their old friends in Rome, while Southwell, hitherto known to Weston only by name, listened to the recollections.

'Early on the 14th they had taken horse at St Giles-in-the-fields and were riding up the Oxford road to Tyburn. At Brentford they took the left fork by Hounslow Heath, and then across the alluvial meadows of the Colne. With the towers of Windsor on their left, they carried on over the Thames by Maidenhead Bridge; and then by a narrow woody way through the Great Frith, or *fruticea sylva*, studded already with early apples, till they saw the river again at a ford called Hurley.'[3]

It was the district where Weston had worked for the past twelve months and had trusted friends. As their party crossed the river they came in sight of their retreat, a house called Hurleyford,[4] two miles upstream from Marlow, on the borders of Buckinghamshire and Berkshire.[5]

[1] H. G. to C. A. 30 July 1586. F.G. 651, f. 211.

[2] R. S. to C. A. 25 July 1586. *C.R.S.*, vol. 5, 308.

[3] Devlin, *op. cit.*, 113–14

[4] By the reckoning of Leland's Itinerary, Hurleyford was exactly thirty miles from London.

[5] The foundations of the Elizabethan house at Hurleyford can be seen in dry weather

This was the new seat of Richard Bold, of Bold near Prescot, a Lancashire squire, who, like his neighbour Richard Shireburn of Stonyhurst, had never ceased at heart to be a Catholic but had conformed for expediency. Nine years earlier he had been sheriff of Lancashire and had joined the Earl of Leicester's household. About 1584 he had incurred his master's violent hatred. It was then he moved from Lancashire to this new mansion in the Chilterns. There he met Weston. He was now a staunch Catholic.

A large group of friends was gathered at Hurleyford to greet Garnet and Southwell, and among them William Byrd, the Queen's musician, who lived nearby at Harlington; probably also Sir George Peckham of Denham, a cousin of Richard Bold and a brother-in-law of John Gerard, who at this time was studying for the priesthood in Rome. Also in the neighbourhood were James Gardiner of Fulmer, a 'receiver of priests', whose sister was a lady-in-waiting to the Queen; Lord Compton of Woodburn, said by the turncoat, Anthony Tyrrell, to be a man 'greatly influenced' by Weston; William Fitton of Bailes, who recently had been reconciled with his family and was now exchanging letters with Byrd on musical subjects.

Weston does not list them; he refers merely to the 'many gentlemen' who had come there.[1] The only man he does name is William Byrd, who at the time was engaged in setting to music the poems contained in his *Psalms, Sonnets and Songs of Sadness and Piety*. This meeting was the beginning of a lifelong friendship between Byrd and Garnet, himself a keen musician, with a fine singing voice; probably also it gave the poet Southwell an opportunity of making himself familiar with the new forms of English verse then current only in manuscripts.[2]

'Mr Byrd', writes Weston,[3] 'the very famous musician and organist, was among the company. Earlier he had been attached to the Queen's chapel, where he gained a great reputation: he had sacrificed everything for the faith—his position, the court, and all those aspirations common to men who seek preferment in royal circles as means of improving their fortunes.'

[1] *William Weston*, 77.
[2] Devlin, *op. cit.*, 115.
[3] *William Weston*, 71.

---

on the lawn adjoining the present mansion, which dates from the reign of Queen Anne. It is on the Buckinghamshire bank of the Thames, opposite the Berkshire village of Hurley and is probably the house described by Weston in his *Autobiography* (ch. 6). The main course of the river, which flowed in front of the house, was diverted in the eighteenth century by Sir William Clayton, to protect himself from observation by river traffic. In the event of a sudden search by Buckinghamshire magistrates, it was possible to make a quick escape into Berkshire, across the river, where the Buckinghamshire pursuivants had no authority to follow.

D

Some ten days were spent together by the three Jesuits. Never again was there such a long period when Garnet was so carefree and manifestly happy. Less than a month later, he was to take on unaided the burden of the entire mission and, later still, many more exacting responsibilities. Now, for a few packed days he was the gay subject of his Superior, Weston, already a veteran after two years of crowded and intense experience, the intimate of noblemen with Catholic sympathy and of common people with simple and tested faith. 'During these days it was just as if we were celebrating an uninterrupted octave of some great feast. ... We were very happy and our friends made it apparent how pleased they were to have us.'[1]

There was a chapel in the house. Their host, Mr Bold, himself 'a skilled musician', had constructed the organ and had trained his household as choristers and instrumental musicians. Sometimes Garnet sang the daily Mass, probably one of Byrd's three Masses and composed for this occasion.[2] The rest of the day was spent in spiritual ministrations. The three priests by turns preached and heard confessions, which were numerous.[3]

Garnet's achievement was founded on Weston's. At the time of the Hurleyford meeting, Weston appears to have had a premonition that his days of liberty were numbered. What he knew of Babington's schemes was slight; what he feared he could not communicate to his new subjects. On every calculation he must have known that the government would attempt to present him as the principal author of the Plot, which was now to be publicised any day; with so many of his circle already caught in Walsingham's net his chance of escape was slender. Now he made his dispositions for the future. To Garnet and Southwell he unfolded the lines on which their work was to develop. In a few simple words he summarised their long conversations: 'the new arrivals', he says,[4] 'explained the instructions they had brought from Father General in Rome, and, on my side, I told them what I knew about conditions in England. Then we discussed our methods of future work and the prospects that lay before.'

Even from this brief narration it is not difficult to piece together what passed at this conference. Both in his *Autobiography* and in his letters to Rome, Weston had described the condition of the Catholic body who looked to him as their leader. In April 1585 at Mr Wyford's house in Hoxton, just fifteen months earlier, he had presided at the conference of Catholic laymen

[1] *William Weston*, 71.
[2] Byrd's three Masses cannot be dated. It may well have been that during this 'octave' one or more of them was rendered for the first time. E. H. Fellowes, *William Byrd*, 53.
[3] *William Weston*, 71
[4] *Ibid.*

no less momentous than this: there, with the help of Lord Vaux, Sir Thomas Tresham and Sir William Catesby, he had met the crisis provoked by the Act of the previous March, designed 'for the utter extirpation of Popery'.[1] Besides making it treason for a priest ordained overseas to return and minister in England, the Act extended the penalty to include all laymen or women who assisted them in any manner. There at Hoxton it was decided that 'all priests should shift for themselves ... in inns and such-like places'; they were to visit Catholic houses only at the invitation of their owners; a fund was raised for their sustenance and administrators appointed.

For the following twelve months, while the lodging houses throughout the country were searched for priests, many Catholic laymen came forward to shelter priests in their homes and give them a base from which they could continue their apostolate. Now at Hurleyford the number and distribution of these houses was discussed, and plans based on them were made for the conversion of England. It is significant that among the first families to offer help were the Vaux and Catesbys, who at the end, as now at the beginning of Garnet's career, were to play a critical part in his fortunes.

From these two meetings, summoned and directed by Weston, sprang the retrieval of the Catholic cause. Between 1581 and 1586 more than 150 young priests had been sent into England from Rheims and Rome; thirty of them had been executed;[2] about the same number lay in London prisons alone;[3] still others awaited trial or execution elsewhere; the few left at liberty were living precariously, mostly around London, while whole areas of the country remained without pastors. 'There are three or four counties together', wrote a priest to Cardinal Allen in July 1586 while this meeting was in progress, 'as yet unfurnished with priests. . . . The tops have been left and only the lower boughs dealt with.'[4] Southwell himself, writing a few days after the conference, made the same comment: 'it is to be regretted that in many counties, containing no small number of Catholics, there is not a single priest. . . . Worse still, the priests actually at work here, make for one or two counties, leaving others without shepherds.'[5]

At the time of the new priests' arrival in England, the government still held the upper hand: the success which it had already achieved was shortly to be consolidated by the discovery of Babington's Plot and the execution of

[1] 27 Elizabeth, cap 2: an Act against Jesuits, seminary priests and such like disobedient persons. G. W. Prothero, *Statutes and other Constitutional Documents (1558–1625)* 4th ed. (1946), 83,

[2] *The Martyrs of England and Wales*, 1535–1680: C.T.S., 11–16.

[3] *C.R.S.*, vol. 2., 241–53.

[4] *S.P.D. Eliz.*, vol. 191, no. 26.

[5] R. S. to C. A. 25 July 1586. *C.R.S.*, vol. 5, 309.

Mary, Queen of Scots, on whom Catholics centred their hopes. Philip Howard, Weston's convert, was already safely lodged in the Tower; the newly arrived Jesuits were all but caught; there was a reign of terror; Weston writes: 'the days were filled with immeasurable suffering: many Catholics were broken'. The government harried them by every device: 'men lay in ambush for them, betrayed them, attacked them with violence and without warning. They plundered them at night, confiscated their possessions, drove away their flocks, stole their cattle.'[1] It might have appeared to many the hour of total victory. The freshness, the youth, the talent of the two new priests from Rome heartened all the Catholics of the Thames valley; in London also their names were already known.

It took years to implement the plans laid at Hurleyford. However, a decade later, in spite of harsher persecution, every county in England was provided with a network of Catholic establishments, served, in all, by more than three hundred priests. Weston belittles his own share in the work: 'I told them [Garnet and Southwell] what I knew about conditions in England. ... Then I gave them the names of Catholic houses, where they might go and make their residence and arranged for reliable guides to take them there.'[2]

It was the Vaux family, Weston's friends, who provided the first homes for the new missionaries: Garnet was assigned to the midlands, to Mrs Brooksby's, Vaux's daughter at Shoby in Leicestershire; Fr Southwell to Vaux's London house at Hackney. It was Weston's plan that while Garnet came to the relief of two most neglected counties, Southwell should remain in London to meet a different problem. With his knowledge of the students who had been under his care in Rome and were now about to enter the country in increasing numbers, Southwell was judged the better qualified to assist them in their first perilous days in England; then, after instructing them on conditions in the country, as Weston had instructed the two Jesuits, to despatch them beyond the capital to centres that it was Garnet's task to establish. What role Weston assigned to himself he does not say.

Before parting, all three priests made their confession. Southwell was the first to leave. 'If all had fallen out as we had wished, we should have sung Mass with all solemnity, accompanied by picked instrumental and vocal music, on the feast of St Mary Magdalen [22 July]. This, however, was put off to the next day, but as I was called away, I could not spend it there.'[3]

---

[1] *William Weston*, 31, and notes.
[2] *Ibid.*, 72
[3] R. S. to C. A. 25 July 1586. *C.R.S.*, vol. 5, 307.

Southwell rode to London on 22 July; he had promised to preach on Mary Magdalen's day to the Catholic prisoners in the Clink. There, a spy reported, 'he catechised the company with the doctrine of Popish repentance, taking for his theme the story of Magdalen and absurdly applying the same to his purpose'.[1] The following day Garnet left Hurleyford. On reaching London he despatched the first of his letters to Aquaviva; then, in the following week, left for Leicestershire. The closing sentences of his letter indicate that he anticipated a long absence, perhaps till the following January or February, when all would meet again for a further period of prayer and conference. 'At present', he concluded, 'I can write no more, nor, in so short a time, could anything have happened to write about. I was anxious to tell you that we are safe. . . . I will not be able to write again for several months. Good-bye in the Lord, and do not forget us.'[2]

Four days after Garnet wrote this letter, about five o'clock in the afternoon of 3 August, Weston was arrested outside Bishopsgate by two of Walsingham's agents lying there in wait, not for him but for Anthony Babington,[3] who was hiding at the time in the same district. Thus in less than three weeks of reaching England, Garnet had succeeded Weston. He was to remain Superior until, after his own arrest, another was appointed in his place.

[1] *Calendar of Scottish Papers*, vol. 8, 542. The sermon, the first that Southwell preached in England, was later expanded and printed secretly in London under the title, *Mary Magdalen's Funeral Tears*; it was dedicated to D(orothy) A(rundell), who, with her sister, visited the Clink to hear Southwell preach.

[2] H. G. to C. A. 30 July 1586. F.G. 651, f. 211.

[3] *William Weston*, 79.

5

FIRST YEAR IN ENGLAND

THE persecution that followed the Babington Plot was widespread and systematic. In spite of the assistants enrolled to help the Justices of the Peace, the county sessions were unable to draw up and engross all the indictments of recusants brought before them: almost every other case of crime went by default. The shock of the assassination of William of Orange was still fresh in public memory; the populace was prepared now to believe any mad story of attempted regicide; at intervals wild statements, picked up by spies in taverns on the Continent, were reported home and given the importance of international plots. On the other side there was a recurrent rumour that a general massacre of Catholics was being planned in London; whenever it gained credence, Catholics would leave their homes and pass the nights in fields outside the city or would hire boats and row up and down the Thames until dawn. Finally, the government was forced to relax its persistent hunting down of Catholics for fear of disturbing the economy of the country. In a letter about this time Weston wrote:

'The sudden hurricane of persecution brought into instant jeopardy not merely the temporal goods of Catholics, but the security of their very lives.... Although it raged for several months in its wild fury and its savagery beyond human endurance, now (I hear) it is less severe. It is not that they are sparing any Catholic, man or woman, but simply that it is impossible for such a violent disturbance of property not to bring with it great disorder in all parts and the imminent ruin of the whole country.'[1]

It was in this atmosphere that Garnet succeeded Weston. As Superior of the Jesuits in England, he had three subjects: two of them, Weston and Brother Emerson, in prison.

Ralph Emerson had been arrested in London just a week after landing with Weston. The Council had kept his place of detention secret, and Weston, after long investigation, had been unable to get news of him: he presumed that he had either died in prison or been sent to solitary confinement in the

[1] W. W. to C. A. 10 May 1587. F.G. 651, f. 48.

38

Tower. In fact he was held a close prisoner in the Poultry.[1] Only in 1594, when Emerson was transferred to the Clink, was he able to meet his new Superior. Meanwhile Weston himself was shut up in a private house on the south bank of the Thames. To keep his whereabouts secret from his fellow-Catholics, his captors gave out that the man who was known to be living there 'behind several barred doors' was a mad and recalcitrant Puritan.[2] It took Garnet nearly twelve months to discover where he was imprisoned.

Thus, with Southwell's help, it fell to Garnet to implement the plans made at Hurleyford. A man of less courage might have postponed the task; but Garnet showed no sign of hesitation. With quiet and methodical persistence he set about his assignment immediately.

It is difficult to follow Garnet's movements during his first twelve months in England: there is no extant letter of his during this period. For the greater part of the time he was absent from London. Reluctant always to write except from London, where his letters could be transmitted immediately to the Continent, he left Southwell to communicate with Rome during his months in the country.

Eleanor Brooksby, Garnet's hostess at Shoby,[3] near Saxenby, in Leicestershire, was the eldest of the three daughters of William, Lord Vaux, who lived in London and was now introducing Southwell to his large circle of friends; her younger sister, Elizabeth, had become a Poor Clare at Rouen; Anne, the youngest of the family was now sharing house with Eleanor. She was to find her vocation in her constant care of Garnet and all the priests dependent on him.

Just nine years before Garnet's coming, Eleanor had married Edward Brooksby, a staunch Catholic well known to the Bishop of Lincoln who more than once had complained to the Privy Council of his obstinate refusal to come to church.[4] Already at that time Eleanor and Edward appear to have kept a chaplain in their house, probably a Marian priest, for Edward contended with the Bishop of Lincoln that he had 'service in his house' and resorted to it himself.

Eleanor's married life had lasted only three years; she was no more than twenty-six when in 1580 she was left a widow with two children, William and

---

[1] *William Weston*, 3

[2] *Ibid.*

[3] The old Elizabethan manor house at Shoby, partly rebuilt and now called Priory Farm, still stands. There is a fine mullioned window at the front, where watch could be kept for pursuivants, and two old fireplaces, behind which Popish vestments are said to have been found. Adjoining the kitchen at the back is an old partly ruined stone building still called the Chapel. Cf. Godfrey Anstruther, *Vaux of Harrowden* (1953), 389.

[4] *C.R.S.*, vol. 22, 52.

Mary. The following year Eleanor's aunt, Maud Borroughs, had died, leaving a large family. Eleanor had immediately adopted one of her aunt's children, Frances, who was a girl of eleven living in the household when Garnet first came to Shoby. 'Being committed to her cousin', as she wrote afterwards, 'she was first taught to say her prayers, then instructed in Catholic religion, for this was a very Catholic household.'[1] There she was brought up as a daughter of the house while her father, nearby at Barrow-on-the-Hill, cared for her brothers and sisters. Eleanor had known Persons and Campion, and during her short married life must have had many days of anxiety as her young husband had escorted them from family to family throughout the midlands, and in London had lent to the Fathers his home in Green Street, where they had set up a printing press.

All four Vaux children were by Lord William's first wife, Elizabeth, daughter of Sir John Beaumont of Grace Dieu, Leicestershire, who had died in August 1562 when Anne was less than a month old. Their stepmother, Mary Tresham, was the sister of Thomas Tresham of Rushton; her father, John Tresham, had married Eleanor Catesby, daughter of Anthony Catesby of Whiston. Both Mary Tresham's parents had died on the same day, 27 May 1546; her wardship had been purchased by Sir Robert Throckmorton of Coughton.

Thus, through marriage, Garnet's hostess was connected with the families of Catesby, Tresham and Throckmorton. Through her and her sister and with their financial aid and their relatives', Garnet started to build up what Gerard later described as the 'churches in those parts'. It was a work of twenty years and the model for every district of England.

Garnet was out of London during the trials of the Babington conspirators; the bells of the city churches had rung out to announce their capture; it was rumoured that Weston had been destined after the *coup* for the bishopric of London. Crowds cheered and made merry in the streets. Looking out on to the road from one side of his cell, and on to the Thames from the other side, Weston watched the street bonfires and the river procession of the victims from the Tower to Westminster Hall. For the space of six weeks he saw Catholics, many of them his friends, 'bound hand and foot, being ferried up and down the river to trial. It was easy to pick them out from all the other river passengers, by the uniforms of the guards and the countless people who took off in light boats, to jeer or comfort them, following them the whole stretch of the river.'[2]

Southwell, meanwhile, was lying hidden at the London home of Henry

[1] Adam Hamilton, *Chronicle of St Monica's* (1906), vol. 2, 165.
[2] *William Weston*, 83.

Vaux. The houses of William Byrd and Francis Browne had been searched, Hurleyford raided and Bold taken to prison. On 8 October the two seminary priests most closely associated with Weston, John Lowe and Richard Dibdale, were executed at Tyburn, along with another of Weston's friends, John Adams — all three selected for execution because their zeal marked them out as 'most dangerous'. Simultaneously a new effort was made to seize Southwell and Garnet, for the plot had given the government the chance of destroying the Society, at least temporarily, in England. As Southwell observed: 'All highways were watched, infinite houses searched, hues and cries raised, frights bruited in people's ears as though the whole realm was on fire.'[1]

On crossing to England, Southwell had not anticipated more than a few months of freedom. During his first days he had led a charmed life. In a letter, written after this date, Garnet gives a picture of his companion shaking off a pursuivant in the streets of London at this time. The man, instead of seizing Southwell at once, 'followed him for a long while, in order to track him to the house where he was going and so make a larger catch'. Southwell however, who liked always to walk at a good pace, suddenly increased his stride and got away.[2]

All this while Tyrrell, still an undiscovered spy in the Clink, was being hard pressed to discover the whereabouts of the two Jesuits. By 4 November he had received information that Southwell was at Lord Vaux's house in Hackney.[3] The next day, Richard Young, the chief magistrate of London, led the search in person. He chose early morning when he was likely to surprise Southwell at Mass. Vaux's doorkeeper resisted, but was overwhelmed: his struggle, however, gave Southwell just sufficient time to hide. 'The pursuivants were ringing all around and seeking us in the very house where I was lodged. I heard them threatening and breaking woodwork and sounding the walls to find hiding places; yet by God's goodness, after a a few hours' search, they found me not, though I was separated from them by a thin partition, not by any wall'; so Southwell wrote on 21 December 1586.[4] And he goes on to say that the house was 'sore watched for many days and I perforce slept in my clothes for several nights together in a very strait, uncomfortable place'.[5]

About the same time there was a raid on the Vaux house at Shoby:

[1] *An Humble Supplication*, 22.
[2] H. G. to C. A. 17 March 1593. Stonyhurst, *Anglia* 1, 73.
[3] Devlin, *op. cit.*, 123.
[4] R. S. to C. A. 21 December 1586. *C.R.S.*, vol. 5, 311.
[5] *Ibid.*

either Tyrrell had given information about Garnet's probable whereabouts or, in the raid on the Vaux's house in Hackney, some clue to his residence had been discovered. Nor was it, in fact, hard to guess. At Hackney two letters had been found signed *Robertus*, which Tyrrell had wrongly presumed to have been written by Robert Persons, who was believed to be at large once again in London. The government was alarmed. There is no official record of the raid at Shoby, but it was foiled by the courage of Eleanors's adopted daughter, Frances Burroughs, then aged eleven: indeed 'her courage was such that she never seemed daunted or feared of anything'.

As at Hackney, the search party broke in at the time Garnet was at Mass in the chamber above the hall, where another priest was also present. Immediately they heard the disturbance below, the ladies, Anne and Eleanor, went down with the child Frances, to 'see what was astir': the pursuivants and constables were already in the hall, their swords drawn. Frances was undismayed. 'Put up your swords', she cried, 'or else my mother will die: she cannot endure to see a naked blade.' Then making to fetch some wine for her mother, she ran back, made fast the doors of the hiding place behind the priests and returned to parley with the pursuivants. On another occasion, possibly in the same year, she barred the staircase after a sudden intrusion. A pursuivant, to frighten her, held a drawn dagger at her breast, then threatened to stab her should she refuse to hand over the priests. With composure Frances retorted, 'If thou dost, it will be the hottest blood that ever thou sheddest in thy life.'[1]

No extant letter from Garnet places these incidents at Shoby, but Frances's age, the time and circumstances make it possible to set it there during Garnet's first year in England.

Now working from Shoby Garnet moved from house to house belonging to the Vauxs' relations, connections and friends; Southwell reported his progress: 'Father Henry toils hard and perseveringly. Till now he has been in the country.'[2] About February they met again in London; at Hurleyford it had been agreed that they should re-unite twice yearly, in February and August, dates that were later changed to Easter and autumn.

At this first February meeting in London, Garnet, drawing on his three years' experience with Tottel and on his contacts with the Stationers' Company, was able to advise Southwell on his project of establishing a secret printing press for the production of his own and other Catholic books. It has been suggested that Southwell had already taken up residence in Arundel House in the Strand, at the invitation of the Countess, and had started his

[1] Adam Hamilton, *op. cit.*, vol. 2, 165–6.
[2] R. S. to C. A. 21 December 1586. *C.R.S.*, vol. 5, 310.

press, not there but at Acton or Bishopsgate, in one of two smaller houses owned by her; and that he was assisted by the Arundels' man, John Charleswood, a former printer. Certainly Arundel House was too central and public for a secret printing apostolate: even Persons' press at Stonor, in a remote fold of the Chilterns, had been discovered. But if Southwell had already moved from Hackney to Arundel House he was only in a remote apartment of the palace, with its own exit on to the river. The rest was occupied partly by the Countess, partly by the Lords William and Thomas Howard, her brothers-in-law, and by the government. The Countess resided on sufferance in her own London palace.

Nothing precise is known of the press or its whereabouts, but two things seem certain: that it was in operation very shortly after Garnet's February visit to London and that it was sited on the outskirts of the city. Certainly Southwell would not have engaged in this enterprise without consulting his Superior. The inspiration was his, the execution Garnet's. With a passion to champion the truth, Southwell, before his re-union with Garnet, had written to Aquaviva on 12 January 1587,[1] aghast at the licence given to the dissemination of anti-Catholic literature: he observed that its effect was cumulative and that lies had to be bolstered by lies: 'What they achieve by lies they will perforce establish and confirm by lies.' This he had learnt after a few weeks in London. Impatiently he had awaited Garnet's visit to find means of combating the spate of tracts, pamphlets and broadsheets written against the Church.

It was barely ten years since Garnet had left Tottel's employment. Certainly there is significance in his assumption at this time of the name Whalley, which he appears to have used mainly in London, for Whalley had been in Tottel's office with him and, after a quarrel with his employer, had set up his own press.

While Southwell moved in secret among the Catholic families of London, Garnet on his February visit acted the part of a printer's assistant, which he was equipped to play. It is unlikely that the press was located for more than a few months at one or other of the Countess of Arundel's two houses on the outskirts of the city: both were known to the Council and could not escape search for long. Moreover, from the beginning Garnet favoured his own independent lodgings in London, which he was free constantly to change. Shortly after this February he transferred his press to a house he himself rented, primarily for that purpose: workmen were engaged through the Earl of Arundel's man. Here both his and Southwell's books were produced. Thus eight or nine months after their arrival in England the two priests were

[1] R. S. to C. A. 12 January 1587. F.G. 651, no. 2.

utilising to the full the faculty given them in their instructions from Aquaviva, to publish without reference to him 'small books' for the edification of Catholics. Only after the press had been active for ten years did Garnet dare to make mention of it in his letters to the General. Writing on 16 April 1596 he assessed its achievement:[1] 'We have equipped at our expense a press which in a short space has filled the kingdom from the end to end with catechisms and other pious books.' When it was seized a few months before writing this letter 'a large stock of many divers books was taken'. Garnet, however, anxious quickly to make good the loss, maintained his employees on working wages until he could establish another press in its place.[2]

Certainly Garnet was at Shoby when his hostess's brother, Henry Vaux, returned home on 22 May 1587 after six months' imprisonment in the Marshalsea:[3] owing to sickness he had been given a short leave from prison to recuperate. He died the same year.[4] He had intended to join the Society and long before his death had made over to his younger brother his title to the barony, 'keeping a small annuity to himself whereby to live in study and prayer all the days of his life'.[5] Garnet, who writes of him with much affection, attended him in his long and fatal sickness.

Little else is known in detail either of Garnet or Southwell during their first year in England. Two things, however, are clear: first, that they worked in the closest understanding, and, secondly, that the activity of the one was complementary to the other's.

In London there was set up what can be best described as a sorting office for incoming priests; in the country, centres were established to which they were sent. The first was Southwell's work, the second Garnet's. Thus by the end of their first year, the two young Jesuits had already played a large part in strengthening Catholicism in England. It was a defiant and far-seeing enterprise initiated at the very time that Walsingham appeared triumphant. As Southwell wrote: 'there is weeping almost unto death among wives who have no husbands and families with no support, where religion has no champion and chapels no loving hands to tend them'.[6]

Southwell acted the 'champion' through his press, while Garnet provided 'loving hands' to tend the 'chapels'. Already there seems something desperate in the actions of both priests. Campion had enjoyed thirteen months of

---

[1] H. G. to C. A. 16 April 1596. Stonyhurst, *Anglia* 2, 16.
[2] *Ibid.*
[3] Cf. *inf.*, p. 209.
[4] November 1587. Godfrey Anstruther, *Vaux of Harrowden*, 182.
[5] H. G. to C. A. 16 April 1596. Stonyhurst, *Anglia* 2, 16.
[6] R. S. to C. A. 12 January 1587. F.G. 651, no. 2.

freedom, Weston two years; neither Southwell nor Garnet had reason to expect a longer term. Southwell's letters now become almost feverish: 'we hang in the balance, not yet safe, but not unduly nervous'; and again, 'they may say as often as they like that I am taken, but I shall endeavour as long as I escape their hands to let them know by my deeds that I am at liberty'.[1]

Southwell, who had come to England straight from the staff of the English College, Rome, was able better than Garnet to identify the increasing number of incoming priests: many of them were his former pupils. Quickly he had them posted either in London or in the home counties where he had many friends and connections whom he had already visited before February. Later, as Garnet consolidated his work, Southwell could send them farther afield, to Leicestershire and the neighbouring counties which were now being opened up. Year by year the system they evolved was to work more smoothly and cover more counties. In a letter of 16 April 1596[2] Garnet surveyed their success. 'When the priests first arrive from the seminaries, we give them every help we can. The greater part of them, as opportunity offers, we place in fixed residences. This is done in a very large number of families through our offices. The result now is that many persons, who saw a seminary priest hardly once a year, now have one all the time and most eagerly welcome any others no matter where they come from.' Hitherto, priests entering England had to shift for themselves and were frequently picked up by pursuivants before they could find a refuge: after landing they had drifted for the most part to London, the only city in which accent or lack of connections did not betray them as foreigners. There they had lived precariously in taverns; not infrequently they had been without means of support. Even now, for a period of a few months, the number of incoming priests outstripped the houses to which they could be despatched.

Frequently priests were required in areas where there were no country houses to maintain them. 'It is necessary also to support priests in a number of rather poor places', Garnet explains,[3] 'and find food and shelter in London for others who have recently entered the country, until they are able to go to their kinsfolk.' Then without exaggeration he continues: 'there is hardly one priest in these last ten years that I have been in England, whom I have not provided with cash' as well as a centre for his apostolate. There was a fund for this charitable work, started by Weston and his friends.

At Hoxton, where Weston had met these friends in April 1585, it had been agreed that laymen of substance should contribute one hundred marks

[1] Devlin, *op. cit.*, 130
[2] H. G. to C. A. 16 April 1596, Stonyhurst, *Anglia* 2, 16.
[3] *Ibid.*

annually to a fund, placed under the administration of Lord Vaux, for the support of incoming priests, and that an appeal should be launched in the country.[1] Now Garnet complained that the more 'negligent' Catholics placed the whole financial burden on these first contributors. The fund soon became inadequate, and Garnet was forced to find means to strengthen it. Always a most reluctant beggar, he obtained from Aquaviva permission to devote to it the patrimony of the increasing number of his own subjects: what was over from this source he sent, again with Aquaviva's connivance, to Dr Richard Barret, President of the Seminary at Rheims, for the support of students there. At the same time Southwell, through his family friends in the counties south of the Thames, assisted his Superior, and to such an extent that Dr Barret declared he had received, during his period as President, more financial aid from these two priests than from the entire body of seminary clergy in England.[2] Indeed it was impossible for Garnet to see a priest in financial need without coming to his assistance. He summed up this important work: his rule was to 'help all, as he had the money in hand and as the need of each individual required, without designating any fixed sum to the purpose'.[3]

In this manner intimate ties were formed between the Jesuits and the priests from Rome and Rheims. Many examples of appreciation could be quoted, but the most touching perhaps is that of the priest from Louth, Eustace White, a Douai student, later a martyr, who from prison in November 1591 addressed Garnet as 'the patron of orphans in these miserable days',[4] appealling to him for money and clothes, since, as he wrote most pitifully, 'I was rifled of all my hose ... of four pounds in money with my rings, a silver pix worth 20 shillings ... and many other things: nothing was left me more than on my back.'

This charity went hand in hand with the systematic relief of prisoners, a work again initiated by Weston and extended by Garnet and Southwell. Under Garnet's supervision it became the principal part of Southwell's apostolate in London: on his very first day there he had visited Catholic friends in the Clink; on his return from Hurleyford he had gained entrance to other prisons. His appearance among prisoners old and new, perpetually stirred fresh hopes. It was the daring, the recklessness of this action that heartened them: the report of his presence among them had started rumours of his arrest. In his letter of 22 December he wrote:[5] 'I am informed by

general talk that I am taken, and hearing this while I was yet free, I smile.'
This may have been a rumour deliberately circulated to dispirit Catholics:
whether so or not, there must have been many occasions when these uncon-
firmed tales gave Garnet days of anxiety. He and Southwell were kindred
spirits. From their first days in England they had depended on each other
for the inspiration and success of their work: their zeal was well-matched,
though Southwell's was more vehemently expressed. Garnet had taken a
calculated risk in leaving his friend in London, the hub of the kingdom: if
London Catholics recovered their shattered hopes then the effect would be
felt throughout the country. Nevertheless it was a daring decision when
Southwell was in the triumphant mood that shows through his early letters:
'I am determined', he said, after he had already twice narrowly escaped
arrest, 'never to desist from the works of my calling though the works, when
done, cannot long escape their notice and will make them aware that there
still lives one of this sort whom they have not yet taken.'[1]

On the brink of his departure for England, Southwell had almost lost his
nerve: now he was exhilarated by results of his apostolate. Faced with danger,
he showed a spirit of steel. In him London had found a true champion of
'religion'.

During February and March Southwell wrote the first pages of his
Epistle of Comfort. Starting from the letters he sent to Philip Howard,
his hostess's husband, imprisoned in the Tower, he later expanded his
message for the spiritual benefit of all sufferers for the Catholic faith. His
tone of exultant confidence, from the first page to the last, must have recalled
to the hard-pressed Catholics Campion's *Challenge to the Privy Council*[2] of
ten years before. There is no Catholic book written in the reign that has
such sustained eloquence. His control of English had suffered little stiffening
from his long absence abroad: his language is crisp and scintillating with
sustained metaphors: every chapter becomes a panegyric of the Catholic
spirit. His message is one of hope, since the Church's enemies, no matter how
much they strive to stifle her, are in fact securing her future, creating
'saints enough to furnish all our churches with treasure when it shall please
God to restore them to their true honours'. Chapter on chapter gives more
compelling motives for endurance — drawn from philosophy, history and
the situation he had found in England; and these motives are re-enforced
by the maxims of mystical theology and prayer: all in language in the tradition of Thomas More and the early Tudor writers on spirituality. Along with
Person's *Directory*, written at the same time, it set the pattern of a self-

[1] *Ibid.*
[2] Evelyn Waugh, *Edmund Campion* (Longmans, 1961), 200–3.

effacing devotion that characterised the English Catholic community of the next two centuries. The *Epistle* gave new heart to the resistance: denigrated though his fellow Catholics were, truth was on their side. 'Our adversaries are so fully persuaded of our good behaviour, that if a man in company be modest and grave in countenance, words or demeanour, if he used no swearing, foul or unseemly speech, he is straightway suspected for a Papist.' Thus in summary he gave his verdict on England that Garnet was to take as the text of many of his own letters to Rome

After setting up the press in London, Garnet returned to the country. Later he summarised his activity between February and midsummer. Writing on 26 August 1587 he told Aquaviva:[1] 'Since the time I was last in London I have visited several counties. There, as the opportunity offered, I have carried out my duties as best I could, to my own ineffable consolation and that of others also. However, one thing spoilt the chance of doing all that I might have done—I was unable to stay any length of time in any single place, for everywhere all the people I met had such a desire to see our Fathers.'

Thus, in a single sentence, he set out his principal problem, which he was to solve by stages during the next nineteen years. For the moment he was merely making a survey of the Catholic situation. It is not known what parts of England he visited: from his mention of the priest, Fr John Mush, it can be assumed that he visited Yorkshire: probably also he was in Derbyshire and Nottingham, for he was never for a long time without visiting his family: certainly either on this tour or during the next twelve months he was in the west country, pursuing the connections made there by Weston eighteen months earlier: always he was quick to see the need of a priest in those parts. Unremittingly on this as on other journeys, he sought out the sick and dying. From his experience between February and August 1587 he makes the general statement: 'If only we had the means of approaching the sick, there is scarcely a man who would not die a Catholic; for while all want to live as heretics, all want to die as Catholics.'[2] Without revealing where the

---

[1] H. G. to C. A. 26 August 1587. F.G. 651, f. 5. This is probably not Garnet's first letter this year. It is the only extant letter in which he uses the Continental as well as the English calendar, dating it 26 August or 5 September 1587. The first phrase, however, contains a reference to a letter written in January or February which has been lost. He opens: 'Living in London from which city we *customarily* send letters to your Excellency....' On the other hand, this may be a reference to Southwell's frequent letters during the year, all of them despatched from London.

[2] H. G. to C. A. 26 August 1587. F.G. 651, f. 5. It speaks much for the work of priests during the next eighteen years that Weston, passing through Canterbury in May 1603 noted 'how attractive even to the ears of heretics is the teaching and practice of the

incident occurred, he gives a single example. Through the introduction of a friend, he had visited a lapsed priest, a man close on eighty, who had been ordained in the reign of Henry VIII, some fifty years earlier. With every change of religion he too had changed his allegiance, 'at least in external behaviour, though in fact he had never renounced Catholicism'.[1] After talking with him, Garnet, to his great comfort, induced him to make one last change and, in his own phrase, 'restored him to Christ'. The poor man was so frail that he had scarcely voice enough to abjure heresy in Garnet's presence: eventually, with help, in a voice full of sincerity, he uttered the words of renunciation. The next day, after Garnet's departure, the old priest lost his speech and died peacefully.

Garnet was out of London still on 15 November 1587 when Southwell received a letter from Aquaviva: 'but we expect him in a short time', Southwell said. 'At present he is going about seeking whom he may save', a phrase playfully adapted from the versicle of Compline and used by Southwell to summarise Garnet's apostolate during his first twelve months in England.[2]

[1] *Ibid.*

[2] *Circuit quarens quem salvet* adapted from 1 Peter v, 9: *Circuit quarens quem devoret.*

Catholic faith, if only it were made known; and how close is our people to accepting the faith if it were possible to preach it freely among them'. *William Weston,* 225

E

6

PASTORAL DIFFICULTIES

On his late summer or early autumn visit to London, Garnet, after consultation with Southwell, was impatient to send a full report of the Catholic situation to Rome.

Aquaviva had given him a most strict injunction not to discuss in his letters politics or questions touching on politics, but to confine himself to matters concerning his own 'trade'. For this reason neither Garnet nor Southwell made any mention of the execution of Mary Queen of Scots at Fotheringhay early in 1587. Garnet's first two extant letters this year are dated 25 and 29 August: the second is a postscript to the first and repeats certain pressing requests made in the earlier letter which he feared might have been intercepted.

Garnet confined himself to a general survey of the condition of Catholics. The fury of the persecution, as he saw it, was unabated: no relief was in sight, but spiritually there was ground for much comfort. He had nothing but praise for his people as he found them in his first year of ministry; his harvest had been abundant; a discernible advance had been made. Bearing in mind the executions of Rheims priests in March and April, he could speak only of the 'supreme constancy' of the community, both priests and lay folk.[1]

The government's answer to the successful mission of Campion and Persons had been the Act of 1581,[2] which made it a treasonable offence to withdraw the Queen's subjects from the religion established by law; it had also imposed a fine of £20 a month on all who refused to attend Church. In March 1587, after Southwell and Garnet had been in England less than a year, this Act was amended to enable the Crown, in default of the fine, to take two-thirds of the property of the recusant, as he was now called, 'leaving the third part only . . . for the maintenance of the same offender, his wife, children and

---

[1] The four executed were: Thomas Pilchard (Dorchester, 21 March), Edmund Sykes (York, 23 March), Stephen Rowsham (Gloucester), John Hambley (Salisbury). The last two were martyred some time in April.

[2] 23 Elizabeth, cap. 1. 18 March 1581.

family'.[1] It was the self-sacrifice of the Catholics who attended his Mass under this dire penalty that won Garnet's admiration. No word of his was exaggerated in his praise of their splendid spirit: here was heroism that Aquaviva could understand, and Garnet was determined to spare him no details of his own experience. The Act, as he explained, covered not only the land but the town houses as well as the country estates of the Catholic gentry. 'At this very moment of writing', Garnet explained, 'orders have been sent to every county commanding this barbarous legislation to be enforced. Would that all foreign Catholics at least appreciated our calamity, if they cannot see it with their own eyes: there would be tears at the sight of anxious widows, orphaned little boys, the break-up of noble families, the almost extreme penury of Catholics. Earlier we had seen this in some measure and it caused us extreme sadness and distress of soul; now we witness still harsher laws. This is the scene outside the walls of prison, at the entrance to the courts. I say nothing of the use of manacles and torture. Imagine what justice means ... and mercy also, when we owe it to the Queen's personal pleasure that we are not annihilated, that we are yet alive and breathing, particularly at a time when any utterly base creature can cast it in our teeth that we are unfitted to have our share of life in common with them.'[2]

Garnet is referring here to a clause in the Act that empowered any person whatsoever to delate his neighbour as a Catholic and thus, for his own pecuniary gain, bring down on him the severity of the law. With cumulative eloquence Southwell described the same enactment: 'We are made the common theme of every railing declaimer,' he wrote, 'abused without means of hope or remedy by every wretch with the most infamous names. No tongue is so foresworn but it is of credit against us: none so true but it is thought false in our defence.'[3] Indeed, Catholics were without legal means of protecting their property, homes or family. On the plea of assisting the local justices, bands of ruffians could rob, housebreak, drive off cattle, take possession of lands as they pleased: Weston had given a picture of the desperate situation even before this Act was passed. Without exaggeration he told how every wretch 'lay in ambush for them [Catholics], betrayed them, attacked them with violence ... plundered them at night, drove away their flocks, stole their cattle'.[4] Now Garnet witnessed yet worse persecution. In

[1] 28 and 29 Elizabeth, cap. 6. 23 March 1587.
[2] H. G. to C. A. 26 August 1587. F.G. 651. The first sheet of this letter is f. 5; the other sheets have been misplaced in the volume as it is at present arranged.
[3] *An Humble Supplication*, 40.
[4] Examples of all these ravages are given with particularised instances in 'An Ancient Editor's Notebook', printed in John Morris, *Troubles* (1887), Series 3, 8–59.

the spring of 1587 Orders in Council enforcing the new fines were sent out to every county: during the summer and autumn assizes Catholics, both prominent and simple, had been summoned for not attending Mass: the records of their appearance and reasons for refusing to attend services are extant in county archives. At York alone hundreds of citizens were imprisoned; their replies before the Bench show a grasp of the fundamental principles of their belief and give deeply moving witness to their sincerity. Only a few among them yielded to pressure; and they, as Garnet explains, were men who had always been timid and were now forced, under duress, to abjure their faith and 'in the presence of the sheriff of their county to attend the profane services'. Those who remained stalwart in their resolution, reported Garnet, 'now await the extreme penalty and all that the worst injustice can devise'.

Nevertheless Garnet was not dejected. He continued: 'Christ's city is daily growing in the number of its citizens; so also is their virtuous life. . . . All priests have the good will of the entire Catholic body: we ourselves are increasingly esteemed'. This so impressed him that he earnestly begged Aquaviva's prayers and the prayers of all the Society that both he and Southwell might live up to the expectation of their people. 'In this way what has been gained hitherto will be held and consolidated. May Christ grant greater strength to his weak instruments so that every day more souls may be gained to Him.'

After his tour of several counties Garnet was now in a position to review the needs of the Church. Before all else, reinforcements of priests were required: if either he himself or Southwell or, worse, both were captured, then the mission would collapse; Catholics once again would feel that their hopes had been raised only to be shattered after a brief spell of glorious expectation. Weston had feared this; and Garnet, even during his first two days in England, before he had actually met his Superior, had appreciated the same danger. 'So I implore your Paternity,' he wrote,[1] 'and in the most earnest manner, send us a supply of men as quickly as you possibly can. They will be able to advance the work we have inaugurated.' The places he and Southwell should have visited, these men would be able to visit, for frequently it had not been possible for these two priests to see all the families who had sought them out.

Garnet's frustration at his inability to follow up his own work had been similar to Southwell's experience. 'Our companion Robert is established in a place where he is gathering a great harvest. However, not infrequently he is handicapped in his work by having nobody to take his place at the house

[1] H. G. to C. A. 26 August 1587. F.G. 651, f. 5.

where he is lodging. If there was another priest who lived together with him, it could be arranged for them to go out in turns and accomplish a very great deal.' But Garnet was thinking not merely, as he said, of one additional priest: there was ample work in Arundel House alone for two or three men: nor did he ask only for Jesuits, but for any available English priest who would not be distressed 'by the clamour and shouting of the enemy, since all the noise they make is to be accounted nothing more than the barking of dogs'.[1] But, like Weston, he was not anxious for any kind of priest; he would rather have none than a difficult or disedifying man, and worst of all, a trouble maker: a priest sent to England was to match the zeal and endurance of the Catholic layfolk. *Est adhuc in Catholicis vigor, est animus*: 'there is heart and vigour in Catholics still'. Priests that cross must be 'reliant on divine providence, equipped with virtue': unless, in St Paul's phrase, they are 'dead to the world' and to personal attachments they will be unfit for their apostolate. 'A wart on the face is observed instantly', Garnet concludes. 'On their example our daily practice of virtue is fashioned; by endurance of hardship lay Catholics become sharp-sighted both in observing and in assessing the actions of priests.' Yet he adds immediately: 'In this matter, however (and it is God's goodness to us), there is no cause of complaint against those who are here with us at present: their modesty is most remarkable, their charity outstanding. They are wonderfully peaceful and eminently hard-working.'[2]

This is the same plea that Southwell had made just six months before: 'For, truthfully, no matter how the storm rages', he had written, 'the bark of Peter ploughs ahead. . . . Any number of people try to board it. Only priests are lacking. Some are due to be sent. Let them come immediately.' No names of particular priests were suggested either by Southwell or Garnet: their petition, however, was heard, although it was another fourteen months before another Jesuit was sent from Rome.

In the same first year Garnet was faced with a connected problem, the case of priests already at work in England who were anxious to join the Society. Although their number soon became an embarrassment to him, during his first twelve months on the mission there was only one applicant. This was John Mush, who at this time was the most distinguished priest in Yorkshire: he had been director and confessor of Margaret Clitherow and her first biographer. Through this association his reputation was deservedly enhanced, for Margaret's death at the tollbooth in York a few months before Garnet's arrival in England had by its sheer savagery made the government reluctant again to implement the law making it high treason punishable by

[1] *Ibid.*   [2] *Ibid.*

death for women to provide a home for priests. Garnet was anxious that Mush should be received into the Society. At the same time the request put him in a most difficult position: if it were granted, Mush would have to leave England to make his novitiate abroad; on the other hand, if it were refused, he might take offence. Moreover Garnet was quick to realize that though Mush was an intelligent and zealous priest, he was not an easy man to handle. All Garnet could do for the moment was to explain his dilemma to Aquaviva and give his own appreciation of Mush's character. In view of Mush's later career and the trouble he was to cause him, it is worth quoting Garnet's appraisal of him at this time: it illustrates his instinctive kindness of judgment that did not lack shrewdness. Mush, he writes,[1] 'has done outstanding work [in England]: and now he is pressing most urgently to be granted his wish; he appears to me most suited to the Society. If at times his character is rather exuberant, the practice of obedience and virtue will prune it. Difficult it is to find anyone in England who has toiled with greater zeal and charity for the salvation of souls. Now the search for him personally, and the fact that he is favoured with the particular hatred (of the government) makes it less inconvenient for him to leave the country at present.'

It is not known what counsels prevailed with Aquaviva. Mush was not admitted into the Society. Before long Garnet had grounds to revise his judgment on this zealous but troublesome priest.

From the two letters that Garnet wrote in the summer of 1587 emerge the kind of problems that had been put to him during his first twelve months in England: some were purely technical; others concerned large and new issues of moral theology peculiar to the English situation. The most acute and urgent touched the behaviour of Catholic priests on trial for receiving orders beyond the seas in contravention of the Act of 1585.[2] This Act had made it high treason for a priest ordained on the Continent to minister within the kingdom or for any lay person to receive or 'relieve' him.[3] If a priest at his arrest or trial confessed that he was a priest it meant not only death for himself but ruin and imprisonment for his protectors: frequently Garnet had been asked for guidance on this question. The answer he himself suggested was no more that tentative; he preferred, through Aquaviva, to get the opinion of the moral professors at the Roman College. 'It is no small

---

[1] H. G. to C. A. 26 August 1587. F.G. 651, f. 5.

[2] Act against Jesuits, seminary priests and other such-like disobedient persons (27 Eliz., cap. 2).

[3] It was under this Act that Robert Southwell and most of the martyrs for the next hundred years suffered.

question among us', he wrote, 'whether, when a priest is asked by a magistrate if he is a priest or not, he is allowed expressly to deny it. To some this denial appears tantamount to denying Christ.'[1]

At a time before the plea 'not guilty' was taken as a challenge of proof, not as an objective statement of fact, this was an intricate question. A partial and controversial answer was later found in the doctrine of equivocation, destined to bring Garnet's name into unwarranted and enduring odium. It was an issue, moreover, that formed part of the larger question of the State's right to demand the truth of a prisoner on trial for his life under an unjust law. An affirmative answer to the direct question was equivalent to the prisoner passing sentence of death on himself.

Only by reading the letters of Weston, Garnet and Southwell is it possible to appreciate the technical problems facing English priests: they ranged from moral dilemmas to intricate points of ecclesiastical law for which there existed no precedent to guide interpretation. Moreover, it was to the Jesuits that other priests, faced with the same problems, frequently turned for direction. Some difficulties required no more than a clear answer from a Roman Congregation, others called for prolonged debate among the most expert canonists. During his two years of liberty, for example, Weston had visited Glastonbury and been shown some remarkable treasures of the old monastery, preserved by pious men against the day of a Catholic revival:[2] in his own travels Garnet encountered the same experience, but over a wider area of the country. Altar furnishings, stained glass windows, church fittings had been preserved in many places by Catholics: by canon law it was forbidden to sell them at a profit. Garnet therefore asked that leave should be obtained from the Pope 'to convert to pious uses, for the benefit of the poor, the church furnishings that have survived from the ancient monasteries and everything else salvaged from the ruins of demolished churches. Very often it happens that church timbers, glass, lead and the like come into the hands of Catholics, who would gladly restore them to ecclesiastical uses if the heretics allowed it. But meanwhile, if they pass them on to their heirs, they may well be put to profane use without the church deriving any advantage from them.'[3] This was a problem unforeseen in the instructions given by Aquaviva to his priests. 'If with permission', Garnet urges, 'we could use them for profane purposes and sell them for their cash value, the money could be spent on the relief of the poor and prisoners.' He confessed that he had given this advice to several persons. For the Catholic poor under the

---

[1] H. G. to C. A. 26 August 1587. F.G. 651, f. 5.
[2] *William Weston*, ch. 13.
[3] H. G. to C. A. 26 August 1587. F.G. 651, f. 5.

legislation of Elizabeth could apply for relief only if they registered as members of their parish church.[1] Nevertheless, Garnet had a scruple of conscience: he preferred the Holy See explicitly to grant priests this permission. 'Since in any case the purchaser stands to gain from the sale of these goods, it is more satisfactory that he should be a Catholic rather than a heretic: at the same time we do not want to be prohibited from selling also to heretics and from enabling them lawfully to turn the goods to profane use.'

Garnet was not thinking merely of ecclesiastical plate but also, he said, of all church and monastic property: timber, lead and woodwork. Plate, consecrated for use at the altar, could not be bought and sold in this way: by canon law the person into whose hands it had fallen was obliged to restore it to the church or monastery to which it had belonged as soon as this was possible. But since 'these monasteries', Garnet pointed out, 'no longer exist and since, after so much disturbance, it is difficult now to trace where the articles originally came from', he sought leave for priests to use their own judgment in each case and, as far as possible, to turn all such goods to Catholic use either by buying them back or without scruple accepting them as gifts.

In the same letter Garnet sought Aquaviva's help on another pastoral problem. Everywhere on his travels he had found a shortage of holy oils, not only for baptism and extreme unction but for the consecration of altars. This was not surprising since there was no bishop in England who could consecrate these oils for the needs of English Catholics. Consequently the oils had to be obtained abroad: moreover, these oils could be consecrated by a bishop only on Thursday in Holy Week. Garnet explains the problem, at the same time offering a solution:[2] 'the holy oils cannot be acquired except with the greatest difficulty, and then only the oils of the preceding year. If it were permissible for priests to bless at least the oils used in the consecration of altars and chalices (not the oils used in the sacraments), it would be worth seeking this faculty from the Pope. Often we have sent to France for oils, but because our messenger has reached his destination after Easter, I think it has happened that no diocese has had a sufficient supply both for our needs as well as its own.' In this event Garnet proposed that a rescript should be given to the messenger, authorising him to collect oil from several dioceses: alternately the Pope should give some foreign bishop the faculty to consecrate oils for England outside Holy Week.

[1] A series of Elizabethan Poor Laws made relief of the indigent in country districts dependent on the parish officials: a poor Catholic was compelled to register himself as a member of the parish.

[2] H. G. to C. A. 26 August 1587. F.G. 651, f. 5.

On a problem of more directly personal interest Garnet sought further advice from Aquaviva: it arose also from the suppression of the ancient convents. On his visits to Catholic families in the country he had met many girls and young women who were anxious to become nuns. Among their number were his own sisters and his hostess's adopted daughter, Frances Burroughs. They and many in a similar situation were faced with obstacles in the path of testing their vocation abroad: the communities they would have to join were foreign. 'Apart from many other inconveniences in the way of carrying out their resolve', Garnet explained, 'there is this: we do not know the state of the convents that are established at Rheims. I mean whether religious discipline can flourish in such penury of temporal possessions.' In his view it was better for young girls not to join communities where the religious spirit was weak, but rather remain in the world, where, under the direction of priests, they would have the opportunity to live truly religious and holy lives.

In the absence of a bishop and of any leader in the Church, it was to be expected that priests should consult Garnet on their pastoral problems. He had been a professor at the Roman College before coming to England. He was on terms of friendship with several of the leading Catholic theologians and canon lawyers in the Church; and, moreover, through Aquaviva, he was in communication with the Pope. Nor was there any other person in England with such personal authority. His own pastoral dilemmas were common to all priests. For the ease of their conscience as much as his own, it was essential that the guidance of the Holy See should be sought.

Garnet soon established a pattern of movement that he observed year by year. In 1587 he came to London in the spring and summer, when the assizes were held. Henceforth he was always in the city at these times, and again for the autumn assizes, unless it happened that no priest was due for trial. Through this self-imposed routine Garnet, perhaps unintentionally, established himself as the most detailed historian of the persecution. His long letters written regularly at these seasons make him for the next twenty years the most reliable informant on all priests who suffered martyrdom at Tyburn.

On his August visit 1587 it was Weston's fate also that agitated him, and in particular, his examinations.

After five weeks' secret confinement in a house adjoining the Clink, followed by another ten months' seclusion in the prison itself, Weston was subjected to a long series of examinations. Garnet's comments on his answers have a particular bearing on his conduct at his own trial. He remembered every detail of Weston's behaviour and took it as a pattern of his own. The Babington Plot in which William Cecil failed to involve Weston was in

Garnet's view a rehearsal for the Gunpowder Plot, in which William's son, Robert Cecil, succeeded in implicating him.

It says much for the accuracy of both priests that every statement made by Garnet at this time corresponds exactly with Weston's account of the same events written nearly thirty years later. Here and there the phrases are actually identical. But while Weston wrote after eighteen years of imprisonment, Garnet wrote within a few days of his visit to Weston in the Clink in August 1587.[1]

The attempt of the Council to find Weston guilty by his answers to hypothetical questions was menacing for the future of Catholics. Garnet was quick to see the implications of the practice. It was one thing to condemn a man for what he had done, another to condemn him for what he might do in a particular situation that would perhaps never occur. The question put to Weston was this: what side would he take and what side would he advise his penitents to take should the Pope invade England? This question, framed by Lord Burghley, was known among Catholics as the 'bloody question', because the prisoner's affirmative reply in favour of the Pope was sufficient ground to secure his condemnation and death. It was not new, but was revived as a legal procedure this year. As early as 1584 Cardinal Allen had made a strong protest against it in his *True, Sincere and Modest Defence of English Catholics*, which answered Burghley's *Execution of Justice in England*.[2] Burghley's attempt to justify this novelty in law had caused alarm both in England and on the Continent. Weston's answers formed the rule for other priests placed in the same dilemma. 'The holy confessors of Christ', Garnet wrote,[3] 'are dragged before judges, not to answer any actual charges that are levelled against them, but in order to forge new charges against themselves. This is done by extracting from them an orthodox answer on the question of the Queen's power and the Pope's.' The summary is exact and precise. Garnet continues: 'These questions, which have been buried for some time past, are now dug out from their grave, for the undoing of Catholics. They have been put to almost all priests, and among others, to Father William. . . . He has shown steadfastness in his confession of Catholic faith, and prudence

---

[1] Compare Garnet's letter 26 August 1587 with *William Weston*. Weston wrote in 1611.

[2] The full title of Allen's book is, *A True, Sincere and modest Defence of English Catholiques that suffer for their faith both at home and abrode, against a false, seditious and slanderous libel, intitled The Execution of Justice in England*. Ingolstadt, 1584. Burghley had his tract translated into Latin under the title *De Justitia Britannica* and published in London and Germany. Allen's work was edited by J. H. Pollen, S.J. (London, 1914); Burghley's is printed in Somers Tracts, vol. I, 189 (London, 1809).

[3] H. G. to C. A. 26 August 1587. F.G. 651, f. 5.

and modesty in his answers. . . . When asked whether the Pope was head
of the Church, he replied, yes. To the question whether there could be any
church over which the Pope was not head, he answered, no: and to whether
the Pope could excommunicate or depose princes, he said that for a just
cause he could.' Thus far there was no difficulty. When Weston was pressed
on his attitude to the Queen, he answered with baffling caution. Out of
regard for the Queen's person, he declined to make any particular application
of these general principles to her; there was no doubt, he said, that the Pope
had power to excommunicate Elizabeth; the debate, as he understood it,
turned on whether, in fact, the Pope had excommunicated her. He could not
answer this for he had not himself read the Bull. When, however, his
examiner produced a copy, Weston could be induced to say no more than
that Elizabeth was undoubtedly Queen.

These were answers that Catholics were now trained to give. But Weston
was in greater perplexity when his examiners turned to the hypothetical
question of the invasion of England by the Pope's force. If the Pope attacked
England with the avowed purpose of restoring the Catholic faith, on whose
side would he stand then? Neither, he answered, for his profession of the
priesthood precluded him from bearing arms. Then, for which side would
he pray success? For neither one more than the other, but for both, that
God's will might be done in heaven and on earth. Hard pressed though he
was, Weston would go no further. Often in war, he pointed out, God for his
own reasons gave victory to the party that had unjustly started it; and so,
for fear of doing an injustice to either side he would pray for neither.

Garnet had reason to be interested in every detail of Weston's examination.
A single indiscretion would have been sufficient to frame an indictment
against him. Still only twelve months on the mission, Garnet would have
been deprived of his veteran adviser, for it is clear from his letters that they
met in secret conference, not only in August, but whenever the opportunity
occurred.

Fortunately Weston was a match for his examiners. Called on to swear that
he would reply directly and truthfully to all questions put to him, he evaded
the demand skilfully: if he accepted an oath from a secular magistrate he
would be infringing his ecclesiastical privilege. To this there was no technical
retort. So day after day, month after month, the examinations continued.

If eventually Weston was incriminated it might well have been the end
of the Jesuit mission in England. Garnet anxiously awaited the announcement of the date fixed for his trial. The delay continued. Garnet could not
explain it. 'I could only presume', surmised Weston,[1] 'that they were anxious

1 *William Weston*, 84

first to have ready at hand all the information they could extort by torture from their other prisoners, and then, at the end of the tragedy, to produce me as a prize-piece convicted and condemned beyond dispute by the evidence of all these men.' Thus 'they would be able to show triumphantly and once for all time that Jesuits contrived the death of princes'. If this were done, the odium in which the name of Jesuit would thenceforth be held might have brought them to ruin in England, perhaps also on the Continent as well. The parallel between the treatment of Weston at this time and of Garnet years later is more than an accident: on both occasions only after all the leading conspirators had been arrested, tried and executed, was attention turned to the Jesuits. Moreover, Weston's reflection on the Babington conspirators was valid also for the Gunpowder plotters. 'As I was afterwards to learn,' he wrote, 'during the space of an entire year, no one who was taken and racked was not closely questioned about me as to whether I knew of the plot or had given advice.'[1]

Weston, finally, cleared himself triumphantly, as did Garnet in a different and yet more difficult manner. The personal conduct of both priests faced with the same charge of plotting the murder of princes is parallel.

While writing his report on Weston, Garnet was interrupted by a messenger. The news he brought was that Weston and his fellow priest prisoners in London were either to be executed or transferred to Wisbech. 'This is an encampment shut off from any communication with men and already made a holy spot by Catholic confessors', including, among others, Abbot Feckenham, the last Abbot of Westminster under Queen Mary. 'We hope', Garnet concludes his paragraph, 'that God will be the merciful and fatherly comforter of those who are now bereft of every worldly comfort.'[2]

Only three days after recounting Weston's examinations Garnet wrote again to Aquaviva.[3] He was about to leave London for the country; he had packed and was attired for the journey, but had been delayed. Walking the streets of the city, probably along or near the Strand, he met Southwell: 'Only yesterday', added Garnet,[4] 'I accidentally met our Robert (in the street). He was reading your Lordship's letter.[5] I am altogether unable to tell you what joy this sight gave me'. The casual encounter illustrated the character of all three priests and their intimate relationship fostered by things

---

[1] *William Weston*, 84.

[2] H. G. to C. A. 26 August 1587. F.G. 651, f. 5.

[3] H. G. to C. A. 29 August 1587. F.G. 651, f. 1.

[4] *Ibid.*

[5] 'Your Lordship', *Dominatio vestra*, was the phrase used by Garnet and Southwell in addressing Fr Aquaviva. It gave no clue to the addressee's identity.

both trivial and grave. It would seem that Southwell, who might rightly have considered Aquaviva's letter confidential, immediately handed it to his Superior. On his side Garnet, with propriety, informed the General that he had read it.[1] His own immediate response was to write thanking Aquaviva for this indication of personal interest in a priest who was at once his closest friend, his confessor and his only subject at liberty. 'I saw from the letter', says Garnet, 'how concerned you were with our safety, with the progress we are making and with our conquests;[2] and how pleasing our poor efforts are to all our brethren, slight though they seem in our own estimation. In our own difficulties we are glad to know that our work gives considerable satisfaction where we most esteem it.'

Both Garnet and Southwell were to derive comfort from their exchange of letters with Aquaviva. By chance the particular letter that Southwell was reading when Garnet met him is extant. Written on 10 February 1587,[3] it is full of personal affection and encouragement, and answers Southwell's two letters of November and December 1586.

Southwell's third letter had gone astray. 'First of all', wrote Aquaviva, 'we congratulate you and our most dear Henry on your safe arrival, on the stations you have established, on your labours, your good health, the escapes you have had from danger, and on the courage with which you are facing the future.' The more often both could write on these matters, Aquaviva continued, the more he would be pleased, for information such as they were giving him made it easier both for him and for their other friends in Rome to maintain their prayers for the mission. And he did not forget messages of compassion for the two prisoners, Ralph Emerson and William Weston.

Southwell was excited. He had written to Aquaviva only two days before receiving the General's first reply. Now with the General's letter in his hands, he was writing again by the same messenger, in a state of exhilaration. His

[1] To appreciate the incident it should be pointed out that any member of the Society has complete freedom to write confidentially to his Superior-General: and that his own Superior (in this case Garnet) has no right to enquire into the subject matter of the correspondence.

[2] The word used by Garnet is *lucrum*, gain. This was part of the mercantile vocabulary he established with Aquaviva; the word must be translated, not according to dictionary meaning, but into the language that the two priests, Garnet and Aquaviva, formed for their secret communications.

[3] Arch. S.J. Rome, *Galliae, Epis. Ger.*, f. 46, printed and translated in *C.R.S.*, vol. 5, 319–21. Although six months is a long time, even in this period, for a letter to reach England from Rome, it is possible that Southwell's secret means of communication were temporarily suspended, for Southwell in his reply on 28 August writes, 'we have received your letter written on 20 February.... What kept this letter so long in transit I do not know, but late as it is in coming, it is more welcome than can be imagined.'

mood reflects Garnet's. He confessed: 'I cannot say in words what joy your letter has meant for me. It was like a longed-for star to sailors tossed by tempest, a timely message to souls suspended in the balance, and, last of all, welcome news of affairs at home for brothers in exile.'[1] Garnet rejoiced to see Southwell's intense elation. After twelve months' toil and the daily hazard of arrest this was the stimulus Southwell needed.

Echoing his conversation with Garnet, Southwell continues: 'We have seen now the fatherly affection of the very best of fathers; we have received the prudent counsel of the most skilled General. . . . God has worked indeed that your Paternity should keep before his eyes and in his heart our unworthy selves, your remote subjects.' He spoke also for Garnet, when he added that the General's letter 'had indeed given fresh courage to men in battle; they could now display bravery in the fight in which the divine goodness has granted such a person as you to spur us on and be our father'.

Then three days later Garnet heard fresh rumours about Weston. 'The news of Weston is uncertain', reported Garnet accurately. By an order of the Privy Council, dated 22 August 1587,[2] Thomas Gray, Keeper of Wisbech prison, had been empowered to appoint overseers to assist him in the transfer of certain priests from London prisons to his custody at Wisbech. Within a few days Gray was in London. The news of his coming quickly reached Garnet, for Gray had provoked much unpopularity with the keepers of the London prisons by selecting the inmates from whom they drew their most lucrative fees. '*Figulus figulum odit*',[3] 'There is no love lost among potters', commented Garnet, quoting the Roman proverb.

Garnet, however, was left uncertain whether Weston was among Gray's party until 21 January 1591, when, in fact, he was marched to Wisbech: only then was his fate settled.

Weston had foiled the government. His conduct had been irreproachable. Too eminent a priest to be executed under the law of 27 Elizabeth that made it treason to minister as a priest in England, his name was already a byword among Catholics for holiness. Eight years later the government, less well advised, executed Southwell, without an attempt to involve him in a plot, and as will be seen, quickly regretted its error. Garnet watched carefully, expecting that any day it would be his turn to stand trial. But the period of waiting was longer than he ventured to expect.

[1] R. S. to C. A. 28 August 1587. F.G. 651, no 4.
[2] *Acts of the Privy Council*, vol. 15, 202.
[3] H. G. to C. A. 29 August 1587. F. G. 651, f. 1.

7
THE EVE OF THE ARMADA

It was Robert Southwell who first established safe and regular means of communicating with Rome, while Garnet had been in the country. Deputising for his Superior, Southwell had written regularly to Aquaviva. The General's reply, full of of affection for his English friend, contained a reprimand for his forthrightness of style and a warning of the dangers it involved. This was the letter that Southwell read and re-read, as he walked the streets of London. It was the greatest event in his first twelve months on the mission. 'Nothing of recent occurence', Aquaviva told him,[1] 'has given us greater pleasure than your two letters. The third letter you sent has gone astray, and I am greatly distressed at this: for I fear the grave harm that may befall should it have got into enemy hands.' To avoid such harm, the General gave detailed instructions which Southwell and Garnet henceforth followed with fidelity. A primitive code was established between them and later extended. 'Do not say much in plain and open terms. . . . The subjects you discuss should to some extent be veiled in allegory, especially if they are important. When individuals are in question, no more than an indirect allusion should be made to them.' Aquaviva then promised to send them a specimen vocabulary, and asked Southwell to warn Garnet that if in spite of these precautions for the safety of their letters there was still likelihood of interception, they should exercise even greater caution in what they put down on paper.

After discussing Aquaviva's suggestions, Southwell and Garnet decided that they should write plainly on all matters that involved no risk, observing the kind of vocabulary suggested by the General — for instance, creditors and debtors should represent persecutors and persecuted; priests should be called merchants, souls merchandise. Whenever possible, devious speech was to be avoided. 'We are not afraid to say openly', Southwell replied,[2] 'even what can well be said secretly, for anything written obscurely, enigmatically or figuratively, is liable on discovery to more close examination

[1] C. A. to R. S. 20 February 1587. *C.R.S.*, vol. 5, 319–20.
[2] R. S. to C. A. 28 August 1587. F.G. 651, no. 4.

and to more perverse interpretation. But we shall never write anything that can cause danger to anyone except ourselves — and our dangers, even if they could be more numerous, could hardly be greater. Already our life hangs on a thread.' Garnet, practising this vocabulary in a letter he sent to Aquaviva the following day, wrote: 'I have no fear of our creditors when I compose my letters, so long as I write nothing apart from what shows me to be a true merchant. This they will see at once.'[1] Southwell signed his last letter simply 'Rob'; others 'Robertus' or 'R. S.': Garnet usually used his initials H. G.; occasionally he signed 'H'., 'Hen'., or 'Henricus'. Frequently he begins by explaining that he has been in the country. Indeed, all but a few of his letters are dated from London.[2]

It is unfortunate that a letter that Garnet sent in February 1587 and Southwell's third letter were lost or intercepted in transit, for both clearly concerned the mission stations they had established. Garnet, starting from Shoby in Leicestershire, had moved diagonally south-west towards Warwickshire. After twelve months Coughton, the home of Sir Nicholas Throckmorton, stood solidly at the farther end of the axis of his apostolate. From there he strove to extend his stations still further west, into Worcestershire. On his first visit to the county he had hoped to install a priest at Hinlip, the home of Thomas Habington, five miles outside Worcester. At his first attempt, however, he was thwarted by Thomas's wife, Mary, an obstinate Protestant and a lady-in-waiting to the Queen.

The work of Garnet during his second twelve months, from August 1587 to July 1588, falls into two periods. Until February 1588 he was in the country. He then returned to London, met Southwell and stayed on there in his place until July. Meanwhile Southwell rode through counties not yet visited by Garnet.

For the autumn and early winter period there is no record of Garnet's activity. In fact there is no extant letter of his between 29 August 1587 and 9 June 1588. When he did write he was unable to speak of his work in more than the most general terms. Through the spring and summer preparations to meet the Armada were hurried on. Garnet, during these months, was

[1] H. G. to C. A. 29 August 1587. F.G. 651, f. 1.
[2] It is not known how Garnet and Southwell got their letters through to Rome. In their first months in England they probably delivered their letters by hand to a messenger from the Spanish Ambassador, who would have sent them under diplomatic privilege either to the Spanish Governor of the Netherlands or to the Papal nuncio there. On the outbreak of war with Spain, Garnet perhaps sent his despatches through the Ambassador of Venice. Aquaviva's rigid injunction that there should be no reference whatsoever to politics in their letters may be explained by his anxiety not to compromise the ambassadors of these countries.

seldom away from London. Throughout England every unescorted or un-familiar figure was suspect. 'We are hoping', he wrote to Aquaviva on 9 June 1588,[1] 'that soon the moment will come which we have long awaited with sorely tried patience, the moment when the persecution will be relaxed just sufficiently to allow us a wider field for our excursions.' Moreover, he he was now awaiting the arrival of two priests from Rome. Until they joined him there was little he could do. He surveyed his work during that winter:[2]

'This is the plan we have agreed on for the glory of God, when there shall be a greater number of Ours[3] here. Two shall be stationed in London — or one in London and one in the environments. The others shall be assigned each one a province or county where they shall toil their utmost to promote religion. Nor will there be lacking other priests, men of outstanding holiness and learning, and we can testify this by experience, who will come to their assistance. The field shall be theirs to take over from our labours, and the harvest shall be beyond measure, thanks to Him who unceasingly guides the work of our hands.'

What had impressed him most during these months was the bond of prayer and sacrifice that united the Catholic community. These were perhaps his most continuously happy months in England. In the face of a common peril there was no distinction or division among Catholics. Embarrassed at times by the number of heroic priests who now begged admission into the Society, he petitioned Aquaviva to include in the prayers of the Society 'all others on whose energy and devotion our life here depends; I mean our hosts, or rather I should say, our protectors and defenders, and also those priests — and their number is great — who wish to become members of the Society'.[4]

With apprehension Garnet and his friends observed how a growing number of people, detached already from Catholicism and not yet attached to the new church, were drifting into paganism. Weston had appreciated this a year earlier, remarking also that 'this people suffer from two principal evils ... heresy and an immoderate pursuit of good living'.[5] It was a recurring theme in Southwell's letters

Garnet and Southwell had met in February 1588; a few weeks earlier Southwell and Weston had been united for a brief private talk, probably in Southwell's quarters at Arundel House. It had been their first meeting since July 1586. Southwell had made the prisons the special sphere of his London

---

[1] H. G. to C. A. 9 June 1588. F.G. 651, f. 14.
[2] *Ibid.*
[3] By 'Ours' Garnet means Jesuits.
[4] H. G. to C. A. 9 June 1588. F.G. 651, f. 14.
[5] W. W. to C. A. 10 May 1587. F.G. 651, f. 48.

F

work, but had never been able to visit Weston, who had been closely guarded
in the Clink prison, on the Southwark bank of the river near London Bridge.
Now in January 1588 the Privy Council, meeting at Greenwich, had given
the keeper of the Clink a warrant to deliver Weston and other priests in
London prisons for conveyance to Wisbech.[1] Shortly afterwards Weston
had obtained from his keeper permission to visit certain friends in London.
Garnet was still in the country. 'The next day I changed my habit for lay
clothes and went out', wrote Weston.[2] 'First of all I visited Catholics
confined in other prisons, priests and laymen alike, and on my side as much
as theirs it was a source of great joy and happiness.' With Weston was John,
the keeper of the Clink. Anxious to see Southwell alone, Weston gave his
parole to return before nightfall. 'You have seen that I can be trusted', he
addressed John, 'and that I am not the sort of person to betray anyone who
has done me a kindness.' His keeper accepted the undertaking.

Weston merely states that he had a 'long conversation' with his friends.[3]
Southwell is more detailed.[4] In his letter recalling the meeting, he reveals
his almost unbounded esteem for the young veteran. 'Before his departure', he
tells Aquaviva, 'Weston was allowed to visit friends and friends were allowed
to visit him. So many requests did he receive to call on Catholics that it
would certainly be unbelievable if there were no proof of it. And this very
high opinion of his saintliness is indeed his due, for he is a true Israelite,
prudent as a serpent and simple as a dove. God grant that we may follow in
his steps.' Weston had received Philip Howard into the Church. Southwell
was still addressing to Philip, imprisoned in the Tower, his regular letters
he was later to rewrite as *An Epistle of Comfort*. Now the two priests spoke
together about their common friend, and about another problem that was
exercising both Southwell and Garnet.

The mere presence of Weston in England, whether in Wisbech or London,
in or out of prison, perplexed the Council. He was incomparably the greatest
priest in England: a figure of veneration among Catholics, an oracle of
wisdom. In four years he had gained a personal renown matched only by
medieval anchorites. The discipline of his life, his charity, counsel, leadership
and learning made him a symbol uniting Catholics with their cherished past,
which, they prayed, might return through his efforts. 'If I spoke with the
tongue of Father Campion, and wrote with the pen of Father Persons and
led the austere life of Father Weston', ran the current parody of St Paul,

---

[1] *Acts of the Privy Council*, vol. 15, 331–2. The warrant is dated 7 January.
[2] *William Weston*, 140.
[3] *Ibid.*, 141.
[4] R. S. to C. A. 22 January 1588. F.G. 651, no. 6. Cf. *William Weston*, 146–7.

'and yet had no charity, it would avail me nothing.'[1] A contemporary writer asserts that he was the 'most esteemed and consulted man in England'.[2]

Southwell and Weston discussed the problem that faced their Superior: it was perhaps the most difficult decision he yet had to make. From the moment Southwell set foot on the coast of Kent he never gave Garnet a moment of concern: Weston, by reason of his prophetic stature, was different.

The problem arose from a proposal of Southwell's hostess, the Countess of Arundel.[3] In disguise she had visited Weston in the Clink, offering to put down a large sum in order to secure his release and exile, which she knew would be acceptable to the Council. Courteously Weston argued with her. 'He was not committed to prison for money, so neither would he be released for money', yet he would have no choice but to accept his liberty if the government spontaneously offered it. Weston was disturbed. After the Countess's visit he wrote to Southwell 'asking him to use every means he knew'[4] to hinder her attempt. Now, at their meeting in Arundel House, Weston again pressed Southwell to dissuade the Countess from her project. A few weeks later Garnet himself, after long consideration, determined the question. Much as he was anxious to see Weston free — if he was exiled he could return at no greater peril than faced his brethren who were still free — it was a course liable to misinterpretation. Briefly Garnet gave his reasons: 'We have already explained', he told Aquaviva,[5] 'that he [Weston] could be bought out of prison for a small sum of money. . . . Hitherto I have not approved of this course. Since he has, as it were, gained an eminent and illustrious position for himself, he is exposed to the observation of all, and it would look shameful for the shepherd to fly from his flock at such a time as this.' Thus Garnet endorsed Weston's own view.[6] Weston remained in

[1] Archives of the English College, Valladolid, Seville 17, B. 686.

[2] William Weston, 16

[3] The lives of Philip Howard and Anne Dacres his wife, by Anne Arundel's confessor, edited by the Duke of Norfolk (1857), 27.

[4] William Weston, 118.

[5] H. G. to C. A. 29 October 1588. F.G. 651, f. 18.

[6] In his Autobiography, written after another fifteen years of imprisonment, Weston still had no doubt that Garnet's decision was right. Release by payment, he says, 'seemed to me a dishonourable course — a course particularly alien to the Society, so many of whose members were daily risking their lives in so many different parts of the world — for a paltry sum to tarnish in a shamefaced manner the confession of my faith. . . . It was not that I did not shudder at the thought of death, nor prize my freedom. I was very much afraid and I would have welcomed my liberty gladly and with open arms. But the thought always obsessed me that it was a despicable method of liberation, particularly unworthy of those times when so many martyrs had been killed for their faith.' William Weston, 119.

prison for the rest of the reign. On 22 January he was led from the Clink under escort on the first part of his journey to Wisbech. Crowds lined the streets to see him, others followed him to the city boundaries. In two years of imprisonment he had become an heroic and emblematic figure: a meek and suffering servant of his people. As Garnet foresaw, his influence was unimpaired and his stature in the land unparalleled when he emerged, years later, a blind and broken man, no more than middle-aged, on the Tower-wharf on the first stage of his journey into exile in May 1603.

Garnet says little of his work between this February and July 1588. During these months he decided to find his own house near London and make it his headquarters. The town houses of Weston's friends had been raided too often to give him sufficient security. The centre of the city was too dangerous, except in the great mansions, like Arundel House, for it was certain that periodic enquiries would be made into their owners or occupiers, and whether or not they 'went to church'. Eventually, Garnet rented a place in Finsbury Fields, probably before midsummer 1588.

It is this house that he described in a letter of 1593.[1] 'Many of the citizens of London', he explained to Aquaviva, 'own small gardens beyond the city walls, and a number of them have built in these gardens cottages to which they resort from time to time to enjoy the cleaner air.' The garden cottage that Garnet rented was divided conveniently into three rooms: a kitchen and dining room on the ground floor, and above it a chapel, which probably served also as the sleeping quarters. Writing later of this house, he says: 'Our priests coming to the city on business, as well as those living permanently in the city, usually visited it; for since it was believed that no one was actually residing there, it was never molested by the officers whose duty it is to make the rounds of every house to enquire whether the inmates are in the habit of attending the heretical church.' For greater security Garnet instructed all using the house not to speak even in 'a natural voice for fear of being over-heard in the road hard by. Nor was it permissible in the day-time to prepare food or to light a fire even in the most bitter winter weather for fear the smoke might be seen. All food was cooked by night and eaten cold the next day.'

To this house Garnet came to write his letters undisturbed; and here also he sought refuge 'when exceptional danger threatened in the city' or when there was need to read or write some particularly secret document or hold conferences either with laymen or seminary priests.

For the last eighteen months Southwell had provided accommodation for

[1] H. G. to C. A. 17 March 1593. Stonyhurst, *Anglia* 1, 73. It is possible that this was Garnet's second, not first, London residence.

priests arriving from Rome and Rheims.[1] Some he had lodged in Fleet Street where he had many friends, others in Gray's Inn Fields, Clerkenwell and outlying districts. However, when Garnet relieved Southwell in February 1588 the excitement at the approach of the Spanish Armada was already feverish. All strangers were liable to scrutiny. Garnet, fearful of sudden raids, at once sought a refuge for incoming priests outside the city. Here he himself frequently hid during the day, emerging only at nightfall, as though, like other citizens, he were returning to the city after enjoying 'the cleaner air' of his suburban garden. While he put this cottage at the disposal of all whom he considered trustworthy, it was only by sheer mischance that it was later raided. It was known to the Council that he had a London headquarters, and it was known also that the operations of the newly arrived missionaries were to a large extent directed from it. No measures were spared to discover it. Here, 'besides books and furniture for Mass, we had all our documents, letters and grants of privilege, which it was extremely important to keep hidden'.

In this small garden cottage the hiding place was in the cellar. It was cunningly constructed behind an untidy store of beer barrels, logs, coal and provisions. Dark and disorderly, it could take six or seven men, and was the work of Nicholas Owen, a mason and carpenter, now in the regular employment of Garnet.

Little foresight was needed on Garnet's part to prepare against an intensification of the search for priests throughout the country: still severer measures were certain to be passed against layfolk who assisted them. Already for two years now there had been rumours of a Spanish attack. As early as August 1586 there were stories of a Spanish landing in Sussex. In the following September, at the height of the Babington scare, the Spanish fleet was said to have been sighted off the coast of Brittany. Then excitement subsided for twelve months until, in August 1587, two hundred and twenty Spanish ships were reported off the Scilly Isles. Nothing came of rumours; but meanwhile Walsingham, to obtain more reliable information, organised an efficient spy service in Spain. Then, Weston wrote:[2]

'The year 1588 now broke, and with it came tense expectations, and large-scale preparation by sea and land to meet the Spanish fleet. It was reported to be approaching in immense strength and the Queen's Council reckoned it would be of little avail to meet foreign arms with arms if they did

---

[1] T. F. Knox, *First and Second Douai Diaries* (1878), 30. In addition to the growing number of priests reaching England from Rome, some thirty priests from the Rheims seminary entered England between January 1587 and December 1588.

[2] *William Weston*, 139

not take timely measures against internal dangers. And since they held the name and race of Catholics in perpetual suspicion, they made provision, in so far as the situation allowed, for a large section of priests and noble lay folk to be herded into remote prisons. They feared that given the opportunity they might go over to the enemy.'

It was manifest to the Council that the personal loyalty of Catholics in a national crisis was beyond question, yet the emergency provided a pretext for stigmatising them as potential enemies of the State, or at least as secret allies of an invading force. In order to foster this suspicion, the Council, early in 1588, interned at Ely and other ecclesiastical prisons, many of the ablebodied among the leading Catholic gentry. Southwell considered this more shameful than ordinary confinement for, as he saw it, these loyal supporters of the monarchy were publicly branded as traitors and held as hostages. Lord Vaux was committed with others to the Archbishop of Canterbury; Sir Sir Thomas Tresham to Lincoln; Sir William Catesby to Ely, their only offence being that they were known recusants.[1]

While at home Catholics behaved with scrupulous loyalty, abroad their leaders played by accident into the government's hands. That, in spite of this, the Catholic body, and the priests in particular, came through the storm even stronger in national esteem, was perhaps their greatest victory of the reign.

In June, a month before the Armada was at last sighted off Lizard Point in Cornwall, a mischance on the Continent brought a lamentable crisis upon Catholics. Walsingham's spies in the Netherlands had, with much cunning, secured a copy of a broadside, written by Cardinal Allen and intended for distribution in England when and if the Spanish forces triumphantly landed. It was a summary of the tract, *An Admonition to the Nobility and People of England and Ireland*,[2] which he had written but not published in the previous April. Both the book and the digest denounced Elizabeth in still more offensive terms than Pius V had done. Yet worse, Allen proclaimed that Philip II was to implement the Bull of excommunication which, through force of circumstances, the Popes had been unable to promulgate.

Both were intended for distribution only in the event of the Prince of Parma's success. But by 12 June Burghley had a copy of Allen's *Admonition*

---

[1] Godfrey Anstruther, *Vaux of Harrowden*, 172.

[2] The full title is: *An Admonition to the Nobility and People of England and Ireland, concerning the present Warres made for the Execution of his Holiness Sentence, by the highe and mightie Kinge Catholicke of Spaine, by the Cardinal of Englande*, 1588. When the Spanish invasion failed, care was taken to burn almost all copies of the work, which is consequently extremely rare. The only known copies are at Stonyhurst, the British Museum and York Minister.

in his hands; and twelve days later a copy also of the *Declaration*.[1] This was his heaven-sent opportunity. As far back as 1583 he had pressed the Queen to frame an oath of allegiance that would split the Catholic body on the hypothetical issue of their stand in the event of a papally-backed invasion. Catholics who took the proposed oath, he argued, would become suspect in their allegiance to the Pope, while 'such priests as would refuse that oath, no tongue could say for shame that they suffered for religion if they did suffer'. The majority, he surmised, would take it. Once their link with Rome was broken 'they would soon fall away from the rest', who would, by law at least, be traitors. None could then claim that they were martyrs.

Garnet did not know of these pamphlets when he left London in July 1588. His hopes were still high. Burghley's counterblast to Allen, although written, was not yet published. Garnet had no doubt that Catholics would be loyal whatever fate the Armada met. There was no mention of the political situation in his two letters sent to Rome on 9 June and 11 July. He was concerned merely with the future of the Church. Thus far this year no news of a priest's execution had reached him; and it was on the number and calibre of the priests that the future of the Church depended. He was anxious only about the supply of more men from the seminaries. Though the ports were closely watched against their entry, the future, in his view, was never more full of hope. 'God does not cease daily to raise up children to Himself', he wrote on 9 June.[2] 'In a short time there would be an infinite number [of young priests] if it were possible to get [youths] abroad'. During his months in London 'very many' had offered themselves for the seminaries and the Society 'and countless others will be coming to us shortly, men prepared to fly [the country] when they can safely do so'.

He was still in London and still confident on 11 July. That day was the second anniversary of his reaching London, and he saw it as a happy augury. Everywhere Catholics were enduring persecution with fortitude; his Jesuit brethren in prison were well; his own heart was full of gratitude to the brave layfolk; he 'could truthfully say that we receive more from them than they from us; for in return for out trivial labours and effort, we are given in return examples of endurance and steadfastness which inspire us and spur us on daily to greater things'.[3]

---

[1] *A declaration of the sentence and deposition of Elizabeth, the usurper and pretended Queene of England*. This is a single sheet of eighty-one lines: there are copies in the British Museum and the Bodleian Library, Oxford.

[2] H. G. to C. A. 9 June 1588. F.G. 651, f. 14.

[3] H. G. to C. A. 11 July 1588. F.G. 651. f. 16.

8

THE CRISIS OF LOYALTY

GARNET was in London again at the end of October 'after a long excursion'. On 29 October he wrote to Aquaviva in altered mood; hopeful still, but oppressed by the weight of the persecution Catholics were now enduring. 'All our hopes turned precipitately into sorrow.'[1] Then taking up a biblical analogy he had used in his previous letter, he explained: 'All things are with us as they were with the Jewish people as they were about to go forth from Egypt.'

In spite of the proved loyalty of Catholics in the national crises, the government celebrated the dispersal of the Armada with an onslaught on priests throughout the country. It began almost before the danger had passed. There was no pretence that the victims were executed on any other charge than their priesthood.

The shock was greater, for no priest had been executed in England since the autumn of 1587. Alexander Crow, the last to suffer, had been put to death at York on 30 November 1587. Now starting in Derby on 24 July, three seminary priests, Nicholas Garlick, Robert Ludlam and Richard Simpson, were executed, all after severe torture. Robert Sutton, another seminary priest, was hanged, drawn and quartered three days later at Stafford. This was while the Armada was still at sea. After its defeat, the number of the executions increased. Between 28 August and 28 November the victims numbered another seventeen priests, nine laymen and a woman, Margaret Ward, who had helped to rescue a priest, William Watson, from Bridewell. It became the policy of the government to induce terror in the public by holding the executions locally: Shoreditch, Lincoln's Inn Fields, Clerkenwell, Isleworth, Kingston-on-Thames, Shoreditch, Mile End Green all saw priests hanging from the gibbets this summer

During this time — that is, between July and October — Garnet appears to have visited the midlands. Probably, once more, he rode through Northamptonshire and Leicestershire. Almost certainly he was also in Derbyshire,

[1] H. G. to C. A. 29 October 1588. F.G. 651, f. 18.

where he saw his family. It is not known whether he was in Derby for the actual execution of the priests captured at the Fitzherberts' house at Padley, though the detailed account he wrote of their death has the stamp of an eye-witness report. After Lancashire, Derbyshire was perhaps the most strongly Catholic county: the city itself was the only enclave held there by the Establishment. The execution of the three seminary priests was a measure of terrorism. Its effect was to drive the people and their leaders into hiding.

In fact, for the next five years the Derbyshire peak district remained an almost impregnable refuge and was used even by priests hunted from their fastnesses in the more remote dales of Yorkshire. In many instances Justices of the Peace were known to be sympathetic. Frequently they gave warning in neighbouring counties when any search was in preparation. Immediately, as Anthony Atkinson, a renegade priest, reported to Robert Cecil,[1] there was a flight into the Derbyshire hills, 'where the papists have their harbours in the stony rocks and are relieved by shepherds, so that the country is a sanctuary for all wicked men'. It was the same situation that Garnet described in his October letter.[2] 'When we might have thought [in June] that we were at the end of the calamities that had already almost ruined us ... now with redoubled energy the chiefs and persecutors of Egypt have turned on us all the wrath they have conceived against Moses and Aaron.'

Garnet goes on to speak of the bitterness of the judges in the summer assizes throughout the country, and as an illustration he takes the fate of the three heroic priests martyred in his native county on 24 July. Fr Nicholas Garlick, from Dinting near Glossop, had been a schoolmaster at Tideswell, and was probably known to the Garnet family: he had already sent three of his pupils to study at Douai for the priesthood before he himself followed them. His companion, Fr Robert Ludlam, was from Sheffield, and the third, Richard Simpson, a Yorkshireman. The activities of the first two were based on the house of Mr John Fitzherbert at Padley, a few miles from Matlock, and here Garnet may well have been a visitor after the disaster that followed their arrest. Padley was a centre of Catholic resistance and Garnet was anxious to link it up with the chain of Catholic bases he had already established to the west and south-west of Derby. But for the tragedy of July 1588 the Fitzherbert house might well have become the hinge between the Catholic houses in northern and southern England.

On this visit to his countryside, Garnet reasserted his claim to be regarded as the principal historian of the persecution. In his October 1588 letter he

[1] Anthony Atkinson to Sir Robert Cecil, 24 October 1593. *C.R.S.*, vol. 1, 221–2.
[2] H. G. to C. A. 29 October 1588. F.G. 651, f. 18.

made his first essay as a martyrologist. Aquaviva had encouraged him to write as fully as possible.

'Three martyrs [writes Garnet][1] obtained their crown at Derby: all men of admirable constancy and contempt of worldly things. In the assizes the last named [Richard Simpson] had fallen away through fear, but he was so angry with himself that he spent a bare twopence every day on his food and always put on a rough hairshirt, which the heretics to their amazement saw he was wearing when he came to the gallows. The day before these men suffered . . . they were imprisoned in the same cell with an heretical woman condemned for the foul murder of her husband or son; and though they had never before seen her they won her to Christ. That night she confessed her sin, and the next day on the scaffold made profession of her faith. The people taxed the sheriff with imprudence for allowing such a woman and these Christian martyrs to share the same quarters for a night.'

Garnet reflected sadly that in the very year the Queen needed the loyalty of such men she should permit their execution, and at the same time pardon murderers and thieves. 'Thus those four souls', Garnet concluded, 'were offered to Christ, and the gallows were kept sacred on that day. Now when wicked rogues have been condemned to death for unspeakable crimes, they are all reprieved. In these turbulent days the Queen considers she has need of such persons. How happy she would be . . . if she realised that she needed far more these others.'

Garnet's own loyalty is never in doubt. It is with a tormented mind that he writes about the Queen in this year. Always a staunch monarchist, he found disobedience in all its expressions utterly odious. Even the death of these priests from his native county could extract from him no word of censure. If fault is to be found with his attachment to the Sovereign, he was conscientious to the point of scruple. Later his speeches before the Council and the Bench and his answers to the Commissioners read like a minute examination of conscience: the heart-searchings of a man who sought and could find no cause of self-accusation in his conduct towards the Crown.

With closer understanding than any other friend, Aquaviva followed the trials of Garnet's conscience. It was Aquaviva also whom Garnet consulted when Cecil, in a last effort to split the Catholic body, devised a form of protestation or oath of allegiance which in a deliberate and subtle manner confused the Queen's rightful authority with her claim to ecclesiastical supremacy. On 22 October, just a week before Garnet wrote to Aquaviva, this oath was offered to his friends interned at Ely. The messenger appointed to receive their oath was Dr Andrew Perne, Dean of the cathedral, an old man

[1] H. G. to C. A. 29 October 1588. F.G. 651, f. 18.

whose own conscience was so readily adaptable to the changes of religion that it was a joke in Cambridge that the letters A.P.A.P. on the weathercock of St Peter's Church could stand for Andrew Perne a Papist, or Andrew Perne a Protestant or Andrew Perne a Puritan. But even Perne was unsuccessful. Not a single prisoner subscribed. Thomas Tresham, Garnet's friend, was prepared to acknowledge the Queen as his lawful sovereign *de jure et de facto* 'in all readiness defending her royal person from violence and preserving this realm and all her Highness' other dominions from invasion, against all persons without exception, be it Prince, Pope or any potentate whosoever, or under what colour or pretext soever the same shall be attempted'.[1] It was the limit to which a Catholic could go without renouncing his loyalty to the Papacy. No government could demand more.

Garnet had been unable to visit Ely. On 29 October, exactly a week after Perne had been there, he opened his letter to Aquaviva with the warning: 'On returning to London after a long journey, I am compelled to write to your Paternity about very different matters indeed than I had anticipated at the time of my leaving.' It is clear that he had already received the text of the Council's protestation of allegiance which Perne had presented to the prisoners: also that he had been asked by them to obtain Rome's consent to a redraft which he had drawn up in consultation with their leaders.

'The Queen's Council', he wrote,[2] 'has drafted a protestation (of loyalty) to which all Catholics will have to subscribe. I shall give it here, with another version altered in accordance with Catholic feeling, in order that you may see both the wickedness of our adversaries and the sincerity of the Catholics. The latter ask your approval and, if necessary, your corrections.'

By Aquaviva's approval Garnet meant the endorsement of the Holy See. In his letter he includes the full text of the Government's oath:

'I, A. B., sincerely and with my whole heart profess that I truly in conscience consider the Lady Elizabeth, her Royal Majesty that now is, to be our true and legitimate Queen, notwithstanding any excommunication or deposition by any Pope, past, present or future. [I believe] that she has and ought to have all superiority, jurisdiction, preeminence and authority over all persons both ecclesiastical and secular in England and Ireland and in her other dominions, and that no external Prince, Prelate, State or Power has or ought to have any authority within her Majesty's territories or dominions. Likewise I sincerely profess that I have and ought to have such a care for her most royal person as to wish with all my might to resist, overcome and pursue unto death all those who in any way attempt to attack her

---

[1] British Museum, Lansdowne MSS. 58, no. 14.
[2] H. G. to C. A. 29 October 1588. F.G. 651, f. 18.

Highness' life or raise a finger against her or spill one drop of her blood or in the smallest way infringe her rights within her dominions, whether it be the Pope or any Prelate or Ruler whatsoever. This I am and will always be ready to prove and justify with my blood.'

The protestation allowed no recognition of the Pope's spiritual power. While Catholics were prepared to give Elizabeth full dominion over all temporal matters and all persons, their conscience could not take them as far as Burghley required. Thus, Garnet, anxious both to save his friends and at the same time settle the issue of obedience once for all, forwarded, at the suggestion of the laity, a modified version of the oath. 'This declaration', he told Aquaviva,[1] 'was modified by Catholics in accordance with the principles on which obedience can be given to Catholic rulers, so long as they do not exceed the limits of their power.' In other words, Catholics were ready to give Elizabeth their obedience in the same manner and measure that Catholics in France or Spain or the Empire gave obedience to Catholic princes. In making their amendment, English Catholics availed themselves of the concession of the Holy See which permitted them to regard Elizabeth as their lawful Queen and honour her as such, on the ground that the Bull of excommunication had never been promulgated.

At the time of seeking Aquaviva's advice Garnet did not know for certain whether any Catholics had in fact subscribed to the form of protestation presented by Dr Perne.

'Just seven days ago [he wrote],[2] commissioners were sent to the prisoners at Ely — that is to the sixteen leading Catholic gentlemen — to interrogate them rigorously on the question of the Queen's lawful dominion and power and on the defence of her person and the kingdom against all foreign invasions whatsoever. We trust the answer of all was such as became Catholics. At this very moment their answers are being put before the Queen. If any of them in his misfortune has done anything that can be interpreted in a good or bad sense, we hope that Catholics of all nations will show sympathy and understanding in their judgment of the words and actions of these unhappy men, for they were not permitted either to consult with priests or have any discussion among themselves on these questions.'

Garnet, however, had no need to fear. The amended version of the protestation was delivered to him before he had finished his letter. Without comment he passed it on to Rome. It ran:

'I, A. B., sincerely and with my whole heart, profess truly in conscience that I consider that Lady Elizabeth, her Royal Majesty that now is, to be our true

[1] H. G. to C. A. 29 October 1588. F.G. 651, f. 18.
[2] *Ibid.*

and legitimate Queen. [I believe] that she has and ought to have all the superiority, jurisdiction, preeminence and authority over all persons, both ecclesiastical and lay, in England and Ireland and in her other dominions, which any other ruler has or ever had in his dominions in Christendom, and that no external Ruler, Prelate, State or Power can or in any way may interfere with the aforesaid superiority, jurisdiction preeminence and authority within these her Majesty's dominions. Likewise I sincerely profess that I have and ought to have such a care for her most royal person as to wish with all my might to resist, overcome and pursue unto death all those who in any way attempt to attack her Highness' life or raise a finger against her, either to spill one drop of her blood or to interfere in the smallest way with her aforesaid rights within her dominions, no matter what their state, condition and rank may be. This I am and will always be ready to prove, etc. . . .'

The revision was rejected by the Council on the ground that it passed over the Pope's excommunicating power. Before the defeat of the Armada there might have been some sincerity in this rejection. Catholics, it is true, could not deny the theoretical power of the Pope to depose princes, but the issue of excommunication was now a dead one. It was the Council that revived it as an instrument to divide and perhaps eventually eliminate the Catholic body. That no Catholic took the oath in its first draft was the measure of their faithfulness to the Holy See. The revised oath was as much as any State was entitled to demand of the Catholic conscience. Its acceptance by the Council would have closed the issue of Catholic loyalty. Instead there was a fresh outbreak of executions. The tormented conscience of the Catholics in Ely and other prisons, on whose family connections Garnet was slowly building up a chain of churches, disturbed him as much as the physical suffering of the prisoners. Besides Sir Thomas Tresham, the prisoners at Ely included Sir John Arundell and Sir William Catesby. Lord Vaux had been committed to the Archbishop of Canterbury; Sir Thomas Cornwallis to the Bishop of London. What irked them more than their confinement was the manner of their treatment, which, as Tresham complained, presented them to the public as 'suspect of disloyalty [and] favourers of the invasion'.[1] No matter in what terms these men expressed their loyalty, it was rejected. Their wives pleaded, as their sons and husbands pined in prison. Severer fines were exacted on the ground that these men should be rendered incapable of assisting another invasion. Sir Thomas Tresham, their spokesman, made a final eloquent appeal:

'When the enemy shall dare attempt any invasion against this realm, . . . then may [we] have that honour done us, as not to be bestowed in the

[1] *Hist. MSS. Commission*, Rushton Papers, 51.

rearward, or in the battle, but in the vanward and before the vanward, to
witness to the world and leave record to all posterity of our religious loyalty
and true English valour in defence of her [Majesty's] sacred person and the
noble realm of England.'[1]

Garnet understood intimately the mind of these men and they knew his.
None questioned his personal loyalty, both to themselves and their sovereign.
If the day should come when the patience of his flock was shattered, they all
knew that Garnet would advise even greater meekness.

The worst of the executions were over when Garnet wrote, but there was
no knowing whether there would be a fresh outbreak any day. The repulse
of the Spanish fleet, as he pointed out, had been a signal for violence. 'It
provided a licence to venture anything in the name of religion established by
law. . . . Then such a tempest arose as there never was from the beginning.'[2]
Only Southwell offered an interpretation. 'The hatred stored up against the
Spaniards they are wreaking with a sort of bestial fury upon their own fellow
citizens.'[3] Yet in spite of the persecution both Southwell and Garnet had
only words of praise for the Queen. They saw in her a compassion that gave
distant hope of relief. Recently she had reprimanded her judges for their
treatment of Margaret Ward. Both priests saw in this a sign of womanly
clemency. Margaret, a married lady from Congleton in Cheshire, had been
hanged on 30 August 1588 for supplying secretly to an imprisoned priest
a rope by which he made his escape. Before her execution she had been
hung up against the prison walls by her hands and scourged. At Tyburn she
declared that she never repented anything less 'than the delivery of that
innocent lamb from the hand of those bloody wolves'. Her condemnation
had been forced on William Fleetwood, the Recorder of London, by the jury,
who had been bullied into submission by the Middlesex Justice, Richard
Young. In self-defence, and equally in disgust, Fleetwood called the Queen's
attention to the barbarous treatment of women in her name.

'The matter', writes Garnet, 'is said to have offended the Queen's womanly
and gentle heart, for she had recently pardoned two women who showed outstanding fortitude at their trial.' She was persuaded to this chiefly by the
entreaty of Fleetwood, the Recorder of London, 'who, while he was hearing
cases in court rounded sharply on Young for bringing in Catholic women to
trial in emulation of his companion and rival, Richard Topcliffe. He told him
that unless he brought along other types of criminals on other charges and
with other witnesses, he would have to find another judge to do his work for

[1] Godfrey Anstruther, *Vaux of Harrowden*, 178.
[2] H. G. to C. A. 29 October 1588. F.G. 651, f. 18.
[3] R. S. to C. A. 31 August 1588. *C.R.S.*, vol. 5, 322.

him.' 'Thus', concludes Garnet,[1] 'this religious man approached the Queen to pardon of her bounty women whom he had iniquitously condemned.'[2]

Among the Queen's judges and courtiers, and still more among the crowds that watched the executions, there was now a reaction against the barbarous manner in which the laws were enforced. Before the end of October 1588 there occured a strange respite, at least in London. The severity of Cecil's policy was defeating its own purpose. 'But now this horrid cruelty has fallen back on itself,' Southwell noticed,[3] 'and though it has not ceased to be cruelty, yet there are degrees in cruelty which make it able to blush at itself.' The more priests and innocent layfolk were executed the more manifest it became on the Continent that the persecution was religious, not political. The England of Elizabeth was a *parvenu* State, anxious for its own good name. In writing to Aquaviva, Southwell expressed this anxiety: he voiced also Garnet's own fears. Both priests were Englishmen to the core and were as anxious as Cecil that their own countrymen should not be judged barbarians abroad, particularly by their own friends.

'I could not make up my mind whether or not to write to you, my dear Father, about the slaughter that has just occurred [began Southwell].[4] Would it not be better to weep alone for the woes of my motherland than to let the misery of one island spread abroad to other nations? I know that the story of our sorrows cannot fail to stir their pity; but I am very much afraid that the tyranny of our persecutors will excite more loathing for the name of England than the bravery of our martyrs will win for her honour.'

He wrote to Aquaviva as to a friend, telling him more eloquently than Garnet the details of these awful months. His poetic appreciation of every situation broke through his Latin prose. 'The trouble of our time', he said in excuse, 'will not be calmed by the uproar of battle, but by the prayers and tears of faithful souls.'[5]

During November 1588 Garnet remained in London. With increasing apprehension he was awaiting the arrival of Fr John Gerard and Fr Edward

---

[1] H. G. to C. A. 29 October 1588. F.G. 651, f. 18.

[2] William Fleetwood (1535–94) as a barrister at the Middle Temple may have met Garnet during his years with Tottel. Although he was well known for his enforcement of the laws against vagrants and Papists, he was scrupulous in his application of them, and reluctant always to pronounce sentence unless the crime was proved in law. Several other incidents show that, in spite of his severity, he was not altogether hard-hearted. Cf. 'William Fleetwood, Recorder of the City, and Catholicism in Elizabethan London' by P. R. Harris in *Recusant History*, vol 7, October 1963, 106–22.

[3] R. S. to C. A. 20 December 1588. F.G. 651, no. 10.

[4] R. S. to C. A. 31 August 1588. *C.R.S.*, vol. 5, 321–2.

[5] *Ibid.*

Oldcorne from Rome. Aquaviva had not dared even to hint to him the date of their coming. Only on 15 August, the feast of the Assumption of Our Lady, did the General personally admit the two very young priests into the Society after the most brief and informal noviceship. It was an uncommon gesture of his appreciation of Garnet's desperate need for more priests. Hence Garnet was all the more anxious to report their safe arrival. At one time he had expected news of them as early as June, for he had written on 11th of that month to Aquaviva:[1]

'So far I have had no word from our men whom we are expecting. Through them I hope to receive some information on matters which I have already raised in my letters and which have given rise to many difficulties in the work we have initiated.' If they had not already left, then, pleaded Garnet, 'we earnestly beg you, for all the concern you have for us, that both these and other matters which we have put to your consideration, be settled before their departure from the city.'

Without a clear answer from Rome on all the questions he had raised about faculties, about the extent to which the decrees of Trent ran in England and the problem of admitting priests into the Society without sending them abroad for their noviceship, Garnet's work was impeded. He waited Aquaviva's answers with almost as much excitement as he waited the priests themselves. On 11 July,[2] he again expressed his impatience: 'I shall be receiving, I trust, many things at the hands of my new companions [Oldcorne and Gerard], but their slow journey is making me suffer their absence far too long.'

Garnet's anxieties increased in the late summer; but before the end of October he seems to have got word that the two recruits were waiting an opportunity to cross, for there is no mention of them in his letter of the 29th of that month. In fact, early in November they embarked at a French Channel port. After three days' sailing they found themselves at dusk off a deserted stretch of coast near Happisburgh, between Yarmouth and Cromer in Norfolk. There was no dwelling in sight and no one to observe their landing. They waited till nightfall and then rowed ashore in the cock-boat.[3]

Gerard has described vividly his first adventures on shore.[4] Like Garnet he had chosen a dangerous time to cross. Vagabonds were roving the eastern counties after the dispersal of the hired levies to meet the Armada; special watches were kept at the entry to villages and towns. For this reason, as well

---

[1] H. G. to C. A. 9 June 1588. F.G. 651, f. 14.
[2] H. G. to C. A. 11 July 1588, F.G. 651, f. 16.
[3] John Gerard, *Narrative of the Gunpowder Plot* (ed. John Morris, 1871), 280.
[4] *Ibid.*

as for the opportunity of making converts, Gerard lingered in Norfolk. Meanwhile Garnet was more anxious than ever. He knew that they had sailed, but he was still without news of them. Only three weeks after their landing did he hear that they were safe. He wrote again to Aquaviva on 24 November: he was depressed, and sent only a few lines, more to comfort himself than to inform his Superior of what was happening.[1] 'I prefer to send a brief letter to your Reverence rather than none at all, for the continuing troubles of the time make a long letter difficult. The two men about whom I wrote in my last letter have arrived safely. We have not yet seen them but we will soon do so.'

Early in November, soon after his return to London, Garnet had sent Southwell on a tour of several counties. 'My companion', wrote Garnet soon afterwards, 'is now out of London, snatching souls for heaven in a freer atmosphere.'[2] His absence and the dilatoriness of the new priests accentuated his loneliness. 'Some of our men expect death; others, who are free, prison, though nearly all of us might be said to be imprisoned. Unless we have urgent business, we dare not go about the city save at night.' Occasionally during these weeks he heard talk of Southwell's activity. Southwell himself had left in high spirits. He was away for seven weeks. With an escort of two, sometimes three, young noblemen, he rode through the southern and midland shires — where he had many relatives and connections — offering Mass, preaching, demonstrating to all that Catholics were not disheartened. 'I have been on horseback round a great part of England', he reported at the end of December[3] ' . . . and have visited a great number of Catholics. . . . I have sometimes called on the Protestant sheriffs to look after secret Catholics in their households; and they, seeing my fine clothes and bevy of aristocratic youths and suspecting nothing as little as the reality, have received me with imposing ceremony and truly sumptuous banquets.' It was a severe winter and the snow was early and deep. His journey had all the dash and glamour of Campion's ride through the north of England nine years earlier. Garnet felt encouraged that he had under him a man capable of emulating Campion's exploits.

As he waited, Garnet got some distraction as he watched and described the celebrations at St Paul's Cathedral in thanksgiving for the defeat of the Armada.[4] In his long eye-witness description of the procession from Somerset House to the Cathedral two notes are discernible: genuine happiness at

[1] H. G. to C. A. 24 November 1588. F.G. 651, f. 13.
[2] *Ibid.*
[3] R. S. to C. A. 28 December 1588. F.G. 651, no. 11.
[4] H. G. to C. A. 5 December 1588. F.G. 651, f. 7.

G

the demonstration of loyalty to the Queen, and hope that the scattering of the Spanish fleet might remove the political grounds for the persecution. Certain features of the pageant — the first of its kind since the coronation of the Queen — appeared a little ludicrous to him. He writes in great detail so that Aquaviva might share his own relaxation.

'On the 24 November this year a solemn procession, or perhaps I should call it a pageant, was held to give thanks to God for the scattering of the Spanish fleet. It was led by noblemen of the Queen's household, all mounted on horses caparisoned beyond my power of description. . . . Behind them rode the Queen's Councillors, and among them the pseudo-bishops conspicuous in their square caps and rochets; then the Queen herself, escorted by her ladies-in-waiting, and followed by the principal ladies of the realm all mounted in like manner.

'The Queen was carried in a gilded chair. High above her head, it was covered with a royal awning: it hung down behind, but was open in front and on both sides. She was drawn by two grey horses royally caparisoned. The unceasing uproar of the vast crowds echoed all round her.'

Here was an opportunity for Garnet to write about the Queen without violating Aquaviva's instructions, and using it to the full, he gives a vivid, perhaps unique, account of the procession. Here and there he interjects his wry observation.

'With all this pomp [the Queen] came forth from Somerset Palace and proceeded to the great cathedral of St Paul's. When the Temple Bar was reached — it marks the boundary of the city, and it is here that the city's jurisdiction begins— she was received by the Lord Mayor and aldermen. Here also she was presented with the sword that is carried before the Lord Mayor only when he is in the presence of the Sovereign.

'Proceeding thence to St Paul's, she was acclaimed by members of the legal profession — with the exception of the judges who, in their robes, already formed part of the procession — a very large and decorative assembly, and by representative merchants and craftsmen . . . from every guild, all accommodated on seats constructed in splendid tiers along the whole route. As she passed there were bands of musicians playing in appointed places. Also there were some charming tableaux.

'Then her clergy came forward to meet her. They looked silly in the eyes of all, dressed up as they were in Catholic copes: copes which heretofore they had burned or cut up in pieces and used for profane purposes. They had been forced to fetch them, in mutilated condition, from the Queen's chapel or from an old armoury in the Tower. The Dean of St. Paul's, who is considered a very holy man by the heretics, roused some measure of sympathy in a courtier who, as he saw him approaching decked up in cloth of gold, said, "My good man, I am sorry for you. Sir, you are the only man whom this cloth of gold does not puff up with pride."[1]

'Entering the cathedral, the Queen knelt and offered her prayers. All then advanced to the place where the high altar used to stand. There the rest of the ceremonies were performed. Very many took communion — whether they were fasting or not I cannot say for certain; it was now close on midday.

'After this the Queen advanced to the cross in the churchyard, where sermons are customarily preached. Here from a raised platform she heard the sermon. From time to time, in the course of it, she applauded the preacher in a loud voice when he was either praising the Queen's clemency or asserting that she was anxious before all else to establish peace.

'After luncheon, given in the palace of the Bishop of London, she proceeded back — it was shortly before dusk — in exactly the same manner. It was most noteworthy that the wife of the pseudo-Bishop of London[2] did not dare to make an appearance before the Queen, who does not so much hate the marriage of her clergy as marriage of any kind.

'This pageant had been long awaited in the city. It had been said that the Queen was afraid to show herself in public — a report confirmed by the order that in every single household along the route no one should be allowed to look out from the windows while she was passing, unless the householder was prepared to stake his life and entire fortune on his trustworthiness.

'However [Garnet concludes his description], there were persons who vouched for me, for they believe I have the Queen's safety more at heart than her own Calvinistic Ministers.'

The celebrations heartened Garnet. His letter to Aquaviva on 4 December becomes more spirited as he draws to its end. He had partially overcome the depression of his days of waiting. Even in events that might then have cast him down, he now finds grounds for hope. The very next day, from the same pulpit at St. Paul's Cross, a priest, William Tedder, made a public renunciation of his faith, but in such a manner that no one doubted that he was an egregious apostate. Within two days, again at the same place, this was to be followed by the second public apostasy by another priest, Anthony Tyrrell, William Weston's former associate. However, Garnet's only comment was that all the efforts of the heretics to discredit the belief of Catholics turned out

---

[1] This was Alexander Nowell, a Marian exile and author of the famous Protestant Catechisms.

[2] John Aylmer, Bishop of London, 1577-94, formerly tutor to Lady Jane Grey, author of many devotional works.

triumphs for the Catholic cause. He himself had an innate faith in the discernment and basic good sense of his fellow-countrymen, and was aware that instinctively they knew when a man was acting from cowardly or unworthy motives. Indeed, his capacity for judging correctly the mood and temper even of a crowd accounted for the success of his own last public appearance. His mind was relieved now that Gerard and Oldcorne were at last safely ashore. But he was still lonely. He continued his letter to Aquaviva with the knowledge that he was writing to a man who could understand him completely — his responsibilities, his torn loyalties, his love for the Queen, his homeland and for his brethren. There is implicit in all he says a confidence that the General, an Italian nobleman and a man of zeal and charity like his own, will sympathise with the outpourings of his heart.

From his description of the thanksgiving service at St Paul's Garnet returned to the question of loyalty: it was more on his mind this year than ever before. He had had further news of the prisoners at Ely.[1] 'The noblemen who were gathered in Ely have now arrived in London to wait on the orders of the Queen, to whom they appear not to have proven their loyalty sufficiently.' Then he continues: 'but if some may have been too extravagant in pledging their fealty, it is because they were far removed from priests who would have advised them willingly in such a critical question'.

Always Garnet manifested understanding charity. It was never for him to doubt the sincerity of those who had given him their trust. The persecution of the recent months had elicited the best from Catholics, seminary priests, and laymen alike. 'This summer almost thirty have been put to death in London and in neighbouring places', he continues.[2] 'Half of them were priests, who were executed because they were priests; the rest because they had sheltered priests or had in some way assisted them.'

Garnet wrote on, exposing his spontaneous and at times half-ordered thoughts as he waited the arrival of Gerard and Oldcorne in London. When eventually they did reach his house, he controlled his impatience. Only then did Gerard realise the anxiety his Superior had suffered on his account. 'When I reached London', wrote Gerard some twenty years later,[3] 'some Catholics helped me to find Father Henry Garnet, who was then Superior. ... My companion, Father Oldcorne, had already arrived. But my Superior had received no news of me and was anxious. On the other hand, for this very reason, he still had hopes that all was well. When I arrived, there was great rejoicing all round.'

[1] H. G. to C. A. 5 December 1588. F.G. 651, f. 7.
[2] *Ibid.*
[3] *John Gerard*, 17

Owing to Gerard's five weeks' delay in East Anglia – it was a short time before Christmas that Gerard reached London — Garnet had been unable to make any arrangements for his winter apostolate. On the other hand, Gerard was able to report the establishment of a new base at Grimston, six miles north-east of King's Lynn and the home of one of the most influential Catholics in Norfolk; also, he claimed a number of converts in neighbouring houses and the promise of more centres. Oldcorne had been in London some-time; Southwell, back from his tour of the shires, later joined them. 'I stayed with the Fathers some time', wrote Gerard,[1] 'and we had frequent discussions on the methods we should follow in our work.' The young priests were particularly interested in the advice given them by Southwell 'who excelled in this work. He was so wise and good, gentle and loveable'.[2]

Garnet was particularly fortunate in obtaining two recruits who could quickly understand the problems peculiar to the English mission. Yet the two new priests could not have been more contrasted in character and upbringing. Gerard, just twenty-two, an aristocrat like Southwell and, like him, with connections at Court, was an adventurer turned apostle, a brilliant swordsman, keen and proficient in all the pursuits of a countryman, simple, shrewd, robust, with an unhesitating faith that was more characteristic of an earlier age. He had all the self-confidence of a young Elizabethan gallant. Already he had set Norfolk astir, and within three weeks of landing had discovered for himself a system of apostolate that over the two previous years Garnet had elaborated with Weston's counsel and Southwell's co-operation.

Edward Oldcorne,[3] a year older than Gerard, was so removed from him in background and temperament that it is improbable that their friendship would ever have been formed if it had not happened that they entered to-gether the Society at Rome on 15 August 1588. Oldcorne came from York, the son of a prosperous bricklayer, well-educated, sturdy in faith, affection-ate and self-effacing. There was something unspoilt and childlike in his character that won him all hearts. His zeal was a match for Gerard's. In the first moments of any encounter his innocence was manifest to all; under the stresses of missionary life in England it developed quickly into a personal saintliness that became a byword in the west country.

Before Christmas the priests were compelled to scatter, for the risk of

[1] *Ibid.* [2] *Ibid.*

[3] Father Oldcorne was born of what Gerard calls 'honest but faithful parents'; his father, John Oldcorne, was a non-Catholic of St Sampson's, York, his mother, Elizabeth, a noted recusant who, like Margaret Clitherow, was several times imprisoned for her faith. In January 1598 she is described as 'old and lame, a recusant'; she died shortly afterwards in a York prison. Foley, vol. 4, 204.

capture was always greater at festal seasons. 'I was sent back, therefore, to the country where I first stepped ashore,' wrote Gerard, after describing his meeting with Garnet,[1] 'and to the same gentleman who first helped me and gave me shelter. [Fr Garnet] provided me with clothes and other things I needed, for he was anxious that I should not be a burden to my host at the start.' Thus equipped, Gerard went about his work like 'a gentleman of moderate means'. Doubtless he was glad, as Garnet had been two years earlier, to be rid of his suiting with a foreign cut that had almost betrayed him on landing.

Before Christmas Gerard was back at Grimston; Oldcorne, for the most part, stayed on with Garnet until March 1589 or perhaps later.

It was only the next year that Garnet expressed his relief and joy at the arrival of the new priests. Writing to Aquaviva on 12 March he explained:[2] 'One [of the Fathers] is with me, the other safe among friends. It was due to their imprudence rather than to any lack of good will that, on their arrival in the kingdom, they went about their business alone with no thought of visiting me. So it happened that without consulting me at all they did things which they had no authority to do and which manifestly they should never have done. . . . And they handed over our own little account book[3] to certain priests who, during their time in Rome, were not considered well disposed to us and are not the persons most fitted for this task.' Deliberately Garnet is vague: but it would seem that both newcomers had been indiscreet. They had used faculties they did not possess and, without authorisation, had communicated these faculties to other priests. Nevertheless Garnet judged that the situation could easily be remedied. He asked Aquaviva to give a more careful briefing to the priests next to be sent from Rome. 'But we hope that things will be put right easily enough and the matter will do slight harm to your interests. But I judged it necessary to write this to your Lordship so that those who are sent hereafter on the same business should properly understand their accounts [i.e. faculties] and seek out some veteran [missionary] as quickly as possible.' Then, perhaps judging that he had been too severe, he concluded: 'but they should pay attention to any profitable business which by chance can be transacted on their journey'.[4]

---

[1] *John Gerard*, 17.
[2] H. G. to C. A. 12 March 1589. F.G. 651, f. 11.
[3] The list of privileges and faculties granted to English Jesuits.
[4] H. G. to C. A. 12 March 1589. F.G. 651, f. 11.

9
TWO RECRUITS

BETWEEN June and December 1588, while awaiting in London the arrival
of the recruits, Garnet and Southwell had frequently visited the prisons in
and outside the city. Catholic confessors were the most favoured of Southwell's flock. 'I managed', he wrote in December 1588,[1] 'to do much work for
our prisoners and was able to help and console those who were not in too
strict confinement.' For them he completed *An Epistle of Comfort*, his
finest prose work after the *Humble Supplication*. Garnet's letters of this time
also describe the most effective apostolate exercised by priests among
prisoners not only in London but throughout the country. At Wisbech,
where Weston had been transferred, the priests were still closely guarded;
but in Norwich gaol, where Gerard had met his first Catholic friends after
landing, a colony of prisoners exercised increasing influence far across the
countryside. It was only in prisons that Catholics were able to live a full
religious life without fear of penalty. 'It is difficult to say', Garnet had written
in June,[2] 'the extent to which Catholics seek us out. A certain Catholic
nobleman, who is in prison, told me — from time to time I am summoned
to prisons on business which cannot safely be transacted by correspondence
— that . . . it was his great desire to have the company of one of our Fathers
in prison: such a priest would make it easier to solve the many problems
of moral theology that are brought there. I judged it right to tell your Lordship this, so that you might clearly appreciate that there is no reason whatsoever to be disheartened should anyone of us be taken and held prisoner by
our enemies; and, besides, to confess Christ is in itself a great privilege.
Inside the ordinary prisons [and by 'ordinary' Garnet excluded Wisbech,
Bridewell and the Tower] it is possible to do more good than outside, for the
priest who remains in prison is always to be found there and he can be
acknowledged as a priest by others in a way the priest wandering here and
there from place to place cannot be.'

[1] R. S. to C. A. 28 December 1588. F.G. 651, no. 11.
[2] H. G. to C. A. 9 June 1588. F.G. 651, f. 14.

Garnet was clearly anticipating Aquaviva's objection that it was wasteful expenditure to send across to England highly-trained men who, after a brief apostolate, would pass their best years in confinement. Possibly also he was correcting the impression made by Southwell's letters that any priest was more than fortunate if he was breathing free air. At this time many young priests sent from Rome were caught either on landing or very shortly after it. Aquaviva would have heard of their fate and been concerned for his own men. 'Please God in a short time', Garnet wrote,[1] 'there will be a supply of our priests who can be posted to different counties, and there, helped by other priests sent from the seminaries, be able greatly to advance the Catholic faith. The position of our own men now is this: if they make some headway with heretics, they cannot win them to the faith in the course of a single conversation; if they are dealing with schismatics, then they cannot wean them from the heretical services in a single argument; if with Catholics, they cannot cultivate in them perfect piety in the space of twenty-fours hours.' Garnet's plan was for the experienced or more gifted men, either seminary priests or Jesuits, to act as pioneers, and then hand over to newcomers the care of the centres they had founded. While the young priests gathered experience locally, their seniors, using these established houses as their base, would ride afield in search of fresh conquests. The execution of this plan is admirably illustrated in the early chapters of Gerard's *Autobiography*.

Meanwhile, however, the scarcity of priests was so acute that he fell back more and more on the assistance of old Marian priests. Now they were brought out of hiding or rehabilitated after a long lapse from their vocation: at least they served quietly to occupy Mass centres in more remote places. It was necessarily a temporary measure, but it had its advantages, for, as Gerard observed, these old men did not go about in peril of their lives 'and could with impunity become known in their districts and more freely administer the sacraments to the dying'.[2] Occasionally misunderstanding arose between the old men and the young, but, for the most part, they worked together with understanding.

Frequently the return of Marian priests to their duties caused Garnet scruples of conscience. He pointed out to Aquaviva[3] that while the Jesuits had the fullest faculties for absolving priests who had lapsed or even made a public renunciation of their faith, this power had not been granted to the

---

[1] H. G. to C. A. 9 June 1588. F.G. 651, f. 14.

[2] *John Gerard*, 20. Marian priests did not fall under the Act (27 Eliz., cap. 2) which made it high treason for a priest ordained overseas to minister in the Queen's dominions. They had been ordained in England.

[3] H. G. to C. A. 5 December 1588. F.G. 651, f. 7.

priests from the Colleges at Rome and Rheims. The example he gives of the confused situation that occasionally confronted him is interesting. Seeking Aquaviva's advice, he wrote:[1]

'A certain priest had fallen away from the Church and had signed with his own hand a public confession, professing himself a heretic. At the same time he betrayed by name all the Catholics who had fed and sheltered him, and also all the priests whom he knew, naming each one of them individually, together with their hosts. So far, however, no one has been condemned to death through his confession. What will happen later we do not know. Since this sin is notorious and egregious, and since the priest has incurred irregularity, I was unwilling to absolve him without consulting your Lordship. Through God's grace he has now returned to a better frame of mind. In prison he made a public profession of his faith; indeed he patiently suffered many hardships there and would never have been released, but he managed to escape. . . . Going to a private house, he lived and still lives like a devout Catholic. The priest who heard his confession absolved him also from irregularity, but had no power to do so.'

Garnet himself had faculties for absolution but was uncertain whether they extended to this case: for both 'ecclesiastical discipline and the edification of the people, to whom the fact was most odious' seem to demand reference to Rome. On the other hand Garnet wondered whether it would not be wiser to leave this man, who had been absolved in good faith, to exercise his orders with an undisturbed conscience.

This was one of many canonical problems that Garnet met in his work for prisoners. In Winchester gaol, which he visited this year, he met a Catholic lady who had never been permitted to see her six-month-old infant. Earlier it had been left without milk: the mother, while willing to pay the cost of her own cell, was unable and unwilling to pay the same sum again for the child.[2] Though Garnet does not say that he himself found the money, the detail with which he tells the story makes it likely that he arranged for the child and mother to be united again.

But there was comfort also in this work for prisoners. About this time, Mr Yates, who had been Campion's host at Lyford and had been arrested about the same time, died after seven years' imprisonment without trial. Among Catholic laymen he was one of the most renowned prisoners, 'both for his gentle birth', as Garnet explained, 'and his long confession of Christ'. 'When he became sick and saw his last day draw near, he was anxious above all things to find for his eldest son a wife from some devout Catholic family. Several were presented and finally, in preference to all

[1] *Ibid.*   [2] H. G. to C. A. 11 July 1588. F.G. 651, f. 16.

others, he decided on Tregian's eldest daughter, and immediately desired to give his son to her, although she had no dowry other than the faith and religion of her two parents.[1]

Unimportant as the marriage might be, it was gratifying for Garnet to see the eldest son of Campion's friend and host marry the daughter of Francis Tregian, the protector of Cuthbert Mayne, the protomartyr of the Douai priests. The marriage, at which perhaps he himself officiated secretly in prison, symbolised the unity that he longed to see established among all working on the mission. Indeed there was no man who appreciated more deeply than Garnet the extent to which seminary priests, religious and lay-folk, had suffered and were suffering equally in the same cause.

About this same time, perhaps in the same month, Garnet had the happiness of comforting in his last hours John James, a Catholic prisoner waiting execution in Chichester gaol. Like Garnet, he came from Derbyshire. He had been a pupil of Garnet's father at Nottingham School.[2] On 1 October 1588 he was executed at Chichester: 'once a student at the English College', wrote Garnet,[3] 'he had a most ardent desire to enter the Society. He sent me frequent letters from prison begging for this and I have no doubt that he is united in heaven with those whose child he desired to be on earth.'

Garnet's universal and practical sympathy for men and women, priests and matrons, under persecution is seen in every page of his letters, and occasionally also flashes of wry humour at the behaviour of heretical ministers. But the stories he heard in prisons reflect every human facet of the fears experienced almost daily by Catholics.

'A certain woman with child [he wrote in his July letter],[4] when her time of delivery drew near, travelled to another county where she might have her child. Catholics have to do this, for if they give birth in their own house the question always arises as to where the child is to be baptised. . . . It is a crime punishable at law for a mother to give birth to a child and not to have it baptised [by the minister], or for her to move about in public before she had been childed by him. So by chance it happened that this woman, after a short labour, gave birth in an open field by the road, without any other woman present; and then she carried her infant son at the breast to the house of a neighbouring [Catholic] lady.'

---

[1] Francis Tregian, a noted Cornish recusant and father of eighteen children, suffered twenty-eight years' imprisonment for sheltering Cuthbert Mayne, the first Douai martyr, at his manor of Golden, Cornwall. He died in exile at Lisbon on 25 September 1608 at the age of sixty. Cf. P. A. Boyan and G. R. Lamb, *Francis Tregian* (1954).

[2] *Liber Ruber*, C.R.S., vol. 37, 22.

[3] H. G. to C. A. 29 October 1588. F.G. 651, f. 18.

[4] H. G. to C. A. 11 July 1588. F.G. 651, f. 16.

It was now no longer possible for Catholics, as it was in the early part of the reign, to perform their own ceremonies in their parish church with their own Marian priest. Now even non-Catholics, who had been brought up in the Catholic tradition, were troubled over the manner in which some ministers carried out the ceremonies of baptism. In the same letter Garnet tells the story of a non-Catholic woman insisting against the protesting onlookers that the sign of the cross should be made on the forehead of her infant. He claimed to have this story from 'a most trustworthy authority'.

Garnet had remained in London with Oldcorne over Christmas. In spring 1589 he left for the country to initiate Oldcorne into the work he had destined for him. Gerard records the events.[1] Garnet, he says, 'took Father Oldcorne with him into the country where he remained. There he employed him in divers missions round about and found him so practical and so industrious that he doubted not to send him on the most difficult enterprises.' This was about March 1589, since Garnet was back in London by Easter.

For more than a year Garnet had planned to make Hinlip Hall, three miles from Worcester, a centre for the recovery of the west of England to Catholicism. It was the home of Thomas Habington, a member of Babington's circle, who had been imprisoned shortly after Garnet's arrival for alleged complicity in the Plot. Over two years he had been in the Tower, an unrelenting Catholic, while his sister, a Protestant, brought up at the Court, refused to meet her husband's wishes and maintain a resident priest in her house. It would seem that Garnet himself failed to convert her; but he saw in Oldcorne, young, naive almost, and inexperienced, the priest for the task. 'The headstrong and petulant woman', writes Gerard after telling the story of her conversion, 'became most humble and pliable in his hands.'[2]

Nearly the whole county, adds Gerard, followed her example. It was the most successful placement that Garnet made. 'For sixteen years Oldcorne lived in her house. It was his work to bring many to the faith in this and neighbouring counties, to support the wavering and lift up the fallen, and to station priests in many places. Many, therefore, who knew him, speak of him in the words St Jerome uses of St John — 'he founded and governed all the churches in those parts'.[3] After Thomas Habington's release from the Tower in 1593, Oldcorne's apostolate expanded still more. Hinlip became a great religious centre — 'so many Catholics flocked there to receive the sacraments, to hear [Father Oldcorne] preach or get his advice'. Within a few years of Oldcorne's arrival Garnet was compelled to send him an assistant, Fr Thomas Lister, a nervous but learned priest, who found in

[1] *Narrative*, 282–3.   [2] *John Gerard*, 44–5.   [3] *Ibid.*

Thomas Habington a man of his own interests.[1] It is not known how much Thomas owed to Lister in the antiquarian researches which he took up after his return to Hinlip and which made him a pioneer in scientific county history.[2]

On 1 May Garnet, now back in London, gives an exact and vivid description of the scene in Westminster Hall at the trial of Southwell's friend, Philip Howard, Earl of Arundel. In April he had written to Aquaviva from the country, but the letter miscarried.

'I have come to London [he now told Aquaviva][3] to transact important business with our creditors at their Easter meeting.[4] On my arrival I found people of every class in a state of alarming affliction and disquiet by reason of the condemnation of a certain noble Earl ... who has spent four entire years in prison, cut off from his family, with no comfort save that of his own good conscience. He ambitioned nothing else than to be a good Catholic and escape to a country where he might live as such. Now at last he has been arraigned, partly on false charges, partly because of his steadfastness in his Catholic faith and practice. He was condemned to death on 14 April to the great sorrow of the heretics themselves.'

Garnet then describes the trial. It is uncertain whether he was actually present at it, but he would seem to have witnessed the London scenes that followed the Earl's condemnation: in fact he is the only person to record them. The injustice of the sentence disturbed the crowd, which made no secret of its sympathy with the Earl.

---

[1] Thomas Lister, a Lancashire man, entered the English College, Rome, on 15 September 1579 at the age of twenty; he was considered a brilliant student. Later he studied theology and before returning to England took a doctorate at Pont-à-Mousson.

[2] Thomas Habington, born 1560, was a godson of Queen Elizabeth, who was served by his father as cofferer. Educated in the universities of Paris and Rheims, he was one of the most cultured persons of his day. Anthony à Wood (*Athenae Oxonienses*, vol. 3, 223, ed. Bliss, 1817) writes of his *Antiquities and Survey of Worcestershire*, which was incorporated largely into Nash's history of that county: 'Part of this book I have seen and perused, and find that every leaf is a sufficient testimony of his generous and virtuous mind, of his indefatigable industry and infinite reading. 'Tis to be wished that some gentlemen of other counties would follow his and the generous example of Dugdale of Warwickshire, Burton of Leicestershire, Thornton of Nottinghamshire etc... and not live like idle heirs of their ancestors' titles.' He died at Hinlip at the age of eighty-seven on 8 October 1647; his son William, a notable poet, was born there on the day before the 'discovery' of the Gunpowder Plot, 4 November 1605.

[3] H. G. to C. A. 1 May 1589. F.G. 651, f. 21. In the Stonyhurst transcript of the Roman autograph the date is wrongly given as 1 September 1589. Stonyhurst, Grene *P.*, 555.

[4] Garnet is referring to the Spring assizes.

'When the people, against all expectation [writes Garnet][1] saw the Earl coming out of [Westminster] Hall with the axe-edge turned in towards him — in the trial of nobles this is the sign that the prisoner has been condemned — suddenly there was a great uproar that was carried miles along the river. Some people in the crowd asked what had become of the Queen's clemency that such a true and gallant gentleman should suffer condemnation. Others were passionately indignant that a man whose only offence was that he had prayed to God should be condemned for that alone.'[2]

The speech for the prosecution, like that at Garnet's own trial, included a summary of every plot since the beginning of the reign. 'Nothing of political significance during the last thirty years, no single person brought to trial — neither Paine, nor Parry,[3] nor Babington nor the Queen of Scots herself, escaped mention. The charges against them were recapitulated both to bring odium on the Catholic name and to secure the condemnation of the Earl'. It was a staged political prosecution, but it was clumsily miscalculated. 'For among the charges brought against him,' Fr Garnet continues,[4] 'the principal charge, and the one on which the whole case turned was this — he had asked a certain priest to pray for the success of the Spanish fleet; whereas in fact all that his enemies could prove against him was that he had asked that prayers should be said every hour of the day and night in the Tower of London and in other prisons, at the time when everyone was expecting a general massacre [of Catholics].' It was abundantly clear that he had not prayed for the success of the Spaniards, but merely for the safety of Catholics. The false charge on which he was condemned caused the horrified cry of indignation that Garnet recorded. It was a spontaneous shout of alarm and explains why Burghley saw that the sentence was never carried out. Six and a half years later, on 19 November 1595, the Earl died in the Tower. His breviary, which he used daily, he gave to Southwell, and later Southwell gave it to Garnet.

Garnet never failed to draw inspiration from his attendance at the trials

---

[1] H. G. to C. A. 1 May 1589. F.G. 651, f. 21.

[2] *C.R.S.*, vol. 21, *Philip Howard* (ed. J. H. Pollen), 214–19. The best short account of the life and trial of Philip Howard is in the pamphlet, *Blessed Philip Howard*, by Margaret Waugh (Farm St., 1962).

[3] At the Earl's trial there was produced a forged letter (corroborated by Elliot, who had betrayed Campion), purporting to commission Paine to provide fifty men with pocket daggers for the purpose of murdering the Queen and certain members of the Council. William Parry, an adventurer and an agent used by the government against Catholics, was eventually caught in the web of his own intrigues and executed in 1585. cf. *The Strange Case of Dr William Parry*, by Leo Hicks, S.J. in *Studies*, September 1948.

[4] H. G. to C. A. 1 May 1589. F.G. 651, f. 21.

of Catholic laymen or priests. Always he found in them some manifestation of popular sympathy with the old religion. All his writing and all his work were based on the belief that some day the country would return to the Catholic religion. With this hope went an humble appreciation of his own failings and a fear that he might disappoint those who had set their trust in him and his brethren. 'Meanwhile we comfort ourselves with the reflection that those who come after us will one day enjoy tranquillity. One thing afflicts not only us who are eye-witnesses,[1] but you also who are with us in spirit — namely, the sight of so many souls falling into perdition, souls that cannot be saved unless it be by the Queen's favour, no matter how much they themselves would wish to be saved.'[2]

Here, in this last phrase, he states the crux of the Catholic conscience. In the uncompromising terms of post-Trentine theology the rescue of souls from hell was dependent in large measure on the religion of the reigning sovereign. Working from this premiss it was not difficult for a simple adherent of the Catholic faith to argue that he was doing a service to God by attempting to substitute for a sovereign professing heresy a ruler of his own religious conviction.

[1] This phrase may be taken as a further indication that Garnet himself was in the crowd outside Westminster Hall at the condemnation of Philip Howard.
[2] H. G. to C. A. 1 May 1589. F.G. 651, f. 21.

THE VETERANS

GERARD, referring to the time of his arrival in London in December 1588, says:[1] 'There were then no more of the Society in England but Father Garnet, the Superior, and Father Robert Southwell . . . and Father Weston, who was then in prison, where he remained until this King's time, for the space of seventeen or eighteen years, and then was banished with divers other priests.' Gerard adds in the same passage that 'by good hap' he had found his Superior in London 'though his ordinary abode were then in Warwickshire almost a hundred miles from London'.

This is the first indication in any source that Garnet had moved his headquarters from Shoby to Baddesley Clinton, a secluded and moated manor four miles west of Warwick. It is probable, though not certain, that this house had been rented by Mrs Brooksby from the Ferrers family.[2] It formed the westernmost station on the axis of the centres built by Garnet. It was here that he took Oldcorne after Christmas 1588, and from here Oldcorne worked his way to Hinlip, no more than half a day's ride south.

After leaving Oldcorne in the west country Garnet had returned to London in March. He was expecting two experienced priests from the Continent: both had left some years earlier in order to join the Society abroad.

In November 1588 he had been restless as he waited the arrival of Gerard and Oldcorne; now eight months later he endured greater anxiety, for the worth of the Jesuits on their way had already been thoroughly tested. Moreover, his letters were not reaching Aquaviva. Since the suspension of diplomatic relations with the Spanish Netherlands it would seem that his link with Rome had been broken. 'Now I have scarcely any hope of sending or receiving letters', he wrote on 12 March.[3] It was with intense relief, therefore, that he welcomed the two Jesuits, Richard Holtby and John Curry,

[1] *Narrative*, 282.
[2] *John Gerard*, 274.
[3] H. G. to C. A. 12 March 1588. F.G. 651, f. 11.

a few days after their arrival in London.[1] Something of his old optimism returned. 'The day before yesterday', he wrote on Mayday, 1589,[2] 'all four veterans met. The recruits were absent, but both of them are well and both making good progress.' The recruits were Gerard and Oldcorne, the veterans, along with himself and Southwell, the newly-arrived priests, Richard Holtby and John Curry.

Holtby already had a reputation for missionary work equal to none in the north. In his lifetime and for many years after his death his name was legendary between the Humber and the Tweed. Garnet had not dared hope that a priest so valued now on the Continent would be released to assist him. In Holtby's return to England he saw another proof of the confidence Aquaviva placed in him and more than a token of his interest in England.

'A little man with a reddish beard', as he was described by a spy two years later,[3] he was perhaps the most accomplished and versatile of Garnet's lieutenants. If he had not been so essential to the structure of northern Catholicism, he would certainly have succeeded Garnet as Superior when some years later Garnet asked Aquaviva to be relieved of his office. By training or by talent he possessed all the qualities required of a leader. A Yorkshireman from Fraiton, he had been a student along with Campion's companion, Alexander Briant, at Hart's Hall, Oxford. Then he had crossed to Douai and, after ordination in 1578, had returned to England. Rather more than two years later he had acted as Campion's guide on his visit to the north-east, and with him had ridden across the moors from house to house, with such discretion that today it is still impossible to trace their movements during the weeks they were together. Then, after Campion's death, he had crossed again to the Continent to enter the Society. His return had been delayed by his appointment as Rector of the Seminary for Scottish priests at Pont-à-Mousson. He was to live until 1640, still active on the Yorkshire mission in his eighty-eighth and last year.

His companion, John Curry, was also a seasoned missionary. Born in Cornwall, he had been in the service of Sir John Arundell, the bulwark of Catholicism in his native county. He had been a priest twelve years when he returned to England in April 1589. Like Holtby he had come strongly under the spell of Edmund Campion, and had been with him in Oxfordshire:

[1] It is only a cryptic reference to two 'veterans' in Garnet's letter of 1 May 1589 (F.G. 651) that makes it possible to date their return to England. It is sometimes stated that Holtby remained abroad until 1590. However, Garnet cannot be referring to any other priests. Henry More (*Historia Provinciae Anglicanae*, 1660, 350) also gives 1589 as the year of Holtby's return.

[2] H. G. to C. A. 1 May 1589. F.G. 651, f. 21.

[3] *S.P.D. Eliz.*, vol. 245, no. 24.

there he had helped to distribute Campion's tract, *Decem Rationes*, which had been secretly printed at Stonor. Just six years later a spy described him as a man 'about forty years old, long, slender-faced, with a black head of hair and a little black beard'.[1] Quiet, beloved, and simple, he worked unobtrusively in the south-west of England until his death in August 1596.[2]

With the coming of four Jesuits from the Continent between November 1588 and April 1589 it was possible now for Garnet to push forward rapidly the plan drawn up at the memorable conference at Hurleyford in August 1586. Never had there been so many priests at liberty in England. Already, since the defeat of the Armada, close on forty newly-ordained priests had entered the country. Yet there is no note of satisfaction in Garnet's letters. He was aware that, with a sudden turn of fortune, Catholic expectations centred on these men might be shattered overnight. Constantly his letters begin or close with the phrase, 'Thank God, we are all alive and at liberty.' Meanwhile, impatiently, almost feverishly, he strove each year to send overseas an increasing number of youths who, after six or seven years' training, would, in the event of fresh disaster, be ready to provide replacements for the present forces.

A lull in the persecution, at least in London, had followed the slaughter of 1588 and the condemnation of the Earl of Arundel. On the arrival of Holtby, Garnet wrote to Aquaviva:[3] 'All classes of person, high, middle and lowest, were astonishingly afflicted and disturbed by the sentence of death passed on the Earl.' Not a single Catholic was executed in London in 1589. Three priests were hanged in York during this year, along with a layman; and a further two priests and another layman at Oxford.[4] But for the present, at least, the severity of the onslaught had abated, and Garnet was able to consolidate his gains throughout the country.

On his return to the north, Holtby gathered about him a group of seminary priests who looked to him for direction and acknowledged him unofficially as their leader. With their help he was able to organise the safe disembarkation of the newly-ordained men crossing from Rheims to north-east England. About this time he established, a short distance up the Tyne from South Shields, two landing places on opposite banks of the river,

---

[1] *S.P.D. Eliz.*, vol. 249, no. 138.

[2] *John Gerard*, 87.

[3] H. G. to C. A. 1 May 1589. F.G. 651, f. 21.

[4] At York, Fr John Amias and Fr Robert Dalby were hanged on 15 March; Fr William Spencer and Mr Robert Hardesty, a serving man, on 24 September. At Oxford on 5 July, were hanged Fr George Nichols, Fr Richard Yaxley with Mr Thomas Belson of Brill, Bucks, and Mr Humphrey Prichard, a Welsh servant man, who had assisted priests.

H

at Hebburn and St Anthony's, where the land was owned by Catholic families. Here, at night, merchantmen on their way upstream to Newcastle secretly discharged seminary priests with a regularity that escaped detection for more than twenty years.[1] After their landing Holtby despatched them to mission stations throughout the north: he provided them also with horses, clothes and cash until they were able to shift for themselves. At the same time he organised the charitable relief of Catholics imprisoned in the northern gaols. He had for the seminary priests the same intense admiration that Garnet expressed so often in his own letters to Aquaviva. 'The true clergy of England are the men whose modesty, fine bearing, discretion, learning and goodness shine out for the whole world to see. In England their number is very great, and they have always shown us the greatest affection.'[2]

With the safe arrival of the veterans Garnet's depression lifted; his faith in the survival of the Church returned; dissensions were in the future. In a single sentence in a letter to Aquaviva, written on 16 January 1590, his companion Southwell describes the expansion during this lull. 'We are all looking after our different counties and working hard for souls with great profit.'[3]

Now, systematically, priests were being deployed throughout the country in places where they were most needed. No experienced missionary expected the respite to continue. While it lasted, full advantage was taken of it. The foundations of the Church were strengthened against worse storms that lay ahead.

It was probably at the end of April 1589, at this first meeting between Garnet and Holtby, that Nicholas Owen, then a layman, joined them for technical discussion. Garnet was aware that the security of centres he had built up depended on protection against the sudden intrusion of pursuivants. Hiding places, sometimes several in the pivotal houses of his system, were now needed if the losses of 1588 were to be avoided in a fresh persecution. Hitherto, as can be seen in the *Autobiography* of Fr Weston,[4] they had been ill-constructed, improvised, badly-ventilated and insecure. The lives of too many priests had been sacrificed through inadequate provision for their concealment.

From this time Nicholas Owen was so constantly in Garnet's company that he became known to the Council and to Catholics as Garnet's man. Owen came from a staunch Catholic family established at Oxford in Mary's

---

[1] For the discovery of these secret places of entry see Philip Caraman, *Henry Morse* (1957), ch. 5.

[2] H. G. to C. A. *Circa* March 1598. Arch. S.J. Rome, *Anglia* 30, II, 364.

[3] R. S. to C. A. 16 January 1590. *C.R.S.*, vol. 5, 329.   [4] *William Weston*, 44–8.

reign. Of his three brothers, two had become priests; the third followed the dangerous trade of Catholic printer — he once set up a small secret press in the White Lion prison while he was detained there. Possibly it was through Henry Owen, the printer, that Garnet first met his brother, Nicholas, who, like him, had already served a term of imprisonment for his bold championship of Edmund Campion's innocence. Certainly they had met in Garnet's first year in England; Gerard states that Owen was principal maker of hiding holes from the year 1587:[1]

'I verily think no man can be said to have done more good for all those that laboured in the English vineyard. For, first, he was the immediate occasion of saving many hundreds of persons, both ecclesiastical and secular, and of the estates of these seculars, which had been lost and forfeited many times over, if the priests had been taken in their houses. . . . How many priests then may we think this man did save by his endeavours in the space of seventeen years,[2] having laboured in all the shires and in the chiefest houses of England.'

Indeed only through research into the activity of Owen is it possible to trace Garnet's own movements. Coughton Hall and Billesley Manor to the south of Warwick, Baddesley Clinton to the west; Huddington and Hinlip in Worcestershire; Rushton, the home of Sir Thomas Tresham, in Northamptonshire; Thrumpton Hall in Nottinghamshire — all belong to this period. How much Holtby in the north owed to this master craftsman is unknown; and no comparison had yet been made between his technique and Owen's. This London meeting in April 1589 complemented the general plan of the Hurleyford conference nearly three years earlier. No details of the discussions are reported, Garnet merely mentions it. Gerard, in his tribute to Owen's work, appreciated its significance.

The lull in the persecution continued through the spring of 1589. Communications with Rome, however, were difficult now that Spain had no ambassador in London. Between 1 May 1589 and 2 March 1590 there is only one short letter despatched by Garnet, dated 12 September. But in the spring 1590 he reviewed in general the situation of the previous six months. It is a story of steady but unspectacular advance.

'Considering the heaviness of this soil and the difficulties of trading, the progress of our work is by no means insignificant. In general, I may say that we owe heartfelt thanks to God. Whether we consider the physical or spiritual health of Ours, or the repute we have among men of good-will or the result of our labours (such as they are), everything is, I will not say

---

[1] *Narrative*, 88–90.

[2] Owen was arrested a few days before Garnet, who was at liberty for eighteen years.

as your Lordship might desire, but such as he has a right to expect. And I am certain that the result will not correspond with your desire until through your prayers and endeavours a way eventually is opened for us to trade more freely.'[1]

Two other things are noteworthy in this year, 1589. Garnet, after expanding his missions over a much greater area of England, now turned his eyes to Wales. In his short letter of 12 September 1589, he wrote to Aquaviva:[2] 'We greatly desire a Welshman of the Society.' Possibly he was referring to an earlier and now lost letter in which he had discussed more fully the difficulties of Catholics in Wales. The following March he returned to his request.[3] 'We are waiting a Welshman, with a companion, whether Welsh or not.'

The second matter was ominous. Without entering into detail, he hinted at the beginnings of divisions among the clergy, and at the trouble raised by priests who were now falling away from their ideals. In his charity he ascribed this, not without reason, to the severity of the persecution in the year of the Armada: 'Everything here is fraught with peril', he explained.[4] 'The fall of some has frightened others. Many of us are wandering homeless. Recently some men have been sent from [the seminary at] Rheims, whom their contemporaries at Rheims judged unworthy of the priesthood: men who, unable to rule themselves but anxious to rule others, cause us much trouble.' It was only with a few of them that Garnet found fault, namely, the men whom Rheims itself rejected: some were worthless, others spies who, with government assistance, had infiltrated into the seminary. 'They are not the clergy of England', he was to write with greater vehemence some years later,[5] 'but seditious men, full of lies and envy.'

Meanwhile, seeing how the situation might and indeed did develop, Garnet showed every kindness to known or suspected trouble-makers. If he met them wandering homeless, he strove to find them houses from which to work; if they were without friends, clothes or cash, he made provision for them. By comparison, troubles with his own men were slight and still in the future. For the present he was intensely grateful for the loyalty of each and all of them. 'Ours, by God's grace, keep their dignity. For this we owe deep thanks to your Reverence for having helped us so much by your prayers.'[6]

[1] H. G. to C. A. 2 March 1590. Stonyhurst, Grene *P.*, 555.
[2] H. G. to C. A. 12 September 1589. Stonyhurst, *Anglia* 1, 41,
[3] H. G. to C. A. 2 March 1590. Stonyhurst, Grene *P.*, 555.
[4] H. G. to C. A. 12 September 1589. Stonyhurst, *Anglia* 1, 41.
[5] H. G. to C. A. *Circa* March 1598. Arch S.J. Rome, *Anglia* 30, II, 364.
[6] H. G. to C. A. 12 September 1589. Stonyhurst, *Anglia* 1, 41.

Garnet promised to write again 'when opportunity offered'. As it turned out, it was seven months before he could get another letter through to Rome. Nor do any letters of Southwell to Aquaviva survive from the second half of this year. The first break in the long silence is a letter from Southwell — Garnet was presumably in the country at the time — sent on 16 January 1590.[1]

After opening with the jubilant cry, *Vivimus adhuc et valemus et vinculis digni non sumus*, 'We live still and are in health and unworthy to be held in bonds', he complains, like Garnet, of his difficulty in despatching letters. Reproachfully he tells Aquaviva that even allowing for the loss of many of his letters, he is writing more than he receives: 'The condition of Catholics is unchanged, full of fears and perils.' His mood was, however, optimistic, for there had been strange portents that he took as forebodings of better times.

'Some very strange prodigies have recently been seen here but whether they are good or bad omens I leave you to judge. On the west coast of England, not far offshore — some thousands gathered to witness the spectacle — was seen either a woman resembling a fish or a fish resembling a woman from the waist up. Both the novelty of its appearance and the sweetness of its singing gave universal pleasure. One of the spectators, however, fired a shot at the singer and wounded it. Thereupon, with a loud and piteous wail, it dived from the rock on which it had been sitting straight into the sea and was seen no more.

'On the north coast five enormous whales — the smallest was about forty-five feet long and the largest about sixty-five — were washed up on a half-mile stretch of beach all at the same time — something unseen for centuries. Furthermore, on the eve of the Epiphany, a storm raged so fiercely that many houses all over the country were knocked down, huge trees uprooted, and in the Queen's own apartment a larger section of the window glass was blown in towards her table by the force of the gale. It broke a very valuable crystal vase and injured one of her courtiers, and would probably have struck the Queen herself had not somebody stood in between and diverted it from her. Also two of the principal royal ships, one named *Revenge* and the other *Triumph*, were sunk in harbour in this same storm.[2]

[1] R. S. to C. A. 16 January 1590. *C.R.S.*, vol, 5, 329–30.
[2] These were the best-known ships in the Queen's navy. When the Spanish fleet sailed up the English Channel in the last days of July 1588 Sir Martin Frobisher commanded the *Triumph*, Sir Francis Drake the *Revenge*. With Sir John Hawkins in the *Victory*, they attacked the rearguard of the Spanish force in the first engagement east of the Isle of Wight.

I have heard of other things no less strange than these, but I pass them over in silence because I have not certain authority for them.'

Portents or no portents, the lull came to an abrupt end with the March meeting of the Jesuits in 1590. During the winter Garnet and Nicholas Owen had been preparing the Ferrers' house at Baddesley Clinton, near Warwick, for a regular meeting of the small but growing Jesuit community. It was remote and ringed by Catholic houses. Although the tenant was a Catholic, the mansion was unmolested. Here the Fathers met in the last days of February 1590. Garnet reported to Aquaviva on 2 March, Southwell on the following day. Their accounts of the reunion underline their differences of character as much as their first letters from England: Garnet is factual, Southwell poetic. 'We all came together [says Garnet][1] during the last few days and conferred on your Lordship's business, earnestly and with great comfort. Since the nature and conditions of our work keep us so much apart, your Lordship can well imagine what a joy it is even to set eyes on one another.' Taking up the same subject, Southwell adds:[2]

'It was a delight to be together again, keeping our ancient custom, helping each other and exchanging views. *We opened our mouths and drew in the spirit.* It seemed to me that I was looking at the cradle of our Society new-born in England, and that we are sowing in tears the seeds whereof others coming after us will gather in sheaves.'

He refers to the solemn High Mass at which Garnet loved to officiate at these gatherings. 'We have sung our songs in a strange land; in this desert we have sucked honey from the rock and oil from the hardest flint.'

The meeting ended suddenly. A pursuivant from the neighbourhood either visited the house or gave some indication of an imminent raid. 'Sorrow pounced on us at the height of our joy', Southwell continues. 'We scattered in alarm but escaped fortunately with more danger than damage.'

With them were the first secular priests, John Nelson and Thomas Lister, whom Garnet received into the Society at this reunion. The number of Jesuits at liberty was now eight. Garnet records their entry into the Society in a letter written six months later.[3] 'There joined our number Thomas Lister, whom I have mentioned in another letter, and John Nelson, most recently sent by your Lordship. As the first days of their apostolate have been admirable, we hope great things from them.'

Lister later was to cause Garnet much trouble; Nelson lived to work in obscurity for six short years. It is not even recorded where he was stationed.

---

[1] H. G. to C. A. 2 March 1590. Stonyhurst, Grene *P.*, 555.
[2] R. S. to C. A. 3 March 1590. *C.R.S.*, vol. 5, 330–2.
[3] H. G. to C. A. 13 September 1590. F.G. 651, f. 32.

A Lancastrian, he had entered the English College, Rome, in April 1585, fourteen months before Garnet started on his journey to England.[1] Ordained just two years later, he had been sent over immediately. He was familiar to Oldcorne and Gerard, who had been students with him; but little is known of his work or character. In December 1596, Garnet, who clearly had much esteem and affection for him, recorded his death: 'Mr. John Nelson, a man of outstanding devotion and holiness, who had been engaged in our business for seven years with very great application and charity and no mean profit, died on 10 July [1596], wasted by a long disease. I beg your Lordship to remember him in your prayers and to commend his soul to the prayers of Ours. I hope they will be all the more generous to this fellow-warrior of theirs in proportion as we are fewer here and deprived of the fraternal assistance of our communities.'[2] In this last, slightly puzzling, phrase Garnet shows himself concerned that prayers should be said for his subjects after their death. In Europe and throughout the Society it had already become the custom for priests of each Province to offer two Masses for the repose of the souls of their fellow Jesuits as soon as their death became known. Garnet's men were few; and under him there were no large communities on whose suffrages his dead brethren had a claim. For this reason he appealed to the charity of Aquaviva for the prayers of the whole Society on behalf of all who died in England. Fr Nelson, who was at Baddesley Clinton at the March meeting, 1590, was the first Jesuit to die a natural death in England, a man not yet thirty, the victim of consumption. If the facts were known, Garnet may well have been reponsible for inspiring an enduring devotion to its dead, so typically medieval and English, in what soon became the English Province of the Society.

At this time, just less than three and a half years after his landing at Folkestone, Garnet foresaw with confidence the expansion of the Jesuits in England. Their first members were men widely different in talent, background and personality; yet all effortlessly attracted to themselves the best of Catholic youth in England. John Gerard, for example, as he moved from house to house in the eastern counties, sent every year as many as half a dozen young men to Sant' Andrea. In his *Narrative* he states that Oldcorne did the same in Worcestershire and the west. Now Garnet wrote for Aquaviva's advice. Many men had asked to join the Society, but the danger of leaving the country secretly was equal only to the danger of entering it. It was possible for youths of the middle class to cover their exit with a plea of business or education. However, the majority who had offered themselves, coming,

[1] *Liber Ruber. C.R.S.*, vol. 37, 57.
[2] H. G. to C. A. 4 December 1596. F.G. 651, f. 98.

as they did, from the family connections and friends, first, of Southwell, and then Gerard, belonged to the gentry. Already their families were marked by the government and listed and watched for their loyalty to their faith. A few years later, with the help of Richard Fulwood, Garnet was to organise an escape route for them — from London to Greenwich and thence to the Netherlands.[1] Meanwhile more young men were clamouring every month to be admitted into the Society.

There was another problem to be solved. In the first years of the Jesuits it had been laid down that candidates, after taking their first vow of poverty, were to keep the ownership, but not the use or benefits, of their worldly property, so that in the event of their not persevering, what they brought on entering might be returned to them on leaving. In England there were several young men who 'were prevented by some undertaking from leaving the kingdom',[2] and yet, explains Garnet, 'while they are still here they want to give over to us their money and possessions'. With the growing commitments of the Society, 'the use [of these revenues] would be very much to our advantage and make it possible to support ourselves by this means alone'; and thus freed in this way from financial anxiety 'we should be able to concern ourselves more completely with the salvation of others'. But until Garnet was in a position to give these aspirants to the Society 'some certain hope of fulfilling their desires', he was anxious not to 'deprive them of what they still needed to live in the world in a manner that was in keeping with their position'.[3] Garnet knew the quality of those who were about to enter; he was desirous to make his own work financially independent of the charity of the families that had hitherto supported the Society and were now crippled by fines for non-attendance at church. It was a typical scruple of a man who was both a just and a zealous leader.

[1] Fulwood's escape route was through Gravesend to Gravelines. It is described in a report of the spy Healy to Lord Salisbury (April 1606): 'The priests of the country command such youths as they make choice of unto him [Fulwood], who placeth them in some blind alley near the water, until the wind serves for passage, which fitting, the vessel (which is some old hoy or suchlike, to avoid suspicion) goeth down empty towards Gravesend, and he provideth a pair of oars and boats, the passengers and carriage, and so ships them into the bark, commonly beyond Greenwich, and conveys the money which belongs unto them afterwards himself. They ship them to Gravelines or Calais and take forty shillings for the passage.' *S.P.D. James I*, vol. 20, no. 47.

[2] H. G. to C. A. 13 September 1590. F.G. 651, f. 31.

[3] *Ibid.*

I I

THE PONTIFICAL PRIESTS

AFTER Garnet had explained the position of young men anxious but unable to enter the Society, he concluded: 'the same also holds for those fitted for the duties of Martha. Already at this time they assist us in many ways with their skill and loyal service'.[1]

Without yet admitting them into the Society Garnet had gathered about him a nucleus of craftsmen, unmarried men devoted to his service, who made it their vocation to assist his priests. To send these men abroad at this time would have delayed, if not disrupted, the work he had planned: Garnet, therefore, kept them in his employment until Aquaviva, accepting their proved loyalty as a substitute for a formal noviceship, consented to receive them into the Society. Owen has already been mentioned: his friend, Richard Fulwood, from Weston in Warwickshire, a man of administrative ability rather than technical skill, appears to have joined Garnet about the same time. The government soon came to discover that 'he was Garnet's agent in nearly all his business',[2] wrote Gerard, 'and offered a large sum for his capture, both before and after they had seized Fr Garnet. In fact they gave him no rest and eventually he had to flee the country.' Among other trusts Garnet gave him charge of his London business during his absences in the country and, in particular, the supervision of the exits and entrances of young students and priests. Only in the first years of the new reign was Fulwood's organisation uncovered.[3]

It is difficult to date with precision the time Owen and Fulwood joined the Society. About the year 1590 occurs a mention also of two other assistants, John Lillie and Ralph Ashley. All were at one time or another captured, tortured and imprisoned; two of them, Owen and Ashley, were to meet death with their masters and in their employment. Along with them also must be grouped Ralph Emerson, who had already been received into the

[1] H. G. to C. A. 13 September 1590. F.G. 651, f. 32.
[2] *John Gerard*, 73
[3] *S.P.D. James I*, vol. 20, no. 47.

Society and had spent many years in prison after his unfortunate arrest in the service of Weston.

In March 1590 the period of comparative tranquillity ended. 'Sorrow pounced on us from the height of our joy', wrote Southwell;[1] ' . . . my companion and I, having avoided Scylla, proceeded to steer into Charybdis; but by a special mercy of God we circumvented both and are now riding safely at anchor'.

During the next twelve months, from March 1590 to March 1591, the persecution intensified. With a few short intervals it lasted for the next five years; it was more fierce and unremitting in the north, until the end of the reign. The rise of Richard Topcliffe, a Yorkshireman of almost un-mitigated evil, dates from this time: tortures worse than any hitherto prac-tised on priests lay ahead for those unfortunate enough to fall into his hands.

Garnet's own problems were made more acute by his isolation from Rome. Another year passed before he was reassured that his letters were regularly reaching Aquaviva. At the end of May 1590 he expressed his personal distress at the breakdown of communications. 'Among the severe hardship which we experience daily in these parts, by far the severest is this, that those above all others whom I desire to endorse what I am doing, I cannot, save most irregu-larly, keep informed of my work.'[2] His depression returned intermittently. He was sad that the best of his own nation were being drawn to the established church in which few really believed. There was a sense of intense tragedy in his letters written in those twelve months after the reunion of March 1590; possibly also there was a fear that if the persecution continued Catholics might break. It is not that he saw any signs of this; on the contrary, the signs indicated perseverance to the end, on the scaffold or in prison or in destitution. But Garnet, now himself the centre of the resistance, saw in the history of the Church no precedent on which he might forecast the future behaviour of Catholics. He was bewildered and in need of guidance from Aquaviva.

Southwell was under the same stress, but accepted it in the gay spirit that had not deserted him since his landing. 'We have written frequent letters to you', he says,[3] 'but, as we have just learnt, only a few have reached you. . . . ' Then he adds characteristically: 'We are tossed around still in the midst of perilous waves. With God's help we have so far escaped with our lives.'

Southwell had returned to London in time to witness the execution of

[1] R. S. to C. A. 8 March 1590. *C.R.S.*, vol. 5, 330.
[2] H. G. to C. A. 25 May 1590. F.G. 651, f. 25.
[3] R. S. to C. A. 8 March 1590. *C.R.S.*, vol. 5, 330.

Fr Christopher Bales, a priest from Rome, a contemporary of Gerard and Oldcorne, who had crossed with them to England on the same ship. He was hanged in Fleet Street on 4 March 1590. He had been Southwell's pupil; his health was extremely frail; he was the youngest priest ever executed in the reign, just six months short of his twenty-sixth birthday.[1] He had been cruelly tortured by Topcliffe — his first victim. The description of his sufferings forms a preface to the last and fiercest phase of persecution, in which Garnet was to lose the best of his subjects and many intimate friends. The warrant for Bales' torture, issued to Topcliffe some time before 1 February 1590, was the first the wicked man received.[2] 'Bales had been hung up off the ground by the hands for a little less than twenty-four hours in order to make him confess where he had said Mass. . . . He stood firm.' He died just two days before Walsingham, who, if the story were known, had perhaps held down Topcliffe: there would seem to be more than a coincidence in the death of the Secretary and the rise of the subordinate. For Catholics the next decade might be characterised as the decade of Topcliffe.

The man's position is difficult to define. He possessed almost despotic power, yet the only official post he held was that of 'Queen's pursuivant'. He appears to have acted with authority deriving directly from the Queen. He had his own gang of followers, a small private army that shared with him the spoils of his conquests; he organised raids and directed them in person; he was the grand inquisitor and torture-master together — with a licence to torture privately on his own premises. At the trial of priests he was assistant prosecutor; at the scaffold, assistant director of their execution. Of all who held such an appointment he boasted, and apparently with truth, that he had the private ear of the Queen. Whenever he sought an audience he was granted it. Even Garnet, who never elsewhere uses terms of personal detestation, speaks of him as 'the most sordid of men': *homo sordidissimus*. They never met face to face, for Garnet skilfully avoided the traps Topcliffe laid for his arrest. 'This most sordid of men', he wrote in 1592,[3] 'has now for some time attained such favour with her Highness that he always has easy access to her, and he need not fear the power or influence of any Councillor or Minister.'

At the start of his inquisitorial career Topcliffe took over an annexe to Bridewell as his peculiar prison where he could pursue his 'practices' without restriction of enquiry. This itself foreboded a more savage persecution. Hitherto torture had been used only in the Tower. Its use was contrary

---

[1] *C.R.S.*, vol. 5, 130.
[2] *S.P.D. Eliz.*, 230, no. 57.
[3] H. G. to C. A. 16 July 1592. F.G. 651, f. 45.

to common law, but was justified by Tudor lawyers on the theory that the
sovereign, by the exercise of his personal prerogative, could by this means
force political prisoners to reveal secrets injurious to the State. Something of
this pretence had been maintained in the devices practised on Campion,
Sherwin and Bryant. But after the Act of 1585 it was no longer necessary
to involve priests in a plot against the State before proceeding to their trial:
now they could be indicted simply for returning to their native country
after receiving Holy Orders overseas. Nevertheless, warrants were now
issued to Topcliffe for indiscriminate torture as a means of extorting from
priests information that would lead to the capture of their brethren. This
was the novelty.

At the same time a new method of torture was adopted: the 'wawle' — a
name derived perhaps from Topcliffe's own atrocious spelling. It was more
efficient, slow, noiseless and merciless than the old-fashioned rack in the
Tower dungeons, for the victim merely hung from a rod passed through
manacles pinned against a wall with his feet off the ground. Thus the body
itself did the work of the weights and pulleys. The method was so simple
that Topcliffe was able to equip his own private torture chamber at a trivial
outlay.

Topcliffe's rise to favour brought with it also a more systematic search
for priests. His own mad zeal inspired local magistrates, particularly in the
home counties, to frenzied activity. He was ubiquitous in the south; on
occasion he was seen in his native Yorkshire. He threatened to delate Justices
of the Peace less active than himself as crypto-Catholics. His success is
described in this same letter, although only later did Garnet associate it
with the person of Topcliffe.

'All magistrates [writes Garnet][1] think now of nothing else but satisfying
their own greed or venting their hatred on Catholics. . . . This indeed is the
agreed opinion of all the brethren. What has happened or is about to happen
is his doing.'

Garnet's work of the last four years was now to be tested. His organisation was well established: the priests from Rome and Rheims were systematically settled on their arrival; old priests from Mary's reign had been
rehabilitated; Catholics were standing firm; there was a shape and strength
in the resistance that gave hope of outlasting Topcliffe's personal power.
Without reference to himself, he contrasts the situation of 1590 with that
prevailing some years earlier. It is a satisfactory picture. None perhaps
summed it up with more detail or accuracy. He wrote:[2] 'We witness and

[1] H. G. to C. A. 25 May 1590. F.G. 651, f. 25.
[2] *Ibid.*

admire the wonderful harvest that, during these few years, God, in his goodness, has brought forth and gathered into the barn of his Church — a harvest
sown by the seminaries established and maintained by the Holy See. While
the present storm of persecution rages in England, this harvest cannot be
concealed.' It was exclusively the work, he claims, of the men he calls
'pontifical priests'; Pope Gregory's men 'who wash their stoles in the blood
of the lamb, who love Christ in their life and imitate him in their death; who
give their bodies to torment for God's sake, who fight unto death for the
law of God, who through faith conquer kingdoms, and, despising the command of princes, merit eternal reward'. The eulogy might have been written
for Aquaviva to read to the Pope, in order to encourage him to increase his
aid to the seminaries. Garnet continues:

'Who can imagine these splendid and illustrious triumphs possible [he is
referring to the Catholic resistance] without these priests ... or conceive
that without the seminaries there could be any priests in England. At the
time the seminaries were founded there were some bishops and very many
priests who not only professed the Catholic faith themselves, but also led
back to the truth others who had strayed from it. But of what avail would
they have been to our cause if, after they had been imprisoned or worn out
by old age or squalor or taken away by untimely death, the care of the flock
had ended with the life of its shepherds? How many old [Marian] priests
did the pontifical priests[1] awaken from the lethargy of schism? How many
priests, who were inert and languid, did they spur on to fight bravely? How
many unlearned and inexperienced priests did they assist with their counsel
and teaching? And, finally, how many stalwart and constant soldiers of the
Lord did they refresh with their company and companionship?'

This is the most complete account there is of the part played by the old
priests, and of the way they were assisted by the new men from the seminaries. In every case the work of rehabilitation was done in the secrecy of
confession. No circumstances or numbers were revealed; only the general
picture is given. Garnet goes on:

'Before the coming [of the seminary priests] many things were perpetrated without any consciousness of guilt. I cannot tell you what supersti-
tions, dissimulations, wicked oaths against the Roman Pontiff and the
religion of Christ, were tolerated even by those who wished to be considered
Catholics. Today the mere mention of these things brings a shudder to the
heart of every Catholic; and now nothing is thought too harsh or inhuman
or barbarous a price to avoid them. For alongside the few whose constancy
in those days of darkness was all the more admirable because it was so rare,

1 Priests from the pontifical seminaries.

there were multitudes nominally Catholics but in fact traitors to their holy
religion and deserters from it. They themselves went to the heretics'
churches, took their children and entire families with them. To be first to
enter and last to leave was considered the mark of a Catholic. They sent their
infants to the heretics for baptism, and their young or adolescent children
were fostered on the preaching and doctrine of the heretics. What wiles of
the devil! From these young people [and Garnet is writing of his own gener-
ation] now grown to manhood, all the responsible offices of the State are
filled; government Ministers and public officials are chosen from their
ranks; clergymen, preachers and overseers are drawn from them; and the
faith which their parents were unable, and their heretical preachers were unwilling, to teach them, none will now confess. No youth could enter a
university unless he was, or pretended to be, a heretic, and this exterior dissimulation was not even thought to be wrong, provided interiorly a man's
faith was sound. Finally, all marriages were celebrated according to the
heretical rite and the sacriligeous Supper was partaken by all — at least all
gave in their names or asserted that they had received it. Moreover, they
thought they could atone for these great evils if they, as it were, blended
things sacred with profane, divine with sacriligeous; I mean, if, after per-
forming the superstitious practices of the heretics, they attended the most
august sacrifice of the Church; served Baal as well as Christ.'

In this letter it is possible to see clearly the widening division between
Catholic and Protestant. Both, in the eyes of each other, worshipped Baal.
If Catholics were to stand out uncompromisingly for the past and refuse
to see their old beliefs diluted, strife was inevitable. This, in Garnet's mind,
was the warfare that Christ came on earth to spread. In England, seminary
priests and the Jesuits were responsible for it. The issues for which they
fought were no longer blurred. Knowing their ground, and sure of it, they
could not yield.

'But now, after the coming of the pontifical priests, everything is different.
Nothing is clearer now in the minds of all than this: that with our heart we
believe unto justice and with our lips we confess unto salvation; not only
that Judas sinned by betraying Christ, but that Peter sinned also by denying
Him and by failing to confess Him. These priests know that the primacy . . .
of authority must be given to the Supreme Pontiff, the Vicar of Christ, and
that it cannot be given to any other ruler without incurring grave guilt
and the sin of apostasy. And this holds if the acknowledgment is made
with dissimulation, or with a thousand ambiguities or with the reservation
that the Sovereign is head of the heretical church, which is indeed not a
church; so that she cannot be considered head of any church at all.'

This is a passage of particular interest in view of the accusations later made against Garnet that he was an equivocator and dissimulated his meaning. In this intimate outpouring of his mind to Aquaviva he speaks without forethought or reflection. He manifests his horror of any form of equivocation. He saw the damage done to the Catholic cause in the past by outward conformity joined to mental reservation of meaning. This had proved the ruin of the Catholic cause. It could be, and indeed was, only a matter of time before the external gesture of conformity induced the whole-hearted acceptance of a position that at first had been considered unacceptable. As he continues, Garnet becomes more emphatic but a little obscure. '[Catholics now] realise that to attend the churches of the heretics, under any pretext of obedience whatsoever, is such a great sacrilege that it is unlawful not only to be present at their gatherings, but also even to hear Mass said there according to the Catholic rite, but with an heretical intention.'

It is difficult to be certain whether Garnet is referring to the early years of the reign, or whether he is recording a practice that persisted even to the date of this letter. Certainly in the religious confusion of the first years of Elizabeth, many Marian priests, after holding a service according to the Book of Common Prayer in their parish churches, then offered Mass in the same place and for the same congregation. Apart from the possible indication contained in this letter, there is no other evidence to suggest that this double-functioning lasted beyond the first decade of the reign. Garnet continues: '[Catholics now] know that they must keep their children from the churches of the heretics and give them positive instruction in Catholic faith and piety, lest they sacrifice to demons those whom they have brought forth into the world. Finally [with the coming of the pontifical priests], there have been granted many smaller blessings that have increased faith and piety in Catholics — although nothing that advances the service of God should be considered small, however small it may seem to those who regard it from a merely human standpoint.' Garnet does not instance these smaller benefits; he hurries on in general terms.

'We have strengthened the faith of Catholics: this is our deed of treason: this is the crime we plot against the strong forces who venture to plunder and profane the vessels of Christ; this is the fruit we offer you; this the harvest you now reap from the seed you have sown so gloriously in the Colleges — a harvest not just tenfold, but thirty-fold, a hundred-fold. Whenever you hear men talk of our crimes and treasons, remember the penny[1] that is given to those who cultivate this great harvest field.'

Unwittingly in this letter Garnet shows the importance of this year 1590

[1] Latin: *denarius*.

for English Catholicism. The excommunication of the Queen twenty years earlier had defined the position of Catholics. Those who followed the old religion were no longer able externally to follow the new as well. The Catholic body was now sharply distinguished and resolute. While many fell away, the nucleus that remained furnished the foundation on which the new priests heroically rebuilt the Church. In the same letter Garnet gives the reverse of the picture — the most bitter phase in a persecution directed, in the north, by the Earl of Huntingdon, and in the south by Topcliffe. Now Catholics were able to withstand it as they could not have done ten years earlier. With mixed horror and equanimity Garnet reviewed the situation. The country was sealed off. Though priests entered secretly from the Continent, they rarely returned: their friends there were left without news of them. 'You will hear from us eventually', says Garnet, 'even if we are silent now . . . for the heretics themselves, if there are some kindly disposed spirits among them, will come to detest this inhuman barbarity.' The flame of resistance 'is burning always more strongly and gives a most comforting light to all who dwell in the household of Christ'. Exceeding afflictions were to be reckoned nothing in comparison with eternity. No extreme of privation could break the constancy of men and women who 'once they have given themselves to Christ, have preferred to lose their lives rather than fail in the enterprise they have undertaken'.

'We are all aware now that the true and orthodox religion is considered treason and stigmatised by that label. As for the name which to Christians is the most honourable of all, as indeed it should be — I mean the name Papist — if it is applied to an heretic or man of the world, he resents it more than the name of murderer or traitor. The loathing in which Papistry is held by the Queen's Council is such that if a man is found in possession of a cross or chalice or missal, and is thrown into prison for this offence, no member of the Council, no matter how friendly or in favour he may be, will dare speak or even whisper a word on his behalf. You know how everywhere men hanker to get news and pass it on to others: well, even those who are exceptionally curious and readily listen to any gossip, whether in London or the home shires or at Court, will not listen nowadays to any other news except that someone or other was captured in such a place with rosary beads in his hand; that somebody else was imprisoned for attending Mass, and has his property seized by the sheriff; that somebody else still was flogged for his faith or made to work at the tread-mill or was kept hanging with his hands tied to a pillar for a whole day to make him reveal the names of Catholics or the hiding-places of priests.'

Garnet was not repeating a cant phrase when he spoke of a fresh impetus given to the persecution. He attempted to define it. He was alert to something new in the situation of Catholics, a further sharpening of their segregation, a new loyalty among them and a still greater heroism they were now showing. His praise of their steadfastness, to some extent, is the measure of his own humility. The sacrifices asked of them were something that no priest, but God alone, could demand of them. Through the fearful passages of his letters there surfaces a satisfaction that exceptional grace is at work in the Catholic flock.

The campaign of defamation became more intense. The charge against Catholics was no longer that they were plotters, but untrustworthy, indeed traitors, by the mere profession of their religion. The slander was accepted, in all but the upper classes of English society and at Court, where their proven loyalty was seldom questioned. As Garnet observes:[1]

'It is the established practice of our enemies to defame with the name of treason the splendid work and dedicated zeal of our priests, whereas the fact is that we are guilty of no treason other than of upholding orthodox Catholic doctrine. . . . We are dragged before the magistrates, questioned, tortured, flayed, we who are plotting nothing, who stay hidden in our homes and attend to our prayers and the concerns of God. We are put to death unless we declare . . . that we are willing to take up arms against the Pope in any circumstances whatsoever.'

Then, with tragic detail, he describes the lot of the simple, unknown Catholics in country places. In a few sentences he speaks of the hardships, unsuspected and unsung, that they endure in order to receive the sacraments. If, in their native county, they were known as Catholics, they were likely to be imprisoned; and 'this is the reason [he continues][2] why many Catholics change their dwelling-place and go, so to speak, into voluntary exile, and live unknown and obscure in remote parts of the country. If only there was some one place where they might be permitted to live in peace, they would consider themselves treated fairly enough. But the faithful are not left to themselves anywhere. It is impossible, save at the greatest risk, to baptise infants, celebrate marriages, give the sacraments or offer the sacrifice according to the Catholic rite. Therefore expectant mothers travel to remote parts for the birth of their infants in order that they may not be asked questions later about the christening of their offspring. When they marry, they ride to some distant place for the ceremony and then return home, to avoid questioning on the celebration of their marriage. At the bi-annual visitations of the pseudo-bishops and the half-yearly general assizes there is nothing into which they enquire more meticulously or punish more severely than the practice of the true

[1] H. G. to C. A. 25 May 1590. F.G. 651, f. 25.   [2] *Ibid.*

I

religion. Consequently when Catholics find any honest method of evasion which they can adopt with a good conscience, they gladly seize it. But if there is not an honest method at hand, they show no inclination to take advantage of loopholes in the law or to answer ambiguously. . . . [1] Who would deny that here is the spirit of God, that God's finger[2] is discernible, that God's power is at work for the salvation of his elect.'

The crux of the letter is an appeal to his friend and Superior, Aquaviva, for a strengthening of the priestly body in England. Garnet is honest. He does not conceal the stark prospect—imprisonment, torture, execution—that awaits priests whom Aquaviva may send. He stresses the urgent needs of Catholic layfolk for the sacraments and leaves the decision in the hands of the General.

'This is the state of things [he concludes];[3] we implore your Lordship, in the charity you have always shown us, to ensure . . . that there will be no failure in our progeny. . . . We beg you always to send us new labourers well-formed in Catholic faith, doctrine and morals, so that we will never lack assistance in snatching from the jaws of the wolf the flock of Christ, that increases daily in merit and number; nor will there be wanting oxen to tread out the wheat. Our Lord is the head of the household: he is now carefully cleansing his wheat. With the winnowing fork of persecution he will scatter the chaff: there will remain among us only clear and clean grain, fit to be ground by the teeth of beasts, yes, ground into pure bread to be placed on the Lord's table. We have no doubt at all that this is for the glory of Christ, that it is pleasing to the citizens of heaven and benefits the universal Church.'

The passage is a blend of Ignatius of Antioch and Robert Southwell. In their account of the persecution both Southwell and Garnet had to go back to the early centuries of Christianity that matched their own: indeed, the Church in Africa at the time of St Cyprian offered the closest parallel with the position of Catholics in England. It is Cyprian's name that occurs more than any other in the writing of Southwell, Allen and Persons; and it was the spirit of St Cyprian, and his devotion to the See of Rome, that principally inspired them.

[1] The manuscript here is worn and illegible.
[2] *Finger of God*, i.e. the Holy Spirit.
[3] H. G. to C. A. 25 May 1590. F.G. 651, f. 25.

12

FINSBURY FIELDS

NOTHING is known of Garnet's movements between May and September 1590. He seems to have summoned the second half-yearly meeting of the Jesuits earlier than usual, probably for the feast of the Assumption. He gives no reason for this but merely records the fact when he writes again to Aquaviva on 13 September.[1] John Nelson was with them; also Fr Thomas Lister. For the present, however, Garnet was happy to see the number of his men slowly increase. 'We derive from these re-unions immense benefit which abundantly compensates for the risk.'[2] Aquaviva in Rome was anxious always for their safety at such times; he seems even to have suggested some alternative to these gatherings, but Garnet set on them too great a value easily to forgo them. They gave his men opportunity not only for the discussion of common problems, but also for confession and spiritual comfort. With the honesty that makes his letters to Aquaviva such intimate and trustworthy documents, he does not hesitate to record, in the same paragraph, the capture and execution of priests almost at the very time his brethren were together: rather than abandon these re-unions, he was prepared to sacrifice the small Jesuit mission in England. The Hurleyford gathering under Weston's directions had meant everything to his own and Southwell's apostolate. This was the experience also of Gerard and the younger men. 'Very recently', he writes,[3] 'four priests captured about Easter time in County Durham were executed. They made such a great impression by their bearing that very many people are eagerly rushing to join the Church. If we had the priests to nurse this fire with tenderness and toil, before it died, the martyrdom of these men would lead to an astonishing increase in the Church.'

This was the report he received from Fr Holtby. The four Rheims priests, Edmund Duke, Richard Hill, John Hogg, and John Holiday — the last

[1] H. G. to C. A. 13 September 1590. F.G. 651, f. 32.
[2] *Ibid.*
[3] *Ibid.*

three of them Yorkshiremen — were all executed on the same day, 27 May, at Durham. Garnet regarded the effect of their death on public opinion as a further triumph for the Church.

The main interest of this September letter 1590 is that it reveals the topics discussed by the Jesuits at their meeting the previous month. They had sought solutions to the difficulties common to them all. Garnet had asked and heard the opinion of his brethren. When it was divided on an important issue, he suggested that they should defer to the judgment of Aquaviva.

The first problems were personal: the disposition of his subjects in prison. Two years earlier he had discussed with Southwell and later with Aquaviva the question of purchasing Weston's release.[1] It had now come up again; and there was a possibility also that Emerson might be freed in the same manner. On Weston, Garnet's view was unchanged and it was shared by his brethren. Emerson's case was different. He was not a figure of eminence; he was not even known to be a Jesuit; he passed simply as Weston's servant, yet he knew the ways of his Jesuit masters. Garnet therefore considered that he would be invaluable now that he was increasingly dependent on skilled and trusted retainers. 'He [Emerson] can return immediately to us. He is deeply loved by us all. So far from thinking that he is fleeing from the enemy, people will see he is making a fresh assault on him with new weapons.' If he could not be employed in England, he could serve in Ireland or Scotland.

It is not difficult to see all the priests gathered at Baddesley Clinton concurring with Garnet's proposal to put Emerson's release in hand. On certain moral issues, however, opinion was not unanimous. Garnet explains the divergent approaches. 'There is not sufficient agreement among us whether a priest sins mortally if he denies he is a priest when he is asked the question publicly or by a magistrate. Some would have it that he commits a mortal sin only if he denies matters touching his faith or his obligations as a Christian: they argue that a particular status freely accepted by an individual does not come into this category.'[2] Then Garnet proceeds to give what would seem his own opinion:

'For if every man is compelled to reveal his status, why would he not be bound also to confess all particulars about his religion: whether or not he attended Mass today; and so on. Others take the contrary view. They hold that the supreme honour due to God is at stake; that without question this honour would be impaired in such a public and notorious issue — and this is the principal argument theologians bring forward for the open confession of our faith. There are others who admit that when a man is bound to confess

[1] Cf. *sup.*, p. 67.   [2] H. G. to C. A. 13 September 1590. F.G. 651, f. 32.

he is a Catholic he is bound also to confess that he is a priest if questioned on the point, for both concern the honour due to God; yet they would have it that this is restricted to the occasion when he is questioned about his religion and priesthood *per se*. Certainly this is not our case, they observe, for here priests are considered traitors by law; and hence to ask a man whether he is a priest is the same as asking him whether he is a traitor; and all admit that he can deny this.

'Nevertheless, whatever is the right view, all who correctly understand the state of affairs here, cannot accept this last solution. It is manifest that priests are considered traitors for no other reason than this, that they are priests. A priest cannot deny his priesthood any more than a Christian can deny his faith, if the Christian is considered a traitor and criminal by reason of "crimes" of this kind trumped up on the sole score of his religion — unless of course his interrogator is so crass as to believe that the charges are true and that a genuine crime is in question and not the religion of the accused. This is never our case, unless some ignorant peasant chances to be the interrogator.'

Garnet's exposition has to be followed closely. It is balanced, detailed, scrupulous; manifestly he is seeking guidance, not the acceptance of his own view. He himself, once again, is leaning to the more merciful opinion that will save the lives of priests: but at the same time he represents the opinions contrary to his own with the exactness and sensitivity of a man who realises that the other side may well be right. He apologises to Aquaviva for putting the arguments of his brethren at such length:

'I have written on this at considerable length. The reason is that some time ago I did receive an answer from Rome, but it was not fully explained or supported by arguments. Moreover, it was not set out in a manner acceptable to all, and was not therefore given the authority it might have deserved. There are still some who cite the opinion of a certain very learned man who was consulted by your Lordship, and now lives in Paris. Without doubt, if the matter had been put to him clearly, he would certainly have dissented from the general opinion.[1] In a question of such importance it is most desirable that all of us here, both Ours and other priests, should be in agreement. Therefore I beg your Lordship to send me a definite and well-grounded judgement on the whole question.'

[1] This is a reference to Garnet's friend, Robert Bellarmine. In 1590, Bellarmine, with Cardinal Cajetan, went as theological adviser to the embassy which Pope Sixtus V sent to France for the protection of the Church's interests there. Garnet, from his personal knowledge of Bellarmine, could claim that he knew what his mind would have been on this subject if he had been fully informed on it.

Indeed it was an issue vital both to the individual conscience of priests, and to the impression they made on the public. . . . In the end, while direct denial of their priesthood was never allowed, priests were permitted to place the burden of proof on their accusers, and at the same time use every available form of verbal evasion short of actual denial. Whether this was Garnet's solution or that of the Roman theologians is not clear. However, it left the conscience of priests uncompromised and contributed to the saving of many lives: it also brought relief and comfort to them. When they knew beyond doubt that their accusers possessed incontrovertible proof of their priesthood, it gave them the intense joy to confess in public what all held to be their incomparable privilege.

Among other questions discussed at this meeting was the ownership of shipwrecked property. It was now two and a half years since the defeat of the Spanish Armada. Catholics, so severely mulcted by fines, felt justified in taking possession of articles washed up along the beaches on to which their estates abutted. By English law such treasure belonged to the Crown. But as Garnet pointed out, there might arise a conflict between civil law and natural law. It was a live issue for Catholics. Many of them had acquired large stretches of coastal property, particularly in more remote parts of England, where they were able to provide safe or at least sheltered landing places for priests. Already, two years before Garnet's coming to England, Weston had been put ashore at a point south of Lowestoft owned by Catholics.[1] Many other priests entered England in the same way.

Garnet considered this question 'of the greatest importance'. He writes:[2]

'Not only by very ancient and established custom but by a statute some two hundred years old, the property of shipwrecked people accrues to the State treasury, so long as no living thing, neither man, nor dog nor cat (as the words of the law have it) survives. Now a large number of Catholics with whom I have occasional dealings seize this property without any scruple on the plea that they hold royal rights over their maritime estates.'

Garnet allowed that the common opinion of theologians and the canon law was contrary to the English statute.

'Nevertheless certain considerations seem to justify our practice (namely,

---

[1] This was the estate of Henry Hubert or Hubbard, south of Lowestoft, at Kitley, Kessingland and Pakefield. In 1592 it was seized by the Crown on account of Hubert's recusancy (Recusant Exchequer Roll 1592–3, *C.R.S.*, vol. 18, 312). All this land either bordered on the sea or stretched towards it. In the north of England Holtby established secret landing places for priests in the Tyne estuary. In Dorset the Arundells had done the same at Chideock.

[2] H. G. to C. A. 13 September 1590. F.G. 651, f. 32.

the Crown's claim to all ship-wrecked property). First, there is the ancient custom of the country, confirmed by statute, which ... would never have been ratified unless the Bishops of the whole country, who have the right to sit in all Parliaments, had duly consented to it. And it is unlikely that anything contrary to divine and natural law would have been sanctioned by statute in a Catholic country by Catholic Bishops. Therefore it can be argued that our custom, and the statute confirming it, are not against the natural law.[1] And if they conflict with the canons, then the tacit permission of the Bishops and of the Holy See, over so many years, should surely deprive the canons of their binding force.'

'What then, should we do?' he asks, reducing the issue to a strictly pastoral one. What is to prevent us sanctioning the custom prevailing here ... without worrying about restitution?' He refers, of course, to those who possess the Crown rights over wrecked goods. Was it licit for them to keep the articles without taking steps to find the owners. It was on this precise point that the canons and the statute conflicted. With good sense Garnet continues: 'Moreover, those who support this view cite the rule and maxim of the illustrious Abbot of St Martin's on the Hills ... that whatever was practised and approved by our ancestors while [the Catholic] religion flourished should by no manner of means be set aside.[2] Reason also gives authority to this law. For since the Sovereign has an obligation to keep the seas free from pirates, it would appear right that he should have the means to do this efficiently, even if the supreme good of the state is the individual's loss.[3]

'Moreover the law lays down that where a man or a dog or a cat escapes alive from a shipwreck, then, provided the owner claims his property within a year, it must be returned to him. The reason for this is that after a year it is very unlikely that the owner can be traced. Therefore it is just, that when the owner is not known, the [canon] law about wrecked goods should be observed. According to this, after the lapse of a year, the goods need not

---

[1] When a ship was lost at sea and part of the cargo washed up, the goods, by the common law of England, belonged to the Crown under the title of wreck. This right of possession was frequently granted to the lords of manors. The strictness of the prerogative right to wreck was relaxed by early charters and by statutes (3 Edward I, cap. 4, 1275, and 27 Edward III, st. 2, 1353) under which owners of shipwrecked goods were allowed to reclaim them within a year and a day, if they could identify them. Earl Jowitt, *Dictionary of English Law* (London 1959), vol. 2, 1884.

[2] This was probably Regino of Prum, who rebuilt the abbey of St Martin's outside Trier, where he died in 915. He made a famous collection of ancient canons on Church discipline in two books; the first treated of the clergy and ecclesiastical property, the second of the laity.

[3] By 'individual' he means the *owner* of the property.

be returned to their owner so long as there has been diligence in seeking him in the meantime. But if the owner, from another ship . . . , saw the ship carrying his goods dashed to pieces before his very eyes, and if he tried immediately to recover his property from the shore, why in this case should everything go to the owner of the [coastal] land, if nothing living is saved from the ship itself?' This was a case covered by Garnet's argument in favour of the statute: 'This is something', he says, 'which we cannot explain, except to say that it is highly probable that a law, which in other respects is based on sound reasoning, does not lack sense also on this point.'

Garnet here shows his knowledge of English law, learned from Tottel in his youth. Later he was to claim, by virtue of this law — for Aquaviva sanctioned his opinion — the right to employ for the English mission two Portuguese Jesuits who were captured at sea and brought to England for ransom. He argued that they were shipwrecked 'goods' and might be used by him until they could be sent to the mission of India for which they had been destined and had indeed set sail.

Other, less surprising, questions arose at this conference. A large number of Catholic squires still held the right of patronage in livings now taken over by the Elizabethan Church. 'Many persons maintain', Garnet writes, 'that this right can be lawfully bought and sold with the property to which it is attached or even without the property.' The argument was the same as in the case of treasure-trove: the practice was allowed by law or at least sanctioned by custom, which over a long period of years received the tacit recognition of 'Bishops, Apostolic Nuncios and the Roman Pontiffs themselves'. Once again Garnet is on the side of the existing practice: there were enough points already on which Catholics were compelled by conscience to take a stand that set them apart from their fellow-countrymen — and it may well have been Garnet's presentation of the case that determined the practice of Catholics who continued for many centuries to hold these rights of patronage.

'It is the accepted opinion of many theologians [Garnet argued] that the right of patronage is not in itself something spiritual. Consequently it can be sold with permission of the Pope. And why should silence not be taken as acceptance? I know that the Pope has in fact allowed the right of patronage to be sold, at least in cases where the money could be used for pious purposes. Here men press this point that patronage can be sold without restriction because it has thus been sold in the past, and that anybody who sells it may keep the money for himself, because this has always been the custom.'

While Garnet himself urged his case with moderation, he was clearly supported by pragmatic canonists like Gerard, for whom past practice was sufficient justification. Garnet's own mind is shown in his summary of the issue.

'These are the questions that give us trouble. Since there are different opinions on them and since, on the one hand, we do not wish to make difficulties about accepted customs and, on the other hand, . . . we do not wish to persist in practices that differ from practices in other parts of the Christian world, it seems essential that we should seek your Lordship's decision.'

The remainder of the letter concerns the problems of individuals, the Society of the Rosary and marriage regulations. Converts made by the Jesuits and seminary priests had often availed themselves of the new English law which permitted marriage within degrees of kindred forbidden by Roman law. Although priests had fairly wide faculties for dispensation, they frequently met cases that required reference to Rome. Garnet himself despatched several to the Roman tribunal. In every instance he showed impatience at the delays: constantly he begged for an answer 'as quickly as possible'. Now, for example, he wrote:[1]

'A certain youth, availing himself of the license granted by the heretics, has married a girl who is his first cousin; indeed she is his first cousin in a twofold degree: the fathers of both were brothers and their mothers sisters. For twelve years now the two have lived together and have had nine or ten children. They were never very hostile to the Catholic faith; and now, through various afflictions, God, as it were, has shown them that their present life is not pleasing to him, so that it would be quite easy to win back one or both to . . . the Church. In order to remove any obstacle in the way of this holy undertaking, I seek permission to dispense them if one or both desire to return to the bosom of the Church.'

In the same letter he petitioned leave to dispense a youth from a vow of chastity that he had rashly made when he had thoughts of leading an eremitical life. With the delays inevitable in obtaining dispensations from Rome, Garnet sought still wider powers. General principle ruled that a dispensation should be given, not direct to the party seeking it, but to the priest handling it. Now he asked for a general faculty to dispense in certain categories of impediments to marriage:

'We wish that a definite formula of concession be sent to us in writing. If it is merely said in general that this or that dispensation has been granted, it remains uncertain whether only the priest who petitions the dispensation can communicate it to the parties, or whether some other Jesuit priest can do this or whether he can empower any priest at all to do so. The last course

[1] H. G. to C. A. 13 September 1590. F.G. 651, f. 32.

is indeed sometimes necessary, when we cannot ourselves seek out the person or persons in the case.'

Garnet concludes the letter with an apology for worrying Aquaviva with these requests: 'and so we never stop harassing your Lordship with our various troublesome affairs. While in your charity towards us, your Lordship attends like a father to these matters, we beg you also to have a care for all things that concern our spiritual well-being and bring us heavenly aid.'

Garnet wrote this letter 'from the diocese of Worcester'. After the meeting he had ridden to Hinlip. Significantly he does not end with the customary report that 'all are well'. Fr Oldcorne was suffering from anaemia. 'His heavy work and his care of all the churches in those parts', wrote John Gerard, 'did not satisfy him. When he was at home [at Hinlip] he studied hard and at the same time did much corporal penance.' Whenever Oldcorne met Gerard, he looked so anaemic that he seemed unlikely ever to recover his strength. Soon after reaching England he had developed a cancer in the throat that was judged incurable. An excision was the only remedy that English doctors could suggest, but this would have deprived him of his vocal organs. As Gerard says, his earnest manner of speech made him an effective preacher, 'though his voice [was] somewhat hoarse and painful unto himself, yet audible unto his hearers'.[1]

It would seem that at this meeting Oldcorne had asked Garnet's sanction to go on pilgrimage to St. Winifrid's shrine at Holywell in Flintshire to seek a cure at the miraculous spring.[2] This he did. His cancer was healed, and he 'recovered also from the anaemia which he thought to be its cause, and . . . came back stronger and healthier than he had been for many years'.[3]

On his return to London, Garnet closed the small London house which he had rented two years earlier in Finsbury Fields. For most of the winter he was out of London. In the spring of 1591, he had grounds for thinking that his place of hiding had been betrayed. In a long letter, written about two years later, he told the story:[4] 'There are many other incidents', he says, 'that

---

[1] *Narrative*, 284.

[2] John Gerard narrates the pilgrimage. As will be seen in the next chapter, it did not take place in 1591, for Oldcorne rode immediately back to Hinlip after the October meeting at Baddesley Clinton. It would seem therefore that it occurred this year. Unless Garnet was 'in the diocese of Worcester' for a considerable period, he would have waited until he was back in London before posting his letter. The urgency of some of the problems it contained made him write immediately. Probably he gave the letter to Thomas Habington to take to London, while he himself waited Oldcorne's return at Hinlip.

[3] *John Gerard*, 48.

[4] H. G. to C. A. 17 March 1593. Stonyhurst, *Anglia* 1, 73.

I could relate at the present moment, but I have been interrupted by the arrival of the man who is to carry this letter to you: it is not safe to retain in my keeping what I have just written. Whenever some means of despatching letters is at hand, I have no choice but to write to you in haste.' Indeed, all but a few of his letters show signs of hurried composition. Frequently his syntax and tenses, occasionally his grammar, become confused. Almost always, he wrote, sealed and despatched his letters before reading them over. Seldom is there a mark of correction. He judged it more prudent not to keep any papers in his hands a moment longer than was necessary.

Although Garnet does not give an indication of the time, the raid on what he calls his 'suburban house' took place probably early in 1591.[1] 'This house might have been of very great use to me', he told Aquaviva, 'if the devil had not begrudged me this great source of assistance.' In his absences from London he left it in the charge of his servant, Hugh Sheldon, who was known in the neighbourhood as 'Mr Gregory'.[2] Hugh had been living there some weeks in the disguise of a gardener, and had looked after Jesuits and other priests on their visits to London. 'But when the inquisition became daily more rigorous', writes Garnet, 'we were compelled to let him go elsewhere.' During that winter the house was unoccupied. The following spring a certain Jesuit, probably Oldcorne, visited London to consult a doctor after his pilgrimage to Holywell. Hugh, who had accompanied him from the country, went ahead to open the cottage. A few days later a priest, Fr James Younger, newly-arrived from the Continent, had gone out there to solicit Hugh's help 'in certain business'.[3] Ignoring Hugh's warning not to visit

[1] H. G. to C. A. 17 March 1593. Arch S.J. Rome, *Ang. Hist.* i, II, f. 27.

[2] Apart from other tasks assigned to him by Garnet, Hugh Sheldon, a Staffordshire man, assisted Nicholas Owen in the construction of hiding places (*John Gerard*, 158). He was eventually captured in 1599 at Kirby Hall, Northants. On the accession of James I he was banished, but he appears to have been in England again in 1606, for Fr Blount refers to him that year in connection with the smuggling of Catholic books into the country. In 1608 he went to Rome, where he succeeded John Lillie as Fr Persons' secretary. (Foley, vol. 7, part 2, 705.)

[3] With reasonable certainty this raid can be dated by Fr James Younger's arrival in England. Early in 1591 (when it was difficult to get priests into England), Fr Persons, then in Spain, devised the bold and successful ruse of smuggling eleven priests (including Richard Blount and John Cecil) through the English ports by persuading a Spanish admiral to equip them as English repatriated prisoners of Drake's expedition against Spain in 1587. On disembarkation at Portsmouth, the priests were taken before the Lord High Admiral, Lord Howard of Effingham, examined and passed with compensation money. When Burghley heard of the deceit, he ordered searches throughout the country, and particularly in London. (Foley, vol. 7, part 1, 64; Morris, *Troubles*, vol. I, 190). Fr Younger, a convert from Durham and a student both at Rheims and Douai, later became an informant against his former brethren.

the city in daytime — an axiom of safety rigidly observed by Jesuits who happened to be in London — Younger left the cottage and returned three days later. 'As he was entering the narrow lane that gave access to our garden, by some astonishing chance a youth caught sight of him, ran up to his mother and shouted, "See, there's a seminary priest! I saw him in Spain. His name is Father Richard". "Get the constable", answered the mother.'[1] The young man ran off. His mother followed the priest to the cottage door. The place was empty. As Fr Younger retraced his steps, he walked straight into the constable. The youth was questioned. He admitted he had made a wrong identification. Meanwhile Hugh Sheldon had returned by a different road. He was inside the house when the constable, 'with a great press of followers whom he had collected in the neighbourhood, knocked at the door'. Garnet continues the story: 'Spying them from a window and seeing their weapons and their prisoner, Hugh was astounded. He demanded to know who the men were. They answered, "The constable, in the Queen's name, is ordering you to open the door." "Open the door to you, why, pray?", Hugh asked. "We must examine the house. The man here whom we have just arrested was coming to it. There is no doubt that he is a priest." "Off with you", retorted Hugh. "You merely imagine he is priest, because you want to cause my master trouble. In any case you did not arrest him here: you are pretending he came from here. How am I to know you are not thieves and want to sack my house. I shall be blunt with you. I am not going to allow anyone in today. If you use force, it will be at your own peril. I shall defend my master's house." Then bolting the doors and barring the windows, Hugh went to the top room which was used by Garnet as his private chapel. There he prayed that God would make dull their senses and understanding, that they should find nothing.'

Garnet goes on to show how this prayer of his servant was answered. Everything had still to be hidden: not only Mass equipment, but all Garnet's papers and correspondence. Hugh spent two hours over the task, 'taking off all his clothes down to his shirt and pants'. Meanwhile the constable, leaving his men to watch the house, had taken Fr Younger into custody. On his return he brought with him the chief justice of Middlesex, Topcliffe's associate, Richard Young. Hugh had now to alter his bluff. He pretended he would have gladly let the constable in, if he had been sure of his credentials: until he was sure, it had been his duty to hold him off. Young was a very different person from the constable. Courteously Hugh continued: 'If it had

---

[1] Garnet's definition of the 'constable' is interesting: he is an officer appointed yearly in each parish from almost the lowest ranks of the people but he possesses very wide powers.

been your Worship who had come in the first instance, I should have opened the door at once in answer to your summons. I am well acquainted with your integrity and with the authority you possess. . . . Yes, the constable's men did say that they had arrested a priest here. This seemed incredible to me. In such a remote, almost uninhabited, spot, I had every reason to fear robbery.'

As soon as his neighbours had gathered and he could rely on them for protection he had come out. Young then questioned Hugh about the priest who had knocked at the door. Hugh answered truthfully that he had not seen him. He had been out of the house. There was a large number of gardens in the district and he may well have come to the wrong one. Young enquired at the next cottage whether anyone had come there and was told a man had in fact been and asked for the garden occupied by a certain Hugh. This, as all were ready to testify, could not have been Hugh Sheldon, for Sheldon was known to everyone as Gregory. 'By the supreme providence of God', says Garnet with relief, 'the neighbours testified that there had been a certain Hugh, a Moor, who had been caretaker of the garden before Gregory. But if [Younger's] enquiry had been for Gregory, that would have been the end, since it was by the name of Gregory that this associate of ours was known to all in the district.' Hugh knew Young's skill as a searcher. He was cautious. Asked whether his master was a Papist, Hugh answered that he was no more than a servant, and it was not his business to enquire into the religion of those whom he served.

Inside, Young saw a huntsman's horn hanging from the wall. 'Who uses this?', he asked. 'I do myself, and if your Lordship orders me I will play you the huntsman's call.' Young was not to be humoured. He ordered the search to begin. Hugh protested that his master had nothing to hide. He offered to find Young an axe and 'to break open, pull down, knock holes through or cut to pieces anything whatever'. Upstairs, in spite of the care Hugh had taken at concealment, Young found a letter written in Garnet's hand, 'which someone had carefully composed for him for the purpose of inducing a brother of his to adopt the faith'. Hugh now thought he was discovered. In desperation he bluffed: 'I don't know whose letter it is. I can't either read or write.' Without looking at the letter, Young put it in his jacket: then he took hold of a purificator. 'Well, what do you think this is?' he asked. 'It is a bib, I think', answered Hugh: 'the kind commonly used to tie round a boy's neck to stop him spoiling his clothes.'[1] Young accepted

[1] A purificator is a rectangular piece of linen used by the priest at Mass to 'purify' the chalice and is decorated (as this was) with a small embroidered cross. Garnet remarks: 'the purificators used in many places in this country are rectangular'.

this. Then he asked to see the cellar where there was a hiding place large enough to take six or seven men. Playing the part of the searcher's assistant — he was afraid Young might sound the walls and discover the hiding place — Hugh poked the coal as if to suggest the stack, the casks of beer, and logs were being used to cover papist stuff. The dust he raised drove Young upstairs. There he offered Young a drink and brushed his silk tunic which was sprinkled with coal dust. Young then left.

Garnet was prepared to lose his furniture: his papers were another matter for, as he remarks, 'they would have revealed our plans and perhaps betrayed some of our friends and caused I don't know what commotion'. Yet the risk of discovery was great. Young left instruction for all the roads leading to the garden to be watched. There was danger that Fr Younger, still in captivity, might make some statement that did not fit in with Hugh's story. Further, while Young was occupied in the search, there had been yet another caller, a friend of Hugh's. However, with presence of mind, Hugh berated him as though he were a stranger, until the man realised a search was on; he had then turned on his heels, been chased down the lane, caught and brought back to be questioned by Young. As he confessed that he had not been to church for twenty-three years, he also was taken to prison.

The arrest and the unconvincing behaviour of both this man and Fr Younger made it urgent for Garnet to act at once. The lease of the cottage had a year to run. No matter how convenient, it was now too dangerous for him to remain there. As soon as Young had left, Hugh burned all Garnet's papers, eluded the watch kept on the house and escaped to friends. Garnet wrote in triumph that 'several weeks later I sent some men there, recovered all the furniture and left the house empty for the owner'.

13
BADDESLEY CLINTON

ON leaving Rome Garnet had been recommended to assemble the priests serving under him twice a year. At the start of the 'nineties not a single Jesuit in England had been in the Society more than fifteen years: none, including Garnet himself, had made his final profession. Gerard and Oldcorne had served less than a few months' noviceship at Sant' Andrea. Neither had more than a brief initiation into the rules and customs of the Society: nor were others who now joined their number more experienced. When, during their first two years in England, Southwell and Garnet met for three days together in London, they spent the time in prayer, preparation for confession and discussion of the problems that faced them both. Regularly before taking leave of each other they renewed their commitments to the Society, and in a short spiritual retreat recaptured the fervour that had first led them to the noviceship at Sant' Andrea.

By turns one or the other priest gave a conference. Southwell suggests also that all gathered in chapel to sing together part of their divine office. Throughout these days Garnet advised, encouraged, and sustained the spirit of the priests working under him. New hopes took shape, fresh plans were formed, adjustments made in the distribution of the priests throughout the country as recruits joined them, or as seminary priests, without entering the Society, put themselves at Garnet's disposition. Always some Rheims or Rome priests joined their Jesuit brethren on these occasions, taking part in all their conferences and discussions. Only then were the Jesuits able to lead a community life. Southwell spoke rapturously about the meetings:

'Through your prayers, my Father [he tells Aquaviva],[1] we hope that . . . springtime will soon be at hand, with the flowers appearing and the vineyards spreading their fragrance. We strive for this as much as we can, in this stony and desert land, by hearing each other's confessions every six months and by renewing our vows. . . . Our small efforts are forming part of that

[1] R. S. to C. A. 20 December 1588. F.G. 651, no. 10.

mighty mountain which is being built up by the good deeds of all just men throughout the universe.'

Gerard was more factual:

'I can bear witness [he says] that these meetings were a great help to all. To speak for myself only (I will tell you my feelings simply) I never found anything that did me more good. [They] braced my soul to meet all the obligations of my life as a Jesuit and all the demands made of me as a priest on the mission. Apart from the consolation I got from renewing my vows, I experienced, after renewing them, a new strength and an ardent and freshened zeal.'[1]

It was the experience of all that these few days together twice a year deepened their attachment to Garnet and increased their admiration for him.

Apart from giving at least one conference, Garnet saw each Father in private. As he wrote to Aquaviva, it was then that 'we forged new weapons for new battles'. Only in one year, 1593, was the risk of arrest too great for Garnet to summon his subjects together. 'The past year', he wrote on 17 March 1594,[2] 'has been so full of trouble both for us and for all Catholics, that, among other hardships, there has scarce been an opportunity for a gathering. However, during this year we met occasionally two or three at a time. But it was never possible for all to assemble to discuss our affairs in common and renew our engagements.[3]

When Garnet wrote this letter he had in mind their October meeting 1591. Now two and a half years afterwards, he recalled every detail of their escape from capture at that time. With his extreme caution he had delayed mentioning it to Aquaviva. Only now, as he explained, could he report on the meeting 'because neither the persons nor the place will be so easily recognized. Had I written earlier it might have brought them into danger, for, as has happened, what I write to your Lordship sometimes by mischance comes to the knowledge of informers, whose number is legion.' While the house was still used by Garnet, he remained silent. After it had changed hands he omitted nothing in telling Aquaviva the story.

Almost certainly the place chosen for the meetings in 1591, as in the years immediately prior to it, was Baddesley Clinton, a moated manor house in Warwickshire exactly a hundred miles from London.[4] Built round three sides of a courtyard and surrounded by trees, it was both secluded from neighbouring properties and difficult for strangers to discover. Gerard refers to

[1] *John Gerard*, 40–1.
[2] H. G. to C. A. 17 March 1594. Stonyhurst, *Anglia* 1, 73.
[3] *Engagements* is Garnet's code word for religious vows.
[4] *John Gerard*, Appendix B, 274–6.

SERMON AT ST. PAUL'S CROSS
Dr. John King, Bishop of London, preaching in the presence of James I,
26 March 1620. Original in possession of the Society of Antiquaries of London

BADDESLEY CLINTON

it as Garnet's country residence. His short description of the search there fits exactly the features and location of the house. The autumn meeting 1591 lasted from 14 to 19 October. 'We had fixed on the same house', writes Garnet,[1] 'which we had previously used for the purpose. It belonged to two sisters, a widow [Mrs Brooksby] and a maiden lady [Anne Vaux]. For emergencies it was furnished with a very safe refuge in a well-concealed cave.' This tunnel, originally the sewer, running the entire length of the back wing, had been converted by Nicholas Owen into a hiding place which could accommodate a dozen or more priests. The old discharge into the moat and the loopholes which lit the tunnel had been camouflaged, and a garderobe turret, into which the sewage was diverted, constructed to project from the wall. The main entrance to it was down a shaft from a room adjoining the chapel. There was a second entrance from the room used by the priests in residence. The only disadvantage of Owen's plan was that the tunnel lay below the level of the moat surrounding the house — an exit had been constructed through a stone slab fitted into vertical grooves in the walls, and it was through this slab that water seeped into the tunnel. In wet weather the priests in hiding were forced to stand in water up to their ankles.

The Fathers met on the evening of 14 October. In the course of the preceding day Oldcorne had ridden from Hindlip, just eighteen miles away; Holtby had arrived from Yorkshire, Gerard from Essex, Southwell from London. Nine in all were gathered. Garnet had chosen the time with care. During the last three years he had observed that the periodic lulls in the persecution usually preceded a worse outbreak; and it was during such a respite that he summoned his priests to meet. Moreover, the country was engaged in parliamentary elections that occupied the attention of the sheriffs, justices of the peace, constables and smaller officials. 'Our adversaries', explained Garnet, 'are engrossed in a general election throughout the kingdom and with devising new methods of persecution.' He warned Aquaviva that the present calm portended no relaxation of the penal laws, 'for the peace which we enjoy here from time to time is not due to any easement of the laws or to greater freedom in the practice of our religion, but to a respite that will usher in a period of even greater harshness'.

Despite the lull Garnet did not remit any of his customary precautions against a sudden raid. No matter what conditions prevailed, danger was always present. Moreover, on this occasion, Garnet had ground for apprehension. Shortly before the meeting a drunken pursuivant had approached the manor and demanded admission. It was the early morning, and he was kept waiting until the vestments and altar vessels had been hidden. When the

[1] H. G. to C. A. 17 March 1594. Stonyhurst, *Anglia* 1, 73.

K

door was opened to him, he announced that he had come as a friend. On finding that he was not courteously received, he threatened to return within ten days 'bringing with him men to break down the doors and demolish the very walls of the house'.

As the pursuivant was resident in the district and familiar to the household, Garnet did not take the man at his word: nevertheless he bore his threat in mind. 'Except from this one foul-mouthed man, who was in the habit of spending days on end snoring in taverns', Garnet wrote, 'there was no danger anticipated from any other source.' Garnet argued that if the rogue really meant to come back, he was unlikely to have advertised his intention. He took a calculated risk, balancing the possibility of a raid against the certain benefits that all would derive from the meeting. If the man did return, it was only a chance that he would hit on one of the three days of the meeting: moreover, there was now a report that he had gone off elsewhere; and, as Garnet wrote, 'he could not come back into the immediate neighbourhood without our friends letting us know of it at once'. In any case it was too late to cancel the meeting; nor if this pursuivant arrived would it be the first time he had been there at these gatherings. 'He had previously visited the place at the very time we were assembled, though he had never actually searched the house while we were together. . . . Nevertheless his proximity always worried us no less than his appearance had frightened us.'[1]

Garnet made his decision unaided. He never failed to face with courage his responsibility as Superior. From this letter to Aquaviva it is clear that he had prayed much for the safety of his subjects: 'We were encouraged by these facts; we also had an exceeding confidence in God, for whose glory we were assembled. Therefore we decided to carry out our full programme. Besides, when so good a work as this was afoot, we never expected to escape the attentions of some evilly-inspired fellow.'

This meeting was particularly poignant for Garnet. Not only was it the largest held thus far, but it was the last that Southwell attended. Never again did he meet all his brethren together.

'We passed the whole of that time in the greatest peace and consolation.' Garnet says no more of their three days spent in prayer and conference for he was anxious not to violate the confidences he had received from his subjects. As his custom was, he himself during these days made his confession to Southwell and sought his spiritual guidance for the last time. A few more details are given by Gerard.[2] 'We held several conferences', he writes, and

---

[1] The passages above in quotation marks are taken from Garnet's letter to Aquaviva, 17 March 1594. Stonyhurst, *Anglia* 1, 73. This holds also for other quotations in the chapter, unless a special reference is given.   [2] *John Gerard*, 41.

the Superior saw each of us for a talk in private.' But he, too, goes no further.

On the feast day of St Luke, 18 October, the priests, at the end of Fr Garnet's Mass, recited before him the formula of their vows. They remained together until lunch. Until that time, Gerard noted, Garnet had shown no anxiety. When, earlier, one of his companions had expressed fears for their safety and had pointed out that there was insufficient space for all to hide, he had answered calmly that it was his responsibility, not theirs, until they had renewed their vows. But at luncheon on St Luke's day, Garnet became agitated. 'I don't know what inspired me', he wrote later, 'to address them as follows. I said that though until now I had taken on myself all responsibility for their security, I was willing to guarantee it no longer.' He then cautioned them all to look to themselves and not to stay on at the manor without good reason.[1]

Out of the party of nine, four took to their horses soon after luncheon. The remainder were then joined by two seminary priests. There was hiding accommodation for seven and no more. 'Unless those four had departed', wrote Garnet, 'eleven merchants altogether would have spent that night in the house.' Southwell, Gerard, Oldcorne and Stanney were there and, in addition to the two secular priests, two Catholic laymen, Gerard's protégés, who had come to seek admission into the Society. Their names are unknown.

The four Jesuits who stayed back were the four senior priests on the mission. They were detained, probably, for two reasons: first, to examine the candidates and report on them to Garnet; then, secondly, to hold a 'consultation' according to the custom of the Society. Garnet seems to say as much when he writes: 'some of us ... stayed up almost to dawn to transact important business.'

Nevertheless the following morning, 18 October, they rose early. At five o'clock Southwell was beginning his Mass. The rest were at prayer, waiting to follow him.[2] At daybreak the house had been surrounded and all the roads leading from it posted with watchers; the stables were astir and the horses saddled in readiness for the priests' departure.

---

[1] Gerard related the incident thus: ' "Yes," said Father Garnet, "we ought not to meet all at the same time now that our numbers are growing every day. But we are gathered for God's glory. Until we have renewed our vows the responsibility is mine; after that it is yours". Up to the day we renewed our vows he gave no sign of being worried; but on the day itself he warned us all to look to ourselves and not to stay on without very good reason. "I won't guarantee your safety any longer", he told us. A number of the party, when they heard this, mounted their horses immediately after dinner and rode off. Five Jesuits and two secular priests stayed behind.' *John Gerard*, 41.

[2] *John Gerard*, 41. Garnet writes: 'Scarcely one of our Fathers had carried out the rites of the liturgy.'

'Inside the house men-servants and maids were busy preparing breakfast, cleaning boots, putting out our cloaks and other things required for our journey (all had previously been kept hidden . . . so as not to give any indication that more persons were present in the house than was well should be generally known.' In the bustle of preparation one of the doors had been left open. At the very moment the chief of the search party approached the open door, a young man who had joined the Fathers the previous day chanced to walk out of the house. Faced with a stranger, this young man locked the door from the outside, took to his heels and hid himself in a wood nearby. At the same time two Catholic stablemen who were saddling our horses got wind of the raid. Armed with farm implements, they rushed out and threatened the searchers with violent treatment unless they left immediately. Garnet remarks that this was the right way to deal with pursuivants. 'If you turn on them, they are abject cowards.'

The method worked. The searchers 'abandoned their fury and resorted to requests'. The constable in charge then begged the stablemen to ask the mistress of the house to open the door: if she did he promised to treat her gently. The servants played for time. On the other side of the gateway the bolts were shot, the alarm was given, books, pictures, rosaries, chalices, vestments, *Agnus Dei*s were hidden away. The company already in the chapel had time to enter the hiding place: the five Jesuits, two seminary priests and the layman still with them. Mrs Brooksby, 'the mistress of the house, hid also in a separate hiding place'. After more than twelve years of intermittent searches, her nerve was broken. 'She was somewhat timid', explains Garnet, 'and unable to face with calm the threatening grimaces of the officer's men.' Moreover, since the house was rented in her name, she was the legal occupier. If the search succeeded, she and her children were certain to be taken to prison. On this, as on other occasions, her unmarried sister, Anne, assumed the role of mistress. Garnet, playing with the Latin words, says that in all crises this brave *virgo* became a veritable *virago*.[1]

The house was quiet again. Anne came to the door, opened it and confronted the pursuivants with composure. To gain time she detained them in conversation: it was vital that there should be left about the house nothing that might indicate the presence of a large number of strangers. For an interval the fierce conduct of the stablemen had kept the searchers at bay: had they not been held at the door, they might have entered the outbuildings, where ten horses were being got ready for the road. 'Our beds', says Gerard,[2] 'presented a problem, for they were still warm and merely covered in the

---

[1] *Whirlwind.*   [2] *John Gerard*, 42.

usual way preparatory to being made, some of us went off and turned the cold side up to delude anyone who put his hand in to feel them.

At the door in her nightgown (Gerard says she was not risen at the time of the disturbance) Anne was a match for the pursuivants. They demanded why she had kept them waiting so long. 'Does it seem right and proper', she retorted sharply, 'that you should be admitted into a widow's house before either she or her maids or her children have risen?'...[1] Then she rounded on them for their discourtesy: what had brought them so early to her house and in such a hostile manner? 'Have you ever found that I was stubborn', she asked, 'or refused you entry on previous occasions when you have knocked?'

The ruse was successful. Faithfully noting every phrase of the conversation as Anne later reported it, Garnet continues:

'The man, turning to his companion, remarked: "Yes, it is true. I have always found this lady courteous. I would have you take my word for it that certainly she had not yet risen when we arrived." But would she graciously tell them who was the man who had fled from the house? Surely he was a priest? They would not leave the place without him, or if they left without him, they would take her with them.'

Momentarily Anne began to fear. She did not know that any of her sister's guests had left the house. She feared that one of the priests had foolishly attempted flight. Quickly she recovered. 'He is a relative of mine.' And then she gave a name that she knew was unfamiliar in the district; 'and I am setting out on a journey with him to-day.' This she said, as Garnet explains, 'because they might see food prepared in the kitchen, and, if they entered the stables (which God however forbade), it would have been hard to account for the number of horses prepared for the road'.

The search began. Gerard describes it briefly:[2] Garnet in greater detail for he stayed behind to hear Anne's account, whereas Gerard rode off the next day.

Nothing was left undisturbed. Every corner, including storerooms and chests, was rummaged. Beds were examined to see whether unwittingly a priest had left a rosary or an *Agnus Dei* or a pious book lying there. Anne compared the searchers to boys playing blind man's buff; they were like children 'covering their eyes and then trying to touch and grasp their comrades', falling over chairs and tables, running into walls, taking no notice of their fellows who stood all round in touching distance. 'You should have

---

[1] Anne was unmarried: but she was now impersonating her widowed sister, Eleanor Brooksby.

[2] *John Gerard*, 42.

seen them', she reported: 'here was a searcher pounding the walls in unbelievable fury, there another shifting side-tables, turning over beds. Yet,
when any of them touched with their hand or foot the actual place where
some sacred object was hidden, he paid not the slightest attention to the
most obvious evidence of a contrivance' made for concealing them. Gerard
calls the men leopards — they tore madly through the entire house: he
says there were four of them. 'One picked up in his hands a silver pyx used
for carrying the most holy Eucharist. As though he noticed nothing, he
put it down at once. Under the very eyes of another there was lying a very
valuable dalmatic. Though the man had unfolded everything else, he did not
touch it.'

There was an interval while Anne offered the intruders breakfast. This
gave the servants an opportunity to go through the rooms, and hide whatever had remained unhidden. On this and other occasions searchers recognised only certain objects as indications of the presence of Catholics: pyxes
were not among them.

At breakfast Anne treated the men with exaggerated and feigned courtesy.
They demanded once more to know who it was that had fled into the woods:
they insisted he should be summoned. At this, Anne exacted a promise that
if the man proved to be no priest, he should be allowed to go free. Only
then did she give an order for him to be fetched. He came. He was believed
at once when he protested that he was not in holy orders: his youthfulness
may well have supported his denial.

The heretics, Garnet added, 'believed at that time that none could deny
that he was a priest without committing sin. However, now that we have
your theologian's answer[1] [this is a reference to a question put to Aquaviva
in his letter of 26 August 1587] that this is lawful, many for the first time are
now acting on this opinion, though some are still nervous of using it:
their reason is that the canons of the apostles contain an instruction that
anyone who denies his priesthood through fear is to be degraded; and they
are uncertain whether this canon is merely human sanction or whether it
asserts a divine principle.'

Satisfied that Catholics always told the truth — as Southwell observed —
the constable set the young man free. The search, nevertheless, was resumed
after breakfast: it lasted four hours in all. 'At the end', writes Gerard, 'they
made off but only after they had got paid for their trouble.' Anne gave them
twelve gold pieces. Gerard expresses his indignation. 'Yes, that is the
pitiful lot of Catholics when men come with a [search] warrant . . . it is the
Catholics, not the authorities who send them, who have to pay. As if it were

[1] Cf. *sup.*, p. 116–7.

not enough to suffer, they have to pay for their suffering.' In Anne's conduct Garnet saw yet another instance of the invincible patience of Catholics,
who, as he put it rather more concisely, 'have to pay for the injuries done
to them'.

The five Jesuit priests hiding in the tunnel were veterans on the mission;
they knew every ruse of the search parties. Only when the men had been gone
a considerable time, so that there was no likelihood that their departure was a
feint, did they answer Anne's call to emerge. Then from the 'den came not
one, but several Daniels'.[1] For the greater part of the morning all had
been standing ankle-deep in water. For this reason Anne had given the
searchers a free hand: they would then finish their work quickly. Since the
roads might still be watched, it was decided that none should leave till
the following day; and then not all together. Gerard and Southwell rode off,
as they had come, in company, leaving Stanney, Oldcorne and Garnet
behind.[2]

The raid had shown the finest qualities in the character of Anne Vaux.
It was not the first time she had faced the pursuivants, but never before had
so much depended on her behaviour. That a lady of her station, in order
to protect the priests in hiding should even condescend 'to wrangle with
unmannerly rogues' won Garnet's admiration. Her resource, chivalry and
prudence never deserted her. Moreover, as Garnet noted, at this time she was
a sick lady, 'very weakened by a long-standing infirmity, with which she was
chronically afflicted'. Her malady, whatever it was, prevented her saying
two or three words consecutively without some soreness. 'Yet whenever
the Queen's officers came, she experienced such a sudden access of strength
that she has been known to spend as much as three or four hours arguing
with them. When she has no chaplain in the house she is especially afraid:
the mere presence of a priest gives her courage, for she is certain then that
the devil has no power in her home.' Garnet was too modest to add that it
was his own particular presence that enhanced this assurance.

The strain of the three days, however, had taxed Garnet's strength. He had
a premonition that disaster was near and considered now that he had guided
the destinies of his brethren long enough. His pioneering days with Southwell were over. After five years the nucleus of the Society in England was
forming. Although he never indulged in false humility, he doubted now
whether in the changed circumstances he was truly the man best equipped to

[1] *John Gerard*, 42.
[2] All these five priests were later captured, but not all together. Southwell, Oldcorne
and Garnet were executed; Gerard escaped; Stanney, who under the stress of the
Gunpowder Plot scare, temporarily lost his reason, was subsequently released.

lead his brethren. Aquaviva knew of the work he had done (more perhaps from Southwell's letters than his own), the mission centres established, the problems solved, the hazards overcome, the courage he had shown and inspired in Catholics who, thanks in great measure to his guidance, had emerged with untarnished loyalty from the tribulations of 1588. First and before all else Garnet was an apostle: the accident of Weston's arrest had made him an organiser: at the same time he was the most sought-after Jesuit in England. It is not surprising that now for the first, but not the last time, he proposed to Aquaviva that he should be relieved of his office, so that he could devote himself single-mindedly to the work of comforting and conversion. There were others now who might succeed him and approach with a freshness of perception the problems that had been with him since he had assumed office. At the end of this meeting, on 18 October 1591, the day the search ended, he wrote to Aquaviva, proposing his own replacement. The request had perhaps been in his mind for many months: 'As far as I am myself concerned', he wrote,[1] 'there is nothing that I could wish for more (if your Lordship agrees) than to hand over the torch to someone more expert than myself, without myself falling out of the course; and be allowed to learn rather than teach, and to run, not by my own discretion, but under the guidance of others.'

During this year, when there were few external events of note, Garnet had built up the strength of the Society, both at home and abroad. Within his own lifetime there was formed the nucleus of a Jesuit Province which, in the esteem of the Church, was to have a record matching even the Provinces of the Indies and Paraguay.

Garnet's character had already emerged clearly in his years as Superior: and fundamentally Aquaviva had been right in his assessment. He was a man who by instinct preferred to obey rather than command, learn rather than instruct, receive impressions rather than impress himself on others. Yet in a crisis he was capable of a determined stand. In the long intimate passages of his letters to Aquaviva, he shows himself a man naturally impulsive yet disciplined; balanced, exact, with a surprising capacity to report any situation objectively as his office demanded. Increasingly he suffered the strain of leadership, and perhaps only in moments of intimate conversation with Southwell could he relax completely. Always he showed himself a man of great heart, energetic by force of office more than by inclination, and an able organiser. For all these reasons Aquaviva decided that as Superior he had no man better to replace him. Garnet continued in office for another twelve years.

[1] H. G. to C. A. 18 October 1591. F.G. 651, f. 35.

14

THE CHARGE OF TREASON

GARNET was right in his prediction that the respite would 'usher in a period of even greater severity'. On the very day, 18 October 1591, that Gerard and Southwell rode away from Baddesley Clinton, the Queen at Richmond signed a new proclamation against Catholics.[1] Its phrasing revealed the ruthless intention of the Council to drive all priests finally and for ever from the realm. What was more sinister, it showed exact knowledge of the strategems used by priests to enter the country and to escape capture. To Garnet it must have seemed that his tactics, so well laid and painstakingly developed, had now been betrayed.[2] On the other hand, the proclamation was also the greatest tribute to his success. Perhaps now, for the first time, Garnet and the Council were matched for a contest that was to last another fifteen years. In the judgment of contemporaries the Jesuit triumphed; in the verdict of history his enemies.

As in 1581 the Act of Persuasions,[3] that made it high treason to reconcile to the Romish religion, followed the mission of Campion twelve months earlier, so this proclamation was a counter measure to Garnet's activity. There was a difference in the fame surrounding the two great figures. Campion was so illustrious that the mere rumour of his presence stirred the entire countryside for miles around and attracted immediate reprisals. For five years Garnet, with the lesson of Campion before him, had been at work quietly. It took time for the Council to realise that he constituted no less a menace to the established religion.

After reciting the dangers to the realm from the king of Spain, the preamble to the proclamation branded all priests his secret agents, 'unnatural

[1] Although the proclamation was dated 18 October, it was not published before 21 November 1591.

[2] Fr J. H. Pollen (*Documents relating to the English Martyrs*, C.R.S., vol. 5, 199) is of the opinion that the 'accusations and information contained in the Proclamation' were due to 'the disloyal and treacherous statements' of John Cecil, who arrived in England with Fr Younger and was now working in collusion with the Council.

[3] 23 Eliz., cap. I.

subjects of the kingdom',[1] and the students in the seminaries abroad 'a multitude of dissolute young men, who partly for lack of living, partly for crimes
committed' had become fugitives, rebels and traitors. In Rome and Rheims
they were instructed in points of sedition and thence secretly conveyed into
the kingdom, 'upon hope by Spanish invasion to be enriched and endowed
with the possessions and dignities of our other good subjects'.

Every phrase of the proclamation was directed to inflame hatred against
Catholics, particularly against priests, as a prelude to a new persecution.
The danger of a Spanish invasion was slight, yet specious. The defeat of the
Armada had not removed the possibility of another attack. Philip II was an
inscrutable politician; the situation in the Netherlands was still uncertain;
more recently the Spaniards had established themselves in Normandy.
There were already rumours that a fresh Armada was in preparation and would
be launched from the newly-occupied French ports. The Council was genuinely alarmed and despatched English forces to aid the French king,
Henry VI, in reconquering his lost province.

In the three years after the defeat of the Armada Catholics had done much
to re-establish their name for loyalty in the popular mind. The death of
priests from the Isle of Wight to Durham, from Dorset to London, had
revealed their true mission. Their reiterated plea that they were dying solely
for religion had been accepted; the phrasing of the proclamation betrays
the Council's concern to rebut it. 'And of this, that none do suffer death
for matter of religion, there is manifest proof, in that a number of men of
wealth in our realms, professing contrary religion, are known not to be impeached for the same but only by payment of a peculiar sum as a penalty
for the time that they do refuse to come to church.' A general muster of the
able-bodied to arms was ordered in every county and instructions given 'to
make all the bands of horsemen and footmen fully furnished with armour,
weapons and munition'. In every 'shire, city and port' special commissioners were appointed to hunt down all persons suspected of loyalty to the
Pope.

The seventh section of the proclamation gives a vivid picture of the
achievement of the priests and of their devices: their secret landings, their
dispersal, their methods of apostolate and what Gerard calls 'the building
up of the churches'. It asserts that they 'do come into the [realm] by secret
creeks and landing places, disguised both in their names and persons, some
in apparel as soldiers, mariners or merchants, pretending that they have been
heretofore taken prisoners and put into gallies and delivered, some come in as
gentlemen with contrary names, in comely apparel, as though they had

[1] For the text see *Harleian Miscellany*, vol. 3 (1809), 96–9.

travelled into foreign countries for knowledge; and generally all or the most part, as soon as they are crept in, are clothed like gentlemen in apparel, and many as gallants, yea in all colours, and with feathers and such like disguising themselves, and many of them in their behaviour [are] ruffians, far off to be thought or suspected to be friars, priests, jesuits or popish scholars.' Masquerading in these ways they make their base in the 'universities and houses of law', and with 'noblemen, ladies and gentlemen' and so 'cover themselves from suspicion' and make converts.

The whole system, so clearly outlined in the life of Fr Gerard,[1] is described with accuracy through the enemy's eyes. A traitor had been at work.[2] There was no secret now in the priests' methods, but need only for greater caution or for new methods of evasion. The last paragraph of the proclamation drew in the net closer. In every parish in the country a committee of eight persons was to be nominated: they were to go from house to house and examine the inmates on their religious beliefs and their attendance at church. None was excepted, no 'nobleman, gentleman, lord, lady, master or mistress or owner whatsoever of any house, family [or] lodging'. If an unsatisfactory answer was given, the individual was to be handed over to the county commissioners for further examination. A list of all who resorted to these houses was to be compiled.

Early in 1585 priests had been hunted out of their residence by the Act that made it treason to give food, shelter or clothing to the 'seminaries and Jesuits'.[3] Thereafter for several months they had lived in taverns. Later they were driven out again into the open. Laymen, on their own initiative, had come forward, risking their lives and possessions to keep the priests secretly in their mansions. The 1591 proclamation aimed to drive them from their places of refuge into the hands of the constables.

There is an interesting comment on the enforcement of this proclamation in a letter to Persons written in March the following year.[4] It hints that, on its publication, a freer hand was given to Topcliffe. After summarising the clauses, the writer adds: 'The servants of recusants they [the commissioners] do either persuade by flattery or compel by torture in hanging them up by the hands to betray their masters in discovering what priests he doth relieve, what persons do frequent the house and the like.'

No official act of Elizabeth's reign had resorted to the kind of language

---

[1] *John Gerard*, passim.
[2] *C.R.S.*, vol 5, 199.
[3] 27 Elizabeth, cap. 2.
[4] Richard Verstegan to Robert Persons, 5 March 1592. Westminster Archives 4, 293–6.

used in this proclamation. The compiler is unknown: certain phrases pointed to Cecil's authorship: in its vituperation it resembles a pamphlet more than an official act.[1] On the Continent, within the space of twelve months, several replies were published, all dated 1592. Fr Persons, Fr Joseph Creswell and Fr Thomas Stapleton wrote in Latin:[2] and all presumed Cecil's authorship.

Only one principal rejoinder, namely Fr Verstegan's, was written abroad in English.[3] As the answers came fast one on another, the good name of England suffered.

Garnet was strangely silent during these months. He did not write to Aquaviva until 11 February 1592,[4] when he made it clear that this was his first letter for four months.[5] Always he was reluctant to send reports to Rome until he had checked the accuracy of his information, or, as in the case of this proclamation, assessed its significance. His October letter had been delayed in the 'hands of those who should have despatched it', and in the end was sent with his February letter. Both reached Rome together. Perhaps the political overtones of the proclamation held Garnet back from comment; only many years later when he had to explain to Aquaviva the circumstances of the publication of Southwell's reply did he refer to it. Thus his reaction to the proclamation is obscure. In his February letter, he refers to the 'terrible storm' and says that Fr William Holt will give a full account of everything on his arrival at Rome. For the moment he judged it safer not to discuss the document; probably he feared he might be quoted by the Catholic pamphleteers; possibly also he was disinclined to give his views on a measure which would certainly bring the Queen into odium overseas. But he makes a reference to Southwell which indicates perhaps that he was giving him leisure to write a reply. 'I am allowing my companion time to breathe:

---

[1] E.g. priests were branded as 'these venemous vipers' and 'unnatural subjects of our kingdom (yet very base of birth)'. Cp. Burghley's description of priests as 'vermin' who 'creep by stealth into the country' in his *Execution of Justice in England* (1583).

[2] Persons entitled his book, *Elizabethae . . saevissimum edictum . . . cum responsione ad singula capita.* The same year it appeared in a shortened English version, *An Advertisement written to a Secretary of my Lord Treasurer's in England.* The title of Creswell's book was: *Exemplar Literarum e Germania ad Dominum Gulielmum Cecilium:* and Stapleton's *Apologia pro Rege Catholico . . . contra varias et falsas Accusationes.*

[3] Richard Verstegan, born in London of Dutch parents, was one of the most notable Catholic exiles. After a brief imprisonment in England, he had escaped in 1582 to Paris where he supervised the printing of Catholic books. He also wrote many controversial and historical works both there and in Antwerp, where he settled the following year. Amidst his other occupations he organised the despatch of letters and books to and from England. He died in 1640 at the age of ninety. *Verstegan Papers, C.R.S.,* vol. 52.

[4] H. G. to C. A. 11 February 1592. F.G. 651, f. 42.

[5] On 18 October 1591. F.G. 651, f. 35.

meanwhile I am living in London.'[1] On the other hand this may mean no more than he was resting Southwell with his friends in Sussex.

In dignity, restraint and nobility of phrase, Southwell's reply to the proclamation was far removed from the rest. It is a prose classic of the decade. Writing in haste he abandoned the stylised manner of his *Epistle of Comfort*. He is more direct in his argument, which loses no force by shunning obloquy; the very form he chose for the book was itself a guarantee that he would observe decorum. Entitling it *An Humble Supplication to her Majestie*, he made it an appeal, not a retort. In contrast with the abuse poured on Elizabeth by other pamphleteers, Southwell addressed her as the 'most clement and sovereign lady under God'. He writes on the presumption that she is unaware of the true facts and would certainly call a halt to the persecution if they were brought to her attention.[2] It is a skilful and at the same time a sincere approach, and it enabled him, without imputation of disloyalty, to refute the charges of the proclamation. Particularly effective, because most keenly felt, is his defence of the seminary priests against the accusation of base birth and dissolute living. Sustained passages of eloquence make it one of the most memorable appeals ever written by a spokesman of a persecuted minority. Southwell's 'most mighty and most merciful, most feared and best loved Princess' was indeed the 'sheet anchor of his last hopes'.

Although the *Supplication* was circulated in a few hand-written copies, Garnet judged it prudent to forbid its publication. Several reasons brought him to this decision. He had hopes that the storm raised by the proclamation would subside sooner if Catholics endured the abuse passively, without attempting to rebut it. He had seen no good come from the vituperant pamphleteering that preceded and accompanied the Spanish invasion. It was the behaviour rather than speech of Catholics that would prove that the allegations against them were groundless; and this view was vindicated within a month of the proclamation, when three priests, Edmund Gennings, Eustace White and Polydore Plasden, were condemned on the sole charge of their ordination abroad. The savagery of their execution had stirred the crowds to sympathy: and it was perhaps at Garnet's suggestion that Southwell inserted in the *Supplication* a reference to their trial.[3] 'We can never be condemned', wrote Southwell,[4] 'upon anything but our own confession of the priesthood.

[1] H. G. to C. A. 11 February 1592. F.G. 651, f. 42.

[2] It was these phrases which later caused such trouble to Garnet when the book was published towards the end of 1600; *inf.*, p. 294.

[3] These three priests were charged on 4 December 1591 at Westminster Hall under the act that made it treason to receive orders abroad and return to minister in England. They were found guilty and executed on 10 December.

[4] *An Humble Supplication*, 31.

And thereof the last arraignment of three priests at Westminster, ever since this Proclamation, gave ample notice; wherein the Lord Chief Justice said,[1] that though many things had been urged, yet he was to pronounce sentence of death against them only upon the Statute of coming into England being made priests . . . since the first [year] of her Majesty's reign.'

This was an approach little appreciated by exiles. Indeed the polemics produced by English priests on the Continent could only have disturbed Garnet, who feared that they would lead to retaliation at home. Although this apprehension did not include Southwell's *Supplication*, nevertheless there was another danger in its appearance. The very form in which it was written, and, in particular, its fulsome praise of the Queen, might lead to further misunderstandings between Catholics at home and abroad. Moreover Garnet knew that its publication would be tantamount to the sacrifice of Southwell's life. Already the search for him was closing in. Garnet was in no mind to hand over his dearest friend to Topcliffe by permitting the diffusion of the book. No priest, not even Campion, had written with such scalding conviction and eloquence. For Garnet, it was a question of balancing the good the publication might do the Catholic cause against the advantages of sheltering the author for a continued apostolate. Only he was in a position to appreciate all that his companion had done for English Catholics since he first stepped ashore with him on the coast of Kent: the sacrifice of Southwell was a high price indeed to pay for the passing exaltation that the *Supplication* would bring the Catholic community.

It has been generally assumed that Southwell had publication in mind. But it is as likely that he wrote on impulse for the private reading of his friends during the short rest that Garnet imposed on him. Even in these months when Southwell suffered from fatigue, he could not resist a compulsion to use his leisure to defend his slandered friends, particularly the English students he had known in Rome who had recently suffered martyrdom in Fleet Street and other parts of London. Whether his work was printed or not, his conscience was now at ease.[2]

Until conditions improved, Garnet considered it wise to hold back on the Continent newly-ordained priests destined for England. 'It is not worth the risk of sending them', he warned Aquaviva, 'unless they are anxious to

[1] Sir Christopher Wray, who died the next year and was succeeded as Chief Justice by Sir John Popham.

[2] The two surviving manuscripts of the Supplication are dated December 1591: distribution of the text took place the following January. A copy that fell into Topcliffe's hands was passed on to Francis Bacon, who commented: 'It is curiously [i.e. finely] written and worth writing out, though the argument is bad.' Christopher Devlin, *Robert Southwell*, 245

rush headlong into peril or dire poverty ... conditions here are so unfavourable. If God does not intervene, all things will reach the verge of ruin; there is no place that is safe.' He was not writing in a phase of depression, but from his personal assessment of the crisis.

The rest of the short letter concerns routine problems and the despatch of novices to Flanders and their financial support. Before the proclamation, two young men had already managed to leave England, but the recent measures against Catholics made it inadvisable to send others after them: 'those who want to go, cannot leave the realm, and it is impossible to help [financially] those already abroad'. He appealed to Aquaviva. 'Even the slightest help of this kind that your Lordship can give us will bring us very great comfort.' With his happy recollections of Rome, Garnet would have preferred to have his novices trained at Sant' Andrea on the Quirinal, where he knew Aquaviva would take a personal interest in them. He hoped that the General would ask to have his latest recruits there.[1]

Meanwhile, with the optimism that sustained him in all but rare moments, he looked ahead with courage. The Queen was getting old. Although there is no phrase in all his correspondence that could be interpreted as an expression of hope that she might soon die, it was understandable that Garnet should expect her end shortly, and with it, some relief from the persecution. 'We are all well', he was able to write almost for the last time, 'and toiling at our native harvest. ... We will reap more abundantly when the Lord grants us still greater blessings. Your Lordship (I hope) will take every care that my sins and shortcomings will not hinder them.'[2]

Garnet's own answer to the crisis was very personal. From the beginning of his missionary work he had encouraged Catholics to enrol themselves in a pious organisation called the Confraternity of the Rosary. At no time did he doubt that the battle for religion was to be won principally with spiritual weapons. From his own experience he set greatest store by the merits and prayers of the martyred priests — and it was this that made him their first and most detailed historian. He treasured also the prayers of his Roman friends. Whenever he sent a letter to Aquaviva, he included a petition, that was no mere formality, both for his prayers and for the prayers of all his brethren in Rome. Throughout his missionary life he exhorted all to patient endurance, which in God's time he believed would pass into triumph.

During his years abroad he had seen an increasing devotion to the Rosary at the very centre of Christendom. When Pius V had summoned a Crusade against the Turks, he had called on all Catholics to support it with the constant recital of the Rosary. Devout persons in all countries attributed the

[1] H. G. to C. A. 11 February 1592. F.G. 651, f. 42.   [2] *Ibid.*

Christian victory at Lepanto, three years before Garnet entered Sant' Andrea, to the widespread use of the Rosary in the churches of Rome and Italy. Garnet himself had witnessed the announcement of the feast of the Rosary by Gregory XIII. Before leaving for England he had received from the Dominican General special powers, reserved commonly to Friars of the Dominican Order, to admit English Catholics into the Confraternity. A Crusader at heart, he believed that this prayer would be as effective against heresy in England as it had been against the Turk.[1]

While Southwell was writing his *Supplication*, Garnet compiled his first published English book, *The Societie of the Rosary*.[2] Its sub-title explains his intention. As the Confraternity, he says 'was first instituted by [that] Holy Light of God's Church, St. Dominicke, against the Albigenses, certaine Heretics of his Age; so undoubtedly will it be a necessary remedy for all Christians to embrace in this miserable time'. At the foot of the title page of the first edition[3] Our Lady is invoked as the conqueror of all heresies; and then the antiphon: *Gaude, Virgo Maria, cunctas hereses sola interemisti in universo mundo: Rejoice, Virgin Mary, since thou alone hast crushed all heresies throughout the world.*

As the rainbow appeared after the deluge, so Garnet saw Our Lady as the rainbow, a token of God's mercy, in the 'present heavily-clouded sky'. Then his preface continues: 'I present therefore unto this my dear country with the same love and affection which I would, if it pleased God, present it my blood, a singular means of winning this Virgin's favour ... the Society of the Rosary.' The book was written, he confessed, for 'the simpler sort', since the 'beads are the unlearned man's book'.

In October 1591, before the proclamation was published, Garnet had written urgently and for a second time to remind Aquaviva that he had already asked for a renewal of his special privileges regarding the Confraternity, for he feared they had lapsed with the death of the Dominican General.[4] Now he added a request that Aquaviva should obtain at the same time

---

[1] At his trial Garnet was charged with praying that heresy might be crushed in England. The Attorney-General, Sir Edward Coke, tried to twist the phrase *Auferte gentem perfidam* (hymn for All Saints) used by Garnet as the text of his sermon at Coughton into a prayer begging God's blessing on the Gunpowder conspirators. Cf. *inf.*, p. 402.

[2] *The Societie of the Rosary wherein is conteined the beginning, increase and profit of the same. Also the orders and manifold graces annexed to it, with divers other things thereunto appertaining.*

[3] There are four known copies of the first edition: in the British Museum; Jesus College, Oxford; Downside Abbey and Oscott. Here I have used the Downside copy.

[4] Sixtus Fabri, Master General of the Dominicans when Garnet was in Rome, died in 1589.

from the New Master General a dispensation from the rule that the names of members should be inscribed in a book.[1] It was one thing to allow Catholics to risk capture by keeping beads secretly in their home, another to draw up lists of names which, if they fell into the hands of priest-hunters, would bring ruin on hundreds of families.[2] To spread devotion to the Rosary more rapidly, Garnet was anxious also that many more English priests should be given the same faculties that he possessed. He, and a few others who were empowered to do so, could not admit into the Confraternity all who were now seeking admission.[3]

Although the book was not published until 1593 Garnet was working on it early in 1592. Printed at his own secret press, it soon became the handbook of the Confraternity in England. The first and subsequent additions carry no date or place of printing. It was already widely diffused when Garnet's press was captured in 1594.[4] In the raid a large stock of the first edition was found. Hurriedly, as has been seen, Garnet re-established the press, retaining meanwhile his workmen on full wages. A new edition of *The Societie of the Rosary* was soon produced.[5] The engraving of the Virgin with her infant Son appeared on the new title page. This was Garnet's hope against heresy: here also was his answer to Cecil. He was 'fully persuaded' that it was for Catholics to enlist on their side the power of Our Lady and 'to obtain from her a new rainbow, which, being a sign of God, cannot signify falsely, but [must] most certainly foretell our comfort and relief'.[6]

[1] On page 19 of the first edition of *The Societie of the Rosary* Garnet wrote: 'This manner of enrolment being not convenient to our country for respects too well known, it sufficeth that after the names be once taken of such that enter they be torn up. Yet it is expedient that when opportunity shall be offered everyone cause himself authentically to be enrolled, that so both God may be in the number of his devout servants more highly glorified and they may also be as it were solemnly accepted and confirmed in that which they have received'. This passage, incidentally, is another indication that Garnet, with the greater part of the people, was expecting a return of the country to Catholicism.

[2] H. G. to C. A. 18 October 1591. F.G. 651, f. 35.

[3] There is record in the Registers of the Master General at S. Sabina, Rome, of permission to found the Confraternity being granted to eleven English priests between 1585 and 1586.

[4] Cf. *Sup.*, p. 44.

[5] The second edition, like the first, is undated. It was prepared probably in 1596. The title page is much improved and bears an interesting engraving. The invocation of Our Lady as the conqueror of heresies is kept, and also the versicle from her Office. To this is added on the title page, *Dignare me laudare te, virgo sacrata, Da mihi virtutem contra hostes tuos. Make me worthy to praise thee, holy Virgin, and give me power over your enemies.* Copies of the second edition are as scarce as the first. It can be seen in the British Museum, Oxford (Bodleian Library) and Ampleforth Abbey.

[6] Preface to *The Societie of the Rosary* (1st edition).

L

15

THE LOSS OF SOUTHWELL

THERE is no evidence of a meeting of Jesuits in the early part of 1592. Possibly Garnet was unprepared for the hazard now that the watch on his priests had been intensified. Already Topcliffe had extended his activities beyond London, while his assistant, Richard Young, Justice of Middlesex, rivalled his partner in his animus against Catholics. 'There is simply nowhere left to hide', Garnet had written in February.

No matter how grave the situation Garnet was never fatalistic, although at times he seems to have had a foreknowledge of imminent disaster. Daily during the spring and early summer of 1592 he appeared to be expecting news of Southwell's arrest. When finally it came, he showed no surprise. 'This was by no means a sudden and unforeseen disaster. For a long time now it had been planned by our enemies.'[1]

It was on Sunday 25 June 1592 that Southwell was captured at the house of the Bellamy family at Uxenden near Harrow. Remorselessly Topcliffe had been tracking him. When he made his descent he made sure that the greatest prize of his career had no chance of escape.

There are two letters that describe the arrest written by Garnet in the same month. In the first, sent to Aquaviva on 16 July,[2] he writes without restraint, expressing spontaneously his deep personal anguish. The second to Fr Persons is curiously reserved.[3] The difference of style is perhaps indicative of his relations with the two men at this time.

Understandably Garnet wrote to Aquaviva before Persons, for Southwell had closer ties with him: and it was characteristic of him that he waited a fortnight before writing, until he had ascertained the facts. Even then he was careful to distinguish what he had learnt himself from what he had heard from others. He was anxious not to spread any false or exaggerated stories.

[1] H. G. to C. A. 16 July 1592. F.G. 651, f. 45.
[2] *Ibid.*
[3] H. G. to R. P. 26 July 1592. Westminster Archives 4, 305.

'Therefore I thought good', he writes, 'to advertise you of the whole truth as far as I could in any way learn it.'[1]

In these letters, written under stress of emotion, Garnet shows the depth of his spiritual character. For his first two years in England Southwell had been his only Jesuit assistant; and though occasionally he refers to him as Robert, he calls him more usually his 'socius'. Southwell indeed had been his 'companion', but also his friend, confidant and confessor. There was no anxiety, decision or hope he had not shared with him since the June day they said farewell to Persons at the Milvian bridge.

On reaching Uxenden, Southwell had intended to ride and see his Superior in London the next day. 'He was about to come and see me,' explains Garnet,[2] 'when at the request of friends he was detained at the house of the Bellamys.' They did not meet again though during the next two and a half years Garnet took every opportunity that offered to catch a glimpse of his companion. When Southwell was transferred from one prison to another, or taken from the Tower to his trial in Westminster Hall, Garnet was there among the crowds and at once reported to Aquaviva on his carriage, dignity and the expression of his countenance.

Southwell was a more scintillating character than Garnet: also he was more of a public figure, moving among nobles, courtiers, poets, while Garnet systematically organised the Catholic centres in the shires. Their work as well as their characters had been complementary. After Southwell's arrest it is possible to discern a change of mood in Garnet's letters. Something of his self-confidence has gone; he is more anxious, hesitating and easily alarmed. Neither Gerard nor Oldcorne, though they were now experienced missionaries, could for a long time replace his 'socius'.

'At length and at last', Garnet opened his letter to Aquaviva,[3] 'it has happened.' Then recalling the day when together they had crossed the English channel, he adds: 'After a peaceful and prosperous voyage lasting six years, we have now encountered fierce and tempestuous seas ... our very gentle dear companion has been captured by pirates, and now in a broken and battered ship we are sailing without a helmsman.'

Compared with all the set-backs he had so far experienced there was none like this. Southwell was the helmsman; Garnet the captain of the vessel. The storm, as he said, had been gathering for several months. Indeed Garnet may well have received sinister reports concerning the renegade Catholic in the Bellamy family who eventually betrayed Southwell. His first reaction to the news must have been relief that he had suppressed the publication of the *Humble Supplication*; for Southwell would now have the comfort

[1] H. G. to C. A. 16 July 1592. F.G. 651, f. 45.   [2] *Ibid.*   [3] *Ibid.*

of standing trial and facing torture and execution with the issue of his priesthood unclouded by politics. Garnet himself felt that he had been 'left over':
Southwell had been chosen before him 'because God did not judge me worthy
of such a contest.'[1]

The Bellamy's house at Uxenden had been one of the oldest and safest
of Jesuit strongholds in England. Persons had met the family on his short visit
twelve years earlier; it was the first Catholic household to give Fr
Weston shelter.[2] Both Garnet and Southwell had visited it frequently. While
Garnet suspected treachery within the household, he was careful to state
that it was not yet established.

Southwell had arrived at Uxenden on the morning of the day following the
feast of St John the Baptist, 24 June. At once, in Garnet's phrase, he 'had
given comfort in his usual manner to "almost all" there present'. The word
'almost' excluded the traitor from sacrilege, for the comforting consisted in
confession, Mass and Communion. It was Southwell's last Mass. Instead of
continuing his journey to London the same day, he yielded, as Campion
had fatally done, to the pressing request of his hostess to remain overnight.
That same night Topcliffe surrounded the house. Never before had he gone
out of London in such strength. On the road he gathered fresh forces. For
six months he had awaited this moment. He took no chances: nor could he.
After all his boasting, failure to capture Southwell would have brought
his hideous career to a crisis. Garnet suspected this, but did not know yet all
that was involved for Topcliffe.

As soon as the alarm was raised, Mrs Bellamy rushed Southwell into a
hiding place. As Topcliffe entered the house, he ordered all the men servants
to be bound hand and foot. Then he told his secret. He knew the exact place
where Southwell was concealed. With Topcliffe's consent Mrs Bellamy
went into secret conference with Southwell, who himself made the decision.
He came out and presented himself in the hall.

Garnet takes much pride in narrating Southwell's demeanour. It was the
last time he was to be seen before his prolonged torture all but crippled him.
Slim, straightly-built with auburn eyes, he was still only thirty, but he looked
yet younger. Topcliffe was twice his age. He recognized his prisoner instantly from the description Anne Bellamy had given him. As they faced each
other for the first time Topcliffe shook with frenzied hatred. He demanded
who he was. 'A gentleman', was Southwell's answer. Then Topcliffe swore,
'No, a priest, a traitor, a Jesuit.' Calmly Southwell asked him to prove each
assertion, for if he admitted his identity he would bring appalling penalties
on his hostess. In his uncontrollable wrath Topcliffe momentarily forgot

[1] H. G. to C. A. 16 July 1592. F.G. 651, f. 45.   [2] *William Weston*, 3–6.

the importance of seizing his prey alive. He ran at Southwell with his sword. Southwell stood his ground as Topcliffe's men rushed forward and held their master back. Impassively Southwell looked Topcliffe, the torturer of his former students, in the eyes. This was more than the villain could bear. He accused Southwell of denying his priesthood through fear; he called him 'the filthiest traitor in the kingdom'. With irony and a masterly choice of words Southwell replied: 'No, it is neither priest nor traitor you are seeking, but only blood. And if mine will satisfy you, then you shall have it as freely as my mother gave it to me; and if mine will not satisfy, I do not doubt but you shall find many more as willing as myself.' He concluded with a priestly warning. 'Only I would advise you to remember that there is a God, and He is just in his judgments, and therefore blood will have blood, but I rather wish your conversion.'[1]

'We came here to arrest you', interrupted Topcliffe, 'not to listen to your prattling.'

As Garnet communicated to Aquaviva his fears and reflections after Southwell's capture, he showed pride in Southwell mixed with sadness. No arrest had caused such distress to Catholics since Campion's. Garnet was confident that now Southwell's example in suffering would be an immeasurable force for good. He feared only for his limbs, now at Topcliffe's mercy. In a simple narrative he tells the rest of the story:[2]

'With the first light of morning he was taken to London. Although they passed through the least frequented streets, the report of his capture had spread already through the whole city. More swiftly than one could believe, it was bruited abroad through the entire kingdom. It is not possible to describe the sorrow of all Catholics, and not only of Catholics; it was as if each of them had lost a dear kinsman.'

Perhaps the rumour had already reached Garnet, and he mingled with the crowd to see his companion ride along the road leading to Topcliffe's house next to the Gatehouse Prison at Westminster. Topcliffe had already despatched a messenger to Greenwich in the early morning to inform the Queen of his prize. He now felt reassured of the royal favour. It was beyond Garnet's comprehension that she could give her protection to such a monster. His testimony, therefore, is all the more reliable, when he writes: 'He feared neither the favour nor the power of any Councillor or Officer of State. At the news the Queen is said to have showed signs of unwonted joy.'[3]

Garnet gives no explanation. If a handwritten text of the *Humble Supplication* was already in the hands of the Council, she had reason to be satisfied

[1] H. G. to R. P. 26 July 1592. Westminster Archives 4, 305.   [2] *Ibid*.
[3] H. G. to C. A. 16 July 1592. F.G. 651, f. 45.

that such a writer was now effectively silenced. She had feared and admired Southwell's pen. Her joy at his capture was no private matter, though Southwell was soon to become an embarrassment to her.[1]

At Topcliffe's house, as Garnet knew, unknown tortures awaited his companion. Here several priests had borne unmentionable suffering, inflicted under Topcliffe's personal supervision. In his rooms, as Garnet notes with apprehension, he had 'erected, as became him, instruments for every type of torture, so that he should lack no convenience for wreaking his vengeance on Catholics'.[2] Indeed the license given to him by the Queen for his evil practices can be explained only by the undertaking given by Topcliffe that he would force all priests to confess that they were traitors. The facts, however, did not fit his contention. No matter how fiendishly he tried all his devices, his victims would, and could, admit only their priesthood. In Southwell's steps were to follow many of his former pupils. Only gradually did Garnet learn the full extent of Southwell's agony.

However, within ten days, from friends connected with the Court and from prisoners at the Gatehouse, Garnet gathered some shocking details. Within twenty-four hours of Southwell's capture, Topcliffe was forced to confess defeat. No word that might be construed as treachery could be extracted from him. In a further message to the Queen, Topcliffe admitted his failure. Stingingly the Queen called Topcliffe a fool and in return sent a message to say that she and her Councillors would take over Southwell's examination.

Among the men chosen by the Queen to continue Southwell's examination was the Clerk of the Privy Council, Sir William Wade, whose wiles were later to deceive Garnet himself. He was given an assistant who was unnamed. 'Nevertheless', says Garnet, 'the prisoner remains obdurate.'[3] On Tuesday night or early Wednesday morning, 28 June, Wade had Southwell removed from Topcliffe's house to the Gatehouse. It was feared, perhaps, Southwell might die in Topcliffe's hands. Now he was examined more systematically, hanged up more frequently and deliberately deprived of sleep.

Garnet could get only fragmentary details of what passed within the walls of Southwell's new prison. He learnt the cell in which Southwell was confined, and noted that the windows had been shuttered from the outside; that his only light entered through a pane of glass set in the ceiling. He could

---

[1] There is a letter, which can possibly be dated 5 May 1592, sent by Francis Bacon to his brother Anthony, along with a copy of the *Humble Supplication*, which he reluctantly praises for its prose style. Cf. Christopher Devlin, *Robert Southwell*, 254.

[2] H. G. to C. A. 16 July 1592. F.G. 651, f. 45.

[3] *Ibid.*

discover nothing about him 'save what his torturers chose to divulge'; yet he did gather one startling piece of news. After Wade had failed to extract a statement of guilt, Robert Cecil himself had taken part in Southwell's examination. He had been prepared by Topcliffe for a display of obstinacy. From the drawn, tortured figure hanging from the wall in front of him, he elicited only a reasoned reply. When the questions touched the lives and whereabouts of his Catholic hosts, Southwell was silent. It was a scene Cecil never forgot. Some years later, as he rode out of London with a friend, he recalled the sight. 'They boast about the heroes of antiquity', he said, 'but we have a new torture which it is not possible for a man to bear. And yet I have seen Robert Southwell hanging by it, still as a tree-trunk, and none able to drag one word from his mouth.'[1] *Semper pertinax* was the summary of Garnet's tribute to his companion. Never had he a moment's doubt that Southwell would remain steadfast.

Garnet's epistolary style changes when he writes of Southwell: he is more direct, unimpeded and hurried. In describing his companion's suffering he reveals himself as never before. There existed in England perhaps no more intimate friendship between two priests, with more bonds of affection and shared trials to secure it. Often they had spoken of Topcliffe; both had written of his iniquities to Aquaviva. They knew also his story; how at the age of sixty with his fortunes ruined, he had striven to re-establish himself at the price of priests' lives. 'Entering now the course of honour', wrote Garnet with sarcasm, 'that you now see him following, he boasts that he gets more pleasure from hunting down priests that he ever got from chasing wild animals or setting snares for birds.'[2]

Now Garnet felt ineffably lonely. Both by temperament and outlook he was separated from other English Jesuits, with the exception of Holtby, whose life was spent entirely in the northern shires. He appreciated the loyalty of all his priests; and on their side, they revered him as their Superior; but none was to take the place of his 'companion'. About twelve years separated him from Gerard and Oldcorne. More than any Jesuit in England Aquaviva was his contemporary in spirit. In his desire for the support of another friendship, he now drew closer to the General in every letter.

At the same time Garnet thanked God that for more years than he expected he had been given Southwell's support. He was comforted that everything had been arranged by Providence: 'While I cannot help myself in my sadness and anxiety . . . deprived as I now am of my companion, my dearest father and my helper [I await] his greatest achievements yet.'[3] Throughout

---

[1] Devlin, *op. cit.*, 288.
[2] H. G. to C. A. 16 July 1592. F.G. 651, f. 45.   [3] *Ibid.*

the concluding pages of this letter he returns constantly to two reflections:

'Southwell is so well prepared', Garnet assured Aquaviva, 'that stricken as we are, we feel that God through the Father's sufferings will enhance his glory, strengthen his Church and confound his enemies. . . . A very special kind of courage is needed to endure these tortures. And I tell myself this, that in the mystical union of one body, in which we are all members one of another, any torture whatever may be endured. And what seems insufferable for one person, when it is shared by all the members, may become sweet indeed, not at all because it is any less severe, but by reason of the love that binds us all together. This truly is to bear one another's burdens; it is the mutual compassion of members whereby the weakness of one is supported by the strength of another.'[1]

Garnet wrote this both to comfort himself for Southwell's loss and to allay his own fears. His physical abhorrence of torture was intense; frequently he had doubts whether he had the courage to endure what others had done. He made no secret of his own fears, as he had no doubts of Southwell's perseverance. 'I draw this great consolation from my companion's position, that never has he been known to disappoint the expectations of his friends.' The physical companionship was now replaced by a mystical fellowship. In his search for some ground of comfort he could give himself, he becomes one of the first Englishmen to develop St Paul's doctrine of the mystical body of Christ. In a hundred problems, great and small, he had sought the advice and criticism of Southwell: now, though separated from him — Garnet noted that from his cell in the Gatehouse he could not even look down on the street — they were still more closely united.

At the end of his letter, Garnet withdrew his last reserves. For the first time he felt that his days of liberty were few; that Providence was indicating that as he and Southwell had begun, so they would end their mission together. He wrote dramatically.[2] He might be arrested perhaps before he had time to sign his letter; indeed perhaps before it came to Aquaviva's eyes his quarters would be exposed as carrion on London Bridge. He expected this to be the last he would write and forewarned Aquaviva that he might well show frailty if he should be treated as Southwell had been. The search for him had been more persistent even than the search for Southwell: public feeling had been stirred up against him. Imploringly he calls on Aquaviva not to relax his prayers. 'While we can never be safe, never free from danger, it is right that your concern for us should never cease; and now more so than ever, because since the coming of the Spanish fleet into these waters, far more than any other priest in the country I am suspect of stirring sedition

[1] H. G. to C. A. 16 July 1592. F.G. 651, f. 45.   [2] *Ibid.*

and raising the Catholics to support the king of Spain. For me and for no other man, tortures are already prescribed. Death itself would indeed be a delight.'

Although Garnet wrote now as his thoughts and fears dictated, he never made a statement without knowledge. He had reason to suspect that Southwell was being racked in torture so that he might reveal his own whereabouts: as indeed were Gerard and others after him. It required very little insight to discern the policy of the government. Burghley had well in hand his plans to detach the Catholic body from the Holy See; then split it brutally asunder. If Southwell or Garnet could be induced to confess criminal plotting, then Burghley had won the day. Once again Garnet admitted that he needed exceptional fortitude not to yield under torture:

'I distrust myself as well I might, and my misery makes me pause. Yet when I consider the goodness of God, the strength my calling gives me, the common tie that binds me to so many saintly men and so many valiant servants of Christ, I begin already to envy my companion and grieve that while he has been taken to receive a crown of immeasurable glory, I have been kept for battles yet unknown. In this spiritual combat God acts like this.'

Then Garnet goes on to contrast Southwell's role as a front-line fighter with his own part that demands organisation in the rear. 'The soldier who fights at a distance remains remote always from victory, which God has decreed should hang in the balance. But when the fight is brought close to the enemy, God assures the triumph of all he choses for this part.'

Garnet had never sought nor relished authority over his brethren. Already eighteen months earlier he had suggested to Aquaviva that he should be replaced as Superior. His only ambition was to help individual souls. Without pressing his request, he again made it clear to Aquaviva that nothing would give him greater comfort that to yield his position to another priest. Before ending his letter, he turns yet again to his fear of torture: it is as though he had endured vicariously all the ten hangings inflicted on Southwell between his capture and the date of this letter. 'If ever God wills it and I am faced with the same torments, may I be able to bear them all with a willing heart. You must give me some special and personal share in the merits of your virtue and of your fatherly affection, love and fortitude. . . . Whenever I have to suffer the extreme hardship, then you must show me extreme understanding.' His comfort, he repeats, is in his membership of the mystical body of Christ. For him, now more than ever, the Society of Jesus, governed by Aquaviva, was a diminutive image of the Church. 'When the harvest of all merits shall be gathered in for the year, then I shall not lack strength to undertake any great work whatsoever or to endure whatever may happen.'

Never before had he written in this manner. The spontaneous affection he had given Southwell was poured out on Aquaviva. His letters became longer, more intimate and unguarded: and he was certain that Aquaviva, on his side, was grateful for the confidence he placed in him. The General's constant promise of prayers was not a barren ecclesiastical formula. Declining Garnet's proposal that he should hand over his responsibilities to another priest, Aquaviva replied by giving him still closer support and sympathy. For several months now there had been ugly rumours of opposition to the Jesuits. To weather the storm, Garnet needed Aquaviva's unquestioning confidence.

Before closing his letter, Garnet dealt briefly with a few outstanding matters of business. He was leaving for the country, uncertain of the date of his return. It was 'too hot' for him, he said, in London. Possibly through his friends who had given him news of Southwell, he had learnt that Topcliffe was in pursuit of him. To capture both within a month was not more than Topcliffe hoped. Southwell had failed to give him a scrap of information; Garnet might. And in any case, by lies and cunning, he could play off the one against the other, as he was later to do when he had both Gerard and Southwell in his hands.

Finally Garnet told Aquaviva that he had now admitted 'Henry' into the Society, with the permission he had just been granted. He was a pious young man and brought up a Catholic by his parents: his health was indifferent but not inadequate for the tasks of a 'merchant'. At Wisbech Thomas Metham, Weston's companion, had recently died.[1] Garnet begged for him the usual prayers said for the dead of the Society. Still a problem was the release of Metham's fellow-prisoners, Weston and Emerson. No confirmation of his view had yet been received. Garnet merely repeated his fears that Weston's liberation might cause scandal.

Before Garnet left London Southwell was transferred to the Tower. Torture had not drawn from him any incriminating statement. The Queen was more than ever disturbed by Topcliffe's failure. Loath always to shed the blood of priests save on a pretext of plotting or treachery, she would not permit Southwell's trial to open. He could be charged only with ordination overseas and unlawful re-entry in the country: that, understandably, did not satisfy her.

---

[1] Father Thomas Metham, a Yorkshireman, son of Sir Thomas Metham, an intimate friend of Thomas Percy, seventh Earl of Northumberland, had been admitted into the Society at Wisbech shortly before his death on 28 June 1592. He had been a prisoner for seventeen years. He was buried in the churchyard of St. Peter's Church, Wisbech. Cf. *William Weston*, 18.

In the seven months previous to Garnet's departure from London, seven priests, with three laymen who had sheltered them, had been executed within the city boundaries. In each case Topcliffe had assisted at the gallows, which, to strike more widespread terror, had been erected in Gray's Inn Fields, St Paul's Chuchyard and other parts of the city that seldom witnessed executions. While this barbarity continued in the provinces, a new policy was sought for London. The following year only one other priest, Fr William Harrington, suffered martyrdom in London.[1] A further twelve months elapsed and Robert Southwell, then thirty-three years old, was executed.

For the present, clemency had been imposed on the persecutors. The Queen, who had first exulted over Southwell's capture, reflected now that the priest at her mercy belonged to a family familiar at her Court. She herself had spent part of her childhood days with Southwell's mother, and with her had learnt the Latin tongue; his father was one of her courtiers. The story of his son's resistance was now the talk and admiration of her friends. After the failure of Topcliffe and her own Councillors to incriminate Southwell, she did not hesitate to use the offices of his own family. At her command, Sir Richard, Robert's father, and Robert's sister, Mary Bannister, separately visited him in the Tower. When they also failed to make him alter his mind, it was judged best to let the clamour caused by his arrest subside. There was no place in England like the Tower where troublesome heroes could be more quickly forgotten by the people.

Garnet's last act before riding out of London was to arrange for a breviary to be sent to Southwell. The Countess of Arundel added a volume of St Bernard's sermons and a consignment of clothes and bedding.

'A Goliath of fortitude' was Garnet's final word in praise of his companion.

[1] At Tyburn on 18 February 1594.

16

RECOVERY

GARNET needed rest and leisure. Life in London was always more perilous than in the shires. Many areas of the countryside were still little affected by heresy and there every month the number of converts increased. Garnet was restless also to be among his friends. He wrote to Aquaviva on 15 August and again on 5 September 1592. Neither of these letters reached Rome;[1] he appeared impatient to receive from Aquaviva some word of comfort. But this summer Aquaviva had left Rome for northern Italy. Garnet did not know this and was unable to explain the delay in his Superior's reply. Nervously fatigued, he took several months completely to recover his health. Writing a third time on 8 October,[2] he realised perhaps for the first time how agitated he had been: 'As every letter I write increases your Lordship's care for me, I try as hard as I can to write more frequent letters. On 4 September I gave you news of my companion. What I said then holds still. He is kept in the royal prison [the Tower] and is quietly hidden from the clamour of his persecutors. He is not allowed to see any of his friends, but this aside, he is now being treated with some humanity by the Lieutenant of the Tower.'[3] Garnet repeated once more that there was never a time when he was more in need of Aquaviva's affection and counsel.

After Southwell's arrest Garnet faced in isolation the most painful problem he had yet encountered, namely, the behaviour of certain priests who sought reconciliation with the government at the price of renouncing their

---

[1] The very long letter written by Garnet in March 1593 suggests that these two letters were lost. There is reference to them in his letter of 8 October 1592. F.G. 651, f. 49.

[2] H. G. to C. A. 8 October 1592. F.G. 651, f. 49.

[3] This was Sir Richard Berkeley, who was succeeded in June 1597 by Sir John Peyton. John Gerard, referring to his own torture and escape in October 1597, writes: 'A gentleman of position told me that he had heard Sir Richard Berkeley . . . say that he had freely resigned his office because he no longer wished to be an instrument in such torture of innocent men [namely Southwell and Gerard]'. *John Gerard*, 114.

loyalty to the Holy See. Not even Southwell, with all his charm and unassailable integrity, could have postponed the storm. However, within just three months of Southwell's arrest, Garnet reported to Aquaviva:[1]

'Two priests who brazenly ventured to countenance an English schism, have now received the deserts of the pride they manifested. One of them went to Rome two years ago to air his fanatical views; but he was captured immediately on his return and sent to prison. . . . It is not yet known how far he has dared or determined to go in the future. The other, who had renounced his [Protestant] ministry, returned to his vomit, and ended worse than he had begun. I enclose with this letter another account of the mournful tragedy. (I cannot now at this moment translate it into Latin.) There are other men also who are said to favour this schism. There is need to act promptly . . . in order to counter it.'

Aquaviva had been kept informed by Persons and others of the harm done by the dissident priests. Quickly Garnet passed on to other matters. In a few sentences he summed up the activity of his brethren. There was nothing new to report; progress continued. 'All are well and although some are experiencing difficulties, they keep to their set course with great profit. Daily to our great consolation we witness examples of constancy in all the courts and assizes throughout the country.'

By October 1592 Garnet was clearly recovering from the personal loss he had suffered in Southwell's capture: his old spirit of enterprise was again awake. During his visit to the country he had time and again seen proof that the perseverence of Catholics was unchanged. One small incident, falsely reported, he interpreted prematurely as a sign of God's intervention in the Catholic interest — the rumoured death of the Chief Justice, Sir John Popham, whom he had known as a regenerate barrister in Tottel's house. Popham, 'the chief prosecutor of our brethren', had tried Campion and his companions; more recently he had passed sentence on the two priests, Eustace White and Polydore Plasden, and on a Catholic schoolmaster, Swithun Wells. Garnet saw 'the finger of God in his unexpected death, at the very time when he was threatening dire measures against the Catholic people'.[2] The report however, was false. Popham was alive. Fifteen years later he was instrumental in securing Garnet's own execution.

Garnet extended his absence from London. It was now his custom to come up for the autumn and spring assizes. This year, however, the plague was raging in the city and the assizes were cancelled. There had been no further news of Southwell. So he ended briefly: 'Wherever we are, we are

[1] H. G. to C. A. 8 October 1592. F.G. 651, f. 49.
[2] Ibid.

always with you in spirit, and we rely on your prayers. We hope therefore that every blessing will be upon us in the future.'[1]

This last letter crossed Aquaviva's, posted to Garnet on 16 July. Aquaviva was then in Mantua: he wrote from there as soon as he heard of Southwell's arrest.[2] It was a letter of personal consolation: he could not settle the questions of business until he was back in Rome. Addressed simply to 'Father Henry Garnet in London', it began with a touching expression of sympathy. He had learnt of Southwell's fate 'with sincere and deep grief' even before he had received Garnet's letter. Garnet surely had suffered calamities enough without having to endure the loss of his companion. The General's own distress was not only for the sudden termination of Southwell's apostolate but for Garnet's deep 'loneliness and grief of mind and heart'.

'But we know this [he adds], no one is crowned save he who has lawfully contested; none receives the glorious trophy unless he has manfully toiled. Assured as we are of this, I know that your personal attachment to him will be all the more ardent and your efforts more sustained: so that if still more bitter trials are ahead, I have no doubt at all that God's grace will be at hand; that you will endure these trials with fortitude and surmount them with glory. I am convinced that, in these storms, and tempests your Reverence is enduring what He endured who, according to the great multitude of the sorrow in His heart, gloried that with them He experienced the joy of divine comfort. And indeed daily and by name I commend earnestly to God the work and perils of all of you who are in England, so that He for whose honour and glory you hazard your lives, may shelter you with his providence and protection.'[3]

The few questions that Aquaviva was able to settle without reference to Rome, he answered with precision. Thomas Metham shall certainly be given the prayers customarily offered for the dead in the Society.[4] He has considered the case of the three Jesuits, Weston, Pound and Emerson, who have been so long in prison: the scandal likely to arise from their release must be given first consideration: 'nevertheless there are also good reasons on the

---

[1] H. G. to C. A. 8 October 1592. F.G. 651, f. 49.

[2] Clement VIII, a great missionary Pope in whose reign Matteo Ricci, whom Garnet had known in Rome, entered China, was elected on 29 January 1592. That year he sent Aquaviva to Mantua, ostensibly to settle a dispute between the Dukes of Mantua and Parma. During his three months' absence from Rome, Aquaviva's enemies persuaded the new Pope to call a General Congregation of the Jesuits with the purpose of obtaining the General's deposition. These months were the most critical in Aquaviva's long period of office. T. J. Campbell, *The Jesuits, 1535–1921* (1921), vol. 1, 210 sq.

[3] C. A. to H. G. 10 October 1592. Arch. S.J. Rome, *Fland. Belg.* 1, 507.

[4] Cf. *sup.*, p. 154.

other side and they have weight and importance. . . . The question demands further thought, which I will give it in time.' Garnet's faculties for admission into the Confraternity of the Rosary are still valid on the axiom that faculties do not necessarily lapse on the death of the person who has granted them. After his return to Rome Aquaviva will go into the other matters raised by Garnet and write again to Garnet.

During this year Garnet was in Hampshire. It is always difficult to trace his journeys; and it is only by his reports of Catholic affairs in the country that occasionally he betrays the places he has visited. In a later letter[1] he gives an account of events in Winchester which probably he himself witnessed this summer. There had been another outbreak of persecution in the city, where the clauses of the recent proclamation had been enforced to the letter. The spring assizes there had been especially brutal; and several Catholic laymen had been brought to trial. Garnet gives a long account of the execution of two of them, James Byrd, a youth of nineteen, and another, John Thomas. The case of Byrd stirred him in a particular manner, and from the way he speaks of him, it would seem that he knew the youth. From the age of nine Byrd had been in prison for he had always refused to go to church. His presence in the city gaol had now become a symbol of Catholic resistance, more striking because his father, a non-Catholic, was a well-known and influential citizen. 'James, who had experience of nearly all the London prisons', writes Garnet, 'and had suffered many whippings (for his recusancy) was unaware that the Lord was preparing for him a crown of martyrdom.' Suddenly he was brought to trial before Judge Anderson and charged with being reconciled to the Church.[2] Normally, Garnet observed, 'reconciliation' was taken to refer only to the first sacramental confession made to a priest on a convert's reception into the Church, but in this case it was extended to include any confession in any circumstances whatsoever. Byrd had never ceased to be a Catholic from the age of eight or nine. This wider interpretation alarmed Garnet. Anderson argued that anyone who confessed his sins to a priest is absolved, and since he is absolved by virtue of authority from Rome, he commits a capital offence.

Byrd was condemned. His execution took place at Winchester outside the West Gate on 25 March 1592 and was followed in August by the execution of the other layman, John Thomas, who, condemned at the same assizes,

[1] H. G. to C. A. 17 March 1593. Arch. S.J. Rome, *Ang. Hist.* 1, II, f. 27.

[2] Sir Edmund Anderson (1530–1605), appointed Lord Chief Justice of Common Pleas in 1582, took part in the trials of Babington (1586), Mary Queen of Scots (1586), the Earl of Essex (1601) and Sir Walter Raleigh (1603); he showed great severity to both Puritans and Catholics.

had later recanted, agreed to go to church on the promise of the Queen's pardon and finally repented. Garnet's account of the incident shows how a sensitive and gnawing conscience could torment Catholics who had weakened under threat of death. 'After his return to prison, the man sent a message to inform the judges, who were then about to leave the city, that he regretted his cowardice and determined henceforth to do nothing unbecoming a Catholic. The judges answered:

' "Why is he in such haste to go to the gallows? Assure him he need only persist in his contumacy and it will not be too late for him to be hanged at the next assizes." But there were some thieves to be taken out to execution; Thomas hastened to join their company. Under his arm he carried a linen cloth wherein he was to be wrapped for burial. He presented himself to the sheriff, who asked him what he wanted. He had been condemned, he replied, and had come prepared to die. "Since you are so keen to be hanged", said the sheriff, "assure yourself that I should be delighted to oblige you if your name were on my list. But since it is not here, go away." He left, weeping bitterly over his sins and his past life, for he had once been a Reader in the Calvinist ministry.'

In August he was executed.[1]

Perhaps it was in this month that Garnet visited Winchester: for in the same letter he speaks of the astonishing constancy of Catholics at the assizes there. He also mentions a Fr Clifton, who, after ten years in Winchester gaol, had recently died worn out by its foulness and stench: also a young priest, Fr John Brushford. He had once been a Jesuit novice but had been dismissed on account of his chronic ill-health. 'Returning to England,' says Garnet, 'he exhausted such bodily strength as he had and, after a long period in prison, laid down his life there for Christ's sake.'[2]

Garnet is careful not to be too explicit in his survey of Catholicism in the country. He speaks in detail only of persons who have been executed or have died in prison for their faith, naming dates and places, and setting down all the information he has been able to gather. When he writes of the living he is jejune, for he is anxious first for their safety. He even conceals the places he visited outside London as carefully as he does his own residence in the city.

[1] Little is known of this man John Thomas: he was perhaps the son of Margaret Thomas, a well-known recusant in Winchester and daughter-in-law of John Thomas, founder of the chantry in St John's Church, Winchester.

[2] An account of Fr Clifton's imprisonment in Newgate is given in the First and Second Douai Diaries (T. F. Knox, 1876), 175. Fr Brushford, one of the first students at the English College, Rome, wrote a short and very moving account of his experiences in England; it is printed in Foley, vol. 3, 276 sq. from Lansdowne Manuscripts (British Museum), 96, 156.

However, his lack of precision in detail compels him to greater accuracy in general summaries. His reflections on this summer and early autumn tour are given at length in his spring letter the following year:[1]

'There are confessors of the utmost constancy [he writes] in every community, in every town, in nearly every country house and parish. . . . Among all the Catholics to be found in England there is none who is not a confessor; there is none who had remained steadfast for the space of a year and has not either made a public confession of his faith or been pillaged of his property, or forced into perpetual hiding, or lives now as a wanderer or exile or is held in prison.'

He then tells a story that illustrates his manner of counselling others.

'A few days ago a young man of very humble station came to me with a view to joining the Church. "Your desire", I said, "is praiseworthy. Certainly, if you do not follow it, you cannot be saved. However, you must consider your decision over again. . . . On no account must you rush into it. The price should be weighed. . . . You know what laws have been passed. . . . More cruel laws are expected any day" '[2]

Garnet gave details of legislation. He was careful always before receiving any heretic into the Church: he was no indiscriminate proselytiser, but wished first to have a moral certainty that his convert would persevere; otherwise incalculable harm might befall Catholics to whom the neophyte was introduced. Always the ultimate decision was left to the catechumen. This man was a servant. Garnet therefore warned him he might lose his position. Was he prepared for this, and to find himself without a livelihood? Once a Catholic, Garnet told him, 'you cannot draw back. If you go forward, you will have to undergo all the hardships that come to you.' On these terms Garnet received him into the Church. Then he gave him a homily that revealed the motives that inspired his own life:

'You must be prepared for every kind of difficulty. You must be persuaded in your own mind that from this day forward you belong to Christ, no longer to yourself. And now that you are Christ's, whether He wills to send you to prison, to afflict you with stripes, to torture you on the rack, to strangle you, to slay you by hunger or lack of all you need to live, no matter; you are wholly Christ's. Henceforth it is not something that is His. This is

---

[1] H. G. to C. A. 17 March 1593. Arch. S.J. Rome, *Ang. Hist.* 1, II, f. 27.
[2] This is a reference to the Act (35 Elizabeth, cap. 2) passed in 1593, 'for the better discovery of wicked and seditious persons calling themselves Catholics, but being rebellious and traiterous subjects'. By this Act the laws against recusants were made more stringent still. Garnet must have received information at the time of this incident that the Bill was being drafted.

M

what you can expect. If things should fall out better, you must count it a blessing.'

From his experience during this recent visit to the country, Garnet claimed (and indeed Fr Gerard and others bear him out) that this was the spirit of all who sought to be received into the Church. 'Some become Catholics every day: old men, youths, girls, noblemen and persons of low station.' And it was this spirit, particularly among the gentry, that sent so many young people to the seminaries, to the Society and to convents abroad. This was the ground of Garnet's optimism. There was now every prospect that within a decade the number of priests working in England would be more than doubled.

While in the year 1592 there were no more than six Catholics (four priests and two laymen, including James Byrd) executed throughout the country, the prisons remained full. In many counties the clauses of the proclamation were being enforced with barbarity. 'London is like a whirlpool. Every day it sucks Catholics into prison and throws them out again: there are now as many as sixty-seven in different prisons. Only one of them is a priest. Persons of higher rank are still kept apart elsewhere; others are living in the custody of private individuals all over the country.'

On his return to London for the autumn assizes, Garnet received further news of Robert Southwell. He was still in the Tower, but not unwell. He had received the breviary that Garnet had sent him. Still no one, however, could visit him or speak with him, nor was he allowed to write or receive letters. Slowly he had recovered his bodily strength, though his torture in the Gatehouse had done him permanent injury. While he was there hanging against the wall, he had suffered an internal haemorrhage: intermittently afterwards he would spew blood. When two and a half years later he was removed to Newgate, his last prison, he 'asked his gaoler not to be too far away in case some accident might happen, or he might need something. As a result of his severe torture, his sides were not strong enough for him to call out aloud.'[1]

On his return to Rome, Aquaviva, as he had promised, wrote to Garnet on certain problems left unsettled in his earlier letter.[2] He had delayed a long time and apologised: the Holy See had been slow in answering the petitions made by the General on Garnet's behalf. A letter had been sent to the Pope beseeching him to settle quickly the schism 'among our friends'. Someone must be given authority to bring the factious priests to order. Aquaviva himself had seen the Master General of the Dominicans, who had confirmed

[1] H. G. to C. A. 22 February 1595. F.G. 651, f. 115.
[2] C. A. to H. G. 9 January 1593. Arch. S.J. Rome, *Fland. Belg.* 1, f. 509.

the statement of his last letter that Garnet's faculties for erecting Confraternities of the Rosary were for his lifetime. Two young Englishmen, brothers, had recently arrived in Rome to start their noviceship, but one of them had died.[1] Aquaviva who had indeed responded immediately to Garnet's request to take into Sant' Andrea as many Englishmen as possible and watch over them personally, feared now that the Roman climate was not suited to them. What caused him most deliberation was Garnet's repeated plea to be relieved of his office:

'And I have hardly anything further to add than this. I have given much thought to the question of substituting in your place another who will have charge of all our affairs in England and direct our work there. It is a serious matter. Your Reverence has now had much practice and experience, and also has other qualities that are needed: you would seem by far the best equipped priest for the office'.

Aware of the disappointment that this decision would cause Garnet, he added:

'You must retain this burden yourself, and with keenness. We have good reason to think that our decision will turn out well. We are ready to send you, if they are needed, more men to help you, discreet persons whom you can trust. We will take no further steps until the time is safe for sailing, and for doing our business. Meanwhile we pray to the Lord that this year may be happy and auspicious for your Reverence and that in his abundant grace and consolation He may turn all to gladness and joy.'

Garnet was comforted with Aquaviva's assurance of prayers and promise of men. It was several years before he raised again the question of a successor. In his letter acknowledging Aquaviva's decision, he pursued the last two points raised by the General: his own position as Superior and the supply of priests.

There was no one, however, who could replace Southwell in Garnet's trust and affection. The two priests had taken it by turns to reside in London. Garnet, when he visited the shires, had always left Southwell with authority to act in his name and on his behalf. By alternating two or three months in London both had been able to elude capture for more than six years. Now Garnet found that his visits to London had to be prolonged. Almost in desperation he tried to make Aquaviva realise the dangers that this involved:[2]

[1] They were Thomas and John Wiseman, of Braddocks, near Thaxted. They entered Sant' Andrea, but the younger brother, John, aged twenty-one, had died when still a novice in 1592. As Aquaviva wrote: 'The Lord not long afterwards called the younger one to a better life; the other continues keenly in his vocation.'

[2] H. G. to C. A. (undated, but between February and March 1593) Stonyhurst, Grene *P.*, 597.

'I beg your Lordship to send me an assistant for I cannot live continually in London except at very great peril. Gladly would I exchange my place with any priest who should become my Superior.... My creditors are pressing me now. It is not desirable that everyone should know when I am in town.' Then he adds insistently: 'Let him [my assistant] be such as your Lordship would send for the highest office. I have already admirable subordinates.' Indeed Gerard, Oldcorne and his other subjects, with the exception of Holtby, who could not be spared from the north, were unsuited to replace Southwell. A newcomer was needed, Garnet pointed out. At once Aquaviva made enquiries concerning an English Jesuit ordained already several years. His name was Henry Walpole.

Garnet, meanwhile, anticipating even fiercer measures against Catholics at the next Parliament, was anxious to send abroad for their training as many novices as possible before the threatened storm broke. But there were difficulties. Two 'recruits', recently sent to Flanders for their noviceship, had fallen seriously ill; priests, anxious to join the Society, had misgivings, for there were no men to whom they could leave the care of the districts of which they had charge; some who had sought admission were in prison; others, 'in hope of martyrdom, begged to postpone for a time the fulfilment of their desires'; and yet others, for peculiar reasons, demanded individual consideration at Rome.

Among the last group was Fr John Cornelius who was stationed with Sir John Arundell of Chideock in Dorset, and was, as Garnet admitted, irreplaceable. He was prepared to go to Flanders if he was so ordered. Even before Garnet's coming to England his ambition was to join the Society; yet if he went abroad for his noviceship, Catholics in Dorset and Devon would suffer, for, as Garnet pointed out, 'he knows everybody there and can go wherever he wishes.' Moreover, Cornelius 'has weak health and for this reason I cannot give him a solid undertaking that he shall be received in Flanders. Some years ago he ruptured himself and is not yet completely recovered. However, he does not allow this to impede his work. Indeed he preaches (he is an excellent preacher) without any fatigue and pursues his studies. Moreover, he can ride about the countryside. He is a humble, pious and saintly priest, the terror of devils; he has recently been exorcising them.' While he asked Aquaviva's advice on this case, Garnet urged that Cornelius would lose nothing by deferring his noviceship. Indeed he should be admitted into the Society and then later, when he could be spared, go abroad for his noviceship.[1]

[1] For several months Fr Cornelius, along with Fr John Lowe, who was executed at Tyburn on 8 October 1586, had worked with Fr Weston. Both Cornelius and Lowe

About three months later Garnet returned to the same problem. After pointing out again that priests of several years' standing on the English mission could not be sent abroad without some disorganisation of the work now in hand, he proposed two solutions: these men should either be dispensed from their noviceship or a noviceship should be established in England, where priests could continue to work during their time of training. Eventually the second solution was adopted. Meanwhile Garnet again and again petitioned Rome for individual exemptions from the formal training of the Society.

A further difficulty was now created by the Belgian Provincial, Fr Oliver Manares who, hard-pressed for space in the noviceship of his Province, was inclined to put the claims of his own country first. 'Mr Oliver', writes Garnet in May this year,[1] 'has written to say that I must not send over any more men until he has returned from his visit to your Lordship.[2] But I have with me now a young man whom I am compelled to send abroad.' Without awaiting an answer, Garnet despatched him to Rome with a letter to Aquaviva.

Garnet's apparent impatience is explained by the threat of worse persecution. There was certain information now that the new penal laws were already drafted. He was anxious to get as many novices away and bring in as many new priests as possible before the new legislation had passed the Parliament.

[1] H. G. to C. A. 15 May 1593. F.G. 651, f. 52.
[2] Oliver Manares as Provincial of Belgium visited Rome this year to attend the fifth General Congregation of the Society, which opened on 3 November and dispersed on 18 January 1594.

(before Garnet's arrival) had written to Aquaviva for permission to enter the Society. Since they could not then leave England, both had taken a vow to join the Society when this should become possible. Many priests (several martyrs among them) were in a similar dilemma.

17

CONDITIONS IN THE NORTH

MEANWHILE Garnet used the interval of comparative quiet to give Aquaviva a survey of the situation in the north. In the winter of 1592 to 1593 his suburban house had been searched. Before finding another home in London he appears to have visited Holtby. The plague was still raging in London: the courts were not in session. It was, therefore, a convenient time for him to view the work being done in Yorkshire and Durham under his lieutenant's inspiration.

In his long letter of 17 March he gives Aquaviva a report of his visit. It constitutes the most detailed and accurate survey of Catholicism in the north of England at this time. The information he did not receive from Fr Holtby he was given by word of mouth.[1] The letter covers Yorkshire, Durham and Northumberland, the counties over which Henry Hastings, Earl of Huntingdon, ruled as President of the Council of the North 'with very ample powers and almost regal magnificence, as though he were a Viceroy'.[2] There the proclamation of October 1591 had been taken as giving unrestricted powers to local authorities in their campaign to eliminate Catholicism. What Garnet observed there made the persecution in the midlands and in the south and west of England mild by comparison. An entire army of pursuivants had been raised with power 'to take into custody Catholics of any and every class. Even noblemen, themselves schismatics,[3] were forced to surrender their Catholic wives and hand them over for imprisonment'; Catholic servants were compelled to go to church, not once a month, but once or twice a week, or alternatively, to 'listen at home to a Calvinist service held by a minister; and they are given a time at which they must take their communion'. The penalty for refusal was imprisonment.

Garnet lists a number of eminent Yorkshire Catholics in prison. He adds:

[1] H. G. to C. A. 17 March 1593. Arch. S.J. Rome, *Ang. Hist.* I, II, f. 27.
[2] *Ibid.*
[3] This term indicates Catholics who conformed exteriorly and went to Church, but remained in heart and conviction Catholics.

'a great many others immediately handed over their wives who, in very many instances, are still kept in such close constraint that their husbands can visit them only by special leave of the Council at York'. Among these Catholic wives were 'Lady Constable, a lady of great piety and resolution, wife of Sir Henry Constable; her sister-in-law, Lady Constable of Everingham, who however eventually fell away; Lady Cholmley of Whitby, and her kinswoman, Lady Cholmley of Bransby, the Ladies Babthorpe, Metham, Lawson of Brough, Palmer, Salvin, Barton of Whenby, Ingleby, Lister, Vaux, Dutton, Holtby and Mistress Catherine Ratcliffe, who, though unmarried, gave herself up'.[1]

This was in Yorkshire: another list followed for Durham. Several ladies with child were delivered in prison: one of them, Lady Bennett, yielded; then from remorse of conscience went out of her mind. Nor, as Garnet pointed out, were the lower classes spared. To accommodate them all, two new prisons were built at this time in York, others at Sheriff Hutton, Knaresborough, Rotherham and Bransby Castle. When Garnet reports that in all of them 'the living expenses (namely, two crowns a week for board) are intolerable', he was probably repeating the complaints he had heard on his visit. In Durham, Tobie Mathew, the Dean of the Cathedral Chapter, was energetic. Every month he arranged for three or four sessions of the Commissioners; and consequently 'such terror took possession of the fickle souls of the people that many forsook the noble cause of religion and joined the heretics in their outward observances, though at heart they were recalcitrant. Garnet anticipated still further terror, for twice already this year, 1593, Huntingdon had himself visited Durham. 'What his intentions are', Garnet ruminated, 'I do not know, but he has created intense apprehension among Catholics. . . . For the least of the troubles he caused was to despatch to different parts of the country pursuivants and many other persons of notorious dishonesty and malice, in order to harass Catholics in their homes, or to make visitations and rob them.'

Speaking of Northumberland, Garnet relates an unusual incident that he either witnessed himself or heard from Fr Holtby:

'Another fearful inquisition [he says][2] was made in Northumberland. It was organised by one of the President's officers with Mr Fenwick, a man who had a great reputation in those parts and whose character made him very

---

[1] For a detailed account of these ladies, see the researches of Dom Hugh Aveling, *The Catholic Recusants of the West Riding of Yorkshire 1558–1790* (Proceedings of the Leeds Philosophical and Literary Society, 1963) and *Post-Reformation Catholicism in East Yorkshire 1558–1790* (East Yorkshire Local History Society, 1960).

[2] H. G. to C. A. 17 March 1593. Arch. S.J. Rome, *Ang. Hist.* 1, II, f. 27.

suited for work of this kind. On a certain night, on very high ground, this man set fire to one of the beacons always kept in readiness on the borders of the kingdom. In this way he summoned a number of men to arms: he made pretence that he was repulsing a raid of the Scots in one of their incursions (for this was the purpose of these beacons), but his real purpose was to maltreat the servants of God.

'Thus there assembled immediately a hundred and forty men, whom Fenwick ordered to march with him in the name of the Queen. He commanded them to surround three Catholic households before dawn. These houses were two or three miles apart from each other, namely, Dishington, Mr Ogle's residence, Rutchester, Mr Thomas Rutherford's, and the Grange, which is the house of Mistress Lawson, the widow.'

Fenwick himself made for all three houses in turn, 'wasting and destroying indiscriminately'. At the Grange, Mistress Lawson, for lack of a hiding-place 'had entered an oven and there stayed in safety. But the excessive heat constricted her breathing and she caught an ailment which was difficult to cure'. So many searches were made at this time, and rumours of others were so widespread, that many people 'were compelled to desert their homes and live in the woods and fields, or fly into the mountains and there live in caves and holes in the ground, toilfully making dwellings for themselves in the earth or in some hole in the rocks. Here they passed their days and nights, some for a month at a time, others for five or six weeks, and others for a shorter period, according to the time that the threat lasted.'

Fr Garnet then illustrates the plight of these poor people with an incident he learnt from Fr John Nelson:[1]

'One nobleman together with his wife, who was with child and due to give birth within a month, lived in this manner for six weeks in an underground place, accompanied by a man called John Nelson. . . . They never judged it safe to emerge save after midday: all the searches were made either in the morning or at night. They constructed two apartments in the cave and prepared two beds, so that they could pass the night there. Also they built a place where they could attend to the daily needs of the body and a recess for storing food which secretly each day was carried to them from their house. The cave itself had been dug under a large oak tree; the entrance was invisible in a cleft root, just large enough for a man to pass through: and it was kept covered with a thin layer of sods. When the rain came and the snow melted, it collapsed on them.'

Other cases that Garnet had witnessed or heard narrated were still more

[1] Cf. *sup.*, p. 103. Father Nelson had been sent to assist Father Holtby. Father Garnet describes him as 'a very faithful servant and a great favourite of ours'.

tragic. There were groups of people in hiding who kept continual watch, day and night, each of them taking certain hours by turn. Some lived for five weeks in this manner in the middle of rushes, in huts built from branches of trees and covered with turf. When the rain came down at night, it soon seeped through the dry sods and at times immersed them almost up to their waists in water. Meanwhile they were never long free from the insidious attentions of the searchers' dogs or the searchers themselves.

'There were yet others who dwelt in ancient ruins, underground, with all their household; there they made separate beds and partitioned off small rooms. For their fellow occupants they had toads, frogs, adders, lizards and such like creatures. On one occasion it was necessary to administer drugs to a maid, who believed that an adder had slipped down her throat while she was asleep.'

Shocked as Garnet was by these experiences, he was at the same time encouraged by the fortitude that the northern Catholics displayed. Like Holtby, he had the spirit of a born leader. As he saw it, the only result of all Huntingdon's activity was that 'the just by faith are winning their kingdom'. He asked: 'What has Parliament in fact accomplished? What have all these proclamations and laws done to crush the spirit of the northern Catholics? War has been waged on a wide front against a few poor priests and unarmed laymen: every bishop, judge and justice of the peace in the north is out to arrest and imprison Catholics.' The expenditure of money and men on foreign wars could not compare with the expenditure on what he calls 'domestic outrages against religion'. Then Garnet expressed the sustaining hope that he carried with him still to the scaffold. In spite of the efforts made to crush the faith, 'it flourishes; indeed it increases, asserts itself and shines more brightly every day, like gold in the furnace': in time 'all will observe the religious conduct of Catholics and, albeit unwillingly, will glorify their heavenly Father and will be ready some day to accept the gifts of his celestial grace'.

It was probably on his way back to London from the north that Garnet visited Wisbech. He was there in the first week of November,[1] and received from the imprisoned priests a welcome that was a tacit acknowledgement of his unofficial leadership of the Church. At their invitation he secretly celebrated High Mass in the prison precincts. This was the brief period between the relaxation of the rigid restrictions on the prisoners and the outbreak of the quarrels among them. Garnet, writing immediately after his visit, described the place as a 'college of venerable confessors'.[2] Hitherto

[1] H. G. to C. A. 12 November 1593. F.G. 651, f. 58.
[2] *Ibid.*

the inmates had lived as solitaries, except at time of meals, which they took
at a common table under the surveillance of the keeper. Their number fluc-
tuated between thirty and thirty-five, as the older men died and others
replaced them, passing through the gates of the prison as though they were
entering a sepulchre,[1] so secluded were they from the traffic of the town.
Their single comfort was that they were able to celebrate Mass, probably on
alternate days, for Weston says that as many as eighteen Masses were offered
each morning:

'They led a collegial and heavenly kind of life, both for inward virtue
and external edification. Their prayer was frequent and earnest, their study
was continual meditation of the holy scriptures and other exercises appertaining to virtue. They lived in common both for their diet and distribution of
alms that was sent unto them; they were present daily at public and private
litanies and at some lesson or conference of controversies and cases of conscience for the better instruction of their judgments. Their conversation was
sweet both in words and countenance, their behaviour holy, and all this by
the direction chiefly of Father Weston.'[2]

Garnet had gone there to discuss with Weston the question of his exile,
which had been raised yet again. His conclusion was that Weston's removal
would cause the breakdown of the communal life he had such a large part
in establishing. Later, perhaps Garnet might have regretted his decision,
but there was no indication at the time that troubles would shortly break out.
Not long afterwards, with the increased freedom allowed to the priests,
persons from all parts of the country visited Wisbech for counsel and
confession and it was argued that Weston, 'the most esteemed and consulted
man in England',[3] was able to do more good in prison than at liberty.
Catholics came to receive the sacraments from him, heretics to consult him
about their doubts and to be reconciled to the Church, and people of every
class to attend the spiritual conferences he gave.[4]

Garnet mentions only this visit to Wisbech and gives no details of it,
save that he was invited to sing High Mass. Weston suggests that it was one
of several visits and that it lasted some days.[5] Five years later when Garnet's enemies tried to represent him in Rome as a man at odds with his own
subjects, and particularly with Weston, his friend recalled this visit. 'I appeal

---

[1] *William Weston*, 162–3.
[2] R. Persons, *A Briefe Apologie, or Defence of Ecclesiastical Subordination in England*
(1601), 64–5.
[3] *William Weston*, 177.
[4] *Ibid.*
[5] W. W. to C. A. 19 May 1598. F.G. 651, f. 163.

to Father Henry himself to say with what great joy and satisfaction I welcomed him and what abundance of affection and comfort we stirred in each other during the several days we spent together. . . . Twice, if not more often, he paid me visits not without great peril to himself and anxiety on my part. . . . He was careful in supplying all my needs. . . . The exchange of small presents between us on many occasions has served greatly to attest our mutual affection and also to preserve and increase our friendship.'[1] Also there were the frequent letters which Garnet wrote to Weston, and were later seized. Indeed, his treatment of Weston was typical of the manner in which he dealt with Catholic prisoners, priests and laity, throughout the country. It earned him the title of 'father of the poor'.

What Garnet had seen in the north made him fearful that in the next Parliament the measures in force there would be extended to the south. On reaching London he gathered all the information he could concerning the proposed legislation. He found it difficult to guess what further measures could be passed, so numerous, comprehensive and cruel were the existing statutes. Nevertheless, before the middle of March, he knew precisely what was contemplated.

'These laws', he tells Aquaviva, 'are as yet in the potter's hands, but without doubt they will be passed.' There had been protests against them: it was argued that if the Papists were really such as the law-makers contended it would be better for the country to exterminate them altogether; if they were fit to live, they should be permitted to live in tolerable conditions. Garnet reported that Lord Grey, a distinguished, though not particularly 'virtuous' man,[2] had remarked: 'I was under the impression that our purpose hitherto was merely to keep the Papists humbled and in subjection so that they should cause no trouble. We have sucked them dry and reduced them to extreme poverty. Now we strive to harass them yet further. It is plain to me that we are persecuting religion.'

In his reflections on the new laws, Garnet, as always, presents the Queen's dilemma with understanding and loyalty. He had respect also for her learning. 'In the last ten days [that is, between 7 and 17 March] our Mistress, the Queen, has asserted that she has perused all the ancient Fathers, Hebrew, Greek and Latin, and some modern Spanish and Italian authors as well, and has been unable to discover anywhere a statement that it is unlawful [for Catholics] to go to [Protestant] churches.' Garnet adds obscurely that he

[1] *Ibid.*

[2] Probably Henry Grey of Enville, Co. Stafford, son of Thomas second Marquess of Dorset and Lord Ferrers. He married Anne, daughter of William, second Lord Windsor, whom Garnet met at Hurleyford in July 1586.

does not know whether this also was the opinion of the Jewish Rabbis, whom he does not count among the Fathers, but he asserts rightly that there are 'great lights of the Church who hold a different opinion'.

The Queen's research had been done for her by a renegade Catholic and published in an anonymous dialogue in England, possibly with the connivance of the government. The author set out to undermine the stand all priests had taken on this question for the last fourteen years. As Garnet remarked, the book was hailed by schismatics as a heaven-sent gift, and drew many into error.

'Every conceivable remedy has been attempted [he wrote]. It is impossible to influence or alter the mind of schismatic layfolk who imagine they are learned and set themselves up as false teachers. Would that they kept their sin to themselves and did not preach to others: they cite a letter of the Pope [Clement VIII] in support of their opinion, and have the impudence to attribute to him the statement that it is only a venial sin to go to church. May God preserve all priests from this sin. Although many doubt it, it is certainly said that a priest was author of the *Dialogue*.'[1]

No one more than Garnet realised the seriousness of the course advocated in the tract, for it threatened to take from Catholics the ground of their resistance. What the Queen could not achieve by Acts of Pariament might still be achieved by dividing Catholics on this issue. 'This is a matter for very grave thought,' Garnet warned Aquaviva, 'since on it hinges the success of our apostolate. *Something must be got from the Supreme Pontiff* [the underlining is Garnet's] which can be promulgated here without any flurry of excitement.'[2]

Before the middle of May Garnet had been troubled again by the unaccountable behaviour of the Belgian Provincial, Oliver Manares. Aquaviva, against Garnet's wishes, had given orders that the English novices should be sent to Belgium. Although the places he had assigned to Garnet's men in the Flanders novitiate were far from all taken, in recent months hardly one of the men Garnet sent over had been admitted. They had crossed in peril of their lives, and it was difficult now to recall them to England. Garnet implored Aquaviva to give the Belgian Provincial strict instructions on the fair treatment of his candidates, and also begged that his novices should be maintained without charge to himself. The severity of the fines on English Catholics made it difficult for him to raise funds. 'We are in debt now, and if we were not at present maintained by the income of two novices, we would be in extreme need. And besides, we are unwilling to make too

---

[1] H. G. to C. A. 10 June 1593. F.G. 651, f. 54.

[2] *Ibid.* Here and later all passages underlined were underlined by Garnet.

free use of novices' money until your Lordship rules how far we can go in this matter.'[1]

At the end of the same letter Garnet made a still more pressing appeal to Aquaviva. He was determined at any price to obtain equitable treatment for the young Englishmen now joining the Society in large numbers.

'I beg your Lordship [he repeats][2] to see that the novices now on their way are welcomed kindly. It will redound in no small measure to your Lordship's credit that you have helped, cherished and with your authority advanced the interests of these young men, who are outcasts from their country and destitute; in God's eyes this credit will be the greater because it is from you alone that these blessings spring, and from your own resources, albeit they are often bestowed on the undeserving, men who become worse the more good you do them. Yet this is only to resemble Him who sends his rain alike on the just and unjust. May God long keep your Lordship safe in his care.'

It is characteristic of Garnet that, rather than blame Oliver Manares for giving preference to Belgians, he appealed to Aquaviva to make good his promise to do all he could to help him personally. The postscript to this letter makes it clear that he had in mind the undertaking Aquaviva had given in his letter of comfort after the arrest of Southwell. 'As I have done earlier, I again plead earnestly with you to send me two veterans as quickly as possible.' Earlier, in mid-May, he had written with the impatience he always showed when he asked for new priests. 'Those two men whom I recently begged of you, I am still eagerly awaiting.' Then ominously he adds: 'No matter how extreme our difficulties are it is not right that our business should fail or languish for lack of men.'

After Southwell's arrest twelve months earlier, Garnet became short of funds. Gerard explains how during his first six years the Jesuits, through Southwell, had depended largely on the benefactions of the Countess of Arundel.[3] Now Gerard's friends came to Garnet's aid. 'Providentially', he explains, 'this happened at a time when the Society was beginning to grow in England.' Among others, the Wiseman family provided generous contributions. Before going abroad, Thomas, the elder brother, had settled his estate on the Society and given Garnet between eleven and twelve thousand florins, which had been used for the support of Jesuit novices and of students at Douai. 'After we had lost Father Southwell', Gerard writes, confirming Garnet's statement, 'we should have been very hard pressed indeed had not these men come to our help.' In the difficult circumstances of the mission Garnet judged it both necessary and just to devote

[1] *Ibid.* [2] *Ibid.* [3] *John Gerard,* 4.

more than half the money he was given to the seminaries abroad. Dr Barrett, the President of Douai, himself admitted that he had received from Garnet and Southwell more money than from the whole body of secular priests in England. Later, when accusations of avarice were made against the Jesuits, Garnet offered to exchange all that the Society had in England for whatever was possessed by any single secular priest chosen by lot. At this time, when he was not visiting friends in the country, he lived on what was offered him from day to day.[1]

In May, after the passage of the new legislation through Parliament, Garnet left London.[2] For some time he had been seeking from the Holy See a plenary 'indulgence' for certain groups of Catholics in England, prisoners and others who had suffered from the persecution. It is difficult to follow exactly the nature of the spiritual favours he was granted, but Garnet expresses more than satisfaction with them, and at the same time asks for an extension of these favours to yet other groups of Catholics. 'The plenary indulgence has marvellously cheered the hearts of all Catholics and stirred them to even greater endeavour. Now it only remains to obtain the same grant under different conditions for all others. This traffic with our Master the Pope has great power to restore and raise spirits that are heavily afflicted or almost prostrate.'[3]

In the worst hours of persecution Garnet never failed to consider the general needs of the Catholic community, and particularly the needs of the seminary priests who, still without leadership, looked to him to transmit their requests to the Pope. This he continued to do for many years until an agent for the clergy was appointed in Rome. Typically he concludes his summary of the situation in England by telling Aquaviva how keen Catholics are to enter the Confraternity of the Rosary, which, he prays, will prove the means of bringing innumerable spiritual blessings on his country.[4]

[1] *Ibid.*

[2] H. G. to C. A. 15 May 1593. F.G. 651, f. 52. 35 Eliz., cap. 2: An Act against Popish recusants. For the text see G. W. Prothero, *Select Statutes and other Constitutional Documents 1558–1625* (4th ed., 1946), 92–3.

[3] *Ibid.*   [4] *Ibid.*

18

WALPOLE AT YORK

DURING his time in London in early May 1593, Garnet had made arrangements for his youngest sister, Margaret, to go abroad and enter the convent of the Canonesses Regular of the Lateran at Louvain. On 1 October he addressed her an affectionate letter to await her arrival there. He had heard that she had reached the Continent safely: he was now waiting for news of her 'happy arrival in that most secure and quiet haven of a religious life'.[1]

An unusually long letter, written in English, it forms a treatise on the religious vocation. There is nothing particularly original in it, but it has great interest as a summary of the private instruction Garnet gave to many young women and men. It shows, moreover, how fresh and unspoilt were his own religious ideals: certain passages might well have been written by him twenty years earlier when he was a novice at Sant' Andrea. 'What greater comfort can there be in this world', he tells his sister, 'than wholly to be severed from the love of the world, and to love Him only who is better than the whole world.' This is something she will fully understand only after she has entered the convent: now she must take it on her brother's word.

Even in England, where sudden raids, the arrest of his brethren and recurrent crises formed the pattern of his life, Garnet followed closely the liturgical scheme of the year, moving prayerfully from feast to feast. He tells his sister: 'In religion you shall continually live and converse with Christ and, as it were, be always brought up with Him: sometimes accompanying Him in the crib, sometimes flying with Him into Egypt, sometimes watching, praying and fasting with Him. . . . Finally you shall die with Him, be buried with Him, rise again with Him and ascend with Him into heaven, where your heart, conversation and comfort must be.'

[1] H. G. to Margaret Garnet, 1 October 1593, Stonyhurst, *Anglia* 1, 76. Garnet's sisters joined St Ursula's Convent. Although a Flemish foundation, it contained many English nuns. When in 1606 a daughter house (St Monica's) was established in the same city for English ladies, St Ursula's then had twenty-two English nuns (six had already died) and had been governed by an English Prioress, Mother Margaret Clement, for thirty-eight years. Garnet's sisters were among the first community at St Monica's.

Thus Garnet, writing to his sister, reveals the secret of his own attraction to the Rosary which gave Catholics, deprived often of the Mass and always of the solemn celebration of the liturgy, a method of following in spirit the calendar of the Church.

Here and there are echoes of St Bernard, Southwell's favourite author, whom now Garnet began to read more frequently in order to keep in spiritual sympathy with his companion. He recalls the words of an ancient English song that was sung at the consecration of nuns: 'Let that song', he urges his sister, 'never go out of your mind. . . . "The kingdom of this world and all the beauty and fairness I have despised for the love of my Lord Jesus, Whom I have seen, Whom I have affected, in Whom I have believed, Whom I have tenderly loved".' Then he gives his sister family news that will strengthen her will to persevere, so that 'you may even touch with your hands the care that God has over those that love Him'. He tells her that on the feast of the Assumption, 15 August last, 'I brought our mother into the union of our spiritual mother, the Church, and left her very hearty and resolute'.

This is the first reference in Garnet's letters to his mother. A little later he told Aquaviva the news. His father had died and been buried at Heanor in 1576; and his brother John in the same year. Nowhere does he reveal his mother's place of residence, but now after seven years in England he had the comfort of receiving her back into the Church. On the death of Brian Garnet, she had married again and unwittingly been led into heresy by her second husband. Recently Garnet had visited her and discussed her religious position. Now all his family were back in the Church into which they had been baptised. At the same time Garnet reported that he had taken Persons' mother, a nonagenarian, into his own house, where contentedly she was awaiting death or another incursion of the pursuivants.[1]

Perhaps repeating the lesson that Father Fabio had impressed on him, Garnet now urged his sister to pray for a humility that would be also an inspiration to bold action. 'You must rise up with great confidence and courage and say with David "My imperfections thy eyes have seen and yet I hope I am written in thy book where thou hast written thy other elect". . . . for [from] the consideration of your own miseries there ariseth a knowledge of the goodness of God; and [from] this knowledge there springeth up a burning love . . . as is able to love them which so little deserve it.' And as though he were exhorting himself to further effort in his own work, he continues: 'Thousands of shields hang over thee, and all manner of armour for valiant soldiers; thou art the field of divine battle, a theatre of spiritual combat, the spectacle of angels, the stage of all courageous fighters.'

[1] H. G. to C. A. 3 January 1594. F.G. 651, f. 60.

Garnet's happiness at his sister's entry into religion had 'carried him further than [he] thought' in this letter. He closed with the suggestion that she should seek leave of her Superiors to write to him from time to time. He, on his side, 'will not fail (God willing) to salute [her] now and then'. One last word he had for her. Although, with the exception of their mother, all the family and friends are in the same state 'both spiritual and corporal' as at the time of her leaving, he has no doubt that Margaret may easily draw 'their other sisters, which are unmarried, unto the like desires'.[1]

Garnet's spirits ran high this autumn. Towards the end of the year he was able to report to Aquaviva that all his subjects were still alive and well, and that the new penal laws proposed in Parliament were never in fact passed: thus their affairs were in no worse state than they were before.[2] 'God with singular love furthers His own work. His hand is not shortened and in all these trials He tightens or slackens the reins as His wisdom judges fit.'[3] Garnet's personal gratitude to Aquaviva overflows. A letter from the General, dated 16 December, had been slow in reaching him; but it was full of comfort, and 'more than paternal solicitude'. Garnet was overwhelmed and felt he could never sufficiently express his thanks. Besides the General's personal affection, which he needed greatly after eighteen months' separation from Southwell, Garnet was granted all the spiritual favours he had sought. He had himself been permitted to determine the conditions for the extension of the Plenary Indulgence for which he had asked. Moreover, through Aquaviva's offices, he received a most favourable reply from Father Manares. Now at last he could send as many men to Flanders as he judged fit for the noviceship. Not all, he now explains, will go at once; some have first to settle their temporal affairs. And he was anxious to act slowly for fear that certain priests, hostile to the Society, might complain that he was 'withdrawing too many labourers from the harvest', though, as he pointed out, 'they will return within a year or two better equipped and more keen to continue the work from which they have been temporarily withdrawn.'

It was a happy time for Garnet. Now he was back in London expecting his new 'companion' any day. 'We are daily waiting for Father Walpole',[4] he told Aquaviva.

[1] Margaret Garnet persevered in her vocation and was professed at St Ursula's Convent, Louvain, on 5 June, the feast of the Englishman, St Boniface, 1595: her sister Helen entered two years later and was professed in 1597.

[2] Among the clauses of the proposed Bill was a penalty of a hundred pounds to be imposed on any person 'permitting their children to be baptised by any Jesuit, seminary or other massing priest'. The draft is printed in Bryan Stapleton's *Catholic Missions in Oxfordshire* (1908), 6–7.

[3] H. G. to C. A. 12 November 1593. F.G. 651, f. 58.   [4] *Ibid.*

N

This was the last of his letters that showed unclouded contentment. Walpole indeed was on his way. Destined by Aquaviva to replace Southwell, he was also the man to whom, when Aquaviva gave the word, Garnet would hand over the government of his brethren.

Yet the year was to close with a bitter loss for Garnet. The same month that he wrote this letter to Aquaviva, Henry Walpole embarked at Dunkerque. Owing to an outbreak of the plague, all the ports on the south coast were closed to foreign shipping. With his brother, Thomas, and another gentleman, Edward Lingham, Walpole secured a passage on one of three French warships sailing for Scotland. The voyage was rough. The party was at sea ten days longer than it had anticipated. Finally, on 4 December, Walpole was landed from a rowing boat off Flamborough Head.[1] With him were his brother and Edward Lingham. Climbing steeply through an opening in the cliffs, they came to the village and were received warmly in a Catholic house belonging to the Constables. Walpole declined an invitation to stay, but walked on to Bridlington where he purchased a horse. That night he reached Kilham. As he was retiring to bed he was arrested by the sheriff. Later it was learned that his landing had been betrayed by a Scotsman, a prisoner on board the French ship, who, to gain money for his ransom, had been put ashore two or three days earlier and had given information to the Council of the North. Instantly the entire north-eastern seaboard had been alerted. It was a piece of ill-luck that neither Garnet nor Walpole himself could have averted. The loss to Garnet was irreparable. Here was a man who in temperament, experience and zeal matched Southwell, and with comparable literary gifts and gallantry.

Two days later, Walpole was identified by the President himself. Until 25 February he was kept in prison at York.

While waiting for Walpole in London, Garnet heard rumours of his arrest; then he received confirmation from Holtby. Partly, as Garnet writes, to comfort him, partly also to find out whether he had brought with him any special instructions from Aquaviva for the Fathers in England, Holtby found means of communicating with Walpole. Walpole's letters to him were later passed to Garnet, who sent transcripts of them to Aquaviva.

It was many years since Walpole and Garnet had met. Garnet had every reason to fear that Walpole might from inexperience be trapped into a statement that would scandalise, embarrass or confuse northern Catholics. Before Garnet's time, the Jesuit, Fr Bosgrave, who had been captured immediately on landing and was unfamiliar with the intricacies of the English

---

[1] Where not otherwise stated, the source of information for Walpole is Garnet's Italian letter (20 June 1595) to C. A. F.G. 651, f. 150.

situation, had stated he saw no reason why Catholics should not go to Protestant services. But Walpole was wary. Holtby, without revealing his identity, did his task of initiation well. 'Your letters are a great comfort to me', wrote Walpole to his unknown friend [Holtby], 'but your presence, even for an hour, would mean more to me than I can say. . . . Remember me. Do remember me.' On several occasions, Walpole was led out to dispute with Anglican divines, for he was Huntingdon's greatest capture: indeed the first Jesuit to fall into his hands. The President of the Council was determined to capitalise his good fortune.

Huntingdon was unsuccessful. With apprehension, Garnet shuddered when he learned that Topcliffe, intermittently still tormenting Southwell in the Tower, had been despatched to York to handle Walpole. After failing with Southwell, Topcliffe now scented the triumph he needed. But Walpole stood the test. He conducted himself like the 'veteran' whom Garnet had requested and with an unspoiled simplicity.

'In the course of these examinations [Walpole wrote to Holtby] I gave in writing an account of my whole life abroad . . . and my intent to glorify God and to spread the Catholic faith, for which purpose I had returned here, desirous to convert not only the people of England but much more the Queen herself and the nobility. I declared that I would spare no efforts to this end. Except to say where I first met them, I refused to answer questions about other persons. This angered Topcliffe. He told me that when I should come to Bridewell or to the Tower of London he would make me tell everything. I replied to him that God could not suffer me to say anything injurious to Himself or to my own conscience.'

Topcliffe's threat was carried out. Walpole was to be tortured even more brutally and protractedly than Southwell. For the present he was bewildered by the attention given to him. No priest since Campion had received so many visits from members of the Council and officials of the State. 'I have always made profession of being the most unlearned priest in our Society', he wrote when he discovered that his friend was none other than Fr Holtby, 'and I marvel that my very common condition makes the Crown so interested in me.' Then wistfully he continues: 'You are with the front-line troops [Walpole had been chaplain once to an English regiment in Flanders], while I stay idly with the baggage-train. Nevertheless our close . . . union with Jesus, our David and King, puts us on an equal standing and everyone of us shares in what all are doing.'

From Walpole Topcliffe had hoped to draw information that would lead to Garnet's arrest. As with Southwell, he failed. Walpole was not as raw as he hoped to find him. 'I was asked', continues Walpole, 'who was the

Superior of Ours in the country; whether it was such and such a person or some other; but Topcliffe knew very well who was Superior and named him.'

In his first encounter with Topcliffe, Walpole had behaved admirably. He asked Holtby that the letter he had sent him should be forwarded to his Superior. "Do me the favour of getting this letter to the rest of the brethren, to each one of them, for to each I should like to give it personally, indeed to all my brethren and fellow-workers in Jesus, from whose trials, prayers and sacrifices I draw such great benefit.' Then this latest recruit to Garnet's staff prepared to pass Lent in prison, sad only that his brother, a layman, who had been captured with him and taken to another prison in York, had gone to church and been released. His second companion, Edward Lingham, in yet another York prison, gave an undertaking that he would be faithful to his religion and (as Walpole commented) 'he will observe this like the gentleman he is and as my brother in Jesus Christ'.[1]

In his last exchange with Topcliffe in York, Walpole, matching the skill both of Southwell and Weston, parried the bloody question. ' "If the Pope were to make war", I was asked, "what would I do?" I replied that the circumstances then prevailing would have to be considered and that I would have recourse to God in prayer. I would also seek advice and would think most carefully before embroiling myself in matters of war whatever the parties involved.'

Walpole was permitted to see certain visitors, who perhaps carried out of prison his letters to Holtby. He knew it was too dangerous to address Garnet directly. Frequently he was visited by Huntingdon and was drawn by him into discussions on points of theology: it was not uncommon then for men of his position to display an interest in divinity. 'Five sheets of paper have been given to me by order of the President which I must fill with reasons for my faith and with answers to questions on the Church, the Eucharist and the Pope.'[2]

Walpole wrote freely. His own conscience acquitted him of any political activity and he judged that no harm would come from saying and writing what was in his mind. 'My actions have been such', he protested, 'that I voluntarily acknowledge them all, and give thanks for them to God, since they are directed to doing good to all and ill to none, to winning peace and

---

[1] Lingham was later sent to the Tower, where in 1598 he occupied a cell adjoining Fr Weston's. In his *Autobiography* (*William Weston*, 207) Weston pays tribute to his steadfastness. Lingham had left England for reasons of conscience and had served as an officer in Sir William Stanley's regiment in the Netherlands; he was at this time returning on business connected with his properties.

[2] Garnet comments: 'After the death of the Father, it was understood that the President was moved by his dissertations considerably more than he had first been, as he himself confessed.'

preserving it, to spreading the Catholic faith and the kingdom of God to the utmost of my power.'

Early in February 1594, perhaps when the Fathers were assembled at their half-yearly meeting, Garnet received a messenger sent post-haste by Holtby. An opportunity had arisen for Walpole to make good his escape. An answer was urgent. Garnet acted as he always did in these cases. He left the decision to the man on the spot, who was familar with the circumstances and better able to judge the chance of success.

Holtby in fact was against the attempt. Walpole, by his mere presence among them, was an inspiration to the hard-pressed Catholics in York. Moreover, it was by no means certain that the escape would succeed. If it did, Holtby feared that 'a general search [throughout the country] ... would follow and that, for one priest at liberty, several might be captured, along with many laymen, some of them perhaps less well prepared to endure torture and death.'

Loyally Walpole accepted Holtby's decision. 'Similar considerations occurred to me. I proposed it only to satisfy others.' True, St Peter had escaped, but he had been given the help of an angel. 'This is to be my Rome, and my *Domine, quo vadis?*' Then fearfully he adds: 'My examiners gave me slight but sure hints of secret torments that awaited me and of death itself.'

Eventually on 25 February Walpole was sent to London. Garnet had gathered every detail of his conduct in York and had reported it to Aquaviva, 'for I know how willingly you listen to even the most trivial affairs of your sons'. To Garnet, however, none of these matters was trivial. With reason he now began to fear for Walpole the same fate as Southwell, for it was Topcliffe, 'old and grey-haired', who supervised his transference to the Tower. No longer would this satanic creature attempt to wean him from his loyalties by smooth devices. Walpole's months at York had been a time of contentment and occupied with visitors and with writing. He had won the Earl of Huntingdon's reluctant respect. In his last month there he had asked the President to allow him a number of books including a Breviary. This, Walpole explained to his captor, is 'the book of the divine office, which contains only Holy Scripture and a number of elucidations of Scripture by the most devout and ancient Fathers of the Church of God'. He was given also the *Controversies* of Bellarmine, and Stapleton's *Principles of the Faith*.[1] 'And I would not object to having along with these books the *Institutes of Calvin* or some other English book that carries authority with

---

[1] Thomas Stapleton's *Principia Fidei*, to which William Whittaker, Dean of Durham, replied, was first published in Paris in 1578. A scholar of Winchester, Stapleton was one of the most noted and prolific writers among the Catholic exiles and, with William Allen, was co-founder of the seminary at Douai.

the Protestants, for if they are going to establish one confession or uniform system of doctrine, as the Catholic church does and has always done, it would make it easier for me to judge where the truth lies.'

With the help of these books Walpole wrote his last works: one entitled *Guard yourself against false prophets* reached Garnet's hands; the other, *On the Invocation of Saints*, was unfinished at the time he was transferred to the Tower. The manuscript never came into Garnet's possession, but he heard that it had greatly pleased the President: others also he had planned, but 'of these', says Garnet, 'nothing is known'.

The letter Garnet wrote to Aquaviva on first hearing of Walpole's arrest appears to have been lost, and it was perhaps for this reason that after Walpole's execution he wrote a full account of his friend's first three months in England. When Garnet wrote again in March, Walpole was already lodged in the Tower and Garnet was searching desperately for information about him. For lack of news he surmised briefly and correctly what had occurred. 'Now he is with Mr Robert', he wrote,[1] 'but he has not been allowed the same quiet, for, as I think, his examinations are not yet over.' At first Garnet guessed, then later established, the facts. Topcliffe had made Walpole his personal prize. This 'most sordid of men had so impressed the mind of the Queen with the danger in which she stood from priests and Catholics that she herself was wont frequently to ask when there would be another execution, since none had occurred for some time'.[2] Playing on her fears of assassination, Topcliffe 'was [now] given authority and a commission to do as he liked'; and he was confident that with Walpole in his hands he would have no difficulty in involving the Jesuits in some plot against the State.

About this time an Irishman named Patrick Collins was arrested and executed at Tyburn for 'intending the Queen's death'. At his trial the Jesuits were maliciously slandered. The incident was followed by a second more specious plot, the madcap scheme of a Portuguese called Lopez, supposedly a Jew, though Garnet remarks that at the time of his death 'he showed himself of the Queen's religion'.[3] This man's machinations were unjustly fathered on the Catholic community. Two other Portuguese who died in the same plot did in fact confess themselves Catholics. In this atmosphere of attempted assassination and fabricated plots, it was not difficult for Topcliffe to persuade Elizabeth that he was her personal saviour. It remained only for him now to implicate Walpole, and with him, the Jesuits.[4]

[1] H. G. to C. A. 10 March 1594. F.G. 651, f. 64.
[2] H. G. to C. A. 20 June 1595. F.G. 651, f. 130.
[3] H. G. to C. A. 6 September 1594. Stonyhurst, *Anglia* 1, 81.
[4] Roderigo Lopez, a Portuguese Jew and an eminent physician, had settled in England

Garnet knew that Walpole had been taken to the Tower for torture *ut tentaretur a diabolo*: so that 'some incriminating tittle touching matters of State might be wrung from him'. Nevertheless Garnet did not allow this set-back to interfere with his wider plans.

Leaving the fate of Walpole for the moment, he again petitioned Aquaviva for experienced men. Clearly he was afraid that the loss of Walpole might deter the General from sending over other English priests who could ill be spared from the seminaries. Anticipating the General's misgivings he wrote: 'The fact that [Walpole] had with him no Jesuit companion, has, so to speak, reduced the loss. His arrest should not deter your Lordship from sending us help, for now is the time we greatly need it.' Then, pressing home his request, he makes an astonishing proposal: 'And help can be sent over without incurring any great hazard, if I am given warning beforehand, so that I can determine what place they are to be put ashore. . . . Or I can send over a messenger and ship so that the crossing can be made more safely.'

Finally he tells Aquaviva that for every priest, like Walpole, lost on the way, he has a large number of young men ready to enter the noviceship: indeed 'I have just sent four to the appointed place.' One of them, George Warford, was well-known to Persons and had a deep affection for him; two others were 'veterans', fine men who had worked a long time in England; the fourth was not a priest. He had no doubt that Aquaviva would return them all as soon as possible. He then speaks of complaints that so many former seminary priests were now joining the Society:

'And there are also two other priests who with highest commendation completed their course of studies a few years ago. But I am keeping them back at present, partly because of the difficulty in getting them over, partly because of the work that they are doing here. Some take it badly when priests are removed from England. If these men were left to lead an idle life abroad, they would be able to join us with the full blessing of our critics. . . . But

---

in 1559 and in 1586 became one of the Queen's doctors. In 1594 he was accused of receiving Spanish bribes to murder her. Although no incriminating evidence was found, he was tortured and made to sign an extorted confession and on the strength of it tried at the Guildhall. The prosecution was in the hands of Sir Edward Coke, who secured his condemnation. Lopez was executed three months later, on 7 June 1594, along with two other Portuguese, Emmanuel Tinoco and de Gama. Patrick Collins, an Irish soldier serving in the Netherlands, was allegedly sent over by Fr Holt to murder the Queen. At Garnet's own trial, Coke adduced these two 'plots' as evidence of Garnet's support of regicide; but, as Gerard says, Lopez 'knew no Jesuit in the world nor was acquainted with any Catholic in England that I know of' (*Narrative*, 234). Garnet also retorted to Coke that he had Holt's sworn testimony that he had never had dealings of any kind with Collins.

soon the matter will be put right. We do not want it to be seen that we are withdrawing too many priests at the same time.'[1]

Probably it was the shock of Walpole's arrest within thirty-six hours of his landing that forced Garnet to organise safer methods of getting priests ashore. With the help of Richard Fulwood he had already perfected an escape route for aspirants to the seminaries and the Society, and also for girls who were now leaving England in increasing numbers to enter the convents abroad. Now with the co-operation of Holtby in the north, and of other priests in the south-west of England, safe landing places were selected and guarded with such secrecy that henceforth, in spite of the close watch kept on the coast, it was rare for a priest to be arrested on landing.

[1] H. G. to C. A. 10 March 1594. F.G. 651, f. 64.

19

EASTER HUBBUB

AFTER the arrest and execution of Collins and Lopez, Richard Topcliffe was confident that it was only a matter of time, torture and trickery before he incriminated Walpole in one or other plot. This was the year of his triumph, and the year also of Garnet's worst losses.

On the advice of Richard Young, Chief Justice of Middlesex, Topcliffe chose cunningly his moment to strike. Much organisation lay behind his plan. Towards the end of Lent, before Catholic gentlemen had left London for their country homes, he organised a descent on all known or suspected Catholic houses in the city and in the bordering counties. The 15 March, the Friday before Passiontide, was the night he chose to strike. The whole city was stirred to tumult. In his letter to Persons, Garnet spoke of 'such hurly-burly as never was seen in man's memory: no, not when Wyatt was at the gates';[1] and writing to Aquaviva, who would not have understood the reference to Wyatt's rising, he draws a comparison from the history of Rome: 'the uproar was such that Hannibal himself might have been at the gates or the Spanish fleet in the river Thames'.[2] The search covered the whole of London. Everywhere Justices of the Peace and city magistrates were called out, with gangs of constables and rabble-soldiery. Suspect Catholics and strangers were dragged from bed. That night the churches of the city were converted into temporary prisons until, the following morning, the arrested persons were examined and identified.

At the upper end of Golden Lane in Holborn there was a house where Garnet had formerly lodged. That night it was raided: but Garnet was not there.

'Nothing [he reported] was found to compensate such an effort, apart

---

[1] H. G. to R. P. 6 September 1594. Stonyhurst, *Anglia* I, 81. Sir Thomas Wyatt, son of the poet, raised Kent in 1554 in an attempt to prevent the marriage of Mary Tudor to Philip of Spain, marched on London but was deserted by his followers as soon as he entered the city, was captured and executed on Tower Hill.

[2] H. G. to C. A. 9 August 1594. F.G. 651, f. 66.

from a tailor's house where, at the time when I was lying in hiding with two other Catholics, I had carelessly concealed books, pictures, crosses and other signs of the Catholic religion. The discovery so elated our enemies that they boasted publicly that in the whole time the present Queen had been on the throne they had made no comparable find. They gave out that they had arrested assassins, sworn to kill the Queen; that a priest's cassock also had been seized; and that this house was a notorious den of priests.'[1]

In this letter to Persons Garnet relates the same incident more briefly. 'No Catholics were found but one poor tailor's house in Golden Lane end, which was esteemed such a booty as never was got since this Queen's day.'[2]

Since his adventure at Baddesley Clinton two and a half years before, this was Garnet's narrowest escape. 'The tailor and divers others taken lie yet in prison. Some of them have been tortured.' More now than ever before Garnet realised how the aim of every planned search was to strike his own place of residence. Southwell had been examined under torture to reveal it; Walpole was soon to endure the same treatment. With much feeling, he wrote of the tailor and those captured and tortured with him. 'That mischance touched us near. They were our friends and chiefest instruments.'[3]

A few weeks earlier Garnet had acquired a house of his own 'four or five miles from London'.[4] The house in Golden Lane he had used while he was negotiating for this new suburban residence, where he was lying on the night of the raid. The previous afternoon Gerard had visited him on business. It was his intention to ride into the city and sleep that night at the house in Golden Lane, which he himself had acquired and later put at his Superior's disposal. 'Just before I mounted my horse', wrote Gerard,[5] 'I went to say "goodbye" to the Superior. He urged me to stay the night with him, but I said that I had business in town and explained what it was and that I had certain appointments to keep [the same evening]. But the . . . Father would not hear of my going, though, as he told me later, he had no idea why he had acted in such a peculiar way. It certainly was not his usual manner and I have no doubt at all that he was guided by the Holy Spirit.'

It was the second time that Garnet had acted on an unexplained but sure impulse that went totally against his customary manner of dealing with his subjects. Gerard had witnessed the same clear premonition of danger on the last day of their meeting in Warwickshire, on the feast of St Luke, 1591.[6] Earlier he had written from Essex asking certain friends to meet him

[1] H. G. to C. A. 9 August 1594. F.G. 651, f. 66.
[2] H. G. to R. P. 6 September 1594. Stonyhurst, *Anglia* 1, 81.
[3] *Ibid.*   [4] *John Gerard*, 54.   [5] *Ibid.*
[6] Cf. *sup.*, p. 131.

that evening in Golden Lane. When his horse was already saddled it was inexplicable that his Superior should ask him to neglect his London appointments and stay overnight with him. 'Early next morning', Gerard continues, 'rumours reached us that Papists had been seized in the house.' Garnet simply observes: 'That very night had been there Long John with the little beard [Fr Gerard] once your pupil, if I had not more importunately stayed him than ever before.'[1] Had Gerard slept in Golden Lane he would not have escaped capture. Through a spy in the household of the Wisemans at Braddocks, it was known where he was then living, that he proposed to spend that night in the house; and it was assumed that Garnet would be with him. As Gerard noted, there was no hiding place at all in the entire building. The tailor, who was captured, was William Suffield, a Norfolk man in the Wiseman service. With him were Richard Fulwood, Garnet's loyal servant, the musician, John Bolt, and John Tarbuck, a Lancashire Catholic. Their examinations, taken under torture, show that they revealed no secrets.[2]

It was not until August that Garnet reported to Aquaviva and Persons the events of 15 March. Although he had received a letter from the General in Holy Week, his acknowledgment and reply were dated 9 August. This alone indicates the intensity of the search for him in the summer of 1594. 'After I had received your letter which was delivered to me in Holy Week itself', he wrote in his August letter,[3] 'I had written an answer to your Lordship's letter and had set out in it a number of questions that required your decision or advice. I had actually given the letter to the courier, but no sooner had I done so than there was a sudden alarm and I had to throw the letter into the fire. Since that time it has been impossible without great danger to send a fresh letter.'

It was, in fact, the first time Garnet had delayed so long in writing; and this was all the more remarkable since he had so much to tell. Now also for the first time, in his letters to Persons, he resorts to a code.[4] Writing on 6 September,[5] he explains his difficulties: 'I had written largely in my letter which I had prepared in answer to your last, but my friend durst not carry it,

---

[1] H. G. to R. P. 6 September 1594. Stonyhurst, *Anglia* 1, 81. Persons had determined Gerard's vocation: hence Garnet's phrase, 'once your pupil'.

[2] *S.P.D. Eliz.*, 248, nos. 37–40.

[3] H. G. to C. A. 9 August 1594. F.G. 651, f. 66.

[4] An example of the Garnet–Persons code can be found in the Stonyhurst manuscripts, *Anglia* 1, 82, in a letter written on 19 November 1594 (cf. Foley, vol. 4, 49). An explanation of the system is given in the introduction to the *Verstegan Papers* (*C.R.S.*, vol. 52, xxiv–xxviii). Used only for individual items that required special secrecy, it was based on numerals which were substituted for vowels or words.

[5] H. G. to R. P. 6 September 1594. Stonyhurst, *Anglia* 1, 81.

and so brought it me again. And in very truth it is a wonder to see how God hath protected our letters of late; for I could write of two or three several escapes almost miraculous if I could declare it without revealing the means of my sending, which I should be very loath should appear in my letter if it chanced to be taken.'

Easter came and with it no respite for Garnet. The capture of Walpole, following closely on that of Southwell, had given a spur to Topcliffe and his associate, Richard Young. Exactly a month after the March hurly-burly Garnet lost Gerard. Tracked by the unfaithful servant in the Wiseman house-hold, John Frank, he was arrested in bed on St George's Day, 23 April, in the same tailor's house in Golden Lane. With him, and sharing the same room, was 'Little John', or Nicholas Owen, Garnet's servant, whom he had loaned for a time to Gerard to make hiding places in this London house and also in East Anglia.[1]

Within the space of five months Garnet had lost Walpole and Gerard, two of his finest priests. Both in their own way were irreplaceable; and with them had been captured Richard Fulwood and Nicholas Owen. In the same April Edward Oldcorne was caught but escaped. Literally he had slipped the grasp of his pursuers: 'Edward Oldcorne, John Gerard's companion, was taken in a garden in the country', Garnet reported,[2] 'but he showed himself nimble, leapt into the house, shut the door and got away.'

About this time, also, some twenty magistrates in and ten miles around London were commissioned to 'search and enquire for coiners, priests and lurking Papists, and to use towards them all forcible means for the dis-closing of their dangerous practices'. 'This', observed Garnet, 'busieth them all day long.'[3]

More troubles followed at midsummer. Eleven young Catholics who had embarked at Chester for the seminaries in Spain were seized and taken to Bridewell, where they were whipped and ill-treated. Then, about the middle of August, two boats lying off Gravesend were boarded before they set sail. Four boys, destined for the seminary at St Omer, and two ladies on their way to a convent in Flanders, were arrested and brought back to London.[4] Garnet had ground to complain that between this Easter and early autumn he had never suffered so many losses. This was the burden of his August letter to Aquaviva. After the raid in Golden Lane End, he writes, 'one danger followed close on the heels of the next, so that from that time hardly

---

[1] For the arrest of Gerard, see *John Gerard*, ch. 10.
[2] H. G. to R. P. 6 September 1594. Stonyhurst, *Anglia* 1, 81.
[3] *Ibid.*
[4] *Ibid.*

a week passed without some great hazard or some exceptional loss. And along with these hardships were the watches kept on the ports, the continual opening of letters, the searching of private houses, so that we were scarcely permitted to breathe, let alone to send letters to our friends.'[1]

This was Garnet's first opportunity of writing to Aquaviva since March. Under the stress of recent events he spoke his mind plainly on the question of admitting priests into the Society. The arrest of Fr Cornelius and his martyrdom at Dorchester on 3 July this year, before he had been formally admitted, exasperated him. For ten years Cornelius had asked to be received; but first Weston, and then Garnet, was reluctant to deprive the west country of his services even for twelve months. In giving a brief account of what happened Garnet spared no detail that might cause Aquaviva embarrassment at the policy he had adopted:

'John Cornelius, loved of God and men, was executed with three laymen on 3 July. This is the man whom I have so highly commended to your Lordship and asked that he should be admitted here in England. While still in Rome he had vowed to enter the Society, but at your own command he returned here for the time being and was allowed meanwhile to share the spiritual benefits of the Society.[2] Thenceforward he never ceased earnestly to beg for admission and took the delay very hardly, particularly after his arrest. . . . I consoled him as much as I was able but it was not in my power to admit him: I would (I said) send overseas to obtain permission. As soon as it was possible to cross, I promised to appoint someone to go over. . . . So with this hope I comforted him at the time he was taken from his London prison to Dorchester, where he was martyred. On his own prompting he pronounced the vows of the Society before three leading Catholics, whom he bound as witnesses to make known the fact to me. I leave over much else which I shall tell you in another letter: I shall mention only a remarkable incident that occurred at the gallows. After the other three men who had lived with him in the same household had been hanged before him, and he himself taken to the ladder, he humbly kissed the feet of the dead men and in front of all there assembled he proclaimed that he died a Jesuit.'[3]

Garnet was distressed. He related the story at length; then petitioned

[1] H. G. to C. A. 9 August 1594. F.G. 651, f. 66.

[2] Apart from certain privileges given by the Popes to the Society, the 'benefits' included Masses offered for his soul after his death.

[3] H. G. to C. A. 9 August 1594. F.G. 651, f. 66. John Cornelius or O'Mahony, born at Bodmin of Irish parents, was a fellow of Exeter College, Oxford, before crossing to Rheims, where he was ordained in 1583. He worked for ten years at Lanherne, Cornwall, and was executed at Dorchester on 4 July 1594, with three laymen, Thomas Bosgrave, John Cary and Patrick Salmon, who had assisted him in his work.

Aquaviva for permission to admit all priests and laymen into the Society if similar circumstances recurred. Personally he was deeply attached to Cornelius and had a great regard for his exceptional holiness. With much feeling he pressed his point. Now at last Aquaviva would surely see what kind of men the Society was losing if he insisted that all applicants for admission had to go abroad for their noviceship. 'Humbly and most earnestly I implore your Lordship to grant the Superior of the Society in England, whoever he may be, the faculty to admit, even in absence, any priest or layman whomsoever, provided he has previously sought admission and has been sentenced to death and is waiting execution. Thus they will be able to proclaim that they are Jesuits; and we shall be both helped and honoured in no small measure by such great and inspiring examples.'[1]

Voluntarily for many years Cornelius had been working under the direction of Garnet. In the same six months both he and Gerard had been lost. Daily Garnet's anxiety increased. Southwell, his 'old' companion, and Walpole his 'new', were still in the Tower. For the moment Gerard's treatment in the Poultry prison and later in the Clink did not make his Superior anxious, though the loss of this 'most active and most useful priest'[2] was something he could never make good. 'He will be stout, I doubt not', he wrote of Gerard. 'He hath been very close, but is now removed from the Counter to the Clink, where he may in time do much good.' In age, breeding and interests Garnet was far removed from his imprisoned subject, who, on his side, had unstinted admiration for his Superior. Garnet speaks seldom of him and then only briefly. While he admired and trusted him and gave him the freedom he needed for his gallant apostolate, he appears at this time never to have been close to him in affection. Yet on his side Gerard considered that he was particularly cared for and loved by his Superior. There could be no finer testimony to the manner in which Garnet treated him.

But for the present it was Walpole's fate that exercised Garnet, who surmised that he had been sent to the Tower for torture. This was soon confirmed: indeed in the frenzied effort Topcliffe was making to involve the Jesuits in plots against the Queen, he had racked him with unbelievable brutality. Nevertheless he failed to extract from his lips any statement that could give the faintest colour to his prefabricated plots. When later Gerard was in the Tower, he gathered all the information he could about Walpole: he was confined in the same cell and from Walpole's gaoler he learned that his fellow-Jesuit had been hung up 'fourteen times in all. . . . And as they tortured him more often than they wanted known, they did not do it in the

[1] H. G. to C. A. 9 August 1594. F.G. 651, f. 66.
[2] *Ibid.*

ordinary public chamber. And I can well believe that he was tortured that number of times, since he completely lost the use of his fingers.'[1]

Garnet had received veiled hints of Walpole's treatment. It was more than twelve months before he was able to piece together the story. In his letter on Walpole's sufferings he gives the first detailed description of the 'manacles'. 'The normal torture they employ is to hang a man up by his hands', writes Garnet,[2] 'and for this purpose they use a piece of iron with two holes about five fingers apart. The iron is tied in the middle by a rope to a beam and the victim is thus left hanging sometimes for five or six hours. Sometimes the iron with the holes is rounded off and polished at the part where it touches the hands. This makes the pain more bearable. Some irons have what resembles a cutting edge that draws blood. But in both cases the torment is excruciating.'

As Garnet heard reports of Walpole's examinations be began to fear for himself. That Lent a Catholic layman, James Atkinson, had been tortured in the Tower in this manner, and had been taken down from the wall for dead: indeed he died two hours later. The purpose of this man's torture had been to get him to accuse falsely his Catholic employer and certain priests.[3] Alarmed by his death, Topcliffe arranged for Walpole's tortures to be spaced throughout the year. While Topcliffe was at work, Garnet was able to gather only scraps of information, so secretly, Gerard says, were the tortures conducted. When, in the following April, Walpole was taken to the scaffold, Garnet noted that 'the middle fingers of his hands were torn loose': anxious not to assert categorically, until he had received confirmation, that Walpole had been racked, he added, 'The rope could have done this, since they say he had not been on the rack. But these men are extremely ingenious at finding new methods of torture not previously used in this country.'[4] Gerard, also, noticed that, on his return to York, Walpole's handwriting looked more like the writing of a schoolboy than of a scholar and gentleman: he himself could barely make it out, for the characters were so ill-formed.

This year Walpole's predicament caused Garnet continuous anxiety. As he remarked: 'certain devilish persons had brought forward false testimony that, on the advice and instigation of this Father, they had determined to murder the Queen. But the whole thing was so absurd that they had not even the effrontery to mention it to him'.[5] Meanwhile in the Tower Walpole's

[1] *John Gerard*, 105.
[2] H. G. to C. A. 20 July 1595. F.G. 651, f. 130.   [3] *Ibid.*   [4] *Ibid.*
[5] This explains the fabricated 'confessions' of Father Walpole (printed in *C.R.S.*, vol. 5, 244–68), which in fact were never used. In an article in *The Month* (November

condition was worse than wretched. For the remainder of his first winter he was without ordinary bedding and clothing until his relatives sent him a few bare necessities.

During this time, Southwell, who had been covered with lice since his entry into the Tower, had already passed through his agony of torture. When Garnet had sent him a Breviary he wrapped it in such a way that Southwell 'knew immediately it came from me'. Desperately during these summer months the two imprisoned priests tried to send messages to each other. When Southwell was given a copy of St Bernard's sermons, he complained that it was poorly bound. Through friends Garnet suggested that he should send it out to be repaired or exchanged 'in the hope that he might write some message for me inside the Breviary. But permission was refused'. After Southwell's death early next year, Garnet recovered the Breviary. Hoping to find there some account of his days in the prison, he 'looked through it with great interest', but, as he wrote:

'I cannot discover so much as one word written in ink, and I must conclude from this that he had nothing with which to write, even secretly. . . . The only thing he wrote that I could see was the word *Jesus*, with a pin, on the fly-leaf. On another page I have made out *Deus meus et omnia*, words so often on his lips, just as he used always to write at the head of everything, *Deus tibise*, *tute Deo*. There are also many numerals written in the same way with a pin. I have studied them most carefully in the hope of finding some relation between them and the pages of the book, for it is sometimes the way of prisoners to write certain numbers in this manner in order to convey their wishes. I have been able to discover nothing. And I have come to the conclusion that the numbers are connected with his examinations of conscience, either general or particular, for he used to encourage his penitents (and he also put it in writing in his *Spiritual Rule of Life*, which is so much appreciated by Catholics), when they had no priest to offer Mass or to hear their confessions, to give some time to both practices.[1] He exhorted them to kneel devoutly every day of their lives and offer themselves to our Lord, assisting in spirit at every Mass being said at that moment in every part of the world. He urged them to prepare themselves every week, and more often, for confession, doing this formally to God as if to a priest.

'I have no doubt', Garnet concludes his surmise of Southwell's activity

[1] Southwell's *Rule of Good Life* was written probably in 1589 for the Countess of Arundel.

1951) Fr W. F. Rea proves conclusively that these confessions were in large measure government forgeries.

in the Tower, 'that he observed these practices himself throughout his time of confinement.'

No wonder Topcliffe was at a loss to find a treasonable charge against Southwell. In a neighbouring part of the Tower, throughout the rest of the year, Walpole was engaged in his own devout practices. It was many years later that Garnet gathered his information, principally through John Gerard, who was later imprisoned in the cell occupied this summer by Walpole. Walpole, Garnet learned, had inscribed his name on the wall, possibly to leave behind him an enduring example of his authentic signature should it be forged (as indeed it was by the Council's agents). Then, nearby, in a recess, he had made a small oratory for himself, chalking on either side of a narrow window the different orders of angels: 'at the top, above the Cherubim and Seraphim, was the name of Mary, Mother of God, and above it the name of Jesus: above that again the name of God written in Latin, Greek and Hebrew characters.'[1]

Garnet must have reflected with pride that no worse treason could be proved against either of his companions than their loyalty to the old faith. Yet, until the end of the year, he was anxious over their fate. The best news he could get of them was that both were still alive.

In his own deep personal distress he wrote intimately to Aquaviva: 'Now indeed I find myself destitute of companions. For although I have very many friends, I cannot confide in them with the same freedom as I can Ours.'[2] He had hoped to send over this summer Fr John Radford, a secular priest for whom he had great esteem and now, since Walpole's capture, destined to become his 'new companion'. But all the ports were guarded and Radford had been forced to turn back. Having lost so many men in the last nine months, Garnet was determined not to let him or any other priest attempt to go overseas.[3] In these straitened circumstances he even suggested to Persons that it might help to have 'some Scotch or Italian Jesuits that could speak English; for such are not subject to the law and many would deal with them that leave us'.[4] He did not explain that these men would be more readily approached by schismatics and that, should they be caught, they were less likely to suffer the same treatment as Southwell and Walpole. Before long, he was to return again to this proposal.

[1] *John Gerard*, 104.
[2] H. G. to C. A. 9 August 1594. F.G. 651, f. 66.
[3] *Ibid.*
[4] H. G. to R. P. 6 September 1594. Stonyhurst, *Anglia* 1, 81.

20

TWO EXECUTIONS

ON 18 February 1595, by order of Lord Burghley, Southwell was transferred from the Tower to Newgate, there to await his trial. Garnet, who was back in London that month, received word of the change. Possibly he watched his companion pass through the London streets that morning. Certainly he saw him two days later, when on 20 February he was taken, again by road, from Newgate to Westminster Hall for his trial. He observed that although during his months in the Tower he had not celebrated Mass or received the sacrament of Penance or had been permitted to speak with any person apart from his gaoler, or to receive any of the comforts of religion, yet he was so tranquil and recollected as he went to Westminster that he might have been walking out of a religious house.[1]

Garnet was taken by surprise at the apparent suddenness of Southwell's arraignment. Unknown to him Southwell had written to Cecil asking him as a favour that he should be allowed either to stand his trial or to be released. At the same time he had begged to see his friends. After examining the facts, Garnet was convinced that Topcliffe had produced the crisis. In what Garnet calls his 'insatiable fury' against Southwell, Topcliffe 'never ceased petitioning the Council to send him for trial: he was hoping always to appropriate the spoils of the Bellamy's house at Uxenden where the Father had been taken and so endow his virtuous bride'.[2] Garnet observed that from time to time the Council would proceed against some Catholic in order 'to create alarm and terror'. The victim, he says, 'is chosen according to the anger or malice of some individual'.[3] However, in Garnet's last analysis, Southwell's fate was governed by divine Providence. Only later did he realize how cunningly the Council had acted. No announcement of Southwell's trial was made: not even his keeper knew the date. Secretly, Southwell was held in Newgate for three days while a diversion was prepared. On the day he was brought to Westminster Hall a notorious criminal was led to Tyburn with

[1] H. G. to C. A. 22 February 1595. F.G. 651, f. 115.
[2] *Ibid.*   [3] *Ibid.*

all the publicity that could be mustered. 'Almost all the city', says Garnet,[1] 'went out to see the execution and knew nothing of what was happening to Father Robert.' Yet, in spite of this, a large number of Catholics attended the proceedings and reported to Garnet.

Although, in common reckoning, Newgate was the most cruel of all London's twelve prisons, yet Southwell's removal there gave Garnet an opportunity to learn something of his condition. Now he was a broken man of thirty-three: his memory was failing: he was afraid of his own physical weakness: yet to the end, he was serene, loving and courteous to all, with the single exception of his tormentor, Topcliffe. 'God forgive me, Mr Topcliffe,' Southwell thrusted at him for almost the last time, 'but I do not think that there can be another man like you in the whole world.'[2] Gerard, who suffered a little later under Topcliffe, could not bring himself to be civil to him when he remembered what Southwell had endured at his hands. By God's ordinance, he writes, Southwell 'was delivered over to encounter hand to hand the cruellest tyrant of all England, Topcliffe, a man most infamous and hateful to all the realm for his bloody and butcherly mind.'[3]

Using his licence to deal as he wished with his prisoners, Topcliffe, without actually maiming Southwell, had attempted to weaken him before his trial. He had him confined in 'an underground place for condemned criminals, without light and company save for some worms that lived there'. The gaoler, who would have treated him with kindness had he been permitted, was never out of call, for Southwell, since his torture, feared to be left beyond shouting distance for help. In fact, his keeper allowed him to receive from a Catholic friend the gift of a bed, fuel for a fire and a permanently lit candle: also a little wine, which he accepted gladly, saying he had not drunk wine for two years. These were the first comforts he had been granted since his arrest.

At the trial the case for the prosecution followed much the same lines that it was to follow at Garnet's nine years later: the judge was the same and also the Attorney-General, Sir Edward Coke. All the alleged machinations and plots of Jesuits from the time of Persons' mission in 1580 were rehearsed. Then Coke strove to discredit Southwell, and with him, the Society, by holding up to odium the doctrine of equivocation. Physically weakened and, as he said himself, 'deteriorated in memory owing to all the tortures I have suffered', Southwell made such an eloquent defence that Coke's only answer was constantly to interrupt him. Garnet, quick to see how the trial was being used to bring detestation on the name of Jesuit, himself supplemented

[1] *Ibid.*   [2] *Ibid.*
[3] *Narrative*, 18.

Southwell's last public vindication of Catholic theology. He wrote and circulated his own treatise in explanation of Southwell's teaching.

The other feature of the trial that stirred Garnet was the open clash between his companion and Topcliffe, who once again took on himself the role of assistant prosecutor. While the Council was determined to use the trial to discredit the doctrine of equivocation, Southwell made it the opportunity to expose Topcliffe. Now he had nothing more to fear at his hands: the brute had already done his worst. To save other priests from the treatment he himself had received, Southwell showed another side to his character, perhaps new also to Garnet himself. The sharpest exchange came when Southwell 'declared upon his soul, as he hoped shortly to answer before God, that he had been tortured more than ten times by Topcliffe and that the memory of these tortures was worse than ten deaths'. Topcliffe denied this. He challenged Southwell to show the marks of his treatment. In one poetic, brief and terrible sentence Southwell retorted, 'Ask a woman to show her throes.' Then with Gerard and Walpole in mind, Southwell made this plea: 'When people are utterly without heart, it would be well to have some means of moderating them, so that through extreme suffering poor men should not reach the point of despair; for this would most certainly happen but for the exceptional help of God.'[1]

In spite of the diversion staged by the Council the trial raised a disturbance in London. After Southwell had been condemned, it was debated whether he should be sent to the Tower by water, to avoid a demonstration of sympathy by the crowd, or returned by road to Newgate. In the end, 'seeing his meekness, the officers decided to send him by road'. Garnet describes the scene: 'his Catholic friends came to meet him at different places on the way; they crossed the road to see him and counted themselves happy if they were able to catch a glance from him. The Father, inasmuch as he was able, indicated that he recognised them.'[2]

The next day, 21 February, Southwell was executed at Tyburn. Garnet was relieved that the sufferings of his friend were at an end. He wrote to Aquaviva. 'Whether I should be sorry now or glad, I do not know. My sorrow is that I have lost my most dear and loved companion; my gladness that the man I have cherished so much has risen to the throne of God, where he will be given the recompense earned by his labours: peace in return for his cares, and the immense happiness of his God in exchange for his unspeakable tortures. And so it is surely more fitting to rejoice, and for the Church, for your Lordship and for me to give solemn thanks to God.'[3]

[1] H. G. to C. A. 7 March 1595. F.G. 651, f. 142.   [2] *Ibid.*
[3] H. G. to C. A. 22 February 1595. F.G. 651, f. 115.

After finishing this letter to Aquaviva, Garnet found time for another the same day. His courier had not yet arrived. In this second letter he speaks more eloquently about 'this unvanquished soldier of Christ, my most faithful subject and the bravest of martyrs, Robert Southwell, once my closest companion and brother, now my patron, lord and ruler, together with Christ in his Empire'.[1] He closed with a request for Aquaviva's prayers that his own sins might not hold him back from the contest or, in the midst of it, make him less brave than his companion.

Southwell's heroic death heartened Garnet. If ever there was a martyr it was Southwell, and Garnet was proud of his intimate association with him. He was convinced that it would be only a short time before Southwell was recognised as one of the great heroes of the universal Church. With this conviction he wrote next month a yet longer letter. Though he addressed it to Aquaviva, he intended it to be passed on to his Roman friends. 'I shall write in Italian', he explained,[2] 'so as to give pleasure to my dear brethren who do not understand Latin', for Southwell's life concerns all, Jesuit brothers as well as priests, and particularly in Rome, for 'he lived and was brought up amongst his brethren there, receiving from them so many loving services'. Moreover this was a way in which Garnet himself could show his own particular affection for them all: he did not forget a single one of them: 'I think and speak of them with the greatest consolation to myself and I still have deep confidence in their holy prayers, for I am assured that they have not forgotten me.' He apologised for the mistakes in his Italian, since 'after my absence of nine years I have forgotten a large part of the little I once knew'.

Throughout the following spring and early summer Garnet's thoughts turned constantly to the good name of his martyr companion. Particularly he was anxious to get assurance that his long Italian letter with the account of Southwell's martyrdom had reached Rome. By 1 May he had received no acknowledgement; he began to fear that the letter had been intercepted; indeed there were rumours that certain papers of his had 'fallen into the enemy's hands'.[3] He had intended to be silent until he knew that his letters were in fact reaching Rome, but now he had fresh details to add. If the government wanted to intercept his correspondence, it could. He said, defiantly: 'We will be no less persistent in writing to you than they are in persecuting us.' There was no need for Aquaviva to fear indiscretion:

'I will uncover nothing that is hidden: I shall not commit secrets to writing

[1] H. G. to C. A. 22 February 1595 (second letter to C. A. of same date), Stonyhurst, *Anglia* 2, 4: also Grene *P.*, 566.
[2] H. G. to C. A. 7 March 1595. F.G. 651, f. 142.
[3] *Ibid.*

nor divulge what is done in darkness: but all the cruel, barbarous and bestial acts perpetrated under the noonday sun, these I shall make known on the summit of the Capitoline hill. Therein is our triumph, our crown and our laurels. Have they intercepted my letter about my dearest Robert? If so, I shall write again. His valour, constancy and devotion are not such as will be lost to memory if a single letter falls into the enemy's hands, unless there is obliterated at one and the same time everything that is written with such splendour in the hearts of all who knew him.'[1]

On the assumption that his Italian letter had, in fact, arrived, Garnet added a postscript. For instance it was noted by onlookers that when they took Southwell down from the gibbet, the executioners, instead of dragging him roughly over the ground to the quartering block, carried him there with much reverence. This was a novel sight in London. Garnet summed up all that he had learnt by saying: 'His manliness, his nobility, meekness and handsome appearance won all hearts, so that in the judgment of the common crowd no man like him had ever been hanged at Tyburn.'[2]

What throws peculiar light on Garnet's own character is his appraisal of Southwell as his subject. Southwell's virtue as a religious priest, he says,[3] was known to all who lived with him; from his own familiarity with him, he could say that Southwell had never lost the first fervour of his religious life. His friends among the layfolk, who knew him well, had often seen him in tears because his Superior had never in his life given a command or even counselled him. This, Southwell had ascribed to Garnet's consideration of his weakness: and he judged that he had not sufficient reliance on his virtue to give him a command. It made him sad. But 'the truth was this, that I never saw in him anything fractious or obstinate. Therefore I allowed him always to act as he himself judged best. And his judgment was always right. Over so many years that we lived together in such harmony of mind and amidst great difficulties, there was never the least shadow of a difference between us: and this I attribute to his virtue.' Although no poet himself or artist in prose, Garnet had appreciated Southwell's literary gifts. Rightly he claimed that Southwell not merely equalled but surpassed many profane authors and poets, and had shown them how they might turn their talent from lascivious to religious and serious subjects. 'I have a rosary', he tells Aquaviva,[4] 'which he threw from the scaffold and also the bone of one of his knees: and these I shall send to your lordship [as relics] when I conveniently can.' Nothing meanwhile would give him more pleasure, he gently prompts Aquaviva, than to learn that his Italian letter had safely arrived.

[1] H. G. to C. A. 1 May 1595. F.G. 651, f. 138.   [2] *Ibid.*   [3] *Ibid.*
[4] *Ibid.*

Garnet says that all the information he gave Aquaviva on Southwell's death was gathered from a Jesuit who was present. Had he been there himself, he would not have dared mention it in a letter. Possibly it was to Garnet that his companion threw his Rosary: a last gift which, he knew, would give his Superior particular pleasure.

This same year Walpole also was executed in York, on 7 April, just a month and a half after Southwell. Throughout May Gerard was daily expecting trial: and there were rumours that the same fate shortly awaited Weston.[1] Garnet realised that his own days of freedom were drawing in. Already, earlier in the year, he had told Aquaviva: 'I do not see how I can escape the enemy's hands any longer.'[2] All his own priests in prison, and others also, had been questioned on his London house; in fact every Catholic recently captured and suspected of knowing him, had been persistently examined on this; some under torture. When Walpole was finally tried at the assizes at York, on 3 April, one of the charges against him was that he had refused to reveal his Superior's place of residence. The prosecutor, Sir John Saville,[3] turned on him: Walpole had been sent by his Superiors to a man called Whalley — this was Garnet's most common *alias* — but never had he said a word to indicate where he lived.[4] Indicted under the Act of Elizabeth that made it high treason for an Englishman to return to his own country after receiving holy orders abroad, Walpole demonstrated successfully that he could not be condemned to death on this count: the Act embraced only priests who did not give themselves up within three days of landing, and he had been ashore less than twenty hours at the time of his arrest. The prosecution turned on him: 'There is no reason why we should stay here all day arguing.' In order that the jury might return a verdict of guilty, Walpole was asked to take the oath of Supremacy, acknowledging the Queen as head of the Church. This he refused to do.

Garnet himself was astonished at the effects of Walpole's execution on Catholics in the north. Although Walpole had only as many hours of freedom as Garnet was to have years, his death was said to have done more for Catholicism in York than any event in the reign. Through his personal holiness and his skill in argument, he had got the better of Huntingdon. The President of the Council was present at the gallows. But it was Walpole's hour. Garnet, who never exaggerated, said that on that day, 7 April, Walpole

---

[1] *Ibid.*

[2] H. G. to C. A. 22 February 1595. F.G. 651, f. 115.

[3] Sir John Saville (1545–1607) was made Baron of the Exchequer in 1598; he was knighted in 1603 and became chief justice of the county palatine of Lancaster in 1604.

[4] H. G. to C. A. 20 June 1595. F.G. 615, f. 130.

drew tears from two thousand spectators: with such effect did he speak to the crowd.[1]

In his long letter describing Walpole's last days, Garnet shows himself the exact historian. There is no detail that he omits: effortlessly he finds some significance in them all. During his last hours in York Castle, Walpole, who had a talent for verse which Garnet did not rate as high as Southwell's, wrote poems on Our Lady and the Angels and addressed others to Christ triumphant in his passion: verses that, as both Garnet and Gerard who saw them say, were scarcely legible since under torture the middle finger of his right hand had been torn out of its socket. Then there were the customary disputations with ministers, wearisome almost beyond endurance to a man preparing himself for death. Garnet noted that Walpole prayed all the night before his execution, leaning against a rough bench: that was his position whenever he fell asleep: then he would wake up and lie on a mat three feet long: his cell-mate said that whenever he himself opened his eyes at night he found Walpole in prayer.

Garnet who, when he writes of the Queen, speaks only in her defence, records Walpole's touching assertion of his personal loyalty to her. At his trial, in phrases that came instinctively to a gentleman, Walpole protested: 'As for my ruler, I love her as a most faithful subject, and I pray God to bless her with his Holy Spirit, and that He may grant her grace to do as she should in this world, so that she may enjoy paradise in the next. And I desire for all here present what I desire for myself, that is, the salvation of our souls, and that we may live in the true Catholic faith.'[2]

Scrupulously faithful to Aquaviva's injunction not to discuss politics or the Queen, Garnet found relief in relating Walpole's public profession of love and loyalty. In conversation and correspondence he himself set an unimpeachable example to his own subjects: never a word of severity or censure tarnished any reference to his Sovereign.

In this long letter concerning Walpole Garnet allows himself a digression concerning his own work. Only rarely, and then most briefly, does he speak of his own apostolate. For this reason the exception to his self-imposed restraint is worth noting in full.

One of the three judges at Walpole's trial was Francis Beaumont, whose mother Garnet had watched with every priestly attention when she lay dying. Beaumont had been reared a Catholic and had attended Mass secretly at home before going to the services of the 'new religion'. This was a common practice in the early years of the reign, but 'since then', Garnet ex-

---

[1] H. G. to C. A. 20 June 1595. F.G. 651, f. 130.
[2] *Ibid.*

plained, 'it was decided that such conduct was illicit: at the instance of English Catholics, the question was decided by twelve Fathers of the Council of Trent (to whom the President of the Council commended secrecy, from consideration of the dangers that confronted Catholics in England: and among these Fathers were our own men, Lainez and Salmeron)'.[1] Meanwhile Francis Beaumont had advanced rapidly in his profession. Though Beaumont was reluctant to implicate himself in religious issues, Huntingdon insisted that he should be appointed to the York division of the Queen's Bench 'so that he should be compelled to sully his conscience with the blood of Catholics'. An intimate friend of his mother and family, Garnet considered Beaumont a person of honour, though weak and ambitious.[2] Huntingdon, however, had a stranglehold over Beaumont. Their properties ran together. If Beaumont as Justice were to 'show any particular favour to priests, the President would then be able to make himself master of his estate'.

Beaumont's mother had died seven years before Walpole's trial, shortly after Garnet had started his missionary work in England. She was the aunt of the two Vaux sisters who had done much to advance Garnet's work. Several times Garnet had been with Beaumont's mother, a pattern of the heroic ladies who came forward to assist the Jesuits. 'It was her pleasure to look after the priests' rooms and to cook their food so that their presence might be kept more secret. And she showed great devotion to me without my meriting it in any way.' Then 'falling ill and making ready for death, she said she desired one thing only: that was to see me before she died. I was therefore summoned and reached her house just ten days before her death'. All the priests who used the house as a centre for their work had left, except one: daily this priest and Garnet celebrated Mass in her sickroom. Throughout her last night Garnet had stayed by her bedside until in the morning the other priest came to say Mass for her. Garnet then left the room. Before he had time to rest, he was called back:

'I came quickly [he says] and said my Mass at which she showed great devotion and received Communion.... After Mass I blessed her ... and I had not taken off my vestments when her death agony began and I read the commendation of her soul to God. Then in the space of four or five *Misereres* our saintly hostess, with the name of Jesus on her lips, went forth to the eternal dwelling prepared for her by her Lord, a dwelling similar to that in

[1] Diego Lainez (d. 1565), second General of the Society, and Alfonso Salmeron (d. 1585) were among the first companions of St Ignatius.

[2] William, third Baron Vaux (died 20 August 1595), married first Elizabeth, daughter of John Beaumont of Grace Dieu, Leicestershire: he was the father of Henry (died unmarried 1587), Eleanor and Anne.

which she had sheltered us. It was the feast-day of that great hostess of the same Lord, St Martha.'

Garnet then gives an account, unique in the writings of the time, of the lady's Catholic burial. That evening the priest with the attendant family carried out the Catholic obsequies for her soul. Shortly after midnight the Mass of Requiem was said. Both priests then left. Until then her death had been kept secret from her son for it was her wish that Garnet should say the Mass for her soul before he arrived. The following night she was buried in the parish church 'without the Ministers saying their prayers over her body'; for this also was her wish.... Several months later her son, Walpole's judge, arranged for a solemn memorial service. At this the Minister preached a panegyric, but, as Garnet says, 'he ruined the soup with one ill-chosen herb', for after praising the lady's virtues, he asserted that 'they had been infected and poisoned by Popery'. Francis was further embarrassed for, under the influence of her mother-in-law, his wife, 'being a confirmed heretic, became a most devout Catholic'.

Only after his own mother's death, so that he should spare her sorrow in her lifetime, did Francis Beaumont accept promotion to the Queen's Bench.[1] Garnet tells the story, not in commendation of his own work but to show 'the cruelty of heretics who make Catholics themselves the instruments of persecution'. Unintentionally he reveals how he himself came to be so intensely loved and trusted by all with whom he dealt.

About the time of Southwell's execution Garnet had been considerably elated by the arrival in England of two new and exceptional men: Fr Richard Banks and Fr William Baldwin. The former had crossed of intent, the latter had been put ashore by a strange accident.

The Spanish vessel in which Baldwin was sailing from Flanders to Spain had been intercepted at sea by a British man-of-war. The boarding party suspected that Baldwin was a priest: but he was also a superb actor. Pretending not to know a word of his native tongue, he sustained brilliantly the part of an Italian merchant with appropriate gestures and manifestations of distress. At Portsmouth, where he was put ashore, he had bluffed his way past the Admiral of the port and was then taken to London. There, through the agency of friends, Garnet raised two hundred gold crowns for his ransom. Baldwin himself, before his release, managed to obtain a safe-conduct from the Council during the length of his stay in England.

Understandably Garnet was delighted to have at his disposition such a resourceful subject, who was also a man of much experience. He lost no

[1] Francis Beaumont died in 1598: he was a serjeant-at-law in 1589 and was appointed Justice of Common Pleas in 1593.

time in explaining his conduct to Aquaviva.[1] While it was against his principles to ransom priests from prison, he had no scruple in paying a large sum for the liberation of Baldwin, whose case was different: he had been brought to England against his will and he was known not as a priest but as a merchant: it was essential that he should regain his liberty before his bluff was discovered. 'But now that he is free', urged Garnet, confronting Aquaviva with a *fait accompli*, 'I should like to retain him. He belongs to me by the law of ransom or acquisition and he himself desires to stay: in any case it would be too dangerous to send him over. Holding, as he does, a safe-conduct, he will be able to move about the country far more freely than the rest of us.'

So Garnet argued in order to keep another priest for work in England. He ended by saying that Baldwin himself would soon write to explain his position to the General.

Arriving direct from Rome, Fr Richard Banks brought with him the personal greetings of Aquaviva and his assurance that he desired nothing more than to promote, as much as he had power to do, the success of the English mission. Garnet was happy to know that, in spite of the loss through death or imprisonment of three inestimable priests, Aquaviva was not deterred from sending replacements. In thanking the General, he observed that while in recent years Aquaviva had given so much evidence of his true concern for England — it was indisputable and Garnet was intensely grateful for it — yet there was still further help the General could provide. The young men who were now being sent to Flanders for their noviceship would fare better if Fr William Holt, the agent of the English Jesuits there, had some watching brief over his English subjects: it was important that they should have over them a person of authority who could speak their own language. English girls in Flemish convents had their own difficulties: it would greatly help them if they were permitted an English confessor. Clearly it was from Fr Baldwin that he learnt these problems which, without delay, he presented to Aquaviva.[2]

[1] H. G. to C. A. 22 February 1595. F.G. 651, f. 115   [2] *Ibid.*

21

THE FIRST SLANDERS

'I F God were only able to unbar the gate, a vast field would lie before us and an unbelievably great harvest.'[1]

This reflection in Garnet's first letter of 1596 was prompted by Gerard's apostolate in the Clink. Although many priests had done work of inestimable importance from their prisons, none developed the technique as systematically as Gerard was now doing. From his cell he arranged for the despatch of young men to the seminaries, boys to the new school started by Fr Persons at St Omer; he heard confessions, offered Mass, received schismatics into the Church, converted his gaoler, gave counsel, carried out the full liturgy of Holy Week, and assisted financially incoming priests, establishing for them a London house where they could reside in safety during their first days in England. 'The work John does in prison is so profitable that it is hardly possible to believe it', was Garnet's message to Rome.[2]

After eight years on the mission Gerard was now mature. Garnet had encouraged him to study, as he did Oldcorne, during the leisure that was at times enforced on them both. The raw, brash but brilliant and loyal recruit, who had landed on the Norfolk coast at the age of twenty-two, was now a seasoned subject. Although Garnet never found him difficult to handle, it was some time before an intimate understanding was established between them. Then quickly it developed into a friendship on which both set great value.

A more recent arrival than Gerard, Fr Thomas Lister,[3] had given Garnet recurrent anxiety; later, there were times when Garnet had doubts about his orthodoxy. Now Lister complained ceaselessly both of his health and of his Superior. Nothing that Garnet did contented him. With his January 1596 letter, Garnet enclosed a note from Lister begging Aquaviva to help him as his Superior had failed to do. Garnet merely commented: 'We hope for better

[1] H. G. to C. A. 17 January 1596. F.G. 651, f. 116.
[2] Ibid.
[3] Cf. sup., p. 91–2.

things from him in the future':[1] he had shown him constant kindness and for two years had kept him at his house and nursed his moods. In November 1595, in an intercepted letter,[2] he had expressed hopes of Lister's recovery: 'that he is improving is apparent even to me'. But Lister did not recover, and Garnet continued to care for him at the risk of his own life. Among his other ills, Lister suffered from claustrophobia, and was unable to endure confinement in hiding holes. For this reason Garnet was reluctant to place him even with his most close friends: he kept him at his side, knowing that by this action he was increasing his own chances of capture in a sudden raid. He wrote to Aquaviva: 'In the midst of the storm of this persecution and in expectation only of battles ahead, I marvel that I have not been arrested. I can think only of this explanation, that I am in the keeping of God and in the shelter of the prayers and Masses of your Lordship.'[3]

Southwell's death in London and Walpole's at York in the space of three months, had aroused in the public such sympathy for Catholics that once again it was rumoured that the Jesuits now in captivity would be exiled. In January Garnet reported the rumours;[4] they became more persistent every day. In order not to be taken by surprise, he made his proposals to Aquaviva for the disposition of these men on the Continent. Unless the General had other plans, Garnet would first send them all to Flanders: there Fr Holt could care for them. Thence they might go on to Spain to help Fr Persons staff the seminaries of Seville and Valladolid. He expected Aquaviva to summon Weston to Rome, possibly to teach Hebrew in the Roman College. But by March the government had changed its plans. 'My hopes have been vain.'[5]

The letter which Garnet had sent on 22 November 1595 had not reached Aquaviva. When he wrote again on 13 March he knew this, since a certain dispensation he had then sought had not yet been granted. It was not the loss of the letter that distressed him. He had told Aquaviva that he wrote nothing that might put him on the wrong side of the law should his letters be intercepted: he feared that this letter might have been passed on to a government forger, and that Aquaviva was now receiving in his name letters he had never written. Already Garnet knew that certain alleged confessions of Walpole had been fabricated. He now thought it timely to warn the General. 'I fear only this,' he wrote in March,[6] 'and I am anxious that your

---

[1] H. G. to C. A. 17 January 1596. F.G. 651, f. 116.
[2] H. G. to C. A. 13 March 1596. F.G. 651, f. 114.
[3] *Ibid.*
[4] H. G. to C. A. 17 January 1596. F.G. 651, f. 116.
[5] H. G. to C. A. 13 March 1596. F.G. 651, f. 114.   [6] *Ibid.*

Paternity should be aware of it: skilled workmen may counterfeit my hand and in my name write to your Paternity things that I am far from thinking. For the present it is enough for me to give you this warning.'

The warning was needed. Now, for the first time, Garnet was suffering, both at home and abroad, from students and a few priests who as secret agents of the government had infiltrated into the seminaries in order to disrupt them from within. In this January letter he had written: 'all priests are working well together here and what a singular blessing of the Holy Spirit this is'.[1] By March the situation had changed. Reports of disturbances at the English College, Rome, had now reached him. What was worse, he had been told that Aquaviva, in order to be quit of this recurrent anxiety, had decided that it was better for the Society to be rid of the government of the College.

The news disturbed Garnet. Confident in the General's professed and proven love for the English nation, he wrote now in more impassioned language than he had hitherto used in his long correspondence. His summary of the situation at Rome and the causes of the 'rebellion' there were accurate:[2]

'I have heard that your Lordship is seriously thinking of handing over to others the College belonging to our nation. But why, dearest Father, are you deserting us now? Why are you leaving us desolate . . . ? These disturbances in very truth are not the work of the devil alone, but, in equal measure, the deceits, guile and machinations of our government. By all means let the men who destroy the peace be removed without mercy being shown them: far better they should return here now with the stigma of sedition that they have earned than later go about in sheep's clothing and stir up trouble everywhere. At present in England there exist among us all a wonderful peace and harmony. Manifestly it would be a most unworthy action if you, most forbearing Father, were now to abandon all that company and with it this entire stricken kingdom. In all these years so many illustrious leaders and brave soldiers have been honoured to serve under your leadership. Now with victory in sight, will you change the standard and emblems that have been so happy and auspicious . . . ? We hope for better things and shall hope for them as long as we live. There are also the obligations contracted by your Lordship after showing to all of us such outstanding love and fatherly affection.'

Although Garnet wrote with much emotion, it is clear that, in spite of all his losses and set-backs, he still hoped for a Catholic recovery. Priests were now entering England in great numbers: instead of one college on the Conti-

[1] H. G. to C. A. 17 January 1596. F.G. 651, f. 116.
[2] H. G. to C. A. 13 March 1596. F.G. 651, f. 114.

nent, there were four. The old reign appeared to be drawing to a close. From his own pastoral experience he had reason to forecast the return of large numbers to the faith, if only conditions were altered. He and others believed that they were at last 'in sight of the port they had so long desired'. Other methods of suppression were needed; and Garnet was quick to see that the government now preferred to make trouble in the seminaries and there to create factions which in time would spread to England.

Garnet himself could no longer expect to remain untouched by the slanders of men working in and among the Catholic flock overseas and at home. This was a critical year both for the Church and for him personally. Although he was the last man to ascribe to his own effort any part of the successes gained in the last ten years, yet, when he heard of the trouble created in Rome between himself and Aquaviva, he felt compelled to give a summary of all that he had done. This he did in his next letter, but reluctantly and with the desire only to save his friendship with Aquaviva, on which so much depended. By April he had learned how wickedly he had been traduced. On the 16th of this month he made a summary statement of all he had attempted to achieve since he had succeeded Weston as Superior in August 1586.[1]

It was Fr William Holt in Flanders who had told him that he had been slandered as Superior of the Society in England, along with Aquaviva himself. The factious students, working with others who had genuine grievances against the Jesuit direction of the seminary, had, as Garnet observed, been sharpening their tongues by practising their calumnies against his friends in Rome, and, in particular, against Fr Persons, who had served their country so well. Now, in search of fresh targets, they have turned on Garnet, 'a little wretch of a man, marked out to die, who day and night thinks of nothing save the rack and gibbet'. In truth, when he set himself beside Southwell and others, Garnet never had confidence that he would behave with the same physical courage they had displayed. Sincerely he dreaded the inevitable day when he would be captured. In his absence from Rome his enemies in the employ of the Council, had slandered him with, 'so to call it, the lash of a scorpion's tail, as though it were not enough to encounter persecution at home without having to suffer crucifixion abroad, and in that city which is the parent of all Christians'.

Garnet, who enjoyed a relationship of peculiar intimacy and trust with

---

[1] What appears to be a draft of this letter is among the Stonyhurst manuscripts (*Anglia* 2, 16). It also is dated 16 April and is just over a third of the length of a letter of the same date, covering the same ground, in the Roman Archives (F.G. 651, f. 106). The phrasing of several passages is similar or identical. Here the Roman letter, which is clearly his final version, has been used.

his own subjects and very many seminary priests, though hurt, was not surprised by the charges levelled against him. He was anxious, not for himself,
but for his work. He feared that if Aquaviva handed over to others the
direction of the English College at Rome, then he might lose his interest in
the English mission. On this, in Garnet's estimation, the Catholic cause
largely depended. He was distressed that the General had to endure such
inhuman treatment from 'ungrateful and ill-bred' men: they were vipers
who endeavoured to destroy the Society that 'had embraced them in their
exile with so much love, fed them at its breast until Christ might once again
be formed in them'. His only comfort came from the reflection that he was
sharing Aquaviva's own anxieties. 'I also am your child,' he told him, 'yes,
a member of the same body, nurtured in the same spirit: on no account
must I be allowed to go immune.'

At first, all that Garnet knew was that he had been gravely calumniated:
he had not been told the details of the charges against him. Fr Holt had merely informed him that his name was deeply involved; Weston, when they last
met at Wisbech prison, had done no more than hint at the trouble, for he was
anxious not to disturb his Superior; he still hoped that the calumnies would
be quashed as quickly as they had arisen. Garnet expressed only a desire
that a day might be appointed on which he might appear before his slanderers
to answer their lies, or be permitted to rebut in writing the heads of their
accusations.

After heart-searching and self-examination Garnet was unable even to
guess what faults had been found in him, although, as he confessed, he had,
in his personal relationship with his God, ample reason to dread the worst of
His judgments. He could honestly say that in his ten years as Superior he had
done nothing in public that gave ground for accusations against him. Clearly
he was torn between his ties to the Society and to his country. As Aquaviva's
subject and as an 'unworthy son of the Society that had given him so many
examples' he should suffer the calumnies with patience; as an Englishman he
could not allow the conduct of these men to lower Aquaviva's esteem of his
nation. His detractors were barbarians, he wrote intimately to Aquaviva,
with no regard for any law, human or divine, men carried to the extremes of
devilment by greed and a sense of their own ineffectiveness; who did not
hesitate to bring odium and ignominy on their own people.

Garnet did not yet know that spies had infiltrated into the college to
kindle in the students an envy of the Society which, in his view, gave no
ground to stir envy in any person. This perhaps, was the hint that Weston
had given him. In placing his finger on the root of this envy, Garnet
modestly reviewed his own achievement in the first decade of his English

apostolate.[1] He refers first to the sad homecoming during his first year in England of Lord Vaux, recalling the words spoken on that occasion by 'that illustrious English nobleman, a shining example of learning, innocence and piety, who died . . . after contracting a fever during his long prolonged imprisonment'. Vaux had sought permission to make a vow that he would enter the Society, which he had greatly admired and assisted. Shortly after his return he chanced to hear his sisters mention certain current calumnies against the Jesuits. Vaux uncovered his head to Garnet and made a formal bow. Then he said words that comforted Garnet greatly when he recalled them now. 'My sisters, I am grateful indeed to you for telling me this. Now I see the mark of divine goodness stamped on men of this Order, and the intimate providence of God who had shown them these tokens of his love. Now I have no doubt that he will be propitious to them; that they in time will reap in this kingdom the same fruit from their labours as they have done elsewhere, for they are not excepted here from the injuries that they suffer in other countries.'

With the outbreak of trouble at the English College coincided the stirs at Wisbech Castle; nor were they unconnected. It was the policy of the government to foster in England a centre of disturbance which could be used to widen the divisions they hoped to open in the Catholic resistance.

From the time access to the prison had been made easy, there had been a constant throng of visitors, and among them a number of troublesome priests, some of whom were later enlisted as agents of the Council.[2] Dissensions broke out. Some twenty priests, anxious for peace, banded themselves into a confraternity, which tied itself to regular devout practices. Then in February 1595 they had begged Garnet to agree that Fr Weston should be appointed their Superior.[3] Addressing Garnet as their 'father and brother, most straitly joined to them all', they urged him to overrule Weston's reluctance to accept authority over them. Already several times Garnet had declined to interfere in their affairs; now, in a very modified way, he agreed to their petition. Weston might be their spiritual adviser, if they so wished, but not their Superior; he might direct the rest by example but without authority over them; if any priest needed correction, it was to be done by a common council, in which Weston should have no voice; finally, to avoid offence to the priests who did not want to bind themselves by rule, both parties should agree among themselves to pursue their own way of life. While making it clear

[1] H. G. to C. A. 16 April 1596. F.G. 651, f. 106.
[2] *William Weston*, 208–10. A summary of the principal incidents that occurred at Wisbech is given in *The Wisbech Stirs*, C.R.S., vol. 51, xi–xxi.
[3] Wisbech priests to H. G. 7 February 1595. Stonyhurst, *Anglia* 2, 2.

P

that he had no responsibility for the division, Garnet defended the priests who wished to form a confraternity. Writing to Dr Christopher Bagshawe, the leader of the party opposed to Weston, he explained:[1]

'Although you think otherwise, I would myself have judged such an arrangement, had mine been the responsibility for making it, one from which nobody mindful of the finest example of Christians need recoil. For, very dear Sir, I have seen what you have often seen in cities that are Christian, Catholic and most renowned, many instances of confraternities among the laity, associations among the clergy and, in Colleges, special sodalities. Furthermore, and this is most to the point, we have both of us seen in the same family of religious examples of different observance and various reforms, all under the same head and the same rule.'

While Garnet defended Weston, he constantly reiterated his desire not to intervene. 'On the management of your household', he told Bagshawe,[2] 'I do not wish further to be heard. . . . I beg you all to be united in this bodily separation. . . . Let silence fall on mention of all past ills, for these, like dangerous wounds, by too much handling do ever open up anew.' Eventually the intervention was successful. Using the offices of two secular priests, Garnet suggested a fresh arbitration, which was accepted. Both parties agreed to live their separate ways of life. On 8 November 1595 eighteen of the Wisbech priests wrote to express their gratitude to him.[3] 'This scandal hath engendered discipline and our separation at table hath conceived unity of hearts; and discord . . . hath brought forth at length peace.'

The peace was to last for nine months. In this interval Garnet wrote to Aquaviva:[4] 'This is what I consider to have been the quarrel among these men; but I earnestly beg your Paternity never to bring the matter to the light of day unless it is essential for our justification. For I am loath both to upset the peace that reigns at present or to make myself odious in recounting the faults of others.' Topcliffe, perhaps a year earlier, had seen the need to perpetuate discord and had convinced the Council that at any price the apostolate of the imprisoned priests must be impeded. In his atrocious hand he had written a memorandum for the Council, complaining that the prisoners had infected much of the countryside with Popery and that 'the seminary at Wisbech' was doing more damage to England than half the seminaries of Christendom.[5] The fresh outbreak of trouble the following year led to

---

[1] H. G. to Christopher Bagshawe. 8 October 1595. Stonyhurst, *Anglia* 9, 45 (now at Westminster).

[2] *Ibid.*

[3] Eighteen priests to H. G. 8 November 1595. Stonyhurst, *Anglia* 2, 7.

[4] H. G. to C. A. 16 April 1596. F.G. 651, f. 106.   [5] Westminster Archives 5, 2.

Weston's removal to the Tower. Garnet was no longer directly concerned in the dispute.

It was partly Garnet's success at Wisbech, partly the high esteem in which he was held by the entire Catholic community that attracted to the Society the attentions of the government no less than the veneration of young Catholics. As Garnet observed, religious discipline flourished among his brethren. From all parts of the country there came young men seeking admission to the Society; in all the shires Catholics rode long distances to visit the Jesuits, hear them preach and receive the sacraments from them. Frequently Garnet had spoken to Aquaviva of seminary priests in England anxious to join the Society. Their number was an embarrassment to him: either he had to refuse them, or, alternatively, deprive the mission for at least a year of much needed priests. 'Very many martyrs on the threshold of heaven itself have wanted nothing more than this.'[1] Garnet thanked God that no scandal had been noted in any of his brethren: none had defected from the Church or betrayed a fellow-Catholic. At the altar and hearth, along with the seminary priests, they had opposed certain men who taught that it was lawful to attend the services of heretics. They had undertaken a number of tasks that others had left undone: that was all. Among Catholics there was rivalry to obtain Jesuits for their homes. In general it was the very success of the Society that was the root of its troubles.

Such was Garnet's analysis. The fierce laws, executions, plots, real or fictitious, financial impositions, imprisonment had failed to check the success of the new priests. The devil and his agents, as Garnet saw it, were trying their utmost to get them expelled from the country: 'that is the crux and summary of it all'. If his enemies really had a charge to bring against him personally, why had they not brought it earlier. There was redress available. He himself was subject to authority and reponsible to others. 'A perfect accusation by factious and contentious men is always suspect. They may not have been instructed earlier what precise charges they were to bring against me.'[2]

Garnet had always left his men free to develop their work on their own initiative and at the same time saw to it that they maintained strict religious observance. In these first ten years he had set a pattern that was to be followed for the next two centuries. It was his achievement to restore in some measure the routine of religious life that had been followed in so many monasteries before the Reformation. This was the strength of the Society.

'We strive our utmost to attain perfection', he wrote: then he listed in this letter his means to this end. First was the Rule, which 'all tried to observe

[1] H. G. to C. A. 16 April 1596. F.G. 651, f. 106.   [2] *Ibid.*

no less fervently than if they were living in a College abroad'; then the mutual help and companionship they provided one another. To this Garnet attached such importance that, even in remote parts of the country, he endeavoured always so to place his men that they could visit each other frequently for confession and counsel. He and Southwell had never for long been far removed from each other; Holtby and Nelson were in close alliance in the north; Oldcorne and (for a time) Lister had both been based on Hinlip. The pattern was extended later, as Gerard opened up Oxfordshire, Berkshire and the bordering counties. 'Hardly a day passes when two or more of our priests do not meet in some place.'

On these exchanges and also on frequent visits to himself Garnet placed great emphasis. He did not consider it sufficient to see his priests just twice a year; at considerable expenditure and hazard, he made himself available both to his own men and to the seminary priests. It meant that he had always to maintain his own house in London where all who wished might visit him. His own priests came as often as they could, either to discuss their problems with him or for a period of study or rest.

Then, as he told Aquaviva in another context, there was the help they all derived from the regular six-monthly meetings: with their prayer, conferences and general confession.

What gave all Garnet's men their greatest stimulus in the pursuit of their vocation was the reliance placed on them by the secular priests: so many of them came, particularly to Garnet, for spiritual discussion and guidance. His house was always open to them: and he received in turn from them much edification and help. These men, and the families that gave shelter to the Jesuits, helped equally to keep them faithful to their ideals: the lives of these holy men and women and their unworldliness inspired them all. In their homes, according to Gerard, only the name was lacking to make them religious houses. There were some places that were already treated with the veneration reserved to sacred shrines in earlier times: so many people came to them from devotion. Embarrassed as he was to write in these terms, Garnet confessed: 'It is commonly said that where one of Ours treads, there follows at once the blessing of God: and certainly if such things were not said, the astonishing changes that have taken place speak for themselves.'[1]

Not merely their Rule and the expectation others had of Garnet's priests kept them faithful to their vocation, but also their persecutors outside and within their fold: 'the sword and torture of the one, the malicious talk and envious eye of the other'. They were compelled to carry their lives and reputations in their hands: 'against the first, they must be armed with the grace of

[1] H. G. to C. A. 16 April 1595. F.G. 651, f. 106.

God, against the second, they must show the light and splendour of their virtues: whatever we say or do is noted and observed'.

In this part of his letter Garnet writes as though he were addressing his own men: 'We are nevertheless very far from being perfect. We are men. We can fail. And I do not know whether we stand or fall.'[1] Rightly he claimed that all he had done, had been done in the open. If in the past year, in his dealings with the prisoners at Wisbech, he had acted in an unfair manner, it would have been shouted from the roof tops. He wrote thus, not because he sought Aquaviva's commendation, or because he set special store by his own work, but because he wanted his Superior to be fore-armed in his defence. All he did now would be scrutinised. The strain on him, particularly without Southwell's help, was worse than any strain imposed by the persecution.

[1] *Ibid.*

22

THE WORKSHOP OF CECIL

MORE insidious and enduring than the personal attack on Garnet was the distrust provoked between the religious and seminary priests. There was no man in England who had worked harder than Garnet for unity and intimate co-operation between all priests. Looking ahead, as he always did, to the day when the clergy, secular and religious, would be permitted to work unimpeded, he had striven to create an atmosphere of mutual confidence. This was the supreme ambition of his life, and after ten years in England he appeared to have achieved it. He never tired of telling Aquaviva that the most perfect harmony and union existed. If he wrote strongly on the damage done by government agents within the Catholic body, it was because he judged that Aquaviva could assist his cause only if he knew the facts.

Before the common privilege of the priesthood and the bond it created, other loyalties and ties, though not insignificant in Garnet's mind, were secondary. He loved his own vocation and the ideal of the religious life, particularly the life of the Society. What he found hardest to endure was the manner in which certain priests 'treat us as though we were not priests like themselves or as if our religious profession excluded us from union with our fellow-priests'.[1] This he was unable to understand. With sadness he remarked that these men acted 'as though every failing in a priest did not cause us the same shame, sorrow and pain as it does them'. Recalling perhaps the stories told him as a child of the Carthusian monks at Beauvale, so near his home at Heanor, he saw religious as much as seminary priests part of the English Catholic tradition. 'It was religious priests who in the past made this island illustrious for its faith. Now the old Orders have for the time been suppressed. All that the country has in their place are a few priests of the Society and two Franciscans, who work with all their strength to confirm Catholics in their faith and to convert the kingdom.'

[1] H. G. to C. A. 16 April 1596. F.G. 651, f. 106.

214

It was a wicked distortion of the truth — indeed it was the work of the Council — to represent religious, and the Jesuits especially, as unwelcome to the men from the seminaries. Garnet knew most of the seminary priests, some of them intimately, and was able to state that, with very few exceptions indeed, they were desirous to see religious, particularly the Society, firmly established in England. They were anxious to receive the help which they considered the Jesuits alone were able to give them: all had been taught in the seminaries that the country could be won back to the old religion only by deeply spiritual men. 'You cannot call it an apostolic vocation', he said with a certain harshness, 'when priests come here merely to seek a living or to amass in a short time sufficient money to keep themselves sumptuously in exile for the rest of their life: the vocation (of true seminary priests) is to devote themselves body and soul to God and his Church: to go out in search of the sheep themselves, not of their fleece.'[1] Happily, in Garnet's survey, very few priests were infected with this vice: the larger number lived frequently in conditions of great hardship and real poverty.

Constantly Garnet insisted that his own men, even if not students by temperament, should each day give time to study whether they were at home or travelling or confined in prison. They were often asked their opinion on many problems; their knowledge must be kept up to date. Already in the well-established centres, Garnet was assembling small libraries of controversial and scriptural works which all missionary priests might consult.[2] Sincerely he pointed out that in the last ten years Jesuits had been placed 'not where they could get money, but where they might help as many people as possible.'[3]

As an illustration of this he sketched the activity based on the houses where his men were stationed. 'There is almost daily a large flow of people to these places just as if they were churches: so large, in fact, we should be in very great danger if God did not protect us. Moreover, in these centres all priests, whoever they are, have a safe refuge. Since both lay people and priests come in such numbers to see us, they are compelled to stay some period of time there: it is not safe for them to leave immediately, since constant arrivals and departures would be observed by the heretics. Moreover we must in some part refund these families from alms begged elsewhere for we cannot expect from our hosts more than they have to give. Their

[1] *Ibid.*

[2] Later this scheme was considerably developed by Garnet's successor, Fr Richard Blount, who gathered at a central place in every large district an important library which served the priests of the area.

[3] H. G. to C. A. 16 April 1596. F.G. 651, f. 106.

revenue, considerable though it may be, is spent on pious but frugal hospitality, while they themselves often go about in worn and patched clothes.'[1]

All these houses were as open to the seminary priests as to the Jesuits themselves; as can be seen from John Gerard's *Autobiography*,[2] they frequently formed a base from which as many as four priests, two Jesuits and two seminary priests, were able to work nearby or even in distant places.

Every favour or gift that Garnet received had been placed at the service of all priests without distinction. Not only did he shelter and maintain them when they first entered the country but he found for them stations from which they could work. Only a handful of them were unprepared to accept his help. Seeking out their own Catholic houses, these men clung to them as if they were benefices. 'Should any other priest so much as set foot there, they take it very badly: and these are places from which ten or twelve priests could make useful journeys into the neighbouring countryside.'[3] One or two such priests had sometimes obstructed work in vast areas which were temporarily lost to the Church. As Garnet pointed out there was far more visiting to be done — and only by visiting can Catholics be kept to the practice of the faith — than any one priest could do himself. Here and there, at the risk of misunderstanding, Garnet had been able to remedy this evil, maintaining at his own expense a second priest in houses that could support no more than one.

Among other services to the clergy, Garnet had established a fund for the maintenance of priests on their first arrival in England, and from this fund he made provision for them until they were able to support themselves. 'We offer them all we can', he said, 'according to their needs and our resources.' It was a development of the policy formulated by Weston's friends at the Hoxton conference a year before Garnet's arrival.[4] Now the fund was taken for granted. The families that had first contributed still bore the main burden of it. Garnet confessed that he would gladly be rid of the task of administering the fund, but it was difficult to do since it was from his closest friends that he collected the money. However, he was able to say that 'I have never neglected the need of any priest so long as I have had the means of helping him.'

His other sources of income were irregular and uncertain. Whatever he was given he regarded as a gift, not to himself or to the Society, but to the

[1] H. G. to C. A. 16 April 1596. F.G. 651, f. 106.
[2] *John Gerard*, chs. 18, 20.
[3] H. G. to C. A. 16 April 1597. F.G. 651, f. 106.
[4] *William Weston*, 28.

Church. To these gifts he had, with Aquaviva's permission, added the patrimony of two Jesuits. All that came to him 'from time to time' he gave away: first to impoverished Catholic families, then to students at the seminaries abroad, and lastly, to prisoners for the faith. That was his chosen order of preference.[1]

There was, however, one point concerning his use of money that needed explanation. All he had received, he had received honestly and in good faith; and he had 'spent it to no man's injury'. Yet, no matter how fair or generous he was, he could not escape criticism. In one matter he asked Aquaviva's forgiveness. There had been so many calls on his purse that he had no choice but to discriminate. Always he put what he considered greater needs first. In acting thus it was inevitable that he should incur displeasure. But 'I have never spent any money', he protested, 'save after prayer and self-examination, and, whenever it was necessary, I have taken the advice of others. With so many Catholics in need of assistance, and very great assistance, it has been impossible to help them without somebody having a complaint against me.' There were six, or at the most seven, devout Catholics who regularly gave him money for the maintenance of his own men. Although the total was barely sufficient for their food and clothing, Garnet managed to find something over for charity. The patrimony of Jesuits that he had devoted to the general needs of the mission amounted to over a thousand pounds or, in Continental money, four thousand gold crowns. 'We only ask to be allowed to live in poverty', he pleaded,[2] 'and to leave all these works of charity to others. If this is done, then nobody should expect help from us when they first come here. Whatever I have to give, I give: when I don't give, it is because I have not got it to give, not because I do not want to give it.' He begged that his critics should be made to 'realise that I am not concealing any treasures, but spend every farthing I have on the needs of all, even to the neglect of my own wants: for some of our own priests have to go without horses, clothing and the books they require'.[3]

Garnet was reluctant to speak of this work, but he was determined for the sake of peace in Rome to inform Aquaviva about it. Nor was it merely financially that he helped all who called on him, but in other ways also. His printing press was available to seminary priests, though he bore the entire expense of maintaining it. Moreover, his craftsmen and messengers served all without distinction.

'We maintain a number of necessary lay helpers, and among them, a

[1] H. G. to C. A. 16 April 1596. F.G. 651, f. 106.
[2] *Ibid.*
[3] *Ibid.*

carpenter.[1] Some time, God willing, he will join the Society: his singular faithfulness and skill make him most suited for its work. He has travelled through almost the entire kingdom, and, without charge, has made for Catholic priests (apart from Jesuits) hiding places, where they can shelter from the fury of heretical searchers. If money is offered him by way of payment he gives it to his two brothers: one of them is a priest, the other a layman in prison for his faith. Some other [lay helpers] accompany both seminary priests and our own men on their journeys; and if it is dangerous to travel, they themselves do all necessary business by carrying their messages or letters. Others look after overseas affairs, that is, they send and receive letters or convey students to the seminaries, ladies to convents and send money over to them and to other poor Catholics. And these services, though they are unbelievably burdensome and fraught with infinite perils and anxieties, are in my opinion the most necessary and useful works we undertake. And do not think they could easily be done by others without our help and support, for we have such friendly and close relations in Rome with your Paternity and his assistants, in Spain with Father Robert [Persons] and Father Joseph [Creswell], in Belgium with Father William [Holt] and others who direct the seminary at St Omer, and indeed with all members of our Society everywhere. Easily and safely we can do what others could not do at all, or do only at very great expense and the risk of deception and betrayal by the very men they should have to employ.'[2]

Were it not for this organisation the new English convent in Flanders, numbering now nearly twenty nuns, could never have been founded. And from this convent 'we look eventually for numerous off-shoots in this realm'.[3]

It is this very work that had brought about such easy, close and perfect understanding between the seminary and Jesuit priests. To Garnet's knowledge there were no more than five or at most six seminary men who were discontented: the rest protested that no greater injustice could be done them than be accused of lack of friendliness to the Society. These few odd priests Garnet himself did his utmost to win over. He relates in detail one case that is not without humour. On a visit to Rome a certain priest — Garnet does not mention his name — insinuated to Cardinals and others in the Curia that the seminary men in England were outraged against the Jesuits. In Roman fashion he was asked to give names and cases. He confessed he could not: he knew scandals unknown to Rome. Pressed further, he gave up, declaring that all he reported he must have heard spoken in a dream.

[1] Nicholas Owen.
[2] H. G. to C. A. 16 April 1596. F.G. 651, f. 106.　　　　[3] *Ibid.*

Another case concerned Garnet more personally. A priest, before return-ing to England, had spread the tale in Rome that no Jesuit had ever been known to assist the young men entering England from the seminaries. Garnet observed that this happened a short time before the death of Cardinal Allen in 1594, as if to associate the outbreak of these troubles with the death of the Cardinal.[1] This man's gossip had alarmed the newly-ordained priests to such an extent that they feared to cross into England. When later 'they found from experience that there was virtually no one to give them help, advice, money, food and shelter on their arrival except our own priests, they were staggered at the man's story and told me so themselves, scoffing at the tales he had told them'.[2] In time this priest himself arrived back during a festal season, perhaps Easter 1595. He lodged at an inn in London.

'It was no wonder [explains Garnet] that he was not welcomed immedi-ately on his arrival, since at that time the houses of Catholics were under strict surveillance and it was impossible to receive a stranger into them. It so happened that the very same day he entered the city, I did too. Before I visited any Catholic, I made for the inn and sought him out in courtesy and friendliness. I could not ask him to come with me, for I was uncertain myself whether any Catholic family would take me in that night. But I had hardly gone twelve yards, when I met a Catholic whom I knew and asked him to have care of this priest, who followed him some distance behind; but the priest got lost in a maze of streets and was unable to find the gentle-man again.... But we have made this priest our friend.'[3]

This priest had just heard the report that the Jesuits were about to hand over the English College. Hastily he sent Garnet a letter imploring the Soci-ety to retain it. In his view it would be a disaster, perhaps the end of the College, if the Jesuits lost its control. The troubles, this priest wrote, were the devil's work.

Here was unpetitioned evidence. Garnet copied the priest's letter and for-warded it to Aquaviva with the comment: 'If such a man, who was once my critic, can write with such affection of me and such harshness of the trouble-makers, what would happen if the matter were put to the vote of all priests here?'[4]

Finally Garnet spoke of the welcome given him by the seminary priests on his journeys throughout the country. Could Aquaviva have witnessed it he would realise that there was no foundation in the reports of hostile or even strained relations with them. 'If all could only see for themselves the happy and wonderful reunions I always have with them on my journeys, and see also the trouble they take to come from neighbouring places to visit

[1] *Ibid.*   [2] *Ibid.*   [3] *Ibid.*   [4] *Ibid.*

me, the warmth of the affection they show me and the most kind letters they
send me from all parts, they would have to say that these priests desire with
their whole heart nothing save the peace and charity of the Holy Spirit.'[1] So
many of them, even those who had not sought admission into the Society,
begged that they should be allowed to act under Garnet's direction. 'I
sincerely and frankly confess', Garnet wrote, 'that nearly half the number of
priests I have met have offered me their complete obedience, but I have
refused absolutely to accept it.'[2]

Garnet knew that the troubles in Rome had been instigated by the
government, contrived, he told Aquaviva, 'in the workshop of Cecil and
Topcliffe'. He added: 'in the eyes of Catholics the quarrels are ridiculous and
undignified'. Whatever happened, Aquaviva must keep his letter secret:
not even were his own men to know that he had written it. 'I beg your
Paternity', he pleaded, 'and most earnestly, never to make these things known
unless it is necessary for my own just exculpation.'[3]

His reason for writing was to prove to Aquaviva that those who clamoured
for the removal of the Jesuits from the English College did not represent
the clergy of England. He was sad for the students' sake, still more for the
sake of the English Church. These men, he said, do not listen to their martyrs, pastors and apostles, but to proud, factious and ambitious priests,
recently recovered from the mire of heresy and even to Ministers and ex-
priests, wandering about without obedience to any man and crying out for
desperate treatment. In the last resort Garnet showed himself not unready
to advise severity. 'Brand these men now with perpetual ignominy — men
who sow sedition and cultivate it. Only in this way will you be rid of the
leaven of Cecil, against which you must watch with infinite care, for if it is
scattered even in small particles, it will shortly affect the whole mass. . . .
Meanwhile I implore your Paternity, never to desert your own sons nor
abandon the house that has nurtured so many martyrs, on account of troubles
caused by a handful of insolent men; but as you have done in the past,
continue to love and cherish it.'[4]

'The leaven of Cecil' was Garnet's anxiety for the remaining nine years
of his life.

[1] H. G. to C. A. 16 April 1596. F.G. 651, f. 106.
[2] *Ibid.*   [3] *Ibid.*   [4] *Ibid.*

23

CLAUDIO AQUAVIVA

DURING the summer of 1596 Garnet continued his pastoral work. There is no record of any incidents of note: there was one grave loss through imprisonment. While on his way to England, Fr John Percy had been arrested at Flushing, tortured, then transported to London, where he was confined in the Tower and again tortured. 'He is happy in spirit and sound in health and expects to be liberated, or at least exiled shortly. If he is exiled, he will return immediately via the port of embarkation.'[1]

There were losses also through sickness. On 10 July Holtby's companion, John Nelson, died. He had been the first of the seminary priests to join the Society after Garnet's arrival in England, 'a man of exceptional devotion and holiness who for seven years had toiled with zeal, success and exceeding great charity'.[2] Garnet begged Aquaviva to obtain prayers for him: his brethren in England, whose suffrages he could claim, were so few in number. Nelson was a young man: his death was caused by the plague. Since Garnet did not give Aquaviva the news until August, it can be assumed that he was out of London from April till the late summer. In the same letter he reported that another of his men, John Curry,[3] an esteemed 'merchant', was lying sick. 'Daily he awaits his death, which may well occur before this letter reaches your Lordship.'[4] Little is known about him, but he was much loved: once he had been the companion of Sherwin, Bryant and Campion and spoke so frequently of them that he came to be called the 'friend of martyrs'. John Gerard says that he died this winter in London and was buried secretly, presumably by his Superior, Fr Garnet.

These three men formed a third of the total number of priests under Garnet's jurisdiction. Immediately Garnet petitioned for replacements. In view of the scrutiny to which his brethren were now subjected by their

[1] H. G. to C. A. 4 August 1596. F.G. 651, f. 98.
[2] *Ibid.*
[3] Cf. *sup.*, p. 96.
[4] H. G. to C. A. 4 August 1596. F.G. 651, f. 98.

critics, he would prefer to go short of assistance than be sent priests who might lack discretion. Therefore he begged Aquaviva to select men who were 'outstanding for their piety'. 'While here all other qualities are an asset, it is piety that is chiefly required.' Then, for the General's guidance, he adds: 'However they should also have good health and average intelligence and capacity for playing the part of ambassadors of Christ before the people.'[1]

Even after these losses Garnet was not unwilling to send back Fr Thomas Lister this year. Later in August there was to be another half-yearly meeting. It had been called earlier than usual because this year a congregation of the Society, with a representative from every Province, had been summoned to Rome.[2] Garnet hoped that Lister would be elected to represent his brethren at Rome.

'When we have finished our own meeting [Garnet wrote][3] we will choose a man to visit your Lordship and he will give you a full report of our business. I should greatly like to do this myself. There is nothing in my life that I want more than to see you again — just once and I should be intensely happy — and to see also the cradle in which I was born to Christ and nurtured in devotion: how glad and grateful I should be.' The demands on him in England made such a journey difficult and the approval of his brethren was required. 'What we shall decide I do not know. I expect the choice will fall on Thomas [Lister] who suffers from headaches and cannot easily find a cure in this country. I hope such a pleasant journey will greatly improve his health.'[4]

The rest of us, Garnet added, 'are alive and well and we campaign on God's behalf with very great peace and tranquillity. There are no feuds between us and the seminary priests, whatever may be happening in Rome.' His old friends in Rome were dear to him, dearer still was that 'union which the Holy Spirit and companionship in the same work brings us'. Nothing, he says, repeating his last letter, 'causes more shame and grief to the seminary priests than they should be accused of thinking or speaking ill of us.' That was the 'very truth indeed' which the testimony of others would endorse.[5]

In his dealings with all priests, Garnet's conscience was clear. Recently he had been much comforted by a kind letter from Aquaviva. Written ten

---

[1] H. G. to C. A. 4 August 1596. F.G. 651, f. 98.

[2] In 1596 there took place at the Gesù in Rome the regular triennial congregation of the Jesuits; it was attended by an elected representative of every Province and important mission of the Society.

[3] H. G. to C. A. 4 August 1596. F.G. 651, f. 98.

[4] *Ibid.*

[5] *Ibid.*

days before his own long letter on the trouble-makers in Rome, it gave him the assurance he sought. Aquaviva did not need to be convinced that Garnet's policy was the right one: he knew what distress the disturbance at the college had caused him and made it clear that he understood its origin correctly. He wrote on 6 April, but it was not until late July or August that Garnet received the letter. The delay is explained by Garnet's own measures of security: it seems that he did not risk having his correspondence forwarded to him in the country. Sometimes he would wait several months before gathering his letters on his return to London; moreover, as he told Aquaviva, it was always easier for him to despatch than to receive letters. He wrote in acknowledgment: 'There is nothing that gives us all so much pleasure in our difficult work than to see just one little scrap written by you.'[1] Aquaviva's letter had restored his zest for work and his happiness at a time when he was dejected. He could not thank him sufficiently for the understanding he had shown him.

At the conference the opinion of his brethren was against sending Lister to represent them: they preferred that Persons, already in Rome, should do this.[2] Nevertheless Garnet instructed Lister to go privately to Rome, where he knew Aquaviva would take special care of his health. In his own opinion Lister's trouble was not any physical weakness or his headaches, but a neurotic condition. The General would be able to see this for himself. Understandably Garnet was reluctant to commit to a letter all that he wished to say about Lister. 'His intentions are good,' he assured Aquaviva, 'he is tractable and has lived a long time very closely to me without giving me trouble.' But he was unfit to live as the other Jesuits did, nor was Garnet prepared to ask that they should share their residence with him. Fortunately Catholic layfolk had noticed in him nothing worse than his excitability and his utter incapacity to rest for any length of time.[3] This was the man with whom Garnet had shared his house for more than two years.

Speaking again of him in this letter, Garnet revealed the extreme kindness he had shown him. 'I have sent to Flanders Thomas [Lister] who for a long time earnestly asked to be sent into voluntary exile. And I could not well refuse him, for he was asking something that he greatly needed.'[4]

The relief Garnet experienced at Lister's departure was great, but he was not rid of him as soon as he had hoped.

Garnet could not risk any scandal, however small, among his own men,

---

[1] *Ibid.*
[2] Fr Persons became Rector of the English College, Rome, on 13 December 1597.
[3] H. G. to C. A. 4 August 1596. F.G. 651, f. 98.
[4] *Ibid.*

for he knew it would be capitalised by his enemies. Aquaviva's April letter
encouraged him to write still more openly. Now he knew there was no fear
that the General would lose his interest in England. While Garnet's troubles
were not yet over, he had now more exact information on the complaints
made against him and his brethren. In a more summary fashion, he wrote again
to Aquaviva, on 10 December this year.[1] As a Jesuit he 'had cause more for joy
than sorrow since, after toiling so many years, after perils and vigils, he had
been traduced and calumniated . . . in that city which is the mother and mistress of all the churches'. Then taking up the points that Aquaviva had made
to comfort him, he added: 'this is a wonderful occasion for imitating Christ
our Leader and putting on his insignia, yet good must be safeguarded not
only with God but also with men'. Lest these disturbers of the peace in
Rome gain the ear of the Pope, it would be well for Aquaviva to be forewarned. Garnet was prepared to be called a liar and even to incur Aquaviva's
displeasure, if his facts were proved false; that is, if he had not manifested the
love of Christ to all priests, loaded them with kindness and good services
and expended on them the patrimony of Jesuits. For his intervention at
Wisbech he could not be blamed: possibly the resolute line he had taken on
the question of Catholics attending Protestant churches might be the explanation of the calumnies. 'Certain priests have had the audacity to defend
illicit attendance at heretical gatherings, even after the decision given by our
most holy Lord Clement[2] *viva voce* to the most illustrious Cardinal Allen,
but I, for my part also, have opposed their wicked endeavours. It is not that
I have oppressed them. Had I acted differently, the Catholic cause would
have suffered severely. There were even some who considered leaving the
Church on this issue.'[3] Then he added that, excluding a large number of
old priests in the kingdom, there were some fifteen seminary priests who
lived scandalous lives, either in manifest heresy or open schism or even in
attempted marriage. These, he declared, were the men who preached heresy,
or wrote books in support of it, or propagated evil doctrines touching the
Holy See or the Society. Yes, he had opposed these men with all his strength.
The personal esteem in which he was held had, in fact, caused jealousy
among a few. If he was able to assist seminary priests, that was neither
to his blame nor to his credit: it was due to 'the devotion of those who, on
entering the Society, have left all they possessed to us . . . or in other ways
have provided us with money to spend on the men to whom I wish to dedicate my life'.[4] Aquaviva had told him he had been charged with oppression.

[1] H. G. to C. A. 10 December 1596. Stonyhurst, *Anglia* 2, 19.
[2] Clement VIII (1592–1605).
[3] H. G. to C. A. 10 December 1596. Stonyhurst, *Anglia* 2, 19.   [4] *Ibid.*

FATHER CLAUDIUS AQUAVIVA
Portrait in former Jesuit College, Valkenburg, Holland
(artist and date unknown)

SIR JOHN POPHAM, *Aet.* 68
Portrait by an unknown artist

After reviewing his conduct, Garnet answered that the accusation was too ridiculous to be entertained, but it provoked from him a noble statement of his personal creed and aspirations. 'The oppression of others is something which I have neither time nor inclination to consider, expecting death as I do daily, and with God's help meditating always on those things which can prepare me to suffer it bravely for Christ's sake: these things are not jealousy, strife, envy, pride and the like, but humility, charity, perfect contempt of the world and wordly honour. Above all things these should be the aim of religious men.'[1]

Reflecting after an interval on Lister's case, Garnet thought fit to warn Aquaviva again that not all English Jesuits now abroad were suited to the mission. No matter how outstanding their talent or learning, they were useless to him unless they were ready to face the hazards of a missionary. It was essential that in their zeal and virtue they should match the lay Catholics among whom they worked and lived. Before any priest was sent over, it was important to assess the spirit in which he was approaching his assignment. Newcomers must be seasoned, not raw, men.

Along with the anxieties that Lister and the Roman College had caused him this year, Garnet also had his consolations. 'After suffering a number of misfortunes which followed fast on one another', he wrote, 'God, in a short space of time, has compensated me abundantly and given me intense joy, for I have been given back safe a number of my friends, who a little while ago were in the direst peril. This was more than I ventured to hope or expect.'[2] Fulwood, imprisoned in Bridewell, had got away. He was the man who had organised the escape line to Belgium and had been used by Garnet 'in nearly all my business'. Arrested while he was escorting a youth to Gravesend, he had met Fr Percy in gaol and with him made a plan of escape. It was so well contrived that these two men, along with two other priests and six laymen, broke from prison together. For the sake of Percy's safety, Garnet immediately sent him to the north, probably as a replacement for John Nelson: soon afterwards Garnet reported he was completely restored in health. Percy, as Garnet confessed, is 'a man I love dearly', and his recovery of freedom gave him great satisfaction. Hastily Garnet explained to Aquaviva that no scandal could be caused by his escape:

'Your Lordship should not be astonished that Catholics sometimes break out of prison. While there are certain prisons in which they are treated with humanity and give a pledge that they will not attempt escape, this prison was utterly barbarous and reserved chiefly for whores and vagabonds. Catholics

---

[1] *Ibid.*
[2] *Ibid.*

Q

were forbidden access to it and there was no communication permitted
between prisoners. Here no pledge was given, for no one had the humanity
to ask it. This escape, therefore, caused no scandal at all.'[1]

Garnet's friendship with Aquaviva was now long-standing: it began in his
Roman days when Aquaviva, the son of the Duke of Atri, was the young
Provincial of the Roman Province. Then he had Garnet among his subjects
both as a novice at Sant' Andrea and as a student at the Roman College.
There was a quality in the English character that appealed to the Neapolitan
nobleman. Before he was elected General of the Society, Aquaviva, as a
very young priest, had volunteered to learn English and cross to England
in Campion's company. In 1579, at the vital Jesuit conference that resolved
to send Persons and Campion to England, Aquaviva, then Roman Provincial, was called in and swayed the Fathers in favour of the mission. As
Persons wrote:[2]

'The Father that was then Provincial of the Roman Province and after-
ward General, Father Claudius Aquaviva, did not a little help in forwarding
the matter, not only favouring the said mission, but offering himself also to
go therein. But Almighty God that had appointed to take unto himself the
very next year that blessed man, Everard Mercurianus [the General], had
designed also that this man should succeed him in his place and perfect that
which the other had begun, which he hath now done with all affection . . .
and hath profited the English mission much more absent by his authority
and favour than if he had been employed there in person himself.'

England and the Indies, where his nephew was martyred,[3] were the missions dearest to his heart. Garnet was not yet ordained when Aquaviva had
been elected General on 19 February 1581 at the age of thirty-six: but, as
Persons justly noted, Aquaviva's high office gave him greater opportunity of
assisting England, which he had aspired to make his adopted country.

When Garnet was a young priest and professor, he was frequently called
to assist Aquaviva in giving communion to the Roman people on Sundays
and the great festivals. 'Our Father General', writes Fr Thomas Stanney,[4]
'when he communicated any great multitude of people, as many times he did,
he would ordinarily choose him [Father Garnet] for his assistant in the Holy

[1] H. G. to C. A. 4 August 1596. F.G. 651, f. 98.

[2] Robert Persons, *First Entry of the Fathers of the Society*, Stonyhurst, Grene *P.*, 8.

[3] Fr Rodolpho Aquaviva, five years older than Aquaviva, was martyred at Cuncolim
in the territory of Goa in 1583.

[4] Memoir of Father Henry Garnet, *The Month*, June 1898, 609. Fr Thomas
Stanney, a native of Salisbury, entered the English College, Rome, at the age of twenty-
three on 18 October 1581; he was ordained in 1585 and went to England the following
year. He entered the Society in 1587.

Sacrifice, for that he used great reverence and devotion, great diligence and dexterity in assisting him.' Only eleven years separated them in age. Their friendship was so close that it was with reluctance that the General allowed Garnet to leave for England in 1586. Two years earlier, Aquaviva, on the ground that Garnet could not be spared from Rome, had resisted Persons' pleas that he should be sent over: he had seen in him a man capable of filling the highest positions in the Society. Rightly he thought that Garnet's conscience and character were too delicate for the rough handling he was certain to receive on his return to his own country. As he took his farewell of Garnet and Southwell in May 1588 he declared that he was sending them 'as lambs to the slaughter': and there is no more penetrating insight into Garnet's character than the judgment Aquaviva passed on him. It is contained in a letter he wrote to Fr Persons, then at St Omer, on 12 July 1585:[1]

'Further, about Father Henry Garnet, I shall have to think much [before sending him to England]. For, not to mention the need I have of him here [in Rome] — this is something I am too easily tempted to put before the advantage of England — a number of reasons occur to me why we should think this Father more suited to a quiet routine than the wandering and ever anxious life that the mission of England means. Yet, as I have said, I will think more carefully about it.'

It was only for lack of substitutes — Southwell was the only alternative person at the time — that Aquaviva gave instructions that in the event of Weston's capture, Garnet should become Superior. What conversations Garnet and Aquaviva had in Rome before June 1586 are unknown: but the understanding shown in the letters of both men was forged in these years. Aquaviva, moreover, knew that Garnet was a person who could do his best work only if he had the unquestioning trust of his Superior in Rome.

After Southwell's execution Garnet, in his letters to Aquaviva, revealed to him many anxieties that previously he had confided only to his 'companion'. Henceforth Aquaviva shared all Garnet's decisions and also the credit or blame attaching to his conduct of English affairs during these years: their friendship had developed into a partnership. Constantly Garnet prayed that God's grace might direct and advance the work which he had begun under Aquaviva's auspices: indeed, these auspices and God's grace were the two supports of his life. Garnet ascribed no limit to the effectiveness of the General's prayers.[2] As every day he saw fresh examples both of God's clemency and of the devil's beastliness, he had no doubt that through the General's prayers, God would increase the former and curb the latter.

[1] Arch. S.J. Rome, *Flandria*, Ep. Gen., f. 83v.
[2] H. G. to C. A. 11 July 1588. F.G. 651, f. 16.

'Your letters', he concluded,[1] 'strengthen me so much that without any wish to appear demanding, I beg you to write frequently. And I hope you will grant my request more readily when you recollect that you have here weak soldiers who, unless they are assisted by your counsel and encouragement, will be unable to hold back the assaults of the enemy.' The day he wrote this was the second anniversary of his landing, and he reflected on the two years' progress: his own safety, the work he had achieved 'beyond any hope and expectation' he then had, he ascribed, after God, to the General and drew up his report for him as 'his due and tribute'.[2]

Garnet had never lost confidence in his Superior's appreciation both of his own and his country's problem; and this allowed him, as he himself said, 'to lay before you both what is good and bad with us, so that the former may be strengthened by your prayers, and the latter more effectively combated'.[3] The despatch of Gerard and Oldcorne from Rome in the late summer of 1588 he had seen as a token of the trust Aquaviva placed in him.[4] The times could not have been more difficult, and Aquaviva had yielded his judgment to Garnet's and risked two valuable men to help him. This had meant more to Garnet than any words, and he had shewn much concern over the safe arrival of his letter of thanks. 'I wrote a letter to your Lordship last month, which was lost. . . . Now I have no time to write again, nor any inclination either, for my letters are exposed to so many different dangers.'[5] There appeared, then, no hope now of getting a letter to Rome. However, less than two months later, he had found a courier.

'We are comforted, now,' he wrote,[6] 'with the hope of future peace: perhaps those who come after us shall enjoy it. These present storms will surely turn out to our advantage, if only we do not fail in our duty. There is but one thing that brings sorrow to me, who witness it with my own eyes, and to you, whose heart is always with us, I mean, the sight of so many who, but for the Queen's pleasure, could . . . be saved and now fall daily into the fires of hell: these souls and the souls of us all are your Lordship's concern. In your charity care for them to the utmost.'

Unburdened by office, Southwell had at first been more spontaneous in his letters to the General: he had written as a friend, recording both trivial and important events without a moment's doubt that Aquaviva would be

[1] H. G. to C. A. 11 July 1588. F.G. 651, f. 16.
[2] *Ibid.*
[3] H. G. to C. A. 29 October 1588. F.G. 651, f. 18.
[4] H. G. to C. A. 12 March 1589. F.G. 651, f. 11.
[5] *Ibid.*
[6] H. G. to C. A. 1 May 1589. F.G. 651, f. 21.

equally interested in both: strange portents in the sea, a mishap to the *Revenge*, the appearance of three 'prophets':[1] Coppinger the 'prophet of mercy', proclaiming terrible judgments; his companion Arthington, the 'prophet of judgment'; the third, Hackett, 'King of the earth, King of Christendom, descended from heaven to execute judgment on those who refuse his mercy'.[2]

The excitement both priests found in their work was heightened by their anticipation of Aquaviva's interest. 'Your Lordship will excuse me if I write less frequently than I should', Garnet wrote once when communications with Rome were difficult.[3] 'You must assure yourself that it is a great pleasure for me to write. No privation can affect me more than the loss of the facilities I once had of writing as frequently as I wished'.

From the time of Southwell's capture to his own last day of freedom, Garnet's letters, some short, others very long indeed, became more frequent. The pleasure his writing gave him compensated in some measure the loss of Southwell's company. Manifestly now, he seldom re-read what he wrote; sometimes he is ungrammatical, nearly always he is hurried and anxious to hand his Roman letters to a courier before the ink is dry: whenever he sees a chance of despatching a letter he takes it.[4] Never is there a doubt in his mind about Aquaviva's personal affection for him. No matter what ill reports of him might reach Rome through his enemies, he was confident that Aquaviva would never falter in his trust and esteem.

[1] R. S. to C. A. 16 January 1590. *C.R.S.*, vol. 5, 329.

[2] Coppinger and Arthington had been respectable Puritans, but both had lost their reason and preached that only those signed on their forehead would be saved. At Cheapside they had produced a mad Minister, Hackett, crowned him as Jesus Christ, and in his name pronounced the damnation of the Archbishop of Canterbury and the deposition of the Queen.

[3] H. G. to C. A. 2 March 1590. Stonyhurst, Grene *P.*, 555.

[4] H. G. to C. A. 13 March 1596. F.G. 651, f. 114.

24

THE SEARCH FOR GARNET

THE YEAR 1597 opened quietly. Yet again there was a lull in the persecution; there were no executions this year in the south. Three laymen and a
priest met their death at the York gallows the same day, 4 July; in late March
another priest, Christopher Robinson, had been hanged at Carlisle. Garnet
gathered details of his death:[1] 'One Robinson, a seminary priest, was lately
in a purchased gaol-delivery hanged at Carlisle. The rope broke twice, and
the third time he rebuked the sheriff of cruelty, saying that though he meant
no way to yield, but was glad of his combat, yet flesh and blood was weak
and therefore it showed little humanity to torment a man so long. And when
they took order to put two ropes, then saith he, by this means I shall be
longer a-dying: but it is no matter. I am very willing to suffer all.'

From experience Garnet knew that no great expectations could be built
on the present respite. The search for him and his men was not relaxed:
in fact, it became more intense with the impending appointment of an Archpriest. It was in the government's interest that a man, pliable to its policy,
should be given a position of authority over the seminary priests and perhaps be prepared to sponsor the establishment of a Catholic national church
that would throw over its allegiance to the Papacy. The primary obstacle to
this scheme was the mass of seminary priests themselves, who looked to
Garnet both as their leader and spokesman.

It is against this background of intrigue that the stirring incidents of
Gerard's captivity must be read. It was in the spring of this year that Garnet
grew in his esteem of this brave priest. Ten years earlier there had been
misunderstanding between them: Gerard was then raw, unscholarly,
immature, a young country gentleman turned Jesuit, but unable for some
time to fill the gaps in his early education.

Garnet was the one priest whose capture might give the Council a
victory that no number of executions could bring about; his fate was in
Gerard's hands. If under torture in the Tower, Gerard remained faithful, all

[1] H. G. to R. P. 7 April 1597. Stonyhurst, Grene *P.*, 548.

might be well. Garnet, who gathered every detail of Gerard's agony, wrote in appreciation of his resourceful, stalwart, loyal subject who, nevertheless, could never quite replace Southwell in his affections.

The aim of Gerard's torturers was to discover Garnet's London lodgings. 'Of John Gerard I have already written where he is', Garnet told Aquaviva on 7 May this year:[1]

'Twice he has been hung up by the hands with great cruelty on the part of others and no less patience on his own. The examiners say he is exceedingly obstinate and a great friend either of God or of the devil, for they say they cannot extract a word from his lips, save that, amidst his torments, he speaks the word, *Jesus*. Recently they took him to the rack, where the torturers and examiners stood ready for work. But when he entered the place, he at once threw himself on his knees and with a loud voice prayed to God that as he had given strength to some of his saints to be torn asunder by horses for the sake of Christ, so he would give him strength and courage to be rent to pieces before he might speak a word that would be injurious to any person or to the divine glory. And seeing him so resolved, they did not torture him.'

Garnet concluded his tribute: 'This Father has indeed always been courageous. . . . May God grant him perseverance and give those that follow him to imitate his example.'

It has never been explained how Garnet received information of Gerard's tortures so soon after they occurred. Although Gerard himself, in his early months in the Tower, had sent out letters written in orange juice, there are details in Garnet's reports that Gerard himself would never have given. Moreover, on being taken down from the rack he was unable to hold a pen in his hands. Probably it was through friends among the officials of the Tower that Garnet gathered his information. In all his examinations Gerard manifested the chivalry all expected of him. Sir Edward Coke, later the Prosecutor at Garnet's trial, was his chief examiner: he was now Attorney-General, appointed in 1595 in preference to Sir Francis Bacon.

'You say', said the Attorney-General,[2] 'you have no wish to obstruct the government. Tell us then where Father Garnet is. He is an enemy of the State and you are bound to report on all such men.'

'He isn't an enemy of the State', Gerard replied. 'On the contrary, I am certain that if he were given the opportunity to lay down his life for his Queen and country, he would be glad of it. But I don't know where he lives and if I did I would not tell you.'

'Then we'll see to it that you tell us before you leave this place.'

'Please God, you won't,' Gerard answered.

[1] H. G. to C. A. 7 May 1597. Stonyhurst, *Anglia* 2, 27.   [2] *John Gerard*, 107.

The entire interrogation during the long day of Gerard's torture turned on Garnet's London residence. Although Gerard was revived by a cordial and hung up again, he retained control of his speech. When at dusk he was conducted by his gaoler through the courtyards of the fortress to his cell in the Salt Tower, his thoughts were still on Garnet's safety.

'On the way we met some prisoners who had the run of the Tower', he writes,[1] 'and I turned to speak to my warder, intending them to overhear.' 'What surprises me', I said, 'is that the Commissioners want me to say where Father Garnet's house is. Surely they know it is a sin to betray an innocent man? I will never do it even if I have to die.'

Gerard continues his story. His concern for Garnet's safety stifled any feeling of self-pity after his five hours on the rack.

'I said this to prevent them spreading a report, as they so often do, that I had confessed something. And I also wanted word to get round through these men that it was chiefly concerning Father Garnet that I had been questioned, so that he might get to hear and look to his own safety. I saw that the warder was not pleased at my talking in their presence, but it made no difference.'[2]

The message reached Garnet, who eight weeks later, on 10 June 1597, wrote to Aquaviva.[3] 'He [John Gerard] had been thrice hanged up by his hands until he was almost dead and that in one day twice. The cause (as I now understand perfectly) was for to tell where his Superior was, and by whom he had sent him letters which were delivered him from Father Persons.'

Gerard's constancy was an inestimable comfort to Garnet; it enlarged also his understanding of one of his bravest subjects; henceforth every year they became more dependent on each other. It was with pride that Garnet again wrote to Aquaviva in June.[4] 'More than once I have written to your Lordship about John: that he was tortured a third time, but overcame everything with an unvanquished strength of spirit. Also recently I have heard of a certainty that the Earl of Essex praised his constancy, declaring that manifestly he could not but honour and admire the man.'

During the spring and summer Garnet regretted that he had not fully appreciated Gerard during the years they were both at liberty. He had been his kind counsellor; he had given him liberty to work as he liked and had shown him every mark of trust; but there were qualities in Gerard that became clear to the Superior only in these months of separation.

[1] *John Gerard*, 111
[2] *Ibid.*
[3] H. G. to C. A. 10 June 1597. Stonyhurst, Grene *P.*, 548.
[4] H. G. to C. A. 11 June 1597. Stonyhurst, *Anglia 2*, 29.

When on 13 May Gerard had been examined by the Attorney-General, he was told that all his statements would be used against him at his trial. Just over a fortnight later, there were rumours that Gerard was to be tried during the current legal term. 'There is speech that Gerard shall be executed this term.'[1] The trial, however, never took place. The next month Garnet again wrote:[2] 'A member of the Queen's Council denies that it is the Queen's wish to have him executed. This John will take hardly.' Garnet was yet to learn Gerard's reaction: but he was right in his conjecture.[3]

It was only later that Garnet was able to guess the reasons for the postponement and later the cancellation of the trial. Since 21 February 1595, three and a half years earlier, when Southwell was martyred, no priest had been executed at Tyburn. The popular outcry against Southwell's death saved Gerard. For the present the bloody persecution had been fought to a standstill. There was better hope now of defeating the Catholic body by subtly fostering internal dissension.

During the very months that Gerard manifested such heroism, Thomas Lister, whom Garnet had nursed in his neuroses, behaved incalculably. 'The Thomas about whom I wrote', he explained to Aquaviva,[4] 'I sent away . . . to Flanders. But just outside the very walls of Antwerp he had such a compulsive desire to return home, that I have him with me here again. He is safe.' Garnet again kept him at his house. All the risks he had taken to get him over to Belgium were in vain. 'I am deeply distressed', he said in a second letter written the same day,[5] 'that his departure came to nothing. He has had no regard for the interests of the mission: both in my judgment and in his own it was essential that he should go. Moreover he had asked for it earnestly both from your Lordship and from me.' The problem appeared insoluble. 'I am tortured in mind over him, uncertain and hesitant how I should deal with him, for the source of his disease is not so much weakness of character as a disturbed mind and lack of responsibility.'[6] Then for Aquaviva's guidance he adds: 'And in case your Lordship might think that his sickness was contracted here, I should tell you that he is now far better than when he first came to me. As you will learn from Mr Octavian,[7] to whom I gave the whole history of the case . . . , I love him and, unless I am mistaken, I am loved by him in turn; but there is certainly great need for prudence and the guidance of the

[1] H. G. to R. P. 28 May 1597. Stonyhurst, Grene *P.*, 548.
[2] H. G. to C. A. 11 June 1597. Stonyhurst, *Anglia* 2, 29.
[3] *John Gerard*, 127.
[4] H. G. to C. A. 11 February 1597. Stonyhurst, *Anglia* 2, 23.
[5] *Ibid.*
[6] *Ibid.*
[7] Fr William Baldwin.

Holy Spirit in dealing with him, and I am sure this will be granted to me through your Lordship's prayers.'

Later in the year, after gentle handling, Lister was persuaded to embark again for the Continent. Freed from the hazards of missionary life in England he recovered his health and for some time did useful work among the exiled English Catholics before returning once more to England. Immediately, however, the risk of Garnet's arrest was reduced.

Again this year there was question of Garnet visiting Rome. This would seem to have been Fr Persons' wish and possibly his directive also.[1] The late delivery of letters from Rome had caused much confusion: only this February did Garnet receive Aquaviva's letter dated the previous August: 'I am now summoned from here by Father Persons and I do not understand clearly whether it is in Rome or elsewhere that he wants me to meet him.' Garnet was puzzled. Already he had provided for the representation of the English Jesuits at the Congregation in Rome; the proposal that he should himself visit Rome had already been raised and rejected: he began to fear that Persons was perhaps out of touch with the English situation. Now, beginning with this year, his letters to Persons became frequent; more frequent even than his letters to Aquaviva. Hitherto he had rarely written to him. In bewilderment Garnet continues:[2] 'But if I should understand that this is what he [Fr Persons] wants, notwithstanding the fact that Father Octavian has gone [to Rome], I shall come . . . unless your Reverence writes as quickly as possible countermanding this. All my fellow priests are opposed to my making the journey. While I have no rea on at all for esteeming myself so highly as to think that everything cannot be safe here without me, to tell you the truth, I cannot find any satisfactory vicar. However when a matter is open to doubt, obedience must have priority over my own judgment.'

This was no hollow profession of his duty. Garnet was prepared to make the journey. 'If I can use gentle persuasion with him, I will take [Fr Lister] with me. I dare not leave him behind without very great misgivings. I shall find him a suitable place in Belgium. Should this course not meet your Lordship's approval, I beg you to write back as quickly as possible, so that I may, at latest, receive your letter in Flanders. After reading it, I can, if need be, return here immediately. And in case your letter should happen to miss me, please also let one of our Fathers know your wishes; but whatever happens he must maintain the most absolute secrecy.'

In the end Garnet did not go to Rome, but he took precautions to keep his possible departure secret in the hope of getting back to England before it was known that he had left.

[1] H. G. to C. A. 11 February 1597. Stonyhurst, *Anglia* 2, 23.   [2] *Ibid.*

As he had been requested, Aquaviva wrote promptly to Garnet, who was then able to reply to Persons:[1] 'I perceive your will is that I should stay here till further orders, which now I acquit myself in. And I could not otherwise leave things here to my own contentment and others, there being none in all respect fit to be left in my room.'

The question of Garnet visiting Rome was not raised again. Aquaviva had accepted completely the construction he had put on the Roman dispute; there was no need now for a personal interview with the General.

Possibly Persons' information on the dispute was not as recent as Aquaviva's and he had judged it necessary to have Garnet in Rome. Persons had been disturbed by a sentence written by Garnet on 18 February 1597: 'Great speeches and joy are in court of the dissensions between English seminaries and the Jesuits.'[2] But this news, that had gladdened the Council, was already stale. Garnet wrote in reply to Aquaviva:[3] 'I have received with great pleasure and joy your Lordship's letter dated 7 July. I clearly perceive from it that your Lordship whom, after God, I most desire and strive to please, has both seen and approved my defence against the manifest calumnies of certain turbulent characters. Two of these men in fact have recently arrived here and have openly proclaimed the charity of our Fathers in England.'

The change of mind and heart in these men was complete. However, a little later in the year, Fisher, the principal dissident student in Rome, came to England. His object was to spread in England the dissensions he had created in Rome. His visit to Wisbech was a failure for he found that peace was temporarily reigning there. 'After travelling through different parts of the kingdom he returned eventually to London' with the Dominican friar, John Sacheverell.[4] Here he over-reached himself: his slanders were too extreme to gain credence. Garnet summarised them under four headings: it was due to the negligence of the Jesuit Rector of the English College that so many students had died; the Rector had drawn off for other purposes the revenues of the Colleges; he had admitted an hermaphrodite — a fact established in ways that Fisher did not hesitate to elaborate; and finally, he had enticed students to enter the Society.[5]

These facts were so far from the truth that they could do little injury to the reputation of the Society either in England or in Rome. But Fisher spread

---

[1] H. G. to R. P. April (no date) 1597. Stonyhurst, Grene *P.*, 595.
[2] H. G. to R. P. 18 February 1597. Stonyhurst, Grene *P.*, 548.
[3] H. G. to C. A. 11 February 1597. Stonyhurst, *Anglia* 2, 23.
[4] H. G. to C. A. 14 May 1597. Stonyhurst, *Anglia* 2, 28.
[5] *Ibid.*

also another calumny which was more difficult to refute, namely, that the Pope had determined to take the government of the College from the Society, but had been prevented by Fr Persons who had obtained the veto of the king of Spain; moreover, the incidents at the English seminary were only part of a larger pattern; the Pope had decided to take all seminaries staffed or governed by Jesuits out of their hands since they were unfit for the task of training priests; indeed in the Archdiocese of Milan alone — and here again Fisher ruined his story by exaggeration — the Pope in the previous twelve months had taken from the Jesuits no less than fifteen seminaries and Colleges.

Reflecting more quietly now that he was assured of Aquaviva's support, Garnet was inclined to minimise the trouble. 'We have worse enemies', he wrote in the same month,[1] 'than those who, being wolves, clothe themselves like sheep.' Their dubious loyalty forced him now to be secretive where before he had been open. With the search for him closing in during the spring and summer of 1597, he knew how 'dangerous it is to tell them our places of resort. But as many Catholics now know them, we can never be sure that our secrets will not be disclosed to some hypocrite or other, and thus, perchance, what we fear will come to pass. Yet God's will be done.'[2]

His personal loneliness betrays itself as he unfolds his apprehensions to the General. If he is betrayed, the guilt will be on others. 'Should it come to pass that we have to suffer for His sake and attain high honour in this way, through the treachery of others, we hope God will turn everything to our greater good, making us more like Him whom it must be our aim to resemble.'[3] Gerard's bravery, which he still constantly mentions in his letters of this year, set for him a personal example which, he confessed, he could follow only with exceptional grace: his example of fortitude, 'besides more ancient examples, is always with me'. It was the subject of his conversation at the May meeting of his brethren this year.[4] Already he began to fear that when his own time came, he would be made a scapegoat, through the machinations of his enemies. 'May the Lord grant that I should be like a stout ass ready to bear any burden for His sake: Catholics here are called "God's fools", since, to their credit, they make themselves simpletons that they may become wise.'[5]

After receiving Aquaviva's letters Garnet was less worried about mischief-makers: his only reason for mentioning them again was that Fisher, not yet ordained, had announced that he had been given a fact-finding commission in England, and for this task had been granted leave of absence from the

[1] H. G. to C. A. 7 May 1597. Stonyhurst, *Anglia* 2, 27.
[2] *Ibid.*   [3] *Ibid.*   [4] *Ibid.*   [5] *Ibid.*

English College. At the end of this mission he was expected to return to Rome and complete his interrupted studies for the priesthood.

'These reports', concluded Garnet,[1] 'though they may disturb you in Rome, seldom disturb me. It is certain that all good men think as we do. If there should be need, we can send their testimony over to you, especially that of the leading priests. But I do not want to propose this unless it should become necessary.... The life and morals of those who accuse us speak eloquently enough on our behalf. Moreover, as all notice, God, too, exercises his own judgment daily on seditious men like these. For one thing I have noted that the instigators of the tumults, when they come from Rome, be they priests or not, seem to be very acceptable to the rulers of this realm and far from odious to our persecutors.'

This was all the more significant since at the moment the persecution appeared to be directed principally against him. 'But it matters little so long as God is on our side.'

Before the end of the year Garnet was re-united with Gerard. When Gerard wrote from the Tower proposing his escape and seeking his Superior's permission to attempt it, Garnet left the decision to him: Gerard was better placed than himself to survey his chances of success. After an initial postponement, which caused Garnet acute anxiety, Gerard with a layman, John Arden, got away from the Cradle Tower by a rope slung across the moat.[2] Garnet noted that it was St Francis's day. Before escaping, Gerard had taken care to arrange also for the escape of his warder, who received an annuity from his former prisoner and ended his days as a Catholic. Wisely, Garnet posted Gerard to a part of the country where he was unknown. During the next seven years, with Garnet's backing, Gerard established new centres in the southern midlands. Starting in Northamptonshire, he moved south and west into Oxfordshire, Berkshire and Buckinghamshire; then he linked these 'churches' with those he had already 'founded' before his arrest.

[1] H. G. to C. A. 10 June 1597. Stonyhurst, *Anglia* 2, 28.
[2] For the story of Gerard's escape, see *John Gerard*, ch. 17.

25

THE ARCHPRIEST

'THERE is no great enquiry after him', wrote Garnet three days after Gerard's escape.[1] The brilliant attention to detail, the note he had left for the Lieutenant of the Tower, the plan made for the escape of his gaoler, convinced the Council that for the present it would be futile to pursue him. Garnet, still in London, was relieved. At the request of Rome he turned his mind to the appointment of a Superior for the seminary priests in England.

It was natural that Garnet's opinion both on the office and on the person to fill it should be asked by Cardinal Cajetan, Protector of England; but it was unfortunate also, since it provided colour to the charge that the man appointed was Garnet's choice, and that Cajetan took his counsel from the Jesuits. Many experienced missionaries had expressed doubts on the wisdom of appointing a priest with the equivalent jurisdiction of a bishop. Dr Bavant and Dr Tirwitt,[2] though ready, as Garnet reported, to accept Rome's decision, 'think there will be great difficulty to have a head here'. Both priests had been trained by Allen and were considered by their brethren the foremost protagonists of the Rheims tradition. Their fears were twofold: if such a man set about organising the Church, 'his place of abode will be subject to dangers and his capture might lead to the disruption of the entire Catholic organisation';[3] secondly, it was thought that the recalcitrant priests might withold their obedience from him. Was it not better to leave them without discipline than attempt to force on them a Superior they were certain to reject? This might well happen, since, as Garnet pointed out, 'no hard course can well be taken here'.[4]

[1] H. G. to R. P. 8 October 1597. Stonyhurst, Grene *P.*, 548.

[2] Dr John Bavant had been one of the first Fellows and the first professor of Greek at St John's College, Oxford, where he had tutored Edmund Campion and Gregory Martin. After ordination abroad he returned to England in 1581, and in 1598, along with Dr Tirwitt, was made an assistant to the Archpriest, George Blackwell.

[3] The treatment of Nicholas Owen, who knew the hiding places of the greater number of priests in England, shows that this fear was not idle. Owen was tortured on the rack until he died, without making any injurious revelation. Cf. *inf.*, p. 366–7.

[4] H. G. to R. P. 8 October 1597. Stonyhurst, Grene *P.*, 548.

Something more than his own anxiety to be relieved of unsought responsibility prompted Garnet to find answers to these objections. His experience of the last twelve months, though it had given him moments of dark depression, had not killed his optimism. 'I think the first [danger] will be remedied if the general body of priests do not have access to their Superior, but some few [only] when he is at home. . . . He can travel once or twice to London in a year and as oft into some one or two counties:[1] and so shall he meet all once a year.' Matters of ordinary business could be done by correspondence. This was his own practice. For eleven years now his system had worked, with his twice-yearly or more frequent visits to London and his secret lodgings in the city, revealed only to a few priests. He had been accessible to all on his visits to the shires, where he was seldom in a single house long enough for the local searchers to get wind of his presence.

In his answer to the second objection Garnet again outlined his own method. 'The second [difficulty] may be avoided by mildness of government or remedied by the fervour and zeal of many other priests scattered throughout the country who undoubtedly will be united to the head': gentleness and tact might perhaps be sufficient to win over the difficult or dissident men. His trust in the fundamental goodwill of all who elected to be priests had not been diminished by a succession of disappointments.

Garnet believed that the man selected to be Superior of the seminary priests would be consecrated a bishop. Writing from his experience in England, Garnet made one proposal: on the assumption that a priest already in England would be appointed, he considered it wiser that the man should not immediately 'go forth from the realm to be consecrated, but that after his election and confirmation, he should begin to practice his jurisdiction and have leave to confirm, and then later at his leisure go [overseas] to be consecrated when and where he will'.[2] It was an obvious measure of caution, for the pending appointment was already known to the Council, who were in touch with Fisher and other seditious priests. If the new Superior left immediately for consecration, he would be watched on the Continent and seized immediately on his return.

The appointment, in fact, came through early the following year. The choice fell on George Blackwell, a Douai priest of experience, who commanded the respect of all parties. Against Garnet's expectation, he was given the jurisdiction of bishop without consecration or the power to confirm. The Brief, dated 7 March 1598, instituting the Archpriest, as he was called, defined his authority over the seminary clergy. He was to direct them, and, when

[1] Either England and Wales, or the north and south of England.
[2] H. G. to R. P. 8 October 1597. Grene *P.*, 548.

necessary, punish them by restricting or revoking their priestly faculties; he could also fix their place of residence to the best advantage of the mission. To assist him was a council of twelve priests, six of them named by the Cardinal Protector of England, the other six by the Archpriest himself. According to his instructions he was to settle strifes and schism among the clergy, call assemblies under his own presidency and pass censures on the contumacious.

In the passage of the Brief concerning the Jesuits, tribute is paid to Garnet's achievement. Though he is not singled out by name, the reference is clear.

'Finally [writes Cardinal Cajetan, addressing all the English priests in the person of George Blackwell][1] you must realise before all else one thing on which I have already touched above: that in these matters the principal concern of his Holiness and of myself is that, as far as the times and circumstances in England permit, ecclesiastical discipline should be upheld, and especially that there should be peace and union of minds . . . between the brethren and priests, and in particular also with the Fathers of the Society of Jesus, who are labouring along with you in the same harvest field. Recently, with his own lips and in my presence his Holiness gravely and earnestly commanded this to some priests who were leaving for England. And not without reason, for these Fathers not only here in Rome and elsewhere toil hard and tirelessly for the cause of England, by founding seminaries, instructing young men, helping the needy, and by varied other means, but also in England itself they carry out the same works of charity; and this even unto the shedding of their blood, as has been shown by the facts. And since they neither have nor claim to have any jurisdiction or power over the secular clergy and do not trouble them in any way, the fact that any Catholic should be envious of them or stir up jealousy against them, seems manifestly attributable to the cunning of the enemy and deceit of the devil working to bring the entire English enterprise to naught.'

Few official pronouncements of Clement VIII had been so frankly drafted. There could be no doubt now in Garnet's mind that his aspirations had been understood correctly in Rome. The concluding sentences of the paragraph are still more emphatic:

'On the contrary they [the Jesuits] ought to be treated with the greatest love and reverence, so that with still greater affection they may favour priests and others (as hitherto they have done) with their service, benefits and most fatherly charity, so that with united mind and activity this most holy work may advance. Consequently if there be anyone who tries to

[1] Litterae Cardinalis Cajetani, quarum vigore Georgius Blackwellus constituitur Archpresbyter in Anglia, 7 March 1598. Printed in Tierney-Dodd, vol. 3, cxix–cxxiii.

SERO SED SERIO

ROBERT CECIL, FIRST EARL OF SALISBURY
A portrait at Hatfield House

ÆTATIS SVÆ. 41
AN D 1593

PRVDENS QVI PATIENS

LORD CHIEF JUSTICE COKE.
CORNELIUS JANSENS PINXIT.

SIR EDWARD COKE, *Aet.* 41
Attributed to Cornelius Jansen
Copyright *Country Life*

undermine this harmony, you [George Blackwell] must, in accordance with the words of the Apostle and the intentions of the Holy See, take note of him in order that he may be admonished or corrected or made to undergo a penalty.'

Garnet's personal relief at the appointment is seen in all his letters of the next twelve months. At last there was a priest with authority over the clergy in England. The Brief left certain questions undefined. Garnet was quick to note them. In the present situation it was imperative that there should be no possibility of questioning the Archpriest's jurisdiction. In a letter to Persons, written about this time, Garnet observed:[1] 'I expect also to know what faculties he shall have given him from the [Cardinal] Protector for himself, what he may communicate to his Consultors, what to others.' Only one thing further Garnet urged: 'I pray you let him have free scope.' He pointed out that Blackwell's jurisdiction should be extended also to the old priests from Mary's reign, for an oversight in the Brief left these men unnoticed. Their position was at least uncertain. The Brief 'sometimes seemeth to include old priests, sometimes to exclude them'. Later Garnet returned to the same point. 'Over old priests it will be necessary that he have jurisdiction; and then he must have a new patent; and yet I doubt not but he will be wary in proceeding with them. But authority is necessary, lest the factious make them their instruments.'[2]

Without reservations Garnet was able to report: '[The Archpriest] doth very well and is generally liked.'[3] The announcement of Blackwell's appointment had met almost universal approval: only a few grumbled against it.[4]

Again Garnet was over-optimistic. It was his own self-depreciation that led him to believe that Blackwell would command the same respect of all as he himself had done. But the ecclesiastical troubles were far from settled by the

[1] H. G. to R. P. 10 June 1598. Stonyhurst, *Anglia* 2, 37.

[2] *Ibid.*

[3] *Ibid.*

[4] Note of letter of H. G. 27 May 1598. Stonyhurst, Grene *P.*, 552. In what is a biography of Garnet I have sought principally to set out Garnet's view. Underlying the appellant controversy that followed the appointment of Blackwell lay the historic antagonism between seculars and regulars that can be seen also in Chaucer and throughout the Middle Ages. Only men of great virtue on either side could avoid partisanship. In the England of Elizabeth the strife was made more acute by the fear of the domination of the Jesuits, then a new and unknown Order, highly organised, backed by the Papacy and with a glamour that attracted to it some of the best men from the seculars. While Garnet was aware of this and did his utmost to allay the understandable fears of the seminary priests, only time could eradicate the suspicion of many good men that the Jesuits were anxious to control the Church in England. This was Garnet's dilemma and it was his genius to come so near to solving it.

R

Brief. True, Blackwell had been well received and by all except those who, as
Garnet observed, had their personal ambition frustrated by the appointment.
Only abroad were lies disseminated on a large scale: at home there was wide-
spread peace, friendship and charity.[1]

For the time, at least, Garnet was relieved. Greater happiness is manifest
in his letters of the spring this year. The strain of the incessant search for him
had taxed his nerves; now that the Archpriest was appointed, he believed that
he would become less harried. The search, however, was intensified.

About this time Garnet took over again a large house, some twelve miles
to the west of London off the road to Oxford.[2] It was the property of his
Northamptonshire friend, Robert Catesby. It was sufficiently near the city to
provide a convenient refuge for incoming priests, yet remote enough to
escape organised searches that were confined to the capital. It was here that
Gerard fled on escaping from the Tower. Oswald Tesimond, a Jesuit
priest newly arrived from the Continent, with his companion, Ralph Ashley,
describes his visit to Garnet there in March 1598.

'It was about twelve or thirteen miles from London', writes Tesimond,[3]
'near a village called Uxbridge and the name of the house was Morecrofts.
I and my companion walked thither and arrived there about an hour or two
before sunset. We were received with the warmest welcome and the greatest
charity imaginable. I found with Father Henry two or three other Fathers of
the Society who had come to confer with him on their affairs.'

Two or three days after Tesimond arrived, an alarm was raised. 'We had
been with Father Henry', continues Tesimond, 'two or three days at most,
when one day towards evening a man came out from London on purpose to
tell us that the Privy Council had had notice of that house and that without
doubt the Queen's officers would come to search it that very night.'

The lines that follow give a most intimate sketch of Garnet, the wise and
imperturbable veteran. They also register an impression of the qualities that
won him the admiration and affection of his fellow-priests and gained for
him an unsought supremacy among his contemporaries.

'It was a perfect marvel, and as such I noted it at the time [he writes][4] to
see the great peace and serenity of soul that Father Henry showed when he
heard the news. In truth he proved himself to be an old soldier and experi-

---

[1] H. G. to C. A. 8 May 1598. Stonyhurst, *Anglia* 2, 35.

[2] Earlier, in 1594, he used this house, then abandoned it when he had reason to
think that it had become known to the government.

[3] 'Father Tesimond's Landing in England', printed in John Morris, *Troubles*, Series
1, 177 sq.

[4] *Ibid.*

enced captain, accustomed to such assaults. Without being the least disturbed, he spoke to all with his usual modest cheerfulness, bidding them recommend to our Lord the necessities of that house, and, after taking some corporal refreshment to enable them to walk during the night, get themselves ready as best they could to go one in one direction and one in another, following either the directions that he gave, or that they knew how to take. There were some, on the other hand, who showed great signs of fear, bringing all sorts of reasons to show how impossible it was to escape so urgent and manifest a danger. Good Father Henry, whom I afterwards saw perfectly calm as he was now on some ten other occasions in dangers greater than this, consoled and strengthened them all by a few grave words.'

Whenever Garnet took command he contented himself with a general instruction that allowed freedom for individual enterprise and responsibility.

'He [Fr Garnet] gave orders to hide in the hiding-places which had long since been prepared for such an occurrence, everything that could show that the house belonged to Catholics: as books, altar vestments, pictures and everything of the sort; and then he stowed away all things of greater value. Lastly, when it was dark, he sent away those that were guests or strangers, that they might return to their usual dwelling places. Amongst these was I, the newcomer, whom he directed until he otherwise disposed of me, to go towards London, with directions that some of us should wait for him at a village called Brentford, about half-way between the house we were leaving and London. His object was that we should go to another house he had in London, which he kept on purpose to be able to retire to it in similar emergencies.'

At this time Garnet had also his house near the Hospital at Spitalfields. It was chosen perhaps because in the hours of the nights he lived alone there, he was able to carry out his apostolate among the dying schismatics of the city: men and women who were prepared to return to the Church only in their last hours. It was to this house, managed by the Vaux sisters, that he directed Tesimond and his companion, Ralph Ashley. It 'served us for some time', says Tesimond,[1] 'without being discovered or known by the heretics. It was a wonderful thing how our Lord constantly set his servants free from the hands of their enemies, just when they made the greatest efforts, and in their opinion were most sure of taking them.'

In the spring and early summer of this year Garnet divided his time between Spitalfields, Uxbridge and Hinlip. While to all outward appearance he remained calm, inwardly he feared more than ever for his arrest.

The house at Uxbridge was probably given up about this time: possibly

[1] *Ibid.*

the evening the messenger came from London was the last that Garnet spent there: he makes no further reference to it. Tesimond gives a picture of Garnet's own last journey from the place. A rendezvous had been fixed at Brentford that night, for London may well have been too distant or dangerous. 'The most of us', relates Tesimond,[1] 'arrived at . . . Brentford, where we waited a good while for Father Henry, not without fear lest he should have met the Queen's officers on the road, for we hoped to have found that he had arrived there long before us, as he was on horseback. However, he and his guide, trying to avoid the high-road, lost their way; and so our joy was all the greater when we saw him arrive at last safe and sound.'

Here also at Uxbridge Garnet had given a home to Fr Persons' mother, to whom he refers always by the code name of 'the old woman'. In a letter of this time he gives the exact date of the search. 'The next day after I last wrote [4 March]', he tells Persons,[2] 'I and all my family were forced to leave all and at midnight to run to London, leaving only the old woman and a maid to look to her.'

The pursuit continued. Missed at Morecrofts, Garnet was hunted into the west country. There was a search at Hinlip for him in the first week of April. For three days the house was invested by pursuivants who beat down walls 'at pleasure' and consumed all the provisions. 'We are constrained to shift often [our] dwelling and to have divers houses at once, and also to keep divers houses at those times when we run away.'[3]

Even at these crises Garnet was never without four or five priests with whom he shared his house, some of them, as he himself admits, often driven to him by fear.[4] He was hunted now, not so much for his life, but as a pawn in the game that the government was playing with the help of the recalcitrant priests. As he wrote himself, there was no priest or layman captured at this time who was not 'asked for Henry, and yet he escapeth, not by any worldly policy but because he is unfit for the combat'. He joked about his importance to the government, recalling his days in Rome, when his natural shyness concealed his calibre, for at the Roman College, amongst the most distinguished company in Europe, he was known as the 'poor sheep'. Now he considered himself 'as much a *pecorella* as ever he was, and so I pray you to tell Benedictus Pereirus,[5] who, as Henry understandeth, should say on a

[1] *Ibid.*

[2] H. G. to R. P. 18 March 1598. Stonyhurst, Grene *P.*, 597.

[3] H. G. to R. P. 9 April 1598. Stonyhurst, Grene *P.*, 551.

[4] *Ibid.*

[5] Benedict Pereira (1535–1616), a Spanish Jesuit, who taught Scripture at the Roman College at the time Garnet was a student and then professor there. He wrote many commentaries on Scripture, notably on Genesis, Daniel and St John.

time, "Io mi meraviglio come quella pecorella ha scapato tanto."[1] I remember him and my other friends oft to my comfort. I sent to Alphonso Agazzari Father Southwell's Breviary that he used in the Tower, but it is taken: he must accept my good will.'[2]

Although there was perhaps no year in which he was more harassed, yet in achievement it was his happiest in England. Hitherto no Englishman, not even Campion or Southwell, had made his final vows as a Jesuit. The year 1598 was marked both by his own and by Weston's profession. For the occasion he chose the feast of St Michael, 8 May, and on the same day Fr William Weston made his profession in prison at Wisbech.

This was their due. But it was also a gesture of the confidence placed in them by the General. Both priests had been the centre of controversy; they had been calumniated, misreported and misrepresented by enemies at home and at Rome. This assurance that they were both highly esteemed by those whose esteem they most valued made the occasion particularly poignant.

Twelve years earlier, on the feast of St Michael, 1586, Garnet had set out from Rome with Robert Southwell. 'The holy angels', he writes, recalling the occasion,[3] 'have not been wanting in my defence, as I trust, for the greater glory of God; for starting from Rome on the feast of St Michael in May, I chose that blessed spirit, with all his comrades, for the special patron of this my mission. Having spent nine years here I began to doubt whether my guardians intended to protect me any longer, for it seemed impossible that I should remain unharmed. However, I am now close to the end of my twelfth year, and having had notice for several weeks to prepare myself for my profession, I was finally instructed by our Reverend Father [General] to make it as soon as possible, and did so accordingly on St Michael's day itself, as if he himself had arranged it.'

The same day, 8 May, Garnet wrote a personal letter of thanks to Aquaviva: the only letter in his long correspondence which he signs with his full name in its Latin form — Henricus Garnettus.[4] It is the most affectionate of all his letters; it touches on no business. He dated it from his 'suburban house', probably Spitalfields, knowing that Aquaviva would at once picture him in his place of hiding. Shyness had prevented his writing sooner, but the emotion of the occasion overcame his inhibition. He had many other reasons for writing, several of them now long standing. Never before had he

---

[1] It is a marvel to me how a sheep like this has escaped so much.
[2] H. G. to R. P. 9 April 1598. Stonyhurst, Grene *P.*, 551. Fr Agazzari was Rector of the English College when Southwell was on the staff there.
[3] H. G. to person unknown (Rome). May or June 1598. Stonyhurst, Grene *P.*, 552.
[4] H. G. to C. A. 8 May 1598. Stonyhurst, *Anglia* 2, 35.

adequately expressed his thanks to Aquaviva: he owed everything to his ineffable generosity. Such a letter as he was now writing had been overdue. Aquaviva had been his personal friend, his protector, a most understanding Superior over him, the director of a dear but comparatively unimportant mission of the Society; for all his own subjects he has shewn a personal love, and for himself a 'more than fatherly indulgence'. The greatest of Aquaviva's many acts of kindness has been his support during the troubles at the English College; and a particular instance of it, his change of mind, at Garnet's insistence, when he had already determined to remove the Society from the government of the seminary. Now, on the most memorable day since he landed, Garnet expressed his gratitude to Aquaviva for his patience in enduring the misrepresentations of the Society there and in England: he had shown his true greatness and nobility of heart in forgiving all who had caused him such pain. It was an action, as Garnet described it, 'worthy of the splendour of his family' and in keeping with the fine work he had done for the entire Church of Christ.

The most touching part of the letter is the statement of his personal attachment to Aquaviva. From his own Roman days Aquaviva's friendship had meant much in his life: since then it had been strengthened beyond measure by his unwavering support, particularly by this last act of confidence — his calling him to be the first professed Jesuit in England. Instead of the formalised sentiments that a priest customarily expressed on such an occasion, Garnet recalled his personal ties with the General and his friendship with his two young nephews, Antonio and Bonifacio, who had attended his classes in Rome. Their intelligence, charm, talent, gaiety, goodness and handsome appearance has endeared them to him and created a private bond between him and their uncle. In conclusion Garnet prayed that Aquaviva might be recompensed for the solicitude he had always shown him and be kept safe many years for the benefit of the universal Church.

Twelve years of work and negotiation had left Garnet's zeal unspoiled All his enthusiasm was rekindled whenever he wrote to Aquaviva. Still there was no place where he could live and for a moment consider himself safe from pursuivants. All this time he kept himself in a state of readiness, both moral and spiritual, for martyrdom: any moment, he told Aquaviva, the trumpet for battle might sound, and the signal for joining the issue be given; 'unless a man is prepared, he stands no chance of victory'.[1]

[1] H. G. to C. A. 8 May 1598. Stonyhurst, *Anglia* 2, 35.

26

EQUIVOCATION

THE autumn meeting of the Jesuits is recorded this year in a unique document: a joint letter to Clement VIII, welcoming with loyalty the appointment of the Archpriest in England. It is dated 30 October 1598.[1] The list of signatories, headed by Garnet, makes it difficult to see how such a small and mixed body stirred such jealousy among any section of the clergy. There are twenty names in all, representing the total strength of the Society in England. Four of these twenty, William Weston, Ralph Bickley, Thomas Pound and Ralph Emerson were in prison: Weston, now a maligned and broken man, and Emerson, his faithful and unworldly servant, might now be left out of public reckoning.

Of the sixteen at liberty few, apart from Garnet, had yet made their mark. Only Richard Holtby, still the principal priest in the north, Edward Oldcorne, still centred on Hinlip, and John Gerard, now lying very secretly in Northamptonshire, could be considered veterans. The rest were newly-joined young men of much promise but little achievement: for instance Richard Blount, later the first and perhaps the greatest Provincial in England, and Edward Walpole, a cousin of Henry. The other names, Oswald Tesimond's excepted, matter little. There is Thomas Lister, back once more in England, Robert Jones, a native of Oswestry, whose work lay mostly in Wales;[2] John Bennet, a devoted priest whose apostolate, based on Holywell, did much to keep North Wales Catholic; Thomas Stanney, John Persons, Richard Cowling, Joseph Pollen and Richard Banks; all honest 'merchants', as Garnet would have described them: none had the stature of Southwell, Walpole or Weston.

These were Garnet's men in England. In the next few years he shaped them to his ideals; ahead were years of glorious expansion.

[1] Vatican Archives, *Fondo Borghese*, Serie 2, 448 A, B, f. 415, 416.
[2] For a short period after Garnet's death, first Walpole and then Jones acted as Superior of the mission. To Jones we owe much of our information about the Welsh Church at this time.

'Hitherto I have never presumed to write personally to your Holiness from England', began Garnet's letter to Clement VIII, 'partly from the respect we have for your very great majesty, partly from the belief that all, or at least the principal things done here by the help of divine grace and the support of your Holiness are known to you through the accounts given by our Father General and the Rector of the English College, and through the letters of others written from here to your Holiness and to the Cardinal Protector.' Garnet then felicitates the Pope on bringing to an end, through the appointment of the Archpriest, 'the disturbances caused by certain of our countrymen in Rome and Flanders'. This was the occasion of the letter, which essentially was a protestation of loyalty by the whole body of English Jesuits.

'There are only two assertions [Garnet continues] we should like to make. Firstly, the appointment itself has given very great satisfaction to Catholics in general and the man chosen for the office [namely, George Blackwell] is the most worthy man to be entrusted with such jurisdiction, since he is unquestionably regarded as the most eminent of all the priests living here, both in learning and holiness, and also in seniority and prestige.[1] Secondly, those few priests of somewhat unquiet disposition who oppose the Archpriest and his authority, established by your Holiness through the illustrious Cardinal Protector (two of them are actually reported to have set out for Rome) seem to be moved by no other purpose than a desire for faction and contention. As a remedy, we think it will be enough if your Holiness, in your great prudence and piety, were to pass your own judgment on them. If further testimony be needed, we have no doubt but that your Holiness can obtain it in abundance, together with opinions on the kind of remedy to be applied, from letters of prominent Catholics sent to the illustrious Cardinal Protector from here, Belgium and elsewhere. The remedy indeed seems to consist in two things: first, that the Archpriest's authority should be confirmed and extended as soon as possible by your Holiness; second, that those two priests who, after first trying to win support here, went to Rome, should be treated with some severity by your Holiness or should be prevented from returning unless they change their temper of mind. But we leave this to be determined by the singular wisdom of your Holiness.'

The letter was a private document, designed perhaps to forestall the slanders of the two priests who had set out for Rome. For this reason it bore the signatures of all the Jesuits in England. It expressed Garnet's personal contentment and indicated means by which English Catholics might enjoy

[1] George Blackwell was exactly ten years older than Garnet. He had been a Fellow of Trinity College, Oxford, then gone in 1574 to Douai, where he became a Bachelor of Divinity before returning to England as a priest in 1576.

the benefits of domestic peace. Instinctively he knew that as the reign drew nearer its close, a fresh wave of persecution would break on them. To withstand it, it was most urgent that the Catholic body should be united.

All this time Garnet strove to win over, as he had so often done, his bitterest critics. Among them was a priest-friend of Campion — indeed he was tried with him but reprieved and exiled — John Colleton, from Milverton in Somerset, an Oxford scholar and convert. He had tried his vocation as a Jesuit, but failed by reason of his ill-health and melancholic temperament. Through the establishment of a technical *alibi* in the Flanders Plot alleged against Campion at his trial — a blunder in the Queen's evidence — he was not condemned with his companion priests. On his return from exile he became embittered. He viewed the appointment of the Archpriest as a device of Fr Persons, and was prepared to 'prove' that his imposition on the secular clergy was a stratagem of the Jesuits. Vehemently he protested that the step was taken without consulting the greater part of the seminary priests in England, who, he claimed, were opposed to it.

This argument was rendered unconvincing by assertions made to support it, namely, that the Cardinal Protector's right to establish such a system of government for a national Church was questionable; that Clement VIII's opinion had not been sought; that appeal to the Holy See had been prohibited until the office of the Archpriest was confirmed; and that the same liberty in the event of maladministration was not safeguarded.

Ten days after writing to the Pope, Garnet attempted to win Colleton to the Archpriest. His letter to him, dated 9 November 1598,[1] opens with a paragraph in which for the first time he touches the eloquence of his companion Southwell: 'If you be sinisterly talked of', he tells Colleton, 'for wronging our Society, blame not him, I beseech you, who for all your strangeness ceaseth not to love you and whom for your hurtful proceedings love enforceth to pity you.'

Garnet was both frank and friendly. Now that the Jesuits had been 'purged from the malicious slanders of some impudent libellers', he desired only that 'all things should as much as possible be forgotten: and if all could not be induced to love and affect us, [they should] bear their aversion with patience and silence'.

It was always Garnet's contention that the appointment of the Archpriest had been received 'with singular liking of the most and best [priests]'.[2] This he reiterated to Colleton as he faced the issue between them. There were certain priests, he told him, who had refused to acknowledge Blackwell, much

[1] H. G. to John Colleton. 9 November 1598. Stonyhurst, *Anglia* 2, 43.
[2] *Ibid.*

less to obey him. Their 'pretences are in everyone's mouth who had heard
of his authority. It is a thing devised by the Jesuits. The Superior is one of
their own choosing: why should the Jesuits appoint us a Superior more than
we a General unto them. It is the fine head of Father Persons that hath invented this. He hath given wrong information to the cardinal and to his
Holiness. The Cardinal was always partial on the Jesuit's side.'

In their belief that the appointment was the result of intrigue, Colleton
and others did not consider it binding until their appeal against it had been
heard in Rome. 'Some of necessity must be sent [there] to inform better.'
That was their contention and it led to the strife, known as the Appellant
Controversy, that was to bring the Church in England near to the verge of
internal collapse. At the start the Appellants aimed secretly at the removal of
Jesuits from all the seminaries abroad and also at their expulsion from England. These aims were openly avowed. Garnet, again careful not to exagger-
ate the facts, did not hesitate to confront Colleton and his colleagues with
them; he charged these priests with setting themselves against the Society 'as
if no other authority were to be liked but that which may beat down the
Jesuits or set them and other reverend Priests together by the ears'.[1]

Yet Garnet was anxious to leave an opening for reconciliation. He went as
far as the truth permitted, when he said that he was persuaded that most of
these accusations could never have proceeded from Colleton's mouth.
Nevertheless it was inevitable that those who kept discontented company
should be reproached with the attitude of their companions, 'it being impossible that all men should distinguish and apply every particular to the
true authors'. As for Garnet's personal loyalty it was pledged to Blackwell:
all who opposed the Archpriest were in opposition also to the Society.

This was Garnet's simple, perhaps naive, effort to quash the controversy
in its infancy. He judged that Colleton was a priest with influence strong
enough to win over the malcontents, and his final appeal to him is noble and
disarming. With fervour, almost in desperation, he insists that the Archpriest 'is the only means to join us together in perfect love and union, which
we had long since enjoyed if his authority had been admitted; [just] as at
present there is no hindrance at all of unity but the refusing of the same'.
Then he cites St Paul's teaching that the body and its members, if they are to
grow, must be subject to the head. 'With the head therefore must I hold . . . to
him must I be united, to him must I cleave . . . and unfeignedly I affirm unto
you that I continually pray in particular for your union unto him [the
Archpriest] in respect of the love I have borne and bear unto you, which
shall not decay.' His conclusion is in keeping with the rest of the letter: 'Thus

[1] H. G. to John Colleton. 9 November 1598. Stonyhurst, *Anglia* 2, 43.

wishing you that which is most to the glory of God and your own soul's
health I cease, your plain friend as you wish, Henry, 9 November 1598.'

The most brazen of Garnet's opponents was a priest named Robert
Benson. Earlier in the year 1598[1] Garnet had pleaded that Benson, then in the
Clink prison, might, after his good behaviour had been tested, be given back
his priestly faculties which had been taken from him by the Archpriest. It was
characteristic of Garnet's manner of proceeding. By kindness he hoped that
he would induce repentance; indeed, Benson had sought his intervention;
'Benson craved my help by Mr Tichburn in the Clink to obtain his faculties
to be restored.'[2] Benson, in fact was reinstated. However, just over a month
later, his conduct proved Garnet's expectations unfounded. In a letter to
Rome that came into Garnet's hands, Benson gave out the most fantastic
reports against the Jesuits. Without concern for the truth, Benson had acted
on the assumption that if he persisted in his slanders, at least some of them
would be given credence. Amongst other charges[3] 'all but proved to demonstration', he contended that the Jesuits in Rome 'had procured the death of
three illustrious persons, of Allen and Toledo, Cardinals of the Holy Roman
Church, and of [Dr Hugh Owen], the most Reverend Bishop of Cassano'. By
saying that this was not absolutely demonstrable, he gave a semblance of
sincerity to his statements. When Benson's assertions came to the Archpriest's
notice he was twice severely reprimanded by letter. 'To the first [letter]',
Garnet observes, 'no answer was sent that touched the points in debate; to the
second nothing of any sort except that by word of mouth he [Benson]
abundantly vented his malice and contumacy in the presence of the Reverend
Mr Tichborne, a fellow-prisoner, of whom the Archpriest had availed
himself for Benson's correction.'[4]

On the evidence of Benson's letter, Garnet for the first time in his career
advised a severe course. Gentleness had always won him the day: now his
patience was at an end. His personal agony is revealed in the simple statement
that, before sending this letter, he had sought the advice of Blackwell and
was writing by his counsel and in his name. The course he recommended was
the only course that could save the institution of the Archpriest and unity
among the clergy. The Pope had already asked the Nuncio in Flanders to
adjudicate the case. Garnet, forwarding this evidence of mischief-making to
Rome, concludes: 'Perhaps it would be worth while showing these words of

[1] H. G. to R. P. 10 June 1598. Stonyhurst, *Anglia* 2, 37.
[2] H. G. to R. P. 31 March 1598. Stonyhurst, Grene *P.*, 551.
[3] Garnet's postscript to a letter of Fr Thomas Tichborne to the Archpriest Blackwell,
13 July 1598. Printed in *C.R.S.*, vol. 5, 344.
[4] *Ibid.*

Mr. Tichbourne [the letter to which Garnet's was a postscript] to his Lordship in order that he, . . . in the care he takes for the authority of the Apostolic See and the Cardinal Protector, may decide and inform the Archpriest
what should be done in this case and whether it is not expedient, when one
finds a man so clearly convicted of so many crimes, to make an example of
him and thereby warn those who favour or follow him.'[1]

While the difficulties over the English College and later over the appointment of the Archpriest preoccupied Garnet, his letters have only incidental
information on the situation of the persecuted Catholics. As his hopes for a
settlement revived, he wrote again more fully about the sufferings and martyrdom of both laymen and priests. Travelling through the shires, he heard
stories of heroism in prison, before the Queen's Bench and on the scaffold.
Bringing comfort to the oppressed was the apostolate he loved best: the
responsibility, which he bore with unflagging courage, was as unwelcome as
it was unsought. Writing in October, he has an unusual story to tell of the
Franciscan priest, John Jones, who was executed at St Thomas Waterings in
Southwark in the previous July. Jones was kept waiting an hour while the
hangman went to fetch the rope which he had forgotten. A friend of Garnet's,
Christopher Blackall, a young law student from the Temple, 'unknown to be
a Catholic to his best acquaintances'[2] while walking in Lambeth fields on a
'moonshine night' took down from a pike one of Fr Jones's quarters. Blackall,
overtaken by hue and cry for robbery, appeared the following day before
the Lord Chief Justice, Popham, accused of removing a traitor's quarter.
Garnet records the exchange in court, where perhaps he was present himself.
'[Blackall] said he knew not that [Jones] was a traitor. "What! was he not
hanged and quartered?" "Yes, for I was by and saw it." "Is he not then a
traitor?" "No, for I heard your Lordship say that you condemned him not
for any treason committed, but because he was a priest; and priesthood alone
is no treason; and therefore I, knowing him in prison and hearing no evil of
him, but loving him, was loth the crows should eat him".' When the Chief
Justice threatened to torture Blackall, the young student replied that he had
'forecast all difficulties'. He was taken to prison, prepared to live off the
common purse should his friends fail to support him. Like Fr Eustace White
Blackall was maintained in prison on Garnet's fund raised from his friends.

Garnet took particular satisfaction in telling Aquaviva the full story of
Jones's martyrdom.[3] Jones had been an intimate friend of the Jesuits; and
Garnet had derived much comfort from his personal loyalty to him when he

---

[1] Garnet's postscript, op. cit.
[2] H. G. to C. A. 21 October 1598. Stonyhurst, Grene *P.*, 545.
[3] H. G. to C. A. 15 July 1598. Stonyhurst, *Anglia* 2, 40.

was most bitterly slandered. Typically Garnet had sought to establish ties with Jones's brethren, for, as he said, he himself was devoted to the whole Order founded by that 'truly seraphic Father St Francis';[1] moreover he had known him first from occasional visits to the Convent of St Cecilia in Rome where Fr Jones had once lived. Three years of work side by side with Garnet, and two years in prison with Gerard, had bound together the new and old Religious Orders. This Garnet interpreted as an augury for the future. Moreover, Jones, like Southwell, had been Topcliffe's special victim, and had gone to his death with a happy countenance. Possibly Garnet was present at his execution, for here as nowhere in his account of a martyr's death he gives details of the disposal of the quarters. The letter ends with a prayer that God might give them all a share in the merits of this most happy Friar.

As the autumn advanced, the search for Garnet intensified. This he had foreseen. While simple, even naive, in his dealings with people, Garnet was uncanny in his prediction of impending storms. Unerringly, with the instinct of a hunted animal, he knew the moment and place of danger, both for himself and others. As early as March this year he had began to fear for Gerard. Taking his own counsel, he resolved to send him abroad. Yet he was open to persuasion: he put his dilemma to Persons.[2] 'John Gerard is much dismayed this day when I wrote to him to prepare himself to go [abroad]. He came to me of purpose. Indeed he is very profitable to me and his going would be wondered at. I hope he will walk warily. You know my mind, if you think it good to desire his stay. All the rest are well.'

In the end Gerard stayed. Henceforth, apart from once in the following year, he walked warily. All the same, Garnet's fears of an intensified persecution — there were few signs of it this year — proved correct. In December he wrote almost in alarm: 'I am uncertain whether ever I shall write to you again, the persecution is so hot and but beginning.'[3]

This *cri de coeur* was made to Persons. During his personal troubles his affection for the maligned Jesuit had deepened. It is not merely that he was casting about for understanding and trust; Persons had proved himself a true friend.

Still Garnet's thoughts went back to Southwell. This year he wrote what he calls *A Treatise of Equivocation* 'to defend Father Southwell's assertion, which was much wondered at by Catholicks and heretics'. At his trial and at the examinations preceding it, Southwell had been charged with 'most wicked and horrible doctrine'. Anne Bellamy, who had betrayed him, had started the

[1] *Ibid.*
[2] H. G. to R. P. 31 March 1598. Stonyhurst, Grene *P.*, 551.
[3] H. G. to R. P. 23 December 1598. Stonyhurst, Grene *P.*, 552.

mischief; she gave out that Southwell had instructed her that, should she be asked whether there was a priest in the house, she was entitled to swear, No. Sir Edward Coke, the Attorney-General, had used this report to bring discredit on the Jesuits. The conflict lay between the claims of charity and the claims of truth. From the Fathers and Doctors of the Church, Southwell had demonstrated that in special circumstances it was possible to deny a known fact when it was understood by the questioner that the truth was being withheld. Some such teaching was necessary to protect not only the secrecy of the confessional but all State secrets as well. He presented Coke with an *argumentum ad hominem* which the Attorney found difficult to rebut. 'Suppose that the French king should invade Her Majesty's dominions and that she (which God prevent) should by her enemies be enforced to fly to some private house for her safety, where none knew her [to be] but Mr Attorney; and that Mr Attorney's refusal to swear [she was not there] being hereunto urged, should be a confession of her being in the house — I say Mr Attorney were neither her Majesty's good subject nor friend.'[1]

This campaign to discredit the current Catholic teaching coincides, though it was unconnected, with the slanders of the faction led by Colleton. Every priest now up for trial was confronted with the doctrine. As likely as not, it was Gerard's report of his own shifts to defend Southwell's argument that finally decided Garnet to write a treatise to champion him. It was a task moreover that he owed to the reputation of his companion whom many, he declared, 'would be glad with their calumniations to fetch out of heaven'.[2]

Indeed, he dedicated the work to him who, as he explains, had written a 'particular instruction on this matter', intended, not as a defence of the doctrine, but as a guide to the conscience of Catholics. But at the time of writing he could find no copy of Southwell's book. 'As for this my small travail', Garnet concluded his preface, 'I think it well bestowed if I may dedicate it unto no other than unto himself [Southwell], and unto himself I doubt not that I may humbly offer it as a token of my ancient affection and present dutiful reverence and honour towards him'[3] Garnet's only regret was that Southwell 'had not had the handling of the matter'. But he was confident that the time would come when Southwell would, 'together with all the saints of God, *stare in magna constantia adversus eos qui se augustiaverunt*'; and at that time Garnet prayed he might 'abide his looks, and find him a more favourable advocate than he has found others here, that we may together at

---

[1] Pierre Janelle, *Robert Southwell, the Writer* (1935), 82–3.
[2] *A Treatise of Equivocation*, edited by David Jardine (1851), 46.
[3] *Ibid.*, 3.

the length meet in the perfect unity of the knowledge and sight of God, and be consummated in Christ our Saviour'.[1]

Although written in this year, the treatise was never printed; at least, there is no extant printed copy.[2] The Roman manuscript carries on the fly-leaf in Garnet's handwriting the title *A Treatise against Lying and Fraudulent Dissimulation, Newly overseen by the Author and published in defence of Innocency.* Garnet's approach to the subject is indicated by his choice of title: he was not writing so much a defence of equivocation, but an advocacy of truth. The 'innocency' he set out to defend was the innocency of South-well. As the threat of a new Spanish invasion became remote, the 'bloody ques-tion' had receded in importance. The Council was determined now to bring opprobrium on the Jesuits and thus widen the breach in the Catholic body by presenting their teaching as perversive of an ordered Commonwealth. The campaign reached its height in the years following Garnet's own execu-tion.

From the first announcement of Blackwell's appointment, Garnet had devoted all his influence to gaining support for the Archpriest. From fear that he might give colour to the accusation that the head of the clergy in England was the agent of the Jesuits, he seldom visited him. Nevertheless he continued to plead in Rome that Blackwell's hand should be strengthened. 'I send you a copy of Mr. Blackwell's letter [to me]. I hope you resolve on him for Bishop.'[3] All the funds he had collected for prisoners and impoverished Catholics were handed to the Archpriest to administer. By agreement with him, however, Garnet maintained his services to incoming priests. In this way he could continue to express his goodwill to all working for the same cause: in recent years it had proved an important means of resolving misunderstand-ings that students, particularly from Rome, might have entertained on entering England. 'We make no public collections', he wrote to Persons,[4] '. . . yet when anything is offered us, which we might well keep for our-selves, we apply it especially to priests first coming in; wherein they best know what we have done.'

For the first time since his arrival in England, Garnet this year makes a

---

[1] *Ibid.*

[2] Two manuscript copies survive: one at the English College, Rome, the other at the Bodleian Library, Oxford. The former is the copy sent out of England to Fr Persons in 1607; the latter, with marginal annotations in Garnet's hand, was used by Coke at Garnet's trial. See A. F. Allison, *The Writings of Father Henry Garnet, S.J., 1555-1606* in *Biographical Studies*, vol. 1, no. 1 (1951), 14-15. There are certain differences in the two texts. Jardine's printed text (1851) is taken from the Bodleian copy.

[3] H. G. to R. P. 31 March 1598. Stonyhurst, Grene *P.*, 551.

[4] H. G. to R. P. 18 March 1598. Stonyhurst, Grene *P.*, 597.

reference to his own health. 'All are well', or 'the rest are well', are phrases that occur regularly in his letters to Aquaviva and to Persons. Now, he refers to an ague: but only after he has recovered from it. 'I wrote to you last week in another hand,' he tells Persons,[1] 'having had an ague and been let blood: now I am well.' His health remained sound: in his last years of liberty he again mentions his health only on two or three occasions, and, once more, after his arrest, following days of confinement in a narrow hiding-place.

[1] H. G. to R. P. 10 June 1598. Stonyhurst, *Anglia* 2, 37.

27

JOHN LILLIE'S DEVICE

WITH persistence Garnet sought from Aquaviva permission, reserved normally to the General, to accept as lay brothers of the Society the craftsmen and skilled workers who hitherto had followed him as servants. His work of organisation had largely depended on a small group of devoted men of this class, tested in loyalty and dedicated to the tasks he assigned them. Ralph Emerson, Campion's companion, who had landed a second time in England with Weston, was the only Jesuit brother in England. Now Garnet asked to receive others into full membership of the Society. The service they had already rendered was proof enough of their loyalty. Constantly he told Aquaviva stories of their fidelity and saintliness: 'I am employing certain people', he wrote in November 1599,[1] 'who wish to be coadjutors [i.e. Brothers]. All are of the highest reputation and they help me as much as if they already had been admitted among us. . . . They serve us excellently in the hope that before they die they will be at least Coadjutors.'

Garnet then lists some of the men he has in mind. 'I keep one joiner for making secret places in which to hide our money and other things of importance; another for doing business of trade and transport; a third for domestic jobs.' Clearly he was referring to Nicholas Owen, Hugh Sheldon and, probably, Ralph Ashley. 'But in addition to all these we have one special man [John Lillie], a person of great courage, humility and devotion'. Apart from attending to all Garnet's most confidential business during his absences from London, he had organised the escape of John Gerard from the Tower. When his first attempt to rescue Gerard had been interrupted by an unforeseen intrusion,[2] Gerard had expected that the plan would be cancelled. Instead he had received from Lillie a letter which began: 'It was not God's design that we should succeed last night, but He mercifully snatched us from our peril — He has only postponed the day. With God's help we will be back to-night.'[3]

[1] H. G. to C. A. 7 November 1599. F.G. 651, f. 88.
[2] *John Gerard*, 132–3.
[3] *Ibid.*

He was as good as his word: he rescued Gerard and continued to serve him with selfless attachment. Lillie was typical of the rest.

Already Garnet had been given a limited faculty to receive into the Society all priests 'on their way ... to Tyburn and other such places of much trading'. Great disappointment had been caused to Fr Cornelius, who had long sought and been refused admission while remaining in England.[1] Now Garnet sought an extension of this faculty to 'our temporal assistants', and a further extension, both to priests and Brothers, *in articulo mortis*. Such a faculty, Garnet pointed out, could not harm the relations between the Society and secular priests, but only bring comfort to individuals among them.

This year Garnet was able to send only a very few men from England to make their noviceship abroad: it was as dangerous to leave England as to land in Flanders. 'Prentices', as he calls them, 'I shall hardly send this year in time because the passing is stopped: yet I will try.' In the previous eighteen months more than one of his candidates, after leaving England, had found himself in a Dutch gaol.[2] This year also Richard Blount finished his noviceship while still working on the mission, and was admitted to the Society on 8 September, a date that has remained the traditional day of admission in the English Province to the present day. In a single short sentence Garnet recorded the event: 'This being the feast of the nativity of Our Lady, Richard Blount has made an end of his two years.'[3]

Towards the close of the year Garnet was still optimistic that the Archpriest would be sufficiently recognised to establish his authority firmly. The priests at Wisbech, with two or three exceptions, had signed a joint letter expressing their loyalty. This, and a large number of letters from other parts of the country, gave Garnet fair ground on which to construct his hopes. Speaking both for the Society and for the laymen who were attached to it, he wrote:[4] 'Our Society is intimately united to him [the Archpriest] and, as for the laity, there has been no event more welcome to them than his appointment.' As Garnet was 'on the point of taking up his pen to write this letter', one of the leading Catholic laymen sent him a message to say that he and all the principal Catholics in England were prepared to write to the Pope, expressing their satisfaction at the choice of Blackwell and their own personal loyalty to him. Garnet, however, advised against this course. Only two weeks later, several letters written by him and the Archpriest were seized in the Gatehouse, in the cell of a priest who was later taken for examination.[5]

[1] Cf. *sup.*, p. 189.   [2] H. G. to R. P. 10 June 1598. Stonyhurst, *Anglia* 2, 37.
[3] H. G. to R. P. 8 September 1598. Stonyhurst, Grene *P.*, 552.
[4] H. G. to C. A. 5 October 1598. Stonyhurst, *Anglia* 2, 42.
[5] H. G. to R. P. 21 October 1598. Stonyhurst, Grene *P.*, 545.

If a manifesto from Catholic laymen, or a copy of it, fell into the Council's hands, it would have furnished it with a complete list of Garnet's friends; and what was more damaging, with incontrovertible evidence of the Catholic profession of all who had signed it. 'There is no necessity', Garnet commented, 'to resort to such dangerous remedies against the schism of a few persons.'[1] However, in support of the Archpriest, he asked Aquaviva not to give credence to those who boast that 'they can bring forward four times as many signatures in objection to the decree [appointing the Archpriest] as might be gathered in its favour'. All his own unsought-for prestige was lent to the support of Blackwell: he pleaded that 'the orders of His Holiness should not hang on or be rendered void by the votes of a few unquiet men.'[2]

This is perhaps the year of the most revealing letters in Garnet's twenty years' correspondence. His hopes for peace ran high in the spring, declined in the summer and rose again in the autumn. With this letter to Aquaviva he enclosed the letter from the Wisbech prisoners. The unhappy dissensions appeared to be healed. Garnet had more time now to tell again in his correspondence of the heroism of the Catholics there; probably he had visited Wisbech in 1597. Anyhow, either from his own experience or from Weston's reports, he narrated the conversion of two gaol-birds to Catholicism on the eve of their execution and the impression their conduct made on the townspeople.[3] 'Two thieves were executed at the assizes at Wisbech and were before reconciled by a priest in the same house, and went forth with great joy through the town, professing their faith till they came to the gallows. Two others in like sort at Shrewsbury were converted by two poor lay Catholic prisoners, and with great constancy rejected the ministers, affirming that heresy brought them to that end which they acknowledged to have been deserved; yet that they would die in the unity of God's Church, and so refused to pray with them, but prayed themselves in Latin.'[4] In his last attempt to convert the thieves, the minister himself succumbed; 'He suddenly fell down on his knees, requesting their prayers and protesting that he believed the same faith, and that Christ was really present in the Blessed Sacrament: that ... he was giving over his benefice and providing for his wife and children, that he might go over and be reconciled.' The thieves in amazement fell on their knees with him 'weeping for joy'. The minister, as a thank-offering, 'gave them money and two Catholic books which he had under his arm, and by which, it seems, he got his resolution'.[5]

---

[1] *Ibid.*
[2] *Ibid.*
[3] *William Weston.* 154–6.
[4] H. G. to R. P. 8 October 1597. Stonyhurst, Grene *P.*, 548.   [5] *Ibid.*

During the winter the search for Garnet did not relax. He was compelled to travel with greater caution than ever, now that the Council was in liaison with certain rebellious priests. In an undated note of a letter written about this time[1] he confessed that he was 'more afflicted then ever' and took 'little comfort in anything'. The affair of the Appellants, he said in this moment of great depression, would 'kill him one day'. In January 1599 he had a very narrow escape from capture but the letter giving details has not survived.[2]

On St Mark's Day, 25 April, a meeting of the Fathers was held. Holtby was present. The question was raised of Garnet's return to the house at Uxbridge where he had received Tesimond and Ashley.[3] After the raid there he had abandoned it as unsafe. Now eighteen months later he considered the conveniences it offered worth the risk of reoccupation. After consulting his brethren he sought Aquaviva's advice, and at the same time strongly advocated his return. Before Aquaviva could answer, he wrote again, repeating his request, on 28 April;[4] then yet again on 2 and 19 May.[5] As his anxieties grew he revised his cypher. On 1 November he felt his pursuers closing on him.[6] A week later he wrote at length to Aquaviva in Italian:[7] he apologised for leaving him so long without a letter: his excuse was that he was certain that Mr Robert[8] had given him news of his affairs from time to time, 'for this is his habit, as well as my own greatest wish. The truth is that we have been so busy getting together our records and gathering into packages all the papers connected with our business . . . that there has been neither time nor place for writing long letters.[9] The amount of information that remains to be given to your Lordship is great.' Then he concludes with the optimism that he recovered whenever he wrote to Aquaviva: 'By the mercy of the Lord victory is already drawing near. Although we have a certain number of Jebusites to worry us, that is nothing of importance.'[10]

In July this year Garnet lost Lillie's services, at least temporarily, for he was captured in July at Gerard's London house, where Anne Line acted as housekeeper. Gerard tells the story in his *Autobiography*,[11] and, in telling it,

[1] H. G. to R. P. no date. Stonyhurst, Grene *P.*, 573.

[2] Note of a letter dated 20 January 1599. Stonyhurst, Grene *P.*, 552.

[3] Cf. *sup.*, p. 242.

[4] Note of letter dated 28 April 1599. Stonyhurst, Grene *P.*, 552.

[5] *Ibid.*

[6] H. G. to R. P. 1 November 1599. Stonyhurst, Grene *P.*, 552.

[7] H. G. to C. A. 7 November 1599. F.G. 651, f. 88.

[8] Fr Robert Persons.

[9] Garnet is referring either to the possible despatch to Rome of papers connected with the recent controversy, or to yet another change of residence.

[10] H. G. to C. A. 7 November 1599. F.G. 651, f. 88.   [11] *John Gerard*, 19.

hints that he himself was a skilled swordsman. At bay in an upper room, without hope of escape, his first instinctive plan was to gather all the men in the house, his friends and retainers, and at the point of the sword force his escape down the stairs, through the door leading into the street. 'We rejected the plan', he explains, 'because we knew that if we were taken in the struggle, the law would fall much harder on the master of the house for contempt and resistance to search.'[1]

It was Lillie who saved him: 'a truly faithful and prudent servant', as Gerard describes him, 'a man full of charity, ready to lay down his life for a friend'.[2]

In order to persuade Aquaviva that he should be allowed to admit such men into the Society as Brothers, Garnet gives a detailed account of the heroic part played by John Lillie in saving Gerard. 'He is at present in prison', Garnet wrote to Aquaviva on 7 November,[3] 'and in the last few days has been tortured twice; he has greatly edified the whole kingdom and it would be most comforting to your Lordship to hear the story in full. I will tell you a little of it.

'This man was taken in the house where they thought they were going to find Mr John;[4] indeed, the officers of the law say that Mr John was definitely there, but this man had graciously hid him away and was then so clever in playing the gentleman in front of the searchers that they really believed they had found their prey.'

Gerard and his servant had been in the same room with a hiding place large enough to conceal only one man. No sooner was Gerard safely in hiding than the searchers broke into the room. Mistaking Lillie for Gerard, they had him taken to prison and called off the search. Garnet continues:

'When they asked him whether he was a priest, he would not reply either yes or no: so they sent him to prison and left the house unmolested. Since then they have resorted to every device and inveiglement to make him tell them of our activity. He confessed that he had helped to free Mr John from prison. . . . "And that", he said, "is all I will confess, because I do not want ever to hurt others, or do anything against charity and the Christian law of friendship." "Very well," they retorted, "if you will not tell us the whereabouts of this and that man and where they have met and spoken, you will go to the torture." "*In nomine Domini*", he answered,[5] "And so (this was

---

[1] *Ibid.* [2] *Ibid.*

[3] H. G. to C. A. 7 November 1599. F.G. 651, f. 88.

[4] Fr John Gerard.

[5] These were the words Gerard himself had used when he answered the same threat. *John Gerard*, 113.

exactly what he said as he wrote in a message he sent out) "they were true to their word and I thank God I was true to mine, for with the grace of my sweet Saviour and the help of the most holy Virgin, it did not so much as enter my head to harm anyone." As they tortured him, they said: "John, look what you are doing. Do you want to kill yourself? Confess, and save yourself this agony." "If you are not to blame if I am killed, certainly I am not", John replied. "My hands and my arms and all my limbs would not belong to me at all unless they belonged first to my Lord. Do as you wish." They tortured him twice; when they took him down they said: "John, you have shown yourself most faithful to your friends. Now it is time to show yourself faithful to God and the Queen by speaking. We shall preserve your good name and keep what you say an inviolable secret." He answered: "You deceive yourselves, if you think I have done this from consideration of any person in this world: I have done it for the love of God alone; as for the respect of this world, I care nothing for it." '

Lillie's examinations were a rehearsal of Nicholas Owen's. As Garnet's years of freedom drew in, events foreshadowed his own last hours: Lillie had saved Gerard by giving himself up in his place; Owen and Ashely were to try Lillie's device at Hinlip in February 1606; but this second time it failed.

Constantly Garnet drew his inspiration from his own servants and subjects. He was happiest when he had the leisure to describe their heroism. 'These are the triumphs we have had which I desire to tell your Lordship', he writes at the end of this letter.[1] 'And what shows still more the gallantry of this soldier is the fact that he wrote to me that he was able without difficulty to forgive his persecutors: indeed he does not bear them any rancour at all. Moreover, such Christian valour must have won the admiration of his enemies, for while one would have thought him likely to receive the severest possible punishment, after helping to free a prisoner from the Tower,[2] he is now in the common prison and full of joy.' Perhaps with a view to his trial and execution, Lillie was transferred this autumn from the Tower to Newgate.

Throughout the summer Garnet had petitioned Aquaviva to leave his present lodgings in Spitalfields and return to Uxbridge: now the decision to moved was forced on him. His residence had been discovered; but he was saved once more by the resourcefulness of Lillie. Garnet makes only a passing reference to this escape: a number of his letters written this year appear to have been lost. The story is told both by Tesimond and by Gerard.

[1] H. G. to C. A. 7 November 1599. F.G. 651, f. 88.
[2] A reference to the part played by John Lillie in organising Gerard's escape: cf. *sup.*, p. 257.

In the course of Lillie's examination, Sir William Wade, the Lieutenant of the Tower, had boasted that he knew Garnet's London house and had planned to raid it within a few days. It was no idle boast. Wade went on to say that he did not mind telling Lillie that Garnet lived in Spitalfields, since there was no chance that his prisoner would communicate with Garnet. Wade was waiting only for Garnet's return to London.

The house had either been betrayed, as Garnet feared it would be,[1] or had been discovered through papers seized in the July raid on Gerard's house. Lillie knew well that Wade was speaking the truth, but he outwitted him. Within a few days he contrived somehow or other to send out from the Tower a parcel to a friend in London.

'It was wrapped in white paper', Gerard explains,[2] 'and was received safely. All his friends knew that if John was given the chance, he would send a letter that way. They read the message, saying that Garnet's house had been betrayed and warning them to let him know at once. This they did. Father Garnet was saved, for sure enough, as Wade declared, he would have been at home within a few days. However, he kept well out of the way, and was able to have all his possessions removed from the place, so that when the house was searched, nothing was found. You can imagine the haul they would have made — Father Garnet himself and all his books, his vestments, everything he had for the altar and heaven knows what else.'

'Under Providence', concludes Gerard, 'this escape was John's good work. He saved Garnet as before he had saved me.' The raid occurred sometime between July, when Lillie was captured, and November, when he was transferred to Newgate. Tesimond says that the house belonged to Anne Vaux and her sister, Mrs Brooksby.[3]

Soon after his transference to Newgate Lillie organised his escape with another priest. The search for him was now as hot as it had been for Garnet. For a time he worked with Gerard; but Garnet eventually judged it prudent

---

[1] This was Gerard's view. *John Gerard*, 156
[2] *John Gerard*, 156–7.
[3] Tesimond's account of the interview between Lillie and Wade confirms Gerard's and is even more vivid. 'One day the Lieutenant of the Tower, a man of great cruelty towards Catholics but above measure hostile to our Society, asked him [Lillie] whether he knew Father Garnet's house ... and he saying "No", the Lieutenant said: "That is right: if you do not know it we do, and we are so certain about it that we expect soon to have him in our hands. I would never have told you this if I were not sure that you were a close prisoner and that you cannot possibly let Garnet know or anybody else.' Then he named the place and the house, being unable to contain himself for joy at the expectation of his speedy capture.' 'Father Tesimond's Landing in England', printed in *Troubles* (ed. John Morris) Series 1, 179–80 (1872).

to send him to safety abroad, where he became Fr Persons's secretary and was admitted to the Society as a Brother. The part he played as the servant of Garnet and Gerard is eulogised in a striking passage of Gerard's *Autobiography*.[1] It was written after Lillie's death. 'During those five or six years he was with me in England', says Gerard, 'and engaged in every kind of business on my behalf in places far and near, with people in every walk of life — for often when I was upstairs with the master of the house and his friends, he was below with the servants, often gamblers and the like — all that time he guarded his heart and his soul with the utmost care.... He was an innocent soul, if ever there was one. And he was so wise and prudent too.'

Garnet ended his letter in praise of John Lillie by explaining that he had 'come to the end of the page'. It is a pity. Although Aquaviva pardoned, as he was asked, Garnet's 'lack of politeness' in finishing so abruptly, many incidents in Lillie's career of faithful service went unrecorded.[2]

After Lillie's arrest and the raid on the Spitalfields house Garnet was homeless; but, again with the help of the Vaux sisters, he found a new residence that served him until his last months of liberty. This was White Webbs on Enfield Chase about ten miles north-east of London off the road to Ware. It was a spacious mansion and could accommodate as many as fourteen priests at a time. Its situation on the fringe of the royal forest provided suitable cover for the constant throng of Catholic gentlemen who visited it. There Anne Vaux and her sister, Eleanor Brooksby, lived privately and shared the charges of housekeeping with Garnet; the landlord was a Mr Hewick, from whom Anne, under the name of Mrs Perkins, rented the house. James Johnson, a faithful servant, acted as caretaker. He arrived about Candlemas 1600; Eleanor and Anne three months later. Before the end of November, Garnet reported to Persons: 'I have had eight more [priests] with me for renovation [of vows]. I cannot keep them away but they will flock to such feasts: all are much comforted.'[3] About this time also Eleanor's son, William Brooksby, now married to Dorothy Wiseman of Braddocks, joined the household. Two children were born to them there. Later Garnet's examiners, in an attempt to denigrate him, sought to father one of the children on to him.

[1] *John Gerard*, 157–8.
[2] Lillie died in Rome of a lung disease on 25 November 1609 at the age of thirty-six. Westminster Archives, 8, 184.
[3] H. G. to R. P. 25 November 1600. Stonyhurst, Grene *P.*, 554.

28

JOHN PIBUSH

AFTER the appointment of the Archpriest, Garnet hoped to be concerned only with his own apostolic work. He was now, as the century opened, a man of forty-five; his health was sound, his zeal unimpaired; in ecclesiastical business his task had been simplified: to give obedience to the Archpriest. This he did with relief.

The old reign appeared to be drawing to its conclusion. Garnet reprobated all Catholic attempts to intrigue for the succession: politics lay outside the brief he had received from Aquaviva. Moreover there was danger that the factious priests would use the uncertainty of succession to foment discord. Garnet was emphatic: 'I think it very expedient', he had written in April 1599,[1] 'that there be an express prohibition and a great censure against any priest which during this schism shall meddle in the matter of the succession.'

His responsibility now was chiefly for his own brethren, few in number, fewer still in outstanding talent, yet marked by a devotion to duty which he himself had largely inspired in them. Never had he considered himself destined for the honour of martyrdom that had been granted to Southwell and Walpole; he expected to spend the remainder of his life unobtrusively building up the Society in England. It was a task that matched what he considered his modest ability, and there was none that could be dearer to him.

As the old century passed without event into the new, Garnet's thoughts turned to his own brethren. In 1598 Weston had been transferred from Wisbech to the Tower.[2] There he had almost lost the use of his eyes, had grown feeble, and in his loneliness had been tempted by the devil to take his own life. No communication is extant between him and Garnet during these years; but it is clear that Garnet kept himself informed of Weston's plight. In

---

[1] H. G. to R. P. 21 April 1599. Stonyhurst, Grene *P.*, 552.
[2] *William Weston*, 21.

January 1600 he wrote to Persons:[1] 'I am in hand to get out our cousin, William Weston. If it be done, it will cost well: his eyes are not well yet, and one he thinketh he shall never use.' Beneath these terse sentences lay a tragic story. It is told in Weston's *Autobiography*:[2]

'Shut again in my cell, I lay there hourly and daily expecting the sentence of death. The time and place were well suited to prayer, and, had not my eyes failed me, to reading and study also. But the sight of one eye was completely gone, and a film, forming over the other, made it more than half blind so that I very nearly suffered complete loss of sight. Moreover, owing to a chronic headache, sleep had become all but impossible. I had, in fact, practically none; and for the space of eight, nine, ten or more days I scarcely had two or three hours sleep — and that only with the aid of sleeping draughts.'

Depression set in, and the increasing burden of endless solitude. As a priest he was useless except for his example of suffering. Broken now, there was no scandal in his exile. Too great a figure for the government ever to bring to the scaffold, yet not aged, his banishment would cause no embarrassment to Catholics: and for this Garnet now worked.

Inexorably, in spite of his hopes, the quarrel made by the troublesome priests persisted. Their aim was now to divide Blackwell from the Jesuits. As long as Garnet lived, the rift could be averted. Nevertheless his position was delicate. If he gave his ardent support to Blackwell, the Archpriest would be represented as his tool; if he stood aloof his attitude would be taken as disaffection. There is a sad note in his letters of 1599 as he came to realise that the decrees of the Pope would be openly challenged. He tells Persons:[3] 'We long for peace here, but yet have no certainty.' And with the end of the reign in sight he continues: 'And we hope that a toleration may be granted, if Christian princes abroad will take pity on us to ask it. If not, at least a peace [that] will mitigate much of our sorrows, for then we hope [that] ... God Himself in time will use His most effectual sword of His inward vocations and motions for the convenience of our country, which is the only thing we seek for.'

Involved against his will in ecclesiastical politics, Garnet sought wholeheartedly 'the convenience' of his country. His lot caused him continual strain and sorrow.

Nevertheless some small consolations came to him during the year. When the Archpriest Blackwell selected the likeness of St Thomas for his

[1] H. G. to R. P. 14 January 1600. Stonyhurst, Grene *P.*, 546.
[2] *William Weston*, 205–6.
[3] H. G. to R. P. 14 January 1600. Stonyhurst, Grene *P.*, 546.

seal Garnet saw in this a blessed augury: it was used for the first time on the feast of St Thomas, 29 December, on a document that deprived a trouble-making priest, Fr Charnock, of his faculties.[1] With mixed distress and relief Garnet wrote: 'The Customer' — this was Garnet's code name for Blackwell — 'taketh St Thomas, his countryman and citizen, for his seal, and a fit seal to be used first upon St Thomas his day against Mr Charnock, as you may see, who besides his general injuries to St Thomas his flock of poor Catholics, publicly exclaimed at Rome, when he was committed in your house, that he was imprisoned for as just a cause as Thomas was put to death, that is, *pro libertate Ecclesiae.*'

Garnet was comforted also by the excellent work done in prison by an Irish Jesuit, Fr Holywood, who had been captured at Dover and taken to Wisbech, then to the Gatehouse.[2] 'There is hope', he reported,[3] 'of getting him at liberty and sending him to his country.' He was concerned also to help Persons in his historical writing. He had obtained, probably in manuscript, a life of Cardinal Fisher, written in English; also a *History of King Henry's Revolt* in Latin; it was incomplete, but went no further than the death of Queen Catherine; nevertheless it contained many things that had escaped Nicholas Sanders's researches.[4] Garnet considered that it was 'excellently done'.[5] He sent also further material on Thomas Wodehouse, the second priest executed under Queen Elizabeth.[6] Wodehouse had sought admission

[1] Fr Robert Charnock, from Leyland, Lancashire, in order to protest against Black-well's government went in 1598 to Rome, where he was put under injunction not to return to England. He did, under the pretext that he was appealing to the Holy See against the command. In January 1603, with twelve other appellant priests, he signed a protest of allegiance to Elizabeth, which was a virtual repudiation of the rights of the Holy See. He died sometime after 1623.

[2] Fr Christopher Holywood, a native of Dublin, organised the Jesuit mission to Ireland on the lines that Garnet had done in England. From 1604 until his death in 1626 he was Superior there. On his arrival there were only five Jesuits in the country; on his death twenty-two. In 1599, on his way to take up his appointment as Superior, he was arrested at Dover and was not released until 1603. In 1617 he wrote to Aquaviva's successor: 'Our brethren are so hotly pursued that in order to keep at large and perform the functions of their ministry, they have to travel by out-of-the-way paths and pass over walls and hedges and through woods, even to sleep on straw in cornfields or old ruins; at which times they always sleep in their clothes in order to be ready to escape.' *Menology of the English-Speaking Assistancy* (1902), vol. 2, 105–7.

[3] H. G. to R. P. 27 May 1600. Stonyhurst, Grene *P.*, 552.

[4] Nicholas Sanders, *The English Schism* (1585).

[5] This material appears to have been used by Persons in his manuscript history of the Reformation preserved at Stonyhurst.

[6] Thomas Wodehouse, a priest in Lincolnshire in Mary's reign, was executed at Smith-field on 19 June 1573 after twelve years in prison for his religion.

into the Society. As there was no priest in England at that time, he had written to Paris. Garnet now suggested to Persons that 'it were good [that] you inquired whether any such were admitted. I heard he was.'[1]

The troubles continued. Garnet felt more keenly for Blackwell than for himself. In the years before the Archpriest's appointment Garnet had been protected by the real or imagined influence of the Society of Jesus in Rome: Blackwell had no backing apart from the goodwill of the greatest part of his clergy. While Garnet could not consider invoking ecclesiastical censures in support of his own position, he advised such means in support of Blackwell's. In March 1600 he wrote:[2] 'Terrible letters and challenges of disputation . . . and threatenings of lamentable ends do continually come to Customer [Blackwell] about the matter of schism. If you define not from thence [Rome] that they sinned, and deserved punishment, we shall never be quiet. They will not be said to have done amiss; but we must confess to have slandered and wronged them. As for the word "schism" we care not for it, if it be censured as disobedience'.

Frequently Garnet had written in confidence to Aquaviva about his work for priests entering England from the seminaries. The martyr, Fr Eustace White, while awaiting execution, had written to Garnet from the Tower for clothing to keep him warm through the winter, for there was no one else on whose help he could call.[3] This year Garnet received a similar plea from another imprisoned priest, John Pibush, a Yorkshireman born at Thirsk and educated at Rheims. 'Twelve years since', Garnet explained,[4] 'on his arrival from Rheims, he was brought to me and I supplied his wants and recommended him to certain friends of mine; and I have been ever most kind to him.' Pibush never forgot this. His letter, written from prison, so deeply touched Garnet that he made a copy of it, and later forwarded it to Aquaviva.[5] It was not that he looked to Rome for commendation of his work. The letter had given him pleasure which he was anxious to share with Aquaviva.

'Dear Father,' Pibush began, 'with all due affection I commend myself to you as to the first and best friend I have met since my return to my country,[6]

[1] H. G. to R. P. 27 May 1600. Stonyhurst, Grene P., 552.

[2] H. G. to R. P. 16 March 1600. Stonyhurst, Grene P., 595.

[3] Cf. sup., p. 46.

[4] H. G. to C. A. 11 March 1601. Arch. S.J. Rome, Anglia 2, 172.

[5] John Pibush to H. G. 26 November 1600, enclosed in letter to C. A. (11 March 1601). Foley, vol. 7, 1351.

[6] Pibush left Rheims for England on 3 January 1589; he worked mainly in Gloucestershire until he was arrested at Moreton-in-the-Marsh in July 1593. He spent the re-next eight years in prison. A few months after writing this letter he was executed at Southwark on 18 February 1601.

a friend whose loving kindness I can never forget if nature, reason and grace prevail in my mind. Well I remember your care for me, your advice that so greatly helped me, and I humbly thank you for your friendly conduct towards me, for your kindly words, for the expectation of me you have raised in others so far beyond my deserts. I beg our Lord to reward you, to make me worthy of your kindness, and shield you from every misfortune on my account. This is ever my earnest prayer to the Lord. It is easy to dissemble in writing, but would to God you could read my heart. . . . I trust I shall leave my testament sealed with the title of a Catholic priest, faithful to my God and to my friends, and earnest in the cause of Holy Church; this is my sole desire. To attain this more surely, I humbly crave from you and your other poor friends the nourishment of true virtue, and that you will daily give me a part in your pious prayers, especially at the time of the divine mysteries, from which I have so often and for so long a time been debarred. For I am convinced that if I have been able to persevere despite my hardships and miseries, it is due more to the devout prayers of others than [to] my own unworthy supplications.'

There existed perhaps something more than friendship between Pibush and Garnet. The next paragraph in the letter suggests that Garnet had perhaps confided in him, as a representative of Allen's priests, some of his own anxieties and hopes.

'My Father', Pibush continued, almost echoing Garnet's own words, 'those who purpose to come to this country and to work profitably therein, must bring along with them vigorous souls and mortified bodies. They must forgo all pleasures and renounce every game but that of football, which is made up of pushes and kicks, and requires constant effort, unless one would be trampled under foot; and in this game they have to risk their lives in order to save souls. On my return to England I found that it was one huge prison for all who, like us, profess the true faith, and for members of your Society who, despite your prisons and bonds, have succeeded beyond hope to our unspeakable consolation.'

Garnet did not know that he was forwarding the letter of a future martyr. To him Pibush represented the 'greatest part' of the seminary priests, devout and prepared for any sacrifice, desirous only to work alongside all who shared their aspirations. Fr Pibush concludes his letter: 'In times past (God knows) no country showed us more favour and left us more free; but now in none are we more straitened. The harmless fledglings who would seek their God here can do so but at the peril of their wretched lives, amidst bird lime and traps on every side, and this they have to do in haste lest the breed be lost.'

Fr Pibush was a countryman and used metaphors more familiar to Gerard than to Garnet:

'The promised land of our Fathers has now for their children become a howling wilderness, over which the hungry fowlers have spread their nets of laws and statutes over the whole country; and they count it a loss if any youth or old men escape their hands since they promise themselves that *omnes ad praedam venient.* You are well aware that many of these snares are set to catch you and your Society. . . . God grant you and other poor Israelites a cloud to hide you from your enemies by day, and by night a column of fire in all your sudden flights; that it may lighten your steps to a place of rest.

'Father, my illness has so far shattered my constitution that I despair of relief by human means. So changed am I from all that I was that some of my friends and acquaintances that come here for other reasons than that of visiting me, and sitting with me in company, have asked: "Who is that man?" and on hearing the reply have sighed deeply. Others have said that they would never have recognised me if they had not heard me speak and tell them who I was. I have lived deprived of religious consolations, banished from human society, parted from friends, debarred from the solace of study, disturbed by those whose company I am forced to keep. My Father, the only keepsakes I can send you are a phial full of bitter smoke, a bundle of filth, lice and fleas. God preserve you from these gifts of Egypt, and heap upon you the figs of his promised inheritance. Your friend to command as long as I live, John Pibush.'

Probably Garnet found ways of getting small comforts to his friend in prison. Only in general terms was he ever able to refer to his organisation for the relief of Catholic prisoners, to which he devoted such a large share of the funds entrusted to him by his friends. Affectionately he followed Pibush's fortunes till his death in the spring of the following year.

As Garnet had foreseen, the persecution now became more cruel. Possibly the government was moving itself into a bargaining position for toleration by a display of its power: otherwise the severe enforcement of the penal laws in the last years of the reign is difficult to explain. Several of Garnet's friends fell victims to the new assault.

He wrote little to Aquaviva this year. 'I have no doubt that Mr. Robert will amply make up for the rarity of my letters.'[1] Only reports of martyrs and questions that required the General's personal decision or snippets of news that would particularly interest him, led Garnet to write. For example, he knew the pleasure his Superior would take in learning that Sir Richard

[1] H. G. to C. A. 1 July 1600. F.G. 651, f. 75.

Southwell, Robert's father, had died a Catholic.[1] He urged Aquaviva to obtain the prayers of the Society for his soul.

The barbarous execution of John Rigby, an impoverished Lancashire gentleman, at Southwark on 21 June, prefaced a sequence of occasional martyrdoms that continued to the end of the year. Garnet described him as a 'noble youth . . . who had a great desire to be admitted into the Society as a temporal Coadjutor'.[2] It was a sadness to him that he could not meet John Rigby's wishes: 'I send him word to say', writes Garnet,[3] 'that, for the present, he should keep his desire, which would be met in due course. He was under sentence of death, but his execution had been temporarily postponed. Then suddenly he was summoned to execution. Had he been forewarned of this, he would have made greater efforts for admission. He had an opportunity of escaping from prison, but he was not ready to forego the opportunity of martyrdom unless he was given a sure undertaking that he would be received into the Society.'

Garnet gave these details in order once more to press Aquaviva to a decision. As the case of Cornelius[4] had led the General to concede a limited faculty to receive priests *in articulo mortis*, the case of Rigby finally induced Aquaviva to allow Garnet to accept his servants into the Society. No noviceship, except the company of the priests whom they served, was demanded. Rigby died a Jesuit brother in all but name; and his execution was recorded by Garnet, who perhaps witnessed the last horrific moments. 'He died under such tortures and with such constancy that I consider his case to be unexampled in the present time. He spoke these words to the executioner as the man was in the act of tearing out his heart: "God forgive thee. My sweet Jesus, receive my soul." He was condemned merely for having been reconciled to our Holy Mother, the Church of Rome, although in truth, he was never out of it; and was a holy man both in life and in death.'[5]

In July four priests were executed, Thomas Sprott and Thomas Hunt at Lincoln; Robert Nutter, a Dominican, and Edward Thwing at Lancaster. The first two, Sprott and Hunt, had been well known to Garnet, who describes briefly their misfortune:

'Upwards of four years ago a very virtuous priest named Sprott (I do not recollect his Christian name), together with nine persons, some being priests and other laymen, escaped one night from prison [at Wisbech]. He had a great

---

[1] Probably early in 1600.
[2] Temporal Coadjutor is another term for Laybrother.
[3] H. G. to C. A. 11 March 1601. Arch. S.J. Rome, *Anglia* 2, 172.
[4] Cf. *sup.*, p. 189–90.
[5] H. G. to C. A. 11 March 1601. Arch. S.J. Rome, *Anglia* 2, 172.

desire to enter the Society. I provided him with a room and all necessaries in London and sent him to some friends of mine in the country. Last year another very excellent priest, named Thomas Benstead,[1] made good his escape from Wisbech and I equipped him and recommended him to the same friends. But both of these good priests going together to introduce themselves to my friends in Lincolnshire were arrested and martyred.'[2]

Garnet followed their story. He wrote on 16 August[3] that he had heard a report that the judge, Sir John Glanville, who condemned the first two priests, had fallen from his horse shortly afterwards and broken his neck. Characteristically he gives this news only as a report, but confirmation came before he had posted the letter. In the margin he added later: 'This is true. He made a feast at his house and went to bring his guests on the way, and had a horse led by, on which getting up to ease himself his man by chance pitched him over instead of helping.' The execution of Sprott had been so expeditious that Garnet had been unable to admit him into the Society. In the fate that overtook Justice Glanville he saw an indication that his friend was among the blessed.[4]

Like Pibush, Thomas Hunt had relied greatly on Garnet's help. When he escaped from Wisbech 'I gave him succour both before and after', wrote Garnet,[5] 'and sent him into Lincolnshire about the beginning of May, to be placed there. But he is in a better place now. He was our very friend.'

In the same summer Garnet received confirmation of his worst fears: the trouble-makers at Wisbech had been in league with the Council and this had been the cause of Fr Weston's removal to the Tower. 'The matter groweth more evident every day', he told Persons.[6] Before his death Fr Hunt had sent Garnet proof of this: now he had confirmation from the keeper himself and the pursuivant who had befriended Weston and his companion, Fr Giles Archer, on the road to London. 'The keeper [of Wisbech] hath confessed it and the pursuivant also; and the keeper hath certain articles drawn up by a workman [i.e. seminary priest] against our friends, and instructions how to procure their trouble. Which articles I was promised a copy of, but he dare not perform it for fear of undoing the keeper, who loveth the better side and feareth the other, and the other him: for they know he hath not kept counsel.'[7]

[1] *Benstead* was an *alias* used by Fr Hunt.
[2] H. G. to C. A. 11 March 1601. Arch. S.J. Rome, *Anglia* 2, 172. The priests were arrested in the Saracen's Head in Lincoln.
[3] H. G. to R. P. 16 August 1600. Stonyhurst, Grene *P.*, 552.
[4] Sir John Glanville (1542–1600), Judge of Common Pleas 1598–1600.
[5] H. G. to R. P. 16 August 1600. Stonyhurst, Grene *P.*, 552.
[6] *Ibid.*   [7] *Ibid.*

It was through the keeper that Garnet now tried to secure the release of Weston and his companions from the Tower. At the same time he feared that Weston's release would expose Bagshawe, 'the workman' mentioned in Garnet's letter, and lead to reprisals that would make the situation worse. 'Mr Southworth [a seminary priest] calleth them bloody fellows and marvelleth that Customer [the Archpriest] punisheth them not. But he dare not accuse them.'[1] The terror they caused was so great that many of Garnet's supporters feared to show themselves friendly to the Society or to make any gesture that would bring on them the hatred of the Appellant faction.[2]

For some weeks towards the end of the year the trouble appeared to die down: then unexpectedly, through John Mush, there were 'new designments' in the north.[3] At this point Blackwell was goaded to action. He withdrew faculties both from Colleton and Mush. But it was soon clear that this was not enough. In the prisons, where the factious priests were most dangerous because, through their keepers, they could communicate with the Council, the quarrels continued. Blackwell ordered copies of his letters of deprivation to be sent to Wisbech and other prisons, but all feared Colleton too much to deliver them.[4] Already Blackwell was beginning to show that he had not the determination of character needed to surmount the crisis. It was only a matter of time before he lost control or compromised.

[1] Fr Christopher Southworth, a seminary priest, was born in 1556, the fourth son of Sir John Southworth of Salmesbury, Lancashire. He had been only four months in England when he was captured in March 1587. In 1598 he was transferred to London with William Weston and confined in the Gatehouse. *William Weston*, ch. 20.

[2] H. G. to R. P. 16 August 1600. Stonyhurst, Grene *P.*, 552.

[3] H. G. to R. P. 22 October 1600. Stonyhurst, Grene *P.*, 536.

[4] *Ibid.*

T

29

SIR JOHN POPHAM

WHENEVER Garnet sent a long news letter for the edification of his Roman friends, he wrote in Italian. It was his intention that Aquaviva, after reading the letter himself, should hand it on to Bellarmine or Persons or his own former novice-master, Fabio de Fabiis, who was now Aquaviva's adviser for Italian affairs. Perhaps also Garnet intended these occasional letters for public reading. In style and content they are distinct from the regular business letters; but they are no less valuable, for in them Garnet takes great pains to gather and order his information both about the condition of Catholics in general and the suffering of individual priests and laymen

His letter of 11 March 1601 is not the longest in this series, though it runs to more than ten thousand words.[1] It was dispatched after the February meeting of his brethren, at which he had checked his information with them and incorporated into his letter their own reports from other parts of the country.

Fr John Pibush, his close friend, was perhaps in the forefront of his mind when he sat down to write. The details of Pibush's story that he adds read as an uncanny forecast of his own fate, for the two chief actors in Pibush's condemnation, Coke, the Attorney-General, and Popham, the Chief Justice, were also to be the principals in his own trial five years later. Although Pibush had been condemned for his priesthood soon after his arrest in 1589, the sentence was not carried out for nearly twelve more years, which he passed mostly in the King's Bench prison, where eventually, as Garnet says[2] 'his right of seniority entitled him to some pre-eminence among the thieves and to a sort of cabin or berth which, as in ships, gives on to the wall and is reached by a ladder'. During this time, Pibush, deprived as he was of Catholic company, advanced greatly in holiness, so that 'everyone noticed in him a great change, although he had always been a well-ordered and good priest'.

Garnet observed every detail of the events that brought Pibush to the

[1] H. G. to C. A. 11 March 1601. Arch. S.J. Rome, *Anglia* 2, 172.   [2] *Ibid.*

scaffold, almost with the foreknowledge that the men who secured his death were soon to secure his own.

Under Coke's wardship was a girl from whose marriage the Attorney-General 'anticipated great advantages'. Garnet tells the rest of the story dramatically.[1] 'It happened that the ward married without the knowledge of the Attorney [-General] who, in order to annul the marriage, sought to prevail on the minister before whom it had been celebrated to acknowledge that he was drunk when the ceremony took place. The minister naturally refused to defame his own character, and was therefore cast into the same prison [as Fr Pibush]. At first he was confined in a solitary cell, where he was all but starved to death; he was then taken to the common day-room of the prison, where the priest made him sit on his own bench and restored his appetite with such delicacies as had been given to comfort him in his own ailments. When the Minister had somewhat recovered, the Father spoke to him in Latin and gave him good counsel for his soul.

'In their malice those imprisoned with him [Pibush] came to an agreement that they should write a letter accusing him of having spoken treason against the Queen and having reconciled many to the Catholic Church. This caused the Chief Justice Popham to propose to the other judges that some priest under sentence of death should be executed. One of them replied that, since so great an interval had been allowed to elapse, it would be fitting to call the priest again to the bar in order to provide him with an opportunity of showing why he should not suffer death.'

On 5 February 1601 Pibush was taken before Popham. On his way through the streets he thought he heard a voice reciting the words of psalm 18: *Their sound is gone forth through all the earth and their words to the end of the world*. After his condemnation he repeated this verse as loudly as his physical feebleness permitted. Back in prison, Garnet writes,[2] 'he frequently begged a friend to recommend him to the prayers of his dear benefactor, Father Whalley (as he called me) and his brethren, that God might give him strength to persevere to the end'.

At his execution in Southwark on 18 February 1601 an unusual altercation occurred. Garnet noted it without enlarging on its significance. Three ministers were at hand, all anxious to dispute with Pibush at the same time: to convert a priest in these circumstances was the surest way to ecclesiastical promotion. Pibush singled out the most intelligent of the three: Garnet recorded their last exchange:

' "I", said the Minister, "and all the Queen's loving subjects are Catholics and we profess the Catholic faith even as Saint Peter and Saint Paul and the

[1] *Ibid.*   [2] *Ibid.*

other Apostles did." To this the martyr replied emphatically, "Would to God that it was so. I am come here to die for the priesthood and the Catholic faith." "Not so", said the Minister. "You are about to die because you went to Rome [he was never in Rome] and were made a priest there, binding your-self by oath to return hither in order to seduce the Queen's subjects from their due allegiance." ' It was perhaps the first recorded occasion on which a minister had publicly claimed that he and all the Queen's subjects were Catholics.

It is possible that Garnet witnessed the execution: he felt safer always in his excursions on the south bank of the river. For many months he had been sending Pibush medicine to give him some relief from attacks of jaundice which, recurring every fortnight, lasted for three days. Pibush, on the morning of his death, had feared that he was about to suffer a paroxysm: he begged all he met to pray he might be given sufficient strength to meet his death. Their prayer was granted.

Pibush's execution in February was the first of several this year. Garnet was surprised that the Earl of Essex's rising had not given the Council enough preoccupation, 'without bothering about the poor Catholics who (like Pibush) had suffered so patiently for so many years'.[1] However, according to the rumours Garnet heard — he said he could not be certain of their truth — the Queen herself had ordered the rigorous enforcement of the penal legislation and had given Popham special powers to this end.

Certainly Popham had been personally responsible for Pibush's death. Garnet, as though aware that he was himself to face him soon, gave Aquaviva this summary of the man whom he had known since his days with Tottel:[2] 'I well know that this Popham is a cruel man of low extraction. The felons he condemns to death tell him brazenly to his face that he deserves the halter far more than they do, since he has been a thief. The Queen, when out of temper, often calls him a "bluecoat", which is the term used for those ordinary servants who attend at their ease on their patrons, and many of whom are the greatest thieves.[3] Be this as it may, Popham is a Privy Coun-

[1] H. G. to C. A. 11 March 1601. Arch. S.J. Rome, *Anglia* 2, 172. In June 1596 Essex, with seventeen ships of the royal navy and another forty-seven warships, carrying about 8,000 troops, had seized Cadiz and sacked the city. Later he was sent to Ireland, but quarrelled with Elizabeth over his conduct of the war there. Brilliant, impulsive and im-perious, he was suspected of attempting to seize power. In February 1601, with a hundred and twenty followers, he tried to raise the city against the Queen and capture the Court, but his way was barred and he was forced to surrender. He was executed on 25 February 1601.   [2] *Ibid.*

[3] *Bluecoat*: formerly the dress of servants and the lower orders, hence used of almoners and charity children. *O.E.D.*

cillor and one of the chief officers of State.' Piquantly Garnet adds that the most influential Councillor with the Queen was always the man prepared to take on himself the odium for executing unpopular measures. Popham offered no objection to filling this role.

Garnet bore Popham something of the intense loathing that an earlier generation of Catholics had shown the Earl of Leicester. In his long letter of March 1601 he recounts an incident that demonstrates how widely this hatred was shared. Lady Rich, the Earl of Essex's sister, was staying in her brother's London house at the time of the rising.[1] There for a few hours four members of the Council, including Popham, were held prisoners in an upper-floor room. As Lady Rich passed through the garden courtyard she called up to their guards, saying (as Garnet reports), that 'if they were true gentlemen, they would throw her down the head of that old fellow [Popham]'. Such, observed Garnet, 'is the general detestation in which he is held by all classes'. Popham, however, was unexpectedly liberated. Piously, Garnet observes that he himself would allow the man time to do penance, 'before a sadder death, were it not that he is prepared to inflict the extremes of injustice on poor Catholics'.[2]

There appeared no limit to Popham's ruthlessness. Among his victims, later in the same month, were two more of Garnet's friends, Fr Roger Filcock, whom he had admitted into the Society, and Mrs Line, who had kept a house for priests in London. For almost ten years this young widowed lady had worked closely, first with Garnet, then with Gerard. In Garnet's esteem she was comparable to the Roman matrons of the early Christian persecutions, and it was with pride that he told Aquaviva that England could still produce such heroic figures. The qualities of her character, as Garnet saw them, made her comparable to Anne Vaux. When the number of incoming priests grew, Anne's work became part of the system Garnet had so carefully constructed for his 'churches'.

As a young girl she had served a lady whose husband was attached to the Court. After her conversion to Catholicism, she and her husband — also a convert — had devoted their lives to the needs of the mission. 'She knew every point of her duty perfectly', says Garnet, 'and was thoroughly conversant in all matters that an educated lady should be.'[3] A needlewoman,

---

[1] Lady Rich was Penelope, the daughter of Walter Devereux, first Earl of Essex, perhaps the greatest beauty of her day and the *Stella* of Philip Sidney's Sonnets. Unhappily and forcibly married to Robert, third Lord Rich, later Earl of Warwick, she divorced her husband and married Charles Blount, eighth Lord Mountjoy. She was a friend of the Wiseman family and took instruction in the Catholic faith from John Gerard, but was not received into the Church. *John Gerard*, 226–7.

[2] H. G. to C. A. 11 March 1601. Arch. S.J. Rome, *Anglia* 2, 172.   [3] *Ibid.*

she worked vestments for the altar. Suffering constantly from ill-health, she made little of it. 'More than once', Garnet wrote, 'I myself have seen her completely exhausted and apparently dead; in fact her infirmities reduced her almost to the extreme stage of physical weakness.'[1]

On the death of her husband she had lost her inheritance since she was known to be a Catholic. Then, under Garnet's direction, she gave the last eight years of her life exclusively and devotedly to housekeeping for the priests of London. John Lillie was with her when he gave himself up to save Fr Gerard; young ladies on their way to convents in Flanders lodged with her until Fr Garnet was able to find transport for them. 'For the purpose of concealment', says Fr Garnet,[2] 'we gave her the name of Mrs Martha: under that name she gained a great reputation and by that name also I believe she was condemned.'

The large number of Catholics who visited her forced Garnet more than once to find her new lodgings 'for fear of false brethren'. In the years before her arrest, she ran three adjoining establishments: her own house, where she kept a number of small children whom she instructed in the faith; a small detached dwelling for a resident chaplain; and a third larger house which formed a retreat for Jesuit and other priests visiting London. Yearly her sickness increased. She herself lived in great poverty. With the services of the Vaux sisters never far from his mind, Garnet was able to write: 'I never knew a woman who equalled her in prudence.'[3]

After the Essex rising, Popham appears to have succeeded Topcliffe as the Queen's personal priest-hunter. Anne, both for her work and her association with Garnet, was an important prize. 'The lodging of this wonderful woman', says Garnet,[4] 'was betrayed by the treachery of some Judas (there are very many of them), and was broken into by a furious band, with the authority of Popham, the Lord Chief Justice, on the feast of the Purification.' The priest, who was engaged in the ceremony of blessing the candles, escaped;[5] but Anne Line, with most of the congregation, was arrested.

Garnet was in London at the time and got letters through to 'Mrs Martha' in prison. He implored her to state her needs. She wrote back saying 'that she was very thankful to me for the interest I took in her, but she wanted nothing'. In the letter, parts of which Garnet quotes, she shows herself a brave woman indeed, anxious only for prayers, particularly Garnet's, that she may be faithful to the end.

---

[1] H. G. to C. A. 11 March 1601. Arch. S.J. Rome, *Anglia* 2, 172.
[2] *Ibid.*   [3] *Ibid.*   [4] *Ibid.*
[5] Francis Page, who was arrested the following year, was tried by Popham and executed at Tyburn on 20 April 1602.

Popham's cruelty at her trial saddened Garnet intensely. On 26 February, the first Thursday in Lent, Anne was called to the Sessions House. She was extremely ill, indeed bedridden: the keepers of her prison testified to this. However, Popham, determined on her death, ordered her to appear no matter what her condition. In the end she was carried to court in a chair between two constables. There was no evidence against her, for it was unproven that she had harboured any priest, let alone a priest ordained overseas. Popham, knowing that she was one of Garnet's principal lay-helpers in London, was resolved to procure sentence on her. When proof of her guilt was not forthcoming he 'warned the jury to be very much on their guard, because the woman commonly received many priests and Jesuits; and in addition he drew their particular attention to the fact that such priests had shown that they knew her very well; and that Catholic articles had been found in her house. And so they condemned her.'[1]

The day before Anne Line's condemnation Popham had gained yet another victory over Garnet; he secured the execution of Roger Filcock. There was no proof of his priesthood at hand; and when it looked as if even Popham was to fail, he introduced into court the Bishop of London,[2] who claimed to have in his possession a letter written by Persons to Garnet, 'in which Persons said that the English seminarians [at Rome] were proud and irreligious, and came to England influenced more by passion than true zeal'.[3]

Filcock challenged the bishop to produce Persons' letter, asking him also to define the sense in which he threw the word 'irreligious' at his fellow-priests. There was no answer: only further charges. 'It was true', Garnet admits,[4] 'that Father Persons, exhorting all here to charity and peace, observed that dissensions among priests would occasion great injury to the Catholic cause; for he had found by his own experience that many eminent and grave persons in Rome, after noticing how stubborn and seditious some of the English scholars were, began to fear lest the greatly renowned martyrdoms in England might be attributed rather to obstinacy against the Queen than to true zeal.' But as Garnet noted, Persons did not state this as a fact but as an apprehension, and observed that until now all the martyrs had been outstanding in their meekness.

When Popham with this fresh charge failed to secure Filcock's condemnation, a pursuivant rose in court and claimed to have found on the prisoner a letter to the Archpriest. Before Filcock could refute this new accusation,

[1] H. G. to C. A. 11 March 1601. Arch. S.J. Rome, *Anglia* 2, 172.
[2] Richard Bancroft, Bishop of London 1597–1604.
[3] H. G. to C. A. 11 March 1601. Arch. S.J. Rome, *Anglia* 2, 172.
[4] *Ibid.*

Popham had directed the jury to find him guilty. They did. Filcock answered, *'Benedictus Deus'*.

There is no extant sermon delivered by Garnet: his style of preaching, however, can be judged by the following extract from this March letter in which he describes the treatment Filcock received on his return to prison; he writes as though he were addressing a Catholic congregation on a journey through the shires:[1]

'All Catholics know well that before the coming of the Son of God into this world and up to the time of his holy Resurrection, there was a place called Limbo. We do not know for certain what has become of that venerable receptacle of the holy Patriarchs and Progenitors of Our Lord, and it has also been disputed whether or not it is now become Paradise. But we have here a Limbo (for so it is called both in Latin and English), a place where they normally confine all those who have been condemned to death. Catholics awaiting execution are sent to that prison unless exempted by special favour, as was granted to holy Martha [Anne Line]. It is an underground place full of horrors, without light and swarming with vermin and reptiles. It is impossible to see there without candles continually burning: and there is neither bed nor chair unless the prisoners make provision for themselves. One of our holy martyrs, a priest [Fr Southwell] was there some years ago after being sentenced to death,[2] and while he was sleeping some poisonous insect entered his body causing him intense suffering until he was transferred to the repose of the saints and just ones of God.'

In Limbo, Filcock met a Benedictine monk, Mark Barkworth, formerly a fellow-student of his at Valladolid and now a fellow victim of the Lord Chief Justice and equally a friend of Fr Garnet, to whom he always 'showed great good will and gratitude on account of some little assistance I had given him'.[3]

Barkworth, Filcock and Line, all Garnet's friends, met their death together at Tyburn on 27 February. Anne Line, to the last, had feared she might be reprieved 'thinking she could not go to heaven otherwise than by passing through Limbo'.[4]

In preparation for death Barkworth shaved his head, as Garnet wrote, 'after the manner of a monk, with a crown': as a token of affection he sent a portion of his hair and of his religious habit both to the Archpriest and to Garnet. 'I am told that our Father Roger', adds Garnet, 'sent me a letter, but I have not yet received it.'[5] As Anne Line was being dressed for execu-

[1] H. G. to C. A. 11 March 1601. Arch. S.J. Rome, *Anglia* 2, 172.
[2] Cf., *sup.*, p. 195.
[3] H. G. to C. A. 11 March 1601. Arch. S.J. Rome, *Anglia* 2, 172.
[4] *Ibid.*   [5] *Ibid.*

tion by her maid she revealed to her fellow prisoners that two days earlier, while she was reciting Vespers of Our Lady, 'she had seen a great light which much surprised her, though she had treated it as a mere superstition. But now, because our Lord was so speedily calling her to Himself, she thought that it was truly from God'.[1]

Since he wrote to Aquaviva describing the martyrdom of Walpole, Garnet had not been so affected by an execution. These were the first martyrdoms at Tyburn for six years. Southwell had suffered there on 21 February 1595; it was now the 27th of the same month 1601. Mercifully Anne, in her state of extreme physical weakness, died quickly, before the procession bringing up Mark Barkworth and Roger Filcock arrived at the gallows. Barkworth was brutally treated. The rope was cut immediately the cart on which he stood had been drawn away. Coming to his feet he made some resistance to the quartering of his live body, crying, 'O Lord, O Lord, O Lord!' While he was being disembowelled, he called out, 'O God!' Filcock, as he waited his turn, spoke to him in Spanish, saying, 'Courage, dear Father.'

Garnet then describes how he was able to gather relics of these martyrs:

'When the crowd dispersed, my agent in London approached the corpse of Mrs Martha. Cutting the sleeve of her gown, he dipped it in the blood of the two Fathers, and he obtained also one of her stockings, notwithstanding the resistance of the executioner, who was himself engaged in the stripping; but he was appeased by a julio.[2] She used to have bandages on her legs, and thus her stockings were large, but they told me that her legs were as thin as the rope with which she was hanged. Perhaps I shall send these stockings to your Paternity if I find the opportunity.

'The head and the quarters of the two Fathers were first buried in a pit dug in the public road, and, later, the body of Mrs. Martha also; and above them all, three or four thieves: I do not know whether they were all women. But the Catholics took away the body of Mrs Martha and buried it in another place not far off in order to inter it with great decorum at some more convenient opportunity. The quarters of the martyrs have also partly been removed, and I believe they have now recovered them all.'

These executions were as many as Londoners were prepared to endure. Two other priests under sentence of death in London prisons, Fr Thurstan Hunt and Fr Robert Middleton, were posted to Lancaster for execution early in March. Before his arrest Middleton had begged Garnet to admit him into the Society, but it is uncertain whether in his strict confinement he

[1] *Ibid.*
[2] A silver coin worth about sixpence, struck by Julius II (1503-13).

received Garnet's message. 'I sent to tell him', says Garnet,[1] 'that his desire had been granted, and I hope for his own consolation and mine that the news reached him.'

It was only before Filcock's death that the reason for this sudden outburst of persecution became public. From a passage of words between Filcock and the sheriff at Tyburn it became clear that the Council was anxious to discredit Catholics by associating them with the Essex rising. The attempt failed. But it was a foreboding of the events that brought Garnet himself to death.

After he had witnessed the butchery of Barkworth, Filcock, awaiting his turn at the foot of the scaffold, had been accused of complicity in the Plot. The sheriff asserted that it was a Catholic contrivance. When Filcock denied this, he was charged with equivocation, for there were Papists who had supported the Earl. Again Filcock protested that there was no Catholic of any position who had been with Essex. 'Upon which', reports Garnet,[2] 'they named one. But [Filcock] replied that he was a youth, and that if he had had any discretion, he would not have mixed himself up with such a crowd of heretics and atheists.' Then Filcock retorted that he died, not for any part in the rising, but for 'being a Catholic, a priest and a member of the Society of Jesus'. He was not permitted to speak further.

Garnet's own view of the folly and fate of Essex was devoutly simple. Essex had been visited by God 'for the outrages, plunder and sacrileges committed at Cadiz in the straits of Gibraltar'.[3] His was a normal case of a fall following inevitably on excessive pride, for, as Garnet pointed out to Aquaviva, there had never been a courtier to surpass him in popularity and influence. He had attained 'the summit of worldly fame and fortune'.

Garnet was more concerned with the unexpected attack of Puritan preachers who tried to fix the blame of the rising on Catholics. It was a smear campaign, fermented possibly by the Council or Bancroft, to divert public attention from the established Church. 'The Puritans strove to fix the blame of the disturbance, of which your Paternity has already heard, on Catholics, and for this end pronounced from their pulpits that the Pope and the king of Spain had been plotting with the Earl.'

A legend was growing that Catholics were behind every political disturbance: within the next five years it was to become almost ineradicably fastened in the English mind. No one was aware of this more than Garnet, the principal victim of a worse plot five years later. Ironically his own trial

---

[1] H. G. to C. A. 11 March 1601. Arch. S.J. Rome, *Anglia* 2, 172.
[2] *Ibid.*
[3] *Ibid.*

was to substantiate the legend to the lasting injury of the Catholic community.

A conversation between two unnamed non-Catholic women on the subject of the Essex rising was perhaps the first recorded interchange of its kind: it represented the prejudice now becoming part of the English heritage. 'A certain noble lady, a bigoted Puritan,' Garnet wrote to Aquaviva,[1] 'calling lately on another lady of the same sect, said to her hostess: "Look, my Lady, I beg you, at what these Papists are capable of doing: for none but Papists could have been implicated in such actions." ' Garnet does not mention either lady's name. With satisfaction he noted that very shortly after this, the lady's own husband, brother and other kinsmen, all Puritans, were themselves arrested for complicity in the Plot and were expecting death on the scaffold.

Catholics, in fact, were compromised in some measure by the Essex rising: Garnet did not deny this. A few very young Catholic gentlemen were cajoled into it: men blinded by the personal glamour of Essex and the 'vain persuasion that if he won the day, there would be an end of the penal statutes against Catholics'.[2] This was a pattern of circumstances that was to reproduce itself later with far more devastating results for Catholicism.

Not even the February executions this year persuaded the people that the rising was a Catholic rebellion. It was a sorry satisfaction to Garnet that the principal actors went to the scaffold professing their staunch Protestantism, one after another, until the day Essex himself was led out. ' "Thank God I am no atheist" ', Garnet reported the Earl's protestations on the scaffold,[3] ' "for I hold that there is a God. Neither am I a Papist, since I do not look to my own merits for salvation." Too true, for he had neither the Catholic faith nor any merits to trust in.'

The last sad moments in the lives of the Essex rebels confirmed the innocence of Catholics in the mind of all save the most prejudiced Puritans. In prison Essex himself had revealed to his 'ghostly Father' the names of all associated with his plot. The minister to whom he made this confession was called up before the Council and repeated there all the information he had gathered in confidence from the Earl. Thereupon an 'infinite [number] was detected'. The Puritans were enraged at this breach of secrecy. Garnet's comment, in view of the cause of his own condemnation, could not be more poignant. 'They say that if a Papist priest had done this, his tongue would have been pulled out, and he hanged.'[4] In fact Garnet was hanged for his refusal to reveal information he had learned under more rigorous secrecy.

[1] *Ibid.*   [2] *Ibid.*   [3] *Ibid.*
[4] H. G. to R. P. 21 March 1601. Stonyhurst, Grene *P.*, 546.

30
FIFTEENTH YEAR

In hours of distress Garnet's thoughts turned frequently to Southwell. He treasured all souvenirs of his 'companion' that came into his hands. Some he kept, others he forwarded to Aquaviva. The breviary that Southwell had used in the Tower he despatched to Rome. When it was lost, he immediately posted, with his letter of 21 April 1601, a piece of material, belonging to another martyr, as a token of gratitude to the General for all the affection he had shown to England. The February executions inevitably recalled Southwell to Garnet's mind. 'I felt great sweetness in so many of the labours we shared together; I have dear memories too of my other Fathers and great confidence in their prayers.'[1]

Among the 'other Fathers', Filcock held a special place. Garnet considered that he had been 'twice martyred',[2] for first he had to watch the barbarous disembowelling of the Benedictine priest, Mark Barkworth, while himself waiting the attentions of the hangman. The material Garnet enclosed in his letter to Aquaviva may have been a piece of cloth given to him by Filcock a few hours before his execution. 'It was sent to me by Father Roger on the very day of his death . . . in true humility without the slightest suggestion of vain glory, simply as a token of his affection and a sign that he was remembering me at that happy hour.'[3] Garnet prayed that Aquaviva would treasure it as the relic of a saint of the Society, 'for while he was not able to live with us, at least he wished to die as one of us'.

Along with this fragment, he sent another relic, a portion of the script that Ignatius of Loyola 'was carrying when he left Monserrat'. It had come into his hands and was now encased in a fine reliquary 'which everyone praises, though it has no great value'.

Garnet was certain that Aquaviva would understand his enthusiasm for these pious objects, although such things were a common sight in Rome.

[1] H. G. to C. A. 21 April 1601. F.G. 651, f. 77.
[2] *Ibid.*
[3] *Ibid.*

'I hope,' he concluded,[1] 'and I beseech Our Lord, that he will allow us to rebuild the Holy Church of God and adorn it with every beautiful object as well as with all spiritual riches.'

These were his hopes. As the year advanced the prospects of peace and unity in the Catholic body diminished. Colleton was in league with another discontented priest, Thomas Bluet,[2] who had told Blackwell to his face that he respected neither the authority of the nuncio in Flanders nor of the Cardinal Protector in Rome, and had asserted that 'again and again he will appeal immediately to his Holiness'.[3] When Blackwell had written to him imploring his submission, Bluet had 'threatened he would come up to London to present [Blackwell's] letter to the Council, and he would enforce a Justice to bring him to the sight of the Queen to discover the treacheries of the Jesuits and the Archpriest'.

It was clear now to Garnet that the support he gave Blackwell was, as he had feared, being used to embarrass the Archpriest. The malcontents insisted that Blackwell was the tool of the Jesuits, and argued that he had therefore forfeited the obedience due to him, since it was well known that the Jesuits had misrepresented the clergy in Rome. The entire group of them was resolved, Blackwell sadly reported, not to obey any censure: no matter in what terms their faculties were withdrawn, they continued to offer Mass and hear confessions.[4] In defence of the Archpriest's authority Garnet could only suggest a drastic remedy — excommunication. He added sadly: 'The Council know all and laugh.'

The malcontents' appeal was made and reached Rome in May. Garnet hastily wrote to point out the dishonest manner in which Bluet and Colleton had sought to give the impression that they spoke for a very considerable number of the clergy. 'Three whose names were added to the appeal absolutely protested that they did not consent. . . . Four more disclaim it: partly they knew nothing, partly they gave their consent only for a supplication to his Holiness to take a sweet order for union and removing of scandal; partly they consented to an appeal, but knew nothing in particular and affirm they have no complaints against any and mislike the contents; [they] utterly

[1] *Ibid.*

[2] Thomas Bluet, a convert Protestant minister from Rogate, was ordained at Douai in February 1578. The same year, on his return to England, he was arrested. In 1580 he was moved from London to Wisbech, where after the death of Fr Metham (June 1592) he became a violent and disorderly character. Later he was one of the leading appellants and went to Rome to plead his case. He was in collusion with Bishop Bancroft and on his return to London spent the last years of his life under the Bishop's protection.

[3] H. G. to R. P. 21 March 1601. Stonyhurst, Grene *P.*, 546.

[4] *Ibid.*

revoke all and wish those who are not quiet were punished. This was the effect of the enquiry made by the Assistants [to the Archpriest].'[1]

Garnet continued to seek action from Rome and suggested some 'excommunication or pacification or edict'. Bluet's constant 'boasting and bragging' that his appeal was being received favourably by the Pope increased 'suspicion of the equity of their cause ... and the number of malcontents'.[2]

During the first part of this year a steady but disturbing flow of books printed at the instigation of the Appellants had entered England from abroad: Garnet was represented as the chief obstacle to peace among the clergy in England; on the Continent, Persons was given a complementary role: both were the subject of unscrupulous abuse. Referring to Fr Persons as 'Mark', Garnet says:[3] 'I wrote that you should not believe what was said against us or against Mark. . . . There is a tale here divulged that Mark's father was not called as Mark is, but because he was a minister's son, who bore that name: and therefore he is so called.' This was the origin of the slander that Persons was the illegitimate son of an Henrician priest, a falsehood that was not only a slur on his origins but on his position also, for ecclesiastical law precluded a man born out of lawful wedlock from receiving Holy Orders without a papal dispensation. Garnet had made little of this slander until it was 'glanced at', as he says, in an answer to Persons' recent controversial work, *The Ward-word*;[4] then later reiterated in a Latin work and finally circulated in gossip stimulated by Colleton.[5] 'We all know the contrary', Garnet assures Persons. Yet the calumny persisted and by constant repetition gained general acceptance. Garnet noted that there were new books in the press against the Jesuits, new journeys to Rome for fresh appeals, a tract in preparation 'on Father Persons' life and irreligious actions'.[6]

Richard Bancroft, Bishop of London, who had tried to secure Fr Filcock's condemnation when the martyr had worsted Popham in court, encouraged clandestinely the disturbances caused by the Appellants. In February 1600 the Council had transferred a number of Catholic prisoners from the Tower,

---

[1] H. G. to R. P. 6 May 1601. Stonyhurst, Grene *P.*, 541.

[2] H. G. to R. P. 6 July 1601. Stonyhurst, Grene *P.*, 537–8.

[3] H. G. to R. P. 20 May 1601. Stonyhurst, Grene *P.*, 596.

[4] *A Temperate Ward-word to the turbulent and seditious Watch-word of Sir Francis Hastings, Knight* (1599).

[5] H. G. to R. P. 20 May 1601. Stonyhurst, Grene *P.*, 596.

[6] H. G. to R. P. 6 July 1601. Stonyhurst, Grene *P.*, 537–8. Persons in answer to this 'lewd slander' appealed to the registration of his birth at Nether Stowey and to the fact that he had required no dispensation either for his entry into the society or for his ordination. *C.R.S.*, vol. 2, 13–14.

Clink, the Gatehouse, Wisbech and Newgate to the half-ruined castle of
Framlingham in Suffolk. On their arrival, the priests were permitted to
select some of their number to go out begging for their sustenance.
Among the collectors of alms was the appellant Bluet. His task had taken
him to London, where he had applied to Bancroft for protection.

With a hatred of Garnet as a common ground, Bancroft agreed to give
Bluet facilities for printing and distributing the books of the factious priests.
Also, Bancroft undertook to commend the cause of the Appellant priests
to the Queen. When the books began to appear, it was said in defence of the
priests that many passages had been written in by Bancroft himself; but
the authors made no public protestation. 'In very deed', wrote Garnet,[1] 'all
moral men, even schismatics and heretics, detest the authors.'

Hitherto, through the influence of his friends, Garnet had prevented any
quarrel among Catholics reaching the Council. Now open controversy was
inevitable. Astutely Robert Cecil, in collusion with Bancroft, demanded that
the Appellants should give proof of their sincerity by publicly denigrating
the Archpriest and the Jesuits. When their first publication, printed in
England under Bancroft's protection, appeared in May 1601, the Council
was left in no doubt about the bitterness and significance of the dispute.
Instantly and instinctively Cecil realised that he had a weapon of disruption
in his hands.

Between May and July 1601 followed another four books in which the
Appellants stated their case. They blamed principally Persons and the Jesuits
for starting the quarrel. Garnet remarked: 'It was Father Weston's observation always that the factions, when they had committed any fault, they
would presently come and exclaim of the other part for the like, though
without any good ground at all. So do they now practice in these books.'[2]
In Garnet's opinion this was open schism: he wished that he could consider
it a less heinous offence, yet 'this is certain that [Pope] Clement [VIII] hath
expressly defined it to be *ex sua natura malum*'.[3] As far as Garnet could see,
the Appellants were as much schismatics as the Donatists or Arians, who,
like them, also attended 'the true sacrifice of the Church'.[4]

The strain of these dissensions taxed Garnet's health. 'On Corpus Christi
day (I think through extreme weariness of business) I was in case that I
thought I should never have been able to write more,' he told Persons,[5] 'but

[1] *Ibid.*
[2] H. G. to R. P. 14 July 1601. Stonyhurst, Grene *P.*, 537.
[3] H. G. to R. P. 2 June 1601. Stonyhurst, Grene *P.*, 553.
[4] *Ibid.*
[5] H. G. to R. P. 30 June 1601. Stonyhurst, Grene *P.*, 539–40.

now (I thank God) I am better than I was this great while.' By 'business' he meant always the work of assisting Blackwell in the defence of his authority. The frustrations Garnet had met, now sickened him. In July his depression was still upon him. His most promising young recruit, Richard Blount, was bedridden with a 'burning ague'. With his eye on anniversaries, Garnet wrote: '[I am] now in the last day of my fifteenth year in this wilderness.'[1]

The front for the attack was broadened. In their writings the Appellants now ridiculed the 'Jesuit' doctrine of equivocation. There could be no more irresponsible behaviour. Sadly Garnet reported that the Appellants were exultant ('very jolly' was his phrase) against Southwell: he sighed at the damage the dispute was doing to the priestly vocation. 'The ancient spirit of workmen is decayed. No marvel their intention is not as in former days.'[2]

Garnet could do no more now than order the prayers of his brethren for the end of the dispute. Before or after Mass each day Litanies were to be recited: twice each week every priest under his jurisdiction was to offer Mass for peace, or to recite the Rosary. If he was prevented from saying Mass, then 'every Sunday, when circumstances allow, there is to be a solemn procession', he ordered,[3] 'and, if it can be done, with the Most Holy Sacrament carried': and all laymen attending houses served by the Jesuits were asked to recite the Rosary twice in the week. The reason for the prayers was made known only to friends. 'I hope Customer [Blackwell] will do as we do', he told Persons.[4]

The collusion between certain Appellant priests and Bancroft, the Bishop of London, made Garnet's personal safety more precarious still. In the summer of 1601 there was a general London raid similar to the March raid seven years earlier. The rumour was that the Jesuits, acting as agents of King James of Scotland, had planned to assassinate the Queen. 'Last week', wrote Garnet on 30 June,[5] 'there was the cruellest search in London there ever was; and some days before and after the Court was guarded and the gates of London. . . . One Justice said he had searched four hundred houses.' Garnet escaped. 'Notwithstanding all our troubles', he ends, 'we sing Mass.'

About two weeks later the reasons for the search became known to Garnet. None of the Council had been informed; the initiative was Popham's, and only the Queen was in his confidence. Popham, Garnet reported,[6] 'is

[1] H. G. to R. P. 6 July 1601. Stonyhurst, Grene *P.*, 537–8.
[2] H. G. to R. P. 30 June 1601. Stonyhurst, Grene *P.*, 539–40.
[3] *Ibid.*
[4] *Ibid.*
[5] H. G. to Thomas Strange. 30 June 1601. Stonyhurst, Grene *P.*, 559.
[6] H. G. to R. P. 17 July 1601. Stonyhurst, Grene *P.*, 539.

said to have promised [her] the taking of twenty Jesuits and the Archpriest and his twelve Assistants. It is very credibly told me that there was hope especially to find Jesuits newly come in.' It was manifest that the Chief Justice had received from lapsed priests information on the whereabouts of the Jesuits. Garnet soon got confirmation of this.

From July until December 1601 there was a fresh stream of pamphlets, tracts and books, in which invective was replaced by uninhibited personal insults. The chief participant in the campaign was a squint-eyed deranged priest, William Watson. In his *Decacordon of Ten Quodlibetical Questions*, published in the second half of this year, he revealed the names and whereabouts of Jesuits throughout the country; also the names of their hosts, converts and friends. On this information Popham had based his confidence in catching at least twenty Jesuits in his June search. Unfortunately Watson provoked Persons to reply. After speaking of Watson's humble origins, Persons wrote that he was 'so wrong shapen and of so bad and blinking aspect that he looketh nine ways at once'. The abuse was more excusable in Persons, who resented Watson's accusation that he was illegitimate. This same summer Persons's aged mother, who had been in Garnet's care for many years, died. 'You will understand', Garnet wrote,[1] 'that those [who] lived long with [her] gave her singular commendation of honesty and gravity. The two gentlemen with whom she died do say that if R[obert] P[ersons] will swear that he is her son, they will swear that he is her husband's son.' Nevertheless the slur clung.

Before the end of the year Garnet received a copy of Persons' book in which the Archpriest was defended and the system of government set up for England by Clement VIII. Persons had begun writing only in the spring of this year, or possibly later,[2] when the first Appellant books reached Rome. The work was entitled *A brief Apologie of the Ecclesiastical Hierarchie*. On 16 December Garnet wrote making a correction on page 201: Persons had confused the priority of two letters written by Benstead. 'Mr Benstead wrote two letters and I sent them over, but that which was written first was sent last and taken to be later.'[3] On the chronology of these letters Persons had argued that Dr Bagshawe was responsible for his fellow-priest's death. Garnet desired that Persons should not overstate his case. He informed him that 'his death cannot be said [to have been] a recompense of his contradiction to the Doctor. Those ten lines should be blotted out.'[4]

[1] H. G. to R. P. 19 August 1601. Stonyhurst, Grene *P.*, 553.
[2] The introduction is dated 20 July 1601.
[3] H. G. to R. P. 16 December 1601. Stonyhurst, Grene *P.*, 554.
[4] *Ibid.*

U

At the same time Garnet maintained his visits to members of the Society in prison. Either in late August or early September he visited Wisbech, where Ralph Emerson, imprisoned all the years Garnet was in England, had been gravely sick. There also was Thomas Pound, a prisoner already when Campion met him soon after his arrival in London.[1] The living conditions of these Jesuits worsened daily. For months they had been allowed nothing but bread and water. Possibly as a result of Garnet's intervention, a small improvement was conceded. 'Now they may have their own meat', he reported, 'but [they] are kept from their chambers and not suffered to have their beds, but in two strait rooms [they] are forced to lie on mats on the ground to the number of twenty.' However, both Emerson and Pound, owing to their physical weakness, were later permitted beds.

[1] Thomas Pound was born at Belmont, Hampshire. His mother was the sister of the Earl of Southampton. On Elizabeth's accession he became one of her favourite courtiers, an eccentric, handsome, cultured youth who acted in plays and masques which he himself composed. In 1571 he became a Catholic, renouncing 'the favours of the Court as the very mermaid's allurements to perdition'. In 1574, when he was about to leave England to join the Society, he was arrested. For the next thirty years he lived in prison; he reckoned that he had been transferred thirteen times to different places of confinement and had spent £4,000 of his fortune in fines. In 1594 he was admitted into the Society but never became a priest. When finally he was released in 1603 he lived quietly in London until his death in 1616 at the age of seventy-six. *The Rambler*, new series, vol. 8 (1857), 24–38, 94–106.

RENEWED PERSECUTION

AT the beginning of 1602 the 'malcontents', as Garnet now termed them, caused fresh ferment, particularly in London, in the precinct of the Bishop's palace, and in East Anglia, where they used the prisons of Framlingham and Wisbech as centres of disaffection. In his first letter of the year[1] Garnet reported that the prisoners who had been given leave of absence to beg for the support of their brethren were resolved to remain obdurate 'until his Holiness be better informed'. One of them vented the question whether it was lawful 'to procure the Jesuits' death' on the ground that they sought to starve the prisoners and it was permissible for a man to kill in self-defence. Garnet, who first with Southwell and later with Gerard and others, had done more than any single priest in England to ease the hardship of Catholic prisoners, felt this fresh calumny sorely. Another itinerant Appellant affirmed that 'Mr Archpriest is Anti-Christ'.[2] At the same time, early in January, there came from the press a book less harmful but more scurrilous than Watson's entitled *An Answer made by one of our Brethren, a secular priest now in prison, to a fraudulent letter of Mr George Blackwell written to Cardinal Cajetan 1596 in commendation of the Jesuits in England.* It appeared under the initials A. P., and was the work of Robert Charnock, a priest who had left the English College shortly after the outbreak of the troubles there in order to stir up discord in England.[3]

Garnet reported sadly: 'These men are detested exceedingly and good Catholics will never have a good conceit of them again.'[4] Watson, on the strength of his betrayal of the Jesuits, was permitted to 'live where he will': Garnet added, 'though he be known generally, yet he goeth in his chain of

[1] H. G. to R. P. 13 January 1602. Stonyhurst, Grene *P.*, 540–1.

[2] *Ibid.*

[3] At Rome Charnock had been forbidden by the Holy See to return to England: nevertheless he did and for his disobedience was suspended by Blackwell. In the following year, with twelve other priests, he signed the *Protestation of Allegiance to Queen Elizabeth*, which virtually jettisoned Catholic loyalty to the Holy See.

[4] H. G. to R. P. 13 January 1602. Stonyhurst, Grene *P.*, 540–1.

gold, white satin doublet and hose and velvet jerkin' — an exact description drawn perhaps from a meeting Garnet had with him in his undying hope of winning over his enemies by his generosity. 'He maketh a common market of redeeming prisoners.'[1]

However, there were signs that might be taken to indicate an end of the schism. Persons's *Apologie* was in circulation early in January: the title explained its aim: *A Briefe Apologie, or defence of the Catholic ecclesiastical hierarchy and subordination in England, erected these later years by our holy father Pope Clement the eighth; and impugned by certain libels printed and published . . . under the name of priests of the seminaries.* The demand for the book was great. Since comparatively few copies were sent over from Antwerp, where it was first printed, it soon became a rarity. On 13 January this year Garnet told Persons that the 'Apology is come and beginneth to go forth'.[2] And without even making a guess at the reason, he noted the fact that the Bishop of London was 'very desirous' to obtain a copy. Possibly it was a tactical error on Persons' part to have written the book at all: the same year Bishop Bancroft himself had it reprinted in London in order to rekindle the controversy.[3]

Inevitably Persons was out of touch with the daily shifts in the Appellants' campaign; yet he was impatient to reply to every fresh tract written against the authority of Blackwell. Copies of his latest work had hardly been in England a few months when two answers appeared: *Certain Brief Notes upon a Brief Apology* by Dr Humphrey Ely, and Colleton's *Just Defence of the Slandered Priests*. Both were able and contentious. Garnet discouraged Persons from replying, for fear he should play into Bancroft's hands. If Persons did insist on answering, then Garnet recommended him not to join battle on the general issue, but to pick out some particular point in each book. Without reserve Garnet approved the *Apologie*. On 17 March he reported:[4] 'From all places I receive great congratulations for the *Apologie*: all marvel how much in particular could be said.'

As early as February the hopes of the Appellant priests to secure toleration through Bancroft were proved illusory. Garnet got word of a discussion on the question in the Privy Council this month: the Keeper of the Privy Seal had 'inveighed against the factious priests, though he said they were of a more scrupulous conscience than those that depended on the traitor Persons. . . . This will alienate many friends who all this while looked for toleration

[1] H. G. to R. P. 13 January 1602. Stonyhurst, Grene *P.*, 540–1.
[2] *Ibid.*
[3] Anthony Rivers: letter of 3 March 1602.   Foley, vol. 1, 21.
[4] H. G. to R. P. 17 March 1602. Stonyhurst, Grene *P.*, 539.

by their means.'[1] Garnet continued to urge strong measures. 'In my opinion', he declared, 'there was no more forcible means to curb the unbridled than, among other things, to determine that, after declaration of their stubbornness, they should lose *privilegium clericale.*'[2]

With individuals Garnet always counselled kindness: only after repeated personal approaches had failed did he propose that Colleton, Bluet and others should be warned against possible laicisation: the threat itself might bring them to realise the harm they were doing to the Church. 'The honour [of the priesthood] would move somewhat; but especially the fear of the laity, if they should unwisely accuse or slander them, which continually they do.'[3]

On their own initiative some eminent Catholic laymen had drafted a Latin letter to Clement VIII, expressing their loyalty to the Archpriest. Garnet judged that if the letter were despatched it would only fan the controversy: he advised that 'it must in no case go abroad for a good while'. Should the dispute again be taken to the papal court, Garnet proposed that certain factual corrections to the *Apologie* should be made in order not to arouse further antagonism. 'Only in common', he suggested, 'may it be said that there was a letter from some principal lay persons, but not in great number': but the letter itself, which was unequivocally phrased, was not to be sent. Garnet had reason for this. If the names of signatories became known 'there may come many examinations and oaths tended to such as may be imagined to have consented: and hereupon dependeth the quiet of all our friends'.[4]

Meanwhile Garnet had been gathering information to kill the slander of Persons's illegitimacy. It had been said that Persons was the son of a priest of Nether Stowey, called Cowbuck. Possibly at Persons's suggestion, Garnet had been in communication with a Mr Walker, the present incumbent and was able to report: 'Mr Walker sayeth that upon his knowledge there was never any parson of Stowey since King Edward [VI]'s time called Cowbuck, which were good to observe: besides the credit of the parties slandered.'[5]

From the flood of Appellant books Garnet anticipated only a renewal of persecution, which would fall most severely on his devoted priest friends from the seminaries and on the laymen who supported them. 'We expect', he wrote in March, 'all manner of persecution here by reason of these books, which will at the last turn to the prejudice of all, through the spleen and perverseness of a few.'[6] Indeed he had reason to be apprehensive, for the books

---

[1] H. G. to R. P. 20 February 1602. Stonyhurst, Grene *P.*, 537.
[2] *Ibid.*   [3] *Ibid.*
[4] *Ibid.*   [5] *Ibid.*
[6] H. G. to R. P. 9 March 1602. Stonyhurst, Grene *P.*, 542.

finally turned Puritans and other non-conformist groups against the Catholic community. There had never been any question of an alliance between Catholics and Puritans: henceforth, for the next hundred years or more, the Puritans became increasingly embittered against Catholics, interpreting this approach by the troublesome priests to the Council as a manœuvre against themselves. A Puritan tract, published in February 1602, and entitled *Humble Motives for association to maintain religion*, made this danger manifest. Immediately Garnet procured a copy and sent it to Fr Persons.[1] He was the first priest to foresee in the controversy a threat of a Puritan persecution against his own people.

Open attacks continued during the last year of Elizabeth's reign. Resort was had to most sinister and underhand methods which involved Garnet deeply, for Southwell's writings were used by the Appellants as an instrument to demonstrate that there was a rift, allegedly concealed for a long time, between Garnet and his brethren.

Southwell's *Supplication*, completed about a year before his arrest, had demolished the calumnies levelled against Catholics, particularly against his pupils at the English College in Rome.[2] It was perhaps the noblest piece of prose written in the decade. At that time, however, Garnet had judged it prudent not to print it, for the unanswerable force of its argument would, in his view, have brought fresh persecution on Catholics.

This year, however, the Appellants printed an expurgated version of the *Supplication*. By omitting certain strands in Southwell's argument, they were able to present the book to Clement VIII in March 1602 as proof that Garnet was unrepresentative of the Jesuits: and to argue that, like themselves, Garnet's own subjects were in favour of accommodation with the government. Already charged in Rome with publishing, in connivance with the government, several books that betrayed the recusant cause, they now determined to demonstrate that, Garnet apart, the Jesuits themselves were in league with the government. All the passages of fulsome praise addressed by Southwell to the Queen were printed in full, but none that thrusted at Cecil, whom Southwell had regarded as the instigator of the persecution. 'As a final piece of cynical bluff, they added the pious hope that the work would be condemned in general terms, without mention of the martyr's [Southwell's] name.'[3]

Garnet reported to Persons: 'Father Southwell wrote a very good answer

[1] H. G. to R. P. 9 March 1602. Stonyhurst, Grene *P.*, 542.
[2] Cf. *sup.*, p. 141.
[3] 'The Patriotism of Robert Southwell', by Christopher Devlin, in *The Month*, December 1953, 351.

to the Proclamation, but it could never be set forth, and when Mr Boswell [an Appellant priest] either for lucre or malice meant to print it, your friend Henry, seeing that now matters were quieted, and . . . that it might breed new troubles, requested Customer [the Archpriest] to forbid it.'[1] Blackwell's view was the same. He prohibited publication, but, as Garnet wrote in understatement, the prohibition 'was little regarded . . . '[2] The printer, James Duckett, for reasons known only to Bancroft, 'was hanged for divulging it, though he were on the malcontents' side, and they in vain sought to save him'.[3] Duckett was hanged at Tyburn on 19 April. 'He died well', says Garnet, 'and asked forgiveness of Customer [Blackwell] and Journeymen [Jesuits] for adhering to the malcontents.'[4]

The Appellants, however, had overreached themselves. Their fraudulence was exposed. In London Southwell's book, even in its vitiated version, was too damning an exposure of the Council for Bancroft to permit it to remain in print. 'The book I will get if I can', Garnet promised Persons, 'for they are all taken almost.'

In spite of the liaison between the Council and Appellant priests, the persecution continued. At the Lent Assizes in York, a Rheims priest, Matthew Harrison, was executed along with a layman, Antony Battie, in whose house he had been taken.[5] The Ecclesiastical Commission was 'very hot everywhere for lands and goods'.[6] In the north there were renewed enquiries, in known Catholic houses, concerning the number of children and servants in each: in London during April, while Garnet was in the country, three priests were executed at Tyburn on the same day,[7] on no other ground save that they had entered the kingdom as priests.[8] Significantly Garnet adds: 'all three, like our Saviour, were betrayed by false brethren'. It had happened before, but rarely: henceforth, hardly a year passed when at least one priest did not meet his death through betrayal by some lapsed priest who had been a fellow-student at his seminary.

The youngest of this group of three priests executed this April at Tyburn was Francis Page. He 'went to the hurdle, not as a slave, but as a commander'. On the day of his execution he was admitted into the Society. Presumably

[1] H. G. to R. P. 5 May 1602. Stonyhurst, Grene *P.*, 547.
[2] *Ibid.*
[3] *Ibid.*
[4] *Ibid.*
[5] H. G. to R. P. 14 April 1602. Stonyhurst, Grene *P.*, 554.
[6] *Ibid.*
[7] Thomas Tichborne, Robert Watkinson and Francis Page: all hanged, drawn and quartered at Tyburn on 20 April 1602.
[8] H. G. to Fabio de Fabiis. 5 May 1602. Stonyhurst, Grene *P.*, 554.

Garnet did not count him among the thirty-one Jesuits in England when he wrote to Aquaviva early in May and recounted Page's death. 'There are already thirty-one of us doing business, even though seven of them are in credit-houses [i.e. prisons], where nevertheless they are able to manage our affairs very well and with much better results than if they were elsewhere.'[1]

At last the Society in England was beginning to show an increase. This small band of Jesuits was to grow more rapidly every year: as the bitterness of attack intensified, more young men were attracted to its ranks.

At the same time Garnet was able to tell Aquaviva that the number of Catholics was growing faster now than at any time during the reign. The policy of Elizabeth had failed. It was perhaps a measure of her despair that fresh executions were ordered as her physical strength ebbed. 'The Catholics are increasing very greatly', Garnet wrote.[2] Then added a morsel of gossip. 'A few days ago the Queen rebuked Canterbury sharply and ordered him to carry out real persecution. This, however, was not necessary since they were already proceeding with the utmost severity in all parts of the country.' He continued — perhaps to nail the lie of the Appellants that their campaign had contained the persecution — 'Many people who think otherwise are deceiving themselves.'

In recent books published abroad about English Catholics many signs, portents and miracles had been narrated. Garnet never gave ready credence to them. 'In all this oppression', he stated, 'our trust is in Him who has conquered the world.'[3] Often, priests fresh from the seminaries, in the flush of their initial zeal, had written back excitedly of their first English experience. Garnet reported: 'I myself have seen here certain letters written by newcomers from Rome reporting various miracles that have occurred in these lands. But be that as it may.'[4] His hope was not based on them, but on the tireless zeal and self-sacrifice of his priests, on their patience and long-suffering. 'My brother Thomas,' he says, referring to Fr Lister, who had been causing him further trouble, 'whom I commended to your Lordship two years ago, is with me and is almost completely cured of his complaint. I hope that ... his native air will soon make him completely healthy. ... Visits to his family will certainly bring him no little benefit.'[5]

The bi-annual meetings continued. Now as many as fifteen would be present. Regularly before they dispersed Garnet would write to Aquaviva to convey the greetings of all his family and beg his blessing on them.

---

[1] H. G. to C. A. 5 May 1602. F.G. 651, f. 82.
[2] *Ibid.*
[3] *Ibid.*
[4] *Ibid.*   [5] *Ibid.*

The Irish Jesuit, Fr Holywood, had been captured and imprisoned at Wisbech. Shortly afterwards two Portuguese Jesuits on their way to Goa had been caught at sea and brought to England. Both were adventurous individuals, and their story supplies a humorous episode in this year of distress.

On their arrival in England they had been placed in the hands of a local constable. Both immediately escaped. Knowing nobody and with no suiting save their religious habit, 'they lived for some days in woods off roots and such things as they could get. But after[wards] they were espied and taken again. Yet one ran away and alighting on a schismatic was by his means apparelled Englishlike and conveyed where he is safe; and I will take order for him.'[1] This was Garnet's first reference to them. While he found a home for the escapee, Garnet kept in touch with his imprisoned brother; and on 4 August reported to Persons: 'A Portugal Journeyman [Jesuit] is escaped out of prison. I hope to see him this night.'[2] The second escaped shortly afterwards.

When Garnet wrote again on 18 October[3] the two Portuguese priests had already been with him 'now for several months'. He was anxious for Aquaviva's guidance, but at the same time pleaded that they should be considered 'treasure trove' and for the time being placed in Catholic houses where they could administer the sacraments until their passage to India was arranged. Garnet argued: 'The Fathers cannot make the journey to India without obvious danger: for what otherwise would be the safest way of travelling can by no means be safe for them, since their appearance and speech betray them as Portuguese.'[4] While ready to suffer martyrdom in India or Japan, the Portuguese did not consider their imprisonment in England in 'the cause of religion'. And Garnet feared that if in their attempt to get back to Portugal they were captured a third time, they would suffer for their previous escape. On the other hand, as he proceeded to point out, 'if they remain and labour in this vineyard and they fall into the hands of the enemy, then, even if they suffer severe imprisonment, it will be all for the sake of the Catholic religion, and they will be able to draw consolation from this. Finally, both have a wonderful desire to remain here, and there is no small fruit to be gathered from their labours, for once they become fluent in English (which they almost understand already) they can be received by Catholics with impunity since they are not subject to the anti-Catholic laws.'[5]

[1] H. G. to R. P. 4 August 1602. Stonyhurst, Grene *P.*, 554.
[2] *Ibid.*   [3] H. G. to C. A. 18 October 1602. F.G. 651. f. 84.
[4] *Ibid.*   [5] *Ibid.*

Garnet, of course, did not mean that the two priests would escape imprisonment: but their hosts would. He pressed his argument: 'They [the Portuguese priests] will not perhaps be able to move so freely from place to place
as their spiritual ministrations or the need to take to flight may require;
but on short and devious journeys, if they are accompanied by a trustworthy
guide, there will be no danger they cannot reasonably avoid.' Then he adds
sadly: 'Perhaps some priests will complain if they see Catholic households
snatched from them as though they were rich benefices. But England should
not be so inhospitable as to deprive them of a home and an opportunity
to preach the gospel, especially as they will be busy in places where it is
almost impossible for our own priests to go. They are men who have been
brought here by duress and forced to live here for a time.'

Garnet awaited Aquaviva's answer. In the interval his brethren came to a
different view. In November he told Persons that in the opinion of all his
friends it was dangerous 'to retain the Portuguese Journeymen'.[1] And in the
same sentence he inadvertently paid tribute to his own warm hospitality
and friendship to foreigners. 'They are unwilling', he says, 'to go.'

At midsummer Garnet went on a pilgrimage to St Winifred's well in
North Wales, a centre of devotion that had continued to draw crowds uninterruptedly through the years of persecution. A devoted priest, Fr Bennet,
frequently imprisoned, had preserved the affection of the people not only of
Flintshire but also of the neighbouring English counties for the Welsh
saint. Oldcorne had been there; Gerard also. Although this may not have
been Garnet's first pilgrimage, it is the first time he mentions it. Miracles
there had never ceased.[2] Possibly Garnet was seeking in prayer a divine
solution of the crisis which now appeared to him beyond means of human
healing. However, he is reticent on this, speaking only of his physical health.
On 4 August he announced: 'I purpose about Bartholomy-tide[3] to travel to
St Winifred's Well for to increase my strength.'[4] In another undated letter
he had written that he feared the palsy, meaning probably Parkinson's
disease, for he had remarked that he would rather 'shake at Tyburn than in
his chamber', and had 'marvelled that he had lived so long'.[5]

Earlier this year he had fallen sick. Now he felt the first signs of shaking
paralysis, the toll taken of his sensitive nature during the dissensions that

---

[1] H. G. to R. P. 17 November 1602. Stonyhurst, Grene *P.*, 537.

[2] An interesting collection of alleged miracles recorded at Holywell in the century of
Garnet's visit is recorded in the *Analecta Bollandica*, vol. 6 (1887), 305–52.

[3] The feast of St Bartholomew was on 24 August.

[4] H. G. to R. P. 4 August 1602. Stonyhurst, Grene *P.*, 554.

[5] H. G. to unknown correspondent. Stonyhurst, Grene *P.*, 554.

threatened to undo the work of the first heroic seminary priests. His sickness explains also his recurrent depression during the last critical years of his life. 'I leave Anthony Rivers to despatch business', he told Persons,[1] and added, 'I shall be absent about a month.'

Garnet's absence from London produced perhaps the most fascinating series of news-letters written in the last months of the old Queen's reign. Fr Anthony Rivers had already begun to write to Persons his own long and regular reports, containing gossip and news of the Court as well as events of national interest or excitement.[2] Now these letters became more detailed. 'The ache in the Queen's arm', Rivers had reported on 12 March,[3] 'is fallen into her side, but she is still, thanks to God, frolicky and merry, only her face showing some decay. . . . Sometimes as she is walking she will put off her petticoat, as seeming too hot, when others shake with cold.' Then, in succeeding letters, throughout the summer and autumn, he followed the course of the Queen's health. Even after Garnet's return to London, Rivers was left to report on national events, while Garnet himself made only an occasional and brief reference to them. On 25 August,[4] for instance, Garnet noted simply that Bancroft, the Bishop of London, planned to license the printing of more books by the Appellants. Rivers is elaborately detailed. On 7 July he reported that Bancroft had denied interpolating passages in the printed works of the Appellants, but had been given the manuscripts, which on his instruction had immediately been 'passed to the press without further censure or examination'.[5]

While Garnet saw no conclusion to the trouble with the Appellants, Persons became more hopeful. On his return from Holywell, Garnet wrote that 'all [were] glad of the good expectation he [Persons] has of a final end of these troubles which have so long molested us all. . . . Here we are very careful not to give any occasion of new complaints, however falsely they complain of us and our friends, whom we warn to be wary.'[6] The Appellants, who had attempted to have Blackwell's authority revoked, did no more than procure a Papal Brief, which re-asserted his jurisdiction on all points. At the same time Blackwell was reprimanded for severity. This second Brief was issued on 20 July.[7] Garnet had been informed of its contents. It was a

---

[1] H. G. to R. P. 4 August, 1602. Stonyhurst, Grene *P.*, 554.
[2] Foley, vol. 1, 1–63.
[3] *Ibid.*
[4] H. G. to R. P. 25 August 1602. Stonyhurst, Grene *P.*, 596.
[5] Foley, vol. 1, 43.
[6] H. G. to R. P. 25 August 1602. Stonyhurst, Grene *P.*, 596.
[7] Westminster Cathedral Archives, 7, 263–5. The text is printed in part in a footnote in Tierney-Dodd, vol. 3, clxxvii.

measure taken in good time. While its immediate effect was a temporary peace, it was peace at a high price. Eventually Blackwell, flying from criticism, fell under the influence of the Appellants and was deposed.

When Garnet got news of the Brief, he immediately sought out Colleton. He found he had left town, but, he says,[1] 'I sent word against Colleton's return, that I would . . . meet him most willingly, but with condition that we would have no reasoning of matters that should be forgotten.' On Monday after Trinity Sunday they met and embraced, 'and I thanked him for his kind letter' and told him that his conformity had taken away the only obstacle to his friendship. Colleton confessed to the calumnies he had spread against the Society and undertook to correct them.

Now Garnet's main concern was the new proclamation that was being prepared. At intervals in the summer months he received rumours of its contents; at the beginning of September he heard that it was drawn up, but not published: 'it lieth still in the dock, and we hope God will cross it'.[2] In his opinion nothing that the Pope might do would prevent it.

It was eventually published on 5 November 1602. In the preamble the Queen declared that she had tried in vain to bring Catholics to a reasonable frame of mind by exercising her royal prerogative of clemency, but had failed. Yet she was willing to distinguish between the traitorous Jesuits and the secular priests allied with them on the one hand, and the Appellants on the other. The former were continually plotting invasion and 'even to murder our person', while the Appellants, whom she called 'other secular priests', not only protest against such action as 'most wicked, detestable and damnable' but offer in their writings and speeches 'to be the first that shall discover such traitorous intentions'.[3] Indeed the charges laid against the Jesuits and their priest friends in the proclamation are identical with the charges made against them in the books written by the Appellants.

In an endeavour to drive a deeper wedge into the recusant body, the Queen further distinguished the treatment she proposed to give the two parties. All Jesuits and secular priests united with them were to leave the kingdom immediately, 'lest they provoke us to extend the rigours of our laws upon them': the 'other sort of secular priests' was given grace until 1 February 1603 to 'acknowledge sincerely their duty and allegiance to us' before the authorities and then be treated in a manner 'thought by us to be most meet and convenient'.

[1] H. G. to R. P. (undated) probably July 1602. Stonyhurst, Grene *P.*, 542–4.
[2] H. G. to R. P. 1 September 1602. Stonyhurst, Grene *P.*, 595.
[3] The full text of the Proclamation is printed in Rymer, *Foedera*, vol. 16 (1715), 473–6; and in Tierney-Dodd, vol. 3, clxxxiv-clxxxviii.

The issue had once again been brought back to the matter of the Royal Supremacy, which had divided Catholics in the reign of the Queen's father: every other pretext of persecution had now been laid bare by the heroism of the martyrs. Here was a question calculated to divide the Catholic body for years to come. It was a triumph for the Council.

Garnet remained serene. The Queen's offer could hardly be considered sincere, for the Appellant priests numbered only a handful. The first steps, however, had been taken to perpetuate the rift: not even the dissident priests were prepared to follow their course to the logical end, which was total schism. 'There is no execution of the Proclamation', Garnet reported on 15 December.[1] By the last week of the year only one priest, whose name is unknown, made his submission and asked for the protection of the law. 'We fear nothing but searches', Garnet added in the same letter. But he availed himself of the facilities the proclamation offered to speed the two Portuguese to the Continent and thence to the Indies.[2] Yet with his unerring instinct he saw in the measure a portent of fresh devices against the Jesuits, and particularly against himself.

[1] H. G. to R. P. 15 December 1602. Stonyhurst, Grene *P.*, 536.
[2] H. G. to R. P. 23 December 1602. Stonyhurst, Grene *P.*, 554.

32

END OF THE OLD REIGN

AT the beginning of the new year, the last of the old reign, Garnet was preoccupied. While Persons was in Rome, Garnet, as has been said, had written less frequently to Aquaviva; but early in January[1] he sent a letter to wish the General every blessing, and in the name of all his subjects to beg the protection of his prayers 'against all the attacks of our enemies, which now indeed begin to thicken'. He was uncertain 'whether it is because the prince of darkness foresees his time will be short, or because all the efforts of the heretics seem to have been thwarted by the prudence of our Holy Father'. For the moment the crisis appeared to have passed; Colleton and Mush had submitted. Garnet's forecast that the proclamation would 'die before it be three months old'[2] seemed exact; he urged Persons to restrain his pen and make no answer. 'If any answer [to the proclamation] be made, we wish the Secretary [Robert Cecil] to be spared as much as may be.'[3]

Unceasingly Garnet worked for peace. His belief was that Catholics had better hope of toleration if they remained fast to the precepts of their faith and gave constant proof of their loyalty to their sovereign, than by behind-stage negotiations that might compromise their loyalty to the Holy See. Only to Aquaviva could he write:[4]

'If in this matter I should take some pride, I shall not, as it seems to me, be unreasonable; for by God's goodness they have nothing to lay to my charge but God's true faith, sincere obedience to Peter's chair and zeal to help my neighbours — if not by bringing them back to the bosom of the Church, then by inciting them to a better life. In truth this is the purpose I pursue with all my strength, and, as far as in me lies, I give to none any ground for offence, though maybe there are some who seek pretexts for estrangement from those who are their friends.'

[1] H. G. to C. A. 19 January 1603. F.G. 651, f. 164; Stonyhurst, *Anglia* 3, 31; F.G. 651, f. 164.
[2] H. G. to R. P. 15 December 1602. Stonyhurst, Grene *P.*, 536.   [3] *Ibid.*
[4] H. G. to C. A. 19 January 1603. Stonyhurst, *Anglia* 3, 31; F.G. 651, f. 164.

His satisfaction at what seemed a settlement was great. He hoped that none would now seek grounds for fresh quarrels: 'only let there be peace within the household of the faith, as we hope there may be'.[1] If that was given him, he had nothing to fear. His and Aquaviva's enemies were shared in common: if they 'should revile us, we will endure it'.

It was certain now that this would be the Queen's last winter. At the end of April the Countess of Nottingham's death sent her into a deep melancholy:[2] she began to complain of many infirmities 'as imposthumation near her head, aches in her bones, and continual colds in her legs'.[3] In Scotland James was making ready to cross the border: he had reviewed his troops in Edinburgh, and it was reported that he could bring fourteen thousand horses into the field, most of them Scottish nags. To prepare against a *coup* by the Spanish faction, Robert Cecil brought the local companies of militia into a state of preparedness. Grain was laid up in London storehouses against a siege: a ditch was planned, between the Tower and Westminster, to include in its circuit the northern suburbs of the city.

None of this news was given in Garnet's letters. He noted, however, that the persecution was unabated. Popham, the proclamation as his pretext, pursued his own almost private persecution; at the beginning of the year Garnet feared another general search throughout London and the suburbs for Jesuits and their priest friends who had not obeyed its clauses. 'The proclamation is read in all parish churches of England', reported Fr Rivers.[4] 'Great persecution is like to fall on the Papists. God send all may turn to the best.'

In February Fr William Richardson, Garnet's friend, was betrayed to Popham and arrested in London: at his trial, Popham acted both as judge and prosecutor. Bursting into the court, he interrupted the Recorder, who was trying some felons, sent for Richardson from Newgate and had him indicted. As there were no witnesses, Popham himself made a deposition to the jury, who, on the strength of it, found the priest guilty. Richardson then spoke: he called Popham a 'bloody man' who lusted for the lives of Catholics.[5]

Among the questions Popham asked his victim was whether or not he

[1] *Ibid.*

[2] The Countess was Katharine, daughter of Henry (Carey), first Baron Hunsdon. She was a lady of the Privy Chamber to Queen Elizabeth and died on 25 February 1603 at Arundel House, which had been granted to the Earl of Nottingham as part of the estate of Philip Howard, the attainted Earl of Arundel.

[3] Letter of Anthony Rivers, 9 March 1603. *S.P.D. Eliz.*, 287, no. 50.

[4] Letter of Anthony Rivers, Foley, vol. 1, 52.

[5] *S.P.D. Eliz.*, 287, no. 53.

knew 'Mr Garnet'. Richardson answered, 'No'. He was executed on 17 February, the last martyr of Elizabeth's reign. 'His conflict is admired by all', wrote Garnet,[1] '[and] he gave also a singular testimony to Jesuits at the bar.' 'His behaviour,' wrote another priest,[2] 'moved many to compassion and to speak against the Chief Justice's cruelty, on whom alone they laid the guilt of his blood. Such spectacles do nothing increase the Gospel.'

On 9 March Rivers reported accurately on the Queen's health: she 'rests ill at night, forbears to use the air in the day, and abstains more than usual from her meat, resisting physic and is suspicious of some about her as ill-affected'. As she approached her end, Garnet got news of the death of Fr Persons's sister and reported it in a letter of 16 March.[3] In his estimation she was 'half a martyr'. On the pretence of seeking for stolen geese, searchers had entered her house on Christmas night and 'looked in her boxes for other manner of geese', and found there *Agnus Dei*s and beads. It was not the first time she had been persecuted for her brother's sake. Some years earlier she had been hunted out of her home by a minister. Now she was too frail to endure the rough treatment she received. She was literally frightened to her death, which occurred on the feast of Holy Innocents.[4] She left a little wryneck boy whom Garnet now took into his care.[5]

Finally, on the vigil of the Annunciation of Our Lady, 24 March, about three o'clock in the morning the Queen died 'easily like a ripe apple from the tree', according to a diarist of the day.[6] Weston, still a prisoner in the Tower, reported the excitement there on her death: he was the single witness to a sinister phenomenon. 'During those few days she lay dying beyond all hope of recovery', he observed,[7] 'a strange silence descended on the whole city, as if it were under interdict and divine worship suspended. Not a bell rang out. Not a bugle sounded — though ordinarily they were often heard.'

On 25 March, at eight or nine o'clock in the morning, James was proclaimed King in London. As the heralds entered the Tower, Weston watched 'the style and order of the proceedings'[8] from the window of his cell. On his way to London, James halted at York, where he knighted Fr Gerard's brother, Thomas, in appreciation of the loyalty that united the two families.

[1] H. G. to R. P. 16 March 1603. Stonyhurst, Grene *P.*, 554.
[2] Anthony Rivers. Cf. Foley, vol. 1, 55.
[3] H. G. to R. P. 16 March 1603. Stonyhurst, Grene *P.*, 554.
[4] *Ibid.*
[5] H. G. to R. P. 11 May 1603. Stonyhurst, Grene *P.*, 554.
[6] Diary of John Manningham. 24 March 1603 (*Camden Society*, vol. 99, 146).
[7] *William Weston*, 221–2.
[8] *Ibid.*

'I am particularly bound to love your blood', the King told Thomas Gerard, 'on account of the persecution you have borne for me.'[1] Gerard did not consider the knighting of his brother any great advancement for a man whose ancestors had been knights already for sixteen generations.

Both Gerard and Garnet cherished hopes of toleration. 'Since my last letter of 16 March', Garnet wrote three weeks after the Queen's death,[2] 'there has happened a great alteration . . . . Great fears were: but all are turned into greatest security: and a golden time we have of unexpected freedom abroad.' He reported that the date of the King's coming was still uncertain: then he continued:[3] 'Great hope [there] is of toleration: and so general a consent of Catholics in the [King's] proclaiming [that] it seemeth God will work much. All sorts of religions live in hope and suspense; yet the Catholics have great cause to hope for great respect, in that the nobility all almost labour for it and have promise thereof from his majesty.' Garnet warned Persons that it would bring disaster on English Catholics if the Papacy, working through princes abroad, should attempt to hinder James from assuming 'the peaceable possession of the kingdom'. It was no time for exiled Catholics to urge the claim of any 'foreign competitors'.[4] The prospects for Catholics had not been brighter since Garnet was a boy at Winchester: he recommended Rome to consider whether a nuncio should be sent to confer with the King. 'I think it would be to good effect', he said,[5] and he saw no reason why a nuncio should not be received; both the Council and the King were anxious for peace with Spain; there was need only for the Pope to assist them in securing it and for goodwill to be established. However, Garnet had one reservation: already the campaign of the Appellants had partially succeeded in stigmatising the Jesuits as disloyal subjects in distinction from the priests in league with the government. 'There are some threats against the Jesuits', wrote Garnet in the same letter, 'as [persons] unwilling to acknowledge his Majesty's title, ready to promote the Spaniard, meddling in matters of state and authors especially of the *Book of Succession*.'

This was one side of the picture: on the other side, Garnet had friends at Court, even in the Council. The principal Catholic laymen, he pointed out, held a different conceit of Jesuits and were working on the Lords to get the King to accept their view. Now, on behalf of the Society in England, Garnet wrote a formal letter, dated 28 March 1603, protesting the loyalty of the

---

[1] *John Gerard*, 213.
[2] H. G. to R. P. 16 April 1603. Stonyhurst, *Anglia* 3, 32.
[3] *Ibid.*
[4] *Ibid.*
[5] H. G. to R. P. 16 April 1603. Stonyhurst, *Anglia* 3, 32.

x

Society to Elizabeth's successor: it was addressed to a high-ranking nobleman, and by him was to be shewn to the King. Only part of it survives.[1]

The nobleman to whom the letter is addressed was unnamed, but he had
sufficient credit with 'divers of the peers and councillors of the realm' to
command the hearing of the King: at the right time and place he was to
declare the loyalty of the Society to James, who would never have cause
to regret the trust he might be pleased to place in its members. On their side,
the Jesuits protested that they would 'most effectually, with words, actions and
hearty prayers to Almighty God always deserve' his regard. The union of
the crowns of England and Scotland was the common happiness in which the
Jesuits wished to share as much as his Majesty's other subjects. Furthermore,
Garnet's friend was commanded to express to the King and Council 'the
very bottom of our inmost thoughts', so that the Jesuits might be protected 'as
dear and not unnatural subjects' of the Crown. 'We therefore,' Garnet
concluded, 'present unto his Highness, as in the sight of God and his saints
and all the world, all the love, fidelity, duty and obedience which can be
desired or yielded by any Christian heart', even though the King has no need
to concern himself with this assurance of 'so small a company of poor, weak
and disgraced religious men'.

While Garnet expressed the sentiments of his subjects, Gerard, now in
touch with those nearest to the King, expressed the hopes of the Catholic
community. What he writes[2] registers the conversation in Catholic houses at
the time and Catholic opinion throughout the country. 'True it is', says
Gerard introducing his comments, 'that most Catholics had great hope and
expectation of King James. . . . And this hope did bring some comfort with
it amidst the many discomforts sustained under the long-continued reign
of Queen Elizabeth.' They had reason to expect that 'the son of such a
mother', who had lived a Catholic and 'died also because she was a Catholic',
would be a friend to Catholics, if not a follower of the Catholic religion.
'Who would think', Gerard asks, 'that the son should join in friendship and
confidence with them, and with only them, that had betrayed and slain both
his father and mother and who had kept himself so long like a ward in his
own kingdom.' There was no reason why James should pursue the policies
of Elizabeth. At the beginning of her reign, Gerard contended, there were
several reasons why the Council should urge the Queen to break with Rome.
'This they pretended to be needful; first in respect of her nativity, which they
knew was not esteemed legitimate by the see of Rome. Then for the favour
Rome was known to have for Mary, the Dowager Queen of France and

---

[1] H. G. to a Catholic Gentleman. 28 March 1603. Stonyhurst, Grene *P.*, 582–3.
[2] *Narrative*, ch. 2.

Queen of Scotland; and the affection all Catholics of England were known to have for her because of her true descent from Henry VII and [for] her constant love and profession of the Catholic faith.' These considerations, however, did not touch James, 'who was the true and hopeful issue of so worthy a mother'. Moreover, there was nothing for the King to fear from Rome, 'who had favoured him much and assisted him in many ways whilst yet he was but King of Scotland'.

Pursuing his hypothesis, Gerard continued: 'Many Catholics, knowing [the King's] wisdom and learning, could not persuade themselves how it would be possible that he would be drawn to any other manner of proceeding', for the toleration of Catholics in England would bring peace abroad and unite the Christian world 'in the firmest league of friendship'. English Catholics, as Gerard observes, were convinced that James had the sagacity to see that any war on the Church at home would be lost unless the Church was eradicated also from Continental countries. This belief was strengthened by the King's own words and promises of toleration, and by his often repeated exhortation to his son to cherish those who had been faithful to his family.

Both Englishmen and Scots at James's court in Edinburgh had expected the King to grant unconditional toleration. The King's own attitude to the Catholic faith was most acutely summed up by Gerard: 'Albeit that for his religion he could be no other than as he had been brought up and instructed, yet was he averse from all severity of persecution against such as were of different religion, especially the Catholic [religion]: granting it to be the ancient mother religion of all the rest, though in some things now amiss in his opinion.'[1] Moreover there were reports that 'out of his own reading he had observed that all his ancestors, kings and queens, both of England and Scotland, without exception had been of the Catholic Roman faith and religion and that himself was the first among them all that ever professed a different religion from them'.[2]

This was the conversation of Catholics. It had been rumoured that the King had sent abroad embassies to proclaim that he would grant toleration to all his subjects. Moreover, on the Queen's death, leading Catholic laymen from England, and certain priests also, had written to Edinburgh to profess their loyalty in the name of the entire Catholic body: and 'at that time and to those persons it is certain that [the King] did promise that Catholics

---

[1] *Narrative*, 22. Gerard is here echoing a sentence of James I's speech to his first Parliament: 'I acknowledge the Roman Church to be our mother Church, although defiled by some infirmities and corruptions. . . .'

[2] *Narrative*, 23–4.

should not only be quiet from any molestations, but should also enjoy such liberty in their houses privately as themselves would desire, and have both priests and sacraments with full toleration and desired quiet'. This was all that Catholics desired. Neither Garnet nor any Jesuit sought more than freedom to administer the Sacraments, for they believed that the grace that came through them would do more to win back England to the faith than any tract, treatise or political intrigue.

Neither Garnet nor Gerard give the names of the priests who were spokesmen of the English Catholics before James VI. Gerard, however, knew them and on their first-hand statements wrote: 'Both priests did kneel before him [James VI] when he gave his promise [binding it with the word of a Prince which he said was never yet broken, and] did protest so much unto divers from whom I have heard it. And divers others, persons of great worth, have assured me the same upon the like promise received from his Majesty, both for the common state of Catholics and their own particular.'[1]

The failure of James, on reaching London, to honour his promise of limited toleration for Catholics was the principal cause of the Gunpowder Plot in which Garnet was to lose his life. Gerard, writing soon after the Plot, had no doubt of this: his words are little known but express the broken and bitter spirit of the Catholic community.

'But now what shall we think to have been the state of all Catholic minds when all these hopes did vanish away; and as a flash of lightning, giving for a time a pale light unto those that sit in darkness, doth afterwards leave them in more desolation? What grief we may imagine they felt generally, when not only no one of these hopes did bring forth the hoped fruit, nor any promise was performed, but when, on the contrary side, his Majesty did suffer himself to be guided and as it were governed by those that had so long time inured their hands and hardened their hearts with so violent a persecution; yea, when he did not only confirm the former laws with which we were afflicted, but permitted new and more grievous vexations to fall upon us than before we had felt, and prepared yet more and more heavy whips wherewith to scourge us?

'Truly the event proved contrary to all our hopes. For first it was observed that some weeks after his being in England, he began to use far different speech of and against Catholics than was expected from the son of such a mother. And when soon afterwards there ensued his first Parliament, he made a bitter speech (now extant in print) against them all; but especially against the See Apostolic, much different from that was expected, where so great favours and tokens of love had been received.'[2]

[1] *Narrative*, 23–4.   [2] *Ibid*, 25.

In London James came under other influences. At first he tried to steer a middle course between mild persecution and limited freedom. There had been alarm at the more open activity of Catholics in the first months of the reign: Mass had been said with less secrecy. Catholics had given the impression of being stronger and more numerous than in fact they were. In alarm Cecil protested to the Venetian ambassador that priests were now openly saying Mass in the country. At Douai Dr Matthew Kellison, who was completing his *Survey of the new Religion*,[1] boldly dedicated his treatise to the King: in his preface he alleged that the Catholics in England were more numerous than any other sect in the realm: and that the King, in adopting his mother's religion, would be on the side of the greater number of his people.

It was not, perhaps, the wisest argument to use with Cecil. James for his part declared that Catholics had no cause to fear for their lives, but that the laws affecting their property would be enforced: moreover, a new proclamation was issued for the banishment of priests and Jesuits. Thus it came about that in May 1603, Weston, who had been a prisoner for all but Garnet's first few weeks in England, was led on the first stages of his journey from the Tower to Dover, where he embarked for the Continent. The scene at the Tower wharf, as he stepped into the boat that was to take him to Gravesend, expressed the mood of Catholics. A vast number was there to salute the figure who had become an emblem of their long-suffering under Elizabeth: some fell on their knees to beg his blessing; some simply greeted him or congratulated him on enduring nobly so many years of solitude and confinement: 'Others sent me messengers with money. . . . One man pressed a purse into my hand, so full that it could hardly be shut. . . . It required almost violence not to accept the gifts that there were offered me, for I took only what seemed necessary to cover the expenses of the journey.'[2]

After several decades of persecution Catholics could not be blamed for expressing, not always discreetly, their belief that at long last their sufferings were over, and that, with freedom to preach, their countrymen would return in large numbers to their old faith. As Weston passed through Canterbury, he had a conversation with the Protestant hostess at the inn where he stayed overnight. 'I do not know', he wrote,[3] 'whether on any previous occasion in her life she had seen a priest or spoken to a Catholic but I record the encounter to show how attractive even to the ears of heretics (excluding, of course, the badly corrupted) is the teaching and practice of the Catholic faith, if only

---

[1] *A Survey of the new Religion, detecting many gross absurdities, which it implieth* (Douai, 1603).
[2] *William Weston*, 223–4.
[3] *Ibid*, 225.

it is made known; and how close is our people to accepting the faith, if it were possible to preach it freely among them.'

At Rome Aquaviva was cautious. He feared that English Catholics would emerge from hiding too soon and too brazenly and thus invite fresh persecution. Writing from Rome on 9 July[1] he exhorted Garnet to extreme prudence: he was to see that his subjects 'in no way meddled in matters that did not concern their apostolate', or permitted others in mistaken zeal to 'attempt anything that by chance might bring considerable distress not only on you and me, but on all Catholics in general'.

It is almost as though both Garnet and Aquaviva had a premonition of the disastrous plot that lay just twenty-six months ahead, almost to the day. Both feared that rash action now would destroy all that had been so laboriously preserved from the ruins of Marian Catholicism; they knew, moreover, that any negotiations to obtain toleration through foreign Princes would be rendered null if there were resort to violence at home. Aquaviva spoke with unwonted severity: his tone of command is unmistakable:

'By the unfathomable mercy of Christ, Our Lord, I implore you to be prudent. Shun every species of activity that might make priests of our Order hated by the world and branded the instigators of tragedy or subverters of peace or the trouble-makers of the world. Divine providence knows how to maintain its order in its own place and time, as St Leo says. For our part we must offer earnest prayers meanwhile that God may assist us with his supporting hand. That is certainly my mind and I am not alone. He [the Pope] who, by God's commission, has in his hands the guidance of the whole ship, has in explicit words ordered me to give you this command in most grave and serious terms. This, on other accounts also, we are confident that you will in your prudence observe.'[2]

In the very first months of James's reign, there was established an even deeper understanding between the Superior of the English Jesuits and his General in Rome. It is in the framework of the Pope's injunction, expressed through Aquaviva, that the actions of Garnet's last years must be interpreted: henceforth all his letters are concerned either with restraining Catholics from violence or with trivialities. 'I hear one say that he thought [the Crown jewels] were worth twelve millions', he wrote to Persons on 3 June; 'others put their value at two hundred thousand pounds. There were also in the Tower fifteen hundred rich gowns of the Queen.'[3] Then, rather more than three weeks later, he continued:[4] 'The jewels of the Crown are certainly

[1] C. A. to H. G. 9 July 1603. Arch. S.J. Rome, Fland. Belg. 1, 2, II, f. 888.
[2] *Ibid.*   [3] H. G. to R. P. 3 June 1603. Stonyhurst, Grene *P.*, 554.
[4] H. G. to R. P. 29 June 1603. Stonyhurst, Grene *P.*, 554.

valued at twelve millions of pounds; the Queen's private jewels were worth five hundred thousand pounds, and the Lady which kept them gave up to the value of forty thousand more than were booked.'

These reckonings, exact or not, distracted Garnet from the work that was to give him no rest, but only increasing sorrow, for the few remaining years of his life.

33
UNREST

GARNET and Aquaviva were of like mind; they exchanged few letters; Persons, still in Rome, was able to explain satisfactorily to the General the needs of the mission: 'and it would be imprudent to multiply letters without need, the post is so uncertain and dangerous'.[1] From time to time, however, it gave Garnet comfort to write directly to Aquaviva and, 'as it were, talk personally to a most loving father and receive from him his most welcome blessing and consolation'.[2] Garnet had with him now in London a Scottish Jesuit, Fr Alexander McQuirrie, well known to James's friends, who had come with him from Edinburgh to London, and he was daily and eagerly awaiting the arrival of Fr William Creighton from France, who 'will be able to get access to the King himself and without any difficulty be able to clear us from any stigma of sedition'.[3]

Garnet feared only that, in their undying hatred, the enemies of the Church should demand that the Jesuits be treated more severely than the rest of the Catholic body; yet he was confident in the representations of the Catholic nobility, 'who know us intimately and love us in a special manner and will, all of them, defend our innocence'.[4]

Now for the first time Garnet wrote with an uncanny premonition that Robert Cecil was determined to involve him personally in a plot against the Crown. 'But if anything is determined against me individually it will come entirely from the fury and hatred that the heretics have against the Church. . . . In that event I must, whatever happens, stand my ground and breast the unbroken strength of these storms with all my constancy.'[5] For the present he and his brethren were enjoying unwonted peace which he prayed might continue.

During the summer months Garnet was optimistic, perhaps for the last time. In spite of his declaration that he would write less frequently to

[1] H. G. to C. A. 20 July 1603. F.G. 651, f. 166.
[2] *Ibid.*
[3] *Ibid.*   [4] *Ibid.*   [5] *Ibid.*

Aquaviva, he sent him in the early autumn[1] another letter, full of affection, in answer to the General's 'loving and solicitous letter' of July: he was comforted that the Pope emphatically forbade Catholics to take any violent measures to secure toleration: they should await in patience the reward of their forebearance. 'There are not wanting restless men', Garnet warned Rome ominously, 'who, even in our own name, entice our most intimate friends to rebellion, enjoining on them absolute secrecy.'

The remaining few years, indeed months, that Garnet survived the new reign, were filled with anxieties such as he had not known in times of the most relentless persecution. Within days of James's arrival in London, Garnet's 'intimate friends' became restive. Their conscience was clear, their loyalty to the King's family beyond cavil; already they were contemplating a bloodless *coup* that would induce the King to observe his promises.

As the first year of the new reign advanced, the hopes of Catholics were cruelly disappointed. Garnet preached restraint; Gerard explained the dejection of his friends:

'For when at the end of the first Parliament the Puritans packed together therein, and urged many new laws to [the] prejudice of [Catholics] for their greater affliction, his Majesty, that with one word might have stayed their fury by saying (as is accustomed in such cases when a Prince will show favour) that he would deliberate and consider of the matter, confirmed first all the most sharp and rigorous laws and statutes which the late Queen or her father or brother had made against Catholics, for afflicting them or shedding their blood. And, secondly, he adjoined new statutes of his own that augmented greatly the grievances of the former. . . . By all which we may plainly see that . . . all hopes were foiled on which Catholics did build their comforts.'

And Gerard had the suspicion that the government was deliberately trying to drive Catholics to desperate measures, and so provide itself with an excuse for their extermination. It was thought, he says, that they were now attempting 'to drive men to despair, presuming perhaps, that some amongst so many thousands would not be so patient as to bear it long, but that despair would urge them to some desperate attempt, whereby the chief causers of this persecution might give the better pretence of the cruelty they intended against them for the satisfaction of foreign Princes'.[2] Then referring to the Gunpowder Plot, he adds: 'Yes, it is verily thought by many of the wiser sort, that these things, with others that followed, were the spurs that set those gentlemen upon that furious and fiery course which they afterwards fell into.'

---

[1] H. G. to C. A. 22 September 1603. F.G. 651, f. 168.
[2] *Narrative*, 29–30.

It was this despair of obtaining any measure of relief from the King that 'did urge them to take the bit in their teeth and run headlong . . . to that desperate course' of setting up in his place one of his younger children, 'a thing very much lamented by all the body of Catholics in England, whose thoughts were only bent now to possess their souls in patience'.[1]

Already, before September, Garnet was agitated. Perhaps it was Gerard who first made him acquainted with what was passing in the minds of their common friends. 'When one of our brethren discovered this, he came straightway to me. At once I sent a message and all was quiet where previously the greatest danger had threatened.'[2]

With the arrival of the new Spanish ambassador, Don Bernardino de Mendoza, in the late summer, the hopes of Catholics momentarily rose: there were indications of a fresh spirit among them. 'As a result of the arrival and pleading of the Spanish envoy,' Garnet noted in the same letter, 'some now allow us more free commerce.' He added that he himself had been delated to the Council as the one man in England on whom war or peace with Spain depended. 'It hangs,' the King had been told, 'on my will and decision.'

'How utterly absurd', Garnet commented, 'I neither saw the person nor spoke to him; nor are the envoys of princes the kind of men who seek my advice. However some friends effectively removed the suspicion and corrected the nonsense.' Significantly he added that there had been a persistent search 'for two of our brethren' and a vast sum of money offered for their arrest.

Garnet was certainly one of 'the brethren'. From the very start of the new reign, Robert Cecil sought particularly to capture Garnet and another unnamed Jesuit, probably John Gerard, and thus make it impossible for them to interfere with the development of his schemes. He knew that the men later to be caught up in the Gunpowder Plot were their friends. From April onwards descriptions of Gerard were being sent personally to Cecil. He is 'a tall black man, very gallant in apparel', wrote Bishop Bancroft of London to Cecil,[3] 'and being attended by two men and a foot boy is exceedingly well horsed'. His movements were watched; he was rumoured to have crossed to Ireland via Westchester: an informant noted, perhaps correctly, that recently he had been in London disguised with 'an artificial beard and periwig of a brown colour, somewhat dark. . . . He was met with in Clerkenwell after this fashion.'[4]

[1] op. cit., 30.
[2] H. G. to C. A. 21 September 1603. F.G. 651, f. 168.
[3] Bancroft to Cecil. 11 April 1603. Hatfield Calendar, 15, 25.
[4] Ibid., 14, 194.

Throughout these years Garnet had drawn closer to Gerard: he admired his subject's loyalty and resourcefulness, and now confided in him, as he had formerly done in Southwell. The respite caused by the arrival of the new Spanish ambassador was short-lived. In the early weeks of autumn the prospects of a bad harvest were confirmed: this could mean only a recurrence of the pestilence. 'Plague will follow immediately on the severe famine', Garnet wrote,[1] ... 'because the poorer people can neither sell their possessions to buy food, nor acquire food by labour, so much does the cruel contagion rage secretly everywhere.'

It was the plight of the plague-stricken that momentarily distracted Garnet from the exasperation of his Catholic friends, on whose houses throughout East Anglia, the midlands and the west country the whole of his work for the Church had been constructed. Starting in early May, the plague raged throughout the summer, declining only in the late autumn: more than 30,000 were reckoned to have died in London alone.[2] Occasionally Garnet noted the official returns: in August, before it had reached its peak, Garnet reported: 'the total of this week of all diseases is 2077 and the total of the four last weeks is 7,247. It is dispersed all over England.'[3]

In the last months of 1603 Garnet was isolated and uneasy. While in the midlands and south of England, Catholics were left in peace, there was a fresh outbreak of persecution in the north: 'intolerable and continual searches' in which 'any base fellow must presently be admitted to search a house and seize on goods'.[4] However, his fears that this violence would spread to the south were unfounded. Within a few weeks he was writing to Persons on the disposition and support of priests in conditions of liberty: 'I have not yet seriously thought or conferred on this point,' he told Persons,[5] but, in so far as he had done, he thought it better that they 'went a-begging'. He considered it would be a mistake to demand their support from the State in any treaty of toleration. But in no case 'let there be any division of parishes as yet: for then someone will plant himself in whole shires and new comers-in will be excluded'. And he ends sadly: 'this we find by experience'.

For the present, Catholics in the south were enjoying what he described as 'some contentment of toleration'.[6] It was not unlikely that the penal legislation would be revoked: it was said that a petition had been presented to the

---

[1] H. G. to C. A. 21 September 1603. F.G. 651, f. 168.
[2] F. P. Wilson, *The Plague in Shakespeare's London* (1927), 141.
[3] H. G. to R. P. 16 August 1603. Stonyhurst, Grene *P.*, 554.
[4] H. G. to R. P. 22 September 1603. Stonyhurst, Grene *P.*, 553.
[5] H. G. to H. P. 26 November 1603. Stonyhurst, Grene *P.*, 596.
[6] *Ibid.*

King, demonstrating the numerical strength of Catholics. With many others, Garnet was against 'the gathering of names', for it exposed the signatories to reprisals if the mood of the government should change. His advice was that Catholics should work through members of the Council who were known to be friendly: they should not ask any recompense, only the assurance that they would get recognition 'when all be done'.

'We desire haste', he urged Persons.

For the next twelve months Garnet remained more silent than he had done since his arrival in England: there is only one letter of his extant for the entire year. Written before the end of January,[1] it is brief, dutiful and largely uninformative. Once again he asked Aquaviva's blessing on himself and his subjects, still increasing in number every month: the work of his priests should meet with even greater success if the domestic situation does not worsen. 'I must not fail to mention', he writes again, 'that what I had in the forefront of my mind, is the joy we derive from the long-enduring care your Reverence has of this very diminutive company. Already over so many years we have had experience enough of your affection. It has never grown less: on the contrary it has ever increased to an extent that nothing almost can be added to it. Mr Robert[2] will explain how this is so . . . . All our good friends acknowledge it, also all those whose eyes were once held in blindness.'

For the rest of the year Garnet remained silent. Between January and October at least he enjoyed peace such as he had seldom experienced for more than a few consecutive days in his eighteen years as a priest in England. There was nothing to report, so in his shrewdness he wrote nothing. By his silence he showed that the government had nothing to fear from the Jesuits: his success was measurable by the contrivances that the Council used to check it. There was a detailed description of his person in their hands: a man 'of middling stature, full-faced, fat of body, of complexion fair, his forehead high on each side, with a little thin hair coming down upon the middest of the fore part of his head: the hair of his head and beard grisled. Of age between fifty and threescore. His beard on his cheeks cut close, and his gait upright and comely for a feeble man.'[3]

Only by ensnaring this tired apostle in a plot could the name of the Society be brought into the odium that would end its influence in England. Meanwhile throughout the southern and south-midland shires, Garnet, like Gerard and his other companions, went about ministering to the spiritual needs of the Catholics. At Easter 1604 he was in Lincolnshire and was reported to have

[1] H. G. to C. A. 29 January 1604. F.G. 651, f. 169.
[2] Fr Robert Persons.
[3] Proclamation for Garnet's arrest (1606).

said Mass at Twigmore, Thornham and Glandford Brigg, a small fishing hamlet twenty-four miles north-east of Lincoln. It was the first time since his arrival in England that his presence in the country had been accurately reported.[1] In November his brethren held their last meeting at White Webbs. On the 21st Garnet wrote: 'Today being the feast of the Presentation of Our Lady, there happened to be here together by good fortune John [Gerard], Blunt, Percy, Cornforth (these three last renewed their vows). . . . High Mass was sung.'[2] About this time, or perhaps a few months later, there is a report of him relaxed at home. A French gentleman, Charles de Ligny, told Sir Thomas Parry, the English ambassador in Paris, that he had been taken out by a certain foreign Jesuit to a house some distance from London. This was presumably White Webbs. There 'he found Garnet in company with several Jesuits and gentlemen, who were playing music: among them Mr William Byrd, who played the organ and many other instruments. To that house came, chiefly on the solemn days observed by the Papists, many of the nobility and many ladies by coach or otherwise'.[3] Suddenly fearing for his safety de Ligny took his leave: possibly he had been informed that Garnet was now sought after by the Council.

[1] Confession of John Healy, servant of Launcelot Carnaby. *S.P.D. James I*, vol. 20, no. 45.
[2] G. Anstruther, *Vaux of Harrowden*, 275.
[3] *Hat. Cal.*, 17, 611.

34

ST WINIFRED'S WELL

At the end of May 1605, after nearly eighteen months spent in domestic labours, Garnet had ground for self-congratulation; he was now entering his twentieth year on the mission. On the day of his landing there was only one Jesuit at liberty; now there were forty-two working in all parts of the country.

His letter written to Aquaviva at the end of this month was the last free from the fear that beset his last year: that the restlessness of his Catholic friends would bring ruin on the Church. It is concerned entirely with the future training of young aspirants to the Society and the expansion of the work he had inaugurated.

No week passed without a new demand being made on his small band of priests; he asked now that he should be allowed to accept ageing or middle-aged seminary men who sought admission into the Society. 'There is a very large number of veteran soldiers here', he wrote to Aquaviva,[1] 'who want to join us and believe that they will be able to fight with more strength and spirit if they wage war in our company.' He continued:

'While I have been engaged here over many years now, I have constantly comforted myself with the hope that it would be but a short time before a house of the Society were established in the kingdom, so that through its acquisition the Society might grow in number and merit throughout England. . . . Now that hope has proved vain and I am forced to turn, dearest Father, to your Paternity, our most firm anchor. By your assistance this mission was first started; by your industry is has continued and expanded; by your prayers (and I reflect on this every day) it was preserved and, unless I am mistaken, sanctified.'

There was no chance yet of founding a house of the Society in England. At their January meeting, 1605, Garnet had sought the opinions of his subjects. Aquaviva had already proposed that Garnet should set up a novitiate in Belgium as the first house of the English Jesuits. In the previous December, a Spanish lady, Louisa de Caravajal of Valladolid, had bequeathed

[1] H. G. to C. A. 29 May 1605. F.G. 651, f. 171.

for this purpose the sum of twelve thousand ducats. Excitedly Garnet listed the advantages such a house would bring to the mission. Apart from giving English novices their own place of training, it would provide also a temporary retreat for old or fatigued priests in England, and enable them to recover their strength without endangering their hosts. Moreover, it would solve also a problem that had exercised Garnet for many years: how to arrange for the regular reception into the Society both of priests and brothers. 'I have here a large number of men who have spent very many years in England; they ask to be recompensed for their labours and will remain unsatisfied until they are admitted into the Society in one or other grade. In my opinion this cannot be arranged conveniently unless, for some period of time, those who have never lived in houses of the Society, go to one: and return to their work after they have made their profession either there or here.'

Still other reasons suggested themselves for such a house. Many young Englishmen had been unable to endure the Roman climate; several had died; others had returned to England sick and incapable of finishing their training; many excellent recruits had been lost to the priesthood. An English house, with English diet and in a country where the climate was not unlike their own, would give these men greater chance of reaching ordination.

'All of us', Garnet concluded,[1] 'most earnestly beg your Paternity to further this most holy enterprise with all your power. But while this house is being established, please grant me special leave to satisfy those who have long sought admission into the Society and in the judgment of all who know them, are considered fit for it. There are some eight or nine such men.'[2]

About Easter time Garnet feared that White Webbs was discovered, and afterwards visited it rarely and for no more than a few days together. To replace it, he rented the manor house at Erith, a small market town on the Kentish bank of the Thames near Dartford. For a few months he was secure there. At intervals of quiet, Catholics resorted to it in large numbers; sometimes on a Sunday five or six coaches, entering through a newly made gate, drew up at the back of the manor; other groups came by water, returning in the afternoon of the same day. It was reported that 'a man and two women kept the house'.[3] During the same months Garnet made use also of a room in Thames Street, an ancient, dark and narrow lane running along the line of the river westward from the Tower.

In early June Garnet was still in the London district. On the 9th at his room in Thames Street he saw Catesby who, in the course of conversation on the wars in Flanders, had asked Garnet a moral question about the killing

[1] *Ibid.*   [2] *Ibid.* The novitiate was eventually founded at Louvain in 1606.
[3] Statement of James Stanley of Cornforth. *S.P.D. James I*, vol. 216, no. 184.

of infants in a lawful attack on an enemy-held city. Garnet had thought no more about it at the time, particularly as Catesby was raising a new regiment for Flanders and might well seek a priest's advice on the ethics of warfare. Only later did he begin to fear an attempt was perhaps planned on the life of 'some great person'.

On midsummer's day, 24 June, he found time for a short letter to Elizabeth Shirley, the daughter of Sir George Shirley, of Shirley, Leicestershire. Garnet had known her at Shoby as a young girl during his first year in England. Now, with Frances Burrows and his own sisters, she was a nun at St Ursula's convent, Louvain. Briefly he gave her news. 'All your friends are well and salute you; though, besides the general affliction, we find ourselves now betrayed in both our places of abode and are forced to wander up and down until we get a fit place; yet we impute to the great providence of God that our persons have escaped through your prayers and others.'

Then he speaks of a procession held a few days earlier at Fremland in Essex.[1] 'We kept Corpus Christi day with great solemnity and music, and the day of the Octave made a solemn procession about a great garden.' The house was watched, but this 'we knew not till the next day when we departed, twenty-five, in the sight of all in several parties, leaving half-a-dozen servants behind; and all is well, *et evasimus manus eorum in nomine Domini*'.[2]

There had probably been no such solemn performance of the liturgy since Garnet's first days in England at Hurleyford; perhaps he saw it as a sign that his days of liberty were numbered. He continues: 'And so you see I must have thus many years rubbed out, not being worthy to suffer anything for His sake in whose affairs I am employed. God grant that we may all one day meet together before His face for to enjoy Him for ever.' Then he adds: 'the time cannot be long'.[3]

The same day that he wrote to Elizabeth Shirley, Garnet, in the form of a long letter to his sister Margaret, addressed an exhortation to her community to remain steadfast in their religious vocation.[4] Mixing new com-

[1] Fremland or Tremnals or Frimnels was the seat of Sir John Tyrrel, whose wife was sister of Sir Edward Sulyard of the neighbouring manor of Berne Hall: both these Catholic houses were in the parish of Downham. In Philip Morant's *History of Essex* (1768) Fremland is described as a 'large old building lying in a bottom a mile and a half from the church'. There is a photograph of the house from the south-west front in the volume of the *Royal Commission* of *Historical Monuments, Essex, South East* (1923), 56: it was destroyed when a reservoir was constructed in the area after the second world war.

[2] *And we have escaped their hands in the name of the Lord.*

[3] H. G. to Elizabeth Shirley. 24 June 1605. Stonyhurst, Grene *P.*, 578.

[4] H. G. to his sister. 24 June 1605. Stonyhurst, Grene *P.*, 576.

COUGHTON HALL

Water colour in the Aylesford Collection, Reference Library, Birmingham

SIR WILLIAM WADE
From Alex. Brown, *Genesis of the United States*

parisons with old, and perhaps recalling recent letters he had given to friends travelling abroad, he writes:

'We may compare a religious life to a bill of exchange, well known to those who have travelled in foreign countries, for they that pass the sea from hence, if they carry great sums of money with them, they do both clog themselves in their journey more than were needful; and if they chance to light into the hands of thieves, they are utterly spoiled of all; only a letter of exchange is neither burthensome to carry nor subject unto the injury of robbers, whereas that letter is of itself little worth and the contents thereof will not avail but him who received it. Even so fareth it with those that seek to obtain such virtues which carry us to heaven.'

The world, as he sees it, is full of 'infinite' robbers, seeking to strip a man of virtue and merit. The comparison continues for the most part in conventional phrases; only in speaking of the effects of divine love on the soul does he come near the traditional language of the English mystical writers and hint that he himself, 'amid the tumult of secular cares', had experienced in his soul some special grace of God; for it is the soul, he writes, 'thirsting after the perfect love of his divine Majesty', on whom he bestows his favours, 'by showing his enamoured handmaid where he feedeth, where he resteth at the noon time of the day, scalding her (if we may term it, for no terms be too vehement for the love of God) with true affection of love'.

Throughout the letter Garnet suggests that 'the end of his earthly pilgrimage' is near; and as if exhorting himself and not his sister to a last heroic effort, he bids her 'fight stoutly in the combat which you have undertaken, which shall gain you an everlasting and particular crown. . . . Love faithfully and constantly Him, which must be your perpetual lover'. Then he speaks of himself, begging the sisters' prayers that he should become 'a perfect religious man who, notwithstanding his unworthiness, hath sought to begin and desireth to see perfect so happy a work in you all'.

This was his last message to his friends' children whom he had sent abroad to enter convents. In the first days of July or earlier Garnet received Aquaviva's answer to his repeated requests for severe papal censures on all Catholics who entered any conspiracy or rising against the State.[1] In 'a very secret manner indeed' Aquaviva had heard what he was sure Garnet already knew, that certain machinations were afoot. 'Any violent attempt whatsoever, especially at a time like this', would bring ruin on the Catholic religion. Consequently the Pope had ordered Aquaviva to write to Garnet in his name. In consultation with the Archpriest and the leading Catholics, he must quash instantly all such schemes which would destroy the negotiations

[1] H. G. to C. A. 15 June 1605. Tierney-Dodd, vol. 4, appendix, cviii.

Y

already initiated at Rome for the relief of English Catholics. 'It is certain', Aquaviva insisted, 'that his Holiness will never abandon them or fail to assist them in their present crisis.' Garnet would have no difficulty in realising how 'grave and urgent' the matter was. As if with foreknowledge Aquaviva concludes: 'should anything happen, which God prevent . . . nobody will be ready to believe that it was contrived without at least the consent of our Fathers'.

Shortly after receiving Aquaviva's letter, Garnet sought out Catesby, who was at Fremland in company with Lord Monteagle and Francis Tresham, and cautioned him most severely against 'rushing headlong into mischief'. Catesby denied that he intended any plot; then Garnet read to him the message from the Pope contained in Aquaviva's letter. Between them it was agreed that Sir Edmund Baynham should be sent to Rome to acquaint the Pope with the situation of English Catholics. Catesby would hold his hand until Baynham returned.

This was the extent of Garnet's general knowledge of a plot; he was now more than suspicious that some 'device' was planned, but he had succeeded in extracting from Catesby a promise that no action would be taken for the present. This was their last meeting. What Garnet now suspected was already known to the government and he had reason to think that the government knew a great deal.

A few days later, 'a little before St James's tide', 25 July, Garnet was visited in Thames Street by Fr Tesimond, and there in confession learnt that Catesby had a plot in hand. Henceforth he could say or do nothing that betrayed the knowledge he now possessed. He prayed, he suffered sleepless nights, he pressed Aquaviva, as earlier in the year he had told Catesby he would, to get from the Pope an excommunication against all who threatened or attempted in any way to disturb the present state of the realm.[1]

---

[1] The above three paragraphs are a mere outline of Garnet's encounters in these months. To avoid overlapping, the details are given later in the account of Garnet's examinations. Here and in the following pages I have told the story of the Gunpowder Plot only in so far as it touched Garnet. The identity of the contriver of the Plot (in its traditional version) remains an historical riddle. Gerard, whose *Narrative* has been my principal source, has not in 350 years been proved wrong in any detail apart from that which I have myself questioned (cf. *inf.*, p. 373). All that controversy on the subject (particularly the brilliant controversy between the second John Gerard and R. S. Gardiner) has shown is that the popular version, which possibly Garnet believed, cannot now be maintained. It is generally accepted that the government played some part in engineering it for its own ends: but the extent of that part is uncertain. As Hugh Ross Williamson (*The Gunpowder Plot*, 1951) and Christopher Devlin (essay entitled 'The Gunpowder Plot' in *Hamlet's Divinity*, 1963, p. 141 *sq.*) have shown, the official version is full of inconsistencies. It would seem that the version of the Plot learnt by

Garnet's remaining letters of this year are the most distraught of his life. On 24 July, about three weeks after seeing Catesby in Thames Street, he acknowledged Aquaviva's stern admonition against involving himself or any of his brethren in machinations against the State. Referring almost certainly to the Watson Plot, Garnet protested that he had in fact already averted certain trouble.[1] Moreover, he felt confident that he would be no less successful in the future 'for it is certain that most Catholics would not wish (save under extreme pressure) to make any attempt of this kind without our consent'. Then he added, with grave misgivings:

'There are two things that make me very anxious indeed: first, that others in some other province [perhaps he is thinking of the Welsh Marches][2] might fly to arms and so through sheer necessity drive others elsewhere to like attempts, for there are some men who cannot be held back by the mere command of his Holiness. In the lifetime of Pope Clement[3] these men brazenly asked whether the Pope had power to prevent them defending their own

[1] H. G. to C. A. 24 July 1605 *S.P.D. James I*, vol. 14, no. 41. William Watson, an opponent of the Archpriest, was released from prison for his services as a spy on his brethren, and worked for a time in collusion with Bishop Bancroft. On the death of Elizabeth, he went with another priest to Scotland to obtain from James a promise of toleration which would justify his courses. When toleration was not granted, Watson lost face and with Sir Griffin Markham and Anthony Copley began to plot against the King: Markham was to seize the person of the King who, yet uncrowned, could be set aside in favour of his son; Copley was to be Secretary of State; Watson, Lord Chancellor. Blackwell, with the knowledge of Garnet and Gerard, gave information of the Plot, which came to nothing.

[2] In May 1605, the dissatisfaction of the Catholics in Herefordshire and Monmouthshire began to show itself in a number of outbreaks of violence. Towards the end of June, Edward Somerset, fourth Earl of Worcester, was sent to the area by the Council to quell the disturbances. The details of the story are to be found in the Cecil Papers at Hatfield House, the State Papers Domestic for 1605 and in a contemporary pamphlet by Thomas Hammond, *The Late Commotion of certaine Papists in Herefordshire*, London 1605. Cf. Roland Mathias, *Whitsun Riot: An Account of a Commotion amongst Catholics in Herefordshire and Monmouthshire in 1605* (1963).

[3] Clement VIII died on 5 March 1605 and was succeeded, first by Leo XI who reigned for seventeen days, then by Paul V, elected on 29 May 1605.

Garnet from Tesimond under the seal of confession was the official version: if this was the case, then it enhances Garnet's innocence and his apostolic simplicity. While Gerard in his *Narrative* would seem to have doubts about it (he raises them only indirectly in his character studies of the 'conspirators'), his account remains one of the most outstanding instances of the manner in which the contemporary history of a controversial subject can be written with impregnable objectivity. There were many Protestants of Garnet's generation who rejected the official version: Archbishop Ussher of Armagh, for instance, is reported frequently to have asserted that 'if Papists knew what he knew, the blame of the Gunpowder treason would not lay on them' (cf. Foley, vol. 4, 143).

lives. Furthermore, they assert that no priest will be made a sharer in their secrets; even certain of my friends complain of me by name and assert that I am an obstacle to their designs. In order to pacify them in some degree and to buy time, so that with delay suitable remedies may be found, I urged them to agree among themselves to send a representative to the Holy Father.'

Then, referring to Sir Edmund Baynham, he says: 'And this was done, and I directed him to the most illustrious Nuncio in Flanders, so that the man might be commended by him to his Holiness: and I also wrote a letter in which I set out their point of view and the position of both sides. This letter, which was long and full, will thus be forwarded with safety.'

This was the first danger, and Garnet had every reason to believe that he had averted it. The second was worse, that violence might be done to the King, and Catholics driven to arms. Without revealing the secret he had heard in confession from Tesimond, that was as much as he could say. In his view 'two things were necessary'. Against the first threat the Pope must make his will plain; against the second, 'he should prohibit under censure all resort to arms by Catholics, and moreover, in a Brief, published to the whole world. The occasion for obtaining it can be the recent tumult stirred up in Wales which in the end came to nothing.' He ends with an entreaty to Aquaviva to get the Pope to act quickly, for every day the situation is becoming more critical.

This was the 'cooling card', as Gerard calls it, that Garnet hoped to elicit from the Pope. Unfortunately the Pope declined to re-enforce his orders with the threat of excommunication. Garnet was homeless; his house at Erith was under surveillance; he continued to travel and at intervals to write pressingly to Rome. His movements and plans are thus described by Gerard: 'Utterly unfurnished of a safe place [he] 'resolved to spend most of the summer in travel, [and] to visit the holy well of St Winifred . . . and to do what good he could at friends' houses', both on his way there and on his return. He hoped that in the late summer 'a house might be provided for him where he might settle for the winter'.[1]

Garnet was at White Webbs for the feast of St Bartholomew, 24 August. He suspected that the house had been discovered 'and durst not remain there past one night or two'. On the 28th he wrote to Persons: 'the increase of Catholics is great and I hope in this journey, which I undertake tomorrow both for health and want of a house, I shall have occasion of much good'.[2] He was optimistic; he had every reason to believe that he had successfully held back Catesby from his design.

[1] *Narrative*, 78.
[2] H. G. to R. P. 28 August 1605: extract quoted by Gerard in his *Narrative*, 79.

With Garnet were Eleanor and Anne Vaux, Eleanor's son, William Brooksby and his wife Dorothy, Nicholas Owen and some servants. There was no sign of military preparations in the houses of his friends; during his weeks of pilgrimage he met many seminary priests and a number of his own brethren; this gave him 'great comfort'. 'In every place', he told Persons, 'I have been exceedingly welcome, more than I deserved.'[1]

On its way through the midlands the pilgrimage was joined by Sir Everard and Lady Digby. A *rendezvous* was made with Father Oldcorne and his servant Ralph Ashley; then with Fr Tesimond; at Harrowden, they met Fr Gerard and Fr Percy. By the time Holywell was reached the pilgrimage numbered thirty, not counting the servants. On the last stages the ladies walked barefoot to the shrine.

On his return Garnet, with the Vaux sisters, spent a night at Rushton in Northamptonshire. Shortly before his visit Sir Thomas Tresham had died, on 11 September. He had been among Garnet's first friends in England and a link with Campion, whom he had entertained and escorted: an eccentric builder, staunch Catholic and versatile author whose devotional life was centred on the Trinity, in whose honour he had built a triangular lodge in his park, a stone's throw from his mansion; his debts, contracted largely through his recusancy, amounted to twenty thousand pounds.

From Rushton, Garnet rode to Gayhurst, Digby's house in Buckinghamshire. From there on 4 October he wrote to Persons:[2] 'We are to go within a few days nearer London, yet are we unprovided of a house nor can find any convenient for any long time. But we must be fain to borrow some private house for a time and live more privately, until this great storm be overblown, for the most strict inquiries are prevised, wherein if my hostess be not quite undone, she speedeth better than most of her neighbours.'

Garnet then described the heightening persecution. 'The courses taken are more severe than in Bess's time. Every six weeks [there] is a general court. Juries are appointed to indict, present, find the goods of Catholics, prize them, yea, in many places to drive away whatsoever they find *contra ordinem iuris*.' Already the now customary steps taken by Catholics to protect their lands and goods were proving inadequate. Hitherto, in many cases, the possessions of Catholics had been registered in the name of Protestant friends or relatives who were not subject to penal fines. Now, reports Garnet, they

[1] H. G. to R. P. 5 October 1605. Tierney-Dodd, vol. 4, appendix, ciii. In the Salisbury Papers there is a list of the whereabouts of most Jesuits and a number of secular priests, drawn up by Thomas Wilson, Lord Salisbury's secretary, from documents in his master's possession. It is dated 20 November 1605. *Hat. Cal.*, 17, 500–1.

[2] H. G. to R. P. 4 October 1605. Tierney-Dodd, vol. 4, appendix, ciii.

'put the owners, if perhaps Protestants, to prove that [the goods] be theirs, and not of recusants, with whom they deal. The commissioners in all countries are the most earnest and base Puritans, whom otherwise the King discountenanceth'. Their inquisition was thorough in a degree hitherto un-experienced; if any recusant, after the forfeiture of his goods, attempted to buy them back again at the price that the Crown could raise for them, the commissioners immediately enquired whether the money he offered was his own; if not, they took that money also, to discourage friends from offering Catholics financial relief. 'In fine, if these courses hold,' Garnet prophesied, 'every man must be fain to redeem, once in six months, the very bed he lieth on; and hereof, of twice redeeming, besides other precedents, I find one here in Nicholas his lodging.'

All the arrangements that Garnet had made with friends for the relief of the priests at Wisbech were now proved inadequate. Again no access to them was allowed. They were left without help from outside: a mark a week for food was demanded of each priest by the keeper, who 'maketh his gain, and giveth them meat but three days a week'.

Openly in court, local justices proclaimed that the 'King will have blood', and particularly in Yorkshire; other judges announced that hitherto the King had 'stroked Papists, but now will strike [them]'. Two priests in the north had been convicted: now, after a 'great stay following their condem-nation' Garnet correctly stated that their execution was certain. This, he said, 'argueth a deliberate resolution of what we may expect'. With the knowledge he secretly possessed, his fears became unendurable: the present condition of Catholics should convince the Pope that 'whatever men give out there' in Rome about the absence of persecution and the 'easy proceedings' was 'mere fable'. Still he put reliance, as he had done for nearly twenty years, on the endurance of the Catholic people. 'Notwithstanding I am assured that the best sort of Catholics will bear all their losses with patience. But how these tyrannical proceedings of such base officers may drive particular men to desperate attempts, that I cannot answer for.'

Yet Garnet continued to plan for the future. Already this autumn he had gathered in London several candidates for the new novitiate in Flanders, 'prentices', as he calls them; but the times were too perilous to send them over. He ordered them back until the spring;[1] and at the same moment he pleaded with Aquaviva for the admission of a secular priest, Fr Sicklemore, into the Society: he had been strongly commended by Fr Holtby. In Garnet's judgment he had 'good talents and strength of body'; he begged Aquaviva to send word if he would have him.

[1] H. G. to R. P. 4 October 1605. Tierney-Dodd, vol. 4, appendix, ciii.

Nine months earlier he had told Aquaviva that the house planned in Flanders would provide a place to rest his veteran missionaries. At that time he had certain cases in mind, men whose mental and physical powers were being taxed by the strain of constant hiding and secret journeyings. As he returned from Wales, Garnet learned that one of his best missionaries, Fr Thomas Stanney, had been taken near Reading in a condition of mental derangement. At the time of writing, Stanney was a prisoner in the Gatehouse. Though closely guarded, he had recovered his sanity and was able to describe to his Superior the events leading to his arrest. He had been tormented by the stone, sick with measles, and suffering from insomnia; he imagined that the house at which he was staying had been invested for a search: he 'went out for fear of hurting the family, came to an inn, where in the morning, after a night of sleeplessness, he imagined that the town was all in armour betwixt Catholics and heretics; and so thought he must do his part and called for a knife and struck the chamberlain'. At his arrest he was closely examined and discovered to be mad. 'All is ended well', Garnet wrote with relief, 'and rather edification taken of all sorts than otherwise; Catholics esteem him as a saint, as indeed his carriage for these twenty years hath deserved.'

Even in the country Garnet was able to keep himself informed of the progress made towards recovery by Fr Stanney, for whom he felt much affection: he had not been unkindly treated in the Gatehouse; on his own initiative, the French Ambassador was working for his release; Garnet was hopeful that permission would soon be granted for Stanney to go restfully into exile.

By October, as Garnet was still without Aquaviva's instructions on the admission of Brothers into the Society, he begged the General to answer him: 'Pray you send word now how many coadjutors you will have.' He pleaded specially for John Lillie: 'I have one, a citizen of London, of very good experience, which may benefit us in buying and selling without taxes.[1] But he is fifty years old — and I think it is not amiss to have, at the first, some ancient men for such.' These 'ancient' men, if admitted as Brothers, would be able to help a younger generation that now sought admission. Impatiently Garnet pressed Persons: 'Send your will herein.'[2]

Unexpectedly, Garnet found space in this letter to report to Persons a joke that was then current. It was said that Persons had secured Thomas Fitzherbert's appointment as secretary to the Pope and had exacted from

---

[1] H. G. probably refers to Lillie's help in sending over students to Flanders and assisting incoming priests.

[2] H. G. to R. P. 4 October 1605. Tierney-Dodd, vol. 4, appendix, ciii.

him an oath to discover and report to him all the Pope's secrets; this oath rendered void Fitzherbert's earlier oath of secrecy to the Pope himself. On the discovery of this at the papal Court, either by torture or threat of torture, Persons instantly fled to Naples. To Garnet the story was ludicrous: he told it to Persons in order to convey to him the reputation he still had among his enemies in England; also, as he said, 'to make you sport. But Mr. Christopher Southworth most confidently reported it'.[1]

From the country Garnet dated this letter 4 October, just a month and a day before the discovery of the Gunpowder Plot. On the 21st, it was returned to him, for the messenger by whom it was despatched to London, was back again in the country: he had been stayed on the way. Garnet took the opportunity to add a postscript: in the interval he had received disturbing news from Ireland in a letter from a Fr Field.[2] Recently a proclamation had been issued against all priests and an order posted throughout the country compelling all Irishmen to go to Protestant churches: what augured worse for both countries was a solemn protestation that King James never did in fact promise toleration nor ever had an intention of granting it. All the news Garnet gathered in Warwickshire suggested that a crisis for Catholicism was not far off.

Yet he made no comment. Faithful to the instructions he had been given on his departure from Rome, he concerned himself merely with the problems of his 'merchandise'. From Ireland the Jesuits had turned to him for help as he had better communications with Rome than his brethren there. His last plea to the General was for them. 'I pray you', he wrote to Persons in this postscript,[3] 'to speak to Claude; grant them, or obtain for them, all the faculties we have here; for so he [Fr Field] earnestly desireth and is scrupulous. I gave unto two of them that passed by me all [the faculties] we have. And I think it sufficient in law, for, being here, they were my subjects, and we have our faculties for Ireland for the most part. I pray you procure them a general grant for their comfort.'

Garnet did not move nearer London. With Eleanor and Anne he stayed at Gayhurst until 21 October, and then, the day he added his postscript, rode to Harrowden, where for the last time he was met by his Jesuit brethren. After their three days of prayer together, Sir Everard and his lady

[1] H. G. to R. P. 4 October 1605. Tierney-Dodd, vol. 4, appendix, ciii.

[2] Fr Richard Field, who died in Dublin at the age of fifty-two in 1606, had been Superior of the Irish Jesuits until he was succeeded in 1604 by Fr Holywood (cf. *sup.*, p. 267). Rising from his sick-bed in 1605, he inspired the heroic stand made by the citizens of Dublin against the enforcement of the laws suppressing the practice of the Catholic religion.

[3] The postscript is dated 21 October 1605.

joined them; Catesby also came. As Everard passed through Wellingborough to Gayhurst, he, Gerard's dearest friend, was inveigled into a plot under oath.

Just over a week later, on 29 October, Garnet, with his same companions, joined by Lady Digby, travelled from Gothurst to Coughton.

35

CAPTURE

At Coughton in the upper room over the Gatehouse there was a large gathering of Catholics for the feast of All Saints. Garnet preached. He took as his text two lines from the hymn of the Office of Lauds that day: *Auferte gentem perfidam, Credentium de finibus*: from the land of believers take away the unbelieving people. It was Friday. The following Tuesday, 5 November, the day appointed for the opening of the new parliamentary session, all London was talking of a diabolical attempt, discovered early that morning, to blow up the Parliament House with barrels of gunpowder placed in the vaults beneath. A soldier who had fought in the Netherlands, a Yorkshireman, John Johnson, *alias* Guy Fawkes, had been arrested as he was standing by ready to ignite the powder in the course of the King's speech. The other conspirators fled to the country, hoping to raise the west of England and Wales; a week later all of them who had not been killed resisting the sheriff in the courtyard of Holbeach House were prisoners in the Tower.

Coughton was within a day's ride or less of most of the houses belonging to the conspirators. Garnet had gone there, it seems, at the suggestion of Anne Vaux. Had he objected or taken any step dictated by the knowledge he had of the plot, he might have betrayed indirectly the secret he had learned in Tesimond's confession. There was no choice for him but to act as he did. On 6 November, still at Coughton, he heard of the plot from Catesby's servant, Thomas Bates. As Bates left to return to his master, Garnet gave him a message: he 'marvelled that they would enter into such wicked actions and not be ruled by the advice of friends and the order of his Holiness given to all'. He refused to 'meddle but wished them to give over'.

Nothing is known of Garnet's movements between 6 and 24 November[1] when, with Nicholas Owen, his 'servant', and the Vaux sisters, he left Coughton

---

[1] In his examination of 6 March (*S.P.D. James I*, vol. 19, no. 16), Garnet says they reached Hinlip 'by St Bartholomew's day, or a day before or after'. St Bartholomew's day is 24 August. Clearly Garnet, who was probably drugged at the time of this examination (cf. *inf.*, p. 372) meant to indicate 24 November.

for Hinlip. Possibly Owen persuaded him that Hinlip was the best equipped house in England to withstand a prolonged siege. Harrowden had been invested on 12 November. After nine days the search for Gerard who lay hidden there was abandoned. It was not unlikely that Coughton would now be attacked. If Gerard had escaped at Harrowden, Garnet had a fair chance of safety at Hinlip.

'Father Garnet', writes Gerard,[1] 'thought best to retire himself to a house of great safety near unto the place he then was. There [he] meant to lie privately till the heat of his persecution were passed, [when] it might be more safe travelling towards London where he meant to settle as he had been accustomed.' Meeting Oldcorne and his servant, Ralph Ashley, near Evesham, they rode to within four or five miles of Hinlip. There they dismounted and went the rest of the way on foot.[2]

Hinlip, standing on high ground about two miles from Worcester, was unrivalled in the district for its size and grandeur, 'so large and fair a house', says Gerard,[3] 'that it might be seen over a great part of the county'. Set in a park overlooking on every side a great expanse of open fields it gave watchers placed on the turrets ample warning of approaching pursuivants. Here Oldcorne had been chaplain for fifteen years; here also Owen had contrived more numerous and cunning hiding-holes than in any other mansion. The Puritans of Worcester 'had often procured warrants to search that house in hope to find some priests there, for which the house and the whole estate of the gentleman [Thomas Habington] might be forfeited to the King'.[4] Hitherto in their sporadic raids they had caught none: 'this being often essayed', says Gerard, 'was never permitted by God until this time, *quae erat hora illorum et potestas tenebrarum*'.[5]

For the space of six weeks Garnet lay quiet. He lived in a lower 'chamber descending from the dining room': Owen made his fire and attended on him; ordinarily he dined and supped with his hostess, in company also with Oldcorne, when he was present.[6] If a stranger was in the house, the priests dined apart. Occasionally Oldcorne was absent, sometimes with Owen.

Alone for the most part in his chamber, Garnet sometime in December wrote an open letter to the Lords of the Council. It was a declaration of his

---

[1] *Narrative*, 149.

[2] *S.P.D. James I*, Gunpowder Plot Book, 2, no. 214.

[3] *Narrative*, 149.

[4] *Ibid.*

[5] *op. cit.* 150. Luke 22: 53. *Which was their hour and the power of darkness.*

[6] *S.P.D. James I*, Gunpowder Plot Book, 2, no. 194. Confession of Nicholas Owen, taken 1 March 1606.

innocence made at a time when the government, engaged in examining the conspirators, was able to test the accuracy of his statements; Garnet himself calls it a 'challenge'. Addressed to the 'very honourable and good Lords' of the King's Privy Council, it was the first such open letter sent to them by a Jesuit since, twenty-five years earlier, Campion had proclaimed publicly the purpose of his coming to England. This was an occasion not for elo-quence but argument. However, his opening appeal for a hearing is not with-out style or dignity.

'After twenty years almost complete in this employment as a missionary' [Garnet began][1] '... being now newly charged, as I understand, with the late most horrible attempt, as if I had been accessory thereunto; and in particular had ... given the Most Holy Sacrament to six of the confederates at their very undertaking so bloody an enterprise, I humbly crave your Honour's patience, if for the honour of God and the Catholic cause, and particularly of the Order of which I am a member and have in this kingdom some special charge, I say somewhat with all possible brevity, for my just purgation: though, I hope, this my disgrace ariseth rather of calumnious reports than of any material accusation.'

He then appealed to be given a hearing 'as an honest man untainted in his loyalty, as a religious bound by obedience to the Pope, even in this particular case, and, finally, as a man who dreadeth the most strict judgments of Al-mighty God'. These were the 'titles and bonds and hopes' by which he pleaded to be heard.

Garnet conceded that in his spiritual apostolate and charitable work 'some of this unfortunate company [namely, the conspirators] may chance to have had [his] help and assistance'; but they never made him privy, still less sought his consent, to the plot, which was 'as unfit for [him] to deal in, as it was bloody in itself'.[2] This was the testimony of his conscience, 'the greatest that can possibly be found or imagined', for it was the testimony of God. To it could be added the 'most excellent witness on earth', namely, the Pope himself, who, as Garnet did not doubt, would testify, if need be, that at the time of 'Watson's plot and other fears', he had procured 'an express prohibi-tion of all unquietness' The phrase 'express prohibition', Garnet underlined in his own hand. Here he revealed the essential simplicity of his character that was to show itself more clearly in his last months in the Tower: he imagined that a motive imperative in his own conduct had equal force over the conscience of the Catholics he served. Yet he was able to plead that he had done more than procure an 'express prohibition'.

He continued: 'But because in so afflicted a number it were to be feared

[1] Stonyhurst, *Anglia* 3, 58.   [2] *Ibid.*

that some persons, forgetting all Christian patience and longanimity, as experience of other countries besides our own hath taught us, might break out into fury, I wished a *prohibition under censures* of all violence towards his Majesty or his officers.' For this was the greatest stay, in his opinion, from all such outrages.

Moreover, since it was possible that a plot might be contrived and kept 'hidden from us and other quiet persons, especially reverend priests, and therefore not possible to be hindered by any industry of our own', such a prohibition would effectively quash it: for it carried with it the 'terror of dying in the most horrible state of *excommunication*, to their utter perdition of body and soul'. For fear that it might be disregarded by desperate Catholics, the Pope had not, in fact, issued such a prohibition under censure. Yet Garnet had no doubt that it would be thus enforced henceforth 'by occasion of this late conspiracy'.

Such was the main argument for his innocence, and it could be supported, if necessary, by the witness of all Catholics who had any dealings with him. 'They will I am assured all testify', he wrote, 'how carefully I have inculcated this commandment of His Holiness upon every occasion of speech.' It was inconceivable that the author of the conspiracy should have dared 'acquaint me or any of mine with their purposes, knowing both this contrary commandment and the special account which, above all other virtues, we make of holy obedience; and I may well say with St Paul: *Si enim quae destruxi, iterum haec aedifico, praevaricatorem me constitui.*'[1]

Then there occurs a passage of intense feeling that sprang from his unshakeable conviction of innocence. It had been suggested that his complicity had been proved by the confessions of the conspirators under torture. Garnet knew that this was untrue; that it was a deceit of Salisbury to entrap him.

'The fourth argument of my innocence shall not be so much a testimony as a challenge. Let the rack, tortures, let the confessions of the conspirators, yea, let all our greatest adversaries utter what they can for my accusation; and yet I know my innocency in anything spoken or done, ever since the first entrance of his Majesty's reign, can never be blemished; and if in any point there may be the least doubt, I humbly beseech your Honours to suspend your censures till I, knowing the exceptions against me, may with my unfeigned integrity clear myself to the satisfaction of all men of honour and wisdom.'

The appeal followed the proofs; but still stronger in Garnet's mind was the argument giving 'a moral kind of certainty'. The affection of the Society for the King, for his mother and family was known to all. It was known also

[1] Galatians 2, 18. Do I put myself in the wrong when I destroy and then rebuild?

how Garnet had intervened to protect the King's life against Watson. 'By my special diligence', he recalled, 'divers were delivered out of the trap. In Wales, though the matters were not so much as was feared, yet I suppose my admonitions were not unfruitful.'[1] And, loyalty apart, how was it possible for him to have a part in a plot which, besides taking the lives of the King, Queen and the two Princes, 'would have included divers lords and ladies and others of special account, so highly honoured and affected by me, that I would rather, for every one severally, have lost my life a thousand times than to have permitted their hazard'. Finally, there was the damage and disgrace that the Society of Jesus would certainly have suffered, had he, as Superior, been implicated in 'these bloody matters'. To say in these circumstances that the conspirators had received the sacrament from his hand, was unbelievable. '*Nescivit servus tuus*', he protests in the words of Achimelech, '*quidquid super hoc negotium, nec modicum, nec grande.*'[2]

There were other proofs and arguments Garnet might adduce, but these sufficed. He concluded with a protestation of 'all fidelity and loyalty', both from himself and all those under his charge, and with the assurance that in their 'prayers, examples, actions and labours' all of them would seek to 'preserve and increase the King's temporal and everlasting felicity' and that of his entire family.

On 15 January the Council replied with a proclamation for the arrest of Gerard, Garnet and Tesimond. The three priests were declared accessory to the Plot and denounced as traitors. 'All England was filled with this new rumour', though, as Gerard adds, 'Catholics did generally believe the contrary of them: and also the wiser and more reasonable sort even of Protestants themselves': for in all the examinations of the prisoners not a single word could be extracted to sustain the charge of their guilt: but on the contrary there were 'many certain reports that the prisoners did all protest that there was no priest at all guilty of the conspiracy or that did anyways assist them therein'.[3]

In his open letter Garnet had misjudged the temper of his enemies. With the inescapable logic of his proofs in their hands, the Council realised that, come what may, a case against him could never be framed until and unless all the conspirators had first been executed, so that none, cognisant of the events, could be cited by him at his trial.

Five days after the proclamation, on 20 January, the long-delayed search for Garnet began. On the 27 he was caught. The news was suppressed for several days. There is every indication that Salisbury, on hearing of Garnet's

[1] Cf. *sup.*, p. 323.
[2] Samuel 22, 15.   [3] *Narrative*, 148–9.

arrest, hastened to eliminate the last surviving witnesses for his defence. On 30 January the first batch of prisoners, including Digby and Bates, was despatched at St Paul's churchyard; the remainder the following day in the Palace Yard, Westminster. There was left now none whose evidence could save Garnet.

According to Gerard, the most trustworthy of all contemporary, and also later, writers on the Plot, the search at Hinlip had been instigated by Humphrey Littleton, who had been arrested for sheltering Robert Wintour. Littleton hoped to save his life by betraying his cousin, Garnet's host, Thomas Habington. Gerard writes:[1] 'Humphrey Littleton being in danger of his life ... and seeing so large promises of favour and rewards to those that would discover any of the three [Jesuits], thought to save himself from a temporal punishment by doing that which deserved an eternal pain. [He] sent up word to the Council, that he had been not long before at Mr Abingdon [Habington] his house, called Hinlip ... where he heard a Jesuit preach called Oldcorne, who did there reside for the most part, and where he thought also Garnet was to be found.' Although this statement is at first sight difficult to reconcile with the date of Littleton's letter to the Council, it is confirmed by Garnet himself. Writing after his capture, he said that the search at Hinlip was primarily for Oldcorne as the abettor of Robert Wintour; that there was no expectation, but merely a chance, of finding him also: 'so that it was only God's pleasure to have it so as it was. *Fiat voluntas tua*'.[2]

Very early in the morning of Monday 20 January the sheriff of Worcestershire, Sir Henry Bromley, according to his own account, horsed himself 'with a seemly troop of his own attendants' and, supported by others specially enlisted for the operation, rode out from Worcester to Hinlip. The party consisted of a hundred men, 'furnished with guns and all kinds of weapons, more fit for an army than an orderly search'.[3]

That Monday, Thomas Habington, after several weeks' absence, returned home. At the gates of his own park Bromley showed him a copy of the proclamation for Garnet's arrest:[4] then he drew out his search warrant. Habington denied that Garnet, Tesimond or Gerard were hiding in his house,

---

[1] *Ibid.*, 150.

[2] Cf. G. Anstruther, *Vaux of Harrowden*, 339.

[3] *Narrative*, 151

[4] The proclamation stated that Garnet, Tesimond and Gerard 'did maliciously, falsely and traitorously move and persuade Catesby and the other conspirators that our Sovereign Lord the King, the nobility, clergy and whole commonalty of the realm of England (Papists excepted) were heretics, and that all heretics were accursed and excommunicated; and that no heretic could be a King, but that it was lawful and meritorious to kill our said Sovereign Lord the King and all other heretics within the realm of England'.

or that he even knew any of the priests named in the proclamation, except for Gerard, whom he had met twenty-four or five years earlier in his youth. 'This liberal and rather rash speech', boasted Bromley, 'could not cause the search so lightly to be given over: the cause enforced more respect than words of that or any such like nature.'[1] Habington, in fact, had no reason to know that Garnet or even Oldcorne was in hiding. His emphatic denial endorses Gerard's statement that Garnet had been betrayed by Littleton.[2]

It was still early morning. The gates to the house had been barred. The usual delaying tactics followed; first a servant, then Dorothy Habington herself, came out to ask the cause of the incursion; meanwhile, priests, books and altar furniture were stowed away.

Gerard continues:[3] 'But Sir Henry Bromley, impatient of this delay, caused the gates, with great violence and force of men, to be broken down; which yet he could not perform in so short a time (by reason they were very strong and answerable to the greatness of the house) before they within had made all safe.' Eventually Bromley forced his entrance; he posted his men in every room; then arrested all he found in the house, servants, family and friends. Only after this did he show Mrs Habington his search warrant. 'She yielded to his authority and gave him full power to do his will.'[4]

Bromley knew the house well; he had searched it before. First he examined the long gallery over the gatehouse. There he found two of the dozen or more hiding places. In his report he pays a generous tribute to the skill of Nicholas Owen: they were 'cunning and very artificial conveyances in the main brick wall, so ingeniously framed and with such art as it cost much labour ere they could be found'.[5]

As the search proceeded three other secret places were found, 'contrived

[1] Bromley to Salisbury, 23 January 1606. *S.P.D. James I*, vol. 18, 38.

[2] There is an apparent inconsistency between Gerard's account (*Narrative*, 150) and the dating of Littleton's letter to the Council. The search started on 20 January; Littleton's letter, containing his offer to betray the Jesuits, is dated 26 January, the day before Garnet's capture. Probably Littleton had supplied the information to Bromley many days earlier, and Bromley held back Littleton's letter until he had Garnet in his hands, as he delayed (or deliberately post-dated) the news of Garnet's arrest. It was only on 30 January, three days after the arrest, that Bromley reported it to Cecil. Both delays are consistent with Bromley's desire to receive the unshared credit for Garnet's capture. He himself claims that he was acting on Salisbury's orders; that when he got no help from Thomas Habington, he relied on his own 'presumpsion' that the priests were there, for early in the search he had found warm beds, 'parcels of apparel and books and writings' that gave proof that 'scholars' at least were in the house.

[3] *Narrative*, 151.

[4] *Ibid.*

[5] Bromley to Salisbury. 23 January 1606. *S.P.D. James I*, vol. 18, no. 38.

LETTER OF HENRY GARNET TO ANNE VAUX,
21 April 1606, with original drawing by Henry Garnet

HENRY GARNET ON THE SCAFFOLD
An engraving by C. Screta taken from Matthew Tanner, S.J. *Societas Jesu usque ad Sanguinis Profusionem Militans* (Prague 1675)

with no less skill and industry' in and about the chimneys, with entrances covered over with brick, mortared and fixed to the planks that formed the entrance, and coloured black like other parts of the chimney. This was Owen's work again. Bromley, who now might have given up the siege if he had not received Littleton's information, himself confessed that 'very diligent search might well have passed [them] by without throwing the least suspicion upon such unsuspicious places'. While in most houses of the time, different tunnels lead from neighbouring rooms into the main chimneys, here Owen had constructed several false chimneys, apparently to carry smoke, but in fact to let air and light into the priests' holes.

No day passed without one or other place of concealment being discovered. 'Eleven secret corners and conveyances were found', Bromley boasted, 'all of them having books, massing stuff, and popish trumpery in them, only two excepted which appeared to have been found on former searches and now therefore had less credit given to them.'[1] But, significantly, there was no mention of supplies of food or drink.

So far no individual had been found. On the fourth day, the Thursday morning, Bromley's persistence was rewarded. He starved out his first two victims. With simplicity and drama Gerard tells the story:[2]

'Two laymen that usually did attend upon the two priests [Garnet and Oldcorne] and were hid in a place by themselves, being almost starved to death did come out of their own accord. For they had placed the priests in another secret conveyance where there was some provisions of victuals laid up for their sustenance a few days; but themselves were forced to go into a place on the sudden, which, though it were safe from finding, yet had no provision at all to eat; and, as I have heard, they had but one apple between them in all those six or seven days.[3] Whereupon they thought it best to come out; and yet . . . not so much to save themselves from death by famine, as for that they perceived . . . the searchers . . . to be staying in the house until they had either found or famished those whom they knew to be within. Therefore these two virtuous men, being in hope that upon their taking the searchers would be satisfied and depart (as either thinking them to be priests or that if there had been any more to be found they would have come out), this hope made them resolve to offer themselves to their enemies' hands, to save the lives of those whom they loved better than themselves.'

[1] *A true discovery of the service performed at Hinlip.* British Museum, Harleian MSS., 360, f. 93 sq.

[2] *Narrative*, 152.

[3] Actually five days, unless Gerard reckons that the search began the previous Saturday.

Z

Gerard adds that the two Brothers planned their exit so as not to endanger their priest companions:[1]

'They therefore, perceiving that some of the searchers did continually by turns watch and walk up and down in the room where they were hidden, which was a long and fair gallery four square, going round about the house, they watched their time when the searchers were furthest off, and came out so secretly and stilly and shut the place again so finely that they were not one whit heard or perceived when and where they came out. And so they walked in the gallery towards the door, which they thought belike to have found open.'

But here their luck ended. The searchers, suddenly turning back on their walk, came face to face with them. At first Owen, then Ashley, tried to pass himself off as a servant of the house and asked to be let pass. They were questioned. Were they priests? Both admitted they were Catholics but refused to give a direct answer to the question whether they were priests, 'no doubt desirous', says Gerard,[2] 'to be taken as such, the better to satisfy the insatiable mind of those blood-suckers. Then being asked where they had been all that while, they answered that they had hid themselves, being Catholics, to avoid taking. And being urged to tell or show the place . . . they absolutely refused.'

Earlier Owen's companion, John Lillie, had saved Gerard's life by passing himself off as a priest.[3] This time the same ruse failed to save Garnet. Bromley knew he had not captured him, but he trusted that one of the two men now in his hands might prove to be Tesimond or Oldcorne.[4] The search was resumed and continued all Friday and Saturday. Clearly Bromley was acting on certain information that Garnet was in hiding. On the same night that the two Brothers were captured, he had written to Salisbury saying that he was still persuaded that there were one or two more in the house and was resolved to 'continue the guard yet a day or two'.[5] All the wainscotting in the gallery was broken down; here and there the walls also. It was assumed that the priests were hiding either in the same or in a neighbouring place. Still none was found.

'We had escaped', wrote Garnet later,[6] 'if the two first hidden soldiers [Owen and Ashley] had not come out so soon, for when they found them,

[1] *Narrative*, 153.

[2] *Ibid.*

[3] Cf. *sup.*, p. 261.

[4] Sir Henry Bromley to Lord Salisbury. 23 January 1606. *S.P.D. James I*, vol. 18, no. 38.

[5] *Ibid.*

[6] Garnet to Anne Vaux. 4 March 1606. *S.P.D. James I*, vol. 19, no. 11.

they were curious to find their place.' Indeed, Garnet would have escaped if Bromley had been content to continue his search merely for two days. It was only on the third day of the renewed search, as he was on the point of calling it off, that he found his prey.

The two priests were resolved to starve to death rather than bring trouble on their hosts by emerging from their place of hiding. 'After we had been in the hole seven days and seven nights', wrote Garnet,[1] 'and some odd hours, every man may well think we were well wearied, and indeed so it was, for we generally sat, save that sometimes we could not stretch ourselves.' In fact the hiding hole had such a low ceiling that even in a sitting position the priests were unable to stretch their legs. They suffered continual pain, Garnet more than Oldcorne; his legs became 'much swollen', he says, 'and continued so until I came to the Tower'. Then tragically he remarks: 'If we had but one half-day's liberty to come forth we should have so eased the place from books and furniture, that having with us a close stool we could have hidden a quarter of a year. For that all my friends will wonder at, especially in me, that neither of us went to the stool all the while, though we had means to do *servitii piccoli*, whereof also we were at a nonplus the day of our taking.'[2]

Every detail of the story told, from both sides of the hiding-place, suggests a betrayal. Had Garnet expected a search, the holes would certainly have been better prepared. It is inconceivable that Owen, who had devoted his best skill to the construction of so many places of concealment in a single house, should have been taken by surprise and that he himself, in such a crisis, should have been forced out by hunger. Moreover, he knew Bromley and his methods. Only positive information that Garnet and Oldcorne were there could have induced Bromley to persist.

'We were very merry and content within', continues Garnet,[3] 'and heard the searchers every day most curious over us, which made me think indeed that the place would be found.'

It was Monday morning, the 27 January, the eighth day of the search, that Garnet and Oldcorne were found. Again Bromley may have been boasting; more likely that he was acting on Littleton's deposition, when he told Salisbury that the place in the chimney where the priests were concealed was discovered, as the rest had been, 'one after another' until the full number of known places had been revealed.

'When we came forth' [says Garnet][4] 'we looked like two ghosts, yet

[1] *Ibid.*
[2] *Ibid.*
[3] *Ibid.*
[4] *Ibid.*

I the strongest, though my weakness lasted longest. The fellow that found us ran away for fear, thinking we would have shot a pistol at him; but there came [a] needless company to assist him; and we bade them be quiet and we would come forth.'

The proclamation had made it high treason for Habington to shelter Garnet in his house. Certainly Garnet would never have sought asylum at Hinlip had he known of the proclamation, which was signed in London exactly four days before Hinlip was invested. This he himself states: 'If I had known in time of the proclamation against me, I would have come forth and offered myself to Mr Habington, whether he would or no, to have been his prisoner.'[1] The surrender of Garnet's person would then have been made by Habington, whom the law could not have touched.[2]

Had the hiding-place not been discovered, it is likely that the two priests would have died within a day or two, not from hunger, but from the stench in the hole. 'The place was so close that those customs of nature which of necessity must be done, and in so long a time of continuance [were] exceedingly offensive to the men themselves and did much annoy them that made entrance in upon them: to whom they [the priests] confessed that they had not been able to hold out one whole day longer, but either they must have squealed or perished in the place.'[3]

Food, however, was ample; marmalade and sweetmeats were not yet exhausted; moreover, through 'a quill or reed taken through a little hole in the chimney that backed another chimney into a gentlewoman's chamber . . . candles, broth and warm drinks had been conveyed in unto them'.[4]

In greater pain than Oldcorne, Garnet was assisted out of the hiding-place. At first he was unable to move his limbs at all. Leaning on his captor, he was led, at his request, to a 'house of office'. There a board in the floor had been removed and Garnet barely managed to save himself from a heavy fall; he reflected that it seemed 'intended of purpose', for if he had come there in the dark, he would have broken his neck.[5]

Gerard could not resist moral reflections on the arrest of his Superior. In

---

[1] Gerard (*Narrative*, 156–7) dates Habington's return to Hinlip two days after the beginning of the search: 'he was presently arrested', says Gerard, 'that he might be in safety if any of these supposed traitors should chance to be taken to his house: because then by the law, he loseth both life and limb.'

[2] As the result of Garnet's capture in the circumstances he himself describes, Habington was confined for the rest of his life to the boundaries of his native county of Worcestershire.

[3] *A true discovery*. British Museum, Harleian MSS., 360, f. 93 sq.

[4] *Ibid*.

[5] H. G. to Anne Vaux. 4 March 1606. *S.P.D. James I*, vol. 19, no. 11.

a dramatically factual narrative he breaks suddenly into a short sermon:[1]

'And so we see that when God will protect, he can hide a Felix between two walls and make spiders His workmen to cover the entry with their webs. And again, when it is His pleasure to deliver up His servants to their last conflicts, no secret, no hide, no defence will serve; but He will deliver them up like sheep to the devouring of wolves, when He hath ordained them to so high an honour as to suffer for His holy name.'

[1] *Narrative*, 155.

36

THE RIDE TO LONDON

As Oldcorne was brought from the hiding-place he was immediately recognised. For nearly seventeen years he had worked in Worcestershire and was well known both to Catholics and Protestants; once, very briefly, he had been under arrest.

Garnet, however, was unknown. His presence at Hinlip had been reported by Littleton, whose information so far had proved correct. Bromley strove to identify him.

'They laboured much to know whether the other were Father Garnet or no,' writes Gerard,[1] 'and though they brought divers unto him to see whether they did know him, yet they could find none for a good while that could and would discover who he was, until at last one poor man was brought, who had drunk too much of that cup of contradiction with which the craft of heresy hath sought of late to infect the minds of some of the weaker sort, thereby to divide and so to destroy the kingdom of faith in our country.'

Garnet was so sick and unshaven that the physical description of him in the proclamation[2] did not help Bromley to identify him. It was his fate now to be recognised by an Appellant priest. Frequently Garnet had feared betrayal at their hands.

Gerard continues:

'This poor man, I hope rather out of simplicity than malice, took knowledge of him, having known him before and been beholden to him, and called him both by his own name Garnet and by other names he had known him to go by, by which he was also described in the Proclamation. And this silly man did utter it with a kind of spleen, as seeming to hope that now the Jesuits would bear less sway than he thought they had done. It is thought he hoped for some favour from the Council for this his good service unto them (though a priest and then a prisoner in Worcester); but I cannot hear that he reaped any fruit besides a wounded conscience *ex hac delatione et accusatione*

---

[1] *Narrative*, 156
[2] Cf. *sup.*, p. 316.

342

fratris sui.[1] And Father Garnet's answer unto him was with great mildness and charity, according to his custom.'

The priest who identified Garnet was Anthony Sherlock. On leaving Oxford he had entered Douai the same year that Garnet came to England. After his return as a priest Garnet had cared for him and then sent him to Stonor Park, where for three years he had acted as chaplain to Lady Cecily Stonor; he had then gone to Brailes in Warwickshire, and finally to Yardley, where he had been captured. In prison he renounced his faith and priesthood.[2]

Sherlock had been lying in Worcester gaol. He proclaimed that his arrest and imprisonment had brought him to his senses: 'my apprehension was the greatest grace and goodness of God to me. *Nam afflictio dat intellectum.*'[3] The identification took place at Holt Castle, Bromley's residence in Worcester. Garnet makes no reference at all to it; he hoped that Sherlock would return to his vocation. However, he told Anne Vaux that he made Bromley's task as difficult as possible. 'I acknowledged not my name', he wrote,[4] and he refused to make a statement about himself until he should meet 'my Lord Salisbury, who would know me'. Yet 'never did I deny my name to Sir Henry, but desired him to call me as he would; for he called me by divers names, but the most common was Garnet'. He insisted that he did not withold his true name from any discourtesy. Although he knew he had no escape, he was afraid that if he revealed himself before reaching London, he would be 'made an obloquy'. Perhaps he had in mind Campion's progress from Lyford and his entry into London with the screed over his hat, *Campion the Seditious Jesuit*. 'When I come to London', Garnet told his captor, 'I shall not be ashamed of my name.'[5]

From Hinlip, Garnet, who was then using the *alias* Humphrey Phillips, was carried to Worcester in Sir Henry Bromley's coach. With him were Father Oldcorne, calling himself John Vincent, Thomas Habington, Nicholas Owen, Ralph Ashley, and two of Habington's servants, Edward Jarret and William Glandish, men judged likely to give information about priests and others who frequented Hinlip. Glandish was the stableman at Hinlip; he had cared for priests on their arrival, unsaddled their horses and prepared for their departure. Jarret attended them inside the house, and hid them in their places of concealment whenever there was an alarm or search.[6]

[1] *From this betrayal and accusation of his brother.*
[2] The examination of Anthony Sherlock, priest, taken before Sir Henry Bromley, Kt. 30 January 1606. *S.P.D. James I*, vol. 18, no. 51.
[3] *Affliction brings understanding.*
[4] H. G. to Anne Vaux. 4 March 1606. *S.P.D. James I*, vol. 19, no. 11.
[5] *Ibid.*
[6] Bromley to Salisbury. 30 January 1606. *S.P.D. James I*, vol. 18, no. 52.

At Worcester there began between Garnet and Bromley a friendship that illustrates the quiet fascination Garnet exercised over others and had gained him friends in Rome and over all England.

It was Bromley's first intention to place his prisoners in the private custody of certain citizens whom he trusted. With them they could be housed in comfort until instructions came from Salisbury. But, as Garnet explained with understanding, 'he [Bromley] said he could not do as he wished, but must send us to the gaol'. 'Very well, in God's name', Garnet answered; but he begged that both he and Oldcorne should not be placed in irons, for they were lame already, and if they were now chained they would be unable to ride to London.

On this pretext Bromley agreed to send them to private lodgings, each with a man to guard him. The other prisoners were despatched about the city. Later Bromley asked Garnet and Oldcorne to be his private guests and prisoners at Holt Castle and sent his coach to bring them there. 'We were exceedingly well used', says Garnet, 'and dined and supped with him and his every day.'

Salisbury delayed. 'On Candlemas day', continues Garnet,[1] 'he [Bromley] made a great dinner to end Christmas, and in the middle of dinner he sent for wine to drink health to the King.' All bared their heads for the toast. With the wine was brought a lighted candle, taken at Hinlip 'with Jesus on one side and Maria on another'. Garnet asked to see the candle. Taking it in his hands and then passing it to Oldcorne, he expressed his pleasure at carrying a candle on such a day. Then again he pledged the King's health, 'yet with favour, as they said, in a reasonable glass'.

Effortlessly, during his days at Bromley's house Garnet's personality impressed his captors' family: they never doubted his sincerity. 'The gentle-women, who were very kind to me, as also all the house ... were with us continually' for the first days: later they were kept apart from the priests, for fear they might be perverted in religion: stricter instructions were given to the guard, but Garnet had already won their goodwill. He made a request of them. 'I desired them all to think well of me till they saw whether I could justify myself in this cause.'[2]

On 30 January Bromley assured Salisbury that he was certainly 'possessed of Garnet and Hall and that he was keeping them at his own house so that they should be able to recover sufficient strength for the journey';[3] he was anxious also to segregate the priests from the other prisoners in Worcester gaol.

---

[1] H. G. to Anne Vaux. 4 March 1606. *S.P.D. James I*, vol. 19, no. 11.
[2] *Ibid.*   [3] Bromley to Salisbury. 30 January 1606. *S.P.D. James I*, vol. 18, no. 52.

Bromley had anticipated that the journey from Worcester to London would take three days. But on the third day, 5 February, he had got no further than Wycombe. Garnet, as Bromley explained, was a 'weak and wearisome traveller' although he had been given 'the best horse in the company'. 'All the way to London', as he gladly admitted, 'I was passing well used at the King's charge, and that by express order from Lord Salisbury.'[1] On the first and again on the last night Garnet suffered a fever and was unable to eat at all; on other days he could take only a little bread, an apple and some wine.

In the party was Sir Henry Bromley's chaplain. 'I had some bickering with ministers by the way', said Garnet.[2] But the full story is told in detail by Gerard:[3]

'It happened by the way that the Minister who went with Sir Henry Bromley as his chaplain or preacher, seeing Father Garnet so modest and to speak so little, especially of matters of controversy, thought belike he had been utterly unskilful in them, and desirous to get some credit in that kind, began to provoke Father Garnet to the combat; but Father Garnet, loth to give offence unto any, and esteeming the example of modesty more fruitful to a proud heretic than to contend with one so likely to resist the known truth, did once or twice put him off with a mild answer, showing only what the other should believe in such a case, and forbearing to allege any further reasons. Whereupon the heretic grew more insolent (as their custom is) and then began in sort to triumph in the hearing of others, which Father Garnet perceiving, and then doubting that his good meaning would be so easily discerned by silence as misconstrued, without giving further answer to the Minister, he hastened his horse a little to overtake Sir Henry Bromley that rode before, and told him how his Minister had divers times provoked him to disputation, which he had purposely forborne, being loth to give offence unto him in whose custody now he was; and partly also because he knew such disputations to be often fruitless where there is no judge of authority to restrain the subdued party from entering into terms of blasphemy and suchlike.' Therefore he thought it better to be silent, 'but that if it pleased Sir Henry to hear the one and restrain the other ... he then, for his part, was ready to give his Minister satisfaction to anything he would or could propound. Sir Henry commended very much his wisdom and government ... and called the Minister presently, willing him to propound all things freely that he would, but yet with modesty. So the Minister began to discourse after their diffuse manner, provoking many things not digested into

[1] H. G. to Anne Vaux. 4 March 1606. *S.P.D. James I*, vol. 19, no. 11.
[2] *Ibid.*
[3] *Narrative*, 157–8.

any good method, nor founded on any sure grounds of faith or learning. Father Garnet suffered him to speak his fill, as long as he seemed to continue in one matter, and then desired leave to speak. Then he in a few words and excellent order related the substance of all the other had said, and then repelled it with so substantial grounds, and with such demonstration of learning, and that even in those kinds which they most esteem and stand upon, which is the Scriptures and Tongues, that it put the Minister to silence and the Knight to admiration; and all the audience were so satisfied both with his modesty and profound learning [that] it was reported presently all over London, to the great commendation of the good Father.'

Garnet does not refer to this incident, but mentions only his encounter with other Ministers; he speaks of four in all. 'I had some bickering with Ministers by the way', he says,[1] and adds: 'Two very good scholars, Mr Abbot and Mr Barlow, met us at an inn; but two others, rude fellows, met us on the way whose discourtesy I rewarded with plain words.'

It was seldom that Garnet used plain words: he was instinctively courteous, but the irritation he was now suffering was excessive. When he met George Abbot, he little suspected that this learned and polite gentleman would strive to calumniate him after his death. Neither Gerard nor Garnet say where the meeting occurred; possibly it was at Oxford, where Abbot, now Dean of Winchester, had been Master of University College and lecturer in Scripture, or at Thame Park, where frequently he was the guest of Sir Richard Wenman.[2]

It is unfortunate that Garnet does no more than say that he met another cleric called Barlow, for this might have been either William Barlow, chaplain to Prince Henry and one of the most accomplished scientists of his time, or Archbishop Whitgift's chaplain, who had recently been appointed Bishop of Rochester. For different reasons both men would have been curious to speak to Garnet, who in the space of a few days had become the talk of all England.

Physically weak, anxious in mind, sick, fatigued and aching in limbs, Garnet continued his journey. His pleasing modesty that had captivated Bellarmine, converted Bromley. On reaching London the Puritan Justice affirmed 'that never in his life had he met the like man to Mr Garnet either for modesty, wisdom or learning and that he would kneel before the king to save his life, if he were not found guilty of the Powder [treason]'.[3]

Garnet and Oldcorne were taken to the Gatehouse prison by the Abbey,

[1] H. G. to Anne Vaux. 4 March 1606. *S.P.D. James I*, vol. 19, no. 11.

[2] It was here that John Gerard had met him at dinner. The amusing encounter is described in *John Gerard*, 170–1.

[3] *Narrative*, 158.

Owen and Ashley elsewhere. News of Garnet's progress had preceded him. As he approached the entrance to the Gatehouse all the Catholic prisoners were gathered there to do him honour. When he came in earshot Garnet called out: 'Is there any of you here that be in for the Catholic faith?' Many answered, 'Yes, yes, we are Catholics and prisoners for our conscience.' Garnet replied, 'Then I am your fellow.'[1]

He was taken to his cell; the door was barred on him. He had only one regret, that he was unable to offer Mass: 'If only', he said, 'I could have my morning delight which cannot be had.'[2]

No such public curiosity had encompassed a captured priest since Campion had ridden into London in 1581. The King, Lord Salisbury and the entire Council were impatient to meet him. During the years of his liberty, as Gerard truly observed,[3] he had established among those who most persistently sought his life a reputation for 'virtue, gravity and learning' that no other man possessed. Moreover, all who were to join battle with him knew well 'how much he was respected by many great persons, and esteemed also by the Ambassadors of the Catholic princes then residing in London'.[4]

The Council now sought ways of presenting Garnet to the country as the arch-traitor, because, in the public opinion, he was considered the arch-Catholic. During the remaining nine weeks of his life the uneven duel was fought. From day to day the issue hung in the balance. In his own shrewd manner Gerard had some perception of the crisis. He noted that Salisbury would not call Garnet before the Council until he was thoroughly prepared for the first interview; the universally high esteem in which his prisoner was held made him 'very wary' and anxious first 'to deliberate much how to proceed with him'. The other Councillors took the same view and 'would not call him . . . before they had informed themselves of as much as they could learn of his words and carriage at his taking and bringing up to London, many of which (to our great grief and loss) are unknown to us'. At the time Gerard wrote this, Oldcorne, Owen and Ashley, who had been with him on the road from Worcester, were all dead, and until their day of execution had been kept close prisoners. 'And the times also have been so troublesome since [then]', Gerard regretted, 'that we could not have such means as we desire to meet and talk with those that were eye-witnesses of many notable incidents, which we hope to do hereafter, and to have many things brought to light which will be greatly to God's glory and all our comfort.'[5]

---

[1] *Ibid.*
[2] H. G. to Anne Vaux. 4 March 1606. *S.P.D. James I*, vol. 19, no. 11.
[3] *Narrative*, 159.
[4] *Ibid.*   [5] *Ibid.*

37

FIRST EXAMINATIONS

ON St Valentine's eve, 13 February, Garnet appeared for his first examination before the Privy Council sitting in the Star Chamber at Whitehall. A large crowd of Londoners watched him leave the Gatehouse: Garnet overheard their comments. 'One said there was a Provincial; another, there goeth a young Pope.'[1]

At the Council table sat Lord Salisbury, Sir John Popham, Sir Edward Coke, Sir William Wade, with the Earls of Worcester, Northampton and Nottingham. Not all attended later meetings, but there were seldom more than two of them absent at any time. By the law of the land the Councillors[2] were also to try the prisoner they had now started to examine. The man among them who knew Garnet personally was Popham; Northampton and Nottingham were perhaps acquainted with Gerard, but there is no evidence that Garnet had met them before this day.

Coke, three years older than Garnet, was a Norfolk man of immense industry and greed. 'Beginning on a good bottom left him by his father, marrying a wife of extraordinary wealth,' he led a thrifty life and sealed his success by making a second marriage into the Cecil family. This was in August 1598 when, less than a month after burying his first wife, he attended old Lord Burghley's funeral and, after it, asked the new Lord for the hand of his daughter, twenty-six years his junior and the widow of Lord Hatton, one of the richest men of his time. His enduring fame as a lawyer came later, first when he stood out against the King's right to make law by proclamation and, then, on the publication of his *Reports*, which established the supremacy of the common law in England.

Wade was now Clerk of the Privy Council and also, as Lieutenant of the Tower, Garnet's official gaoler. He was feared only less than Popham for his venom against Catholics. The son of Amagil Wade, the 'English Columbus' who had sailed to Newfoundland in the reign of Henry VIII, he

---

[1] H. G. to Anne Vaux. 2 March 1606. *S.P.D. James I*, vol. 19, no. 11.
[2] With the exception of Wade, who was Clerk of the Privy Council.

had been in the service of the Cecils since he was twenty and on Garnet's arrival in England was at the centre of the spy system organised by Walsingham. He was a past master of intrigue and as indispensable to Salisbury as he had been to his father.

Charles Howard, Earl of Nottingham, had sat in trial on the Gunpowder conspirators. While he was the least active of the Councillors, his kinsman, Henry Howard, Earl of Northampton, son of the poet, the Earl of Surrey, was the most enigmatic. Always a suspect Catholic, he was described by the King as a 'tame duck with whom he hoped to catch many wild ones'. He was sixty-six years old when Garnet confronted him, an ambiguous, incalculable and distrusted man. More concerned with grand living than with religion — he built both Audley End and Northampton House — he nevertheless wrote in his will, dated 14 June 1614: 'I die a member of the Catholic and Apostolic Church, saying with St Jerome, *In qua fide puer natus fui, in eadem senex morior.*' He appears to have played a minor part in the examinations of Garnet, but spoke at the trial. His position in the government was strong, for he had worked with Salisbury to secure the succession of James I.

Worcester's role among the Councillors was perhaps the most sinister. The Earl Marshal of England and a Catholic, he had nevertheless received a commission in 1602 to expel the Jesuits from the country. He had worked closely with Popham and had been very active against Catholics at the time of the disturbances in Herefordshire. After Garnet's trial he had received a monopoly for making gunpowder and saltpetre. He was one of Salisbury's most useful tools.

It is a measure of Garnet's intelligence that throughout the examinations he was a match for Salisbury himself. Machiavellian in practice as his father had been in theory also, Salisbury knew when to flatter or threaten to secure an advantage, and was an adept in dissimulation, a practice which he claimed made Garnet and all Jesuits unfit to breathe their native air. In Garnet's trial he saw the opportunity to secure and strengthen his position.

The Councillors treated Garnet with a great show of respect; in fact, the first interview opened with punctilious courtesy on both sides. 'When I came to the Council, I kneeled and I was bid stand', wrote Garnet.[1] Gerard adds: 'The Lords themselves would seldom speak unto him but they would put off their hat and sometimes hold it off for a good while'; before asking him any question, they addressed him as Mr Garnet.[2] One piece of abuse Salisbury, however, could not resist. He had intercepted a letter from 'Mrs

---

[1] H. G. to Anne Vaux. 2 March 1606. *S.P.D. James I*, vol. 19, no. 11.
[2] *Narrative*, 160.

Vaux to me, subscribed, "Your loving sister, A. G." My Lord Salisbury said, 'What, you are married to Mrs Vaux. She calls herself Garnet. What, *Senex fornicarius* [old fornicator].' At the next interview, however, Salisbury asked Garnet's forgiveness, 'and said he spoke to me in jest'. He put his arm round Garnet's shoulders and held it there a long time. The other Councillors said that 'I was held for exemplar in those matters.'[1]

There is a report of this examination, signed by Garnet, with marginal annotations in the handwriting of Sir Edward Coke,[2] and a shorter account, written by Garnet to Anne Vaux, three weeks later.[3] No attempt was made to implicate him in the Gunpowder Plot. The examination was exploratory. To the question of his true name he confessed that it was Henry Garnet and that at times he had used also the names of Whalley, Darcy, Farmer and others, as a measure to protect his friends. He admitted he had been Superior of the Jesuits for the last twenty years and had been continuously in England during that time.[4]

After these preliminaries Garnet took the initiative: he asked the Councillors whether they had received his letter, protesting his innocence to the King and Council. When they denied any knowledge of it, Garnet repeated his protestation. 'They wished I would not so earnestly protest', he reported. They claimed that there was proof of his complicity in their hands.

Little more was said of the Plot. Garnet merely admitted that he had been at Coughton and on 6 November had received there a letter from Digby and Catesby. 'The effect of the letter', the examination reports Garnet as saying,[5] 'was to excuse their rashness. [They] requested my assistance in Wales... My answer was that they should not enter into so wicked actions but be ruled by the advice of friends and the order of his Holiness.'

Garnet was believed. His denial of complicity confirmed the emphatic testimony of the conspirators themselves. Digbys' letter, Garnet pointed out, contained not one word of powder in the Parliament house: he had heard it mentioned only by the messenger, Bates.

Neither now nor at any later time did the Council explain the character of the evidence they claimed to possess against him. For the greater part of three hours they questioned him on points of doctrine, particularly on

---

[1] H. G. to Anne Vaux. 13 April 1606. Hatfield Calendar, vol. 18, 111. There is no way of dating this incident exactly, for it is mentioned by Garnet in a long letter that gives 'the whole state of his cause'. Salisbury's purpose was not directly to insult Garnet, but to observe his reaction. He was anxious to use Garnet's relationship with Anne Vaux to lower his esteem in the public mind. As will be seen, his apology was insincere.

[2] Examination of Henry Garnet. 13 February 1606. *S.P.D. James I*, vol. 18, no. 87

[3] H. G. to Anne Vaux. 2 March 1606. *S.P.D. James I*, vol. 19, no. 1.

[4] *S.P.D. James I*, vol. 18, no. 87.   [5] *Ibid.*

equivocation. 'I was glad to have this occasion', wrote Garnet later to Anne Vaux, 'to be accounted a traitor without the Powder-house, rather than within.' In his innocence he did not suspect that he was already providing Coke, his chief examiner, with material he would later use in the preamble to his speech of prosecution. Unable to implicate Garnet, Coke's aim was to demonstrate that Jesuits, and particularly this arch-Jesuit, confessed to doctrines that subverted the good order of the State.

Salisbury then took over. 'His interrogations and my answers,' wrote Garnet,[1] 'with some intermingled disputations, especially of equivocation . . . lasted three hours almost.' The mutual courtesies continued. Salisbury made the point that he was not there to question Garnet on matters of religion or on the priesthood or the real Presence, though these were touched on, but on the doctrine of equivocation, for on this turned the vital issue whether Jesuits could be trusted as subjects of the Crown. Cecil said: 'This is the high point in which you must satisfy the King, that he may know what to trust unto.'[2]

Open on the Council table lay a manuscript copy of Garnet's treatise on equivocation.[3] The title was discussed. Garnet said that he had called it a 'treatise against lying and fraudulent dissimulation' because no use of equivocation could justify lying: this had been emphasised in a marginal note he had inserted in his own handwriting on page forty-seven and by other emendations he had made.[4] While Garnet answered, Coke took notes. At Garnet's trial Salisbury argued that this treatise, which, as he was now told, had never been published, formed the main part of the 'visible anatomy of Popish doctrine', which he declared was the principle reason why the government had proceeded against the conspirators. Robert Abbot, who as royal Chaplain may have been consulted before this examination, later wrote that the author was *sacerdos quidam Satanae.*[5]

---

[1] H. G. to Anne Vaux. 2 March 1606. *S.P.D. James I*, vol. 19, no. 11.   [2] *Ibid.*
[3] Cf. *sup.*, p. 255. This copy is now in the Bodleian Library, Oxford.
[4] Examination of Henry Garnet. 13 February 1606. *S.P.D. James I*, vol. 18, no. 87. Coke did not call Garnet's attention to the alteration made on page 57 of the manuscript before him. It is the passage that follows (the words in brackets are added in Garnet's hand and the words underlined deleted by him): 'Besides other strange and barbarous torturing of men after they be apprehended, not for (to utter) any (treason to our country or) danger to her majesty's sacred person who we wish with tears did know our loyal and most faithful hearts, but only to wring out with divers cruelties the names of Catholics and such actions as may be subject to penal laws. . . .' For the words deleted Garnet substituted: 'whose princely heart detesteth hard procedings'. At this place a small piece of paper is pasted on to the margin as a catch-marker: on it is the letter *B* in Coke's hand.
[5] Robert Abbot, *Antilogia adversus Apologiam Andreae Eudeamon-Joannis pro Henroic Garneto, Jesuita, Proditore* (1613).

For the rest Garnet answered, to use his own words, 'plainly and modestly and with great moderation'. Coke knew that he was dealing with a prisoner who had knowledge of the law. Garnet's training at Tottel's press was manifest in the precision of his mind that Coke saw in the treatise. On page thirty-eight of the manuscript Garnet had explained that every man is bound to answer directly a direct question, no matter what he is asked: this was his legal as well as his moral obligation, and when questioned by a lawful authority under which he lawfully fell on a matter subject to the law, he had no alternative but to reply truthfully if the law itself was a just law.

Throughout the three hours Garnet was careful to say nothing that might bear an offensive construction. This became clear when Salisbury touched on the question of heresy: he was anxious to know whether the King, the Council and all adherents of the State religion were, in his view, heretics. 'I said' Garnet replied. 'that the religion was heretical: of the persons I would not judge.' To be formal heretics 'they must have sufficient knowledge to the contrary'. Though pressed, he would not pronounce on the King 'out of reverence for him'. This finally they allowed.

After an interval Garnet was brought again before the Council for another hour. Now Coke took up the questioning. He achieved little. His hope was that Garnet would implicate his friends. But Garnet refused to name any person whose life or property might be endangered. When Coke examined him on the activity of the conspirators, Garnet, with manifest honesty, disclaimed all knowledge of their designs.

That afternoon Garnet was taken back to the Gatehouse. He was now the talk of London. 'The expectation touching Father Garnet', wrote Gerard who was in London at the time,[1] 'was great in every place, and the conceits of men very divers and their discourses different.' The citizens were quick to notice that he had been handled with great respect; and this was interpreted variously both by Catholics and Protestants. Some thought that he would be pardoned; others that his friends would be permitted to ransom him. Already it was rumoured that the Council could find no ground for proceeding against him. The same or the following day a devout Catholic lady offered a courtier of influence five hundred pounds to obtain his release.

Between now and his death, and indeed after it, Garnet's name was mentioned both by Catholics and Protestants in tones of veneration. Even his enemies, Gerard noted as he mixed among the crowds, 'could speak no other but much good of him'. Already after his first examination the starting-point of speculation on his fate was that he was one of the most 'notable' men in the country 'famous for learning, piety and modesty'.[2] His first

[1] *Narrative*, 160.   [2] *op cit.*, 161.

encounter with the Councillors had baffled them: his behaviour left them uncertain how to proceed, and doubtful perhaps whether they should proceed at all. Yet, as examination followed examination, the case of the prosecution took shape.

The following day, 14 February, Garnet was transferred to the Tower. This itself was an indication that the government would prosecute. All through the evening and night the speculation had continued.

'Briefly,' says Gerard,[1] 'the general report was that he was free from the Plot, and not to be touched with this conspiracy, which even Protestants affirmed to be most likely, in that he was not accused by any of the conspirators, as might easily be seen in their printed examinations, for that, above all the rest, would have been printed, if by favour or force or fear it could have been wrung from them. Now as for Catholics, it was generally their opinion that he was innocent, for they knew very well he could not be guilty who had so often and so effectually laboured to stay them from all attempts or disobedience, though in matters of much less moment than this so cruel intention against the Parliament House.'

While 'all London and England' speculated on Garnet's fate and 'every man gave his judgment ... according to his several humour and opinion',[2] Garnet, on St Valentine's day, was taken to the Tower. The Lieutenant, Sir William Wade, received him with abuse. He called him the 'plotter of all treasons'. Garnet made no answer. Wade then took offence. Garnet replied that 'he was not moved with his words, for Christ his Master had taught him by His own example to bear quietly such contumely'.[3]

Garnet was given a comfortless but spacious and well-lit room. On the first two nights he was very weak with what he described as 'ill-lodging'. In the Tower, luxuries such as a bed or chair had to be provided by the prisoner himself. All Garnet could obtain from his gaoler was a little straw to lie on. Though he had many friends in London, he had to be very wary. He could make his request only through an intermediary who was held in some other prison. There Garnet's friends brought bed, chairs, fruit, money and wine. They used 'great circumspection' for, as Gerard says, they would certainly be 'watched narrowly and perhaps dogged to their homes, which is an ordinary practice in all such cases'.[4]

Even in the Tower, Garnet, though alternatively insulted and flattered by Wade, suffered no exceptional hardships. At the expense of his captors he was permitted certain luxuries he appreciated. 'I am allowed with every meal

---

[1] *Ibid.*
[2] *op. cit.*, 162.
[3] *Ibid.*   [4] *op. cit.*, 163.

AA

a good draught of excellent claret wine', he told Anne Vaux.[1] It was Wade's intention to draw from him by friendly talk some statement that could be used against him at his trial.

For his first days in the Tower he had no fire. Then through Anne Vaux he received money to purchase coal.[2] On 26 February, in a letter to Anne,[3] he acknowledged the receipt of the linen she had sent him, namely, 'two pairs of sheets, two pillow-bears, and one handkerchief'. And he added: 'God reward all our benefactors. I would gladly you sent me direction how to send to some good friends in the Clink for such things as I shall chance to want, for the Gatehouse is too far off. I pray you try if any there will or may undertake to help me. I want a pair or two of socks, also a black nightcap and I will send out this to be new lined. I think I shall shortly send for some money, for we have not yet paid our fees, and I would gladly have all things even.' Then he asked for another pair of spectacles 'to see things afar off; for to read I need not'.

Garnet's first examination in the Tower took place soon after he had been transferred from the Gatehouse and before he made these requests to Anne. He does not give a full report of this examination; nor does he mention whether it took place in his cell or in the Council chamber in the Tower. Salisbury was again present, with Coke, Wade and Popham, the Chief Justice. For the most part it was conducted in the same atmosphere of friendliness. What passed is recorded merely by Garnet.[4] He confines himself largely to what he calls their 'pleasant discourses'. Either at this or a later examination he told the Councillors: 'I cared not for my life; but whether innocently to die as I hoped (and yet am sure) or guiltily, death was welcome.' Coke said that this was a pity, for he was a 'fit man to live and serve' his country. Asked what day he had reached Hinlip, Garnet said that if he was given a calendar he could tell; but he thought it was 'St Sebastian's day or next to it.' At this Coke interjected that Garnet had saints for every day. 'We have for the most', said Garnet. 'Well then' Coke sneered, 'you shall have no place in the calendar.' 'I am not worthy', answered Garnet quietly, 'but I hope to have a place in heaven.' 'Yet', admitted Garnet, 'he is very courteous.'

Garnet was aware that anything he said to his examiners might be used against him when they sat on the Bench as his judges. They passed from one topic to another in the hope that their prisoner might be trapped into an

[1] H. G. to Anne Vaux. 2 March 1606. *S.P.D. James I*, vol. 19, no. 11.

[2] Writing on 2 March (*ibid.*) he added, 'For now fire will shortly be unnecessary, if I live so long: whereof I am very uncertain and careless.'

[3] H. G. to Anne Vaux. 26 February 1606. *Hat. Cal.*, 18, 60.

[4] *Ibid.*

unguarded admission. Gerard succeeded in gathering much information, but with difficulty. Deliberately Coke spread the report that he would not prosecute Garnet for contravening the statute that made it high treason for an Englishman, born in the realm, to minister in his native country after receiving orders abroad. Gerard heard this, and also that Coke had put Garnet many questions which, had he answered either weakly or unwisely, would certainly have brought ruin on his friends: 'for instance, [he was asked] where he had lived for a long time, how he had been maintained, what places he was at in that last journey, what company he had met at the places which they affirmed he did stay in, and finally, whom he knew and had had any dealings withal'.[1] Garnet revealed nothing. 'He acquitted himself wisely and answered . . . resolutely. No one of high or low degree came into trouble by his default or oversight.'[2] The friendliness of his examiners did not deceive him. Only when he was certain that the government was already fully informed on any place, person or subject was he prepared to speak.

'They asked me whether I did not christen a child at White Webbs', Garnet wrote in his own account of these early interviews in the Tower.[3] 'I said such a thing might be, but I remembered not.' On hearing mention of an infant, Wade interjected an indecent observation. 'The other two reprehended him, and said the father lived in the house and was one Brooksby, with a bald head and a reddish beard.' Garnet protested to Wade: White Webbs was a 'place of justice and such calumniations were unfit'; Coke took his side. Garnet wrote of the Lieutenant: 'He is very kindly in his usage and familiarity, but most violent and impotent in speeches when he entereth matters of religion.'[4]

The conversation turned to Jesuits. Wade forecast that their Order would be dissolved by the Pope, as the Templars had been, and, as a first step, they would be sent out of England. Garnet answered with dignity: 'I said that if it pleased the King to grant free liberty to other Papists, I would presently send away all Jesuits.' Popham interrupted: surely this was more than Garnet had authority to do. 'I would try', replied Garnet, who said he feared that, in any case, measures would be taken against them in the course of the present Parliament. 'My advice is that they hire themselves private lodgings and help their friends abroad,[5] and say they are dismissed for a time by the Superior. This I think best till Father General's will be known.'[6]

---

[1] *Narrative*, 163.   [2] *Ibid.*
[3] H. G. to Anne Vaux. 4 March 1606. *S.P.D. James I*, vol. 19, no. 11.
[4] *Ibid.*
[5] i.e. in the country.
[6] H. G. to Anne Vaux. 4 March 1606. *S.P.D. James I*, vol. 19, no. 11.

With every interview Garnet's adroitness increased. Constantly Coke returned to the subject of equivocation. On this, Gerard noted, Garnet 'was much and often urged, and ever gave them such satisfaction as in reason they could wish no more'.

From all these early examinations the only material Coke could extract for his prosecution speech was Garnet's teaching on equivocation; and this he possessed already in Garnet's annotated copy of the book.[1]

Thus far the attempt to implicate Garnet in the Powder treason failed: his honesty had baffled them. 'They verily thought that I was at White Webbs with the conspirators', he wrote to Anne Vaux.[2] And he admitted that if it could be proved that he had been there after the end of August 1605, he might find it difficult to acquit himself of the Powder action; hence they urged him to make this 'very protestation'. Then they questioned him on the time of his going to Coughton. Garnet maintained rightly that it was only accidental that his visit coincided with the Plot, about which he was ignorant. All Catholics knew it was a necessity 'that he should be there'.[3] Nothing he said about the movements of the conspirators was any help to the Council in framing an indictment against him.

Humbly he revealed to Anne Vaux his own surprise at the manner in which he had stood up to the interrogations. 'In truth I thank God I am and have been *intrepidus*. And herein I marvel at myself, having such great apprehensions before.' Frequently, when he had written in praise of the martyrs he had fears that the same courage would never be given to him: now he reflected sincerely, 'I often fear torture. Yet it is the same God, and I cannot be tortured but for justice; that is, either to wrong myself or others, as I cannot be condemned but for justice.'

After the failure of these first interviews in the Tower, the Council altered their strategy: Gerard was quick to observe it. 'The Council', he writes,[4] 'finding that no advantage was to be gotten of him in his examinations, either against himself or others in this chief matter, they committed the care and charge of proceeding with him in that kind unto the Lord Chief Justice and to the Attorney-General, to wit, Popham and Coke, both professed enemies to Catholics and their religion.'

---

[1] In Gerard's manuscript of the *Narrative* there is a sentence which he later erased. As it indicates the care Gerard took to get his facts correct, it is worth noting. Speaking of Coke's discourse on equivocation in his speech of arraignment, Gerard first wrote: '[Coke] must needs have a fling at it [equivocation] because his place was not to speak much before, when the Council did examine him [Garnet].' Later he scored out this sentence (*Narrative*, 164).

[2] H. G. to Anne Vaux. 2 March 1606. *S.P.D. James I*, vol. 19, no. 11.

[3] *Ibid.*   [4] *Narrative*, 164.

A new phase now opened: relentless, unscrupulous and unremitting. It was reckoned that if this process was continued it was only a matter of time before the Council could produce against him a case on which a jury, suborned or bullied, would find him guilty.

Popham was ambitious. He was determined to have Garnet hanged for the Powder Plot. Correctly Gerard assessed the menace.[1] These 'professed enemies' of the Church, the judge and the prosecutor at his trial a few weeks later, 'were so forward, or rather so desirous, to undertake the business that (as it is said) they offered, if they might have their full scope to deal with him as they thought good, they would undertake to prove him guilty in the Plot of Powder'. Even Gerard was shocked and begged God's forgiveness for them. 'I pray God that the saying of the prophet David be not proved against them. *Veloces pedes eorum ad effundendum sanguinem*,[2] when they shall be cited to a higher tribunal, where neither the one [Coke] shall plead nor the other [Popham] be judge, but both be judged *secundum mensuram qua mensi fuerint*.'[3]

[1] *Ibid.*
[2] *Their feet are swift to shed blood.* Psalm 13: 3.
[3] *According to the measure they themselves have meted out to others.* Matthew 7: 2.

38

THE INTERLOCUTIONS

THE remaining Councillors waited on the work of Popham and Coke. 'Garnet was delivered to their pleasure and it pleased them to examine him very often.'[1] For several days the examinations continued. Popham gained no advantage. He resorted to lies. Then with Coke's collusion he attempted to get Garnet sentenced without trial by Act of Parliament. Garnet knew nothing of this, until he came to trial.[2] The source again is Gerard's *Narrative*, the incident is told from first-hand information:

'After three or four examinations, they [Popham and Coke] were so bold as to give out that he had confessed all. But this was for another end. For hereupon presently the Attorney spake in the Parliament House to have eight Jesuits condemned of this treason by the High Court of Parliament, *vidlt.*, Garnet, Hall, Greenway, Gerard, Hamon, Westmorland (there being no such of the Society), Creswell and Baldwin. But the Parliament refused to condemn these men without better proof of their being guilty, and therefore willed the Attorney (seeing he had Garnet's examinations) to lay down the next day the proofs before them, which he promised to do in so clear a manner as their Lordships should rest satisfied of their guiltiness, and that by Garnet's own confession. At the time appointed he brings his proofs, which all proved no confession of Father Garnet (as he had promised), and indeed nothing else but mere conjectures, imaginations, and inferences of his own, and that with so little colour of likely truth as no man applauded the motion, although there were very many that were no friends to the parties accused (to speak the least), and so Mr Attorney his motion died, and was never revived.'[3]

This story, unnoticed by historians, may explain the general disbelief of the country in Garnet's guilt and the efforts made by the Council after his

[1] Gerard was scrupulous to avoid exaggeration; he added and then erased the following phrase: 'as Job to his accusing enemies to persuade by bloody interrogations and other vexations also, as they should find it needful, reserving his life'. *Narrative*, 164.

[2] Cf. *inf.*, p. 397. [3] *Narrative*, 164–5.

death to justify itself in proceeding against him. Gerard continues: 'Yea, a nobleman coming from the Parliament at that time, said to his friend, that these lawyers were so accustomed to lie that they could say truth in no place. But indeed Mr Attorney must be excused for this time, the cause and case being very particular and a thing much sought for and long desired.'

Resolutely Parliament refused to convict on the mere word of the Attorney-General. Coke was foiled; his reputation suffered while Garnet's was enhanced. He had overstated his case, and in the Bill of Attainder had included two non-existent English Jesuits. 'There were also', says Gerard, 'some questions sent unto Father Garnet from the Parliament itself, and he answered to all their demands by writing in such sort as gave good satisfaction.'[1] These answers appear not to be extant. They convinced the House. Popham and Coke renewed their efforts. Daily they visited Garnet in his cell, not, however, Gerard observes with sarcasm,[2] in the manner calculated to bring them the blessing promised in the gospel for this work of mercy: *I was in prison and you visited me*.[3] 'They did daily vex him with subtle examinations and cruel interrogations, but finding they could win nothing by these means, they devised by treacherous stratagems to discover the secrets of his heart if any were concealed by him of which they might take advantage.'

The stratagem was Garnet's partial undoing. His gaoler was made Popham's instrument. This man, Gerard writes,[4] 'was directed to affect himself much moved by Father Garnet his behaviour and words (as indeed they were sufficient to move a better and wiser man than him that had not been without grace) and to pretend that he began to be much inclined and almost won to the Catholic faith, and, in the meantime, to show himself very friendly, and promise to be faithful to Father Garnet in anything wherein he might do him service'. The fellow was very 'cunning in this art of cozenage and . . . set a fair gilt upon his copper'.[5] Garnet believed him sincere, 'though he meant not', Gerard adds hastily, 'to trust him so far as might greatly endanger either himself or others' until he had tested the man.

It has been common to blame Garnet for fatal simplicity in trusting his gaoler. Certainly he gave nothing away in any of the letters he sent out from the Tower: just one phrase from them was cited against him at his trial. While his inquisitors scrutinised every line for some indiscretion, Garnet was able to communicate with his friends, who received counterfeit copies made after Coke had read the originals. Even Gerard, who was shown these copies by Anne Vaux, did not detect the forgery.

[1] *Ibid.*
[2] *op. cit.*, 166.
[3] Matthew 25: 36.   [4] *Narrative*, 166.   [5] *Ibid.*

Precisely because Coke found in all these letters nothing 'but either spiritual comforts or the relation of his [Garnet's] estate and examinations'[1] he fell back on another 'subtle craft'.

Carey, the gaoler, was instructed to show Garnet how, through a hole in the wall, he could talk with Oldcorne who had been placed in the neighbouring cell. Gerard tells the story with drama and accuracy.[2] First, on the instructions of Coke, Carey 'placed Father Oldcorne in a chamber near unto Father Garnet. [Then] this sly companion and cunning or rather cozening keeper, making show of great love to Father Garnet, told him there was a thing wherein he knew the Father would take great comfort, and which he would be willing to grant .. but that he durst never as yet tell him of it, lest it should be espied by others; and then he was undone.'

Garnet had now been in solitary confinement for four weeks. He was anxious to speak with Oldcorne if no danger was involved: it would be helpful to them both in future interrogations if each knew what the other had said: moreover, he desired to make a general confession of his life before his death, which, as he now saw, nothing could prevent: the Council was determined on it.

Carey extracted from Garnet a promise to tell no one, and to see that Oldcorne gave the same undertaking. He then showed Garnet the cleft in the wall, and said that the two priests 'might speak well together and might hear one the other' if they spoke 'with any loudness'.[3]

Two eavesdroppers were then placed in hearing distance. Gerard says[4] that one was the keeper himself, but this would seem incorrect, for they signed their names on the report as Edward Fawcet and J. Locketon.[5] Gerard suggests that the place had been specially built as a trap for Garnet. It was, he says,[6] 'so contrived . . . that sound of their words must needs be carried to another place not far off, where this keeper would stand and some other with him, to have a double witness in their double dealing'.

Their account of the first 'interlocution' between the two priests is dated 23 February.[7] For his convenience Coke set marginal capital letters, from *A* to *N*, against each paragraph of the document. The eavesdroppers were honest in their statements: both admitted that there were many parts of the conversation that they could not catch at all and other parts that were obscure, fragmentary or confused. 'They are honest men', said Garnet, 'but they did not hear well.'

[1] *Narrative*, 168–9.   [2] *Ibid.*
[3] *Ibid.*   [4] *Ibid.*
[5] *S.P.D. James I*, vol. 18, no. 117.
[6] *Narrative*, 169.   [7] *S.P.D. James I*, vol. 18, no. 3.

The priests, writes Gerard, 'thinking themselve secure . . . took some fit time (as they thought) to have each other's help in the sacrament of confession'. More details are given in the report of the spies. 'As soon as they came to speak together, they seemed to confess themselves one to the other. First Hall [Fr Oldcorne] and then Garnet.'[1] The spies noted that the two priests, before hearing each other's confession, said a prayer in Latin,[2] and that there was a 'beating of hands on their breasts',[3] a detail that proves they were in sight as well as within earshot of Coke's spies. The amount of Garnet's confession that the spies heard in this first meeting disappointed the Councillors: 'Garnet confessed that he had a great suspicion of one (whose name I could not hear), but said he found it but a mere suspicion, and that he hath been subject much to that kind of frailty.'[4]

This statement has the authentic self-accusing character of a confessional statement made by a penitent with an uncommonly sensitive conscience. In the self-scrutiny that preceded his actual confession of sins, it is understandable that a man in Garnet's circumstances might well have judged that he had harboured unwarranted suspicions. Now, in the ear of his confessor, he accused himself of this in so far as he might be guilty. His last years of liberty had been beset by clerical quarrels. On occasion he may wrongly have thought an innocent party was to blame: certainly he is likely to have told Oldcorne that he was 'subject to that kind of frailty'.

Correctly the eavesdroppers stated that the mutual ministrations of the two priests were brief: their notes on this part of the first 'interlocution' occupied one of the fourteen paragraphs of their report. When the contents of the remaining thirteen paragraphs (*B* to *N*) are scrutinised, they reveal nothing. All that passed between the two priests on 23 February, the date of their first meeting, was trivial talk that might well have taken place in the presence of their keeper. Garnet said nothing that was not already known either to him or to his examiners.

After confessing to Oldcorne, Garnet gave him his news: that he had heard from Rookwood of Tesimond's escape, and from Fr Gerard of his own plan to go abroad. 'I hope if he be not taken', Garnet was reported as saying, 'he is escaped: but it seemeth that he hath been put to great plunges.' Anne Vaux was in town. He had written her a note explaining how she might

---

[1] *Ibid.*

[2] Presumably the prayer said customarily by a priest before his penitent starts to confess: *Dominus sit in corde tuo et labiis tuis ut rite et perfecte confitearis omnia peccata tua. In nomine Patris etc. May God be in your heart and on your lips that correctly and perfectly you may confess all your sins. In the name of the Father, etc.*

[3] *S.P.D. James I*, vol. 18, no. 3.

[4] *Ibid.*

meet his gaoler who would 'convey . . . anything unto her': she in her turn would 'let us hear from all our friends'.[1]

The remainder of their talk is more pathetic than revealing. Garnet, who spoke in a clearer voice than Oldcorne, said: 'I gave him [my gaoler] an angel[2] yesterday, because I will be beforehand with him, and he took it very well, with great thanks. And now and then at meals I make very much of him and give him a cup of sack and send his wife another; and that he takes very kindly. So I hope we shall have all well. You should do well now and then to give him a shilling, and sometimes send his wife something.'

This was authentic but harmless reporting. For Oldcorne's guidance Garnet told him certain statements he had made before the Council: for instance, that he had admitted his presence at White Webbs. Coke, he said, had been very friendly in his manner and had undertaken to 'make the best construction to the King of my examinations, to do me good'; Wade was unpredictable: 'he will sometimes scarce speak to me, and yet sometimes will sit down as he passeth through my chamber and use me with very good words: but when he falleth into speech [about] Jesuits, Lord! how he inveigheth against them and speaketh the strangest[3] things that can be; and he told me that we were the lewdest people': then Wade had uttered calumnies so gross that he could not have believed them himself.

It was useful to Oldcorne to know what treatment Garnet had received from his examiners and what points he had been pressed to answer. If it could be proved that he was at White Webbs at the time the plotters were making their final plans, the coincidence would be of inestimable importance to Coke. 'I think it not inconvenient to deny that we were at White Webbs', he was overheard to say, 'they so much insist on that place. Since I came out of Essex, I was there two times, and so I may say I was there.' But he added that they 'press me to be there in October last', which he would not confess, for it was untrue.

All this Garnet had already stated in his interviews with Coke. His object in repeating it now was to make it easier for Oldcorne in his next interview with the Council: he told him also that he expected to be pressed on certain prayers he had said at the time of the meeting of Parliament 'for the good success of that business which indeed is true'.

---

[1] H. G. presumably refers to his first letter sent from the Tower to Anne Vaux. It is undated, and is printed in *S.P.D. James I*, Gunpowder Plot Book, 2, no. 241. The first sentence is written in ink and concerns his ill-fitting spectacles. The rest of the note is in lemon juice.

[2] An old English coin worth between seven and ten shillings.

[3] The text has 'straingliest'.

The underlining is Coke's. Garnet was speaking of prayers for the relief of Catholics from further penal legislation. Nevertheless, he had used words that could be twisted to illustrate a desire that the conspirators should be blessed by heaven. It was the most damaging, though still disappointing, 'confession' that emerged from their first meeting. 'Hark you, hark you, Mr Hall', Garnet said at the close, 'whilst I shut the door, make a hawking and a spitting.'

No word was said of Nicholas Owen. It was clear that neither priest had received news of him.

Four weeks later, when Oldcorne was told that this interlocution had been overheard, he wrote his own account of it:[1] he found it a difficult task after the lapse of four weeks. 'It is a very long time', he says,[2] 'since those speeches first passed between us.' At the time, Oldcorne, 'hearing but slightly', had taken no care 'to commit them to memory, supposing I should never have occasion to repeat them again'. Oldcorne adds nothing to the report of the spies save trivial details: for instance, that it was in the Gatehouse, before his transference to the Tower, that Garnet received a message in orange juice (he did not reveal the sender) giving him news that Tesimond had crossed the seas and that Gerard was to follow presently. The rest of Oldcorne's summary, as might be expected, consisted in a comparison of the questions they had both been asked by the examiners. Truthfully he observes that the Councillors already had these answers in their hands, 'wherefore [he] will not trouble . . . here again to repeat them'. It is not surprising there-fore, that a second interlocution was staged two days later, on 25 February.

The same 'two worthy gentlemen were in ambush'.[3] They overheard no more than an intimate conversation between friends. Both priests were inno-cent of the Plot and both, as now clearly appeared, were anxious only to help each other in their examinations. It was important not only for them but for all who had sheltered them, that neither should give information likely to bring their friends to torture. Here was an opportunity, which both used guardedly, to preserve others from the agony the faithful Owen was enduring while they were yet conversing speaking to each other.

Certain small details have some interest. Garnet, for instance, had learned from Wade that his indictment had been framed. He was concerned to know whether this had been done before or after the proclamation issued for his arrest: 'if before, it will be the worse for Mr Habington; if since, it is no great hurt to him'.[4] In phrases that were not heard with precision Garnet

---

[1] *S.P.D. James I*, Gunpowder Plot Book, 2, no. 214. It is endorsed 25 March.
[2] *Ibid.*
[3] *S.P.D. James I*, vol. 18, no. 117.   [4] *Ibid.*

touched on the theoretical issue that had been put to him 'in Queen Elizabeth's time' and discussed in all the moral text-books of the age, as to whether
it was lawful in warfare to take the lives of innocent citizens.

At one moment in their second conversation the expectation of the spies
rose high, for Garnet introduced the names of Lord Mounteagle and the
Earls of Northumberland and Rutland, but they could not hear 'to what
effect they were named . . . by occasion of a cock crowing under the window
of the room and the cackling of a hen at the same instant'.[1] Garnet told
Oldcorne that he was still being pressed on the reasons for his coming to
Coughton at the time the Plot broke, since the prosecution was manifestly
anxious to prove a connection between his presence there and the Plot. This
made Garnet fear torture, for his examiners 'went away unsatisfied, and
therefore we must expect at the next time either to go to the rack or to pass
quietly with the rest', meaning perhaps, to pass to execution with his martyr
friends.[2]

Again, there was no mention of Nicholas Owen, though they had heard
that other servants of theirs had been racked. Garnet promised to get Oldcorne
more money to pay for his small comforts in prison. At the end 'Garnet bid
Hall take his shovel and make a noise among the coals whilst he might shut
the door'.[3]

The councillors persisted in their ruse. It is unlikely that Garnet did not
now suspect eavesdroppers, for on the two occasions that he confessed to
Oldcorne, he had spoken in a whisper that was almost inaudible. The very
ease and regularity with which the meetings were now arranged may well
have put him on his guard. But there was nothing he had to conceal except
the names of friends who had helped him in his apostolic work.

The third interlocution took place on 27 February. The report of it is
much shorter. At first, after mutual greetings and the discussion of their
examinations the previous day, Garnet told Oldcorne that the Council had
done with examining him and that now he would be arraigned. Yet should
he be examined again, he told Oldcorne, he would ask for proof of his guilt:
this he was entitled to do since the Council claimed to possess 'three or four
witnesses' who could convict him.

Garnet reported that Wade had again railed against the Pope and the

[1] *S.P.D. James I*, vol. 18, no. 117.

[2] Oldcorne is more detailed: 'He [Garnet] told me also that my Lord Chief Justice
threatened him with torture, and Mr Garnet answered him with the words of St Basil to
the Emperor Valens: *Minare ista pueris* [keep these threats for children]. So that I think
said Mr Garnet to me, the next time they come they will try my courage. *S.P.D. James I*,
Gunpowder Plot Book, 2, no. 214.

[3] *S.P.D. James I*, vol. 18, no. 117.

Society, and had again accused him of fathering the baby he had christened at White Webbs; again he had been pressed on Coughton, the exact time of his going there, the company he was in and the purpose of his visit. The meeting closed with Oldcorne shaking a 'great fire shovel among the coals'.

Before their last meeting on 2 March it would seem that either Garnet or Oldcorne had been told that they would not be allowed to converse again. This was perhaps a trick to get the priests to confess once more, since the spies were instructed to keep their ears strained for any mention of God. Garnet began: 'Let us go to confession first, if you will.' Oldcorne was first to confess. His hoarse voice which Gerard mentions several times made his speech inaudible. The eavesdroppers claimed to hear no word that he said. Garnet followed. Instinctively, he spoke to be audible only to his confessor, 'more softly than he used to whisper in these interlocutions'.[1] He was brief. He had examined his conscience already; he confessed, not that he had been party to the Plot, but [so the spies overheard him] that he had drunk more than he needed — the word he was reported to have used was 'extraordinarily'. For this reason he 'was fain to go two nights to bed betimes'.

There is no ground for thinking that Coke's spies misheard or misconstructed Garnet. What he said did not amount even to a confession of drunkenness; probably no more than to drinking a glass of sack above the glass he ordinarily took with his food, but sufficient to induce drowsiness. Nothing was made of the statement at the time, nor at his trial. Only later, after his execution had won sympathy both for him and the Church throughout the country, was this confession used in an attempt to defame his character.[2]

Garnet had conceded nothing. A few days later the Council could do no more than charge him with 'divers conferences' with Oldcorne: they placed before him Oldcorne's account of them.

The first friendly treatment Garnet had received from the Council had failed to win from him a confession of guilt. Coke had failed to get him condemned by Act of Attainder; he had failed also to ensnare him into indiscreet conversation with Oldcorne or into a careless phrase in his letters sent out of the Tower. In desperation he decided, as Garnet feared, to employ the 'mannacles'.

[1] S.P.D. James I, vol. 19. Interlocution between Garnet and Oldcorne. 2 March 1606.

[2] Robert Abbot, at this time chaplain to James I and later Bishop of Salisbury (1615–17), seized on this statement and in his book, Antilogia adversus Apologiam Andreae Eudaimon-Joannis pro Henrico Garneto, Jesuita, Proditore (1613), spread the calumny that Garnet was a habitual drunkard. With equal malice and less foundation he asserted that Garnet had been expelled from Winchester for gross immorality and an incurable propensity to plots, unknown in the annals of English schools. Cf. 'Contributions towards a Life of Henry Garnet', by J. Gerard, in The Month, January 1898.

39
ANNE VAUX

MEANWHILE, inside the Tower walls, Nicholas Owen was being tortured to death. No specious civility was shown him: day after day he was taken to the rack. 'He hung in the torture seven hours together, and this divers times,' wrote Gerard, 'though we cannot as yet learn the certain number.'

He was racked for the last time on 1 March, the day before Garnet's final conversation with Oldcorne. Coke had given instructions that the questions put to him should turn principally on his presence at White Webbs and at Coughton. All that Garnet's heroic servant stated under torture Coke already knew: nothing was drawn from him to assist the prosecution of his master. Owen admitted that he had often been at White Webbs with Garnet and was with him at Coughton also at the beginning of November, 'when ... by the watch that was in the town they did understand that Catesby, Percy and the rest of the conspirators were up in arms',[1] and he confessed that on All Hallows Day Garnet had offered Mass at Coughton, which he had attended with many other Catholics.

This was redundant and useless information. It was extracted at the cost of Owen's life. For many years he had suffered from a rupture which, by the custom of the time, exempted him from torture. Coke, in his determination to find Garnet guilty, disregarded the convention. Inevitably Owen died. In Gerard's words 'his bowels gushed out': but his torturers, 'minding yet to continue that course with him, girded his belly with a plate of iron to keep in his bowels, but the extremity of pain (which is most, in that kind of torment, about the breast and belly) did force out his guts, and so the iron did serve but to cut and wound his body'.[2] Taken down from the wall where he was hanging with great weights fastened to his feet, he lingered in unspeakable agony until the next morning, 2 March. To cover their crime, the Council gave out in London that he had taken his own life. A Catholic

[1] The confession of Nicholas Owen, taken on 1 March. *S.P.D. James I*, Gunpowder Plot Book, 2, no. 194.
[2] *Narrative*, 188.

gentleman, James Fitzjames, was arraigned before the Star Chamber for denying the report.[1]

'Little John, [writes his biographer] lame, ingenious, silent, died as secretly as he had lived. We have no memorable sayings of his to ponder. His handiworks, which were his wordless prayers, remain. With the years some were put to less notable uses than he had planned; some were forgotten, rediscovered and exhibited as quaint survivals of a ruder age. Nicholas in his agonised, furtive death had finished with all concealment and disguise and had been welcomed by Campion and all the martyrs into a fellowship where there is no use for human language.'[2]

Owen's torture had produced no incriminating statement; nor had the interlocutions. Now it was a matter only of time before both Oldcorne and Garnet were racked. For a week or more Garnet had been writing regularly to Anne Vaux. Although his letters were read, copied and scrutinised before they were delivered, the Council gathered nothing from them. The first series of these letters are dated 26 February, and 2, 3 and 4 March; a fifth letter was probably written on 1 March, certainly before the 5th.

Garnet lists his personal requirements in prison: socks, spectacles, handkerchiefs and a Bible. 'They say I am obstinate,' he adds, 'and they have nothing against me but presumptions.' Through Anne he transmitted his instructions to his brethren. He appointed Anthony Hoskins temporary head of the Jesuits until Aquaviva himself should choose his successor; he gave faculties to Fr Jones to deputise for him at the next meeting of Jesuits.[3]

Then, as if to clarify his own memory on the sequence of events, perhaps to let his friends know what had happened, he narrated all that had passed since his arrest to the time of writing. It is his longest letter sent from prison. As Coke read and annotated it, he could only have admired Garnet's accuracy of statement. Once again Garnet had achieved his aim, which was to scotch 'evil reports or untrue' which 'do myself or others injury'.[4]

What he said to Anne about the threat of torture corresponds exactly with the report of all that he had told Oldcorne. He added, however, that torture had been mentioned because the Councillors were 'nothing satisfied in my last two examinations'. He made no mention of Owen. He asked Anne

[1] Anstruthers, *Vaux of Harrowden*, 347.

[2] Margaret Waugh, *Blessed Nicholas Owen* (1961), 23.

[3] *Hat. Cal.*, 18, 60. As these instructions did not concern Anne, Garnet wrote them in Latin, explaining in a later letter (3 March): 'The Latin was for Mr Blunt [Father Richard Blount] or any of the Society. Show it them if you have it still or I will write again.' *S.P.D. James I*, Gunpowder Plot Book, 2, no. 242.

[4] *S.P.D. James I*, vol. 19, no. 11. Many of the details in this letter have been used in earlier chapters.

to help James, John, Harry, his imprisoned servants from White Webbs and Erith, by begging 'bedding for them or by money if there be to spare'. His last thoughts were for Fr Thomas Strange who had been captured. 'I know not how Mr Strange is provided.'[1] He needed to say no more, only to beseech Anne 'in her charity to others to have a care for her own necessities'.

This letter was despatched on the day of his last talk with Oldcorne. The following day, 3 March, he wrote again to Anne:[2] 'I have received two bands, two handkerchiefs, one pair of socks and a Bible. God reward all my friends. I would you could make shift to borrow eleven pounds. I shall be able to repay at least half again when I send to a friend. I and Mr Hall have not yet paid our fees, whereof I am ashamed.'[3]

These instructions were written in ink: there was a postscript in orange juice: 'Take heed no more of our friends come in danger. It will breed new examinations.' Then he repeated his requests on behalf of his servants 'who all have been tortured'. He concluded: 'Master Catesby did me much wrong, and hath confessed that he told them [the Council] that he said he asked me a question in Queen Elizabeth's time of the powder action, and that I said it was lawful. All which is most untrue. He did it to draw in others. I see no advantage they have against me for the powder action.'

Catesby had not in fact made the statement attributed to him by the Council; but it was now the Council's stratagem to put out false reports in order to ensnare Garnet in his replies.

It is surprising that Garnet troubled to write in orange juice; possibly he was practising the craft; more likely he sought to inculcate caution in Anne Vaux.

It was during these days that Garnet in an undated letter released Anne from all the obligations she had undertaken to him, both as his friend and as his penitent. Whether she chose to stay on in England and serve Garnet's successor or cross to the Continent, he advised her and 'your sister [also] and your nephew, [to] look to yourselves till the bruit be passed'.[4]

Oldcorne in a dream thought he had seen prepared for himself and Garnet

---

[1] Fr Strange had been captured on the way from Harrowden to join Fr Garnet at Coughton. He was now in the Tower where the severe racking he endured dislocated his limbs and left him with pain in his head and loins till his death in 1627.

[2] H. G. to A. V. 3 March 1606. *S.P.D. James I*, Gunpowder Plot Book, 2, no. 242.

[3] Garnet is probably referring to the bill for his confinement in the Gatehouse. Cf. Gatehouse Bills: 'Garnet a Jesuit, oweth... for one week and three days for himself and for one that did attend him in his chamber and for other necessaries as . . . fuel, candles, wine and fees, three pounds five shillings.' *C.R.S.*, vol. 53, 273.

[4] H. G. to Anne Vaux before 5 March 1603. *S.P.D. James I*, Gunpowder Plot Book, 2, no. 245.

'two fair tabernacles or seats ... and so he awaked and falling asleep again had the same dream'.[1]

In the end the Council used these letters to bring against Garnet a calumnious charge of moral misconduct with Anne. The relationship of trust that had existed now for twenty years between the Jesuit Superior and his devoted friend was well known both to his examiners and to the Catholics of England. The letters written to each other during these months are the only letters known to have passed between them; if others were exchanged they have not survived. Had Garnet written, not to Anne, but to Gerard or Blount or some other Jesuit who was in or about London, he would have betrayed their places of hiding. Anne's whereabouts were known to the Council. By using her as an intermediary with his brethren he was bringing no one into danger, and at the same time was able, through her, both to transmit his instructions to his priests and to provide for the comfort of his servants in the Tower. Before all else he was anxious to protect his friends' retainers from arrest and torture: and this he succeeded in doing by means of these messages to Anne. Once again Garnet, seemingly foolish, was as Gerard says, not only 'simple as the dove, but cunning as the serpent'. Only one phrase in all the letters he sent from the Tower was used against him at the trial. After he realised that he would certainly be convicted he had quoted in a letter not to Anne, but to Thomas Garnet, then in the Gatehouse, the saying of Our Lord, 'It is necessary that one should die for the people.'[2] In his speech of

---

[1] *Ibid.* Gerard narrates this incident thus: 'I could thereunto add a vision which both of these blessed Fathers had in the Tower the 7th of March before their martyrdom, the very night before they were hung upon the torture. It happened in this manner. Father Oldcorne in his sleep did seem to behold a very sumptuous throne set up, with great care and cost adorned, at which sight when Father Oldcorne much admired, not knowing to what end it should be prepared, it seemed unto him that there entered into the room the most Reverend Father General, and with him some other ancient Fathers; and that Father Oldcorne did demand of Father General what should be the meaning or intention of that throne so much adorned; and that the Father should answer that both Father Garnet and himself should presently be professed. To which Father Oldcorne made answer that Father Garnet was already professed. Then Father General replied, he would now have him make a more excellent profession than before. This vision Father Oldcorne the next morning told unto his keeper, desiring he would tell it unto Father Garnet, which he performed; and Father Garnet assured him the very same thing, in the same manner, had also that night appeared unto him. But Father Oldcorne did see it again the next night after. This was so generally spoken of in the Tower about that time, that if there had been no other means afterwards to know the truth, that alone had been sufficient to publish it.' *Narrative*, 306.

[2] H. G. to Thomas Garnet. 26 February 1606. *Hat. Cal.*, vol. 18, 60. Garnet wrote: 'Yet they [the Council] know all the persons [in my households] and so I wish all be wary till their malice be wrought on one: *necesse est ut unus moriatur pro populo.*' (Jn. 11, 50.)

prosecution, Coke, taking the phrase from its context, charged Garnet with blasphemy for applying to himself words that Our Lord had used to explain his own passion.

Nor could anything be gleaned from Anne's replies, which show only her devotion to Garnet and a loyalty that had already been tested in more perilous times: her letters are difficult to read, ill-punctuated and in places obscure. 'Though it be greatest comfort I have had in the world', she wrote in answer to Garnet's first letter, 'to hear from you: yet this is the greatest grief except your taking that I ever had, for it seemeth you leave me unto myself: and that is so great a grief as nothing in the world can be more. . . . Mr Hall [Oldcorne] his dream[1] had been a great comfort, if at the foot of the throne there had been a place for me.'[2]

In a postscript Anne added that she was sending Garnet an 'hose and doublet'. It was her last letter. Garnet replied on 4 March. Already Coke had resolved to arrest and imprison Anne in the Tower and there see whether under examination she could be brought to implicate her friend. This was tantamount to an admission that he had failed thus far in every ruse he had employed to make good his undertaking that he would prove Garnet guilty, provided he was permitted to use what means he pleased.

Since the middle of Elizabeth's reign it had been the pious custom among devout Catholic women, on some pretext of business or by bribery, to seek entrance into the Tower precincts and there, by arrangement with imprisoned priests, to obtain their blessing, which would be given on a pre-arranged sign of recognition.[3] Anne desired the comfort of seeing Garnet and receiving his blessing. In his letter of 3 March Garnet had told her that she would be given directions through the mother of Carey, his keeper: 'but come not hither except with good guides', he cautioned her,[4] 'and when Wade is abroad; for he is often with me or in the gallery hard by. You may see me, but not talk.'

Once again through the services of his keeper the Council attempted to ensnare Garnet. Carey fixed a time 'when [Anne] should come to the Tower privately'; he would then take her to a place from which she could at least see Garnet. Anne 'failed not of her time, but coming thither [she] found such signs and causes of distrust that she returned sooner than she intended, and was followed by persons prepared for the purpose, to see whither she would

[1] See sup., p. 369.
[2] Anne Vaux to H. G. S.P.D. James I, Gunpowder Plot Book, 2, no. 246.
[3] Gerard in his Autobiography (120) describes how during his own imprisonment in the Salt Tower Francis Page had sought his blessing in this way.
[4] H. G. to A. V. 3 March 1606. S.P.D. James I, Gunpowder Plot Book, 2, no. 242.

go to take her lodging, thereby not only to bring her but her friends also in question'.[1]

Anne suspected a trap. Gerard continues the story: 'Perceiving herself to be dogged, [she] would not go to her own lodging nor to any Catholic house: but wisely intended to have gone into the prison of Newgate, where there was a great store of priests and other Catholics, unto which many of all sorts had continual access.

'Thus far they let her pass, but when they saw she intented to go no further, they presently staid her, and with some rough usage carried her back unto the Tower, from whence she came.'

The date of her arrest is unknown, but it was after 6 and before 11 March.

Gerard was right in asserting that it was a very unusual procedure to commit a woman to the Tower. However, it was convenient since Anne could be examined there by Coke and Popham, and if necessary, be made to confront Garnet. There was also another reason.

In despair of bolstering up his case Coke believed that he could smear Garnet's character by insinuating into the mind of the public an unsavoury relationship between him and Anne. Already more than once Wade had hinted at this to Garnet's face, and it was perhaps he who persuaded Coke to this new course. Gerard does not mince matters. He says expressly that malicious calumnies were spread about London as soon as Anne was imprisoned and unable to refute them.[2] Among other things 'it was reported in many mouths that Father Garnet was married to this gentlewoman and such like stuff'. Her attempt to see Garnet in the Tower was taken as proof of their carnal acquaintance: otherwise she would never have been 'so forward to adventure for him', the gossip said, 'and to go and see a man in so great danger as he was'.

Gerard commented: 'It was not understood how much more force true charity hath than fond affection, but *animalis homo non percipit ea quae Dei sunt.*'[3]

Before Anne came before the Council for examination, Garnet was taken to the torture. Gerard describes how he was prepared for it. 'He was in very strange plight', says Gerard, when he was brought before the Council on 5 March.[4] Unable to speak for a strange thirst he had on him, he called for beer and drank two glasses; he was so drowsy that he could not hold up his head; he complained that he had not slept for five nights. And 'it was

---

[1] *Narrative*, 171.
[2] *op cit.*, 172.
[3] *Ibid. A man with animal instincts does not appreciate the things of God.*
[4] *S.P.D. James I*, vol. 19, no. 15.

reported', writes Gerard,[1] 'by divers of good intelligence in London, that he was watched of purpose and kept from sleep to make his head light and himself less able to bear that which was imposed upon him; also that he had some mixture of intoxicating drink given him which should obscure his understanding and distemper his body.'

Gerard's story perhaps explains the self-accusation made by Garnet, in his confession to Oldcorne, that he had drunk 'extraordinarily' and 'was fain to go two nights to bed betimes'; it would also date the first application of drugs before 2 March.[2] Garnet had no suspicion that his drink was tampered with. Later, when questioned in public on his treatment in the Tower, he did not complain. Gerard, however, observes: 'I for my part do rather think it was done, but in such manner as himself could not perceive, by mixing his drink or meat with such confections as might work both those effects, to distemper his body and hinder his sleep, and yet the Father did not know when and how it was procured.'[3]

On 5 March there is a most brief report of a further examination before a full session of the Council.[4] Garnet was charged with 'divers conferences' with Oldcorne; no other matter was raised, for it seems that it was this meeting to which Gerard refers when he writes: 'The Lords permitted him to go to sleep an hour, and then being awaked, he was brought unto them again, but was little better.'[5] Salisbury, Suffolk, Worcester and Northampton were present, as well as Coke and Popham, and it was probably from Northampton, his friend and Garnet's admirer, that Gerard obtained his report of Garnet's conduct.

On the 6th Garnet was examined yet again. This time only Coke, Wade and Popham were present; in their report there are indications that his mind was still far from clear. He spoke of reaching Hinlip about 24 August, whereas he clearly meant 24 November, confusing the saints' days for the first time.

It was his last examination before his torture. Again the questions turned on White Webbs. No point was gained. For more than two weeks Coke and Popham had tried every trick they could contrive: Garnet had defeated them, had remained courteous to his enemies and loyal to his friends.

---

[1] *Narrative*, 173.
[2] Cf. *sup.*, p. 365. It was on 2 March that Garnet confessed he had 'drunk more than he needed'.
[3] *Narrative*, 174.
[4] *S.P.D. James I*, vol. 19, no. 15.
[5] *Narrative*, 174.

40

THE CONFESSION

IT was probably on 7 March, the day following his examination before Coke, Popham and Wade, that Garnet was taken to torture, for his long letter to the Council, dated 8 March, was written after he had been taken from the rack.[1]

In his *Narrative* Gerard, without giving the source of his information, makes a statement that has been accepted uncritically by all writers on the Plot. Speaking of Garnet's 'secret' conversations with Oldcorne he says[2] that, when asked whether he had been 'pressed with this matter of the Powder Treason', Garnet admitted that he had, and added that there was none who could prove 'such matter against him' but one man: a phrase which Gerard took to imply that there was only one man who could implicate him in the Plot.

Gerard continues:[3] 'This, lo, was the word that afterwards bred him so much trouble, and others of his friends so much grief, until by his public answers he had cleared their doubts.' The phrase, says Gerard, was overheard by the 'keeper and another easing-dropper, his companion, in that listening and cony-catching office' and was carried at once to the Council 'with no small joy'.

There is no support for Gerard's statement either in Oldcorne's account of the conversations, or in the more brief, less exact and in part confused reports written with conscientious accuracy by the two eavesdroppers themselves. But, believing the story true, Gerard asserts that this was the reason why Garnet was put to the torture, for it was hoped by this means 'to wring out of him who this person was that only could accuse him and how far he could be accused'.[4]

Gerard did not know that Garnet had already been threatened with torture more than five days before his last interlocution with Oldcorne. Only two

---

[1] H. G. to the Council. 9 March 1606. Hatfield MSS., printed in *English Historical Review*, vol. 3 (1888), 510 sq.

[2] *Narrative*, 170.   [3] *Ibid.*   [4] *op. cit.*, 171

points had to be proved in order to make the case of the prosecution against Garnet appear plausible: first, that he had been at White Webbs after the end of August 1605 and, secondly, that he had gone to Coughton in late October in order to assist the conspirators. Coke was still determined to present Garnet as the instigator of the Plot and Garnet, as his conversations with Oldcorne prove, knew this. Thus far Coke had failed to construct his case. Now he persuaded the Council to issue a warrant authorising the use of the mannacles.

This explanation is borne out by Garnet's own statement of March,[1] from which the true sequence of events emerges. In his exasperation that the talks had yielded no incriminating evidence, Coke determined to bluff. 'Expressly and falsely' he charged Garnet with 'discovering' himself guilty of the Powder Plot to Oldcorne, and on this pretext ordered him to the rack.[2] Only after he was taken down, did Garnet in fact tell the Council that 'no man living (one only excepted) could touch [him] therein or [in] any way suspect [him] so much as to have been privy to the same'.[3] This statement could not have been made before Garnet was taken to the torture, since, until that moment, he was bound still by the seal of confession, as he himself explains later in the same letter.

Coke's deceit was twofold: first, he claimed that Garnet's statement was made before torture; secondly, he deliberately suppressed Garnet's explanation of the statement. Gerard himself was deceived:[4] drawing merely on the report current in London, he had no means of testing the sequence of events during these two days. Had there been any truth in the story, Coke would certainly have used it devastatingly in his speech of prosecution at Garnet's trial. Although, in fact, he produced the minutes of the interlocutions and extracted from them trivial advantages, he made no mention whatever of this crucial phrase which was allegedly overheard.[5] Moreover, when Garnet was again examined after torture on the interlocutions, still there was no reference to it:[6] the Council had at once accepted the explanation he had given.

[1] H. G. to the Council. 9 March 1606. Hatfield MSS., printed in *E.H.R.*, vol. 3, 510 sq.

[2] Garnet states: 'I [was] falsely charged expressly to have discovered myself herein [the Plot] to Mr Hall [Oldcorne] by a witness of great honesty, though herein indeed deceived, for he misunderstood me.' H. G. to Lords of the Council. 9 March 1606. *E.H.R.*, vol. 3, 510 sq.

[3] *Ibid.*

[4] And also all subsequent historians of Garnet's role in the Plot.

[5] Cf. Foley, vol. 4, 176, where Coke's speech is printed from Additional MSS. (British Museum), 21203.

[6] Examination of Henry Garnet. 12 March 1606. *S.P.D. James I*, vol. 19, no. 40.

Gerard is the only writer to give details of the torture. Significantly he is uncertain of the date. He writes that he thought 'they did not torture him for long',[1] and that on the rack Garnet declared that 'he would utter the matter [his knowledge of the Plot] justly as it was, that being the time wherein he might lawfully do it, and before he could not, the knowledge that he had being a secret committed to him in confession, which the penitent did only license him to utter to save himself from torture, but not in any other case'.[2]

'Then being taken down from the torture he was demanded how far he was of counsel and a furtherer of the Plot of Powder. He answered he was never any furtherer of it, but did ever both mislike it in his heart, and, in what he could did hinder it. And being asked how it was, or by whom he might then be accused, he answered that he could not be otherwise accused of it, but that he had only a simple knowledge of it, and that also in so secret a manner as that it was never lawful for him to utter it, being in confession. They asked him how it came to be more lawful now to utter it than before. He said, in respect that now he had leave granted by the penitent, who had licensed him to utter it rather than endure torture for keeping his confession secret. And being urged by some of the Lords why it might be lawful to utter the secret of confession to save himself from torture and not lawful to utter it for the saving of so many great persons from death, he answered it was lawful in neither case, but by the license of the penitent, who could *dilatare* or *restringere sigillum secreti*,[3] which appertained to himself.'[4]

On 8 March Salisbury in triumph added a postscript to a despatch he had addressed to Sir Thomas Edmunds, the English Ambassador at Brussels. He asserted, not that Garnet had confessed all, but that Edmunds was now in a position to affirm confidently that Garnet 'is guilty *ex ore proprio*, this day confessed, of the *Gunpowder Plot*'. He added: 'he saith he devised it not, only he concealed it when Father Greenway (alias Tesimond) did impart to him all

---

[1] In the original, Gerard added and then erased the words: 'but the time [length of torture] we cannot certainly learn' (*Narrative*, 174). Since Garnet was able to use his hand to write a letter to the Council less than twenty-four hours later, Gerard is almost certainly right.

[2] A priest hearing confession is bound by absolute secrecy, from which only the penitent can release him either absolutely or on conditions laid down by himself. As Gerard observes, Garnet was free to speak only if he were threatened with torture: that concession Catesby had permitted. Garnet might have acted correctly, but less rigorously, if he had chosen to make a statement on being taken to the torture room. Instead, he waited until the threat was implemented.

[3] *Extend or restrict the seal of the secret.*

[4] *Narrative*, 174–5.

the particulars, and Catesby only the general. Thus do you see that Greenway is now by the Superintendent[1] as guilty as we have accused him.'[2]

In a letter written the next day,[3] Salisbury laid bare his machinations: 'Whether Garnet lives or dies is a small matter', he wrote, 'the important thing is to demonstrate the iniquity of Catholics, and to prove to all the world that it is not for religion, but for their treasonable teaching and practices, that they should be exterminated. It is expedient to make manifest to the world how far these men's doctrinal practice reacheth into the bowels of treason, and so, for ever after, stop the mouths of their calumniation that preach and print our laws to be executed for difference in point of conscience.'

All this Salisbury hoped to deduce from Garnet's declaration of 8 March, with his further notes written the following day: two documents that set out in a precise narrative the extent of Garnet's acquaintance with the Plot.

The endorsements of these papers are revealing. The first endorsement reads, 'original all in his own hand'; the second, written by Salisbury, 'this was forbidden by the K[ing] to be given in evidence'.[4]

What were Garnet's motives in making this confession? No doubt he was exhausted by incessant examinations. Already, before going to torture, he had heard reports of Nicholas Owen's death; all his servants from White Webbs had been racked; also George Chambers, Oldcorne's servant, better known as Brother Ralph Ashley; and now Oldcorne himself, several times. He had perhaps learnt also of the arrest of Anne and feared that she too might be brutally handled. In greater or less measure all these persons had endured suffering because of him, that they might yield evidence on which a charge of complicity could be laid against him. Only a complete and truthful statement, which now, after torture, he was free to make, could stop the long procession to the rack.

Garnet's own conscience was clear. Whether or not the Council accepted his explanation, he did not now mind: he knew that Catholics would, and with them the greater part of his fellow countrymen. He began: 'For the full

---

[1] Presumably Salisbury meant the 'Provincial', i.e. Garnet.

[2] Stowe MSS. (British Museum), 168, 366.

[3] Salisbury to the Earl of Mar. 9 March 1606. *S.P.D. James I*, vol. 19, no. 27.

[4] It has been argued that the first endorsement makes the document suspect as a part-forgery on the ground that the Council would have stressed its authenticity only if there had been doubt about it. Since it is impossible to establish the hand of the forger (if there was a forger at work) it is here assumed to be genuine. The argument that Salisbury filed at Hatfield all documents (Garnet's statement among them) that were tampered with by forgers, in order to protect himself, is largely *a priori*: it could be argued the other way that he was anxious to keep in his own hands all documents that demonstrated Garnet's innocence.

satisfaction of your Lordships and his Majesty I here sincerely set down how I have carried myself.'[1]

As Gerard relates, Garnet was criticised at the time for his simplicity. 'This acknowledgment of Father Garnet was afterwards censured by many, and even by some of his friends and well-wishers was esteemed weakness in him.'[2] But Gerard, after weighing 'the causes that moved him thereunto (as they were no doubt considered by him)' maintains that Garnet 'will not be found to deserve any imputation of fear or imprudence'.[3]

First Garnet acknowledged that hitherto he had 'dealt very reservedly with their Lordships in the case of the late powder action'. Now he would speak openly 'for two respects: first, for the saving, as much as might lie in me, of the credit of my own person, my profession and religion'; secondly, since there had been 'such a settled conceit' that he was privy to the treason, 'the disclosing of the naked truth could only turn more to his advantage than disadvantage'.[4]

Garnet had not seen the report of the eavesdroppers. Either when Garnet was on the rack or in his last examination before he was taken there, Coke without any statement of the spies to support him, claimed that Garnet had declared to Oldcorne that he had been privy to the Plot. Coke spread this story abroad in London. It justified the interlocutions (they had succeeded) and also the use of torture. Garnet fell for his bluff. He believed that he had been misreported. Gerard heard the story and recorded it. After many weeks Coke had scored a victory.

By dint of lies he had placed Garnet in a dilemma. 'If he [Garnet]', Gerard observes correctly,[5] 'had then insisted upon denial, that would neither have saved his life nor his estimation touching the matter; yea rather, it would have left him suspected of further practices as a principal plotter of the matter, and withal would have made all the rest of his true assertions more distrusted. Whereas, by telling the plain truth that he only heard it in confession, he did both show himself and the party from whom he heard it to be free from being either principals or parties in the action.'

Garnet's full statement is unexceptionable. It falls into two parts: his vague knowledge of some trouble in preparation, and his specific knowledge of Catesby's plot under the seal of confession.

[1] H. G. to Council. 8 March 1606. Hatfield MSS., printed in *E.H.R.*, vol. 3 (1888), 510 sq.

[2] *Narrative*, 175.

[3] *Ibid*.

[4] H. G. to Council. 9 March 1606. Hatfield MSS., printed in *E.H.R.*, vol. 3, 510 sq.

[5] *Narrative*, 176.

'About the beginning of Trinity Term',[1] Garnet wrote, 'Mr Catesby asked me whether, in case it were necessary to kill a person or persons, it were necessary [also] to regard the innocents which were present, lest they should perish withal.' To this question, which he had considered theoretical, Garnet had given the usual answer of the moralists, that it was lawful practice in just wars 'to beat down houses and walls and castles, notwithstanding innocents were in danger', provided such battery was necessary for victory. He had believed that Catesby had asked an 'idle question' which any layman might casually put to any priest in the course of conversation. Then, with exemplary honesty Garnet continues his narration:

'After this I began to muse with myself what this should mean, and fearing lest he should intend the death of some great persons ... I thought that I would take fit occasion to admonish him that upon my speech he should not run headlong to so great a mischief, which I did after at the house in Essex when he came with my Lord Monteagle[2] and Francis Tresham. For walking in the gallery with him alone, my Lord [Monteagle] standing afar off, I told him that upon that question lately asked, I had mused much with myself and wished him to look [to] what he did, if he intended anything.'

With suspicions in his mind, but nothing more than suspicions, Garnet had been able to act only as he now states he did. If Catesby intended anything, Garnet told him, 'he must first look to the lawfulness of the act itself, and then he must not have so little regard of innocents that he spare not friends and necessary persons for a Commonwealth'. He added that Catesby no less than himself was in conscience bound to remain quiet and keep others quiet: as Catesby knew, he had sought from the Pope a special Brief that would expressly prohibit all plots. 'I was at that time to write to Rome to inform the Pope of the state of Catholics, and, upon occasion of the little tumult in Wales,[3] desired that the Pope would expressly prohibit all commotions; so now I thought to write again to confirm the Pope in that course which verily he desired.'

Before writing, Garnet had pressed Catesby for more definite knowledge of what he had in mind; then, in Catesby's presence, had implored Monteagle and Tresham to be more precise: 'I asked what they three thought of the force of Catholics, whether they were able to make their part good by

---

[1] Garnet means the Trinity Law term, starting at the end of April or early May, after the Easter recess. Garnet usually came to London during sessions of the criminal courts. Cf. *sup.*, p. 323.

[2] Lord Monteagle was the brother of Dorothy Habington. His role in the Plot is most ambiguous.

[3] Cf. *sup.*, p. 323.

arms against the King. My Lord Monteagle answered, if ever they were, they were able now, and then added the reason: "the King (saith he) is so odious to all sorts." ' Garnet had refused to accept any 'conditional proposition'; he had insisted on a 'direct answer', since he 'would write to the Pope a certainty'. All replied 'negatively', that is, that they intended no Plot. In confirmation Tresham, on behalf of them all, declared that they must wait till the '*end* of the next Parliament' and then 'see what laws are made against Catholics'. Only then would they consider seeking 'the help of foreign princes'. This could only mean that there was no danger of action for a long time. Nevertheless Garnet strove to restrain his friends. ' "No", said I, "assure yourselves they [foreign princes] will do nothing." "What", said my Lord Monteagle, "will not the Spaniard help us? It is a shame." ' In conclusion Garnet had assured them all that he 'would write to the Pope that neither by strength or stratagems we could be relieved, but with patience and the intercession of princes'. Then for exactness he added: 'When I say I wrote to the Pope, I mean to my immediate Superior [Aquaviva] who should inform him.' At the time he had then no reason to distrust the word of Catesby, Tresham or Monteagle, and indeed had every reason for thinking that he had in fact dissuaded his friends from all desperate actions, at least until after the end of the next Parliament. Meanwhile, as he had hoped, the Pope's condemnation would remove the danger of all tumults.

Very shortly after this meeting Garnet had received from Aquaviva a 'very earnest letter . . . where he saith that he writeth *ex mandato Papae*, that we were expressly commanded by his Holiness to hinder by all possible means all conspiracies of Catholics. . . . The effect of this letter was published to all Catholics by the Archpriest, Blackwell.'

At this time Catesby was seeing Garnet frequently. 'He was seldom long from us for the great affection he bore the gentlewoman [Anne Vaux] with whom I lived, and unto me.' When Garnet first met Catesby after receiving this letter (he actually sought him out), he showed it to him and at the same time severely 'admonished him of the Pope's pleasure'. He admitted also his suspicion that Catesby 'had some device in his head', and told him that, whatever it was, 'it would not prosper for it was against the Pope's will'. In reply Catesby brashly asserted that if the Pope knew the situation of English Catholics he would not hinder it for the general good of the country. Garnet had protested: the Pope expressly forbade all violence in all circumstances whatsoever. When Catesby retorted that he was not bound to 'take knowledge . . . of the Pope's will' through a third person, Garnet had answered: 'Indeed my own credit was but little, but our General [Aquaviva], whose letter I had read unto him, was a man everywhere respected for his wisdom and virtue.' He had begged Catesby before he attempted anything to 'acquaint the Pope'. Catesby refused: he 'would not for all the world make this particular project known to him [the Pope] for fear of discovery'. Garnet pleaded. Through some laymen Catesby should inform the Pope, at least in general terms, of the dangerous situation of Catholics: this he said, knowing that the Pope could only reiterate to Catesby, personally, the prohibition he had made to Garnet through Aquaviva. The debate continued. At its conclusion Garnet had reason to be satisfied. Catesby promised that 'he would do nothing before the Pope was informed in general by such a messenger' as both agreed to send him.[1]

Garnet himself had proposed that Sir Edmund Baynham might act as messenger, since he was already about to leave for Flanders, but he refused actually to sponsor Baynham's journey from Flanders to Rome 'for the Pope would not take [it] well that we should busy ourselves in sending messengers'. Catesby agreed. 'Sir Edmund came to me', Garnet continued. 'I desired him to go to the Nuncio in Flanders and inform him how things went, but not in my name.' As for Baynham's journey to Rome, Garnet 'took no knowledge of it' or of its purpose, beyond Baynham's intention to obtain the Pope's advice. Garnet declined to give Baynham a letter to carry to Rome: he had only 'very short conference with him'[2] during which he had reminded the messenger of the continuing persecution, for it had been given out that there was no persecution in the country: thus Salisbury had hoped to remove any excuse for plots. Garnet put Baynham 'in mind of some points, as of two laymen executed in the north;[3] of expectation of severe laws in the Parliament'. 'Our meeting was but once and brief', Garnet repeated, but what instructions Baynham later received from others, he did not know.

At both meetings between them Catesby had offered to tell Garnet of his plot. On the first occasion Catesby said 'he had not leave, but would get leave'; on the second, Catesby had got leave, but Garnet, considering the prohibition he had, refused to listen.

[1] Garnet repeated this statement in his examination of 12 March 1606. 'He [Garnet] confesseth that at his second conference with Catesby at Fremland, Catesby did faithfully promise him that he would not proceed in the matter before he had acquainted the Pope generally with the state of England and taken his advice and directions therein; and this examinant named Sir Edmund Baynham to be used by him [Catesby] to the Pope in that behalf, which accordingly Mr Catesby did. And Catesby told the examinant [Garnet] that the matter was such as he thought the Pope would not hinder it.' S.P.D. James I, vol. 19, no. 40.

[2] This and other details in the remainder of this paragraph are taken from Garnet's second statement on 10 March 1606. Cf. E.H.R., vol. 3 (1888), p. 517 sq.

[3] In 1605 two laymen had been executed in the north: Thomas Welbourne at York on 1 August, and William Browne at Ripon on 5 September.

This has been the extent of Garnet's 'general' knowledge of the Plot. The only ground on which an indictment might now be framed was this, that, after these two conversations with Catesby, Garnet had not delated his hot-headed friends to the Council.

It was with the help of these friends—Tresham, Catesby, and Monteagle — and on their relatives and connections, that Garnet had built almost the entire chain of Catholic centres throughout the midland counties. All these men were bound by ties of blood or marriage with Anne Vaux. It was as his spiritual child that Catesby sought his counsel, first in a veiled manner, and then less hypothetically. As soon as Garnet suspected a 'device', he had sought and been given an undertaking that nothing would be done without the Pope's approval, and that nothing was contemplated until after Parliament had closed.[1]

In the breathing space he believed that he had gained, Garnet had every reason to hope that the Pope would reiterate his prohibition of plots yet more emphatically: and that, once again, the danger of violent action, which he had feared since the beginning of the reign, would be averted. Of the details of the plot Garnet knew nothing. 'Moreover, until this very instant,' Garnet concluded the first part of his statement, 'I assure myself that all I have conversed withal, would take it upon their conscience that I was never acquainted *in particular* with the action of the powder.' Then he added: 'except him of whom I now begin to speak'.

This was Fr Tesimond. 'Within a few days' of seeing Catesby for the second time, Garnet had been visited by Tesimond: instantly Garnet noticed his restlessness. Tesimond paced up and down Garnet's chamber. He 'seemed much perplexed [and] said he had a thing in his mind which he would fain tell me, but he was bound to silence and it was about some device of Mr Catesby'. Garnet replied that he 'had an inkling of some matter intended by him'; then he added that Catesby had been anxious to tell him the details, but he had declined to listen 'in respect of the prohibition we had from Rome and of the danger of the matter at home'.

For a long time Tesimond walked with Garnet 'as it were in a balance whether he should tell and I give him a hearing'. Garnet made the decision. 'I told him', he writes in this statement, 'that if he [had] heard the matter out of confession, he might tell it me with a safe conscience, because Mr Catesby

---

[1] Later in the same statement Garnet writes: 'Mr Catesby's promise of doing nothing until Sir Edmund [Baynham] had been with the Pope made me think that either nothing would be done, or not before the end of Parliament; before what time we should surely hear, as undoubtedly we should, if Baynham had gone to Rome as soon as I imagined.'

had offered to tell me himself, and so it might be presumed that it should not be an injury to him or a breach of promise.' Then Garnet added: if he was to know, it must be in such a way that Catesby and others should never hear he had been told. By this he meant that if Tesimond did tell him outside confession, Garnet should consider himself free to take whatever action he judged fit to thwart Catesby.[1]

Tesimond then stated that he had promised Catesby complete secrecy; that since 'he was not master of other men's secrets he would not tell it me but by way of confession, for to have my direction'. Garnet continues: 'Because it was too tedious to relate so long a discourse in confession, kneeling; if I would take it as in confession, walking, and after take his confession kneeling either then or at any other time, he would tell me.' Thus in this manner Tesimond 'discovered unto [Garnet] all the matter as it is publicly known abroad'.

Before writing his account of this interview,[2] Gerard, who had spoken to Tesimond's friends, explains Garnet's dilemma and his reasons for seeking confession. Tesimond abhorred Catesby's plan and had refused to assist him in any way, 'either by counsel or otherwise'. Yet, explains Gerard, 'doubts and scruples fit for confession might arise in his mind two divers ways': he might have doubted whether in fact he had done enough to dissuade Catesby from his plot, or whether he had used the best and most effectual arguments against it.

'Whether he feared he had done too much or too little . . . his fear on either side might be cause sufficient for confession. . . . For either he must confess he had hindered it or not. If that he had hindered it, then he was no furtherer of it; if that he had not hindered it sufficiently, then it was apparent that he misliked the plot and meant to hinder it. But the truth indeed was (as I have heard it) that he had sought to hinder it by persuasion; but was doubtful whether [he had done so] in so earnest and effectual a manner as might be likely to prevail with so absolute resolutions.'

Garnet listened 'amazed'. He protested that it was a 'horrible thing and he had never heard of the like': he charged Tesimond to hinder it if he could. In answer Tesimond promised to do his utmost; he had already protested to Catesby; he 'knew well enough what prohibition we had'.

'So we parted, yet with this compact, that if ever I should be called in

---

[1] In all his statements Garnet restricts himself to what in fact he did or said. Nowhere does he say what he might have done or said had circumstances been different. It is interesting to speculate what action Garnet would have taken had Tesimond found it possible in conscience to tell Garnet of the Plot outside confession.

[2] *Narrative*, 176–7.

question for being accessory unto such a horrible action, either by the Pope, or by my Superiors beyond, or by the State here, I would have liberty to utter all that passed in this conference, which he gave me.'[1]

On the assumption that all parts of this statement are authentic, the Plot revealed in confession to Garnet was, as he wrote, similar in outline to the story as 'it is publicly known abroad', save only in one detail, that it was first mooted, not by Catesby, but by Percy.[2] At that time, according to Tesimond's statement reported here by Garnet, there were no more than seven persons privy to it: Bates, Robert Wintour, Grant and Digby were not then involved. Tesimond also had told Garnet this detail. After the action, Percy 'would carry the Duke[3] in his arms and so ride post [-haste] into Worcestershire, and that they would have the start of all which might pursue them'. On the other hand, 'if the Duke were in the Parliament House, then they would surprise the Lady Elizabeth, and proclaim her'. No thought had been given to the choice of a Protector: this decision was postponed 'until the noblemen came together which should be left alive'. Then, finally, Tesimond revealed to Garnet the fanatical resolution that had inspired Catesby. While Catesby 'had a design to save all noblemen whom he did respect, yet he was of mind, rather than in any sort the secret should be discovered, not [to] spare his own son if he were there'.

In two short paragraphs Garnet describes his horror at the revelation.

'Now I remained in the greatest perplexity that ever was in my life and could not sleep a-nights, so that when I saw [Fr Tesimond] next, I telling him so much, he said he was sorry he had ever told me.

'Every day I did offer up all my devotions and Masses that God of his mercy and infinite providence would dispose all for the best, and find the best means which were pleasing unto him to prevent so great mischief; and if it were his holy will and pleasure, ordain some sweeter means for the good of Catholics in our counry; and this and no other was the end of all my exhortations and prayers.'

Throughout the rest of the summer Garnet claimed that he had 'ceased not to commend the matter daily to God'. The tenor of his letters to Rome was the same. 'So did I not omit to write continually to Rome, for to get a prohibition under censure of all attempts':[4] this he had told Catesby he would

---

[1] Neither the Pope nor his Superiors beyond were to call him in question, only the State. This permission (given by Catesby through Tesimond) applied only if he was examined under torture or threat of torture.

[2] Cf. Garnet's second statement, 10 March 1606. 'I never was told nor can imagine when or where Percy moved the matter first, for all my knowledge came by a sudden and short relation of Mr Greenwell.' *E.H.R.*, vol. 3 (1888), 517 sq.

[3] The Duke of York, afterwards Charles I.   [4] Under the penalty of excommunication.

do. He sought to 'hinder all' plots in general; 'particulars I durst not mention' for fear of violating the seal of confession. He believed that Catesby, hot-blooded as he was, possessed simple faith enough to hold back from his enterprise should it be condemned at Rome.[1]

'As for my life,' Garnet concluded, 'I esteem it in the King's hands already; and I also voluntarily offer it to his Majesty, either to be taken away at his pleasure, or to be reserved wholly to his service in anything which may stand with my religion and duty to God, whom I am assured his Majesty preferreth before himself.' He begged the Council to be 'suitors to his Majesty' to restore 'the former calm of all Catholics'.

The King was impressed. By opening what Gerard calls 'the plain truth of the matter', Garnet did not, 'in any way prejudice, but rather relieve, both his own and his penitent's case as things then stood'.[2]

Even with Garnet's full statement in its hands, the Council was unsatisfied: the King, who had scrutinised it as a theologian, was convinced that Garnet had acted correctly and forbade the use of his confession as evidence in his trial. For these reasons the examinations under torture continued.

Oldcorne, who so far had escaped the rack, was the first to suffer. The exact dates of his racking are unknown. 'In the meantime', says Gerard,[3] 'Father Oldcorne was called in further question ... but they found him always alike himself, both virtuous and wise. . . . [He] endured the extreme torments they put him unto, as I have heard, five hours every day, four or five days together, which was a greater extremity than one will easily believe that hath not tried it.' Also Ralph, his servant, was racked at the same time: the 'number and measure' of his torture Gerard could not learn.[4] Neither from him nor from Oldcorne did the Council get the name of a single person who might be called in question to provide evidence against Garnet. 'But above all they were most troubled and tormented that were known most to belong to Father Garnet',[5] particularly John Grissold, 'an honest, faithful man', who kept house for Anne Vaux. He suffered even more than Oldcorne and Ashley 'almost every day for a long time together'. With this bad usage he was brought close to the same death that Owen had already endured.

[1] 'Catesby protested at his death in the field, and Digby at the bar, that not for them-selves, but for the cause of Christ, not for their wives and children, but for the Church, the spouse of Christ, and [for] saving so many thousand souls, the children of God, from eternal flames, they attempted with fire to cut off the chiefest heads and only causes of that greater ruin.' *Narrative*, 11.

[2] *op. cit.*, 179.

[3] *op. cit.*, 181.

[4] *Ibid.*   [5] *Ibid.*

While Coke was writing his speech for the prosecution, he prepared the public to receive it. Already he had given out the story, unfounded in fact, about the interlocutions. Now he spread the report that Garnet was guilty by his own confession. In his letter to Brussels,[1] Salisbury had alerted the Continent to receive the news of Garnet's condemnation. Now in a letter to the English Ambassador at Venice he continued his work. Without even an allusion to the fact that Garnet's knowledge of the Plot was under the seal of confession, he wrote: 'Garnet, the Provincial, hath confessed both his own privity and Greenway's in the treason of gunpowder . . . not sticking to allow the action justifiable by divinity.' Then he continues: 'Thus you see now what these men be, that under the mantle of holiness and piety do countenance the foulest and most abominable treason that ever was conceived against their prince or country. But I doubt not but they shall shortly have their just reward, as their fellows have lately had before them.'[2]

Gerard was still in London. He saw nothing but good result from Garnet's statement. Had Garnet continued to conceal his knowledge, he writes,[3] greater troubles might well have fallen on Catholics who would have endured still more 'examinations, searches and vexations', and particularly on all who were acquainted with him personally. Immediately Garnet himself was relieved that he had ceased to be 'the cause of trouble to many'.[4] Certainly he succeeded in removing suspicion from the mind of the King, 'who could not fear any further power or practice in Father Tesimond'. He hoped also that, while preventing worse persecution, he would at the same time free both himself and Tesimond from the stigma of consent to the Plot as well as all other Jesuits from 'so much as the least knowledge that any such thing was intended'.[5]

After the torture of Oldcorne and of Garnet's own servants there was no further action that the Council could take to extract material for the prosecution. It had already been decided to bring Garnet to trial. It remained only

[1] Cf. *sup.*, p. 375.

[2] *S.P.D. James I*, vol. 19, no. 59. After the execution of Garnet, the Gunpowder Conspirators were described in government publications as, 'Garnet, a Jesuit, and his confederates'.

[3] *Narrative*, 178.

[4] Assuming that the story spread abroad in London by Coke was true, viz. that only one man living could incriminate Garnet, Gerard argued: 'to name any other man than Tesimond was unlawful, because it was untrue. Moreover, the fact that Tesimond had mentioned the Plot to Garnet in confession, extenuated rather than aggravated the part played by Tesimond, who strove his uttermost to dissuade and divert [the conspirators] from their purpose.' By his statement, Gerard argued, Garnet had shown that Tesimond 'was neither contriver nor counsellor, nor yet consenter to the Plot, of all which he stood then accused in the proclamation'. *Narrative*, 178–9.   [5] *Ibid.*

to determine the date. London was not yet fully prepared. Gerard describes vividly how Garnet's statement was used to make ready the public for his condemnation:

'So they left Garnet for a time, but carried with them matter enough, as they thought, to convict him of this treason in show of the world. To which end it was presently[1] given out through the whole town that he had confessed all, and [that] now they could prove the Jesuits to be the principal plotters of the treason, and him [Garnet] and Greenway to be the chief authors and devisers of the same; and it was in most men's mouths that all this was under Garnet's hand confessed. And this [was] presently carried unto the Ambassadors there residing, that by them it might be divulged in other States; and so [that] a falsehood first grounded, might be more hard to be removed by sequent information of the truth, and their proceeding against Father Garnet . . . seem more justifiable. This report, though it troubled the Catholics of England much, until they knew the contrary, yet could they not believe it, being so well acquainted with the giving out of such things, as the chiefest do desire to have believed, though the truth be often found on the contrary side.'[2]

Even with Garnet's confession in their hands, the Council was not satisfied: again torture was threatened. Popham was the spokesman this time. 'After I had acknowledged all that was true', wrote Garnet,[3] the 'Lord Chief Justice said that they must have more.' Garnet must confess himself deeply in the Plot and in the intended invasion from Spain. 'For these two points I was to go to the torture a second time upon Friday [24 March], which was Good Friday beyond the sea. But I pleaded that I was hardly dealt with, having told all I could, and bade them set down what they would have me confess; and, so far as it concerned only my own credit, I would acknowledge it without torture, whether torture were appointed as a punishment or as a trial.' Then, almost broken, he pleaded on: 'What if I confessed nothing in my next torture, must I be tortured again? This was against the course of the common law. But they said: "No, not in cases of treason" . . .' I entreated that in respect of my conference with the three Deans all that forenoon and in respect of my long examination that afternoon,[4] I, being wearied, the torture might be deferred to another time, and desired Mr Lieutenant to be a mediator. They all said they were sorry, but it was so commanded. "Well then," quoth I, "this is the day in which my Saviour

---

[1] *Immediately.*
[2] *Narrative,* 180.
[3] *Hat. Cal.,* 18, 108.
[4] There appears to be no account of this interview.

died for me. I am contented and will appeal to a higher Judge. So I went to my chamber, but afterwards Mr Lieutenant told me that he had obtained a delay till the next coming of the Commissioners, though the Council's commandment was most peremptory. . . . My Lord of Salisbury told me that more than I had told would be brought out of my fingers' end.' Then Garnet protested: 'I told them that verily I knew no more . . . and that I could utter no more than I had done.' He begged them to hasten his arraignment that he 'might be quiet'.

41

THE KING'S QUESTIONS

BETWEEN his confession and trial Garnet was examined at least four times, and made to write answers to another five sets of interrogatories drawn up by the Council.

His first examination after torture was on 12 March. On the previous day Anne Vaux had stood before the Commissioners.[1] From her replies, set alongside Garnet's,[2] it is clear that the Council sought to play the one off against the other, or to trap her into a statement of conflicting detail. They failed. A note written in Anne's rounded hand at the foot of her examination, shows that Coke was again resorting to subterfuge; he had told Anne that Garnet had now confessed that he had been privy to the plot. 'I am sorry to hear', she wrote discreetly, 'that Father Garnet should be any least privy to this most wicked action, as he himself ever called it; for that he made to me many great protestations to the contrary divers times since.' Just twelve days later, on 24 March, Anne was examined again. This time the questions turned on what had passed between Francis Tresham, Garnet and herself: their purpose was to force from her an admission that Garnet, sometime, either at the close of the old reign or the beginning of the new, had made a remark to Tresham that could be interpreted as an incitation to rebel. Anne had nothing to conceal. She protested that, according to her knowledge, Garnet would always exhort his friends to patience. 'She remembereth that he used these words: "Good gentlemen, be quiet. God will do all for the best. We must get it [toleration] by prayer at God's hands. In his hands are the hearts of princes." '[3] Garnet, asked to endorse Anne's statement, wrote: 'I do acknowledge these meetings and required Mr Tresham to be true, as is above contained.'

Meanwhile, on 12 and 13 March, Garnet was handed lists of questions

[1] Examination of Anne Vaux. *S.P.D. James I.*, vol. 216, no. 184.
[2] Examination of Henry Garnet, Jesuit, 12 March 1606. *S.P.D. James I*, vol. 19, no. 40.
[3] Declaration of Anne Vaux, 1606. Gunpowder Plot Book, 2, no. 212.

intended to settle certain doubts in his oral replies;[1] they touched principally on papal policy towards England in the last years of the Queen, and on his dealings with Catesby and his friends both then and in the first months of the new reign. In answer, apparently to the question whether he had copies of Aquaviva's letters to him or of his letters to Aquaviva, he said 'he never kept copies of any [letters] that he sent to Rome. And such as he received from Rome, he used to take brief notes out of them, and presently burn the letters themselves'.

On the 14th he was called before the Council;[2] no new ground was covered and no additional information gathered. The purpose of this examination was to get a statement on the Pope's policy which would enable Coke to demonstrate that Garnet as Superior of the Jesuits was the principal agent of an hostile foreign power. This is clear from the final set of interrogatories put to him on 23 and 26 March.[3]

On the table before his examiners lay copies of three papal documents: two Briefs, both dated 12 July 1600 and addressed, the first to Blackwell, the second to the laity of England, and a copy of another letter to the Papal Nuncio in Brussels.[4] Garnet was asked to recall the contents of these letters, though, as he told the Council, he had destroyed his own copies on the accession of James I. Vainly Coke sought to get from Garnet some admission that he had meddled in politics at that time, but Garnet was alert and answered adroitly. Recalling from memory the substance of all three letters, Garnet explained that there was nothing in these Briefs 'directly against his Majesty'; on the contrary, James was 'without all exception the most desired on all sides'; the Briefs were written against 'divers Scottish competitors within this realm' who might cause divisions and even civil strife. To the Catholic laity the Pope had expressed his hope that their long-suffering would now be rewarded with a grant of toleration. The effect of the letter to the Nuncio was to commend unto him the care of 'countries adjoining to England'; he was to divulge the Briefs only when the moment for their publication came. As Garnet justly observed, this moment never, in fact, occurred, for the letters 'were even worn out before the Queen's death'; their purport was never divulged. As for his own copies, he had burnt them on the day James I was proclaimed; the King's promise of toleration had made them meaningless.

[1] *S.P.D. James I*, vol. 19, nos. 40, 41, 42.

[2] *op. cit.*, no. 44.

[3] *op. cit.*, no. 87; vol. 20, no. 1; Gunpowder Plot Book, 2, nos. 205, 206. Cf. Foley, vol. 4, 159–63.

[4] The Brief to the Nuncio in Belgium, dated 12 July 1600, is printed in Tierney-Dodd, vol. 3, lxx–lxxi; that to the Catholics of England (*Anglis Catholicis*), dated 5 July 1600, in the same work, vol. 4, cvi–cvii.

Garnet then makes a prayer for the King, 'whom [may] Almighty God establish here, with his posterity for ever, and incline him to extend his favour towards poor Catholics that they may enjoy long their life, liberty and worldly goods, to his Majesty's perpetual service'.[1]

James was kept informed of the proceedings: the report of every examination was sent to him. He himself was anxious to take advantage of Garnet's presence in the Tower to put before him a number of theological questions concerning the royal prerogative, and particularly the rights claimed by the Pope over sovereigns. There are two series of the King's questions and of Garnet's answers: both are undated and it is impossible to determine whether the exchange occurred before or after Garnet's trial on 28 March. The internal evidence would suggest that they belong to the pre-trial period, probably to the ten days, 13 to 23 March, during which Garnet was left comparatively undisturbed by the Council. As Gerard says, 'they left Father Garnet for a time', indeed, to the eve of his trial, for 'they carried with them matter enough, as they thought, to convict him of this treason in the show of the world'.

The first set of questions was put to Garnet by the King's learned friend, Sir Henry Wootton,[2] the second by James himself.[3] There is no reason to think that anything other than doctrinal curiosity inspired them: the second set of questions, which enter with greater detail the same theological arena as the first, are framed with admirable brevity and exactness; Garnet's answers are respectful but uncompromising.

'*Question:* Whether our Church be heretical, holding the doctrine of the Scriptures, the three Creeds,[4] and the four first Councils?[5]

'*Answer:* The Church of England is heretical, not for holding the things above, but for holding many things contrary to the definition of the Church of Rome, now and heretofore; for whatsoever is held contrary to the Church of Rome is heretical, which definition is either in General Councils confirmed by the Pope or in his own decrees. . . .

'*Question:* Whether there is anything to be believed now that was not necessary [to be believed] in the time of the Apostles?

'*Answer:* There is nothing to be believed now that was not necessary to be believed in the time of the Apostles, but yet they might be so believed as not necessary *de fide* at that time. . . .

---

[1] A Declaration of some special points of the Pope's Bulls, 26 March 1606. *S.P.D. James I*, vol. 19, no. 87.
[2] *S. P. D. James I*, vol 20, no. 1   [3] Stonyhurst, *Anglia* 7, 4.
[4] The creed of the Apostles, Nicaea and Athanasius.
[5] Nicaea (325), Constantinople (381) Ephesus (431) and Chalcedon (451).

'*Question:* Whether a priest is bound to reveal a treason dangerous to King and State if discovered unto him in confession, the party signifying his resolution to persist.[1]

'*Answer:* The party cannot be absolved, but if he come to submit himself *clavibus Ecclesiae, tunc obligat sigillum confessionis*, but he [the confessor] is bound to find all lawful means to hinder and discover it, *salvo sigillo confessionis.*'[2]

Other questions showed the King's interest in purely theoretical issues. Thus he asked whether Garnet would 'allow of worshipping God in the devils'. Garnet replied that it was 'a purely metaphysical conceit', which he disliked. James also desired to know whether Garnet knew Vasquez, the eminent Jesuit theologian, personally; what he thought of the doctrine of equivocation, whether it was *de fide* that transubstantiation took place and that Christ was truly present in the Eucharist, since the priest's ordination and intention in Mass, on which transubstantiation depended, were themselves not *de fide*. All these questions had no bearing on Garnet's knowledge of the Plot. There was only one that did. Through Sir Henry Wootton, the King asked whether the late treason had been endorsed by his 'authority, advice and knowledge'. Garnet denied the suggestion, and the King accepted the denial without pressing Garnet further.

The trial was fixed for 28 March. As Gerard points out, the Council had no hope of proving Garnet 'guilty of any help or furtherance at all given by him to this Powder treason': instead they resolved 'to proceed against him only upon his simple knowledge thereof which he had received in confession'; for, he rightly explains, they were unwilling 'to let go this opportunity since no greater advantage could be gotten'.[3]

Not to bring Garnet to trial after so many examinations would have been an admission of failure. London and the whole country, as well as parts of the Continent, were 'full of expectation'. It was certain that no matter how correctly Garnet had acted in not revealing a secret learnt in confession, he would not be able to 'justify it before the world: it being accounted treason by the laws of England to know of treason intended and not to reveal it'. On this ground Coke hoped to secure his condemnation: the law, as Gerard points out, could make no exception for knowledge acquired in confession, 'because confession itself being in England rejected, the good and necessity

[1] Since this question was raised also at Garnet's trial, it is probable that it was first put to him privately by the King.

[2] Garnet here means that a confessor, after hearing of a plot in confession, cannot use his knowledge in any way; on the other hand if he also hears of it later out of confession, he is not released from the obligation on his conscience as a citizen to hinder it, provided in so doing he does not use his knowledge gained in confession. [3] *Narrative*, 224.

of the secrecy thereof is not so much esteemed as their public peace and prosperous proceedings in their worldly estate'.[1] Here also Salisbury had 'matter
enough against Father Garnet to make him odious to the people' and, with
him, all Jesuits. 'Therefore', continues Gerard,[2] 'it was intended that his
trial should be performed in the most public and solemn manner they could
devise, thereby to disgrace more both him and his religion.' Coke once, and
Salisbury twice, in the course of the prosecution confessed that this was their
purpose.

What the Commissioners lacked in evidence they would make up with
pomp and solemnity in the proceedings: on this day 'God's saints would be
vindicated'. On the eve of the greatest triumph of his career, Salisbury
assumed a humble, pious air, declaring himself privileged to be an assistant
in the protection of God's honour. By fair means and foul he would discredit
the arch-Jesuit.

That is how Gerard, still in London, viewed the preparations. Garnet was
to be condemned for his fidelity to the seal of confession. 'So . . . one may
see plainly',[3] says Gerard in summary, 'the whole day's work was bent
against religion, and whatsoever was pretended against Father Garnet in
this matter, all was directly intended *in odium Catholicae fidei*. And so we may
see in the process of the accusation, when the Attorney brought against
Father Garnet all other former matter that had been forged against the martyrs
in Queen Elizabeth's time, with which (if they had been true) . . . they
could no more have charged Father Garnet with them in justice than the
child that was yet unborn.'

Yet until the very hour the trial opened there was a lingering anxiety in
the Council. It was feared that there might be a demonstration in Garnet's
favour; Coke now had misgivings about the success of his campaign of
defamation, which he had considered essential to the success of the prosecution; at all costs he must avert a public show of sympathy such as Garnet
himself had witnessed and recorded at the trial of the Earl of Arundel:[4]
should this occur, then even if the Council secured his condemnation, it
would hesitate to proceed to Garnet's execution.

Two days before the trial, Sir William Wade, Governor of the Tower
and Garnet's official gaoler, wrote to Salisbury asking his instructions for
taking the prisoner from the Tower to the Guildhall, where the trial was to
be staged.[5] It was the custom, Wade pointed out, to bring prisoners to their
arraignment on foot, but he doubted whether it would be wise to adhere to
this usage in Garnet's case, for 'the way is long from the Tower to the

---

[1] *Narrative*, 224   [2] *Ibid.*
[3] *op. cit.*, 225.   [4] Cf. *sup.*, p. 93.   [5] Gunpowder Plot Book, 2, no. 216.

Guildhall'; moreover, 'Garnet [is] no good footman', suffering as he still was from the effects of his ten days' concealment at Hinlip. But, before all else, Wade was anxious to deliver him 'safe'. Thus he asked Salisbury whether 'it may be done better than in a slow march on foot'. Wade himself was anxious for a seat at the trial: he put his difficulty to Salisbury: 'there is a place provided in the Guildhall for the prisoner, but none for me': he might stand at the bar, but this would be a recognition of the City's claim, which he did not acknowledge, that Garnet, once he had left the precincts of the Tower was in the custody of the City. It was 'quite contrary', Wade protested. 'He is in my hands till the court ordain otherwise'; for this reason Popham had suggested that there should be a place railed in for him close to Garnet where he could sit as acknowledged custodian of the prisoner.

Salisbury agreed. 'Therefore the day appointed being come, which was a Friday, 28 March, about eight of the clock, he was taken from the Tower in a coach with the Lieutenant of the Tower, Sir William Wade, and another Knight, the curtains being close drawn about them.'[1] Gerard rightly noted that this manner of conducting a prisoner to trial was altogether 'very extraordinary', a departure from the treatment given to Digby and the other conspirators and altogether without precedent. Gerard, who may have watched the progress of his Superior to the Guildhall, noted the astonishment of the crowd. 'The people did much wonder at it', he writes,[2] 'and thought it strange that he should be so carried, considering that most of those that were indeed conspirators in the treason were men of better birth (which by them is much respected) and yet were used in [a] much different manner. But some did more truly guess that this was not done for any grace unto him (whom they sought to disgrace in all they could), but to grace their own cause, by making him seem a man of the greatest account amongst the Papists, against whom they meant to object and hoped to prove the Powder Treason, and so all Papists to be, as it were, proved guilty in him they chiefly esteemed and followed.' Then he adds: 'but the curtains were doubtless kept close that the people might not be moved with the sight of so reverend a man, or he moved on any occasion to speak unto them in his own clearing'.

A large crowd jostled at the entrance to the Guildhall. Garnet arrived at 9 o'clock; the Commissioners took their place half an hour later. Along with the Lord Mayor of London,[3] who *ex officio* was the King's Lieutenant for

---

[1] *Narrative*, 225. [2] *Ibid*.

[3] Sir Leonard Halliday, a merchant tailor. The pageant in the year of his office was written by the renegade Catholic, Anthony Munday. On his death in 1612 his widow married Sir Edward Montagu, the Recorder of the City.

the city, there sat on the Bench, Charles Howard, Earl of Nottingham, Thomas Howard, Earl of Suffolk, Henry Howard, Earl of Northampton, Lord Somerset, Robert Cecil, Earl of Salisbury, with Sir John Popham, the Chief Justice of the King's Bench, Sir Thomas Fleming, the Chief Baron of the Exchequer, and Sir Christopher Yelverton, a Justice of the King's Bench. They were the most eminent men in England.

Wade brought forward his prisoner to the bar, then placed in the hands of the Council the writ by virtue of which he had kept Garnet prisoner. The formality of reading the writ was not observed.

The indictment was then read by Sir John Croke, Sergeant-at-Law. Its phrases echoed the purpose of Cecil in staging this climacteric trial of the Plot.[1] It was to the effect that 'Henry Garnet of the profession of the Jesuits, otherwise Whalley, otherwise Darcy, otherwise Roberts, otherwise Farmer, otherwise Philips (for by all those names he called himself)' stood charged with the most barbarous and damnable treasons, the like whereof were never heard of. 'This man had conspired with Robert Catesby and Oswald Tesimond on 9 June last (in the parish of St Michael in the ward of Queenhithe in London) to depose the King, to kill him and his son [and here he struck the note that was to be taken up by Coke] and such a king and such a prince, such a son of such a father, whose virtues are rather with amazed silence to be wondered at than able by any speech to be expressed.'[2] Furthermore he had conspired to stir sedition and slaughter throughout the kingdom, to subvert the true religion of God and the whole government of the realm, to overthrow the commonwealth; it was he who had determined with Catesby and Tesimond, that Wintour, Fawkes and others should blow up with powder the Parliament House, the King, the Prince, the Lords Spiritual and Temporal, the Judges of the realm, the knights, citizens and burgesses and many other subjects and servants of the King, without respect of majesty, dignity, degree, age or place.

[1] A masterly digest of the indictment is given by Gerard in his *Narrative*; the full text is printed in *A True and Perfect Relation of the whole proceedings against the late most barbarous traitors, Garnet a Jesuite, and his Confederates* (1606). This (in its various printings) is the official account of the case for the prosecution, reported almost verbatim. It was published by the King's Printer, Robert Barker, and, as the title shows, is a propaganda document. While it gives fully the case for the prosecution, it abbreviates and selects Garnet's replies. The most detailed account of Garnet's defence is in the *Narrative*. Gerard was able to obtain his report 'from two or three sufficient men that were present and did carefully observe' all the speeches (*Narrative*, 227). Among the other accounts, the most important is that printed in Foley, vol. 4, 164–90, from the Additional MSS. (British Museum), 21203, Plut. ciii, *F*.

[2] All citations of the indictment and prosecution are taken from *A True and Perfect Narration*.

Rehearsed perhaps by Salisbury, Croke spoke 'with fear and trembling'. He observed that a plot 'so inhuman, so barbarous, so damnable, so detestable . . . was never before read or heard of or ever entered the heart of the most wicked man to imagine'.

In the first months after Garnet's return to England, just twenty years earlier, Lord Burghley, at the time of the Babington Plot, had tried but failed to indict Fr Weston as the arch-conspirator.[1] Now his son, Salisbury, produced Garnet as the contriver of the 'most damnable' plot in history. As the indictment was read every judge on the Bench knew that no word of it was true. But this was Salisbury's hour. He would distort the facts he had extracted from Garnet's examinations and set his distortions against a long tale of plots and treasons, so that when Garnet came to speak it would be impossible for him to reply satisfactorily on all points; if at any moment, Garnet, tired and perhaps doped, appeared to be endangering the case for the prosecution, he would interrupt and reiterate his lies. This is what happened. Salisbury's directions were clear: 'It is the cause, not the person. He [Garnet] is a poor seduced priest: returned not with a heart of an Englishman, but as one *alieno mundo natus*. He quits fidelity for an unnatural and unjust supremacy. We are now therefore not to arraign Garnet the Jesuit nor Whalley the Provincial; but to unmask and arraign that misnamed presumptuous Society of Our Saviour Jesus Who if He were on earth again would say as God doth to the wicked: why dost thou take my name on thy mouth?'[2]

To the indictment Garnet pleaded 'Not guilty'; for his trial he referred himself to God and the country. Then a jury of twelve was impanelled. Garnet was asked whether he took objection to any member, and replied, No. The twelve swore to try the issue between the Jesuit and the King impartially and according to the evidence produced against the prisoner. This done, the indictment was read a second time. Then Sir John Croke promised the jury that in support of the indictment they would be given proofs *luce clariores*, clearer than daylight, so that every man among them might read it 'running'; and to this evidence would be added witnesses, to say nothing of confessions and testimonies, so overwhelming that all would point to the prisoner and say, 'thou wicked subject, thou wicked servant, condemned out of thine own mouth'.

At this the Sergeant-at-Law made way for the Attorney-General, the man best fitted to prove the indictment in a manner calculated to 'stop the mouth of all contradiction'.

[1] Cf. *sup.*, p. 59. [2] *Hat. Cal.*, 17, 595.

42

PROSECUTION

The material for the prosecution had been gathered laboriously from the twenty-three recorded examinations endured by the prisoner at the hands of the Council, who now sat in judgment on him. From day to day the trial had been postponed while Coke polished his speech: even after this laborious preparation he had to resort to dishonest use of the information he had collected. Every paragraph in his speech contains a deliberate distortion of the evidence or an unwarranted insinuation drawn from it. Yet, by brilliant invective and consummate eloquence, the sheer cumulative effect of this method succeeded in clouding the mind of listeners for long enough to secure a verdict of guilty. Indeed his speech was a masterpiece of malicious misinterpretation.

Rising and facing the Council Coke began in a low voice. He claimed that the court was now witnessing the last act of that 'heavy and doleful tragedy which is commonly called the Powder treason'.[1] Before them stood a man on trial for that same treason; he excused himself, therefore, if he should be compelled to cover again, at least in part, the matter adduced in his prosecution of the other conspirators. This was inevitable, and indeed pardonable, because the 'access of people at the former arraignment' made it impossible for more than a few persons to hear the government's case: *nunquam nimis dicitur quod nunquam satis dicitur*.[2] Moreover, what he now repeated would be 'mingled with such new matter as shall be worth the hearing'.

---

[1] Unless other references are given the quotations from Coke's speech are taken from the official report printed in *A True and Perfect Relation of the whole proceedings against Garnet* (1606). This book was printed several times between June and December 1606, and the extant copies contain small but insignificant alterations. It is the official government version of the trial, and there is no doubt that Coke polished up his speech before publication. There is more than one manuscript report written from notes by men present in the Guildhall, the most important being that among 'Papers relating to the English Jesuits', British Museum, Additional MSS. 21203, Plut. ciii, F. Where I have used this I have put a reference thus: B.M., *Add. MSS.*

[2] *Too much cannot be said if there is always more to say.*

The preamble raised expectations that the story of the Plot would now be completed. As prosecutor, Coke was to be excused for the 'procrastination and delay of proceeding', especially against such a person. While the impatience of the people could well be understood, on the other hand the matter with which the prisoner stood charged was so 'transcendent and exorbitant' that there was need for a full revelation, which took time to secure. Thus Garnet 'being first examined on the 13th of the last month hath since then been again examined and interrogated above twenty several times, which lasted unto the 26th March, within two days of this arraignment'. Developing this plea, Coke, still engaged in his preamble, committed his first deliberate suppression of the truth: he blandly claimed that although Garnet's treason was 'without precedent or example' and could well have been met by deed of Attainder, yet it was the wish of King and Council that he should be 'indicted, arraigned, publicly heard and proceeded withal in a moderate, ordinary and just court of law': thus, when a Bill of Attainder was 'exhibited in Parliament concerning this traitor and this treason', it was deferred, not (as was the fact) 'for want of just and sufficient proofs', but in order to give the prisoner a fair trial.[1] Now that the time had come to open proceedings he prayed that the judgment would 'tend to the glory of God and the honour of religion'.

Coke then exposed the lines that his speech would follow: he would deal with Garnet's offence 'before, with and after' the Plot; the offence itself he would term 'Jesuits' treason', for it was something belonging to them *ex congruo et condigno*, their proprietary thing'.

He then enunciated the principle. *Plus peccat author quam actor*, illustrated in Genesis by the different treatment given by God to the serpent the *author*, and Eve the *actor*: 'the serpent, because it was the first author of that temptation, committed three sins, Eve that tempted Adam, two sins, and Adam that was the chiefest actor, but one'.[2] All treasons plotted by the Jesuits since Garnet's coming to England in July 1586 could be set at his door as *author*, as Adam's sin sprang from the serpent's, for Garnet was Superior of the Jesuits. Insinuating that there was a connection between the date of Garnet's coming and the preparations for the Armada, he pointed out that Garnet was a traitor 'in his very entrance and footing in the land', since he had contravened the statute of 1585 which made it a treasonable offence for a priest ordained after the first year of Elizabeth's reign to return to England: 'a bloody, cruel, unjust and new upstart law', according to the Papists, but in fact 'a mild, merciful, just' measure, 'grounded upon the ancient fundamental laws of England', indeed a retaliatory act against the Bull *Regnans in*

[1] Cf. *inf.*, p. 358.   [2] B.M., *Add. MSS.*

Excelsis (1570), which had excommunicated the Queen, and made all her Catholic subjects traitors on two scores: first because they had infringed the law of Edward I which made it treason for one subject of the realm to bring in a Bull against another; and secondly, because (in spite of later interpretations) it had withdrawn her Catholic citizens from the Queen's loyalty. Before the Bull there were no recusants in England. All came to church (however Popishly inclined or persuaded in most points) to the same divine Service. 'Till that time Sir Henry Bedingfield upon my knowledge went to church; till that time Mr Plowden *quem honoris causa nomino* (for excepting his recusancy he were otherwise a learned and good man) refused not to go to church. Nay till that time there was none of your great recusants in England but went to church.'[1] But '*thereupon presently* they refused to assemble in our churches or join with us in public service, not for conscience of anything there done' . . . but because the Pope had cursed those who should obey her Majesty.[2]

Garnet, Coke foresaw, would retort that it was a new and barbarous law that made priests traitors; they came simply to preach the old faith against the new-fangled Lutheran doctrines.

'You will ask, perhaps,' he said, embarking on a novel theory of the established religion,[3] 'where our Church lurked before Luther's coming . . . but I say it makes no great matter where it was, so long as I am certain it was, for as a wedge of gold, if it be dissolved and mixed with a mass of brass, tin and other metals, does not lose its nature, but remaineth gold still, although we cannot determine in what part of the mass it is contained, but the touchstone will find that one; so though our Church hath ever been since Christ's time in the world, yet being mixed and covered with innovations and errors, we cannot tell in what part it was.'

The Bull to which he had just referred was the beginning of open rebellion in the north. Following on it came Campion to form a Pope's party; then, as a harbinger of the Armada, Garnet himself. 'Note here', urged Coke, that since 'the Jesuits set foot in this land, there never passed four years without a most pestilent and pernicious treason, tending to the subversion of the whole State.' Garnet, as the *author*, was more to blame than all the *actors*.

[1] B.M., *Add. MSS.* It was Coke's purpose to mix truth with untruth throughout his speech so that it would be impossible for Garnet to answer all his points. Certainly Edmund Plowden (1518–85), who for religious reasons refused Elizabeth's offer of the Chancellorship, never went to church services.

[2] Unwittingly Coke in this passage testifies to the success achieved by the Bull, for, on his own admission, had it not been issued, the Catholic body would have soon lost its identity and the process of absorption of Catholics into the new religion continued unchecked.   [3] B.M., *Add. MSS.*

From this opening Coke passed to the recital of all the plots, from the Armada to the end of the reign, reinforcing his point by stressing what he alleged to be an association in each instance with the Jesuits.

This occupied more than the first third of his speech. The Armada of 1588 was followed in 1592 by the plot of Patrick Collins who, declared Coke, was incited (amongst others) by the Jesuit Father Holt, then in Belgium, to kill the Queen, 'for which purpose he received absolution and then the sacrament at the hands of the said Jesuit, together with his ghostly counsel that it was both lawful and meritorious to kill her': a brilliantly developed prologue to the unfolding of the treason in which he was to prove Garnet had played the leading part. He continued: then 'anno ninety-four came Williams and Yorke to the same end, *viz*, to kill the Queen, being wrought to undertake so vile and detestable a fact by Father Holt the Jesuit and others his accomplices. And thereupon the said Williams and Yorke in the Jesuits' College received the sacrament together of Father Holt and other Jesuits, to execute the same.' After another interval, 'anno ninety-seven came Squire from Spain, to poison her Majesty, incited, directed and warranted by Walpole a Jesuit, then residing there: at whose hands, likewise after absolution, he received the Sacrament, as well to put the practice in execution as to keep it secret'.

These were the treasons laid to Garnet's door as *author*. Not only, as Gerard says,[1] was Garnet as innocent as a child yet unborn, but both Coke and the Judges on the Bench knew that he was innocent.

The back stage was set now for Garnet's role as *actor*. 'In 1601 when these practices had failed, then force again was attempted'. Thomas Wintour, together with the Jesuit, Tesimond, furnished with letters from this prisoner to the Jesuit, Joseph Creswell, went to Spain to offer the services of English Catholics to Philip II; he promised to have ready against his landing both men and horses to join him. This treason was accompanied by two Briefs sent to Garnet: their drift was studiously summarised for the benefit of the Council, who, in fact, had already read them when, a week earlier, Garnet had been examined on their contents.[2] Catholics were to give their support only to a claimant, no matter how remote from the throne by blood or marriage, who would tolerate the Catholic faith and further it in every manner. This gave Coke an opening for a flamboyant panegyric of the King, whose propinquity and antiquity of blood, descended as he was from both St Margaret

---

[1] Coke had faithfully adhered to Salisbury's instruction to make plain that the Plot had its origins in Elizabeth's reign, and to implicate the Catholic exiles in Flanders. Cf. C. D. Bowen, *The Lion and the Throne, The Life and Times of Sir Edward Coke* (1957), 228. [2] Cf. *sup.*, p. 389.

of Scotland and from Margaret, the daughter of Henry VII, raised him to such eminence that made Garnet's treason almost unimaginable. In James's person were united the Lions of two 'famous, ancient and renown kingdoms', lions 'noble and magnanimous . . . and able without any difficulty or great labour to subdue and overthrow all the letters and Bulls (and their calves also) that have been or can be sent into England'.

Coke proceeded. These Bulls were timed to coincide with the invasion, to take place on the death of Elizabeth, 'that miserable woman', as Papists called her, but 'a bright morning star' to her loyal subjects. He was nearing his climax: 'And now, since the coming of the great King James there have not passed, I will not say four years, but not four, yea, not two, months without some treason', all of them inspired, instigated or directed by Garnet. This he strove to demonstrate. In March 1603, before James's entry into London, Christopher Wright was employed in Spain by Garnet, Catesby and Tresham (a significant trio of names) 'to continue the former negotiations of Thomas Wintour'; and Garnet wrote again to commend Wright to the Jesuit Creswell; then in June, Father Baldwin, a Jesuit, sent Guy Fawkes from Flanders to Creswell in Spain to procure the despatch of the expedition; and the same month Garnet, in England, working in co-operation with other Jesuits and 'Jesuited Catholics' — a phrase coined by Coke and soon to slide into common currency — 'laboured not only in providing horses' to join the invading army, 'but did by force of the said two Bulls or Briefs, dissuade Roman Catholics from yielding true obedience to his Majesty'. The same month, on 9 June 1603, the treason of Watson and Clarke was discovered. This was the crisis: 'the Jesuits . . . having advertisement . . . that the king of Spain did now distaste their propositions', realising at last that there was 'no further hope left for force . . . fell again to secret practice'. Here was the reason why Garnet had burned the Bulls: now they had no importance.

Thus, by ingeniously constructed stages, Coke approached the Gunpowder Treason. Expounding first the question of the 'slaughter of innocents',[1] which Catesby had proposed to Garnet, he declared that the solution given by the Jesuit Superior 'was the strongest and only bond, whereby Catesby afterwards kept and restrained all the traitors in that so abominable and detestable confederacy'. For in the following March all of them took their oath of secrecy, 'were confessed, had absolution, and received thereupon the sacrament by the hands of Gerard, the Jesuit, then present'.

From now to the end of his speech there were facts in abundance that might be twisted to his purpose. In June 1604 Catesby and Tesimond conferred

[1] Cf. *sup.*, p. 378.

about the Powder Plot, and at midsummer, with Garnet, who agreed with them that 'it was so secret that it must prevail'.[1] After this conversation 'Garnet seemed to desire that the Pope's *consent* might be obtained, but Catesby answered that he took that as granted by the Pope in the two Bulls or Briefs before'. On 11 December the mine was started: then in March Fawkes was sent over to Sir William Stanley in Flanders, with letters from Garnet to Baldwin, to arrange that, at the time of the blow, 'forces might be brought near to the seaside, to the end that they might suddenly be transported into England'. Moreover, Garnet wrote now to Rome, in May 1605, after the 'Welsh broil',[2] to stay all commotion in order to concentrate the whole Catholic effort on the Gunpowder Plot and in the meantime 'to lull us asleep in security [with] their dissembled quietness and conformity': Garnet thus schemed in order that the 'least impediment might be offered to this main plot by reason of any suspicion of the stirring of Papists or of enquiry after them upon occasion of any petty commotions or broils'. Then in a masterly mixture of lies with truth, Coke proceeded: 'but when he further desired that it might be so enjoined upon censures, that latter request was not granted, lest it might indeed be an impediment to the Powder Plot'.

The facts, as Coke and all the judges knew, could not have stood more nakedly in contradiction to his argument. Hence inevitably he passed to the confession made by Tesimond (he calls him Greenwell) to Father Garnet. Cleverly he transposed the initiative: note, he exclaimed, 'the politic and subtle dealing of Garnet', who, Catesby alone excepted, would not confer with any layman, but only with another Jesuit, because it was undignified for Garnet 'in a cause of so much blood' to seek a lay opinion. Thus the matter was discussed between the two Jesuits in a 'disguised, fictitious and ambulatory confession'. The very same month there was a conference between Garnet, Catesby and Francis Tresham on the strength of Catholics in England in order to persuade the Pope that they could muster 'sufficient force to prevail'. Only after this did Garnet 'appoint' Baynham to carry his letters to the Pope, not as Pope but as a temporal Prince, begging him to 'stay', under pain of censure, all commotions; yet he knew well that 'before his letters could be answered, the house of Parliament . . . should have been blown up'. The lies rolled on. Where could he find a comparison fit for this consummate Jesuit intrigue?

'But this trick he used like a thief', Coke persisted with mounting

---

[1] Cf. *sup.*, p. 378. With deliberate intent to deceive, Coke placed the crucial meetings between Garnet and Catesby exactly twelve months before they occurred, and made the laying of the mine (December 1604) consequent on these meetings, which (Coke knew) did not take place till June 1605.   [2] Cf. *sup.*, p. 323.

eloquence, 'that going to steal and take partriches with a setting dog, doth berate his dog for questing or going too near, until he have laid his net over them, for fear the game should be sprung and the purpose defeated.'

The journey to Sir Winifred's Well in August had given Garnet opportunity for undisturbed and unnoticed conference with his fellow-conspirators. 'And what business was this, trow you? Marry, even the blowing up of Parliament house with powder. And to this effect also he made a prayer for the good success of the great business in the beginning of the Parliament, and most maliciously misapplied two excellent verses in his speech he made on Allhallows' day last, which are these:

> Auferte gentem perfidam,
> Fidelium de finibus,
> Ut Christo laudes debitas
> Persolvamus acriter.[1]

'And how did he apply this? Marry, to the blowing up of us all, I warrant you.'[2]

On the 5th November the Plot was discovered: on the 6th Catesby sent his servant, Bates, with a letter to Garnet at Coughton, asking him to raise Wales in open rebellion. Garnet, who was there 'of purpose' with Tesimond, hearing that the Plot was discovered and knowing that he and Tesimond were 'the chief authors thereof, prophesied the overthrow of the whole order of the Jesuits, saying that they feared the discovery and miscarrying of this practice would utterly undo and overthrow the whole Society of the Jesuits.' Tesimond, who was anxious to raise Lancashire, urged Oldcorne to stir up Worcestershire and the bordering counties. Still worse than this was the prevarication that accompanied and followed the Powder action. On being taken to the Tower, Garnet wrote a letter to a friend in the Gatehouse:[3]

[1] Cf. *sup.*, p. 330.

[2] B.M. *Add. MSS*. Garnet had used the text, but had not 'applied it', as Coke knew, to the blowing up of Parliament.

[3] From the Tower Garnet did in fact write letters to his nephew Fr Thomas Garnet, then and at the time of trial a prisoner in the Gatehouse, and he used him as his intermediary with Anne Vaux. But he wrote no such letter as Coke now adduced as evidence of his complicity; the document was forged on the instructions of Coke and the Council, and then delivered to Thomas Garnet. This is known, not from examination of the letter itself, but from the statement of Thomas, who was sent into exile shortly after Henry's execution. As he was being led to the Thames wharf for embarkation Salisbury sent a messenger with this very letter, asking him to acknowledge it as Henry Garnet's. This he utterly refused to do, and declared he could do it only 'to his damnation', for he would 'lie against his conscience by asserting that Father Henry sent it to me'. He asserted also that he had never received the letter from Garnet and that it was certainly not in his handwriting. Cf. Foley, vol. 2, 481.

'there was nothing to be seen therein but ordinary matter, but in the margin, which he made very great and spacious, and underneath where there remained clean paper, he wrote cunningly with the juice of an orange or a lemon, to publish his innocency, and voluntarily confessed . . . that as for the Powder treason he hoped for want of proof not to be touched by it. . . . Wherein note his prevarication and equivocation. For before the Lord Commissioners, he truly and freely confessed his treason. And to prevarication he added unspeakable blasphemy for he applied to himself the words which Caiaphas spoke of Christ, "it is necessary that one man should die for the people" '.

This prevaricator and blasphemer, who was he? 'He is, as you have heard, a man of many names, Garnet, Whalley, Darcy, Roberts, Farmer, Phillips: and surely I have not commonly known or observed a true man that had so many false appellations. He is by country an Englishman, by birth a gentleman, by education a scholar, afterwards a corrector of common law print with Mr. Tottel the Printer, and now' — here was a touch that Popham, sitting on the same Bench, would relish — 'and now is himself to be corrected by the law. He hath many gifts and endowments of nature, by art learned, a good linguist and, by profession, a Jesuit and a Superior as indeed he is Superior to all his predecessors in devilish treason, a Doctor of Dissimulation, Deposing of Princes, Disposing of Kingdoms, Daunting and deterring of subjects, and Destruction.'

And now he expounded each member: in the first part of his speech he had asserted without proof that Garnet was the instigator of the Plot: now he turned in detail to doctrine that inspired him, demonstrating that men who held such doctrine were unfit to have room in the kingdom. Dissimulation meant equivocation, on which Garnet had written a treatise: Coke dwelt longest on this. 'The law and sanction of nature hath, as it were, married the heart and the tongue, by joining and knitting them together in a certain kind of marriage; and therefore when there is discord between the two, the speech that proceeds from them is said to be conceived in adultery, and he that breeds such bastard children offends against chastity.' Then he adduced a tampered statement of Francis Tresham, written by him as he lay dying in the Tower, to the effect that he had not seen Garnet for sixteen years before the Plot, which, when Garnet was shown it, he passed off as equivocation.[1]

[1] What Tresham wrote was tha the had not seen Garnet for fourteen years before 1602. Coke deliberately distorted this statement (Tresham had died in the Tower) and made him say that he had not seen Garnet for sixteen years before 1605. When confronted with Tresham's alleged statement, Garnet had answered that he must be using equivocation. For the details of the deceit, see Anstruther, *Vaux of Harrowden*, 360–1.

From the, Deposing of Princes, he moved on to the 'Daunting and Deter-ring of subjects'. Jesuits, whose doctrines he had expounded, were no res-pecters of persons; they practised it against the King, the Queen 'great in birth, greater in marriage, but to all posterity greatest in the blessed fruit of her womb',[1] against the Prince, then, finally, against the Council, the Nobility, the Clergy, nay, against religion, itself, and specially against the city of London'.

He was speaking in the Guildhall and nearing the end of his speech. Here was an opportunity for an appeal to the jury to act in the interests of the city they represented, by finding Garnet, the eminent Doctor of Daunting and Deterring, guilty of the charges in the indictment. 'This city of London', Coke's admirable eloquence was unabated, 'that is famous for her riches, more famous for her people (having above five hundred thousand souls within her liberties), most famous for her fidelity and more than most famous for her true religion and service of God. Hold up thy head, noble city, and advance thyself, for that never was thy brow blotted with the least taint or touch of suspicion of disloyalty. . . . And for thy comfort and joy this day Britain's great King hath honoured thee' with these proceedings against Garnet, for when the Plot was discovered, the fidelity of the city appeared: as he himself witnessed, the people cried, 'Our city, our country, our religion is safe, for our King James is in safety.'[2]

Little now remained to be said. Coke had presented both the 'facts' and the doctrine: a few observations were perhaps necessary to guide the jury. Garnet's conspiracy had intended the destruction of the kingdom: now was the occasion to make sure that the Jesuits were destroyed, and with them the Catholic religion. 'We shall never have a Bull more to come from Rome to England, because they shall never have a party strong enough to encounter the King.' It was for the citizens of London, through their representatives on the jury, to advance God's cause. Coke foresaw that the fall of Catholics was 'near at hand'; both divinity and philosophy indicated this. 'There are now in England about four hundred priests'; the same number was in Israel at the time of Achab. These undertook, through dissimulation, the fall of Achab. 'Their fall was near when once a lying spirit had possessed the priests,

---

[1] This phrase was perhaps a sneer at the *Hail Mary*.

[2] According to Coke the King had ruled that Garnet's trial was to be held at the Guildhall and not Westminster, because he could rely on the loyalty of the city which, Coke said, could be called 'the King's chamber'. 'For as a man accounteth himself safest in his chamber, so doth the King deem himself most sure in this city.' He was lying, however, when he said: 'well experienced soldiers do affirm that such a quantity of powder was gathered with so many crowes of iron, it must necessarily have shaken a great part of this city'. B.M., *Add. MSS.*

according to the vision of Micheas, as now it hath possessed the Jesuits. The imitation of good for the most part comes short of the pattern: but the imitation of evil ever exceeds the example. Now no imitation can exceed this fact [the Powder Plot], and therefore their time is at an end.' It was an ineffable providence of God that had discovered this Jesuit Superior to be party to the treason. This Coke proved in five stages, summarising with even wilder distortions the tenor of his argument. Finally he brought forward non-existent 'proofs for every particular accusation', drawn from the 'explicit and voluntary confessions' of Garnet and his accomplices. Then, as he closed, he produced the two men who had overheard his conversations with Oldcorne. Garnet was asked to acknowledge their identity. This he did. The eavesdroppers swore that Garnet had confessed himself guilty of the treason.

The case for the prosecution was over.

43
THE DEFENCE

GARNET rose, then bowed respectfully to the Bench. Calmly he began his speech in his own defence. First, he asked pardon for the weakness of his memory if he should fail to give satisfaction on any particular point that had been objected against him. Though certain that he was already condemned, he spoke with confidence. He held no notes. The plan of his speech was clear. 'Considering the whole discourse of Mr Attorney, I find the things by him treated . . . may be reduced to four principal heads: the first, concerning our doctrines in general; the second, concerning recusants in general; third, concerning Jesuits in general; the last, concerning myself in particular.'[1]

It was easy to show the learned and illustrious Bench that Coke had misrepresented the doctrine of equivocation, less easy to persuade the jury and onlookers. So far from breaking the bonds of human society, equivocation, if properly understood and safeguarded, was, in fact, necessary for its preservation. 'We do not teach, as Mr Attorney affirmeth, that it is lawful to equivocate in matters of faith; but most expressly we teach the contrary, rejecting that doctrine as heresy, condemned long since in the Priscillianists.'[2] There was no passage of eloquence: only clear reasoning, inexorable logic and the cumulative force of persuasion. Feeling underlay what he said, but it was controlled. 'Yea, some Catholics have suffered death for answering directly to questions which they might have avoided, but that they feared they should then equivocate in matters of faith, or seem to deny their religion.' He would not dwell long on this.

'And, my Lords, because I have discoursed to your Lordships of this point heretofore and to other learned men sent to me in the Tower, I will

---

[1] Unless other sources are indicated in the footnotes, the citations from Garnet's speech in this chapter are taken from Gerard's *Narrative*, 243, sq. This is the fullest account.

[2] It was commonly believed that the Priscillianists, fourth-century Spanish heretics, were allowed to tell lies for a worthy end. It was against this doctrine that St Augustine wrote his treatise *De Mendacio*.

be the shorter at this present: and, as I say, it is never lawful to equivocate in matters of faith: so also in matters of human conversation it may not be used promiscuously or at our pleasure, as in matters of contract, in matters of testimony, or before a competent judge, or to the prejudice of any third person: in which cases we judge it altogether unlawful.' The cases in which equivocation might be used were restricted. If a judge, exceeding his competence, 'should examine me of the secrets of my heart or the secrets I have heard in confession', there he might lawfully use equivocation because these secrets were not liable to any external court, but, even then, only if its use 'is in no way prejudicial to others', but, on the contrary, can shield them from harm. This was the doctrine of the Fathers and St Thomas of Aquinas, who explains it in many places, 'and specially in that place where he teacheth that if a confessor should by any man whatsoever be examined concerning points which he knoweth only by confession, he may lawfully, yes, he is bound to, disavow them'. In two places in the Scripture Our Lord manifestly used speech to conceal the knowledge he certainly possessed: for instance when he was asked when the day of judgment would occur.[1] Hence equivocation, in the terms of Garnet's definition, could not be equiparated with lying, for lying could not be tolerated, 'much less practised by Him that is the rule and measure of all truth'. Augustine, who distinguished eight kinds of lies, did not place equivocation, justly employed, among them. 'Seeing that this saying of our Saviour cannot be verified otherwise ... but with this secret reservation that He knew it not to reveal it, it cannot be denied but these reservations in some cases are lawful.'

At this point Salisbury interrupted him. He would ask just one question. 'You teach it', he said, 'to be unlawful to equivocate before a competent judge, and I trust you take us to be such. At the least I do. Now did you not deny in the Tower unto me with earnest asseveration that you had not any conference with Hall [Oldcorne] until the witness was produced against you, and you confessed it. Is not this to equivocate before a competent judge?'

To this Garnet answered that, until the proof of them was produced, he did in fact equivocate, because he thought the conversation secret, and therefore not liable to the questioning of any judge, however competent.

This was an honest answer. He continued. 'The second point of our doctrine that Mr Attorney greatly inveigheth against is the deposing of Princes and excommunicating of Kings.' Although he could discourse at large on this subject, 'I am unwilling', he said, 'in this honourable assembly, to speak anything which may be offensive to his Majesty. ... I will only say a word or two in just excuse of myself and my brethren, the Catholics of England.'

[1] Mark 13, 32. Cf. Mt. 24, 26.

This was Garnet's opportunity: he used it to defend, not himself — he knew he was pre-judged — but the Church which he represented. The doctrine of the deposition of Princes was held by all divines of his day. 'Therefore I cannot see why,' he urged inexorably, 'why we, concurring with them and with all our predecessors in this kingdom, without innovating or changing any one principle . . . should be so severely branded with such notes of infamy.'

His next point was no less valid. 'For clearing our case the more,' he said, advancing his argument a stage further, 'I will observe a great difference to be made between our Sovereign that now is and other Princes that have once embraced and professed the Catholic faith and do afterwards revolt and decline into heresies, parting themselves from that body unto which they were before united, dividing themselves from that Head . . . by whom they were governed; for they incur the censures which those authors, cited by Mr Attorney, do speak of and are punishable by that power which in precedent times they admitted. But his Majesty's case is different from theirs.'

Garnet spoke not knowing that the King was in secret attendance at his trial. He continued: 'the King maintaineth no other doctrine than that which from his cradle he hath been nourished and brought up in. And therefore those general sentences are not by any private man to be applied to this case in particular.'

Salisbury again interrupted: 'Can the Pope excommunicate King James?'

As Salisbury well knew, this was a controverted point among Catholic theologians and had little to do with Garnet's personal guilt. 'I cannot deny the authority of his Holiness', Garnet answered.

'If he should be excommunicated, then would it be lawful for his subjects to rebel?' 'My Lord,' Garnet parried, 'I have already answered that point. I beseech your Lordship to press me no further, You have my opinion in the Canon *Nos Sanctorum*, which I before alleged.'[1]

Coke then produced the Canon, which was read out amid jeers and derision.

Garnet was unperturbed. He passed to the second part of his defence, namely, that of recusants in general. Their recusancy, Coke had urged, was grounded upon Pius V's excommunication of Elizabeth. The inference from this, Garnet pointed out remorselessly, would be that since King James is not excommunicated, it would be lawful to repair now to the churches and

---

[1] This was a canon issued by Gregory VII in the Roman synod of 1075 (*Nos, sanctorum predecessorum nostrorum statuta tenentes* . . .) It released from their obligations all who were tied by oath of allegiance to excommunicated persons, until such time as the excommunicated made satisfaction. Cf. *Corpus Juris Canonici*, ed. Aemilius Friedberg (1879), vol. 1, 756.

services of England. 'But if this were lawful, doubtless Catholics would have done it before this, thereby to avoid the penalty of those statutes which in that case are enacted. Neither it is true, as Mr Attorney constantly avoucheth, that till the eleventh year of Queen Elizabeth all Catholics did resort to their churches. For I knew many Catholics at that time living that I am certain never went to Protestants' churches in their lives. And Sir Thomas Fitzherbert of my knowledge did not only refuse it before that time himself, but also had written a treatise to prove that it could not be tolerated in any Catholic; and it is apparent to the world that before that time many Catholic priests and bishops were imprisoned for their refusal. Whereby it is evident that their recusancy is not founded upon any excommunication, but only upon mere matter of conscience.' This doctrine went back to the time of the Arian heresy: 'for even then the Catholics refused to communicate *in divinis* with the Arians, albeit they had priests, Masses, altars and their whole service the same both in substance and ceremony'. Moreover it was the very doctrine defended by Protestant divines, by Calvin, Luther, Beza and others, 'who all teach it to be unlawful to be present at our service, not only Mass, which they count idolatry, but at Evensong also'.

'Yet I grant', Garnet concluded the second part of his defence, 'this point was not so clearly understood by Catholics here until the Council of Trent, where twelve most grave and learned men were appointed to consult and conclude of this matter; who, without controversy, determined that it was in no case lawful to communicate with the heretics in their service, no, not to avoid any torment whatsoever. And their decision was by the whole Council approved; although the same was also concluded of by the Council of Nicaea above thirteen hundred years ago.'

Garnet was manifestly gaining the advantage.

'You go about to seduce the people', Salisbury interjected. He then turned to appeal to the City of London represented by the jury. Here in their own court uncovered before their eyes was the anatomy of Popish doctrines. Garnet resumed. He advanced to his third section: the Jesuits in general.

As he spoke, he knew that the Council would use this trial to brand his brethren with infamy.

'The third thing I was determined to speak of', he said, 'was the Jesuits in general', accused by Coke of undertaking treasonable attempts against the Sovereign. The Attorney had mentioned by name the plots of Collins, Yorke, Williams and Squire. 'I can say no more than this,' Garnet answered, 'that I have had the hands and protestations of those Fathers that are accused, as Father Holt and Father Walpole, who on their salvation affirm they never treated with the parties concerning any such matter; and it was very unlikely' that they would have done, since these conspirators were 'no Catholics, or but feigned Catholics, as Yorke and Squire were, who died Protestants. . . . And howsoever they might in time of torture or for fear be brought to accuse themselves, yet at their death some of them . . . protested that they died innocent of the facts for which they suffered, as Williams and Squire did. And for Father Sherwood, accused also by Mr Attorney, there neither is nor was any such Father of the Society. Indeed there was one of that name that entered the Society, but he died before he came to be a priest.'[1]

When Garnet came to rebut of the charge of personal treason, he was convincing and moderate. 'Now for myself in particular. First, I protest I am clear from approving, and much more from fathering, either this or any other treasonable attempts, and have ever thought and taught them to be unlawful; and have by all my best endeavours laboured to divert and suppress them.'

'True it is', and here he came to the crucial point in his speech, 'that I did understood in general by Mr. Catesby, that he would have attempted something for the good of Catholics; which I dissuaded him from so effectually that I well hoped he would have desisted from all such pretences. And this I revealed not, because as a religious Priest[2] I thought to suppress it between him and me, which course our Saviour prescribed, warning us, that if our brother offend in any, we should admonish him between him and us: and if this prevail *lucratus es fratrem tuum.*'[3]

'Now, my Lords, because I was persuaded upon this admonition he would give over his former designs, I held myself in conscience discharged from making any further discovery of that practice. Howbeit that in your common law I think that insufficient in that it deemeth it not convenient to leave the safety of the commonwealth depending on the discretion or peculiar provision of any private person.'

'But yet, my Lords, that I did dislike such proceedings, and as much as I could did endeavour to reclaim them, your Lordships may gather by the express commandment which I procured by means of our Superior, whereby were expressly forbidden all attempts against the King in general, and also by the endeavours I used, as seriously as I could, to procure the like prohibition . . . under pain of some heavier censure: which I would never have endeavoured, if I had in any way approved it. And I know very well his Holiness much disliked all such courses; and, as I was informed, commended

---

[1] John Sherwood, born in London 1559, entered the English College, Rome, in 1581. Two years later ill-health forced him to leave Rome for Rheims. Thence he went to Paris, where he became a Jesuit in 1585; but he died before receiving orders.

[2] i.e. a priest who was a member of a Religious Order.

[3] *Thou hast gained thy brother.* Mt. 18, 15.

my care and vigilancy in seeking to repress the former stirs wherein Watson and Clarke did join with others the first year of King James's coming into England': moreover, he knew that such activity 'was contrary to our religious obedience', a virtue held in 'special account' by the Society, 'by which we were expressly forbidden to meddle in any such causes'.

The only way in which Garnet's defence could be weakened was by constant and unfair interruption: it was Coke's turn. There was no other proof, he urged untruthfully, of such protestations apart from the word of the defendant, who was known always to speak well of himself. As for 'the prohibition which you procured, I do not think you did it for love of us, but for your own ends, lest ... by some matter of small importance your main plot should be prevented and hindered'.

Garnet answered that all plots, without exception, were prohibited, and that he could not possibly favour any one in particular. And, as Gerard points out,[1] he could have urged that, so far from seeking the prohibition in order to ease the way for the powder plot, he had obtained it before he knew anything at all of that plot.

Now Garnet spoke with some show of irritation.

'And, Mr Attorney, howsoever you labour to misconstrue my intentions, my meaning was so as I have said. And to proceed further, I am blamed also for giving letters of commendation to Mr Thomas Wintour and Fawkes and others that went over (as now it appears) for the accomplishing of treasons. And to this I answer, that I gave them indeed letters of commendation. But I protest I knew not that they went over about matters of treason, for I never inquired of their business. But I knew them to be Catholic men and of good conversation, [and] without further enquiry I gave them letters to testify so much to my friends beyond the seas, desiring their favour and furtherance for them in any ordinary matter of courtesy and charity. And the like letters I have given to divers other Catholics that were no ways to be touched with any treacherous attempts.'[2]

It was Salisbury's turn to interrupt. 'Did you give them the letter without knowing the end why they were sent over?'

'Yea, my Lord', answered Garnet.

'Why,' Salisbury retorted, 'did you not yourself tell me that you did nominate Sir Edmund Baynham as a fit man to go over to the Pope?'

---

[1] *Narrative*, 251.

[2] In December 1601 Thomas Wintour went to Spain. At his trial it was alleged that his purpose was to get the King of Spain to send over an army to England on the death of Elizabeth: what he actually did remains uncertain. Garnet, who knew nothing of his intentions, gave him a brief personal letter of introduction to his friends abroad.

'My Lord,' said Garnet, 'I told your Honour thus much: that it was thought convenient that someone should inform his Holiness of the estate of our country, and that it was a great charge to send over one of purpose for that business. Knowing therefore that Sir Edmund Baynham was going over and had been so resolved for above two years, I thought it better that now he might discharge that care and save that charge than that one should be sent over to the Pope of set purpose to inform him of the state of England.'

'Nay,' objected Salisbury, 'you said that Sir Edmund Baynham went over to acquaint the Pope with this Plot of Treason, and that therefore you would not have him said to be sent by you, because the Pope would be offended that you employed a layman in that business.'

'My Lord,' Garnet answered, 'at the going over of Sir Edmund Baynham I did not know of that treason myself, and therefore could not think that Sir Edmund went to acquaint the Pope with it.'[1]

The argument continued. Garnet was still gaining ground; unjust insinuations from the Bench punctuated his speech more frequently now; but truth was on his side. He reiterated more cogently the points he had made to the Councillors during his examinations.

After his conversation with Catesby, Garnet continued, it was inconceivable that Catesby should ask the Pope's approval for a plot such as Tesimond later revealed to him in confession. 'I imagined within myself that peradventure Mr Catesby, by means of Sir Edmund Baynham, might intend to acquaint his Holiness with some pretence in general for the Catholic cause, which they should undertake if his Holiness should approve it. And ... Mr Catesby promised me that he would not go forward with any attempt till the Pope had been acquainted and made privy to it.'

All this Garnet could prove. Coke knew it. Now he produced the confession made under torture by Guy Fawkes, and read out the statement, ascribed to Fawkes, that Garnet had sent Baynham to Rome to acquaint the Pope with the Plot and seek his assistance.[2]

Garnet could only reply that if Baynham went to Rome to inform the Pope about the Plot, he himself knew nothing of this.

The exchange continued.

[1] Here Gerard inserts a comment: 'Note the modesty of this Father that would not contradict the Earl, although the matter touched him very near; but rather proved, by a necessary consequence, that he could not say so unto him, than he would seem to aver that the other had misreported his words.'

[2] All historians have cast doubt on the authenticity of the crucial parts of this confession. Garnet had not been confronted with it before. No doubt this was what the Councillors had in mind when, at Garnet's first examination, they claimed to possess undoubted proof of his guilt. Cf. *sup.*, p. 350.

'You see, my Lord,' Coke again interjected, 'that he saith he did not approve or consent to it. But I will prove that he did both.' First Garnet had told Catesby that as a general principle it was lawful to kill innocent persons; then he had prayed for the success of the Plot 'about the time it should have been put in practice, he having known thereof in particular' from Tesimond in confession.

Garnet was a match for the Attorney-General. He admitted that the case was proposed to him in general, whether, 'if a town could not be taken, or a wall beaten down without the death of some innocents', their death might be permitted. 'But that Mr Catesby misapplied this general question, was neither fault nor approbation of mine; which when I heard of, I conceived a great horror at the thing itself, and thought it would be a scandal and disgrace to Catholics.' In his prayers he had begged God to suppress it, and that it might be God's will to grant toleration by milder means.

Salisbury rejected this. 'Nay, you prayed not with that condition; for you said to me in the gallery, that although we did not approve of your Masses, yet you did think assuredly that they had done us good; for you prayed heartily that it might not come to pass, except it were for the good of the Church.'

Garnet denied that he had said this. 'And as for the prayer on All Hallows Day, wherein you note the words so precisely, *Gentem auferte perfidam*, you must understand that it was the hymn of the same feast. . . . I admonished the hearers to reiterate this unto Almighty God for the Catholic cause, the Parliament being then at hand, and great fears in us for more severity ensuing for us. . . . I meant to desire God that he would put in the mind of his Majesty and the Lords there assembled in the Parliament not to permit those rigorous laws to be passed against us.'

The witnesses who had overheard the interlocutions were called. Coke spoke in commendation of Fawcet, 'a great linguist', he called him, 'a learned man, and one who would do wrong to no man'. Because the Tower was so full of prisoners, he told the jury, the Lieutenant had been compelled to lodge Garnet and Oldcorne in adjoining rooms. Their gaolers, who happened to be passing through the Tower to other prisoners, overheard the two priests talking and subsequently were placed nearer the priests to catch their conversation. Distinctly Fawcet had heard Garnet admit that he had prayed for the success of the Plot. Again Garnet denied it: no matter what he was reported to have said, he meant only that he had prayed that the laws would not pass Parliament. Turning to Fawcet, he asked: 'And how say you, Mr Fawcet, were you not mistaken?'

'No', he answered, 'we both understood it so[1] and writ it down so, and

---

[1] *viz.* that Garnet admitted he had prayed for the success of the plot.

we have had so great care to do you no wrong, that we omitted divers things, wherein we agreed not; and nothing was set down, but with both our consents.'[1]

Salisbury re-entered the debate. If the evidence of one eavesdropper, not both, was admitted, 'we could charge you', he said hypocritically, 'with further matters than these; but we will not do so, that the world may see what mildness and mercy we use in the execution of justice, and to this end my Sovereign determined that your trial should be in this honourable assembly'.

He continued addressing the Bench:

'For who is Garnet that he should be called hither, or that we should trouble ourselves in this court with him, which I protest were sufficient for the greatest Cardinal in Rome, if in this case he should be tried?'

'No, Mr Garnet, it is not for your cause that you are called hither, but to testify to the world the foulness of your fact, the error of your religion and His Majesty's clemency. For these causes His Majesty ordained your trial should be in this court before this honourable assembly, wherein you may glory as much as if the greatest Cardinal in Rome were pleading at the Bar. The witness, Mr Fawcet, is a man of reputation and . . . would do you no wrong.'

Garnet replied that he thought so, but he might be mistaken.

'No,' rejoined Salisbury, 'he was near you enough to understand your words: for Hall and you, of policy, were lodged so near one to the other and in such a place where your interlocution might be easily heard.'

There the collusion between Coke and Salisbury broke down. Gerard was quick to notice this. 'Here it appears', he says in one of his rare comments, 'Mr Attorney his speech was idle when he said it was . . . by chance they were overheard', for he did not realise that Salisbury meant to tell the truth in order to satisfy the Ambassadors present. Such devices, he admitted, were

[1] Between the interlocutions and the trial Coke had suborned Fawcet, who now deliberately lied. In his report Fawcet made no such statement as he now claimed to have written. What he wrote was this: 'Garnet said [to Oldcorne] that he was charged about certain prayers to be said for the success of the business at the beginning of the Parliament, to which he answered that if they would shew him any such prayers he would confess if they were done by him, which was refused to be done. Then they pressed me whether, if it could be proved that I made such a prayer, I would yield myself privy to all the rest. Indeed upon All Hallows Day we used those prayers, then I did repeat to them two Latin verses, which both prayers and verses Garnet did now rehearse to Hall [Oldcorne] confessing that he had made them both.' (Interlocutions between Garnet and Hall. 25 February 1606. *S.P.D. James I*, vol. 18, no. 117.) The 'prayers' and 'verses' were those appointed by the Church for the feast of All Hallows. Garnet admitted to using or saying those prayers that day, and this is what Fawcet correctly noted in his report.

not to be commended in a Christian commonwealth, but 'if we should not use such courses, I know not how we should deal with such people as you.' There was no mention in the report that Garnet had been overheard to tell Oldcorne that but one man living could incriminate him in the Plot. This surely was the time to produce the statement, if it had ever been made.

Again, for the benefit of the Ambassadors, Salisbury asked Garnet whether he had been treated with consideration in the Tower. Garnet replied that he had.

So far Garnet had answered all the charges with satisfaction. Both sides knew that the verdict of the jury was already determined; Garnet had still to be shown guilty before the people. Coke had done his work. Salisbury now took charge and came to the only ground on which Garnet could be held guilty before his countrymen. Since Tesimond's confession, he pressed, was no sacramental confession by the Church's laws, for he had no contrition and the matter of his confession was *de futuris*, Garnet was bound to reveal the Plot.

Garnet answered: Tesimond was his spiritual child; he had no doubt at all that his penitent had all the disposition needed for the sacrament: yet even if he had no contrition, Garnet, as confessor, could not reveal anything he had heard in confession.

Northampton, more learned in theology than Salisbury, spoke for the first time: 'Mr Garnet, Tesimond, in his reservative clause was more careful of you than of the King or commonwealth, in giving liberty to you to reveal it in time of your own danger rather than the danger to the King and commonwealth.' Tesimond who made the confession, Garnet replied, was himself restricted by confession. The restrictions he imposed on Garnet had been imposed on him; and as confessor in this particular confession, Garnet had no more liberty to extend the permission than the penitent himself had.

It was Nottingham's turn. He took a theoretical case.

'Mr Garnet, if a man should tell you in confession that he would stab the King with a dagger to-morrow, are you not bound to reveal it?'

'My Lord,' said Garnet, 'unless I could know it by some other means, I might not.'

The prosecution was achieving its end. 'Hereupon', says Gerard, 'the people fell into a great laughter, not understanding that the secrecy of confession concerneth a greater good in the life of many souls than the corporal life can be of any particular man.'

The laughter died down. Garnet proceeded: 'In that case, my Lord, my duty were to dissuade the party from it, to refuse to give absolution, and to labour to divert it by all means which might not open the confession.'[1]

[1] By this Garnet meant that he could take no action based on his sacramental knowledge, for this would be equivalent to a violation of the seal.

Northampton returned to the case. 'Mr Garnet, you were consenting to the Powder Treason, for you did not forbid it': then he quoted the principle, *Qui non prohibet cum potest, jubet.*[1]

'My Lord,' answered Garnet, 'I did prohibit it, as much in me lay.'

'Why did you not then make it known to those that could and would have hindered it?', Northampton urged.

Garnet answered as before, that he could not because he knew it only in confession.

Coke made his own theological point. 'Although you could not discover Tesimond, by whose confession you knew it, yet you might have well discovered what you understood concerning Catesby and his associates, whose confession you heard not.'

Garnet answered: 'What sin soever is heard in confession, although it concern not the penitent, but some other, cannot lawfully be revealed.'[2]

In this exchange on sacramental confession, Garnet had triumphed. Yet the Bench, by choosing its questions skilfully, had been able to hold up the doctrine of the seal to the mockery of the jury. This was the most they could hope to achieve. Now, until the end, Garnet's defence became a debate.

Coke again urged that Garnet's presence in Warwickshire at the time of the discovery of the Plot itself indicated complicity. On his return from St Winifred's well, Garnet explained, he passed through that county and 'by the entreaty of some of his friends and some occasion also of business, he was detained there for a time, not suspecting any such troubles would have happened in that place'. Had he been endowed with foresight, then his judges 'could well imagine he would in discretion have been a good way off from that place and country'.

'But', said Salisbury, 'what did you, Mr Garnet, on the 6th day of November, when Bates came to you with a letter from Catesby, after the Plot was discovered and they in open rebellion?'

'My Lord,' said Garnet, 'I said I would not meddle with him that had wrought himself into such treasonable attempts, and thereby endangered himself and his friends.'

'Yea,' answered Salisbury, 'but did you not sent Tesimond to Catesby, who went to raise the countries abroad.'[3]

'My Lords,' said Garnet, 'he went without my knowledge; neither could I gather from any speech of his that he had any such intention, as Bates could testify if he were alive.'

---

[1] *If a man does not forbid something, when he is able to forbid it, he orders it.*
[2] The sin of a third person, mentioned by a penitent in confession, is as rigidly covered by the seal of secrecy as the penitent's own sins.   [3] The neighbouring counties.

The Council had a letter from Bates, in which he had cleared Garnet of guilt. Garnet did not know this.[1]

Fatigue was telling on the prisoner. There had been no adjournment since proceedings had opened at 9.30. Now it must have been past four in the afternoon. Throughout his defence, possibly also during Coke's long speech of prosecution, Garnet had been standing. There were no signs of mental or physical collapse; but he was less alert now. Coke saw his opportunity. He asked the licence of the court to read the letter written by Francis Tresham as he lay dying in the Tower.

In this letter Tresham had cleared Garnet of what was now called the 'Spanish treason', the alleged conspiracy, supposedly involving Garnet, to put a Spanish claimant on the throne after Elizabeth's death. On his salvation, Tresham, in the last letter of his life, protested that he had wronged Garnet by stating that he was privy to it and that he 'had not seen Garnet for fourteen years before'.[2]

'Now,' said Coke, 'to prove this untrue, here is a confession of Mrs Anne Vaux, who, though likewise a very obstinate woman, yet in this she confesseth plainly, that within these three years Tresham had been several times at her house with Father Garnet, and twice this last year, at which times Father Garnet had given him very good counsel. So you see', he concluded, displaying his ace card to the jury, 'they will swear and forswear anything.'

Coke's effort was now to show indisputably that, since Garnet could not be trusted, his defence was worthless. Salisbury came to the Attorney's support, repeating the same accusation.

Anne Vaux's confession[3] did not, as Coke knew, contradict Tresham's statement. Tresham had written that he had not seen Garnet for fourteen years before the Spanish treason; 'as his words are plain', comments Gerard,[4] 'and the cause also of his writing doth make it plain, for his intention was only to clear the Father of the Spanish treason, which he had wrongly accused him of, and therefore it was a very material proof that he had not seen him of fourteen years before that business.'

Here was a deliberate misconstruction with the aim of proving Garnet guilty of equivocation. Indeed, as Gerard observes, had Tresham written

[1] Bates's letter is printed in Gerard's *Narrative*, 210-11. He wrote: 'I thought Mr Greenway knew of this business but I did not charge the other [Garnet] with it.'

[2] Francis Tresham had died in the Tower on 22 December 1605. It was in his cell that Coke discovered the copy of the treatise on Equivocation, which he used in his examinations of Garnet.

[3] Examination of Anne Vaux, 2 March 1606. *S.P.D. James I*, Gunpowder Plot Book, 2, no. 212.

[4] *Narrative*, 259. Cf. *sup.*, p. 403.

EE

anything else, his words would have been 'unproper'.[1] Coke had distorted
Tresham's sentence to his purpose. He had also damned Tresham's good
name after his death, 'as though he had been found to have protested an
untruth'.[2] Following up quickly, Coke claimed that if Tresham's protestation of innocency was false, then, 'other protestations were also like to be
untrue which divers of the conspirators had made before their death to clear
the Fathers'.

Yet, as Gerard saw it, this attempt to discredit Garnet turned in the end
to his credit, though not to his immediate advantage. 'It is worthy to be
noted how Almighty God did permit them now, at the end of this long
day's trial of Father Garnet, to bring forth this letter, (whereby they thought
so clearly to disprove such testimonies as might be afterwards brought for
Father Garnet) which letter did indeed so clearly prove him innocent in that
former dealing with Spain, whereof there were more likely presumptions
against him than about the Powder Treason.'[3]

Garnet did not see the deceit, or know how to meet it. He had been put
in the dilemna of accusing either Tresham or Anne Vaux of equivocating.
He was silent. It was the only occasion throughout the trial that he had not
satisfied the Bench. Gerard ascribes his silence to fatigue. 'This was not
surprising after so many hours standing at the bar.' He had answered endless
questions unfairly framed and pressed amid constant interruptions. Though
some onlookers had jeered at him earlier when he had explained the Church's
teaching on the secrecy of confession, now, at the end of the day, there were
many in the Guildhall whose sympathies were on his side; and among them,
the King, 'who was there in private'.[4]

From his secret listening point James sent Salisbury a note, instructing
him to allow the prisoner to speak without interruption. Immediately
Salisbury ignored it. Rather he made it the excuse 'to speak at large, and
said that, though he would not meddle with Mr Garnet in matters of divinity,
yet .. he desired to demonstrate with what sincerity and moderation his
Majesty's justice was carried in all points.' So far from giving Garnet the
opportunity to speak uninterruptedly, he himself 'discoursed of the manner
of the proceeding [at the trial] and said it was not performed with such
solemnity in respect of Garnet, who was but a private man, but to discredit

---

[1] Gerard argues that had Tresham meant to say he had not seen Garnet in the last
fourteen years, he would have written 'this fourteen years', but since he said 'I did not
see him of fourteen years before' he clearly meant fourteen years before the time in
question, namely, the Spanish treason.

[2] *Narrative*, 259.

[3] *op. cit.*, 260   [4] *op. cit.*, 261.

in his person his religion, and to credit the Gospel'; and also to demonstrate the King's just proceedings to the world, and withal to favour the city of London in doing it in the sight of the city. Then he showed how gently Fr Garnet had been used, 'more like a nurse-child than otherwise, and that in this arraignment divers things had been permitted to be read, which made for Father Garnet; as namely, this testimony of Mrs Vaux who, said the Earl, would sacrifice her life to do him good. And he concluded, affirming that the whole course of proceedings ... had been mixed with such clemency, as he thought there was none so malicious that could calumniate.'[1]

Salisbury was followed by Northampton, who made a short speech to the same effect: to 'show the foulness of the Plot of Powder, the just and merciful proceedings of the King and the presumption of Garnet being guilty.

To satisfy the King's command, Salisbury spoke: 'Good Mr Garnet, whatever you have to say, say in God's name, and you shall be heard.'

Garnet addressed the jury. He begged them to take such things as he denied to be justly and truly disavowed, unless they had evidence to the contrary. And he asked them to give their verdict only upon what was acknowledged to be true and not to condemn him upon circumstances or presumptions. 'Is that all you have to say?' asked Salisbury, when Garnet had finished speaking. 'If not, take your time. No man shall interrupt you.'

'Yea, my Lord', answered Garnet.

Coke, turning now to the Bench, asked the Lord Commissioners to tell him whether he had overlooked any point in his prosecution. Salisbury, speaking for them all, assured him that 'he had done well, painfully and learnedly'.

Coke then asked the jury to consider their verdict.

[1] *Ibid.*

44
THE DAYS OF WAITING

THE jury was absent less than fifteen minutes. They found Garnet guilty of treason for not revealing the Powder Plot.

Then Lord Salisbury informed the prisoner that it was the King's pleasure that he should have leave to speak.

'Only this I have to say. I am unwilling to dispute your verdict. The day shall come when this same cause will be tried before the tribunal of Christ, in the presence of all these bystanders, not upon fallacious conjectures and ill-founded arguments, but in the light of conscience. Meanwhile, may God preserve the King. My life and death are in his hands. I fear not death, which will be an end of all my miseries. If my life is spared, I shall, saving my faith and religion, strive to merit it by every duty in my power.'[1]

The Serjeant-at-Arms, Sir John Croke, prayed judgment might be given. The crier was asked to proclaim silence. Sir John Popham, the Chief Justice, pronounced the sentence against Garnet, that he should be hanged, drawn and quartered.

The Earl of Northampton then rose and made a long speech. It formed the epilogue to what Salisbury had made the greatest drama of the reign. With chosen texts from Scripture, passages from the Fathers, maxims of law, parallels from history, he showed that no power on earth could dispossess a prince. It was only recent Popes who had claimed such authority: in the Middle Ages, Pope Gregory called the Emperor his Lord.[2]

It was now between six and seven in the evening. When Northampton finished, the court broke up. Garnet was returned to the Tower to await the day appointed for his execution. As the King left the Guildhall, he was heard to say that the Commissioners 'had done the prisoner wrong to interrupt

[1] H. More, *Historia Provinciae Anglicanae*, 324.

[2] Northampton's speech as printed in *A True and Perfect Relation* was expanded for publication. As the editor notes, Northampton gave him a version 'amplified and enriched . . . with greater variety of arguments'. A synopsis of the speech, as it was delivered, is given by Gerard in his *Narrative*, 263.

him so often', and he added that if he had been in Garnet's place 'he could have defended himself better in some points'.[1]

While the King was dissatisfied with the justice done, the Councillors themselves, who had done the justice, were concerned about the impression they had made on the public. It was not Garnet's conviction they were anxious to secure — they could have secured it merely on proof of his priest-hood — but his conviction on the ground of complicity in the Plot. On their success all the Commissioners had their reservations. Moreover, Garnet's defence, and his carriage in the dock, had undoubtedly won him much sympathy.

Gerard is the only writer to record the impression that Garnet made at his trial. Understandably, he speaks only for Catholics. 'It did comfort them much,' he says,[2] 'that he was condemned only for concealing the treason that he had heard only in confession.' Had his complicity in the Plot been proved, the Council would have shown no further interest in him save to appoint the day of his execution. More than five weeks were to pass before the sentence was carried out. After all their efforts the Council had still failed: in the eyes of Catholics Garnet appeared a true martyr. 'Consequently', continues Gerard in the same place, 'his condemnation was only for conceal-ing confession, which is a most happy cause, and the case of a martyr, as all the Catholics did then account him, and as the justice of his cause did then approve him.'

Just over a week later, on 4 April, in a letter to Anne Vaux, Garnet gave his own verdict on the manner in which he had conducted his defence.[3] His condition was weak; doctors were in attendance on him. From them and from William Wade, clearly acting in concert, he had learnt that his speeches 'had given great scandal'. He had been told that after his trial 'five hundred Catholics turned Protestants, which, if it should be true, I must needs think that many other Catholics are scandalised at me also'. Yet he suspected now that this was yet another rumour circulated to trap him, into a lying con-fession of guilt that the Council was still anxious to extract from him.

In depression Garnet pleaded: 'I desire all to judge me in charity, for I thank God most humbly, in all speeches and actions, I have had a desire to do nothing against the glory of God.'

Then he turned to the different phases in his speech.

'For the matter of the Pope's authority, of the *sigillum confessionis*, of equivocation, I spoke as moderately as I could and as I thought I was bound. If any were scandalised thereat, it was not my fault, but their own.'

[1] *Narrative*, 264.
[2] *Ibid.*   [3] H. G. to Anne Vaux. 4 April 1606. *S.P.D. James I*, vol. 20, no. 11.

He continued: 'The *Breves* [Briefs] I thought necessary to acknowledge for many causes, especially Mr Catesby having grounded himself thereon, and not on my advice.'

There was nothing else he could remember that might have scandalised Catholics. 'But I was *in medio illusorum*, and it may be,' he added, searching for possible grounds of scandal, that 'Catholics also think it strange we should be acquainted with such things.'

He continued to his humble conclusion. 'But who can hinder, but he must know things sometimes which he would not. I never allowed it. I sought to hinder it more than men can imagine, as the Pope will tell. It was not my part (as I thought) to disclose it. I have written this day a detestation of that action for the King to see. And I acknowledge myself not to die a victorious martyr, but as a penitent thief, as I hope I shall do.'

Then he asks Anne what anyone else would have done in his condition, after he 'had been twenty-three times examined before the wisest of the realm', not taking into account 'particular conferences with Mr Lieutenant'. The conspirators, thinking him safe, had used his name freely, 'though, I protest, none of them ever told me of anything'. The paragraph ends: 'Yet I have hurt nobody.'

This, he thought, was his farewell to Anne. Without restraint he expressed the affection that the ties and trials of twenty years had created between them.

'However, I shall die a thief, yet you may assure yourself your innocency is such but I doubt not, if you die by reason of your imprisonment, you shall die a martyr. *Tempus est ut incipiat iudicium a domo Dei. Vale mihi semper dilectissima in Xto, et ora pro me.* The time is come for judgment to be made from God's house. Farewell, my ever dearest in Christ and pray for me.'

It was the measure of Garnet's greatness and of the esteem he had among his subjects that he could write such a valedictory sentence to his dearest friend among the Catholic laity without fear of misinterpretation. He knew that what he wrote from his heart at that moment would never be misconstrued by the men whose loyalty had sustained him as Superior.

In the same letter Garnet gave Anne his spiritual testament. 'I write now more particularly a direction for you, what I think best when it shall please God to set you at liberty.'

In an early letter to Aquaviva, Garnet had pointed out that there were in England many ladies who could serve the Church more profitably in their country homes than in convents abroad.[1] Anne, by private vows, had bound herself to administer to the Church in obedience to Garnet. Now there was

[1] Cf. *sup.*, p. 57.

need for Garnet to give her advice. 'If you can stay in England and enjoy the use of the sacraments in such sort as heretofore, I think it absolutely the best', he continued. 'And do I wish that, if it may be, you and your sister live as before in a house of common repair of the Society, or where the Superior of the mission shall ordinarily remain. Or if this cannot be, then you and your sister to make the choice of someone of the Society, as you shall like, which I am sure will be granted you.[1]

'Secondly, if you go over[-seas], then do I wish you stay a while at St Omer's and send for Father Baldwin, and consult with him where to live, for I think St Omer's not to be as wholesome as Brussels. And then in respect of your weakness, I think it best for you to live abroad [i.e. unenclosed] and not in a monastery.[2]

'Your vow of obedience, being made to the Superior of the mission here, when you are once over[-seas], ceaseth. And then you may consult how to make it again.' Garnet then reminds her that while no member of the Society can accept a vow of obedience made to him in person, yet anyone 'may vow as he wish', with the advice of a ghostly father, and follow his direction as a confessor.

'For poverty', he tells her, 'you may also do the like; but this I would have you know, that all that is out for annuities, I always meant to be yours, hoping that after your death you can leave what you can well spare to the mission.'

After further suggestions for the disposition of her money Garnet passes on through her his instructions for his brethren. Until a new Superior is appointed by Aquaviva, Fr Anthony Hoskins, Fr Richard Holtby or Fr Holland are to take charge of the younger priests at their six-monthly meetings. They may 'hear at any time the confessions of such as shall please to use them, with full authority as much as I myself have. I desire they know that I leave the Society charged with an annuity of twenty pounds yearly to Mrs Mary Grene, and the like to a gentleman, a bachelor, whom you call uncle.

'Also I owe (though not in rigour) to Mr Thomas Wintour four pounds two shillings, which I wish paid to his sister.[3] I wish also some consideration of Mr Yates for his horse he gave me.'

Finally he gave Anne directions for the disposal of all that belonged

---

[1] This is not altogether clear. Probably Garnet means either that the Superior will grant her a priest as her chaplain if she cannot live in a house sufficiently large to be used as the headquarters of the mission, or, alternatively, he would appoint a Jesuit priest to act as director to her and her sister.

[2] Cf. *sup.*, p. 135, where Garnet speaks of Anne's delicate health.

[3] Thomas Wintour was executed for complicity in the Plot on 31 January 1606.

to him in the house at Erith. Earlier, when he suspected that the place was under surveillance, he had given orders for the books to be taken away, since there was no suitable place in the house where they could be hidden. If any should be found, you must challenge them as yours', he told Anne. 'Otherwise let all things lie as they are hidden till fit opportunity, and let God work his will.'

From the restlessness of the Council in the weeks following Garnet's trial, it was clear that the speeches made by Coke, Salisbury and Northampton at the Guildhall had not carried the conviction of the masses. Had the Commissioners won an indisputable victory, then Garnet would have been taken to execution the following day, or at least, in the same week. Yet over five weeks passed before the sentence was carried out. Meanwhile, as day by day Garnet waited notice to prepare himself for the scaffold, his former judges by insinuation, by rumour, by further trickery and still more examinations attempted to trap him into a confession of the crime of which he had already been found guilty. And with this went a last attempt to break his resistance. Garnet was not allowed even the comparative comfort of preparing peacefully for death.

On the day following his trial, 29 March, Garnet was compelled by Wade to make a fresh statement on equivocation.[1] This he promptly sent to Salisbury. It may have been that Salisbury hoped to obtain from him a restatement of his teaching in loose phrases that he could twist for purposes of propaganda. His motive is not clear. But Garnet was still alert. Nothing in his written answers weakened his position: on the contrary, his definition is more precise and convincing. The main interest of his last examination on this subject is his view on Tresham's alleged statement. Still ignorant of the manner in which he had been tricked — for Tresham as he lay dying had not equivocated at all[2] — Garnet defends the good faith of his friend. 'As for Mr Tresham's equivocation, I am loth to judge', he writes with caution and charity.[3] 'Yet I think ignorance might excuse him, because he might think it lawful in that case to equivocate, for the excuse of his friends. Yet would I be loth to allow of it, or practise it', for (according to the Council's distortion of the instance) Tresham had made this confession voluntarily, and in a case that concerned manifest treason. This point Garnet repeats in another form at the end of his statement: 'in cases of true and manifest treason, a man is bound voluntarily to utter the very truth, and no way to equivocate, if he know it not by way of confession, in which case also he is bound to seek all lawful ways to discover it *salvo sigillo*'.

[1] *S.P.D. James I*, Gunpowder Plot Book, 2, no. 217.
[2] Cf. *sup.*, p. 403.   [3] *S.P.D. James I*, Gunpowder Plot Book, 2, no. 217.

It was Salisbury's last attempt to draw from Garnet a formulation of doctrine that would enable him to represent the Jesuits as practiced and professional liars.

Three days later Garnet was made to answer a second questionnaire: this time on the Catholic teaching concerning civil laws. A single loose phrase might be construed as a defence of rebellion. With admirable clarity Garnet set out the Catholic position. It was as though, at the end of his life, he was occupying again the professorial chair he had briefly held in the Roman College. Possibly, in this instance, it was the King, not Salisbury, who was anxious for elucidation on points of Catholic doctrine. The questions concerned the nature of obedience to the law. All just laws had to be obeyed, but any law that conflicted with God's law was unjust by definition and therefore void. This was the teaching 'not only of divines, but of Aristotle and all philosophers'.

From this premiss Garnet proceeded to explain what Catholics held. It was his last piece of apologetic writing, and it was admirably phrased.

'Thereupon it ensueth that no power on earth can forbid or punish any action which we are bound unto by the law of God, which is the true pattern of all justice. So that the laws against recusants, against the receiving of priests, against confession, against Mass, and other rites of the Catholic religion are to be esteemed as no laws by such as steadfastly believe these to be necessary observances of the true religion.

'Likewise Almighty God hath absolute right for to send His preachers of His Gospel to any place in the world. *Euntes docete omnes gentes.* So that the law against priests coming into the realm sincerely to preach is no law, and those that are put to death by virtue of that decree are verily martyrs, because they die for the preaching of the true religion.'

Garnet had not been indicted under this law, that had made all the true martyrs of the years he had worked in England. Seeking another category in which he could place himself, for lack of anything better, he had described himself as a thief. This is how he constantly refers to himself from this day to the end of his life — a thief who had the honour of dying besides the martyrs in the service of his Master, penitent, not for any part he had taken in the Gunpowder Plot, but for his personal sins, which, as he saw them, merited God's punishment. It was the approach of a man of intense humility.

This second questionnaire had yielded nothing. One last trap was set. Garnet, who had been correctly informed that Tesimond had escaped safely to the Continent, was now assured, on the word of the Council, that he had been arrested and had sworn that the revelation of the Plot he made to

Garnet was not under the seal of confession.[1] This was told him in an effort, first, to break his spirit, for he had spoken of Tesimond's association with the conspirators only because he believed him safely out of their hands, and secondly, to elicit from him another confession which might enhance his guilt in the eyes of the public. Instead, the ruse drew from Garnet a most humble letter of apology to his former subject. Believing now that he had wronged him, he did not hesitate to say so. 'My most dear and loving sir', he began,[2] 'I am sorrier for your taking than for my own.' Then he explains how, after his conversations with Oldcorne had been misheard he judged it better to tell the very truth, with less discredit to our Order, than to permit them to have harder conceits of us, as of contrivers and authors of all this conspiracy.' After repeating to Tesimond (as he thought) what he had told the Council, he added: 'We both conspired to hinder it, and to this purpose I wrote continually to Rome, procuring censures, but not expressing particulars.'

Thus far the Council had got nothing new. Indeed Garnet's letter was a defence of Tesimond as much as of himself. 'I said that you, at the house in Essex, told me of the matter in confession, yet walking and after confession, because it was too tedious to hear all kneeling. . . . I never approved it, nor, as I think, you.' Again he apologises, this time in a more stricken manner. 'Because I assured myself that you were beyond the seas, I laid part of the blame upon you, you being already touched very deeply, for which I heartily ask your forgiveness.' The 'blame' was no more than the truth that Tesimond had told him of the Plot in confession. This revelation did no discredit to Tesimond; but had he, in fact, been arrested, as the Council gave out, it would have added to his difficulties.

Nothing indeed could have distressed Garnet more than such 'news': the Council knew it and deliberately lied in the hope that in a moment of mental derangement he might confess that he was the instigator of the Plot, or at least an accomplice. But Garnet had spiritual strength sufficient to master his sorrow. 'Almighty God send us plenty of his heavenly comforts', he concluded his letter to Tesimond, 'for your apprehension hath made my sorrows to be renewed. *Fiat voluntas Dei, et mihi parce.*'

Outside the Tower the campaign of slander intensified. Gerard gathered

---

[1] Soon after the Gunpowder Plot, Fr Tesimond was caught in the streets of London reading a description of himself appended to the Proclamation for his arrest. There were many people about and he allowed himself to be taken off quietly. But in a deserted side street he threw off his captor, escaped to Suffolk and crossed to the Continent with a cargo of dead pigs.

[2] H. G. to Oswald Tesimond. 4 April 1606. *Hat. Cal.*, 18, 95.

and recorded the rumours. At first there was much speculation as to whether the sentence would in fact be carried out.[1] Only the Council knew, Gerard remarks, but it is doubtful whether their decision was finally taken before the last days of April. 'In the meantime the whole afflicted company of his friends and spiritual children did join in earnest prayers unto God for him.'[2]

'In the meantime, also, there was of purpose spread many false rumours ... that forsooth he would yield and go to church with heretics, and that they should see him preach publicly heretical doctrine, and such like; all which things God knows were far from his thoughts, as he showed by his great constancy and in express words also when he came to die.'[3]

From 4 April, for nearly three weeks, there was little heard of Garnet. During this time his sadness was increased by the news of Oldcorne's execution.

In prison Garnet was given only information that was calculated to depress him. Had he been told of the admirable behaviour of his fellow-prisoner, he would have found comfort in it, as he had done in the death of so many martyr priests he had known. Oldcorne rode out of London through Holborn with John Wintour, already condemned, and Humphrey Littleton yet untried, a company selected to suggest that he was guilty of the Powder Treason. This Garnet would have heard. But he did not know how, by his brave defence and manifest innocence, Oldcorne had defeated the aim of the Council. No one in the west country believed in his guilt: and this accounted in part for the sympathy the crowd was to show Garnet at his own execution a few weeks later. Far from reviling him as a conspirator, the people of Worcester revered him as a saint, and were happy 'to have him a patron of their country for time to come, who had been a pattern to them in the way of virtue whilst he walked among them.'[4]

At the bar Oldcorne's management of his own defence was as sound as Garnet's but more successful. He was tried at the Lent Assizes in the Shire Hall at Worcester. The indictment, as Gerard points out, was framed, 'to draw him within the compass of some participation in this late treason', on the ground that he had sent 'letters up and down to prepare men's minds for the insurrection'.[5] Also he was accused of 'a sermon made at Christmas', in which, it was said, he had excused the conspirators or extenuated their guilt, and about the same time in conversation had told his friends not to condemn the conspirators, for 'God doth not always give present success to such causes as yet He doth approve and will afterwards prosper'.

[1] *Narrative*, 265.
[2] *Ibid.*
[3] *op. cit.*, 287.
[4] *op. cit.*, 266.
[5] *op. cit.*, 269.

No proof could be alleged in support of the terms of the indictment. When Oldcorne utterly denied that he had said any such things, his reputation in the county was such that the court was forced to accept his denial. The indictment was then reframed, and he was condemned as 'a priest and Jesuit, well known to have gained many souls to the Catholic faith'.[1] After sentence had been pronounced, Oldcorne spoke of his time in the Tower, where he had been tortured to draw from him information that could be used for the conviction of his Superior. 'He received the sentence with joy', writes Gerard,[2] 'and told them there in public that he had been tortured in the Tower five hours five several days together, one after another, which if it were five hours at a time even one of the days (as his words were understood), then was it a great extremity that he sustained.'[3]

Oldcorne, followed by Ralph Ashley, John Wintour and Humphrey Littleton, was executed at Red Hill, Worcester, on 7 April. As the rope was fastened round his neck, Oldcorne commended himself to St Winifred, at whose shrine in Holywell he had been cured of cancer in the throat during his first years as a priest.[4]

Garnet in the Tower knew only of Oldcorne's death. None of the details were told him: and doubtless he was given lying and degrading accounts. His sorrows were complete. False reports, calumnies, deliberate lies were spread in London about him and about his closest friends. He was in no position to check the information that was fed to him, nor had he any reason for disbelieving it. Now he was told that Richard Fulwood and Habington's servant, Robert, had been captured with a cypher;[5] that his house at Erith had been raided: also his lodgings in Thames Street. He begins his last letter to Anne Vaux: 'It pleaseth God daily to multiply my crosses. I beseech him give me patience and perseverance *usque in finem*.'[6] Then he lists the items comprising his sorrow. All his life he had prayed that when the moment of his arrest came, none should suffer for it; yet he had been taken at 'a friend's house', and Habington had been arraigned for harbouring him; in the Tower his confessions to Oldcorne had been overheard and his letters intercepted. Then followed, he told Anne, 'the taking of yourself afterwards; my arraignment; then the taking of Mr Greenwell; then the slander of us

---

[1] *Narrative*, 270.

[2] *Ibid.*

[3] From his own experience (Cf. *John Gerard*, ch. 15) Gerard adds: 'For one hour's torture will make the hands so swollen and so sore (besides the pain in other parts of the body) that it is a very cruel thing to put a man to the like the next day after.'

[4] *John Gerard*, 64–8.

[5] Possibly his own, but certainly belonging to one of his brethren.

[6] H. G. to Anne Vaux. 21 April 1606. *S.P.D. James I*, vol. 20, no. 39.

both abroad; then the ransacking anew of Erith and the other house; then the execution of Mr Hall [Oldcorne]; and now, last of all, the apprehension of Richard and Robert with a cypher . . . and that which was a singular oversight, a letter written in cypher, together with the cypher, which letter may bring many into question.'

Yet with Job he praised God that his sufferings had not been brought on by any folly or negligence on his part. '*Sufferentiam Job audistis*'; he concluded, '*et finem Domini vidistis, quemadmodum misericors Dominus est et miserator.*[1] *Sit nomen Domini benedictum.*'[1]

It was his last letter. He signed himself: 'Yours *in eternum*, as I hope, H. G.'

One final questionnaire he was made to answer, on 25 April, just five days later. Still the Council hoped that in his condition of extreme mental fatigue and anxiety he would be induced to contradict himself. To the same questions Garnet gave the same answers, with no less clarity than before.[2] His paper was scrutinised. He was then made to add a paragraph stating that he wrote without 'equivocation'. This was endorsed by Northampton, Suffolk, Worcester, Nottingham and Salisbury.

[1] James 5: 11
[2] Gunpowder Plot Book, 2, no. 44. Examination of Henry Garnet at the Tower, 25 April 1606.

45

EXECUTION

ONLY when the Council was resigned to the failure of its last efforts to implicate Garnet in the Plot, was it decided to proceed with his execution. The day first appointed was 1 May. Garnet, when he was told, 'misliked the choice they made'.[1] It was a public holiday and the crowd was likely to be riotous, for it had long been the 'custom in England upon that day in the early morning for the people to go into the fields and come home with green boughs in their hands in sign of joy, and to spend most of that day in triumph and pastime'.[2] Even if the revellers were not uproarious they were unlikely to be sympathetic. Garnet was determined to use the criminal's privilege and speak to the people: there had been slanders spread about him and he would quash them before he died: this he owed not only to himself, but also to Anne Vaux, to his Jesuit brethren and to the Catholics of England.

'What, will they make a May game of me?', Garnet asked William Wade, the Lieutenant of the Tower. The remark was repeated to the Councillors, who agreed that the day 'was not fit'. As Dudley Carleton, the diplomat, wrote on 2 May: 'upon better advice his execution is put off till to-morrow for fear of disorder among the 'prentices and others in a day of misrule'.[3] Saturday 3 May was the feast of the Finding of the Holy Cross, 'and the day no doubt assigned by Almighty God for his martyrdom: for, of all other days of that season, the martyr himself was most affected unto that, having ever had a special devotion unto the Cross and Passion of Christ; wherefore as he misliked the unfit choice of the other day, so he rejoiced exceedingly at this election, and prepared himself gladly to find this cross which God would send him upon that day; and by that cross to find the way to heaven. He showed himself a true disciple and follower of the Apostle *et gloriatus est in cruce Domini nostri Jesu Christi, in quo est salus, vita et resurrectio ejus, per quem salvatus et liberatus est.*'[4]

The place appointed for the execution was St Paul's churchyard, at the west end, opposite the bishop's palace. When in January it was announced

---

[1] *Narrative*, 288.   [2] *Ibid.*   [3] *S.P.D. James I*, vol. 20, no. 4.

[4] *Narrative*, 288–9. 'And he gloried in the Cross of our Lord Jesus Christ, in whom is his salvation, life and resurrection, by whom he is saved and delivered.'

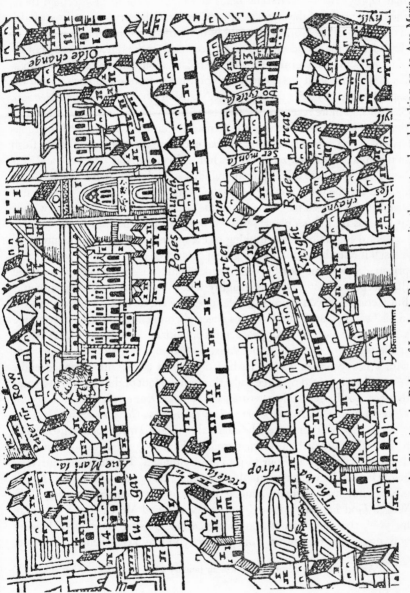

PLAN OF ST PAUL'S Showing the Bishop of London's Palace opposite the west end and backing on to Ave Maria Lane and Pater Noster Row. From Ralph Agas' Plan of London.

that Digby, Robert Wintour, Bates and Grant were to be executed there, the impropriety of the site was pointed out to Salisbury. 'In my poor judgment', Sir Arthur Gorges had told him,[1] 'I did not think it a fit place to be defiled with the blood of such wretches, nor to make butchery in a churchyard and almost under the eaves of the most famous church of our kingdom. ... Besides it is an ill presage to have blood and execution approach so near the capital house of God's divine service.' Salisbury had ignored the objection. St Paul's, in more recent times, was associated with the great day of national thanksgiving for the defeat of the Armada.[2] Garnet had described to Aquaviva the procession and sermon on that occasion; the memory of it was fresh in the mind of adult citizens; Gorges himself had seen the 'late dread and dear Sovereign Elizabeth offer up in all humility upon her knees her thanksgiving to God for the great victory upon the Spaniards'. But it was precisely this visible link between the Armada and the 'arch-plotter' that Salisbury wished to impress on the people. He was a propagandist to the end.

Gerard could not learn anything of the manner in which Garnet prepared himself for death, 'all things being kept most close in that most close and strict prison, where none but his only keeper could possibly come to him; and that keeper a most malicious naughty fellow, as before hath been shown'.[3] But Gerard believed it was possible to see the effects of his prefatory prayer in his 'well prepared mind and his cheerful countenance which, in so grave a man, was a sign of great peace and contentment of mind'.[4] On 21 April, at the foot of a letter to Anne Vaux, he had drawn the sacred monogram with a heavy brush. Above he had depicted a cross with seraphed ends: below a heart pierced by three nails: through the foot of the emblem in a hand that was not forged he had written the words, *Deus cordis mei: et pars mea Deus in eternum. God of my heart and my inheritance, God for eternity.*[5]

As he was led from his cell, he chanced to meet a Tower cook, who begged to take his leave of him. Garnet smiled, 'Farewell, good friend Tom, this day I will save thee a labour to provide my dinner.' Through the courtyard below his cell he walked to the hurdle, where had gathered not only Tower officials but many others. Among them was the Lieutenant's wife, Lady Wade. 'God be with you and comfort you, good Mr Garnet. I will pray for you', she said. Garnet acknowledged her greeting cheerfully. 'I thank you, good madam, and for your prayers you may keep them at this time;

[1] Sir Arthur Gorges to Lord Salisbury. 29 January 1606. *Hat. Cal.*, 18, no. 36.
[2] Cf. *sup.*, p. 81.
[3] *Narrative*, 289.
[4] *Ibid.*
[5] *S.P.D. James I*, vol. 20, no. 39.

and if it pleaseth God to give me perseverance I will not forget you in my prayers.' Then, suddenly, from the crowd rushed Anne Vaux. Wade, angry and amazed, ordered her immediately back to her cell. No speech passed between her and Garnet: no opportunity was given for a farewell word. Wade lashed at Anne's gaoler with oaths. 'I was only carrying out your orders', the man protested.[1] Wade had, in fact, told him the previous day that he might permit Anne to watch from a window in the Tower as Garnet was taken to the hurdle; instead he had brought her to the courtyard. Anne was unperturbed. Salisbury had spoken truthfully when he told Anne that she would sacrifice her life for Garnet.

'Then being brought to the hurdle, there he was laid, as the order is, having a black cloak somewhat long upon his other clothes, and a hat on his head. All the way, as he was drawn (with three horses), he held his hands together, lifted up somewhat towards heaven, and kept his eyes shut for the most part as a man in deep contemplation.'[2]

Unlike Sir Arthur Gorges, Gerard considered the choice of St Paul's appropriate, indeed 'provided so by God, that as by his virtuous life and doctrine, [Garnet] had confuted heresy, so by his constant death he might confound both it and the teachers thereof'.[3]

The previous day carpenters had been engaged in erecting outside the west entrance a great scaffold with a gibbet in the middle of it. There were 'such multitudes of people', writes Gerard, 'noble and ignoble, so many standings set up ... to hire out for money that a mere place to stand on would cost twelvepence well; and the party from whom I have many of these particulars (being a priest of great credit and estimation) was glad to give twelvepence only to stand upon a wall. All windows were full, yea, the tops of the houses full of people, so that it is not known the like hath been at any execution.'[4]

Garnet was lifted from the hurdle. Below the scaffold waited the Deans of St Paul's and Winchester,[5] 'with a company of other Ministers, to greet him and continue with him an argument begun in his last days in the Tower. Coming up to him, they held their hats in their hands with a great show of reverence.

'Mr Garnet', began Overal impressively, 'I am sent unto you from his

[1] *op. cit.*, vol. 21, no. 5.
[2] *Narrative*, 289–90.
[3] *Ibid.*
[4] *Narrative*, 290.
[5] Dr John Overal, later Bishop of Lichfield, and Dr George Abbot, later Archbishop of Canterbury.

Majesty, to will that now being in the last hour of your mortal life, you will perform the duty of a true subject, to which you are obliged by the laws of God and nature. . . . Therefore disclose such treason as you know intended towards his Majesty's danger and the commonwealth.'

This confession he had attempted to wring from Garnet several times in the Tower and failed to do.

'Mr Dean', answered Garnet correctly, 'it may please you to tell his Majesty that I have been arraigned, and what could be laid to my charge I have there answered and said as much as I could; so that at this place I have no more to say.'[1]

Garnet desired only to die quickly. The Deans would not permit it: they tried to convert him to their beliefs. Garnet cut them off sharply. There was no need, he said, to trouble either themselves or him; he could do without their instruction on the state of his soul; he came 'prepared and . . . resolved'. These last words, says Gerard,[2] were enough to kill the slanders that he had become a Protestant in prison. Finished with argument, as he thought, Garnet was led to the scaffold. The Deans and other Ministers followed him. The two sheriffs of the city, and the recorder, Henry Montagu, took charge of the prisoner.[3] Garnet saluted them, and then greeted 'some Catholics of reckoning' who stood by the gallows. He was 'very kindly and cheerful'.

First he asked whether there was some place where he might be allowed to pray privately, but the Recorder answered that he and others were there by order of the King to get him to acknowledge his treason and beg his Majesty's forgiveness. Garnet protested: he had not committed any treason, nor any offence against the King; he was not guilty of the Plot in the least degree, 'but had earnestly dissuaded and sought to hinder both that and all other attempts against his Majesty':[4] there was no ground on which he could be condemned save that he had not opened the secret of confession, since it was only in confession that he had knowledge of the Plot. All that could be said against him was that 'he had done according to his function' and for that he 'could not justly be condemned'. If this manner of concealing the treason (and he was bound in conscience to it) had in any way offended his Majesty

---

[1] *Narrative*, 290–1.

[2] *Ibid.*

[3] The two Sheriffs of the city were Sir Clement Scudamore and John Jolles, draper, who was knighted shortly after Garnet's execution, on 23 July 1606, on the expiration of his term (cf. G. E. Coykayne, *Some Account of the Mayors and Sheriffs of the City of London, 1601–25* (1897), 27–8, 72–3. The Recorder was Henry Montagu of the Middle Temple, who later became Chief Justice of the King's Bench, and was subsequently created Earl of Manchester.

[4] *Narrative*, 291.

or the State, he asked forgiveness with all his heart. In no other way had he hurt the King.

For his last defence Garnet expected a fairer hearing than he had been given at his trial, but the Recorder, snatching at his words, turned to the crowd:

'Gentlemen, do you hear? He asks the King's forgiveness for the Powder treason.'

'You are wrong', Garnet was abrupt. 'I have no cause to ask forgiveness of that whereof I was never guilty, nor was I privy to it in such sort that it may justly be imputed to me for concealing it.'

Montagu regretted his sally: the crowd was clearly with Garnet.

Now the Recorder made good his former speech 'with facing down the Father'.[1] 'What', he retorted, 'will you deny your own hand? We have it under your hand that you knew of it by other means than confession; that Greenway [Tesimond] told you of it by way of consultation, and that Catesby and Greenway came together to be resolved of you.'

'No', Garnet answered. 'Mr Catesby never told me of any particular. And for Mr Greenway I knew it only, as I have said, by confession, which therefore I could not lawfully open, until ... I had leave so to do.' Then he repeated what he had already told the Council: 'Neither would I have named him [Tesimond] as I have done, but lest any might think him guilty of counselling or furthering in the matter, and to the end the very truth might be known, because false reports make him thought more guilty than he is.'

Garnet believed that Tesimond was in prison; that these words would be reported to him.

'What is under my hand', Garnet said, parrying the Recorder's final thrust, 'that I will not deny; but you shall never show my hand contrary to what I have spoken.'

Montagu did not take up the challenge. Later, as Thomas Garnet, Henry's nephew, was being taken through the streets of London on the first stage of his journey into exile, Salisbury's messenger, running up to him, produced the forgery, and beseeched him to acknowledge his uncle's hand. Thomas protested on his eternal salvation that Henry had not written it nor had he received it.[2]

'You do but equivocate', Montagu returned to the debate. But there was no other argument on which he could fall back. He threatened Garnet: 'And if you will deny it, after your death we will publish your own hand, that the world may see your false dealing.'

Garnet answered with some show of impatience: 'This is no time to talk

[1] *op. cit.*, 292.　　　　[2] Cf. *sup.*, p. 402.

of equivocation; neither do I equivocate.' Then he swore an oath, as he was justified in doing, that he had made no such confession.

'But in troth, in troth, you shall not find my hand otherwise than I have said.'

This double asseveration, as Gerard calls it,[1] satisfied his hearers, though none would 'be satisfied that was resolved and prepared to contradict'.

In this category was the Recorder: he turned to a man standing by him: 'Let him see his own handwriting.'

Garnet was calm.

'You cannot', he said, 'show me any such writing of my own hand.'

Gerard gives the conclusion of the exchange.[2] 'He that should have had the note, said it was not there. It was left at home.'

At this 'many of the standers-by laughed in their sleeves'.[3] Garnet had already won over the crowd; the last word was his: 'Neither here nor at home have you any such.'

By law Garnet was permitted to speak to the people. He was asked whether he had anything to say. 'His voice was low', he told the Sheriffs, 'and himself weak.' He doubted whether he would be heard.

But strength came to him: there was no likelihood of interruption now: it was a moment he could claim as his own.

'Upon this day is recorded the Invention of the Cross of Christ', he said; 'and upon this day, I thank God, I have found my cross, by which I hope to end all the crosses of my life, and to rest in the next by the grace and merits of my Saviour. As for the treasons which are laid against me, I protest now at my death that I am not guilty of them: neither had I knowledge of the Powder but in confession, and then I utterly misliked it and earnestly dissuaded it. Yea, I protest upon my soul I should have abhorred it ever, though it had succeeded. And I am sorry with all my heart that any Catholics had ever any such intention, knowing that such attempts are not allowable, and, to my knowledge, contrary to the Pope's mind.'

He pleaded for the last time. 'And therefore I wish all Catholics to be quiet, and not to be moved by any difficulties to the raising of tumults, but to possess their souls in peace. And God will not be forgetful of them or of his promise, but will send them help and comfort when it is most to his glory and to their good.'

This was his last message. Still he was interrupted. A man near the scaffold called out to him:

'But, Mr Garnet, were you not married to Mrs Anne Vaux?'

Turning from the crowd, he addressed the interjector:

[1] *Narrative*, 292.   [2] *Ibid.*   [3] *Ibid.*

'That honourable gentlewoman hath great wrong by such false reports. And for my part, as I have always been free from such crimes, so I may protest for her upon my conscience that I think her to be a perfect pure virgin, if [there] be any other in England or otherwise alive.' Then he reiterated his statement: 'She is a virtuous good gentlewoman, and therefore to impute any such charge unto her cannot proceed but of malice.'

Garnet did not resume his speech. Already he had carried himself with an instinctive integrity that had won total conviction. Now he made his last preparation for death.

He asked the Recorder whether he might still be permitted to pray. At the foot of the ladder he knelt and stayed there 'for a good space in a devout and religious manner'.[1] Then, to save others the task, he stripped himself to his shirt, 'which was somewhat long': during his last hours in his cell he had 'sewn down the sides thereof almost to the bottom', that the spring breeze round Ludgate Hill 'might not blow it up, which was noted by many as a sign of great modesty'.[2]

A zealot from the throng of Ministers came forward: he was anxious to make a last attempt to convert Garnet, 'but the Father desired him to hold himself contented and not to trouble him any further'.

He was then taken to the ladder. He made the sign of the Cross and asked the prayers of 'all good Catholics'. There was another shout from the crowd.

'Mr Garnet, it is expected you should recant from your religion and become a Protestant.'

The man had revealed a further reason for the choice of St Paul's churchyard for the execution: as Gerard had noted, it had been given out in London that Garnet would recant, and afterwards preach at St Paul's Cross. Garnet ended any speculation that was still abroad:

'God forbid it. I had never any such meaning, but ever meant to die a true and perfect Catholic.'

Devout and undaunted he turned for the last time to the crowd: to them he gave his last spiritual message. 'He wished them to consider well the state of their souls, assuring them, upon his conscience and salvation, there was no other way to their eternal bliss but to live and die in the profession of the Catholic faith.'

Yet again he was interrupted. This time it was Overal, the Dean of St Paul's.

'But, Mr Garnet, we are all Catholics.'

'No, no,' Garnet was emphatic, 'you are not, for such are only Catholics

---

[1] *op. cit.,* 294.
[2] *Ibid.*

as live in unity and profession of one faith, under one supreme head of God's Church, which is the Pope's Holiness; and you must be all of the Roman Catholic Church or you cannot be saved.'

The remaining moments were his own. He prayed for the King, for whom he had not lost his regard, for the Queen, soon to be received into the Church by one of his brethren; then for the Council, together and individually; and finally for the whole State. So that he might have some moment to pray for perseverance to the end, he begged the hangman to give him warning before he cast him off the ladder.

After making the sign of the cross, *In Nomine Patris et Filii et Spiritus Sancti*, he prayed. 'We adore Thee, o Christ, and we bless thee, because by thy holy cross thou hast redeemed the world.' No longer was he a public figure: so he permitted himself to pray in Latin, joining his suffering to Christ's: his thoughts moved from the cross to Christ's mother, and then again to the cross. Gerard tells the rest of the story.

He prayed: *Maria, Mater gratiae, Mater misericordiae, tu nos ab hoste, protege et hora mortis suscipe*;[1] then *in manus tuas, Domine, commendo spiritum meum.* This he repeated two or three times: then his thoughts turned again to the Cross. He signed himself: 'By this sign of the Cross [he spoke still in Latin] may all that is wicked fly far away. O Lord, fix thy cross in my heart';[2] then he repeated *Maria, Mater gratiae*, etc.

His prayer finished, he told the hangman he was ready. 'Being desirous to carry the cross with him out of the world imprinted on his breast, he crossed his arms over his heart on his breast, and so was cast off the ladder.' His arms remained crossed: he made no struggle against death, he hung motionless.

His behaviour, his protestation of innocence and constancy had so conquered the 'hard conceits' the people formerly had of him, that 'they prevented the hangman with a loud cry that he might not cut him down too soon'.[3] It had been proposed that he should be quartered alive and quickly. When he was presumed to be half-dead the hangman again made to cut the rope, but again the people cried out, 'Hold, hold'; and a third time also. 'Yea, and one of the citizens took him by the legs and pulled him, to put him out of pain, and that he might not be cut down alive.' Gerard noted the import of this action, for these 'kind of favours are nothing usual when people do presume men die for treason'; they 'were not used to the gentlemen that suffered

---

[1] *Mary, mother of grace, mother of mercy, protect us from the foe, and receive us at the hour of death.*

[2] *Per crucis hoc signum fugiat procul omne malum. Infinge crucem tuam in corde meo, Domine.*

[3] *Narrative*, 296.

before, although men of good sort and much beloved and esteemed before this enterprise.

'And it was much marvelled how the people durst do this publicly, seeing the State so generally bent against Father Garnet in this cause. But most of them proceeded much further than this. For when he was cut up and his bowels cast into the fire, and his heart pulled out and showed unto the people with these words, that are ever used in such cases, "Behold the heart of a traitor", there was not heard any applause, or those that cried, "God save the King", which is always usual when the heart or head is held up in that kind.'[1]

'Yea, so strange and unexpected an alteration there was in the very heretics themselves, that some of them said without doubt he was in heaven; and other said, he died like a saint; others, that he looked not like a contriver of treason. Yea, and some ministers themselves were heard to say that questionless he was in heaven. And, generally, the people went away much satisfied of his innocency and sanctity.'[2]

The priest, Gerard's informant, who had paid twelvepence to stand on a wall near the scaffold, approached Garnet's remains in the hope of obtaining a relic of a martyr, 'and found divers there looking for the same prey'. A Catholic gentleman was given the shirt Garnet was wearing at the time of his execution; other Catholics acquired different parts of his apparel, 'which are now esteemed of more than their weight in gold'.[3]

The very hour that Garnet died, Gerard escaped to the Continent. He saw in his safe-passage a sign that his late Superior was already protecting him before God. 'Twice on the 3 May, the day on which Father Garnet went to heaven, I received signal favours, which I believe were due to his intercession. The first was this. When I arrived by arrangement at the port from which I was to pass out of England with certain high officials, they took fright and said they could not stand by their promise.[4] Right up to the time I was due to embark with them, they refused to let me come. Then, just at that moment, Father Garnet was received into heaven and did not forget me on earth. Suddenly they changed their mind. The ambassador came to fetch me personally and himself helped me to dress in the livery of his attendants so

---

[1] Garnet, in his letter to Aquaviva reporting Southwell's execution, had noted that the crowd had refused to respond. 'Aye, aye', when the executioner held up his companion's head, saying, 'Behold, the head of a traitor.'

[2] *Narrative*, 296.

[3] *op. cit.*, 297.

[4] Gerard had planned to cross from Dover in the suite of the Marquis of St Germain, the Spanish Ambassador, and Baron Hobach, the Ambassador of the Netherlands, who came to England in April on a special embassy to congratulate James I on the preservation of his life in the Gunpowder Plot. *Hat. Cal.*, 18. 117.

that I could pass for one of them and escape. I did escape and in my own mind I have no doubt that I owed this to Father Garnet's prayers.'[1]

There was needed a century of unceasing slanders to soil the impression of innocence that Garnet made at St Paul's. While Persons told his brethren that nothing worse could be proved against Garnet than some knowledge of the conspiracy, Aquaviva, with a surer inspiration, consented to the proposal of Garnet's Roman friends that the cause of his canonisation should be brought forward: an example to the world of a priest's fidelity to the secrets confided in the sacrament that was the true cause of his execution.

---

[1] *John Gerard*, 209. The second 'favour' was his profession as a Jesuit, three years later, 3 May 1609. 'It seemed that God wanted to show me that I owed this also to Father Garnet's prayers, for there was a strange similarity in the circumstances of my profession and his martyrdom. The day originally fixed for both was 1 May, the feast of the Holy Apostles, St Philip and St James, but in both cases unforeseen delays postponed the event until 3 May.'

Appendix A

Garnet's first objective was Canterbury. From the Folkestone area there were two recognized routes which the shepherd probably pointed out to him. If Garnet took the longer route, he would have left the rising ground on his left, passed north of Folkestone along the escarpment until he came to the entrance of the Elham valley at Etchingwell. Then he could either have followed up the valley past the villages of Lyminge and Ottinge till he came to Elham, a fair-sized place at this time, and then on to Barham and Kingston. Alternatively he could have taken a parallel track on the high chalk ground to either the east or west of the valley. These were old routes established by pilgrims to Canterbury landing at Folkestone Stair and known as the Caseway. Beyond Kingston he would have struck the old Roman road from Dover to Canterbury at the point marked by the fourth milestone out of the city. Here he may have mingled with the crowds going from Dover to St Thomas's Fair and continued along this route: or he might have left it two miles further on at Milestone Farm and followed a track that joined the pilgrim route from Canterbury to Hythe. Since Garnet was on foot, this seems more probably his route rather than Southwell's. It was perhaps outside Elham that Garnet rested.

On parting company the two priests, in order to reduce the risk of joint capture went different ways. It is likely that Southwell went north-east, along Capel Street which followed the ridge past Radigund and Kearnsey Abbeys before reaching the Dover–Canterbury road two miles outside Dover. From there he could either have continued the eighteen miles along the road to Canterbury or, to avoid other travellers, have crossed the road to hit a bridle track that ran parallel with the road through Whitfield and Coldred. A short distance from Canterbury this track joined the old pilgrim way from Hythe.

Appendix B

THE WRITINGS OF HENRY GARNET

A critical list of the printed books of Henry Garnet was made in 1951 by Mr A. F. Allison of the Department of Printed Books at the British Museum and published in *Recusant History* (then entitled *Biographical Studies*), vol. 1, no. 1, 7–21. Garnet's known printed works are the following:

1. *A summe of Christian doctrine.* This is a translation of Peter Canisius's famous catechism. Garnet added to the original work three supplements on the veneration of images, on pilgrimages and on indulgences. It was printed at his secret press in London.

2. *An apology against the defence of schisme.* This deals with church-going. It can be dated approximately by the controversy on this subject. It was printed at the same press.

3. *A treatise of christian renunciation.* A small compilation principally from the Fathers of the Church in elaboration of the text: 'Unless a man have leave father, mother, etc.' There is an appendix which returns to the subject of church-going. At the end of the book there are six pages written by Garnet by way of preface to the 'Declaration of the Fathers of the Council of Trent on the frequentation of (heretical) churches'. The decree is printed both in English and Latin.

4. *The Societie of the Rosary.* Cf. *sup.*, 144. There were four editions of this book.

5. *Briefe meditations of the most holy Sacrament and of preparation for receiving the same.* This is a translation of Luca Pinelli's *Libretto di brevi meditazioni de santissimo sacramento* (1597). For English readers the main interest of this book is the translation of the *Lauda Sion* made by Robert Southwell, and certain short prayers he composed and left among his papers. This book was also printed at his secret press.

Garnet's treatise on equivocation (cf. *sup.*, 253) circulated only in manuscripts.

Appendix C

GARNET'S HEAD

John Gerard (*Narrative*, 305) says that when Garnet's head was placed on a pole near London Bridge, his face, according to many witnesses, 'did continue so comely and with so pleasing a countenance, as it seemed rather the head of a man alive than separated from his body; and also his quarters also so purely white that it was much admired by all that did behold them'.

The strange phenomenon is reported more fully in an anonymous narrative (Papers relating to the English Jesuits, British Museum, Add. MSS. 21, 203, Plut. clii. F):

'After that Father Henry Garnet, Superior of the Society of Jesus in England, was executed by commandment of James now King of that realm, the third day of May, being the feast of the Invention of the Cross, in the year 1606, his head appeared in that lively colour as it seemed to retain the same hue and shew of life which it had before it was cut off, so as both heretics and Catholics were astonished thereat, and so much the more, in that according to custom being cast into hot water it received no alteration at all; as neither it did after it was placed upon London Bridge, and set up there upon a pole. Whereupon there was such resort of people for the space of six weeks as that was admirable, the citizens flocking thither by hundreds to see so strange and wonderful a spectacle, as the head of this glorious martyr did exhibit, whose face continued without any change, retaining a graceful and lively countenance, and never waxed black, as usually all heads cut from the bodies do. Whereupon the magistrates of the city, and Council confounded with the miracle, and displeased with the continual resort of people to behold the unexpected event, gave order that the head should be put so as the face should be turned upwards, and the people thereby not able to view the face as they had been accustomed. There have been so many to see it at once sometimes, what from the bridge, what from places near thereunto, as from the water and houses, as divers there present have thought them to have been to the number of 400 or 500 persons.'

Appendix D

GARNET'S STRAW

There is an astonishingly large literature on a curious incident, perhaps trivial in itself but important in its repercussions, viz. the appearance of Henry Garnet's likeness on an ear of corn which was stained with his blood. This likeness is shown in the illustration on page 445.

John Gerard (*Narrative*, 301–5) writes: 'The first sign by which it pleased God to show the merit and glory of this His martyr was concerning his relics, which were eagerly sought for by many Catholics at the very time of his martyrdom. Amongst the which there was one young man,[1] who stood

---

[1] This was John Wilkinson, who afterwards became a student at St Omer and on his death-bed in that College dictated a narrative of Father Garnet's execution and the finding of the straw. Cf. More, *Hist. Prov. Angl. S.J.*, lib. vii., n. 35.

by the block where the martyr's body was cut up, with great desire at least to get some drop of his holy blood. And whilst he had these thoughts, not daring to take where he desired for fear he might be espied, it fortuned that the hangman having cut off the martyr's head and showed it to the people (as the custom is), he cast it into a basket standing there of purpose, full of straw, to hold the head and quarters when they were divided. Out of this basket did leap a straw, or ear void of corn, in strange manner into the hand of this young man, which he beholding, and seeing some blood upon it, kept it with great care, and no little joy that he had obtained his desire. He carried it away safely and delivered it unto a Catholic gentlewoman[1] of his acquaintance, who kept it in a reliquary with great devotion; and after three or four days, a devout Catholic gentleman coming thither, she showed him the bloody straw, which he was also glad to see and reverence; but beholding the same more curiously than the others had done, he saw a perfect face, as if it had been painted, upon one of the husks of the empty ear, and showed the same unto the company, which they all did plainly behold, and with no small wonder, but with much greater joy did acknowledge the mighty hand of God, Who can and doth often use the meanest creatures to set forth His glory, and is able both out of stones and straws to raise a sufficient defence for His faithful servants.

'They put up the straw again with great admiration, and kept it now with much more reverence and devotion than before. This was quickly published to many of the chiefest Catholics about London, who much desiring to see this wonder, it was carried unto divers, who all are witnesses of this truth. At length it came to the Council's ear, and some of them desiring much to see it, it was granted, being now in the keeping of a great person,[2] but with promise to have it safely restored; so that some of them did see it, and did much admire it, affirming that it must needs be more than natural. Others often desired to see it and to seize upon it, because now the fame did grow so great of this image of Father Garnet drawn by the hand of God, whose image and memory they sought to deface in all they could, that they feared the evidence of the miracle would plead against their proceedings and prove him innocent whom they had punished as guilty. Therefore the Bishop of Canterbury[3] sought to have the miraculous straw into his hands, but it was denied, and none would acknowledge where it was to be found.

[1] Her name was Griffin.

[2] Father More says it was the Spanish Ambassador, and he gives the attestation of the Baron Hobach, dated in 1625, that he had seen it in 1606, when he was in London as Ambassador of the Princes of the Netherlands.

[3] Dr Richard Bancroft.

Spica Wilkinſoni.   *Spica Ieſuitica.*

GARNET'S STRAW

From *Antilogia adversus Apologiam Andreae Eudaemon-Joannis,* by Robert Abbot (1613)

He learned out the party to whom the keeping of it was first committed, and sent for her husband, who was a known Catholic and a virtuous man. He examined him strictly how it came to pass, and where the straw was. The Catholic affirmed the truth of the thing, and described it unto him in words; but said it was not now in his keeping, and he knew not where to find it. And when they could get no other answer of him, they committed him to prison; but afterwards, having sundry and great friends in the Court, he got out upon bonds to appear again at certain days' warning.

'The Council afterwards understanding that this miraculous picture in the straw had been showed to divers painters in London, they sent for the painters, and willed them to make the like portrait to that which they had seen in a like empty ear of corn; but they all answered it was not possible for them to do it: neither could the draught of that face, in so little a room and so loose a groundwork as that empty ear, be otherwise drawn than by supernatural power. And this testimony they gave of it that had both skill to judge and no will to favour the Catholic cause (being in opinion heretics), but only convinced in their understanding by the evidence of the miracle.'

The same details are given in the paper cited in Appendix B from *Papers relating to the English Jesuits* (British Museum. Add. MSS. 21, 203, Plut. clii, F). This account is printed in full in *John Gerard*, Appendix *G*, 274–6. The only difference between the two reports is this: Gerard says the face was first seen three or four days after Garnet's execution, the writer of the British Museum account that the likeness appeared on the straw when the head, pinned on London Bridge, was turned face upward. However, Gerard would seem uncertain of the time, for he first wrote 'two or three months', then substituted the words 'three or four days'.

Fr Richard Blount, who saw the straw, writes in a letter dated March 1607: 'It cannot be a thing natural or artificial. The sprinkling of blood hath made so plain a face, so well proportioned, so lively shadowed as no art in such manner is able to counterfeit the like.' Further information about the straw is given by John Wilkinson, the silk-mercer, who first acquired it, in a deposition printed in Foley, vol. 4, 195–201. Mr Hugh Griffin, a tailor and the husband of Mrs Griffin, to whom Wilkinson gave the straw, was examined about it before the Archbishop of Canterbury on 27 November 1606. The report of this examination is printed in the same volume of Foley, 127–8. Fr Henry More in his *Historia Provinciae Anglicanae* (1660), 330, says that the straw was kept at the house of the English Jesuits at Liège. The last mention of it is by the Abbé Feller in his *Dictionnaire Historique* published at Liège in 1797 (after the suppression of the Society of Jesus).

In the article *Garnet*, the Abbé writes: 'L'epi est adjourdhui entre les mains d'un de mes amis, qui le conserve soigneusement.' It has since been lost.

In the illustration (p. 445), the drawing on the left represents the actual straw, that on the right the straw as the Jesuits were supposed to represent it.

Appendix E

EQUIVOCATION

Since this is an historical biography, a theological discourse on equivocation would be out of place, particularly as there is a book in preparation on the subject by Mr A. E. Mallock, who has made available to me the result of his researches into the moral theologians of the time. My task has been merely to record the line of defence taken by Garnet and to explain his reasons for taking it. His exposition of what Coke called this 'most wicked and horrible doctrine' was based on the same arguments that were used by Southwell and Gerard (cf. *John Gerard*, second edition, 1956), Appendix E (Fr Southwell's Defence of Equivocation), 279–80, and Appendix F (Report of Fr Gerard's Examination concerning Equivocation), 281. All three made it clear that equivocation could be used only when the obligations of charity overrode the demand to give information that was wrongfully sought. While in the years after his death Garnet was pilloried for his teaching, and most notably by Shakespeare in *Macbeth*,[1] yet the position he defended was later incorporated into common English ethical teaching. Milton, for instance, in his *De Doctrina Christiana*,[2] writes: 'All dissimulation is not wrong; that only is blamed which is malicious. I do not see why that cannot be said of lying which can be said of homicide and other matters, which are not weighed so much by the deed as by the object and end of acting. What man in his senses will deny that there are those whom we have the best of grounds for considering that we ought to deceive?' Dr Johnson perhaps stretches the use of equivocation further than Garnet would have done; certainly he defends it with the same absence of hesitation and for the same reasons. 'The general rule', he writes,[3] 'is that truth should never be violated. . . . There must, however, be some exceptions. If, for instance, a murderer should ask you which way a man is gone, you may tell him what

---

[1] Cf. Act 1, scene 2, 'Faith, here's an equivocator that could swear in both the scales against either scale; who committed treason enough for God's sake, yet would not equivocate to heaven.'

[2] Lib. 2, c. 13.

[3] *Apud* Boswell, ix, 277.

is not true, because you are under a previous obligation not to betray a man
to a murderer. It may be urged, that what a man has no right to ask, you may
refuse to communicate; and there is no other effectual mode of preserving a
secret, and an important secret, the discovery of which may be very hurtful to
you, but a flat denial; for if you are silent, or hesitate, or evade, it will be held
equivalent to a confession. . . . Supposing the author had told me that he had
written "Junius", and I were asked if he had, I should hold myself at liberty
to deny it, as being under a previous promise, express or implied, to conceal it.'

It seems hardly necessary to adduce more examples of a moral teaching
that has been defended by all English ethical philosophers from the time of
William Paley.[1] It was the same teaching that Garnet used in his defence;
and it was used also by the Council to defame him and his brethren. There is
no need here to trace the genesis of the teaching among the works of the
Roman theologians of the later sixteenth century.

Appendix F

SOUTH MIDLAND CATHOLIC HOUSES

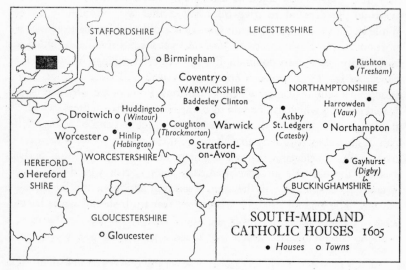

---

[1] Cf. Works, iv, 123.

INDEX

Abbot, George (1562–1633), Archbishop of Canterbury, 346; and Garnet's execution, 433 and n. 5, 434

Abbot, Robert (1560–1617), Bishop of Salisbury, 351 and n. 5; slanders Garnet, 365 n. 2

Agazzari, Alphonso, Rector of the English College, 245 and n. 2

Aglionby, Edward (1520–*c.* 87), 9

Agnus Dei, 21 and n.

Allen, Cardinal William (1532–94), 251; and the English College, Rome, 17, 20, 238; meets Garnet at Rheims, 23; and the Seminary at Douai, 181 n.; *True, Sincere and Modest Defence of English Catholics*, 58 and n. 2; *An Admonition to the Nobility and People of England and Ireland*, 70 and n. 2, 70–1; *A declaration of the sentence and disposition of Elizabeth*, 71 and n. 1

Amias, John (*d.* 1589), 97 n. 4

Anderson, Sir Edmund (1530–1605), 159 and n. 2

Appellants, aim to remove Jesuits from England and foreign Seminaries, 250; Garnet and, 250–2, 260; seek to divide Blackwell from the Jesuits, 266, 273; defy Blackwell's authority, 285; their publications in England, 286, 287, 291, 292; in collusion with Bancroft, 288; Garnet advises deprivation of clerical privileges, 293; make use of Southwell's *Humble Supplication*, 294–5; secure a Papal Brief, 299–300; the Queen's Proclamation (1602) and, 300–1; identify Garnet, 342–3

Aquaviva, Claudio (1543–1615), General of the Society, relations with Garnet, 12, 18, 19, 226–9; urged to send more priests to England, 20, 52–3; his instructions to English Jesuits, 20–2, 50; and the support of his priests in England, 46; Garnet's dependence on, 60–2, 84, 151, 152–4, 156, 223, 226–9, 245–6; establishes a mercantile vocabulary, 61 n. 2, 63; admits Oldcorne and Gerard, 80, 228; and wastage in sending priests to England, 88; accepts Garnet's novices into the Society, 105; anxious for the safety of his men, 115; and Southwell's arrest, 158; his attempted deposition, 158 n. 2; refuses to replace Garnet, 162–3; sends English novices to Belgium, 172; and the English College, 206, 208; favours the English mission, 226; his high opinion of Garnet, 226–7; instructs Garnet to take his final vows, 245–6; allows Garnet to accept his servants into the Society, 271; implores English Catholics to be prudent, 310; proposes an English novitiate in Belgium, 318–19; conveys papal censures on Catholic conspiracies, 321–2, 323, 379; proposes Garnet's canonisation, 440

Arden, John, 237

Archer, Giles, 272

Arch-confraternity of the Holy Trinity, 15

Aquaviva, Rodolpho (*d.* 1583), his martyrdom, 226 n. 3

Armada, the Spanish, preparations to meet, 64, 69–70; excitement engendered by its approach, 69; rumours concerning, 69; intensifies persecution of priests, 72–4, 78; thanksgiving for its defeat, 81–3; ships engaged in, 101 n. 2; ownership of

GG 449